W9-BRL-055

WYATT EARP

WYATT EARP

THE LIFE BEHIND THE LEGEND

CASEY TEFERTILLER

**FOREWORD BY ANGUS CAMERON,
WINNER OF SEVEN WESTERN HERITAGE AWARDS**

John Wiley & Sons, Inc.
New York • Chichester • Weinheim • Brisbane • Singapore • Toronto

Frontispiece: A stern young Wyatt Earp as he appeared in the mid-1870s, at about the time he became a deputy in Wichita. (Charles W. Dearborn Collection/Courtesy of C. Lee Simmons)

This text is printed on acid-free paper. ∞

Copyright © 1997 by Casey Tefertiller. All rights reserved.

Published by John Wiley & Sons, Inc.
Published simultaneously in Canada.

No part of this publication may be reproduced, stored in a retrieval system, or transmitted in any form or by any means, electronic, mechanical, photocopying, recording, scanning, or otherwise, except as permitted under Section 107 or 108 of the 1976 United States Copyright Act, without either the prior written permission of the Publisher, or authorization through payment of the appropriate per-copy fee to the Copyright Clearance Center, 222 Rosewood Drive, Danvers, MA 01923, (978) 750-8400, fax (978) 750-4744. Requests to the Publisher for permission should be addressed to the Permissions Department, John Wiley & Sons, Inc., 605 Third Avenue, New York, NY 10158-0012, (212) 850-6011, fax (212) 850-6008, email: PERMREQ@WILEY.COM.

This publication is designed to provide accurate and authoritative information in regard to the subject matter covered. It is sold with the understanding that the publisher is not engaged in rendering professional services. If professional advice or other expert assistance is required, the services of a competent professional person should be sought.

Library of Congress Cataloging-in-Publication Data

Tefertiller, Casey
    Wyatt Earp : the life behind the legend / Casey Tefertiller.
      p. cm.
    Includes bibliographical references and index.
    ISBN 0-471-28362-2 (paper : acid-free paper)
    1. Earp, Wyatt, 1848–1929. 2. Peace officers—Southwest, New—
Biography. 3. United States marshals—Southwest, New—Biography.
4. Southwest, New—Biography.   I. Title.
    F786.E18T44 1997
    978'.02'092—dc21
    [B]   97-2932

Printed in the United States of America

V10005095_100918

To my mother, Ruby Dunlap Tefertiller,
who has always believed that miracles
can happen with enough hard work.
With love and affection.

CONTENTS

FOREWORD

ALMOST ALL OF THE BOOKS on Wyatt Earp and his brothers, from Stuart Lake's 1931 "biography," *Frontier Marshal,* until this book by Casey Tefertiller, have been, alas, regrettable examples of all that is the worst in the western myth. For this writer it has been a most enjoyable experience to watch (through several manuscript versions) how Mr. Tefertiller has produced a book that is not romantic nonsense but rather honestly derived from sources and much of it from new sources never used before. To write a book evading the cliches of the western myth is a most difficult task and that task has been made infinitely more difficult by the added smokescreen of misinformation laid down by a succession of ridiculous motion pictures. In these movies the complicated lawman that Wyatt Earp really was has disappeared completely from view and Earp has emerged as a classic movie hero.

When modern readers survey the evidence provided by Casey Tefertiller they will discover that the real Wyatt Earp was an infinitely more interesting man than the trashy "heroes" who have emerged from the books and movies made since Wyatt Earp died. And they will discover a host of other things, including an account of the famous (or infamous) shoot-out at the O.K. Corral (a favorite episode for purveyors of western myth) that explains that violent episode without doing violence to the truth in the process.

Tefertiller is unsparing with his hero; he presents the data and readers can reach their own conclusions. Some may look upon the moody Wyatt as a brave peace officer; some may concede that but reserve the judgment that if he was a "bent cop," as we would put it today, he probably was not bent much, no more perhaps than a modern cop on the beat who though a good officer is not above "liking the best of it," as a con man might put it.

Tefertiller makes no bones about making clear that in seeking private revenge for the assassination of one brother and the crippling for life of another, Wyatt indeed became an outlaw. Mr. Tefertiller leaves it to readers to decide what they themselves might have done had they been in Wyatt's place.

Like any reliable scholar Casey Tefertiller gives the readers the facts about Wyatt Earp as the sources—many of them newly uncovered— reveal them, and lets the readers make up their own minds.

It seems unlikely that a future writer will soon feel like tackling another biography of Wyatt Earp unless much more material is unearthed about Wyatt Earp's later life.

ANGUS CAMERON

ACKNOWLEDGMENTS

A WORK OF THIS SCOPE required much assistance, and this book is really the combined effort of many people who have sought the truth about one of America's great mysteries. I am most thankful to Carl Chafin, who opened to me his collection of Tombstone materials, provided access to previously untranscribed sections of George Parsons's diary, and helped in all ways possible. Jeff Morey, historical consultant for the movie *Tombstone*, freely shared material and insight to help shape much of the thinking and understanding in this book. Dr. Gary L. Roberts of Abraham Baldwin College has pursued a better understanding of the frontier throughout his academic career and shared information and insight. Writer-historian Jack Burrows has been researching Arizona history for more than four decades and gave invaluable support. Angus Cameron provided invaluable help in shaping this book and clarifying the thinking on complex issues. Historian John Boessenecker provided detail on the activities and operations of Wells, Fargo and other information about the West. Historian/lawyer Bob Palmquist freely shared much information and legal knowledge on obscure Arizona Territorial statutes. Roger S. Peterson, who has spent years researching the Earps and interviewing family members, shared his tapes and notes of conversations. Barbara Grcar investigated the life of Josephine Earp in San Francisco and provided information. Historians William Seacrest, Bob McCubbin, and Craig Fouts have been most generous in their assistance and support; Writer Harriet Rochlin provided her research on Josephine Earp; Lee and Marlene Simmons opened their extensive Earp files, part of which is the former Al Turner collection; Jeanne Cason Laing, a friend of Josephine Earp's whose mother and aunt prepared the Cason MS., has shared her memories. I am very grateful to the descendants of Charles Welsh—Major Lois C. Welsh, Elena Armstrong, and Grace Elizabeth Spolidoro—who freely shared their most interesting personal memories of Wyatt and Josephine Earp's later years.

Hugh O'Brian was most generous in sharing recollections and knowledge from his days portraying Earp on television. Kate Edelman and Susan Chadwick of Edelman Productions provided material on the television show. Hana Lane and Seymour Kurtz of John Wiley & Sons brought this together. Literary agent Gerard McCauley provided considerable help.

Many others have also been of great help, including Earp researcher Michael Campino; Robin Gilliam and Candy Carlson of the Southwest Museum in Silver City, New Mexico; Tombstone researcher Gary McLelland; Peter

Blodgett of the Huntington Library; Josephine Earp descendant Gary Greene; Megan Hahn of the New York Historical Society; Christine Rhodes, Cochise County Recorder; Lois Jermyn and Mel Patterson of the *San Francisco Examiner* Library; Richard Buchan of the Southwest Museum; Debbie Savage of the San Bruno Public Library; Thelen Blum of Pinkerton's; Seymour Rothman of the *Toledo Blade;* Christine Marin of Arizona State Special Collections; Linda Sue McCleary of the Arizona State Library; Jim Bradshaw of the Haley Library; Judy Mullins of the Harvard Law Library; Leslie A. Morris of the Houghton Library, Harvard University; Mario M. Einaudi of the Arizona Historical Society; Brad Koplowitz of the University of Oklahoma; Champ Vermillion and John P. Vermillion, descendants of Texas Jack Vermillion; Idaho historian Judge Richard G. Magnuson; Bonnie Hardwick, Dean Smith, Richard Oger, and the staff of the Bancroft Library; Brandon Bowen for assistance with photography; Robin Vidaurri for computer assistance; Bob Boze Bell; Carolyn Lake; Don Chaput; Pat Jahns Clark; Ray Robinson; Jack Castel; Tom Wilson; Gloria Atwater; Steve Ellis; Brad Newcomb; Margaret Harding; Cynthia Pridmore; Earp descendant Reba Young; Brooks and Joan White; Arvo Ojala; Dr. Chris Carroll; Richard Lapidus; Janel Cook of the Ellsworth County Historical Society; Dan Geller; Susan Caulfield; Keith Lieppman; Nick Cataldo; Irene Shipman; Rich Freeman; Jim Dunham; Leslie Auerbach; Robert K. DeArment; McLaury reearcher Paul L. Johnson; Stilwell family descendant Virginia Card; Carina Roter; Bob Candland of the *Tombstone Tumbleweed;* Allen Barra; the late Richard Erwin and the late Frank Waters.

The following libraries and repositories have graciously shared information: The Southwest Museum: Bancroft Library; Iowa State Historical Society; New York Historical Society; Idaho Historical Society; San Francisco Public Library; Oakland Public Library; San Bruno Public Library; Albuquerque Public Library; Tucson Public Library; Huntington Library; Arizona Historical Society; University of Arizona Special Collections; Arizona State University Special Collections; Arizona Historical Foundation; University of Oklahoma; Houghton Library, Harvard; Harvard Law Library; Nita Stewart Haley Memorial Library, Midland, Texas.

Helldorado copyright 1928 by William M. Breakenridge
Copyright renewed 1956 by Fred E. Adam.
Portions reprinted by permission of Houghton Mifflin Company.

Undercover for Wells, Fargo copyright 1964 by Carolyn Lake
Published by Houghton Mifflin Company, Boston.
Portions printed by permission of Carolyn Lake.

Wyatt Earp: Frontier Marshal copyright 1931 by Stuart Lake
Published by Houghton Mifflin Company, Boston.
Portions reprinted by permission of Carolyn Lake.

INTRODUCTION

WHEREVER WYATT EARP APPEARED, the world seemed to go mad around him, and it forever baffled him that history would not just leave him alone. Other men had killed and left their pasts behind, but controversy followed Wyatt like a detective in a pulp novel. He could run fast and far, but he could never escape from Tombstone and the five months when his actions stirred the conscience of a nation. Tombstone, with its web of ambiguities and uncertainties, would haunt Earp for the rest of his life.

It troubled him deeply to see his name smeared in newspapers, magazines, and books. By the time he reached his seventies in the 1920s, many writers had rediscovered the old stories of Tombstone and were telling lies, accusing him of crimes he never committed and wrongs he believed were morally justifiable. Earp had spent a quarter of a century refusing to discuss Tombstone, simply trying to leave the past behind. But when the writers began filling the magazines with lies, he knew he had no choice but to tell his story or forever be branded as the worst type of criminal: a mankiller.

He had killed only when he saw no other choice, and his victims had been criminals who deserved bullets, not sympathy. He believed, as strongly as a man can believe, that he had done everything he could to avoid killing. He never imagined that for generations to come his righteousness would be the subject of debate, and his courage would be the substance of legend.

"He was not an angel," former Tombstone resident George Parsons wrote in 1928, "but his faults were minor ones, and he never killed a man who did not richly deserve it."

Earp had been a tough officer, tough to the point of brutality during his days behind a marshal's star in the Kansas cattle towns and in Tombstone. But most striking about his law enforcement career is how diligently he avoided killing. He always preferred fists and pistol-whippings to pulling a trigger. He even refused to carry a gun much of the time he wore a badge. He did not need one; he was man enough to stand tall without a pistol in his hand.

Bat Masterson, a frontier legend in his own right, wrote a series of essays in 1907 on western gunfighters. He chose his old friend as a subject:

> Wyatt Earp is one of the few men I personally knew in the West in the early days, whom I regarded as absolutely destitute of physical fear. I have often remarked, and I am not alone in my conclusions, that what goes for courage in a man is generally the fear of what others will think of him—in other words, personal bravery is largely

1

made up of self-respect, egotism, and an apprehension of the opinions of others. Wyatt Earp's daring and apparent recklessness in time of danger is wholly characteristic; personal fear doesn't enter into the equation, and when everything is said and done, I believe he values his own opinion of himself more than that of others, and it is his own good report that he seeks to preserve. . . . He never at any time in his career resorted to the pistol excepting in cases where such a course was absolutely necessary. Wyatt could scrap with his fists, and had often taken all the fight out of bad men, as they were called, with no other weapons than those provided by nature.

Earp's weapons of choice were always those provided by nature, his fists. Earp had no compunction against beating up troublemakers. He assiduously stopped short of killing them. He had always done this; always, that is, except in Tombstone. For this and for a series of old rumors, he was branded a mankiller and a badman.

The real Wyatt led a life that was authentically Western. He was a gambler and a saloonkeeper, and he enjoyed the charms of several women, even leaving his common-law wife to take up with a dancer. Most of all, he was as tough as men came when toughness earned respect. He was loved and hated, a man who drew strong allegiances and made devoted enemies. Wyatt Earp was a natural leader with a coterie of followers and friends who always believed he did right. He believed it, too.

He was not a mankiller who delighted in death, and he was never a gunfighter, at least in the sense that later movie generations would understand the word. He fought only two standup gunfights, one with a pistol and the other with a shotgun. There were no fast draws, no fancy shooting. Wyatt Earp faced a challenge and responded. He never really understood what he had done by becoming a law unto himself, and he did not spend much time analyzing the issue. His heart told him he had killed to save lives, and that did not make him a man killer. History, and history by Hollywood, would pass its own judgments.

By the time he reached his seventh decade, the old stories returned to torment him. Magazine tales and books appeared accusing him of horrible crimes, and he finally told his story. He could never know that nothing he could say or do would end the controversy over Tombstone. He had become the fulcrum of an issue that would be passionately argued for generations after his death. Wyatt Earp could never escape the legacy of Tombstone, and Tombstone remained ingrained in the American consciousness.

COWTOWN JUSTICE

NICHOLAS PORTER EARP, a widower with one son, married Virginia Cooksey in 1840, and five years later moved the family from Kentucky to Monmouth, Illinois. He arrived about the time the Mexican War broke out and quickly enlisted in the company commanded by Wyatt Berry Stapp. His military career ended abruptly with a kick in the groin from a mule. Returning to Illinois a wounded veteran, he worked in Monmouth as a farmer, harness maker, and sometimes justice of the peace, never really finding contentment while all that empty land in the West seemed to be calling as the family kept growing. On March 19, 1848, with the birth of his fourth son, Nick paid tribute to his old captain, naming the baby Wyatt Berry Stapp Earp.

Two years later the Earps moved again, landing in Pella, Iowa, where Wyatt's younger brothers, Morgan and Warren, were born. The growing family remained settled until the Civil War broke out. Elder brothers James and Virgil and half-brother Newton went off to fight for the Union, and James took a musket ball through the left shoulder and spent seventeen months in military hospitals before returning to the family. Wyatt would later tell stories of how he tried to run away and join the army, only to have his father find him and bring him back. Nick had made enough contributions to the cause. He was taking his family away from the action. Wyatt was 16 when the family, including wounded brother James, headed to California in 1864, leaving older brother Virgil fighting in the Civil War. Young Wyatt assumed a man's role on the trip, serving as a hunter and helping to fend off two Indian raids on the train of forty wagons.[1] With all this moving, Wyatt had little time for formal schooling, although he did learn reading and writing along the way.

Virgil returned from the Civil War and joined the family in southern California's San Bernardino County, where Wyatt learned to hate plowing, hoeing, and just about everything else connected with farming. Obviously, this did not much please his father, and the teenaged Wyatt knew it was time to leave farming and find another way to make a living. He joined Virgil working on freight wagons between southern California and Salt Lake City, and on another line to Prescott, Arizona. Young Wyatt worked as a swamper, doing the menial tasks, helping with loading, and probably took a few turns at driving the teams.[2]

The ever-restless Nicholas decided to move the family back to Iowa in 1868, then on to the little town of Lamar in Missouri. Wyatt, after completing his contract with a freighter, dutifully returned to plowing and hoeing, at least temporarily. In this midwestern farm town he found a job much more to his liking. For the first time, he pinned on a badge. On March 3, 1870, he received the appointment of constable in the tranquil little town. His life seemed headed in the right direction. Two months earlier, on January 3, he had married a local woman named Urilla Sutherland, whose father owned Lamar's hotel.[3]

The biggest controversy Earp faced as constable was a civic dispute over whether the lawmen should be responsible for herding away hogs that ran loose on the street. Nicholas Earp ran for the board of trustees on a ticket opposed to shutting up the pigs. Nicholas won, a victory for both the Earp and porcine families. There were other problems in Lamar. At one point an arsonist set the school on fire, and shortly after Wyatt Earp's appointment he had to handle two inebriated brothers. The duo got roaring drunk on a June night, then went wandering the streets until the young constable "found one of them upon the street incapable of taking care of himself and took him down to a stone building which he has appropriated for the use of just such customers. As Mr. Earp was about turning the key upon his bird the other one came staggering up, enquiring for his lost brother. Mr. Earp opened the door and slid him in."[4]

Leaving the makeshift jail, Wyatt met "another hard case in the shape of a tramping butcher who asked Mr. Earp to purchase him a lead pencil in place of one he alleged Mr. Earp had borrowed from him some time previous. Mr. Earp enticed him down to the stone building and procured him a pencil, and of course he shared the fate of the other two. There being a hole in the roof of the building, the three caged birds managed to crawl out before morning, and the stranger not liking the reception he met with here, left for parts unknown. The other two were brought before Esq. Earp, and fined $5 and costs, each. A few more examples, and the town will be better for it."[5]

Wyatt declared his intentions to run for his constable's post, and surprisingly his older half-brother, Newton, emerged as his top opponent. In November, Wyatt won, 137–108, the only time he would ever run for office. Wyatt's tranquillity in Lamar was disrupted shortly after the election. Less than a year after his marriage—the exact date is unknown—Urilla died suddenly. The cause is uncertain; some reports say typhoid, others say she died in childbirth with a stillborn baby. For reasons obscured by time, Wyatt, with brothers James, Virgil, and Morgan, engaged in a street fight with Urilla's two brothers, Fred and Bert Sutherland, and their friends the Brummett boys, Granville, Loyd, and Jordan. Both sides emerged bruised, battered, but alive. The cause of the brawl has never been determined.

A few months later, Earp left town and left behind a mystery. James Cromwell charged that he had paid Wyatt $75 for an execution of the court, and that Wyatt erased the "7" and replaced it with a "5". The implication was that Wyatt pocketed $20, a significant sum in those days. Cromwell brought charges against Wyatt and his bondsman, James Maupin, plus Nicholas Earp and his Methodist minister brother Jonathan. Records do not indicate why Nicholas and Jonathan would be involved in the action. When the court ordered the new constable to find Wyatt and Nicholas for a hearing, they had already sold their property and left Lamar, never to return. Jonathan Earp and Maupin did show up at the hearing, and were found not guilty. The case was appealed and dismissed. It has never been established whether the legendary lawman was guilty or innocent of a $20 fraud, and as with just about everything else in Lamar, details are sparse and rumors rampant.[6] Wyatt Earp never said much about his Lamar days, going to the extent of writing relatives not to talk to biographer Stuart Lake about the events. He had a secret, and he succeeded in keeping it.

Wyatt Earp, now 22, left Lamar, either grief-stricken over the loss of his wife or escaping possible prosecution for fraud, and wound up in Indian Territory, now eastern Oklahoma. Almost immediately he became entangled in an incident that would trouble generations of researchers with the question of whether or not the future lawman was a horse thief. A warrant was issued on March 28, 1871, charging that Earp, Edward Kennedy, and John Shown had stolen two horses from the Keys family. The three defendants were arraigned April 14. On the same day, Shown's wife, Anna, gave a sworn statement to a U.S. commissioner charging that Earp and Kennedy had gotten her husband drunk near Fort Gibson, Indian Territory, then instructed him to ride ahead while they took two of Jim Keys's horses and hitched them to a wagon. When Earp and Kennedy caught up with John Shown, they exchanged horses, and Earp went toward Kansas. Shown was left with the two Keys horses, as he and his wife stayed behind. Jim Keys caught up to the Showns and reclaimed the horses. Anna Shown claimed that Earp and Kennedy had told Keys that her husband stole the horses. Then, ominously, Anna Shown said that Earp and Kennedy had threatened to kill her husband if he turned state's evidence.[7]

Earp and Kennedy were indicted; Kennedy stood trial and was acquitted. Earp never went to trial. Apparently the law lost interest after Kennedy's acquittal. Records of the case are so sketchy it is impossible to determine Earp's exact role and whether an actual crime was committed, although the incident in Lamar with the erased digit, the flight, and the apparent horse theft do create the suspicion that young Wyatt Earp may well have engaged in certain dubious activities after his wife's death. The records are too ambiguous to be conclusive, and Earp never discussed the incidents, but it seems likely that 23-year-old Wyatt Earp nearly found himself bound for a career that would have landed him inside a jail cell instead of guarding one.

Earp followed his year of misfortune with a period of adventure, serving as a hunter for a government surveying crew one season and a buffalo hunter another. He wintered on the Salt Fork of the Arkansas River in 1871, where he met two young brothers, Ed and Bat Masterson, both future lawmen, and began a friendship that would continue for years. While Earp lived the life of a foot-loose wanderer, a new industry emerged on the frontier, trade in cattle spurring the creation of towns dedicated to cow commerce. As the railroad tracks stretched westward, little towns seemed to burst from the prairie as the meeting points for the cattle trails and the railroads. Longhorns would be driven north from Texas to hit the burgeoning towns, then allowed to graze and fatten up before being loaded on trains bound east or driven to other points for sale. The cattle trade quickly became a high-profit business for merchants with enough foresight and luck to locate their saloon or dry goods store in the town that would become a hub of commerce; it also had its rough side, with dozens of Texas drovers roaring into town after months on the trail, where they were greeted by an element more than eager to take their cash.

"Saloons, gambling-joints and honkey-tonks of the northern towns had one main purpose in view—the taking of the visiting cattleman's money as quickly as possible," recalled drover Frank Murphy. "The games were crooked; the cowboys, whose wages were but a dollar a day, were charged 50 cents a dance and every dance was short. It needed but a day or two in town and the cowboys would be picked clean by these human vultures. Fed the most horrible whisky ever distilled, cheated at every turn, it is little to be wondered at that the Texans, none too even of temper at best, were now and then prone to be quarrelsome."[8] In the infancy of the cattle trade, the toughest, wildest, and most prosperous town at the end of the trail was a little spot in central Kansas named Ellsworth.

The cow trade happened quickly to Ellsworth. Little more than a trading post in 1868, by 1871 the town had become the primary shipping and receiving point for Texas longhorns, and the home, at least temporarily, of the gamblers, prostitutes, and others who fed off drovers with a few dollars in their pockets. The merchants knew they had to have tough officers to keep order in a town primed for trouble. In June of 1873, a few drovers awakened the town by shooting at a few signs, and the officials beefed up the police force to five officers, all reputedly experienced gun hands, under Marshal John Norton, called Brocky Jack because of his pockmarked face. "Every man on the force was a bribe taker and a villain. Every man on the force would kill on the slightest provocation, if he felt his hide was safe in doing so," Ellsworth lawyer Ira E. Lloyd recalled in his memoir. Norton's oddest deputy was a sour and dangerous drifter named John Morco, nicknamed Happy Jack. He was evading criminal charges in Portland, Oregon, apparently for killing four men who tried to interfere when Jack was beating his wife.[9] Morco had been arrested for vagrancy on June 9 in Ellsworth. "Happy Jack was a drunkard, a brawler, and brave where there was no danger," Lloyd said.[10] The only officer who developed a rapport with the Texas drovers was John DeLong, whom Norton laid off when he had to cut the force from five to four in July.

Brocky Jack's aggressive crew made violations out of minor infractions and began arresting gamblers with regularity. Among the cardplayers arrested were brothers Ben and Billy Thompson, English by birth and Texans by choice, who were charged with somewhat vague infractions—carrying deadly weapons, being drunk, conducting themselves in a disorderly manner, disturbing the peace—and escorted roughly across the town plaza to draw fines ranging from $15 to $35. This surprised many, since the Thompsons were already notorious as tough gun hands and had tangled with Wild Bill Hickok in Abilene, the first of the cattle towns. The Thompsons were not alone in drawing the wrath of Norton's police force. "Daily from five to thirty men were arrested and brought before the police magistrate," Lloyd said. "Many were fined. Many were discharged. But it is safe to say that perhaps many or most were arrested with an idea of blackmail." The biggest targets seemed to be gamblers who had won money from the officers.

The other law enforcement officer in Ellsworth was 31-year-old county sheriff Chauncey Beldon Whitney, who enjoyed far more respect among the Texas drovers and upheld the law with a more even hand. Whitney had served as a civilian scout for the army in a celebrated Indian fight at Beecher's Island in eastern Colorado. Since Whitney's primary duty in Ellsworth was to keep order in the outer areas of the county, he played a secondary role to Brocky Jack within the confines of Ellsworth. Whitney had little control over a situation that was daily growing more explosive through the hot summer. One day in August, the anger came to a climax when Billy Thompson had too much to drink.

The brothers Thompson were gambling in Brennan's saloon with policeman Happy Jack and John Stirling [or Sterling]. Stirling and Ben Thompson had a dispute over the game, and Stirling struck Ben in the face. A voice, probably Happy Jack's, yelled out, "Get your guns, you damned Texas sons of bitches, and fight." Both sides grabbed their iron and started arguing. Outside, they walked the streets, firing a couple of errant shots. The confrontation was about to erupt into a battle when Sheriff Whitney rushed in to defuse the situation. Whitney, along with former policeman John DeLong, approached Ben Thompson and said, "Boys, don't have any row. I will do all I can to protect you. You know John and I are your friends."

In typical frontier fashion, Whitney invited the Thompsons to join him for a drink at Brennan's to talk out the trouble. According to Ben Thompson's story, Billy kept his shotgun, agreeing to put it up when they reached the saloon. Billy carried it with the hammers up, ready to fire if the need arose. Happy Jack suddenly stepped out, toting a six-shooter in each hand, then ducked behind a building as Ben pulled his gun, fired, and missed. The drunken Billy lifted his shotgun and fired, hitting Whitney in the shoulder.

"My God, Billy, you have shot me," Whitney yelled.

Ben Thompson, in shock, looked at his brother and said, "My God, you have shot our best friend." The wound would prove fatal.

Ben tried to get Billy to leave town quickly. Billy rode out slowly, seemingly inviting a fight. Mayor James Miller ran out and ordered Ben to surrender his arms. Ben kept his guns, and the streets filled with armed Texans ready to defend him. For more than an hour, the band congregated on one side of the street, awaiting a move from the remaining Ellsworth lawmen. Marshal Brocky Jack and policemen Ed Hogue and Happy Jack just stood and watched, and Mayor Miller responded by discharging the entire force.[11]

What happened next is one of the great murky points of frontier history. Stuart Lake, Earp's biographer, told a glorious story of Wyatt accepting the appointment of town marshal on the spot and boldly heading up the street to Thompson, surrounded by a horde of Texas gunslingers. Showing no fear, Wyatt walked forward alone into the nest of gun barrels, threatening yet conciliatory as he talked Thompson into surrendering.

> "Come on," Wyatt ordered. "Throw down your gun or make your fight."
>
> Ben Thompson grinned.
>
> Wyatt Earp's guns were still in their holsters. Now, for the first time, his hand went to his right hip.
>
> "You fellows get back!" he ordered the Texas men. "Move!"

As they obeyed, Wyatt stepped up to Thompson and unbuckled his prisoner's gunbelts.

"Come on, Ben," he said. "We'll go over to the calaboose."

With the famous Thompson six-guns dangling from their belts in his left hand, Wyatt marched his prisoner across the plaza to Judge V. B. Osborne's court. Until he reached the entrance, no onlookers spoke to him, or moved to follow.[12]

By Lake's account, Ben Thompson got off with a $25 fine, and a disgusted Wyatt Earp turned back his badge when offered the permanent job of marshal. "Ellsworth figures sheriffs at twenty-five dollars a head. I don't figure the town's my size," he said.

Almost immediately after Lake's book appeared in 1931, this incident began troubling researchers. Floyd B. Streeter, the dean of Kansas historians, began checking and found the newspaper records and all the trial data when Billy Thompson was arrested three years after the shooting. The name of Wyatt Earp never appears. In 1950, Streeter made his feelings clear in a letter to University of Oklahoma professor Walter S. Campbell, who wrote under the name Stanley Vestal: "I question the accuracy of Lake's book, so do not use it to any extent. I checked up on his Ellsworth and Wichita stories and found a considerable portion of the narrative was fiction."[13]

While Lake probably embroidered the episode in Ellsworth, there are reasons to believe that Wyatt Earp did step in and mollify a tense situation. William Box Hancock, who helped drive herds to Kansas, said he had heard the story that Earp "was appointed city marshal by the mayor of Ellsworth, Kansas, when the notorious Ben Thompson had threatened to kill everybody in town. [Earp] arrested him and put him in jail."[14]

There are other clues of Earp's involvement in Ellsworth: Wichita deputy Dick Cogdell would say in a story picked up nationally in 1896 that Earp had been marshal in Ellsworth, and Earp would make reference to arresting Ben Thompson in a 1928 letter to Lake. Earp's pattern was to cover up his misdeeds, not to create false glory. And, before Earp's death, Lake wrote letters to Kansas to try to find details on the Ellsworth affair.

When Sadie Earp, Wyatt's third wife, was consulted on her biography in the late 1930s, she said she asked her husband about his encounter with Ben Thompson. "Well," she quotes Wyatt as saying, "I thought he would shoot me. I really expected to be killed unless I could see his wrist move in time to draw and fire before he would pull the trigger. But that's the chance any officer has to take, and for the time being I was taking the place of an officer. But I wouldn't stop for that because I couldn't bear to see him get away with what he was doing. People have a right to live in peace and he was protecting the getaway of his brother who for pure meanness had killed a good man."[15]

When Sadie asked him for further details, he said only, "Oh, I just kept looking him in the eye as I walked toward him. And when he started talking to me I was pretty sure I had him. I tried to talk in as pleasant a voice as I could manage and I told him to throw his gun in the road. He did and that's all there was to it."

Sadie Earp said she heard the story from Bat Masterson, who talked with Thompson and said the English gambler never held a grudge against Wyatt.

Sadie also described a cordial meeting years later when Wyatt and Ben Thompson exchanged friendly words in Texas.

While the exact story is unclear, it seems likely Wyatt Earp did in some way intercede to prevent a showdown between Ben Thompson and the citizens of Ellsworth, and the newspaper failed to accurately report the story, possibly because in the frenzy of activity the details never came clear or because the editors were intimidated by the police force. Earp is not mentioned in the court documents of Billy Thompson's trial, but prosecutors did not concern themselves with the events after the shooting of Whitney: the details of Ben Thompson's arrest were not relevant to the trial and were not discussed in court.

The disarming probably was not nearly as dramatic as Lake's version of the story. Perhaps Earp simply walked over to talk with Ben Thompson, telling him the only thing that made sense was to surrender and avoid bloodshed. Thompson obviously did not want problems and probably just sought a face-saving way out of the mess. Wyatt Earp likely gave him one. Thompson came out the big winner, having to pay only a small fine for standing off the town.

The story apparently circulated among the drovers so that young William Box Hancock would hear it from other Texans and repeat it as fact a half-century later. While the details and absolute authentication still lurk in the mists of history, it seems Wyatt Earp's reputation began as a peacemaker in Ellsworth.

TEXAS CATTLE COULD TURN TO GOLD along the railroad lines of western Kansas, and cowtown entrepreneurs wanted their share of the business. Every herd that graced their town meant more dollars flowing into the dry goods stores and restaurants, the saloons and brothels. Every herd delivered helped make the cowtown grow as a center of commerce rather than remain a little prairie hamlet selling seed to farmers. Growth would bring business, business would bring prosperity. By the mid-1870s the trade became so lucrative that towns began competing, sending out salesmen to lure the cattle bosses with promises or payments.

First Abilene, then Ellsworth boomed and faded as the rail lines cut across Kansas. By 1872 another dusty little town emerged with aspirations of grandeur. From the horizon, Wichita seemed to rise from a sea of grass on the prairie, a collection of buildings straddling the banks of the Arkansas River. Wichita proper sat on the east bank; across the river was Delano, with a cluster of saloons, gambling dens, brothels, and dance halls to attract the drovers looking for a way to rid themselves of the money they earned on the trip north. For a town to become a cattle hub, it needed entertainments to amuse the boys, and Wichita's suburb had its share of vice, technically beyond the control of town police. The *St. Louis Republican* described the scene: "Wichita resembles a brevet hell after sundown. Brass bands whooping it up, harlots and hack drivers yelling and cursing; dogs yelping, pistols going off; bull-whackers cracking their whips; saloons open wide their doors, and gayly attired females thump and drum up pianos, and in dulcet tones and mocking smiles invite the boys in and night is commenced in earnest."[16] Among the town's sundry other excitements were races staged by naked belles of the demimonde, dashing through Delano as the on-lookers bet on the winners. There were wild nights in this corner of the wild West, all to keep the drovers entertained and spending their cash.

Into this scene came young Wyatt Earp. He had never seen this type of wildness, the kind reserved for few places outside San Francisco's Barbary Coast, and he must have been taken with the opportunities. By 1874, Wyatt's older brother Jim and his wife, Bessie, along with Wyatt, settled into the cow-town life of Wichita. It is likely that here Wyatt learned the skills of gambling, a natural for a young man who was unusually quick of hand and mind, brimming with the nerve to make the big bet. He was 26 years old and filling out to 6 feet and 180 pounds with an athletic build and natural strength. Rugged, bright, and clever, he was the image of a frontier lawman with at least some reputation trail-ing him from his dealings with Ben Thompson. Despite his relative youth, he had an aura of authority about him, a solemnity and bearing that commanded a situation. He rarely laughed or even broke a smile. He was all business when he was going about his business.

Wichita deputy Jimmy Cairns recalled that town marshal Bill Smith saw Earp and chose him for an officer because of his physique and appearance. Cairns said that when he and Smith approached Earp to discuss the job, Earp quickly agreed to wear a deputy's badge.[17] While official records do not show him appointed to the force until April 21, 1875, there is evidence that he served in some capacity during the 1874 cattle season. The farm boy quickly found him-self a deputy in a tough town, where the police faced a complex task. Officers had to preserve peace and keep some degree of order without becoming so tough they would scare off the trade. Obviously, cattle bosses would be less in-clined to choose a shipping point so dangerous that they could expect their drovers and perhaps themselves to wind up in jail or even dead. Merchants wanted the trade, and dead drovers were bad for business. Ellsworth's mistakes in hiring the two Jacks for their police force had brought more problems than solutions, and Marshal Smith seemed to have a far better comprehension of the situation. His officers were tough, not deadly.

In May of 1874, Wichita resident Charley Sanders, an African American hod carrier, returned to his house to find two Texans bothering his wife. Sanders responded by beating the drovers badly and tossing them bodily from his house. According to Cairns, the cowhands were wild with rage: taking such a beating from a black man was unthinkable. They returned to their camp outside town and gathered a group to plan retribution. A cowhand referred to as Shorty Ram-sey received the "honor" of being the triggerman. The next day, May 27, the group drifted into town, two at a time to avoid drawing attention. Sanders was working on a building being constructed in the downtown area. Ramsey stepped forward, shot Sanders twice, one bullet grazing the skull and the other going through the rib cage, mounted his horse, and rode out of the city yelling and flourishing his revolver. A gang of Ramsey's Texas friends followed him to the bridge across the Arkansas River, quickly located Smith, and held their drawn revolvers on the helpless marshal to prevent him from taking action. Smith's in-action led the *Wichita Eagle* to call for a reorganization of the police department, which may have led to adding young Wyatt Earp to the force. The marshal's helplessness in the situation also apparently disappointed Earp and led him to question Smith's competence in a tough situation.[18]

A few weeks later, Wyatt Earp would meet a major test as a peacekeeper when a few drovers decided to take out their revenge on the town. As Earp biographer Stuart Lake told the story, a brothel keeper known as Ida May, "the high priestess of the Cyprian Sisterhood in Wichita," purchased a piano in Kansas City for $1,000 and paid the first $250 before turning away all other visits from bill collectors. Earp took four tough men into the saloon and began to repossess the piano, chastising the Texans for being too cheap to help their hostess pay her debts. This led to the assorted patrons passing the hat to collect the remaining $750. Earp left, warning the drovers not to head into anything they couldn't buy themselves out of. Earp's comment and manner infuriated the drunken drovers.[19]

Cairns could never forget the events that followed. A mob of nearly fifty men, made up of cattle bosses and their hands, banded together in Delano, across the bridge from Wichita, while Earp and the other officers led a group of citizens through the streets of town to meet them. As Earp's party approached the bridge, the Wichita defenders scattered so as not to be easy targets. Mannen Clements, a cousin of gunman John Wesley Hardin, served as leader of the cattlemen. According to Cairns, Clements was "by no means classified as a 'bad man,' but had the peculiar psychology of most of the early day cattle handlers that caused them to use violence at times in an effort to have their own way."

The Texas men rode onto the bridge, their horses clapping hooves against the wooden planking. Clements saw Earp's spread-out force across the river, and Cairns recalled the cattlemen drawing their guns, ready for action. The two forces halted within speaking distance, the cowboys defiant and the townsmen determined to hold their ground. Any wrong move could have led to a deadly battle. Earp stood in the center of the line of defenders and calmly called for Clements to put away his guns. When Clements failed to comply, Earp said, "Mind me now, Mannen, put up those guns and go on home." Clements paused for a moment, then slipped his pistol back in the holster before turning his horse back across the bridge. What could have been war ended quietly, defused by Earp's steadiness under pressure and calm in a tense situation. "Wyatt certainly had a way with men," said Cairns.

Wyatt Earp understood his duty as a lawman was to prevent trouble, not ignite it. Law enforcement meant keeping the peace more than solving crimes or hunting down wrongdoers, because the cowtowns were not so much centers of criminality as they were wild areas subject to the instant outbreak of disorder. The police had to keep the drovers and townsmen from killing each other at night so they could do business the next day. The Wichita police would not tolerate man killers on the force.

Earp did branch out into a little debt collection in October of 1874 when a cattle outfit left Wichita with a mass of unpaid bills. M. R. Moser, who lost a new wagon to the drovers, either hired or convinced Earp and John Behrens, both identified as officers, to trail them. "Those boys fear nothing and fear nobody," the *Wichita City Eagle* said. Earp and Behrens rode across the prairie almost to Indian Territory, when they caught the indebted drovers. The *Eagle* reported: "To make a long and exciting story short, they just leveled a shotgun and six-shooter upon the scalawags as they lay concealed in some brush and told them to 'dough over,' which they did, to the amount of $146, one of them remarking that he was not going to die for the price of a wagon. It is amusing to hear Moser tell how slick the boys did the work."[20]

Earp's exact role as an officer during 1874 is unclear. Records do not identify him as a member of Marshal Smith's police department, though several newspaper stories refer to him as "Officer Erp." Wyatt could have served as a part-time officer, appointed for work during the cattle seasons, or he may have been a member of the special reserves that served almost as an auxiliary of the police force. Both Morgan and Virgil joined their brothers Wyatt and Jim at times in Wichita, and Virgil apparently acted as a member of the special reserves.[21] During his first year in the cowtown, between police duties, Wyatt probably worked in one of the keno parlors, gambling houses where bettors played a bingo-like game. It was common for the parlors to hire tough dealers capable of keeping order.

Jim Earp and his wife, Bessie, had their own activities to keep them busy. Jim worked in saloons while Bessie engaged in the brothel business, not an unusual situation for cowtown couples of the saloon crowd. Court records show that Bessie and a Sally Earp were repeatedly prosecuted for prostitution, with arrests starting in May of 1874 and continuing for nearly a year. On June 3, 1874, Sally and Bessie were arrested on the complaint of Samuel A. Martin, who swore that they did: "Set up and Keep a bawdy house or brothel and did appear and act as Mistresses and have the care and management of a certain one story frame building Situated and located north of Douglas Avenue near the Bridge leading across the Arkansas River used and Kept by Said parties as a house of prostitution in the City of Wichita." The 1875 census lists Jim Earp's wife as Bessie, in the profession of sporting—a common way of referring to prostitution—and it is most likely the Earps were supplementing their income with a few brothel-house transactions. Mysterious other women identified as Earps—or Earbs—also show up on the docket books. Eva, Kate, and Minnie all identified themselves as Earps on court records.[22] The assumption must be that the women of the house took the madam's name to protect their own identity, not an unusual ploy for women in this trade.

Prostitution played a strange role in Wichita. Officially, it was illegal, and in fact there was a concerted effort to isolate it in the vice district of Delano across the river. Wichita proper did have two legal brothels, Bessie's not among them, and several freelancers. Most prostitution arrests were considered simply the equivalent of licensing fees, an unpleasant necessity of the business. The civic leaders of these freshly born cowtowns understood that such activities were necessary to keep the herders finding their way to Wichita.

Wyatt's role in brothel activities is open to speculation, but he could not have been happy about the arrest of his sister-in-law and her sisters in sin. He may also not have been pleased with Marshal Smith for never naming him officially to the police force, although he was serving in some capacity. And Smith's handling of the Shorty Ramsey flight had been unimpressive. Whatever the reason, Earp and Smith would not remain the best of friends.

Wichita faced an important election in April of 1875, with Smith trying to keep his job in the race against former marshal Mike Meagher and the assistant marshal, Dan Parks. Meagher had been appointed city marshal in 1871 and served until April of '74, when a new city council decided to replace him with Smith, whose impressive detective work in solving a murder case had drawn much local praise. Meagher spent a year serving in the low-paying job of deputy U.S. marshal before returning to Wichita to run for his old job. Meagher won easily, drawing 340 votes to Parks's 311 and only 65 for Smith. On April 21, the new city council approved a police force of Assistant Marshal John Behrens and deputies Jimmy Cairns and Wyatt Earp. Cairns was dropped from the force at the end of the cattle season.[23]

Deputy Earp piled up an impressive list of achievements during his tenure as a Wichita lawman; and, most important, there were no major outbreaks of violence or rowdyism. For the most part, cowtown violence flared up after too much whiskey and too liberal a use of six-shooters. There were shootings and few killings, and planned crime was a rarity. There was only a trickle of crime, not a wave, and the police were always ready to act. In May of 1875, Deputy Earp called the bluff of a horse thief.

While making his usual nightly rounds, Earp ran across a man whose appearance and dress answered the description of W. W. Compton, wanted for stealing two horses and a mule in Coffey County. Wyatt asked the stranger's name; "Jones" came the stranger's unconvincing response. Earp took "Mr. Jones" to a saloon called the Gold Room to make a more complete examination under lamplight. The stranger turned and ran out, with Earp in pursuit. Earp paused and fired a warning shot; the stranger stopped immediately. As Earp escorted his prisoner to jail, he acknowledged his true identity as Compton, wanted for horse theft. Investigation showed Compton had stored a black horse and a buggy, which he had traded for the stolen horses. The *Wichita Beacon* editorialized: "He will probably have an opportunity to do the state some service for a number of years, only to come out and go to horse stealing again, until a piece of twisted hemp or a stray bullet puts an end to his hankering after horse flesh."[24]

The young deputy earned civic acclaim in December when he found a drunk in the street carrying $500. The drunk awoke in jail the next morning, with his bankroll intact. The *Beacon* said: "He may congratulate himself that his lines, while he was drunk, were cast in such a pleasant place as Wichita as there are but few other places where that $500 roll would ever been heard from. The integrity of our police force has never been seriously questioned."[25]

The two incidents say much of Wyatt Earp as an officer. He would have faced little recrimination for shooting Compton, a criminal in flight. Instead he fired a warning shot and took the horse thief to jail. In the incident of the drunk, Earp could easily have taken the cash, with the potted victim none the wiser. He was neither dishonest nor murderous when he patrolled the streets of Wichita, and he was alert enough to be aware of criminals who might be passing through the area. He was both competent and effective.

Most of Earp's police duties in Wichita were far more prosaic than facing down Clements and the cowmen. He inspected chimneys, swept the sidewalks, and dragged out dead animals. He and the other officers also tried to control the packs of wild, yapping dogs that infested the area. The police were charged with doing sidewalk repairs, so Earp—the low man on the force—would have to haul out his hammer and nails to replace broken planks in the sidewalk. Being a cowtown cop was not always glamorous. Earp also had a moment of true embarrassment. On January 9 of 1876 Wyatt Earp nearly shot himself when his pistol dropped from his holster. He was sitting in the back room of the Custom House Saloon when the gun fell out, hit a chair, and sent a ball through Wyatt's coat.[26]

Earp's police term in Wichita ended dramatically on April 2, 1876, when he took a too active interest in the second marshal's race between Meagher and Bill Smith. Apparently Smith had said that if Meagher was reelected, he would place Earp's brothers on the police force. Virgil and Morgan had both been in Wichita during the past year. What else Smith said is subject for speculation, but he could have tried to turn Bessie's brothel into an issue as well. He may have chosen to run his campaign against Wyatt Earp, since he knew he would have little chance of beating Meagher without a campaign issue. Wichita's citizens were growing discontented with the thriving vice trade, and a deputy with family in the flesh business would have been enough to draw attention. The *Beacon* said, "The remarks that Smith was said to have made in regard to the marshal sending for Erp's [*sic*] brothers to put them on the police force furnished no just grounds for an attack, and upon ordinary occasions we doubt if Erp would have given them a second thought." Meagher ordered Earp to stay away from Smith, but Wyatt decided to go see the former marshal and settle things. Earp was settling them with his fists when Meagher arrived to pull the young officer off Smith before Wyatt did serious damage.

Meagher had no choice but to fire Earp and arrest him for disturbing the peace. Wyatt received a hefty $30 fine—about two weeks' wages. In reporting Earp's firing, the *Beacon* said: "It is but justice to Erp to say he has made an excellent officer, and hitherto his conduct has been unexceptionable."[27] Meagher easily won reelection and two weeks later, with a new city council in place, tried to reappoint Earp to the police force. On April 19, the council voted two in favor and six against Earp's reinstatement. Apparently Meagher or a councilman spoke in Earp's favor and convinced the body to reconsider young Wyatt. This time the vote tied at 4–4, and the measure was tabled with Earp unemployed. Wyatt apparently remained with the police in some capacity through part of April, since the council approved payment to him of $40 for 20 days' work, but the board also ordered an investigation of unauthorized persons collecting money due the city.

On May 10, the council ordered that the vagrancy act be enforced against "the 2 Erps" and that Wyatt Earp and John Behrens not be paid until all cash collected by them for the city was turned over to the city treasurer. Apparently they complied, because no further effort was made to collect. The identity of the two Earps is not specified—it could have been two of Bessie's doves or an attempt to move Wyatt out of town. Within two weeks he was gone, with a job offer from another cowtown. The cattle trade had diminished in Wichita in 1876. The railroads were again moving west, and settlers kept filling the prairie around Wichita to plow the ground that had once served as grazing land for Texas cattle moving north.

Wyatt Earp's stint as a Wichita lawman had been impressive. Dick Cogdell, who succeeded Meagher as police chief, would say twenty-one years later: "Earp is a man who never smiled or laughed. He was the most fearless man I ever saw. . . . He is an honest man. All officers here who were associated with him declare that he is honest, and would have decided according to his belief in the face of an arsenal."[28]

Cairns also paid him tribute: "Wyatt Earp was a wonderful officer. He was game to the last ditch and apparently afraid of nothing. The cowmen all respected him and seemed to recognize his superiority and authority at such times as he had to use it."

Quiet, unsmiling, and ever nervy, Wyatt Earp had been a highly competent deputy in a tough situation. He had helped keep the peace in Wichita, and he never had to take a life in the process.

WITH THE RAILROAD TRACKS PUSHING WEST through Kansas, two liquor dealers saw a chance to turn a quick profit by building a little tent store near the Arkansas River, out in the midst of buffalo country, to provide drinks for both the railroad men and the hunters. The village in the southwest corner of Kansas boomed quickly, developing into a center for buffalo hunters by 1872. With the cattle trade moving west as settlers filled the land around the other cowtowns, Dodge City emerged by the mid-1870s as the new site of cattle commerce. A collection of wooden saloons, stores, and houses sprouted on a gentle bluff that rose above the Arkansas River, looking out on a seemingly unending expanse of buffalo grass spreading in all directions.

The town had been established by liquor dealers and saloon owners, and whiskey merchants controlled its politics. Texas drovers could find just about any pleasure they could imagine in Dodge, from enough cheap liquor to keep up a two-day drunk to cheap women ready to entertain them. Almost immediately, and probably inevitably, Dodge fell into political factionalism. A group called "The Gang" seemed to dominate local politics and controlled most of the early elections. Bob Wright, a hotel and dry goods store owner, acted as a political power who rarely chose to intercede but carried authority when he did. The day-to-day running of local politics fell to James H. Kelley, nicknamed Dog for the band of racing greyhounds he owned. The Irish immigrant had served with the Confederacy during the war and fought Indians with Custer before arriving in Kansas. He presented an unkempt appearance, wearing a handlebar mustache over his receding chin; an often-ratty top hat was his usual choice of headgear. Kelley and his partner Peter L. Beatty ran the Alhambra Saloon, one of the most popular dens in Dodge. Liquor dealer George Hoover led the political opposition, which carried no title, and drew the support of the growing German population that had settled around Dodge and begun farming sparsely settled Ford County. Three-hundred-pound Larry Deger, the son of a German immigrant, stood as one of the leaders of the community and held some political strength.

Dodge would soon wear the label "Queen of the Cowtowns," but it was still a princess in April of 1876 when a reporter for the *Atchison Daily Champion* arrived in the four-year-old town brimming with saloons, brothels, gambling dens, and dance halls. If Wichita was wicked, Dodge was Sodom itself, with no pretense of being anything else. The reporter tried to capture the city in a poem:

Did you ever hear of Dodge City,
   Where nearly every house is a shanty,
And the roughs sing this queer little ditty
   "Take a hand pard? —quarter ante."
Where killing a man is no sin,
   And stealings are branded as jokes.
Where the principal commerce is gin,
   And the law is but a terrible hoax.

Lawlessness reigned beyond the control of the weak police force, which had changed marshals several times. The Atchison reporter described a town "infested principally with gamblers, horse thieves, prostitutes and murderers, who look upon the law as a huge joke. . . . The arm of the law is palsied and hangs powerless by the side of Justice, who stands away in the background like the statue of a forlorn and helpless exile. Horse thieves, burglars, peace disturbers and even murderers go at large."[29] Young and wild, Dodge City had become a town spinning out of control.

With German immigrant support, George Hoover won the mayoral election in April of '76 and immediately appointed the gigantic Deger as marshal in the town where law enforcement had become a "terrible hoax." Hoover apparently had another plan to strengthen the police force. In May he sent out the call for the well-known deputy who had just been fired in Wichita. Earp said he had been recruited to take the marshalship, not the deputy job.[30] However, the only surviving issue of the *Dodge City Times* for 1876 lists Deger as marshal and Earp as "assistant marshal." Lake's version would say that the mayor had appointed Jack Allen to serve as Deger's assistant, but Allen was run off quickly by Texans hurrahing (shooting up) the town. Lake said Earp then received the offer to become marshal, but Hoover wanted Deger to finish the term for political reasons while Earp served as top enforcer. No other substantiation or explanation survives, but there is probably some truth to this story. The mayor, not the marshal, appointed the assistant marshal; and Deger apparently held the post more as a political plum than out of respect for his crime-fighting competence.

Earp said he insisted on the right to name deputies for the first big cattle season in Dodge, and he chose to retain Joe Mason and added Jim Masterson, one of Bat's brothers. About a week later Bat Masterson came into town, still limping from a bullet he took in a gun battle when he killed Corporal Melvin King, a U.S. Cavalry soldier and noted troublemaker. Bat Masterson had already received some degree of fame for his role in the 1874 Indian battle at Adobe Walls, where about twenty-eight buffalo hunters and traders held off the onslaught of a combined force of Kiowas, Cheyenne, and Comanches at a small trading post about 150 miles from Dodge City on the Texas Panhandle. Masterson was a native of the Canadian province of Quebec, born in 1853 and christened Bartholomew, later shortened to Bat. As a young man he changed his name to William Barclay Masterson.[31]

The spring and summer of 1876 would be Dodge's first major cattle season. No records remain to tell the story or to show Earp's exact role in Dodge City law enforcement. He is listed as assistant marshal in the October 14, 1876, *Dodge City Times*. He shows up again as assistant marshal in the next existing copy on March 24, 1877, and again on March 31 before his name is dropped from the directory of city officers. This all becomes confusing because Earp told Lake that he left the force on September 9, 1876, and traveled to Deadwood with his brother Morgan.[32] Wyatt said he spent the winter selling firewood, at a good profit, and was hired to ride guard on an ore shipment coming from the Black Hills in June.[33] The *Times* may just have left Earp in its directory after the cattle season, or Earp could have been granted the equivalent of a leave to go off cutting firewood. By June, Dodge had a new assistant marshal—Ed Masterson, another of Bat's brothers, had accepted the post as Deger's enforcer. Earp returned to Dodge City in July of '77 to an endorsement by the *Times*:

> Wyatt Earp, who was on our city police force last summer, is in town again. We hope he will accept a position on the force once more. He had a quiet way of taking the most desperate characters into custody which invariably gave one the impression that the city was able to enforce her mandates and preserve her dignity. It wasn't considered policy to draw a gun on Wyatt unless you got the drop and meant to burn powder without any preliminary talk.[34]

There is no official indication that Earp was either offered a job on the police force or served during the cattle season, although he may have been asked to help with the festivities during the Fourth of July celebration. The only other mention during the summer came later that month when Earp had a row with a noted local woman of the demimonde. "Miss Frankie Bell, who wears the belt for superiority in point of muscular ability, heaped epithets upon the unoffending head of Mr. Earp to such an extent as to provide a slap from the ex-officer, besides creating a disturbance of the quiet and dignity of the city, for which she received a night's lodging in the dog house and a reception at the police court next morning, the expense of which was about $20.00. Wyatt Earp was assessed the lowest limit of the law, one dollar."[35] While the cause of the incident remains a mystery, the sight of Wyatt Earp slapping ever-feisty Frankie Bell must have set the local tongues wagging.

By October, Earp was gone from Dodge, apparently to chase train robbers Mike Roarke and Dave Rudabaugh, perhaps as a freelance bounty hunter, perhaps at the behest of the Santa Fe Railroad. His exact role during this period is unclear, but he seems to have engaged in hunting fugitives, a lonely and dangerous way to make a living.[36] The chase took Earp through Indian Territory and into a little Texas town called Fort Griffin, where he ran into a saloonkeeper named John Shanssey, an old acquaintance from Cheyenne, Wyoming. Apparently Earp asked Shanssey about Rudabaugh and was directed to a slender man, a dentist who spent more time at the card table than over a dental chair.

This would be the first meeting between Wyatt Earp and Dr. John Henry Holliday, one of the most unusual characters of the frontier. This frail, tubercular man with ash-blond hair and deep-set blue eyes would emerge as a legendary figure even in his own lifetime. He was a peculiar combination of ruthlessness, loyalty, and good humor, jovial one minute, morose the next. Educated, intelligent, and gentlemanly, he could fly off into rages that climaxed with gunfire. No one really quite knew what to make of Doc Holliday.

"Holliday had a mean disposition and an ungovernable temper, and under the influence of liquor was a most dangerous man," Bat Masterson wrote in 1907. "Physically, Doc Holliday was a weakling who could not have whipped a healthy fifteen-year-old boy in a go-as-you-please fist fight, and no one knew this better than himself, and the knowledge of this fact was perhaps why he was so ready to resort to a weapon of some kind whenever he got himself into difficulty. He was hot-headed and impetuous and very much given to both drinking and quarreling, and, among men who did not fear him, was very much disliked. He possessed none of the qualities of leadership that distinguished such men as . . . Wyatt Earp, Billy Tilghman and other famous western characters. Holliday seemed to be absolutely unable to keep out of trouble for any great length of time. He would no sooner be out of one scrape before he was in another, and the strange part of it is he was more often in the right than in the wrong, which has rarely ever been the case with a man who is continually getting himself into trouble."[37]

San Francisco Examiner correspondent Ridgely Tilden, writing in 1882, called Holliday "as quarrelsome a man as God ever allowed to live on this earth."[38]

Life had always been one rough deal after another for Doc Holliday. Born in 1851, he grew up in Valdosta, Georgia, during the Civil War. Rumors survive of a troubled adolescence—that he shot his pistol over the heads of several former slaves swimming in a waterhole and that he participated in an aborted plan to bomb the local courthouse—but these stories cannot be documented. When he was about 18 he went off to dental college in Philadelphia, then began the practice of dentistry in Atlanta. Soon after, he moved to Texas, where he was diagnosed with consumption, the deadly disease now known as tuberculosis. The rest of his life became a race against death.

"I settled in Dallas and followed the dentistry for about five years," Holliday later said. "I attended the Methodist Church regularly. I was a member of the Methodist Church there and also a prominent member of a temperance organization till I deviated from the path of rectitude."[39]

Doc deviated about as far from rectitude as a man can go. By the time he met Wyatt Earp in Fort Griffin, he had a nasty drinking habit and a disposition that varied from playful to just plain mean. He may also have had a killing or two on his hands by the time he arrived in Fort Griffin. Holliday said he "fixed one or two" drunken Mexicans with whom he had scrapes. Holliday had also picked up with a prostitute going by the name of Kate Elder, later called "Big-Nose Kate" by Earp and his friends, most likely because she nosed into areas that were none of her business. She was actually a native Hungarian named Mary Katherine Harony who moved to Iowa before seeking a life of adventure on the frontier.

Holliday asked Earp many questions about Dodge and seemed to consider moving to the gambling mecca on the prairie. Soon after Earp left, a series of incidents would make it necessary for the dentist to find a new home. According to Earp, Holliday sat in at a faro game with a gambler named Ed Bailey, who was "monkeying with the deadwood, or what people who live in the cities call discards. Doc Holliday admonished him once or twice to 'play poker' which is your seasoned gambler's method of cautioning a friend to stop cheating—but the misguided Bailey persisted in his furtive attentions to the deadwood. Finally, having detected him again, Holliday pulled down a pot without showing his hand, which he had the perfect right to do. Thereupon Bailey started to throw his gun around on Holliday, as might have been expected. But before he could pull the trigger, Doc Holliday had jerked a knife out of his breast pocket and with one sideways sweep had caught Bailey just below the brisket."[40]

According to Earp, Holliday waited under guard in the hotel as a crowd of gamblers approached. When Big-Nose Kate learned that a lynch party was gathering, she procured two pistols, led two horses into the alley, then set a shed afire to divert attention. The plan worked perfectly. The crowd raced to douse the fire, leaving only the small guard on Holliday. Kate boldly walked in and tossed a six-shooter to Doc so they could escape with guns pointed at the constables. Doc never hesitated, and the couple rode off for Dodge City. There is no other report of this story, and Kate flatly denied it: "Just think of it! A woman weighing only one hundred and sixteen pounds standing off a deputy, ordering him to throw up his hands, disarming him, rescuing her lover and hustling him to waiting ponies. It reads fine, makes me a regular heroine, but there is not a word of truth in that fairy story."[41] The tale probably grew with the retelling as Earp or writers provided dramatic enhancements years later. There were no newspapers in Fort Griffin or records of warrants for a fleeing dentist and his paramour. But Doc and Kate were soon headed for Dodge City, where they would meet again the man who would so affect their lives.

Wyatt Earp rode on to continue his hunt for the robbers, stopping in various Texas villages before apparently trailing Mike Roarke to his hometown in Joplin, Missouri. Earp said he found a telegram waiting for him there, asking him to again pin on a badge.

JOHN BENDER, A CONDUCTOR ON THE SANTA FE RAILROAD, walked down the aisle of the train taking tickets when he came upon two toughs. Bender looked down and asked for the tickets.

"Ain't got no tickets," one of the toughs said.

"Where are you goin'?" Bender responded.

"Goin' to hell," came the insolent reply.

Unfazed, Bender had his retort ready: "Give me a dollar, cash, and get off at Dodge."

By the spring of 1878, Dodge City had matured into what a Chicago editor called "The beautiful, Bibulous Babylon of the West," a cowtown with an attitude. The village on the bluff above the Arkansas had grown to become the central shipping point for nearly all the Texas cattle coming north, which brought more business and more entertainment to the wickedest little town in the West. The railroad tracks ran down Front Street, dividing the town into two almost separate villages. To the north were the dry goods stores, boot shops, markets, and haberdasheries, the places of commerce where residents and drovers alike could find the makings of a good dinner or the clothing that would keep them warm for the winter. To the south, on a little patch of land between the tracks and the Arkansas River, a few buildings housed the entertainment trade, keeping the saloons, brothels, bawdy theaters, and dance halls separate from the more orderly sections of town and giving the Texans a place to circulate the silver dollars they had earned for two or three months in the saddle. A ramshackle wooden bridge at the end of town crossed the Arkansas to provide the route of departure for the Texas men who had spent their money and quenched their thirsts.

Comedian Eddie Foy, later to become one of America's premier vaudeville entertainers, arrived in Dodge in '78 and told of "an ugly but fascinating little town. . . . One of the most vivid of my first impressions of Dodge yet remaining is that of dust; heat, wind, and flat prairie, too, but above all dust! It had been dry for some time when we arrived, and the wind was driving clouds of yellow dust along the main street; the buildings, the horses, people's hats and clothing were covered with it."[42]

Foy settled into a cattle-season-long engagement at Ben Springer's Comique Theatre, called the "Commy-Kew" by the Texans south of the tracks. He grew to know the saloon men and the women of the brothels and dance halls, almost always dressed in ginghams and cheap prints rather than the silks and satins of big-city courtesans. Bat Masterson bought a share of the Lone Star Dance Hall, where the herders could pay outrageously for a dance with a woman who might, or occasionally might not, be doing a little body work on the side. Many of the businesses took on Texas-style names, a blatant lure for the cattle drovers coming north.

Drover William Box Hancock made his way to Dodge in the late '70s and recalled the sight: "Dodge City . . . was a wild frontier town of about thirty-five hundred people; probably the roughest little city in the United States. It was the terminus of the trail and was full of tin horn gamblers and wild women. Almost every house on the south side of the railroad was a saloon or house of ill-fame."[43]

The Gang regained control of Dodge City politics in April of 1877 when Dog Kelley won the mayor's race. He then pulled something of a surprise by reappointing Deger as marshal despite his loyalty to the Hoover faction. This may well have been a political concession to the fast-growing German population, which had become a significant voting block in rural Ford County. Kelley made sure a Gang member would be prominent in the marshal's office by appointing Ed Masterson assistant marshal. The Masterson brothers had emerged as the Gang's enforcement arm, efficiently keeping the peace and boosting the Gang's politics at the same time.

However, law enforcement became a mess during the summer of 1877. Deger ran afoul of Kelley in July, when the mayor ordered the marshal to release a prisoner. When Deger refused, Kelley immediately fired him. Deger arrested Kelley for interfering with an officer, and the two wound up in police court. The situation was smoothed over, but Deger found himself in an uncomfortable position as marshal without the support of the mayor. Ford County sheriff Charlie Bassett's term expired in November, and he could not seek reelection because of term limits. Deger and Bat Masterson emerged as the two top candidates for the job, and Bat, not quite 24, won by a 166–163 margin to take control of the most important enforcement office in the county. Bat always had an air about him, a blend of cockiness and charisma that charmed just about everyone he met, and a style that seemed to invite good times. Burly and strong, with a mustache that always appeared barber-trimmed, he usually wore citified duds topped with a derby hat.

Kelley and the council officially fired Deger in December and replaced him with Ed Masterson, then hired former sheriff Charlie Bassett as assistant marshal. Marshal Ed Masterson apparently had a difficult time preserving order. The Ford County *Globe*, which had supported Deger, wrote:

> We have heard more complaint during the past few days about parties being "held up" and robbed on our streets than ever before. How long is this thing to continue? We have one more policeman on the force now than ever before at this season of the year. It therefore seems strange that midnight robberies should be more prevalent than ever before. There is something wrong somewhere, and the people are beginning to feel that there is no legal remedy. We would like to see the town smell worse of dead highway robbers than hell does of sinners.[44]

The carrying of firearms had been banned in Dodge, and it was the marshal's duty to enforce the rule. The drovers seemed to flagrantly ignore the law in the early weeks of the 1878 cattle season. Try as he might, control of the rowdy elements seemed to slip away from Ed Masterson. His loss of control would prove fatal.

As Ed went about his usual rounds on the night of April 9, 1878, he came upon two drunken drovers named Jack Wagner and Alf Walker outside the Lady Gay dance hall on the south side of Front Street. Ed began struggling with the drunken Wagner, and from the darkness came the yell, "Ed, shove him away from you." It was Bat Masterson, off in the distance. Wagner managed to unload one shot, dead into Ed Masterson's stomach, the flash of the gun setting Ed's shirt afire. Walker, Wagner's boss, joined the fight, and five more shots quickly sounded. Onlookers dived for safety as Ed Masterson staggered through the streets. Attorney Henry Gryden stepped out of George Hoover's saloon on the north side of Front Street and saw a light flickering through the dark. He remarked, "That cigar he's smoking is burning remarkably lively." As the light grew closer, Gryden could see it was no cigar. Ed Masterson staggered, his clothes ablaze, and brushed past the attorney. Unsteadily, he stumbled into Hoover's and said to bartender George Hinkle, "George, I'm shot," then slowly dropped to the floor.

Back on the street, Wagner and Walker lay badly wounded. Wagner had taken shots to the chest and arm; Walker had a ball penetrate his lung and took several hits in his right arm. Wagner would die the next day, while Walker survived his injury. Newspapers would erroneously report that Ed Masterson had recovered to shoot his own killers. But Bat Masterson and other Dodge citizens knew Bat had entered the gunfight. In an 1885 court hearing, Bat would testify: "I shot those parties who killed my brother there in 1878—in the spring of 1878."[45]

Kelley and the town council quickly appointed Charlie Bassett to take over the marshal's office. While there is no confirmation of Earp's report that he arrived in Joplin to find a telegram from Kelley asking him to return to Dodge, calling for tough enforcer Wyatt Earp to help quiet the town follows the logic of the situation. Earp returned immediately to some public notice. "Wyatt Earp, one of the most efficient officers Dodge ever had, has just returned from Fort Worth, Texas. He was immediately appointed Asst. Marshal, by our city dads, much to their credit," the *Ford County Globe* wrote on May 14. The news spread to Wichita, where his position became exaggerated by the *Wichita Eagle.* "Wyatt Earp, well known in this city and for a long time connected with our police force, received an offer of $200 per month to take the Marshalship at Dodge City, which he went up to accept, with all its dangers and responsibilities last week."[46] Both marshals and deputies were commonly referred to simply as "marshal," which has led to general confusion. He did not receive $200 a month; he started at $75 and moved up to $100. But there were bonuses that made the job more lucrative.

In Dodge, business still revolved around the cattle trade, and officers still faced the challenge of enforcing the law without inhibiting the franchise. Earp, Bat Masterson, and the other officers developed the not so gentle art of head-banging violators with a pistol. They called it "buffaloing," and it certainly provided a more reasonable means of law enforcement than trigger pulling. Dead drovers could not drink whiskey, contribute to the faro banks, or enjoy the company of those fine taxpaying women south of Front Street.

Earp seemed to serve as the top field officer while Charlie Bassett took care of the office duties. Wyatt made more money than Bassett because city officials paid a bonus of $1 for every arrest and another dollar for every court appearance. Dodge City police records show Wyatt and policeman Jim Masterson, another of Bat's brothers, repeatedly making arrests for such offenses as carrying a pistol, drunk and disorderly behavior, and acting in an angry and violent manner. Preventive law enforcement was their means of avoiding problems. This may not jibe with today's approach, but it surely worked to keep troublemakers from acting up. The drovers came to understand quickly that they could enjoy any kind of sin they wished in Dodge City, but they could not cause trouble or they would wake up with a nasty headache and a fine from the police judge.

Andy Adams, a young rider with a cattle drive, recalled an old-timer coming into camp one day near the end of a trail drive. The veteran cowman briefed the young drovers on the rules in Dodge City:

> I've been in Dodge every summer since '77, and I can give you boys some points. Dodge is one town where the average bad man of the West not only finds his equal but finds himself badly handicapped. The buffalo hunters and range men have protested against the iron rule of Dodge's peace officers, and nearly every protest has cost human life. Don't ever get the impression that you can ride your horses into a saloon, or shoot out the lights in Dodge; it may go somewhere else, but it don't go there. So I want to warn you to behave yourselves. You can wear your six-shooters

into town, but you'd better leave them at the first place you stop, hotel, livery, or business house. And when you leave town, call for your pistols, but don't ride out shooting; omit that. Most cowboys think it's an infringement on their rights to give up shooting in town, and if it is, it stands, for your six-shooters are no match for Winchesters and buckshot; and Dodge's officers are as game a set of men as ever faced danger.[47]

Adams, writing in 1903, followed this recollection by listing the names of Dodge City's most noteworthy law officers, including Earp, the Mastersons, and Doc Holliday, and then observing: "The puppets of no romance ever written can compare with these officers in fearlessness. And let it be understood there were plenty to protest against their rule; almost daily during the range season some equally fearless individual defied them."

Earp met all challenges, without bloodshed and rarely by drawing a pistol. Always, he had that way about him of calmly taking charge of a situation and cooling tempers before they exploded. The *Ford County Globe*, which had complained about police inefficiency the previous summer, wrote on June 18, 1878, "Wyatt Earp is doing his duty as Ass't Marshal in a very creditable manner. — adding new laurels to his splendid record every day."

By early June, Doc Holliday had arrived in Dodge, showing all indications of pursuing his hand-in-mouth profession. Holliday may have been a drinker, a gambler, and a shooter, but being a dentist had a priority in his life, and he always liked the job. On June 8, 1878, he took out an ad in the *Dodge City Times:*

DENTISTRY

J.H. Holliday, Dentist, very respectfully offers his professional services to the citizens of Dodge City and surrounding country during the summer. Office at room No. 24, Dodge House. Where satisfaction is not given money will be refunded.

Earp and the dentist who offered refunds were little more than casual acquaintances when Doc and his lady friend Big-Nose Kate rolled into Dodge that spring. Earp later would say, without giving details, that Holliday saved his life. As the story can best be pieced together, in late August a Texas herder named Tobe Driskill, known to Earp in Wichita, and his partner, Ed Morrison, got drunk and started making trouble at the Comique Theatre on the south side. The drunken drovers tried to take possession of the bar when Earp and another officer entered and began pistol-whipping the Texans, clubbing wildly to take control of the saloon before the drovers took control of the whiskey. One of the Texans drew a gun and pointed at Earp's back. Holliday yelled, "Look out, Wyatt," then drew his gun and fired, most likely scaring the Texan enough to back off.[48] This would mark the beginning of a strange and remarkable friendship between the quiet, unsmiling Earp and the volatile, puckish, and often drunken dentist with a bent toward danger.

That summer of 1878 would be the most memorable of Earp's Kansas cowtown days. For the first and only time in Kansas, he may have drawn blood with his pistol. By late July the cattle season was in full swing, with the saloons serving all night and the drovers keeping the cash flowing. By three o'clock on the morning of July 26, the celebration was going full blast with the clicking, clattering poker chips in the gambling rooms and the songs from the stages. Eddie

Foy called a square dance at the Commy-Kew, while Bat Masterson dealt Spanish monte in the corner, with Doc Holliday sitting in at his table. After a long night of drinking, one of the Texans apparently had an altercation with Earp and called on his pals for assistance after he left the theater. The drovers responded with a six-gun fusillade that perforated the theater with bullets. Holliday, Masterson, and everyone else in the Commy-Kew went stomach-to-floor instantly. "The firing kept up until it seemed to me that the assailants had put hundreds of shots through the building. They shot through walls as well as windows, for a big .45 bullet would penetrate those plank walls as if they were little more than paper," Foy recalled.

The barrage of gunfire brought Earp and Jim Masterson running into the street. Earp arrived in time to make a lunge at one of the mounts, but his attempt to grab the tail missed. A couple of shots went in the direction of the marshals, and Earp, Masterson, and possibly several others returned fire. The Texans dashed over a bridge across the Arkansas, and one fell from his horse. A posse assembled, but the Texans had too much of a lead. All they found was young George Hoy lying on the ground, badly wounded in the arm. The men helped Hoy back to town as the denizens of the Commy-Kew checked for carnage. None killed, none wounded. Foy did suffer a casualty of his own: he had just purchased an $11 suit, and he left the coat hanging in his dressing room on that hot night. He found three bullet holes in the garment, one still smoldering from a ring of fire.[49]

Badly injured, Hoy lingered on until August 27, when he died of his wounds. The *Ford County Globe* mourned his passing:

> George was apparently rather a good young man, having those chivalrous qualities, so common to frontiersmen, well developed. He was at the time of his death under a bond of $1,500 for his appearance in Texas on account of some cattle scrape, wherein he was charged with aiding and assisting some other men in "rounding up" about 1,000 head of cattle which were claimed by other parties. He had many friends and no enemies among Texas men who knew him. George was nothing but a poor cow boy, but his brother cow boys permitted him to want for nothing during his illness and buried him in grand style when dead, which was very creditable to them. We have been informed by those who pretend to know, that the deceased, although under bond for a misdemeanor in Texas, was in no wise a criminal, and would have been released at the next setting of the court if he had not been removed by death from its jurisdiction. "Let his faults, if he had any, be hidden in the grave."[50]

There is no certainty whether it was the bullet of Earp, Jim Masterson, or some other unknown shooter that landed in George Hoy's right arm and led to his death. This was probably the first time, other than in the Indian raids when he was a boy, that Wyatt Earp shot at a man. He had always found other ways to deal with troublemakers, usually more often garrulous drunks than criminals. This time, he fired in what he considered self-defense. The shooting had an unexpected side effect—for the first time Earp's name appeared in a national publication. The *National Police Gazette*, which emphasized the more sensational stories, found the cowtown shooting just perfect to titillate the folks back east:

Wyatt Erpe, a good fellow and brave officer, had an altercation with a "cow-boy," when the latter getting worsted, went for assistance and revenge, which was obtained from a number of mounted Texans who rode by a variety hall . . . and fired a volley into the hall, which is a frame "frontier theatre," and was beautifully perforated with bullets. At the time of the firing a banjoist was giving his performance on the stage, and a number of girls and men were seated in front and in the boxes. The audience was thrown into considerable consternation at this unexpected episode in the performance, but numerous six-shooters were promptly drawn and the fire of the "cow-boys" was vigorously returned from the windows, one at least of the attacking party falling from his horse as the result. . . . The only reason for the attack on their hall was a reckless whim on the part of the "cow-boys."[51]

Just past his thirtieth birthday, Wyatt Earp had a touch of national praise and attention. This would not be the last time Eastern readers would find his name in print.

Wyatt Earp would come to believe Hoy's attack had really been an attempt on his life, paid for by Bob Wright, the town's leading merchant, a political boss and a representative in the Kansas state legislature. Earp said the feud started when he arrested Bob Rachals, a prominent trail leader who drunkenly shot at a German fiddler. Wright tried to block Rachals's arrest rather than anger the cattle boss, who was one of the top financial contributors to the Dodge economy. Wright even threatened to have Earp thrown off the force. Earp refused to free Rachals and threw Wright in jail as well. The papers never covered the story; Dodge City's newspapers missed much of what occurred and were not eager to embarrass the most influential man in town. There is little confirmation[52] beyond Earp's statements, and the supposition initially sounds like paranoia until further analyzed. Earp's action in jailing Wright is entirely in character—he did something similar in another dusty town two years later, and he never put great stock in authorities who interfered with the law. Earp had been vigorous in pistol-whipping the Texans, and his often arrogant manner could well have irritated Wright to the point of at least trying to scare the assistant marshal out of town. It was often the pattern in these cowtowns to bring on the tough lawman, then drive him away before he got in the way of business. Wright may well have quietly tried to do this on his own without involving the city council.

As Earp told it, the next attempt on his life came when notorious Texas gunman Clay Allison arrived, probably in early September, shortly after Hoy's death.[53] Allison owned a reputation as a killer, making him just the right man to come and throw a scare into an overeager assistant marshal. It did not quite work out that way. Earp said Allison arrived in town and behaved well for the first day, but the next morning a policeman came and awakened Wyatt with the word that Allison carried two six-shooters and was making threats against him. Earp picked up his guns and located Bat Masterson, who retrieved a shotgun he kept at the district attorney's office, near Wright's store. Masterson stayed across the street, hiding the weapon and appearing unconcerned. Other Earp allies stood casually in doorways, guns at the ready. Earp began his search of the saloons, first heading into Ab Webster's place. When he came out, he stepped face to face with Clay Allison, perhaps the most dangerous gun-thrower of the frontier. They greeted each other, then leaned against the wall, calmly measuring each other with sideways glances. Most onlookers might have taken it for a casual chat between old friends.

Finally Allison said, "So, you're the man that killed my friend Hoy." Earp responded: "Yes, I guess I'm the man you're looking for." Earp had a firm grasp on a pistol in his pocket as he watched Allison's hand slowly reach toward his pistol pocket. The deputy planned to use his left hand to grab Allison's gun if he drew. Allison studied the situation, saw Masterson, and said, "I guess I'll go around the corner."

"I guess you better," Earp replied, then watched the gunman turn the corner. From across the street, Masterson could see that a dozen tough Texans had assembled, armed with Winchesters, to cover Allison's retreat. Earp turned the corner but saw Masterson's signal to keep out of range. Earp stepped back as Allison rode up on horseback.

"Come over here, Wyatt, I want to talk to you," Allison called.

"I can hear you all right here," Earp replied. "I think you came here to make a fight with me, and if you did you can have it right now."

Wright came running down the street. Apparently he had changed his mind about having Allison challenge Earp because Masterson, shotgun in hand, had quietly told him, "If this fight comes up, Wright, you're the first man I'm going to kill." Wright decided he would rather call off Allison than find himself ventilated with buckshot.

"Well, I don't like you any too well," Allison said to Wright. "There were a lot of your friends to be here this morning to help me out, but I don't see them round now." Allison then turned to Earp and raised his voice. "Earp, I believe you're a pretty good man from what I've seen of you. Do you know that these coyotes sent for me to make a fight with you and kill you? Well, I'm going to ride out of town, and I wish you good luck."

The incident ended as little more than a conversation on the street, with ominous undertones. Allison could quickly recognize that Masterson would never have let him leave town with all his body parts intact had the gunman made a play against Earp. Wright had not provided the promised backup, and cocksure Bat Masterson was just crazy enough to kill Allison despite the Winchester-toting Texans.

Earp said Allison returned ten days later and sent a messenger to town asking Earp's permission to come into town and attend to business regarding his cattle. Earp welcomed him, and Allison behaved. "It was a fourteen days' wonder, for Allison had never in his life before conducted himself like a Christian," Earp said. "Indeed, it had been his practice to force every store, saloon, and bank other than those he patronized to close up during such time as he honored a frontier town with a visit."[54]

The local papers noted only that Clay Allison passed through town on his return from East St. Louis. The Dodge papers were not about to accuse Bob Wright of conspiring to murder, and the incident itself happened so quietly it could have gone unnoticed by most townsmen. It had all been typical Earp/Masterson law enforcement—one worked as the point man while the other served as backup, providing the real force. Earp may have been brave, but he was not stupid enough to go up against Clay Allison without the threat of guns behind him to throw a scare into a potential adversary. It was a pattern he would repeat. As for Wright's murder plot, it seems probable that the legislator thought he could scare Earp out of town with little fuss. The rumor that Clay Allison was packing guns and backed by Texans would be enough to drive most sane marshals out of town on the fastest horse in the stable. Instead, Earp handled the situation quietly, backed by the shotgun-toting Masterson. Earp said Wright came to him to apologize and told of his conspiracies with Hoy and Allison. Eventually they grew to be friends of sorts.

Days after the episode, Masterson picked up the shotgun he had held ready to blast Allison and the Texans and went out for a little target practice. Much to his surprise he found the gun contained not buckshot, but a load of fine birdshot that would have done little more than sting the drovers. Apparently, someone had borrowed the gun for hunting and left it loaded when it was returned. Bat grumbled about the shotgun, "It would have been a shame if a good man's life had depended on the charge in that gun."[55]

The cattle season slowed as winter approached, with fewer herds crossing Indian Territory to the shipping point at Dodge. Bassett, Earp, and Jim Masterson made only four arrests in three weeks as Dodge City settled into its winter stupor by early October. It had been an eventful summer, with Deputy U.S. Marshal H. T. McCarty shot and killed in the Long Branch saloon in July, the Hoy incident a couple of weeks later, and the flight of Dull Knife and a small band of Cheyenne from the reservation. Winter usually turned wild Dodge into a peaceful village for a few months before the herds would again come bellowing north after the spring thaw.

One drover had had more than his share of trouble in Dodge during the summer and fall of that year. Darkly handsome Jim Kenedy came north with the herds, but he was no common cowboy. Called Spike by his Texas pals, he was the son of Captain Mifflin Kenedy, one of the wealthiest and most respected ranchers in Texas and the owner of the large Rancho de Los Laureles in Nueces County. Young Spike loved the wild life of saloons and brothels, and he already had had run-ins with the law. In 1872 he lost money to Texas cattleman I. P. "Print" Olive in a saloon card game in Ellsworth, then accused Olive of cheating. Kenedy challenged the unarmed Olive, who remained calm in the tense situation. Frustrated, Kenedy left, but later that afternoon entered the Ellsworth Billiard Saloon, where Olive was again playing cards. Kenedy grabbed a pistol from a gun rack at the bar and turned loose on Olive, hitting him in the hand, groin, and thigh. Jim Kelly, an African American cowhand working for Olive, dashed into the saloon and shot Kenedy in the leg. Police arrested Kenedy, but he escaped with the help of friends, leaving Ellsworth in the dark of night.[56]

Spike Kenedy spent most of the next five years in Tascosa, Texas, running his father's two-thousand-head spread with a full crew of men. He seemed to mature past his reckless youth and earned the respect of his men. That was before he heard the siren song of Dodge City. Dr. Henry F. Hoyt, a Texas friend, wrote about him, "In the course of time he drove a herd to Dodge City, Kansas, sold them, and, unable to withstand the temptations of the underworld there, he 'stepped out.' "[57]

Spike's transgressions were fairly routine, at first. He seemed to think being the son of a Texas cattle baron made him exempt from the law, and he drew an arrest and a fine from Wyatt Earp for carrying a pistol on July 19, 1878. A month later he was back in court, fined for disorderly conduct after an arrest by Marshal Bassett. Kenedy obviously did not enjoy his relations with Dodge's police force. He found Mayor Dog Kelley in his Alhambra Saloon and bitterly laid out his grievances. Kelley offered no solace. Instead he told Kenedy the officers were acting under his orders and that he damned well better behave in Dodge. The enraged Kenedy threatened the mayor and then rode out of town. But vengeful Spike Kenedy was not done with Dodge yet. He went off to Kansas City and lingered there a while, looking for and finding one of the fastest horses in the city. Again he made the trek west to Dodge.

Back in Dodge, Mayor Kelley became ill and went to Fort Dodge, the military outpost, for treatment. In his absence, he allowed two actresses to use his little frame house. Fannie Garretson, of the Commy-Kew, slept in the front room. Dora Hand, who worked under the stage name Fannie Keenan at the Varieties Theater, rested in Kelley's bedroom. At about four in the morning of October 4, Spike Kenedy guided his sleek racehorse through the quiet streets of Dodge and up toward Kelley's shack. Four shots exploded through the still night air, one slashing into the bedpost a few inches from Fannie Garretson's head to awaken her in terror.

Quickly responding to the shooting, Jim Masterson and Wyatt Earp heard the sound of sobbing from the little house behind the Western Hotel. Beside the splintered door of Kelley's house they found Fannie Garretson scared and shivering in her thin nightgown. The horrified actress pointed into the house, where Earp and Masterson discovered the beautiful Dora Hand lying dead in Kelley's bed. The bullet had entered under her right arm and crashed into her chest cavity, apparently killing her in her sleep. Garretson said her friend gasped once or twice, then dropped back onto the pillow without regaining consciousness.

Earp went to the Long Branch Saloon seeking information and saw Kenedy sitting at the monte table. Earp asked the bartender if Kenedy had been inside when the shots erupted. "For God's sake, don't say anything here," the bartender whispered. "Come into the back room and I'll tell you." The bartender said Kenedy had left shortly before the shooting and returned afterward for a big drink of whiskey. Earp stepped back into the bar to find that Kenedy had departed. Earp and Bat Masterson located a friend of Kenedy's who had been with him before the shooting. The lawmen threw the unnamed friend in jail and started the interrogation. The friend confirmed that Kenedy had fired the shots but insisted he himself had not been involved.[58]

The townsmen began grieving the next morning. Hand had been popular for her kindness and generosity as well as her acting. In death, her townsmen glorified her. Sheriff Bat Masterson put together what the *Dodge City Times* called "as intrepid a posse as ever pulled a trigger," with Marshal Bassett, Assistant Marshal Earp, and deputy sheriffs Bill Duffy and Bill Tilghman. Their difficult assignment was to find the fugitive in the vast prairie lying to the south and west of Dodge. They picked up Kenedy's trail and followed it for two days until a heavy rainstorm wiped out the hoofprints. Stopping at a ranch for the night, the posse was told that Kenedy had gone by the previous day, "and he seemed in a hurry, too." Masterson's posse picked up the trail only to lose it again to another rainstorm.

Finally they decided to rest their tired horses, and turned the animals out into the grass to graze. As they settled in, they caught sight of a horseman four or five miles away. They watched with idle curiosity as the rider approached. Bat said, "That's Kenedy. I know him by the way he rides, and besides, I know his horse." The sharp-eyed Masterson proved correct. By then the horses were scattered over the pastureland, too spread out to be quickly assembled for a chase. It would have been unwise to wait until Kenedy came close enough to recognize the law, so the possemen prepared for an ambush behind a little mound. They formed a plan: If Kenedy tried to escape, Earp would kill the horse; Masterson would shoot the man.

Kenedy approached within about seventy-five yards when the posse arose in full force to face the killer. Spike grabbed for his gun and fired as he wheeled his mount. Earp fired, downing the horse. Masterson's bullet landed in Kenedy's shoulder and dropped the man. The racehorse fell atop Kenedy, forcing the posse to extricate him. Masterson said he could hear the bones "craunch" as he pulled him out. All the angry Kenedy uttered was, "You sons of bitches, I will get even with you for this."[59] The posse hired a team and took him back to Dodge, where the newspapers immediately exaggerated the story. In their accounts the accidental capture of Kenedy became a well-plotted attempt to deceive Kenedy into thinking he was in no danger by allowing the horses to graze so they would not appear to belong to a posse. The capture owed more to luck than to pluck, but it became distorted into a tale of glory and cunning.

For two weeks Spike languished in his jail-cell bed recovering from the wound, which apparently had sent his body into shock. Finally he was well enough for Judge R. G. Cook to hold a preliminary hearing in the sheriff's office, a room too small to accommodate spectators. Cook ordered Kenedy's release, prompting the *Ford County Globe* to write: "We do not know what the evidence was, or upon what grounds he was acquitted. But he is free to go on his way rejoicing whenever he gets ready." The *Times* reported only, "The evidence being insufficient, the prisoner was acquitted."[60]

Earp would later credit Mifflin Kenedy's money as the reason Spike never faced a jury. The captain came to Dodge on December 9 to join his son at the Dodge House. Spike Kenedy needed another surgery, and doctors removed a four-inch piece of bone from his shoulder. When Spike could travel, Mifflin Kenedy took his son back to Texas, where Dr. Henry Hoyt said the shoulder and arm were shot to pieces. Young Kenedy never fully recovered. According to Hoyt, he lived only a year or two more.[61]

Dodge rewarded Bassett, Earp, and Jim Masterson by cutting their salaries that December. The three officers, who normally drew a combined total of $250 per month, were reduced to dividing $200 at a time when there were few arrests to add to the coffers at two dollars a bashed head.[62] Public service did not always have its rewards.

The winter of '78 passed quietly. In April, Earp and Jim Masterson received raises from $50 to $100 a month, decent wages for the frontier. The two deputies had an adventure in May when a drover rode off without paying an African American workman for services rendered. Earp and Masterson delivered the writ demanding payment for services only to find seven drovers lined up against them. According to the *Globe* report, Earp and Masterson "showed no sign of weakening" and delivered the writ, then received full payment before returning to town.[63]

As the summer progressed, all was not well in Dodge. Drought reduced the available grazing land near town, and Ogallala, Nebraska, emerged briefly as a shipping point to provide competition. In 1879, only about half the number of cows wended their way to Dodge as had the previous year. The reduction in business led naturally to a reduction in illegal activity—Earp made only nine arrests between April 13 and July 24. The wildest moment of the summer came in early September when a summer festival turned ugly, the cowhands brawling and fighting with the locals. Earp stepped into the middle and began his customary head-banging. According to the *Globe*, "The 'finest work' and neatest polishes were said to have been executed by Mr. Wyatt Earp, who has been our efficient assistant marshal for the past year."[64]

Wyatt Earp had gained more in Dodge than just a little experience banging Texans around. Some stories suggest he had several romantic interests during his time there, and he apparently settled in with a woman named Celia Blaylock, always called Mattie. She grew up near Fairfax, Iowa, and ran away from home at 16 to head west, stopping in Scott City, Kansas, before reaching Dodge. She left no records, and there is no real hint of her employment. Much later, she would become a practicing prostitute, and it can only be surmised that she followed that ancient trade before settling in with the assistant marshal in the West's most wicked town.[65]

Dodge may not have had much character, but it certainly had more than its share of characters. Earp met several men there who would remain his friends for life; many of them he would meet again in another frontier town down the trail. In Kansas, he met and befriended Luke Short, a gambler/gunman whose name would also become a legend like Earp, Masterson, and Holliday. Johnny Tyler, another gambler/tough, sat in on card games in Dodge.[66] Bill Tilghman, who rode with horse thieves in his youth, emerged as a sterling example of a frontier lawman.

Dodge also had its good times. Masterson and the boys were dedicated practical jokesters, pulling prank after prank with sophomoric glee. Masterson usually operated as the instigator, with the dour Earp at his side to lend authenticity. The favorite gag, constantly repeated, was to take a tenderfoot on a ride in the country and have a group of "wild" Indians surprise the party. The Indians, of course, would be Dodge folks dressed in native attire for the sake of a good scare. This worked quite well until someone tipped a tenderfoot, who took along a pistol and began shooting wildly over the heads of the fake Indians.

Earp apparently played a key role in one of the classic gags. The Reverend O. W. Wright had come to Dodge to lead the sinners away from perdition. He received a cordial welcome as Bat and Wyatt helped collect the funds to raise a church. In early June of 1879, the Ladies Aid Society decided to have a Beautiful Baby Contest to raise a missionary fund. Only Dodge-born infants less than a year old were eligible, with ballots to sell at six for a quarter. The winner would receive a hundred dollars in gold, donated by Luke Short, manager of the gambling concession at the Long Branch. The mothers campaigned intensely for their progeny, soliciting the townsmen to buy ballots and show their support. Sales intensified as voting drew to a close, with the gamblers buying ballots in $20 lots. At the church supper that evening, the Reverend Wright rose to announce that the contest had brought in more than $2,000, drawing the applause of Dodge's unusual congregation. The minister then read the name of each child, starting with the contestant with the fewest votes. One by one, the children of all the doting mothers were eliminated. Wright paused before naming the winner, then called out a name unknown to the churchgoers. The sports in the rear began laughing as the reverend asked if anyone knew the woman. Masterson and Earp stood with proper solemnity and said they knew her and would bring her. They returned a few minutes later, escorting a very large African American prostitute from a dance hall on the south side of the tracks. After protests from the mothers and laughter from the gamblers, the minister turned over the money.[67]

Earp gained some distinction as a cowtown Christian. He would leave Dodge with a bible presented by two local lawyers and inscribed, "To Wyatt S. Earp as a slight recognition of his many Christian Virtues and steady following in the footsteps of the meek and lowly Jesus." Earp served as a deacon in Wright's church, a rather odd position for a gun-toting deputy cohabitating with a woman. But this was Dodge City, after all, where old-fashioned morality was usually on holiday. Earp learned the job of lawman in the skewed reality of Dodge. Enforcing cowtown law meant preventing trouble so that the saloons would not be closed and the brothel business would not be slowed. The troublemakers were usually good-time boys out for a little fun, rarely real criminals who stole as a profession. City and county officers worked together almost as one force, and the offices were virtually interchangeable. Earp and the Mastersons worked together more as one unit than as separate forces. All this was about the worst preparation possible for what Earp would face not far in the future, where nearly everything would be different.

The Wyatt Earp who left Kansas had matured markedly from the boy who found himself in trouble in Indian Territory. He had become a most self-assured man who stoutly believed in right and wrong—and in his ability to determine which was which. He loved to be amused, yet almost never laughed; his dour countenance covered an air of supreme confidence in his ability to deal with just about any problem. He attracted followers, drawn by his strength; others were repelled by his self-assured ways. He was a saloon man, tolerated and respected by the better classes though never really accepted.

Wyatt Earp did draw the antipathy of many Texans, who left Dodge with bruised skulls that hurt more than their hangovers. Wyatt was often excessively rough in keeping the peace, but keep the peace he did, along with the Mastersons, Bassett, Tilghman, and the other officers whose job it was to prevent rowdyism from interfering with whiskey sales. Earp had even earned something of a national reputation for the Hoy shooting and the capture of Spike Kenedy. When young Texan William Box Hancock reached Dodge with a cattle drive, he made it a point to get a look at Earp and recounted his impressions to his wife when she wrote his memoirs. He may not have spelled the name correctly, and he confused Wichita with Abilene, but he knew the story of Wyatt Earp:

> Wyatt Erps was the city marshall. He held the town down and controlled the bad actors with an iron hand. Having heard a great deal about this noted peace officer, I was very anxious to see him.
>
> When he first came to my notice, I had heard of him as a great buffalo hunter. Later, he was appointed city marshal by the mayor of Ellsworth, Kansas, when the notorious Ben Thompson had threatened to kill everybody in town. Erps arrested him and put him in jail. Later, he served as city marshall of Abilene, Kansas, and finally drifted west and became the marshal of Dodge City.
>
> I found him a man perhaps thirty years of age, tall, erect and athletic, light hair, blue eyes and blonde mustache. He seemed very quiet in manner, but old settlers of Dodge told me he was the most fearless peace officer in the entire western country.[68]

One of those Dodge City settlers was a young lawyer named John Madden, who had enlisted the help of Earp and Bat Masterson to protect a client from attack by the Texas men. The two officers quietly prevented trouble, just by their presence. "They were in the vanguard of law and order in the early days of Kansas," Madden wrote. "God Bless old Wyatt Earp and men of his kind. They shot their way to heaven."[69]

Wyatt Earp had had his impact on the cowtowns of Kansas. He may have spent much of his time at the gambling tables, but that was expected since his job was to protect the business. Masterson and the rest did the same. He certainly made his mistakes—beating on Bill Smith, the man who once handed him a badge, was not a prudent decision. He was no plaster saint with a spotless record, but he was the kind of man the citizenry wanted walking in front of the procession during dangerous times. Men like Earp were also the men whom the "good" citizens wanted out of town during peaceful times. Earp seemed most at home with the gambling crowd, surrounded by prostitutes, with men whose morals would not meet high standards. Wyatt Earp had been an honorable and effective lawman, one of the best of a generally unsavory lot. His fling with recklessness in his youth seemed to end, and his honor and honesty never came into question as he fit well into the easy morals of the trail towns.

Dodge City had already started to change by 1879. The cattle trade had fallen off dramatically, and settlers had moved into much of the prairie land that had once been used for grazing cattle. The temperance unions had started a drive to dry out Kansas, which would certainly dry out Dodge as a center of wickedness. Earp had served his time as a lawman, and he was ready to become an entrepreneur. He was later quoted as saying: "In 1879 Dodge City was beginning to lose much of the snap which had given it a charm to men of restless blood, and I decided to move to Tombstone, which was just building up a reputation."

Brother Virgil had settled in Prescott, Arizona, and began hearing stories of the fabulous silver mines that were just starting to boom. He wrote Wyatt about the possibilities, and the two looked to more profitable enterprises than bruising Texans. A cowtown assistant marshal would never be rich, and Wyatt Earp was to spend his life trying to join the ranks of the wealthy. On September 9, the *Ford County Globe* reported that Earp had resigned and was headed to Las Vegas, New Mexico. If he could translate his skills to business, he could expect to make more than the meager wages of a lawman.

A NEW TOWN,
A NEW BADGE

IN THE FACTORIES OF THE EAST, on the farms of the South, and in the mining camps of California, a certain breed of Americans awaited the call their parents had heard before them: opportunity built on a foundation of optimism. Somewhere, sometime, every little guy would have his chance to become a baron of enterprise; whether he made his stake by running a cowtown saloon or hitting a vein of silver, opportunity waited just one right decision away. The Earps knew this, as did the many adventurers-in-waiting who bided their time behind a mule or working for wages, hoping for that chance to come. It had happened before, in the gold fields of California and the silver strikes of Nevada. America's West had been built on gold, silver, and illusion, built on the beliefs of the masses that they might be the lucky ones to strike it rich. Certainly there were enough examples to make this dream plausible. It was a lottery mentality—take a risk and hit the jackpot. The risks were big and the stakes high, but dreams could come true in America. Success would come to those with the guile, ambition, and grit to turn risk into riches, and these would-be moguls awaited the next opportunity. There were always strikes and even more rumors, but by the late 1870s the stories began circulating about a mining region that truly held the promise of becoming the next Comstock Lode. Down in the hills of southern Arizona, just a few miles from the Mexican border, in a dry, dusty area filled with Apaches and scorpions, a lone miner made a find that would echo across a nation.

When Ed Schieffelin went prospecting in southern Arizona, he was told by soldiers at Fort Huachuca that all he'd find would be his tombstone. With Apaches roaming the hills and long stretches of desert, the area was simply too dangerous for one man alone. But Schieffelin, with his long beard, waves of black hair, and tattered, patched clothing, made his strike. Filing the claim in the fall of 1877, he recalled the soldiers' warnings and gave the locations as Tombstone and Graveyard. Schieffelin collected a few rock specimens and was down to 30 cents in his pocket when he arrived at the Signal mine in northwestern Arizona where his brother, Al, worked. Al Schieffelin showed three of the samples to Richard Gird, the assayer at the Signal. After looking at two of the three, Gird supposedly said, "The best thing you can do is to find out where that ore came from, and take me with you and start for the place." The third sample tested out even richer, at $2,000 to the ton. Gird and the two Schieffelins returned to the site quickly and Ed made his biggest strike, a silver vein so rich he could press a coin into it and leave an exact imprint. Gird assayed the sample from this location at $15,000 to the ton, and supposedly said, "Ed, you lucky cuss—you have hit it." The mine was called the Lucky Cuss. It turned out to be a small vein, but the Tough Nut, Grand Central, and Contention all proved bigger strikes, and the rush began to America's new mining center. Miners would be followed by merchants, gamblers, and prostitutes also seeking their fortunes in the frontier boomtowns, if not with the turn of a shovel, then perhaps on the turn of a card or the growth of a business. It had happened in the rushes of California, Virginia City, and Pikes Peak before, and it would all burst forth again in a Tombstone filled with hope and promise.

The first-rush boomers pitched their tents and built their shacks atop a hill that rose from a plain of tall grama grass. In one direction, they could look out upon the mighty rock formation called Cachise's Stronghold, where the Apache leader later called Cochise had eluded capture by cavalry troops. Turning in the other direction, the miners could look past the miles of grassland to the Huachuca Mountains, standing like temples in the desert; far in the distance stood the taller San Joses across the border in Mexico. The first silver rush brought miners and the elements that fed off them—gamblers, prostitutes, and whiskey peddlers. Merchants and settlers who would replace the tents with buildings and turn the rough settlement into a community soon followed.

Tombstone sprang up so quickly there was little room for planning. Almost immediately a scandal erupted with a force that struck just about everyone in town. In March of 1879, five men organized the Tombstone Town Site Company, ostensibly to establish proper title to the town's lots, many already occupied by buildings that were going up in a haze of sawdust. The founders of the Town Site Company knew that controlling real estate in a boomtown would be almost as lucrative as owning a silver mine, and far more secure. Their moves, though of questionable ethics, had some legal basis under the laws of that time. Soon after its founding, original member James S. Clark and an associate named Mike Gray, a local justice of the peace, bought out the other members of the company. The company would approach the owners of the lots and offer to sell clear title with the price based on the value of improvements, which, of course, the owner had done himself. In essence, the Town Site Company was selling the property back to the landowners. There were stories, though unverified, that an owner who refused payment would be visited by local thugs acting as enforcers. Much to the shock and outright anger of the townsmen, Mayor Alder Randall and the town council backed the Town Site Company and provided official sanction. The real estate mess would constantly be hanging over Tombstone, tearing apart its political structure and dividing the residents into separate camps.

Clark and Gray were scorned by some and respected by others. Irate citizens assailed them in public and threatened their lives. It was the first big political issue in town and proved to be an ongoing controversy. Tombstone's first newspaper, the *Nugget*, started on October 2, 1879, virtually avoided the issue as editor Artemus Fay simply chronicled events without engaging in controversy. A few months later, on May 1, 1880, fiery young editor John Clum brought a more adversarial style of journalism to town when he opened the *Epitaph* with the financial backing of Richard Gird, the former assayer now wealthy from his share of the mines. Clum, with experience both as the Indian agent at San Carlos and as the former editor of the *Tucson Citizen*, mounted a crusade against the Town Site group and condemned Mayor Randall for signing the Town Site documents.

Tombstone and several smaller mining camps sprouted in the southern end of huge Pima County, about seventy-five miles of rough road from the county seat of Tucson. Pima officials had little reason to pay attention to the wild, remote regions to the south until the new camps demanded courts, government, and police. Almost from the start, policing became a problem in an area that drew misfits of all types. Law enforcement had three tiers: the county sheriff held jurisdiction over all crimes in the district and county; the city marshal, an elected official, was responsible for the village of Tombstone; and the U.S. marshal had authority over such federal offenses as stagecoach robberies and violation of the mails. Jurisdictions often overlapped, officers disagreed over their responsibilities; the situation was primed for chaos. This structure helped make Tombstone one of the most intriguingly complicated stories in frontier history. At different times, the lawbreakers were the lawmen, and the line between good and evil blurred in the eyes of the community.

Into this maelstrom of opportunity and excitement came Wyatt Berry Stapp Earp, carrying some reputation from Kansas as a tough, competent lawman. At 31, he had filled out into a lean, powerful man with sandy blond hair and a drooping mustache. He owned a booming, authoritative voice, so deep it seemed almost a growl, and a self-assured swagger that as many men would find irritating as would find uplifting. Wyatt and Mattie left Dodge in early September, accompanied by brother Jim, his wife Bessie, and two children from Bessie's earlier marriage. They stopped briefly in then-booming Las Vegas, New Mexico, to collect Doc Holliday and Big-Nose Kate. Doc had run a gambling house and gotten into some trouble for killing a gambler named Mike Gordon in July, but was not convicted. The party went on to Prescott, Arizona, to meet up with Virgil, now 36, a town constable who had earned a reputation of his own for participating in a shootout against two Texas desperadoes. Wyatt and Virgil looked so much alike that even acquaintances would confuse the two. Jim, 38, the wounded Civil War veteran, was shorter and slightly darker than his brothers. Kate liked Prescott, and she and Doc decided to remain. The Earps had come West for opportunity, and all the talk was of the burgeoning little boomtown down near the border. Wyatt, Jim, Virgil, and their wives outfitted their wagons and headed south, into the most promising silver field in America.

Wyatt Earp brought with him a wagon he planned to convert to a stagecoach. "I intended to start a stage line when I first started out from Dodge City," Earp said in a 1925 court deposition. "But when I got there I found there was two stage lines and so I finally sold my outfit to one of the companies, to a man named Kinnear."[1] He found the two established stage lines—Kinnear's and Ohnesorgen & Walker—in the midst of a price war that had led to passenger rates being cut to $4 for the trip from Benson to Tombstone, hardly enough to make the run profitable.[2] The Earps realized quickly there would be no future in stage coaches, so they sought their fortunes in whatever appeared most fruitful, whether gambling or speculating in mining claims or real estate. Virgil had already chosen another path. Before leaving Prescott, Virgil visited U.S. Marshal Crawley Dake and received the appointment of deputy U.S. marshal, a prestigious though low-paying position in which his job was basically to support other local agencies and investigate crimes against federal law.

There was a freshness about Tombstone when the Earps arrived in the final weeks of 1879, their wagons loaded with supplies to start a new life. They found a village of about nine hundred residents with far more tents than buildings. Already the gambling parlors were running full bore, filled with the smells of wood-stove heat, whiskey, and tobacco smoke and the sounds of men yelling numbers, punctuated by the occasional cry of "Keno!" A large tent housed a dance hall with four bored-looking women taking turns entertaining the miners. Freighters carried fresh lumber from the distant mountains for the legion of Tombstone craftsmen to turn into saloons, businesses, and cabins. All around was the banging of hammers and whuzzing of saws, cutting and crafting to build a boomtown. The village with the odd-sounding name had a constant bustle about it: noise, excitement, anticipation. Optimism always flowed as freely as whiskey, for only the most optimistic would chance their lives on an unproved hope of new riches.

The Earps quickly went about staking mining claims, hoping one would become a big producer. The village grew rapidly around them as an army of boomers brought their hopes into the Arizona hills. Stagecoaches arrived daily with a dozen or more people jamming the rig and hanging from the top. They came to escape an economic depression that had hit much of the country; by 1878 more than eighteen thousand companies had gone out of business and many railroads were in receivership. In February of 1880 George Whitwell Parsons walked into town, bursting with visions of speculating on mines that would make his fortune. Parsons had another passion, keeping a diary that recorded the movements, emotions, and vibrancy of the town. Four months after Parsons arrived, Clara Spalding Brown came to Tombstone to keep house for her husband, mining engineer Theodore Brown, and to serve as correspondent for the *San Diego Union*. She promised her readers a "woman's view" of Tombstone and wound up describing bloodstains on the street.

"Thinking a few notes regarding Tombstone and the journey thereto, from a woman's point of view, may be entertaining to some of the ladies of San Diego, I take this opportunity to address you," Brown wrote on July 7, 1880, her first dispatch. After describing a long, dusty trek to southern Arizona Territory, Brown told of what she found:

> We beheld an embryo city of canvas, frame and adobe, scattered over a slope. . . . It is a place more pretentious than I had imagined, and full of activity, notwithstanding the hundreds of loungers seen upon the streets. The only attractive places visible are the liquor and gambling saloons, which are everywhere present and are carpeted and comfortably furnished.
>
> The ladies of Tombstone are not so liberally provided with entertainment, and find little enjoyment aside from a stroll about town after sunset, the only comfortable

time of the day. The camp is one of the dirtiest places in the world . . . and one is never sure of having a clean face, despite repeated ablutions. It is time to talk about dirt. The sod lies loose upon the surface, and is whirled into the air every day by a wind which almost amounts to a gale; it makes the eyes smart like the cinders from an engine; it penetrates into the houses, and covers everything with dust. I do not believe the famous Nebraska breeze can go ahead of the Tombstone zephyr.

The mercury gallivants around in the nineties, with altogether too high-minded ideas. One could stand two or three days of that sort of thing with tolerable grace, but it taxes one's endurance to receive no quarter at all. . . . We cannot obtain desirable food for hot weather; fresh vegetables are scarce, and the few fruits in the markets require a very large purse. . . . The camp is considered a remarkably quiet one — only one murder since my arrival. . . . Religious services are held in a furniture store, and attended by the few who know when Sunday comes around; in about two months, an adobe church will be completed. As far as I can ascertain, every one from San Diego is doing well and making the best of everything. All feel that this is a place to stay in for a while; not a desirable spot for a permanent home.[3]

From her first article, Clara Brown understood a critical point of life in southern Arizona. Tombstone would be a town of sojourners more than settlers; boomers who came to find fortune, then escape to more hospitable climes that offered such luxuries as fruits and vegetables. Most of the people who came to this desolate spot were not looking for a home in which to raise generations of little Browns or Parsonses — they were coming to make money then leave. This sojourner mentality would quickly establish an antagonism between the transitory townsfolk and the cattlemen who came to Arizona to build ranches and start families that would populate the Southwest for generations.

Tombstone at first burst resembled the other mining towns of the time, filled mostly by rough men and the marginal characters who fed off them. It was an intemperate little town loaded with dust and toughs, typical of most mining communities where whiskey drew bigger crowds than God. But the town would change quickly and often, forever in transition. As early as 1880 a trickle had begun of a better-educated, refined element; mining engineers, lawyers, and political opportunists nestled into the growing village, to walk the streets filled with loungers and cardsharps. Parsons provides a good example of the new settler. A well-bred native of Washington, D.C., he grew up in Brooklyn, went West to work at a bank in San Francisco, then joined the boomers for the trek to Tombstone. The more refined settlers were a minuscule minority at first, living amid a world of roughneck miners and saloon dwellers.

The sojourners found a wild country brimming with conflicts in waiting. The remnants of the Apache Nation were spread through the hills and on the San Carlos reservation, feeding a constant apprehension of attack; the unsavory loungers in town were not above fleecing miners in crooked card games or committing a few robberies; and the backcountry began filling with another breed of troublemaker, ruffians who rustled cattle and highwaymen who preyed on travelers using the roadways. Most of the boomers were so caught up in their rush to riches that they barely paid attention to the rising crime until the problems became immediate and demanded tough law enforcement.

With the stage business already locked up, Wyatt Earp went back to work, as an employee, not a boss. He spent eight months carrying a shotgun and sitting atop other men's stagecoaches serving as a guard—called a shotgun messenger—for Wells, Fargo. With Virgil working as a deputy U.S. marshal, Jim tending bar, and Wyatt guarding shipments, the Earps settled into Tombstone. They had arrived seeking fortune, not wages, and they gambled and sought out opportunities by filing mining claims, amassing land holdings, and acquiring water rights. Wells, Fargo records, although incomplete, show that Wyatt had received only one month's full pay when he passed the job to veteran Wells, Fargo employee Bob Paul. Wyatt's brother Morgan, 29, arrived from the family home in California in mid-July, stepping in immediately as special deputy to his brothers and often filling in as a shotgun messenger. The youngest brother, Warren, 25, would occasionally move in and out of Tombstone as well. Always on the horizon was a mining claim that might hit or an investment that might pay off.

The family set up residence in three houses on Fremont and First Streets, with three couples, plus two of Jim Earp's stepchildren from Bessie's first marriage, sharing the rooms. The families had come from a world of Western saloons and brothels, where moral codes were far less rigid than in the East. The boomers had better ways to spend their time than to speculate on the marital or nonmarital status of their neighbors. It is likely that only Jim and Bessie had enjoyed the formality of a marriage ceremony, though Wyatt and Mattie, Virgil and Allie, and later Morgan and Louisa were all living as husband and wife. Before Louisa's arrival, Morgan often bunked with a man named Fred Dodge, a sometime gambler and saloonkeeper who often rode with posses and generally sided with the Earps in most disputes. It was not for nearly half a century that Dodge would disclose to the Earps his true reason for residing in Tombstone—he was a secret agent for Wells, Fargo, sent to Tombstone to look after the company's business.[4]

Such proper Easterners as Parsons found the situation shocking: a town almost devoid of traditional morality, with 24-hour-a-day saloons, brothels, and dance halls operating openly. For the men and women with frontier experience, this was business as usual, no wilder than most mining towns and certainly not as wicked as Dodge with its city-of-sin atmosphere. Early in his Tombstone tenure, Parsons sat down in moral shock to write: "How men of good family and connections East can come here and marry prostitutes—take them out of a dance house—I can't see." [5] Men of good breeding and men of marginal breeding, such as the Earps, did take women out of dance halls, and they did lead lives outside the accepted bounds of morality, but morality was bent to accept the independence of this frontier free-love generation.

Parsons found another sight even more disgusting. "This place holds some of the most depraved—entirely and totally so—that were ever known. I have seen hard cases before in a frontier oil town where but one or two women were thought respectable, but have never come across several such cases as are here. It would be impossible to speak here of some or one form of depravity I am sorry to know of—for bad as one can be and low as woman can fall—there is one form of sin here (fortunately confined to two persons) which would I almost believe bring a blush of shame to a prostitute's cheek. Such persons, if the facts were generally known it seems to me, would be run out of town. One of the two I saw tonight in the ball room; also other depraved women and men, of course.

Others wore the garb and appearance of gentility. Good manners and good was, but there was a sad mixture."[6] He apparently referred to the remarkable sight of a lesbian couple, something he had never seen in the East, or even in San Francisco.

The Earp brothers and their common-law wives fit well into this loose lifestyle; they lived on the margins of society amid the world of saloons and brothels in a place where such pursuits were generally accepted. Jim's main occupation had always been as a saloon man, Wyatt aspired mostly to success, Morgan loved his good times, and Virgil seemed to have an honest commitment to law enforcement. These would not be the type of men invited to the fancy parties of high society in Boston or San Francisco, but they fit into a frontier society where most boomers accepted the differences. Even the proper Parsons would come to take men at their mettle.

The Earp wives went about setting up house in the little cottages on Fremont. Allie Sullivan Earp, Virgil's third wife, claimed a distant relationship to prizefighter John L. Sullivan and by most descriptions was just about as pugnacious. The feisty little woman of Irish ancestry gave strong-willed support and absolute loyalty to her beloved Virgil. They would stand together as husband and wife, marriage ceremony or not, with a bond stronger than a wedding band. Bessie Earp came from the brothels and made certain Jim and her children had a home. Louisa, beautiful and delicate, stayed behind at the Earp family home in rural San Bernardino County, California, until late summer of 1880, when she joined Morgan. Mattie Earp, dark-haired, quiet, and unassuming, left little trace on the records.

AS TOMBSTONE GREW INTO MORE OF A TOWN, a new breed of badmen in the Arizona backcountry grew into more of a problem. They started as a small collection of misfits, disenfranchised cowhands who drove the herds in from Texas, fighters from the Lincoln County wars in New Mexico, and sundry social castoffs fleeing the law from Wyoming or the Dakotas. They were an odd mixture of rabble bent on living by their own rules and prospering outside the boundaries of society. They were not all Texans, but they took on the appellation of "cowboys," a word that came into use in the Kansas cowtowns to describe the drovers. Gradually, the townsmen took to referring to all the backcountry troublemakers as cowboys, distinct from the ranchmen who raised cattle.

Tom Thornton ran a hotel in Galeyville, near the New Mexico line. He knew the cowboys and lived with them. He said: "There are some who have followed the frisky longhorn herds over the Texas plains, but nine-tenths of them never saw Texas in their lives. They are wild, reckless men from all over the world. They do not claim a home, a business or close affiliation with civilization. Some are miners from Colorado, and the Black Hills, others are escaped criminals and refugees from all portions of the world. Some are mere reckless adventurers who have followed the line of new railroads since the first rail was laid from the Missouri River or in the Sacramento Valley. They do not work, and they are never without money. They live in a style that you city folks would despise no doubt, but still they are never actually without food, a good horse, arms, ammunition and blankets. They are not all brave, and often sneak away from danger, but in my twenty years' intercourse with them I never knew one of them to whine and squeal when he knew he had to die. They will run away from death, but when cornered will look into the muzzle of a six-shooter with defiant indifference."[7]

The cowboys created quite a scene in the southern Arizona mining camps. By late 1879 and early 1880 they had barely begun an activity that would lead to much greater trouble. Southern Arizona had been shaved off Mexico in the 1854 Gadsden Purchase, and the cowboys used the area as a base to ride across the border, rustle Mexican cows, and bring them back to sell to Arizona ranchers. Thornton explained, "Whenever a man wants a herd of cattle and notifies any of the leading spirits among them that he wants a bunch of stock, and a price is agreed upon, the cattle are forthcoming." The cowboys even did a little rustling on the northern side of the line, taking American cows from the big ranchers and selling them to friendly Mexicans.

The rustling game became tiresome for the honest ranchers. T. W. Ayles wrote to the *Epitaph* that he often supplied beef to his neighbors, "and could do so always if I had not to divide with the unknown and irresponsible partners viz: 'Cow Boys,' or some other cattle thieves. . . . There seems to be an organized band, and their connections seem to extend to and over the Mexican border and to the borders of New Mexico and across both. . . . Honest dealers in stock must either have protection or join the band of robbers and their accessories, the purchasers and hiders."[8] While the cowboys engaged primarily in rustling during the early days, other avenues to ill-gotten gains were being explored. The first-known attempt at a stage robbery in the Tombstone area occurred nine miles east of San Simon in May of 1880, when two men leaped into the road in front of the coach and began firing, killing Silver City resident Antonio Chaves and wounding driver John Henry in the leg. The horses bolted, but Henry guided them to San Simon.[9]

The cowboys had their defenders, however, and for good reason. Cowboy pal Thornton said they made mighty good Apache fighters at a time when the backcountry citizens were far more afraid of losing their lives than of seeing the big ranchers lose a few cows. In the early days, the cowboys pretty much confined their activities to rustling and looting in Mexico. By the morality of the day, many Arizona boomers did not consider this stealing, exactly. The Mexican War had ended only thirty years earlier, and hard feelings still lingered among a populace that not only remembered the Alamo but benefited from the reduced prices of beef that stealing cows made possible.

The cowboys were romanticized, even then, and were occasionally seen as somewhat heroic for helping small ranchers by contributing a few head of cattle. John Pleasant Gray, son of Mike Gray of the Town Site Company, ran the family ranch and spent much time with the outlaws, a necessity in the backcountry where getting along meant survival. "Among the rustlers were undoubtedly some pretty tough characters—men who knew crime as a business, and being sought in other states had drifted to the southwest frontier as their last refuge," Gray wrote in his unpublished autobiography. "But such men most always had a strain of honor in their hearts which placed them several notches ahead of our present-day criminals. For one thing, they would not kill an unarmed person as so often occurs in our so-called civilized world of today; nor would they rob the hand that fed them. In short, the rustler was much of a gentleman even when playing the role of Robin Hood."[10]

Estimates of their number varied from several dozen to upward of two hundred, and it is likely the totals fluctuated and grew notably as time passed. These cowboy-outlaws ranged from the southwestern New Mexico areas of Shakespeare and Silver City over through southeastern Arizona, moving into Tucson at times. They made their headquarters mostly in the smaller towns, away from the burgeoning population of citified newcomers. Shakespeare became a popular haunt, as was Galeyville, about seventy-five miles east of Tombstone, and the small town of Charleston about nine miles to the southwest of Tombstone, where a mill was established to turn silver ore into bullion.

The cowboys made friends among the merchants and became enemies of much of the other citizenry. Deputy U.S. Marshal Virgil Earp said: "The most of them are what we call 'saddlers,' living almost wholly in the saddle, and largely engaged in raiding into Sonora and adjacent country and stealing cattle, which they sell in Tombstone . . . to some of the butchers practically in partnership with them, and I know of cases where the finest cattle in the country have been sold at a dollar a head. When cattle are not handy the cowboys rob stages and engage in similar enterprises to raise money. As soon as they are in funds they ride into town, drink, gamble, and fight. They spend their money as free as water in the saloons, dancehouses, or faro banks, and this is one reason they have so many friends in town. All that large class of degraded characters who gather the crumbs of such carouses stand ready to assist them out of any trouble or into any paying rascality. The saloons and gambling houses into whose treasuries most of the money is ultimately turned receive them cordially and must be called warm friends of the cowboys. A good many of the merchants fear to express themselves against the criminal element, because they want to keep the patronage of the cowboys' friends."[11]

They were a rip-roarin', fun-lovin' bunch of boys when they had money to spend, and most of the saloonkeepers wanted the cowboys to spend it at their bars, even if they paid with Mexican pesos and dirty money. The citizenry had an even more difficult problem—they could not tell the cowboys from the honest ranchers. The two dressed about the same, and a few of the toughs had done stints as ranch hands on the spreads. Southern Arizona's sojourners could not distinguish between the ranchers who came by their herds honestly, and those who bought illegal Mexican beeves from the cowboys for resale, most notably two of the better-established families in the area, the Clantons and the McLaurys.

The Clantons reached Arizona in the mid-1870s, led by patriarch Newman Haynes Clanton or "Old Man," as just about everyone called him, and his sons, Joseph Isaac (known as Ike), Phineas, and Billy. The Clantons had ranged the West, coming most recently from California and settling in Arizona at Lewis Springs, about a mile south of Charleston. Ike even ran a restaurant in Tombstone for a short time. The McLaurys built a ranch on the Babacomari River, about fifteen miles west of Tombstone. They later moved another twenty miles east of Tombstone to the Sulphur Springs Valley. To most of the new townsfolk they seemed indistinguishable from the likes of Henry Hooker, T. W. Ayles, or dozens of others running legitimate cattle ranches, but the Clantons and McLaurys had a dirty little secret: they were cooperating with the backcountry rustlers on highly questionable cattle deals.

Brothers Frank and Tom McLaury served almost as middlemen between the cowboys and the community. The rustlers stole cows in Mexico, then drove them to the McLaury ranch on the Babacomari River for sale and rebranding. The McLaurys were the fences of the frontier, taking "hot" cows for resale at big profits. The stolen beeves would then be driven into Tombstone. The McLaurys enjoyed a certain veneer of respectability as honest ranchers by the community, which was mostly unaware of their activities. Many of the townsmen who did know the truth cared little about an activity that profited most of those concerned and usually hurt only a few Mexicans.[12]

"These boys were plain, good-hearted, industrious fellows," John Pleasant Gray wrote of the McLaurys in his memoirs. "They may have harbored passing rustlers at their ranch, but what rancher did not? and it would have been little of a man who would have turned away any traveler in that land of long trails and hard going." Being uncooperative would have meant courting danger from the rustlers.

The cowboys did get out of control on occasion. In mid-July, Ike Clanton apparently caused problems when he, Joe Hill, and a German cowboy tried to sell cattle, believed stolen, to the San Carlos Apache reservation. When the purchasing officer hesitated to make the buy, Ike and his companions got mad and moved on to Maxey, down the road from the mill town of Safford, and fired a few random shots into the houses. Mill supervisor Jerome B. Collins took away Ike's pistol and told him he would shotgun them if they caused further trouble. Moving on to Safford, Ike and his pals started by shooting out the lights in a saloon. Then they shot into a house. Continuing their rollicking good time, they broke into a store and used the merchandise for target practice. They went to a nearby saloon and stirred their drinks with the barrels of their pistols before turning the guns on a man and commanding him to dance. Then they fired off random shots into the Safford mill, while forcing the workers to provide the cartridges. The angry Collins tried to assemble a posse to arrest the troublemakers, but found not a single man willing to join him in the effort. Collins finished his report on the incident with the words, "It will be a God's blessing for this valley to get rid of them."[13]

In 1880, such troublemaking was rare. The cowboys were more often involved in rustling than rowdyism, and few of the first-wave boomers paid much attention to them. But the cowboys just could not confine themselves to looting the Mexican herds. A few of them decided to take on the U.S. Army. In late July, Wyatt was recruited along with Virgil, Morgan, and Wells, Fargo agent Marshall Williams by Lt. J. H. Hurst to join an army search party for six mules that had been stolen from Camp Rucker, seventy-five miles east of Tombstone. They rode with four soldiers to the McLaury ranch on the Babacomari River on July 25. Virgil Earp, as a deputy U.S. marshal, held the position of authority. A cowboy told Virgil the theft had been carried out by the McLaurys, Billy Clanton, and Pony Deal, another known rustler. When the posse arrived at the

McLaury ranch, they found the mules. The thieves were in the act of changing the "U.S." brand to "D.8." A rancher named Frank Patterson seemed to be overseeing the operation. Lieutenant Hurst conducted the negotiations, and Patterson stipulated he would return the mules if no arrests were made. Patterson told Hurst bloodshed was certain if the posse tried to take the mules, so he would deliver them to Charleston the next day. Hurst accepted the compromise and went to Charleston. He waited two days before the McLaurys, Billy Clanton, and Patterson rode into town and laughed at him, saying they had offered the compromise only to get clear of the Earp party. According to Virgil Earp's story, the mules were never returned. Hurst reacted angrily. Notices he posted describing the stolen mules identified the thieves as Pony Deal, A. T. Hansbrough, and Mac Demasters, and charged that Patterson and Frank McLaury were among those helping to hide the mules.[14]

An irate McLaury came to town and responded to Hurst with a paid advertisement in the August 5, 1880 *Nugget* in which he gave his side of the story, saying he was not involved in any mule stealing and had at Hurst's request tried to find the missing beasts. "The next thing I heard of was the placard . . . wherein my name is spoken of as a thief. If J. H. Hurst was a gentleman, or if I could appeal to the courts for protection, I would proceed differently in this matter. But Hurst is irresponsible and I have but one course to pursue, and that is to publish to the world that J. H. Hurst . . . is a coward, a vagabond, a rascal, and a malicious liar. This base and unmanly action is the result of cowardice, for instead of hunting the stock himself he tried to get others to do it, and when they could not find it, in order to cover up his own wrong acts, he attempted to traduce the character and reputation of honest men. My name is well known in Arizona, and thank God this is the first time in my life that the name of dishonesty was ever attached to me. Perhaps when the matter is ventilated it will be found that the Hon. Lieut. Hurst has stolen those mules and sold them, for a coward will steal, and a man who can publish the placard that bears his name is a coward. I am willing to let the people of Arizona decide who is right." McLaury had cleverly tried to blame the army officer for stealing his own mules, a strategy of misinformation that would appear again.

According to Virgil Earp, McLaury did more than take out his ad. Both McLaury brothers came to Virgil and asked if he had anything to do with placing the newspaper notice. When Virgil said he did not, Frank McLaury spoke threateningly: "If you ever again follow us as close as you did, then you will have to fight anyway."

"I answered that if ever any warrant for his arrest were put into my hands I would endeavor to catch him, and no compromise would be made on my part to let him go. He replied that I would have to fight, and that I would never take him alive," Virgil said. "And he said that he had only come in to find out if I had anything to do with the notices, and if I had, to kill me. But they were satisfied that I had not."

The stolen mules were only a small matter in the course of daily life in Tombstone, but the confrontation between Virgil Earp and Frank McLaury marked the beginning of the animosity between the Earps and the cowboys. Now, the situation had changed, and Wyatt Earp was ready to make wages. In late July he received a serious job offer. Charlie Shibell, the sheriff of Pima County, wanted to make him a deputy for the area around Tombstone. Since Shibell would be based in Tucson, Wyatt and another deputy could pretty much run their own show in the area, receiving a cut of the taxes and a regular salary. It was a good job, and Wyatt Earp needed something steadier than turning cards in other men's faro banks. The offer came at a time when the cowboys were just beginning to grow into a threat, both to the Earps and to the community at large. The Earps never much liked being threatened and forced to take guff, and Wyatt may well have believed he was ready to become part of the action.

The *Epitaph* lauded the decision: "The appointment of Wyatt Earp as Deputy Sheriff by Sheriff Shibell, is an eminently proper one, and we in common with the citizens generally congratulate the latter on his selection. Wyatt has filled various positions in which bravery and determination were requisites, and in every instance proved himself the right man in the right place."[15]

But nothing was ever quite that simple in the complexities of southern Pima County. Almost from the time Wyatt Earp pinned on his new badge, he was in the midst of controversy.

TOMBSTONE SEEMED TO CHANGE DAILY. By mid-1880, wooden and adobe buildings replaced the tents that had lined the main business streets of Tough-nut, Allen, and Fremont. Restaurants, saloons, butcher shops, and many types of mercantile stores moved into the newly crafted buildings that sprouted in the business district. The Bilicke family opened a premier hotel in September of 1879, starting small and adding rooms. By the time the Cosmopolitan was completed in 1880, the two-story brick building had fifty guest rooms, all furnished with bedroom sets of black walnut and rosewood. The Grand Hotel sprang up in mid-1880, its sixteen rooms fitted with walnut furniture. Around the perimeter, cabins were built to house miners and merchandisers who would call them home, at least for a time. Burgeoning Tombstone offered an odd combination of grandeur and grit. Dust and garbage blew through the streets in front of fine hotels and new shops, always with more buildings under construction. Mining engineers from San Francisco bumped shoulders with Texas cowhands on the streets of the village on the hill above the grama grass.

It was from this wicked, dirty town that deputy sheriffs Wyatt Earp and Newton Babcock were charged with trying to control crime in the area, a challenge beyond realistic expectations. Earp assisted city marshal Fred White in keeping the town somewhat peaceful, but there were problems. As with most frontier towns, whiskey primed the order of things. In hard-drinking times, Tombstone was a hard-drinking town, and miners took their liquor stiff. Drunks caused constant problems, some minor, some murderous.

Death came for the strangest reasons in Tombstone. One July day in 1880, Tom Waters purchased a blue-and-black-checked shirt and proudly wore it into the saloon, where he quickly received a heavy dose of ribbing for the unusual garment. Soured by the criticism and bolstered by a few shots of whiskey, Waters vowed revenge on the next man who jested about his new shirt. "Now, if anyone don't like what I've said let him get up, God damn him, I'm chief, I'm boss. I'll knock the first son of a bitch down that says anything about my shirt again."

E. L. Bradshaw, Waters's close friend and cabin mate, came up and saw the shirt for the first time, then made a disparaging comment. Waters laid into him with his fists. Bradshaw left to bandage a cut above his eye and returned armed. "Why did you do that?" Bradshaw asked. Waters made some remark and apparently turned away. The angry Bradshaw, described as "very reserved and peaceable," fired four shots into his friend; two entered the center of Waters's back.

In a twist of irony, the *Epitaph* ran the story next to an advertisement for a local merchant who "has just received a large supply of checkered shirts."

Two weeks later, shots rang through Tombstone again, and the crowd raced to an alley behind the Headquarters Saloon to find Tom Wilson with a gunshot through his heart. Witnesses had seen Roger King approach the door of the saloon, fire one shot, then race in. Wilson ran out the back door with King in pursuit. King fired again, and Wilson fell. King calmly walked up the street and turned himself in to an officer, saying he had killed Wilson for robbing him.

King, employed as a stable-keeper, had already received some notice in Tombstone as leader of the anti-Chinese movement, an outgrowth of the Workingmen's Party in San Francisco, which advocated an end to Chinese immigration. The movement protested against the railroads, which brought in shiploads of Chinese workers to take the jobs of other workers, often Irish immigrants, at lower salaries. King quickly found support in Tombstone, where many of the boomers came because of the paucity of jobs elsewhere.

Wyatt Earp had the responsibility of delivering Roger King to Tucson for trial. He held him in town for several days to await orders to proceed. Much to his surprise, Tombstone resident John Pace came up to Earp and handed him a telegram directed to Deputy Babcock stating, "You will please deliver prisoner to J. J. Pace. C. Shabell." The message and misspelled signature puzzled Earp, and he told Babcock he thought it was a forgery. Babcock believed it genuine and advised Earp to give the prisoner to Pace. Earp followed his own hunch and wired Shibell, who affirmed that the message was a forgery. The *Nugget* praised Earp and made it clear that Wyatt Earp was nobody's fool.[16]

Temporarily, at least, the anti-Chinese fervor quieted in Tombstone, and the city received a report and a reprimand from *Nugget* owner and editor Artemus Fay.

> The anti-Chinese movement seems to have entirely disappeared along with its leader, King, who is presumably expounding his favorite doctrine to the inmates of the jail at Tucson. The usual bonfire was lighted last Saturday night and the President stated that no means save violence could be devised for rooting out the pest and as that was not for a moment contemplated, the matter had better be dropped, an opinion that was met with no signs of dissent. The legitimate workingmen of the camp had better fight shy of the next self-constituted leader who comes along and endeavors to induce them to make asses of themselves.[17]

Oddly, neither King nor Bradshaw, also tried in Tucson, was convicted. The *Epitaph* blamed politics for King's going free; apparently the county magistrates feared losing the votes of Anti-Chinese League members.

Perhaps the most celebrated murder of 1880 occurred just before Earp stepped into the role of deputy sheriff. Frank Leslie, a bartender and part owner of the Cosmopolitan, wore buckskin clothing and claimed to have served as an army scout. He was one of the most colorful characters in a colorful town and a well-known ladies' man. After chambermaid May Killeen separated from her husband, Mike, a bartender at Lowry and Archer's saloon, she began devoting her affections to Buckskin Frank Leslie. This did not sit well with Mike Killeen.

On the evening of June 22, Leslie and his friend George Perine stopped off at Lowry and Archer's for a drink and were greeted pleasantly by Mike Killeen. But later in the evening, Leslie told Perine that Killeen had threatened to kill both him and May if they attended an upcoming ball. About midnight, May Killeen showed up at the saloon and saw Leslie and Perine talking. She invited Buckskin Frank to sit on the porch of a nearby hotel. "Wait, I won't be gone over three minutes; wait in the barroom," Leslie said to Perine.

While Frank and May sat on the porch, two shots cut through the darkness, one creasing Leslie's scalp. Leslie said he wrestled with his opponent, drew his gun, and shot the assailant in the chest. Mike Killeen fell back mortally wounded. When the police arrived, Leslie claimed self-defense. May Killeen backed up his story, but Mike Killeen in a dying statement said that he had seen the couple on the porch and was leaving the area when Perine yelled, "Look out, Frank, here is Mike!" With that, both Leslie and Perine started shooting at him. He grappled with them and beat them both over the head with his pistol but was shot by Perine. The first judge to hear the case ruled out Killeen's dying statement and discharged Buckskin Frank. Free and happy, Leslie wed May Killeen August 8 at the Cosmopolitan Hotel, the ceremony officiated by Judge James Reilly. Six days later, Deputy Sheriff Earp received a warrant to arrest George Perine for murder.

E. T. Packwood, who heard Killeen's dying statement, testified at the hearing, and Dr. Henry M. Matthews contended that the position of the wound indicated that it could not have been inflicted by Leslie. Judge Reilly presided over a long, tumultuous hearing and held the prisoner to await the grand jury on charges of manslaughter. Perine, unable to raise the $5,000 bail, spent two months in a Tucson jail before the grand jury failed to return charges against him.[18] Community opinion considered Leslie responsible for the killing, but four decades later Earp would make clear that he believed Perine had fired the shots.[19]

Judge Reilly became the focus of much controversy in Tombstone during the Perine hearing. Before his appointment to the bench, Reilly and a local lawyer named Harry B. Jones had been opponents on a case. The case came up again—in Reilly's court—and Jones protested Reilly's serving as judge on a case where there might be a conflict of interest. When Jones arrived in court, Reilly ordered him to leave until he apologized for questioning the judge's integrity. Jones refused. But Jones had another problem. He was serving as George Perine's attorney, and the preliminary hearing was held before Reilly on August 17. Jones entered the court and sat beside Perine. According to the *Nugget* report, "Upon this Reilly, with the majesty which would have shamed a Roman

Emperor, thundered forth, 'Mr. Jones,' and pointed with a massive finger in an unmistakable manner toward the door. Jones understood the signal, and replied that he was there as an attorney and had a constitutional right to remain. Reilly ordered the officers in attendance to remove the offending attorney."[20]

Wyatt Earp, who was in the courtroom, hesitated, and Reilly rose and started toward Jones. But Jones drew a pistol and refused to leave. As Earp tried to step between the two, Reilly reached around and grabbed Jones by the coat collar. Jones responded by slugging Reilly on his judicial cheek. Earp leaped in to take control of the situation, arresting both judge and barrister, then leading them to the court of Justice Mike Gray. Jones was charged with assault and released on his own recognizance. He immediately returned to Reilly's courtroom, where the judge fined him $25 for contempt of court and sentenced him to 24 hours in the county jail.

The sentence meant Earp would have to waste his time taking the otherwise law-abiding lawyer to Tucson to sit in jail overnight. The sentence hardly warranted the trip, and Earp released Jones on his own recognizance before the two took the stage to Tucson. Reilly ordered Earp back to court the next day to show cause why he should not be fined for contempt for not immediately removing Jones to Tucson when Reilly made the order. In typical Wyatt Earp style, just as he had done with Bob Wright two years earlier in Dodge, the deputy sheriff turned the tables on Reilly by telling him to consider himself under arrest on a charge of assault as soon as he adjourned his court. It was typical of Earp to arrest a judge in his own courtroom. Wyatt would mollify saloon fights and negotiate when needed, but he would not take any guff from a petty politician whose silliness wasted his time. Earp escorted Reilly to Mike Gray's court, where the truculent judge was released on his own recognizance. Earp's case was postponed, then dropped. The situation seemed so absurd that the *Tucson Star*, after hearing the story from Jones, scoffed, "We think Harry Jones must have given the *Star* reporter a fill at Earp's expense."[21]

With a dandy bit of prognostication, the *Nugget* wrote: "Thus endeth the first chapter but it is more than probable that there will be succeeding ones of accumulating interest."[22] The succeeding chapters grew increasingly interesting as Earp made a powerful enemy whose revenge would echo for a century. Reilly, a first-class eccentric who had been humiliated by Wyatt Earp, would emerge as a premier spokesman of the anti-Earp group nearly two years later, when the circumstances in Tombstone would be much different.

On the afternoon of Earp's court appearance a petition began circulating around town calling for Reilly's resignation. The judge responded by running an ad in the *Epitaph* stating he would resign his office if a petition to that effect were signed by "forty or fifty names of men who make an honest living, as business or professional men, or as mechanics, miners or laborers." He obviously did not include Earp's pals in the saloon crowd. Tombstone responded. The next day the petition appeared in the *Epitaph* bearing 115 signatures calling for Reilly's resignation. Among the signers were Wyatt and Morgan Earp, city marshal Fred White, businessman Pete Spence, Mayor Alder Randall, Judge Bryant L. Peel, the owners of the town's two largest hotels, and numerous merchants. Reilly answered by chastising the businessmen for being "misled by the statements of persons in whose truth, integrity, and disinterestedness you had no good reason to rely," and for acting unfairly and without dignity.[23] Reilly refused to resign and, apparently, held a grudge against the Earps for years to come.

In about September of 1880, an old Earp friend from Dodge drifted into town. After his stay in Prescott, Doc Holliday found himself ready for a new array of gambling tables. His life in the territorial capital had been fairly quiet. Strangely, census records taken in June show that Holliday wound up living in the same rooming house as John J. Gosper, territorial secretary under Governor John Fremont, before making the trek south. The dentist brought along Big-Nose Kate for an investigation of the booming new mining town.

"I did not like it in Tombstone," Big-Nose Kate wrote in 1940. "I went to Globe, I wanted Doc to go with me, [but] the Earps had such power I could not get Doc away from them. I used to get letters from Doc to come to Tombstone, begging to pay him [a] visit. I went to see him three times."[24] More than a year would pass before Kate again visited Tombstone.

The unusual friendship between Earp and Holliday can never be fully understood. Earp would say Holliday saved his life in Kansas, which created a bond. Kate would say the friendship really grew on the trip West. Perhaps for Holliday, a factor was simply that Earp accepted the tubercular dentist at a time when many people feared the disease and would not think of coming near anyone who had it.[25]

On the evening of October 10, 1880, Holliday made his first trouble in town, engaging in a dispute with John Tyler, both described by the *Nugget* as "well-known sports." Holliday had probably known Tyler from Dodge. He and Tyler were gambling in the Oriental Saloon when an argument broke out. Several men stepped between the two, and Tyler left the saloon. Owner Milt Joyce chastised Holliday for creating a disturbance. When Doc argued back, Joyce threw him out of the saloon. The belligerent Holliday returned, demanding his pistol from behind the bar, where it had been placed by the officer who disarmed him during the shouting match with Tyler. The bartender refused to return the gun. Holliday left, only to return a few minutes later. Walking toward Joyce, Holliday swore lustily and fired a pistol from not more than ten feet away. Joyce leaped at the dentist and crashed a pistol against Doc's head. Marshal Fred White and a deputy raced in to pull Joyce off the bruised Holliday and confiscate the pistols. When the disruption ended, Joyce had taken a shot through the hand, and William Crownover Parker Jr., a 19-year-old partner in the bar, had been nicked in the big toe of his left foot. The shot totals were uncertain, but bartender Gus Williams was accused of firing in the melee.[26]

Charges were quickly dismissed against Williams, but Holliday was not so fortunate, receiving a $20 fine and $11.30 in court costs, the sentence handed down by Judge Reilly. Court records show that prosecuting witnesses failed to appear, and Doc plea-bargained from assault with a deadly weapon to assault and battery. The shooting began a stormy relationship between Holliday and Joyce that would affect the Earps. Joyce would become a political player in the area and align himself solidly against the Earps in coming months. Tyler would also become a nuisance around town; he would have a run-in with Wyatt Earp some weeks later.[27]

During his few months as deputy sheriff, Earp developed a reputation as a competent officer. A young lawyer named William J. Hunsaker practiced law in Tombstone during 1880 and early '81 before moving to Los Angeles and earning a reputation as one of the top legal minds in southern California. Hunsaker wrote about Earp: "His conduct as a peace officer was above reproach. He was quiet, but absolutely fearless in the discharge of his duties. He usually went about in his shirtsleeves without a coat and with no weapon in sight. He was cool and never excited, but determined and courageous. He never stirred up trouble, but he never ran away from it or shirked responsibility. He was an ideal peace officer and a law-abiding citizen."[28]

Summer and fall of 1880 proved most eventful in southern Pima County, and newspaper reports show Wyatt Earp dealing busily with all kinds of criminal activity. He chased horse thieves, arrested lot-jumpers, foiled petty criminals, and hunted killers, with Morgan often serving as his deputy. Morgan earned particular distinction in August after a horse theft in Contention. Wyatt dispatched Morgan and Virgil, serving as deputy sheriffs, to chase the horse thieves, when they came upon another band of rustlers with stolen army mules in their possession. One thief resisted, "but gave up when a six-shooter was run under his nose by Morgan Earp," the *Epitaph* reported.[29] The Earps just kept getting in the way of rustlers trying to earn a dishonest living.

Morgan had another odd moment in September while he was riding shotgun messenger on the Benson stage. Ten bars of silver bullion rode on the stage, with two in the hind boot. Much to Morgan's dismay, upon arrival at Contention, he and the driver discovered the boot had broken, and the two bars had fallen out somewhere along the road. They turned the stage and went hunting for the silver, finding the bars a mile apart down the road.[30]

Enforcing the law in the Tombstone district proved a far different experience from taming Texans in Dodge. These were no longer good ol' boys getting rambunctious after a party, these were real criminals: hard cases out rustling, stealing, and even killing on occasion. While Earp had tasted crime-solving in Dodge, his main job had been keeping the peace. Most problems could be solved by bruising a skull or letting a troublemaker sober up. Now he was facing off against the likes of Pony Deal, career criminals who lived outside the boundaries of society. The job called for a different level of skill than had been demanded in Dodge and Wichita. Earp met the challenge.

Wyatt Earp had already spent four months wearing his badge when another former lawman showed up in town in September of 1880. Nobody could help but like Johnny Behan, who had served in the territorial legislature and as sheriff of Yavapai County. He was the image of a budding politician, always bustling but never too busy to stop for a quick chat or to pass along a good story. Unlike the quiet and somber Earps, Behan had that good-guy, everyone's-pal quality that enabled him to make friends easily. He had already heard talk back in Prescott that a new county would be carved from Pima, meaning a big share for county officials who would get a piece of the tax money raised from mines, railroads, and other operations; Behan had the right political connections to wrangle an appointment when the time was right. Meanwhile, he served as a bartender at the Grand Hotel and became a partner with John Dunbar in a livery stable known as the Dexter Corral. In the past, Behan had gone through a bitter divorce, held government jobs, and built political alliances. He could spin stories, make friends, and influence just about anyone he met. These abilities would serve him well in Tombstone, at least for a time.

WHISKEY TINGLED THE TONGUE and addled the brain, and for some reason shootin' and sippin' seemed to go just fine together when the boys joined up for a night on the town in Tombstone. Shortly after midnight on October 28, a few rowdy sorts assembled to tipple at a saloon, then decided to take the fun outside and try to shoot the moon and stars out of the sky, the *Epitaph* reported. It was all good fun, the rowdies believed, rousting the townsfolk in the middle of the night. City marshal Fred White had a different idea. He came to break up the fracas and chased one of the boys into a vacant lot. The man he pursued would turn out to be Curley Bill Brocious, one of the leaders of the cowboy crowd with a reputation as a dangerous man with a gun.

Wyatt Earp, unarmed as usual, had been at Billy Owens's saloon when he heard three or four shots fired. Earp dashed into the street and saw the flash of a pistol through the darkness. Several more shots sounded as he sped toward the flashes and ran into his brother Morgan and Fred Dodge. Morgan pointed and said he saw several men run behind a building. Wyatt borrowed Dodge's pistol and chased after the shooters, passing a man named James Johnson as he ran. As Earp approached, he heard Fred White's voice saying, "I am an officer, give me your pistol." Curley Bill pulled his gun from the holster, and White grabbed the barrel.[31] Earp said he threw his arms around Curley Bill to check for other weapons. White yelled out, "Now you God-damned Son of a bitch, give me that pistol." The marshal gave the gun a quick jerk, and the pistol discharged. White held the pistol as he fell to the ground, a ball through his groin. He screamed, "I am shot," as his clothing caught fire from the muzzle blast. Earp immediately crashed his pistol onto the shooter's head, knocking Curley Bill to the ground. Stepping over Bill's body, he picked up the six-shooter, then grabbed Bill's collar and ordered him to get up. "What have I done? I have not done anything to be arrested for," Curley Bill protested.

Earp remained calm in the midst of chaos. Fred Dodge would write: "In all that fusillade of shots, Wyatt's voice sounded as even and quiet as it always did."[32]

As the townsmen took White to the doctor, Wyatt and Morgan Earp, along with Dodge, took charge of the prisoner. Everyone acquainted with the law feared that such a deed could lead to a lynching on the streets of Tombstone. They hustled him to the small jail, where Dodge and Morgan Earp stood guard while Wyatt, Doc Holliday, Virgil, and Turkey Creek Jack Johnson checked out the town. Dodge and Morgan Earp questioned every person approaching the jail to prevent any attempt to avenge the shooting of the town's marshal.[33] With the threat of a hanging in the air, Curley Bill went before justice of the peace Mike Gray and waived his examination at his lawyer's suggestion. Wyatt hurried Bill out of town and up to Tucson before the good citizens could put together a lynching party.[34]

Two days later Marshal Fred White, 32, died. The *Epitaph* estimated that a thousand people turned out for the funeral, the biggest showing ever in the new mining camp. All gambling was stopped and most stores closed on November 1, the day of the funeral.

White's death caused the town council to change the existing gun ordinance from prohibiting the carrying of concealed weapons to prohibiting the carrying of deadly weapons. This new law, that only police officers could carry guns in Tombstone, became a fitting memorial to Fred White. The council also appointed Virgil Earp acting city marshal and called for a special election on November 12. Virgil lost to Ben Sippy, 311–259, and Sippy won easily in the January general election when Virgil did not run.

Wyatt Earp took Curley Bill to Tucson for the hearing, and along the way picked up an interesting story. As Wyatt told the *Epitaph*, the outlaw asked him where he could get a good lawyer. Earp suggested the firm of Hereford and Zabriskie, but Curley Bill said he could not because James Zabriskie had prosecuted him in El Paso, Texas, for waylaying a stage, with one man killed and another wounded.[35] The citizens of Tombstone were not aware they had a man of such exploits in their midst, and it would not have been a comforting thought. Curley Bill, notorious rustler and robber, would have months of waiting in a Tucson jail cell to learn whether his life would end at the bottom of a rope.

Politics in Tombstone began to polarize in late 1880 and early '81 as the town grew rapidly. Less than two decades earlier, the Civil War had torn the fabric of the Union asunder, and many Northerners were still suspicious of Southerners, even believing another war might be needed to quiet the rebels who still insisted on following their own ways, sometimes in defiance of the government. The old animosities carried all the way to Tombstone.

"The Republican Party saved it [the nation] and must perpetuate it. It is too soon to trust it to the hands of the party seeking its destruction 17 years ago," ardent Republican George Parsons, Tombstone's intrepid diarist, wrote on September 1, 1880. "I have some fears of a Solid South from the action of that South—their words, policy, fraudulent census returns—thereby increasing their representation and general action. The old issues are not forgotten. I can now see the hollowness of Southern Chivalry. It is a name and nothing more. What other government under heaven would have granted amnesty to its traitors, given them their lands back and put them in power, and what is the result. . . . Perhaps the Republican Party will be called on again in an emergency."

The ranchers and cowboys of southern Arizona were mostly Democrats of Southern origin or sympathies. Many came West from Texas, looking for a new start and opportunity. The townies were mostly Republican, often from the Northeast or San Francisco, and involved in mining ventures or businesses. The townsmen charged the cowboys as the source of crime, responsible for robberies and rustling in the hinterlands. Many small ranchers blamed the town toughs— some called tinhorn gamblers—for the disorder. These were the cheap schemers, loungers, and con men, many of whom fancied themselves real gamblers. Both sides had their supporters, who would pass on stories for generations. The Clanton and McLaury families were perceived by many as prominent ranchers; the Earps belonged to the town faction. This was a situation filled with lingering animosities, with Northerners against Southerners, townies against ranchers, and Republicans against Democrats.[36]

Arizona had a history of Southern sympathy and had once been declared a territory of the Confederacy. Between the town's two newspapers, the *Epitaph* voiced the Republican view while the slightly older *Nugget* leaned toward the Democrats. Pima County was heavily Democratic, but many of the new miners and merchants in Tombstone voted Republican. Many Southerners held some sympathy for the displaced Texas cowboys; Northerners tended to see them as unholy scum terrorizing their towns. But business took precedence, and some of the riffraff actually contributed to commerce in their own unruly way.

"The Tombstone country is of a peculiar character, the community being unsettled and dangerous," Virgil Earp said. "Most of the business men there stay simply to make money enough to live somewhere else comfortably, and, of course, the greatest object with them is to have as much money as possible spent in the town and to get as much of it as they can, careless of the matters of dispensation or the results of rough manners. Aside from the legitimate business men, the bulk of the residents are idle or desperate characters, most of them coming into town broke and depending upon the gambling table or criminal ventures to supply them with means of livelihood and dissipation."[37]

A little rustled stock helped keep meat prices down, and stolen Mexican gold and silver streamed across the gambling tables and into the saloonkeepers' pockets. The cowboys were good business, even if they were bad trouble. In contrast, the mine operators wanted a safe Tombstone to attract investors, and to protect their own lives.

Almost every election in the post–Civil War era held the fervor of a religious crusade, and the first Tuesday in November of 1880 caused high fever in the West. Republican James Garfield and Democrat Winfield Hancock battled for the presidency, while Pima County's most contested race centered on Bob Paul's bid to unseat Sheriff Charlie Shibell. Garfield won the presidency by fewer than 10,000 popular votes and an edge of 59 votes in the electoral college. The race in Pima County proved even more complex. Democrat Shibell, despite appointing Wyatt Earp as his Tombstone district deputy, was perceived as more an administrator than a tough lawman and received the support of the cowboys. Oddly, outlaw John Ringo served as a delegate at the Pima County Democratic convention despite a question of his legitimacy because he had no legal residence. The Democrats chose to avoid problems and seat Ringo. In another strange note, the expected division of the county played no role in the election, and the residents of the southern portion of the county voted for candidates who would serve them for only a few weeks.

Shibell, a slight man of average height, could barely make a shadow against big Bob Paul, who earned a reputation as a tough officer, building an impressive record in California. He had often worked for Wells, Fargo. Earp sided with Paul against his boss, although he remained as Shibell's deputy sheriff. Shibell won reelection by a close margin as rumors ran through town of massive election fraud. The San Simon Cienega precinct recorded 103 votes for Shibell and one for Paul, in a district that had no more than 50 eligible voters. All but one of the 23 Democrats on the ticket received those 103 votes, including Mike Gray, while nearly all the Republican candidates polled only one vote each. The *Epitaph* noted: "The odd vote is said to have been cast by a Texas cowboy, who when questioned as to why he was voting the Republican ticket, said: 'Well, I want to show those fellows that there wasn't any intimidation at this precinct.'"[38]

Election officials for the district included Ike Clanton and John Ringo, two characters whose names did not exactly inspire trust. More puzzling was that the district votes were certified by a Henry Johnson, a name no one seemed to recognize. To complicate matters further, Clanton and Ringo had been appointed to oversee the San Simon results, then had their appointments revoked a few days before the election because of uncertainty whether they actually resided in Arizona Territory. Despite being relieved of their duties, Clanton and Ringo acted as election officials.[39]

Paul sought a recount, and the disputed election went before the district court in Tucson. Investigation showed that "Henry Johnson" was actually James K. Johnson, who had been with Curley Bill on the night of the shooting of Marshal White and did not quite qualify as one of Arizona's leading citizens. The situation became suspicious enough that Wyatt Earp apparently intervened. Earp officially resigned as deputy sheriff of Pima County, effective November 9. He would later say that he did not think it right to work in Paul's behalf to overturn the election while serving under Shibell. The ambitious Earp had little to lose with this decision. If Tombstone remained in Pima County, Paul would certainly reappoint Earp to the deputy job; if Tombstone became the seat of a new county, Governor John C. Fremont would appoint a new sheriff and Earp would be considered a prime candidate by the Republican governor, or so he must have thought.

Wyatt's resignation also came as the Earps made their biggest financial strike in Arizona. The brothers finally started succeeding as capitalists, selling a set of lots for $6,000, of which they received $1,000 down in August. In early November, Wyatt and partner Andrew S. Neff sold the Comstock mine for $3,000, a tidy sum at a time when lawmen made about $125 a month. They also sold an option on the adjoining Grasshopper mine. The Earps seemed to be finding their bonanza in land deals. Working as deputy sheriff would only get in the way of making real money. However, Earp would say he took an active role in helping Paul win the election fraud case. Earp's exact role is unclear, but he apparently struck a deal with Curley Bill: He would tell the accurate story of the Marshal White shooting in exchange for Bill's convincing his rustler pals to tell the truth about the San Simon fraud—trading one truth for another. Election judge Ike Clanton, Shibell's key witness, avoided the problem altogether by eluding the subpeona and never testifying.[40]

In Tucson, the debate continued. For two months, both sides in the election fraud put together their cases before arriving in court on December 28, 1880. It quickly became clear that there had been problems on both sides. Leslie Blackburn testified that he had seen votes for Shibell that had been inaccurately tabulated for Paul. Johnny Behan supported the statement. Johnson testified that he had shown up and Clanton told him to vote and sign his name "Henry Johnson." Other witnesses showed a pattern of deception.[41] The election results stank so badly that the *Arizona Weekly Star* remarked: "There is evidently 'something very rotten in Denmark,' or in plain language there has been some big cheating somewhere, and by some persons. The evidence is very straightforward and to the point and unless an earth, or some other kind of quake, occurs to upset the testimony given yesterday, why it looks to us like a very plain case, that out of 104 votes cast in San Simon, about 100 were fraudulent."[42]

The decision came January 29, when Judge C. G. W. French ruled the entire vote for Shibell at San Simon invalid and declared Paul the winner, with 1,684 legal votes to Shibell's 1,628. But Shibell's attorneys acted quickly, filing an appeal that automatically kept Shibell in office until a final decision by the territorial supreme court. Finally, on April 12, 1881, the court dismissed the appeal and Paul was named sheriff of Pima County. By then, much had changed, both in Tombstone and in the life of Bob Paul.[43]

WITH WYATT EARP'S RESIGNATION and return to private life in November of 1880, Shibell appointed genial Johnny Behan, already one of the best-liked men in Tombstone, as his new deputy. Through his various government jobs Behan had made many friends among the state politicos, and his contacts would serve him well through the coming months. Everybody's pal Johnny Behan began a cordial relationship with the Earps, and even sought Wyatt's political support.

Talk had grown serious of trimming the southern portion of Pima County to form a new county. The sheriff of the new county would also serve as tax collector, taking a cut of the revenue from mines and railroads. It would be a posh job with easy pickings for a big paycheck. Both Earp and Behan wanted the position, and Earp said that Behan had a deal to offer: If Earp would not seek the sheriff's job, Behan would name him undersheriff and split the lucrative tax-collecting profits. They would hire office help and deputies on salary, then share the profits. Behan could collect the taxes and Earp would serve as top enforcer, just as he had in Dodge under Larry Deger and Charlie Bassett.[44] Earp said he never applied for the sheriff's job, which would be awarded by Territorial Governor John C. Fremont. Behan said that he promised Earp the job whether Earp withdrew or not, which seems either unlikely or unwise.

Earp had other business at hand. One of his horses had been stolen shortly after he arrived in Tombstone, and he often heard rumors that the mount had wound up at the Clanton ranch. One night in late December an unusual series of events set off a confrontation. According to Behan, he had to deliver a subpoena to Ike Clanton in Charleston to testify in the Paul–Shibell case. After asking Virgil Earp how to locate Clanton, Behan set off for Charleston with his deputy sheriff, Leslie Blackburn, and another man. As they were riding in the dusk, they were passed by two speeding horsemen, one of whom Behan believed to be Virgil Earp. At roughly the same time, according to Wyatt Earp, he and Doc Holliday were returning from the Huachucas, where they were checking a water rights claim, when they ran into Sherman McMasters. Earp would later say that McMasters was one of several informants the Earps had among the rustler crowd.

"He told me that if I would hurry up that I would find my horse in Charleston," Earp said. "I drove into Charleston and seen my horse going through the streets towards the corral; I put up for the night at another corral." Wyatt said he wired back to brother Jim to get the proper paperwork to reclaim the stolen horse; Warren Earp soon after left Tombstone to deliver the documents. "While I was waiting for the papers Billy Clanton found out I was in town and went and tried to take the horse out of the corral. I told him that he could not take him out, that it was my horse. After the papers came he gave the horse up without any service of papers and asked me if I had any more horses to lose. I told him I would keep them in the stable after this and give him no chance to steal them."[45]

Behan said he arrived in Charleston after dark and found two familiar faces: "I . . . met Wyatt Earp and Doc Holliday there. I think I asked them what they were doing, or what they were on. Earp told me he was down there after a horse that had been stolen from him. Nothing more was said between us, and I came back to Tombstone. I was in Tucson a few days afterwards. I was told there that I came very near getting myself into a hell of a fuss. Ike Clanton said to me there that Earp said I had sent a posse of nine men down there to arrest him and take him to Tucson. Then he told me that he had armed his crowd and was not going to stand it."[46]

It would be typical of Earp to run such a bluff on Ike Clanton — to preempt the situation before it became a problem. Earp succeeded in regaining possession of his missing horse and avoided bloodshed, confrontation, or serious incident. But Ike was not forgiving. The Clantons had been shown up in their own town, and they would hold a grudge. This also proved the beginning of difficulties with the deputy sheriff. Behan apparently believed the Earps had come to warn Ike of the subpoena so Clanton could hide out and avoid testifying. Only Ike's testimony could preserve the votes of the San Simon district for Shibell, and Ike faced the choice of testifying accurately and going to jail for election fraud or lying and sending Curley Bill to the hangman. Behan apparently thought Earp had interfered with serving the subpoena and resented the intrusion. Very soon, however, they all would have something else to occupy their minds.

After having one mount stolen, Wyatt Earp hated to let anyone else ride his favorite racehorse, Dick Naylor. But on the morning of January 14, 1881, Dick Naylor needed exercise, and Virgil wanted to take him for a ride. Wyatt relented and allowed Virgil to ride off and check a mining claim called the Last Chance, about three miles south of Tombstone on the road to Charleston. Virgil rode out of town on the powerful, high-strung horse, and nearly reached the claim when he heard a commotion coming up the road. He saw a buckboard racing forward, with nothing else in sight, and recognized George McKelvey, the constable of Charleston, with a young, white-faced, manacled prisoner.

"Help us," the constable yelled. "They're after him to lynch him."

Virgil Earp told the prisoner to jump behind him on the back of Dick Naylor, and they raced into town, stopping at the Wells, Fargo office where Wyatt Earp watched their arrival. Wyatt recognized the prisoner as a little tinhorn gambler called Johnny-Behind-the-Deuce, for his favorite faro bet. Johnny told Wyatt he had killed a man in self-defense, and a mob from Charleston was on the way to lynch him.

What followed would become one of the more spectacular episodes in the Earp legend, with most agreeing that Wyatt's courageous actions that day impressed many of his townsmen. By the most plausible accounts, Wyatt took a shotgun from the Wells, Fargo office, then hustled Johnny into Vogan's bowling alley and saloon across the street, where Jim Earp tended bar. A throng of men from Charleston filled Allen Street, in front of the bowling alley, and Deputy Sheriff Behan and Marshal Sippy arrived. Wyatt ordered Virgil, Morgan, Doc Holliday, Fred Dodge, and three or four others to circle the gambler as he led a march across town to the livery stable. Wyatt, with a shotgun in hand, led the posse and rarely spoke, saying only, "Stand back there and make passage. I am going to take this man to jail in Tucson."

The mob halted their progression, and Earp looked at mine operator Dick Gird and told him to back off. Gird may have been a leader or, more likely, Earp selected him because he knew that Gird commanded much respect in town and was no troublemaker. Earp made it clear that Gird would die if the mob attacked the posse. Gird moved back. Others in the mob edged backward and off to the side to allow Wyatt's posse to pass and reach the livery stable, then take Johnny-Behind-the-Deuce to Tucson. Wyatt risked his own life to save that of a no-account tinhorn gambler. "They could have gotten me easily, but no one fired a shot," he said years later.[47]

The dramatic tale of Johnny-Behind-the-Deuce has fallen almost into the realm of legend, spawning several different versions. The *Epitaph* described the incident without even mentioning Wyatt Earp, instead crediting Virgil, Behan, and city marshal Ben Sippy for standing off the crowd. No period record survives telling of Wyatt Earp walking into a maddened mob to save the life of a scared young man. Yet there is really no doubt that it happened: even Billy Breakenridge, an Earp foe, credited Wyatt with the deed, as did townsman Robert Boller, who said Earp rushed into the milling crowd and ordered everyone to disperse: "As no one in the crowd was armed or knew what had been going on, they did as he demanded."[48] Certainly, much of the throng was made up of townsfolk who wandered onto the scene out of curiosity and made a few angry millhands appear to be a massive mob.

Parsons, usually the best observer, wrote: "A gambler called 'Johnny-Behind-the-Deuce,' his favorite way at faro, rode into town followed by mounted men who chased him from Charleston. . . . The officers sought to protect him and swore in deputies, themselves gambling men (the deputies that is) to help. Many of the miners armed themselves and tried to get at the murderer. Several times, yes a number of times, rushes were made and rifles leveled, causing . . . me to get behind the most available shelter. Terrible excitement, but the officers got through finally and out of town with the man bound for Tucson. . . . This man should have been killed in his tracks. Too much of this kind of business is going on. I believe in killing such men as one would kill a wild animal. The law must be carried out by the citizens or should be, when it fails in its performance as it has lately done." Fred Dodge, the Wells, Fargo spy, told virtually the same story.

Parsons did not mention Wyatt Earp at the time, but twenty years later he wrote to the *Los Angeles Mining Review*, "A day that I recall, one that Tombstoners now living will not forget, was one during which 'Johnny Behind the Deuce' was brought into town from Charleston. That was the day that saw the Earps and Doc Holliday stand off the crowd bent on hanging. . . . That was a gallant preservation of law and order on the part of the intrepid Earp posse and the nearest approach to a wholesale killing that Tombstone ever saw."[49]

Nearly a half century after the event, Parsons wrote to Wyatt Earp's biographer Stuart Lake: "Wyatt, I could see him now as his team went down the street, he backed his horse down the street fronting the mob and lowered his rifle every now and then on them when a rush was attempted. Several others were with him and kept the crowd back from a would-be lynching. . . . It was a very nervy proposition, particularly on the part of Wyatt."[50]

Wyatt Earp seemed to see the whole event with far less complexity. He matter-of-factly told writer Walter Noble Burns that Virgil rode into town with Johnny mounted behind him, "and turned him over to me, and miners came swarming in, and I faced five hundred of 'em and just didn't let them get him. That's all."[51]

While details are sketchy, the incident began when 18-year-old Johnny-Behind-the-Deuce, whose real name was probably Mike Rourke, killed Philip Schneider, the manager of the Tombstone Mining and Milling Company's San Pedro smelter. The *Epitaph* reported that Schneider was angry over a robbery at his cabin and believed Rourke responsible. Schneider went to Smith's Restaurant, moved near the stove, and commented on the cold weather. Rourke supposedly said, "I thought you never got cold." Schneider, according to the *Epitaph*, said, "I was not talking to you, sir." Rourke responded, "God damn you, I'll shoot you when you come out," and left the room.

The *Epitaph*, in graphic prose, wrote, "After eating his dinner, Mr. Schneider passed out the door, and was proceeding to the mill, when, true to his promise, the lurking fiend, who had desecrated himself with hell in his heart and death in his mind, drew deadly aim and dropped his victim dead in his tracks."[52]

A *Tucson Citizen* reporter stopped by Rourke's cell the day after his arrival in Tucson and described him as "rather under the average size, has a fair face, slight black mustache and well-marked eyebrows, blue eyes and black hair and seemed quiet and self-possessed." Rourke told the paper the incident started when Schneider made a remark about the weather and Rourke answered by saying, "Yes, it is cold." Schneider then said he was not talking to the young gambler and called him an obscene name, which Rourke resented. Rourke was hustled out by another man, and Schneider followed.

"I looked around and said, 'I don't want you to throw out any more insults to me.' He says, 'I wasn't talking to you.' I said, 'Well, that's all right, then, if you wasn't.'

"'Supposing I was,' says Schneider, 'what are you going to do about it?' I says, 'I ain't a-going to do anything about [it].' Schneider seemed to get mad, and kept coming nearer and nearer. I kept stepping back, and finally he got so close I put my left hand against him, as he got nearer. I said, 'Go away from me; I don't want any trouble with you.' He had a knife in his hand. I was excited, of course, for the man was twice as big as I was. I'm not certain whether the knife was open or not, for his hand was sideways to me and I could only see the end of the handle. He continued to crowd against me, and I pulled my gun and shot him." Rourke paused in his story and illustrated the motion of drawing a pistol.

"I was so excited when I shot him that I dropped my revolver and ran a little ways. I always tried to keep out of such trouble, and when I saw the blood— well I didn't hardly know what I *was* doing, I guess."[53]

A week after the incident, the *Citizen* reported:

> The accumulating evidence is more and more corroborative of Rourke's own story . . . in which case those newspapers which called loudly for the prisoner's gore should feel rather "cheap." More particularly the Tombstone Epitaph, which published a most ridiculously furious and improbable account of the affair. The Citizen now learns that to Deputy United States Marshal Virgil Earp and his companions the credit of saving the young man from the fury of the miners is due. There is too much inexcusable killing in this county, but if the statements of the arresting officers are to be credited there are a dozen men in our county jail who deserve lynching much more than does young Rourke.[54]

Rourke never stood trial. He escaped from jail in Tucson and headed for parts unknown.

The story grew in Tombstone lore, with numerous versions and added exploits. It has been told, retold, and dramatized to the point where fact and fancy mix into legend. It has been the grist for numerous movie plots and glorified to one of the bravest feats accomplished by a Western lawman. But at the time, this remarkable standoff by Wyatt Earp did not receive a line of newspaper coverage, and Wyatt did not even include the Johnny-Behind-the-Deuce story in his memoirs that appeared in the *San Francisco Examiner* in 1896. Wyatt Earp never seemed to believe this was much of a big deal at all.

CURLEY BILL SPENT MOST OF NOVEMBER AND DECEMBER sitting in the Tucson jail awaiting the court hearing that would make him a free man or send him to the hangman. He had maintained from the start that the killing of Marshal Fred White had been absolutely accidental, the result of White's trying to jerk the gun away from him on that October night when the cowboys tried to shoot the moon.

Wyatt Earp testified on December 27, 1880, in the court of Judge Joseph Neugass. Earp told his story of the events that night, detailing how White had indeed pulled the barrel of the gun before it went off in Curley Bill's hand. Earp said he examined the pistol and found only one discharged cartridge, with five remaining unfired. Morgan Earp told virtually the same story of the events.

James Johnson took the stand and said he had been out with Curley Bill and a few others when one of the band pulled a pistol and fired. Johnson said Bill even yelled, "Don't do that" to try to stop the shooting, but the revelers fired off several more rounds, which drew a rush of townsmen. He said he saw from about ten feet away that White demanded the pistol by saying, "You damned son of a bitch, give me the gun," then jerked the weapon as it went off. Johnson was certain Bill had not drawn his gun before White demanded it.

Gunsmith Jacob Gruber examined the pistol and found it could be fired at half-cock, meaning it could have gone off accidentally as White grabbed the gun. Also introduced was a dying statement from the marshal saying he believed the shooting had not been intentional. Judge Nuegass reviewed the case and ruled accidental homicide. He discharged Curley Bill from custody, with Wyatt Earp's statements playing a major role in the decision. While Earp may well have made a deal with Brocious on the Paul–Shibell election, he still delivered on his end. The former deputy sheriff had the opportunity to lie and rid the community of probably the most dangerous man in southern Arizona—to go back on his deal—but he chose instead to tell a straight story. It is one of the great ironies of this saga that Wyatt Earp's honesty would lead to the exoneration of a man who was to become one of his key adversaries over the next seventeen months of what came to be called the Arizona War.[55]

Little more than a week after Curley Bill went free on the murder charge, he decided to do a little celebrating with a spree that became notorious across the West. On Saturday night, January 8, 1881, as told by Wells, Fargo detective Jim Hume, Curley Bill and a friend walked into a crowded Mexican dance hall in Charleston, and each cowboy placed his back against an exit door. At a given signal, they drew their guns and yelled for the music to stop.

"Strip, every one of you," shouted Bill. They did so without hesitation, according to Hume. "Now, strike up a tune," Bill said to the musicians.

For about a half hour, a mad fandango was danced, with Bill and his accomplice holding pistols as the dancers swayed and glided to the Mexican music. The restrained newspaper reports avoided description and left Curley Bill's naked fandango to the imagination of their readers, who could envision bouncing breasts and dangling organs, all boldly displayed for the entertainment of the two drunken cowboys.

A local officer passed by the ballroom and looked in the window at the strange scene. He quickly organized a posse of four or five men to try to capture Curley Bill. They decided it would not be a good idea to race into the hall with pistols blazing, so they hid in a corral where the cowboys had left their horses, with plans to shoot them down when they came out. As the cowboys were on their way to the corral, one of the pistols of the officers' posse went off accidentally. Bill and his companion at once raised their pistols and began firing into the corral. Under cover of darkness the not too heroic preservers of law and order crawled out of the enclosure and made good their escape. The horses of the cowboys had not been injured, but several other horses in the corral had been wounded by the shots. The next day Bill sent a friend over to Charleston with money to pay for the damage done.[56]

Curley Bill followed his Saturday-night indulgence in mass nudity with a little piety on Sunday morning. According to Hume, the two cowboys rode up the road three miles to Contention. They kept drinking and were well fueled by the time they reached a church with an itinerant preacher pounding out a sermon. The two cowboys stalked up the middle aisle of the church, with guns drawn and the congregation frozen into silence. Curley Bill spoke out. "You're a pious sort of man, I've been told, but I want to test it. You just naturally think of the Savior while my bazoo [gun] works, and at the same time pay a little attention to me." The minister agreed.

"Now stand perfectly still and you won't get hurt," Bill said. "Don't move a peg or this congregation will be without a gospel sharp. Do you take?"

The two cowboys began firing, with the shots striking the side wall above and on either side of the pastor's head, some coming within an inch of his cranium. The minister never flinched, only to lift his head toward the roof for a prayer.

When the gunfire stopped, Curley Bill spoke out. "You have given us an evidence of piety which shows that you have chewed the Bible to good advantage. I'm damned if I don't like your style, and if you don't climb up to the good place, it's because the seats are already filled. Now step down on the floor, my pious friend, and we will have the doxology.

"Come right down," Curley Bill said when the minister hesitated. "It shan't cost you a cent, and Pete, my Christian friend here, will provide the music." He pointed to his pal. The minister stepped to the floor and folded his hands as Curley Bill laid out his next command.

"Now dance a jig, and see if you can't discount Solomon in all his glory."

The minister finally protested. "I can't dance. You know not what you ask."

"Oh, that's all right," Curley Bill responded. "Do the best you can. Dance anything, only dance you must." Curley Bill pulled his gun and the minister began shuffling his feet, continuing until Bill ordered him to stop.

"My friend, your piety is of the right stripe. It pleases me to find that this congregation has such a worthy man to guide its spiritual affairs. Now go right ahead with your gospel chin music and proceed with your bible lessons to the kids."[57]

With that, Curley Bill and his friend left the church and headed for Tombstone. There were more adventures ahead.

Neither the nude dance nor the preach-and-pray incident can be confirmed by the few extant Tombstone newspapers for that week, but diarist George Parsons wrote obliquely on January 10: "Some more bullying by the cowboys. Curly Bill and others captured Charleston the other night and played the devil generally, breaking up a religious meeting by chasing the minister out of the house, putting out lights with pistol balls and going through the town." He provided further confirmation with his May 13 entry when he encountered an itinerant preacher he called McKane, actually Joseph McCann, this "rough, uncouth dominie, is a strange, original character. He is the one Curly Bill made dance and commanded to preach and pray, shot out lights, etc., at Charleston recently. He won't discuss the matter."

After the wild night of nude dancing and the less than reverent Sunday morning in church, Parsons recorded that Curley Bill showed up in Tombstone Monday night to continue the rampage. "They captured the Alhambra Saloon here and raced through the town firing pistols."

A little more than a week later, Curley Bill was back in action in Contention, according to a letter-writer to the *Arizona Star.* On January 18, Curley Bill and a companion identified only as George took a few shots at an innocent citizen, stole $50, and generally were a nuisance. When Deputy Sheriff T. B. Ludwig came forward to make the arrest, Bill and George warded him off with Henry rifles. A citizens' posse went out after the troublemakers, and shots were exchanged without injury before Bill escaped. The writer railed against the Pima County sheriff's office for failing to take control of the situation: "The Sheriff and his deputies have the authority to call out a force sufficiently strong to take in small bands of evil doers—or large ones either. It is disgraceful that this 'Curly Bill' should occupy the gate to Tombstone—Waterville—for two days after such an outrage as that of the 18th. This bravado sent messages to some of the deputy sheriffs 'that he was there and to come and take him.' He was seen and at the time had on two belts of cartridges, a revolver, and a Henry rifle in his hand. The time has come to make this community too hot to hold them. The terror these men have caused the traveling public, as well as the residents along the San Pedro, is having a serious influence, and this scab on the body politic needs a fearless operation to remove it. Let the Sheriff and his deputies see to it. It is no trouble to find the rascals, for they are not hiding, and they defy the law."[58]

Curley Bill had emerged as a Grade A frontier badman, with a reputation to match. In the coming months, he would draw national publicity in the *Police Gazette*, which printed a version of Hume's story, and his activities would be covered in the San Francisco papers. Through 1880, he apparently confined his nefarious activities to cattle rustling and looting Mexican pack trains moving through Arizona and Sonora, but he would gradually extend his range of operations. He had arrived in Arizona from Texas with a mysterious past. Even his real name is uncertain; one of his friends spelled it Brosciou, though court records list it as Brocious. His deeds were later confused with those of another Curley Bill, Curley Bill Graham, who occasionally rode in Arizona, but the two were different desperadoes. Most references to Brocious were simply as "Curley Bill." In Arizona, that was enough.[59]

Deputy Sheriff Billy Breakenridge described him as "fully six feet tall, with black curly hair, freckled face, and well built."[60] In one of the truly peculiar parts of the Tombstone saga, Breakenridge describes how he befriended Curley Bill and recruited him as assistant tax collector.

The idea of my asking the chief of all the cattle rustlers in that part of the country to help me collect taxes from them struck him as a good joke. He thought it over for a few moments and then, laughing, said, "Yes, and we will make everyone of those blank blank cow thieves pay his taxes."

Next day we started and he led me into a lot of blind canyons and hiding places where the rustlers had a lot of stolen Mexican cattle, and introduced me something like this:

"Boys, this is the county assessor, and I am his deputy. We are all good, law-abiding citizens and we cannot run the county unless we pay our taxes."

He knew about how many cattle they each had, and if they demurred, or claimed they had no money, he made them give me an order on their banker [George] Turner. Curly had many a hearty laugh about it. He told them that if any of them should get arrested, it would be a good thing for them to show that they were taxpayers in the county.

I was treated fine by all of them, and I never want to travel with a better companion than Curly was on that trip. He was a remarkable shot with a pistol, and would hit a rabbit every time when it was running thirty or forty yards away. He whirled his pistol on his forefinger and cocked it as it came up. He told me never to let a man give me his pistol butt end toward me, and showed me why. He handed me his gun that way, and as I reached to take it he whirled it on his finger, and it was cocked, staring me in the face, and ready to shoot. His advice was, that if I disarmed anyone to make him throw his pistol down.

I learned one thing about him, and that was that he would not lie to me. What he told me he believed, and his word to me was better than the oaths of some of whom were known as good citizens.[61]

The bizarre sight of Behan's deputy riding around the backcountry with the most noted desperado in the territory could not have been comfortable to the honest ranchers in the area, and undoubtedly it cut into Behan's public support in the community. But it did raise the tax revenue, with Behan getting a percentage. And money always mattered to Johnny Behan. For Curley Bill, death and taxes had become his business.

As with many badmen, Curley Bill had a charm about him that seemed to win friends. Emma Muir recalled the rustler from her childhood in the New Mexico mining town of Shakespeare. She described him as more than six feet tall and of massive bulk, with a heavy beard, and often wearing a red tie. When he got drunk, which was often, he would shoot quarters from between the fingers of anyone willing to hold the target. Most were willing, because few would risk becoming the victim of his temper. Bill had a reputation to match his temper, with the locals believing he had recorded many kills. Despite all this, Muir and her family liked Curley Bill.

"Desperadoes, when not working at their business, were like anybody else, considerate, honorable, good neighbors," Muir wrote. "I remember the first time I met Curly Bill. . . . Only Mother, my sister and I were at home. Someone knocked at the door. Mother opened it. There stood Curly Bill. We knew him by sight, but had never been so close to him. He had at that time incurred the wrath of Shakespeare, which had added to the price on his head. But that did not bother mother. She just saw a stranger at the door, and supper was ready."

Emma's mother greeted the outlaw by saying, "Good evening. You're just in time. Emma, lay another plate."

Bill responded cordially. "Thanks, ma'am, but somebody might see me here and it would go hard with you. I have a clean flour sack and I would shore appreciate it if you put some of those biscuits in it. I haven't any money now, but I'll drop by some time and pay you."

She declined the offer for payment and filled a flour sack with biscuits, a package of Arbuckle's coffee, and a large piece of steak, carefully wrapped in paper. As they filled the sack, the outlaw went over to inspect an Estey organ the family had brought from Virginia City. "That," he said, "is the first organ I have seen since I left home, where my mother had one. She used to play it and sing to us kids. Never thought I'd do this sort of thing then. Well, ma'am, thanks. And don't tell anyone I was here, please."[62]

Tom Thornton, the Galeyville hotelkeeper who catered to cowboys, blamed most of Curley Bill's reputation on bad press. "You newspaper men have given him an undeserved notoriety. He ain't half as bad as you paper writers have made him out to be," he told the *San Francisco Examiner.* "Curly Bill is a bad man when he gets riled up, but he is neither a robber nor a murderer. . . . The worst trick I ever knew him to do was to go into a restaurant once, while the people were at dinner. He was drunk and pulled out his two revolvers and laid them beside his plate, and ordered every one at the tables to wait until he was through as it was ungentlemanly and impolite to rise before all had finished their meal. Of course, everybody in the restaurant sat and waited until Bill got done eating, but he was so 'full' he laid down his head upon his arms and fell asleep, and the folks were so afraid of him that they supposed he was just shamming sleep so as to get a chance to shoot the first one who rose from the table. They all waited until he awoke, when he paid the bill [for everyone in the crowd] and left.

"Another time Bill came into my place of business," Thornton continued. "I saw that Bill was drinking, and, of course, said nothing to annoy him. He seemed to be annoyed at my lamps and said, 'Tom, ain't your lights a little too bright. They hurt my eyes some. Shall I put out some?' I told him he might put out one, just to satisfy him. He then pulled out a pistol and shot the light out without breaking the lamp. He then went out and shot out as many lights as he imagined gave him offense."[63]

Curley Bill had become a pain in the neck for the local constabulary, and in May he had more than a pain in his own neck. Thornton said the hard feelings began because Curley Bill jokingly shot the horse of his partner, Jim Wallace, and rode into town while his rustling buddy had to walk. On May 19, Curley Bill, Wallace, and eight or nine of their pals were drinking in Galeyville when Breakenridge rode into the little mining town in the mountains of southeastern Arizona. Galeyville sat in a small valley between two sharply rising peaks, with mines scattered up and down both sides and a few stores near the bottom. The small saloon district sat on a flat outcropping on the bank of Turkey Creek, facing the magnificent rise of a mountain across the trickle of a stream. The village had boomed quickly in late '80, and its residents included a woman blacksmith named Mrs. M. E. Harrington.

When Deputy Sheriff Breakenridge entered the bar, Wallace pulled his revolver and yelled out an insult, according to a published report. The deputy paid little attention and quietly left the saloon. Curley Bill, clearly a friend of Breakenridge's, ordered Wallace to go find the deputy and apologize. Wallace did as told and brought Breakenridge back to the saloon to find Curley Bill in a quarrelsome mood. Bill laid into Wallace, ending with, "You damned Lincoln County son of a bitch, I'll kill you anyhow." Wallace started toward the door of the saloon with Bill in close pursuit. Just as they stepped out the door, Wallace turned and fired his pistol, the ball entering the left side of Bill's neck and crashing out through his right cheek, breaking his jawbone.

From all directions miners and residents came running. Curley Bill's friends threatened a lynching, while the law-abiding sorts stood in the background, willing to let the outlaws go to war among themselves. Breakenridge stepped in and arrested the shooter, preventing further bloodshed on the streets of Galeyville. After a brief hearing, Wallace was discharged. The cowboys carried Curley Bill to a nearby house, believing him close to death. A doctor arrived and said the wounds were "dangerous, but not necessarily fatal," with about a 50–50 chance of recovery.

The *Arizona Star* provided the comment, "A great many people in southeastern Arizona will regret that the termination was not fatal to one or both of the participants. Although the wound is considered very dangerous, congratulations at being freed from this dangerous character are now rather premature, as men of his class usually have a wonderful tenacity of life."[64]

Thornton, the cowboys' pal, claimed to care for the injured outlaw for the next two months. "He was shot clean through the head, and it seemed almost impossible for him to live through it. He says he just lived so that he could kill his cowardly partner." When asked in October if Bill had met up with Wallace, Thornton answered, "Not yet, but they will and when they do someone will drop, for Bill will surely kill him on sight. I would advise him to keep out of Bill's tracks, but he is likely to run across him some day."

Before the outlaw had recovered enough to stir up more trouble, he was in the news again when time ran out on Tom Harper. Harper had been convicted of the 1880 murder of an unarmed John Talliday, described as an old man, in a dispute over money. On July 8, all Harper's appeals ended. Under Pima County sheriff Bob Paul's order, he dropped through the gallows floor, dying on the end of a rope. His last message had been directed to his friend, Curley Bill, telling him: "Curley, you are aware that I am not in the habit of lecturing any man, but in this case you may remember the words of a dying man (for I am all to intents and purposes such), and perhaps give heed to them. . . . Curley, I want you to take warning by me. Do not be too handy with a pistol. Keep cool and never fire at a man unless in the actual defense of your life. You must stand a heap from a man before you kill him. Words do not hurt, so you must never mind what is said to aggravate you. As I said before, don't try and hunt a row. Give my kind regards to any of my old friends who you may chance to meet, and tell them to take a warning by me. I bear no ill will, and I think I am going to die in peace. Hoping you will take heed of what I write, I am, as ever, your unfortunate friend. THOMAS HARPER"[65]

Curley Bill had been forewarned, but the warning was ignored. As soon as he recovered, he rode out to cause more trouble. His wound and the wisdom of avoiding a tangle with Marshal Virgil Earp kept him away from Tombstone for most of '81. Much happened during those months.

Fate had finally favored Wyatt Earp in January of 1881. His mining ventures had just sold for a goodly sum of money, and he and his brothers had other promising sites just waiting to be picked up. It would not be long before Johnny Behan officially received the appointment as sheriff for the new county, which they had agreed would give Earp the job of undersheriff. Earp had always preferred enforcement to the mundane duties of tax collecting. From the beginning, he had shown a keen interest in accumulating money; building a significant stake that would allow him and Mattie some degree of future independence. With just about everything else going right in his life, another opportunity found Wyatt Earp.

Shortly after the Johnny-Behind-the-Deuce affair, he went into partnership with Lou Rickabaugh in the gambling concession at the Oriental Saloon. Earp would be a good man to have at hand if there was trouble at the most spectacular saloon and gambling palace in the region. "The 'Oriental' is simply gorgeous and is pronounced the finest place of its kind this side of San Francisco," correspondent Clara Brown wrote back to the *San Diego Union*. "Every evening music from a piano and a violin attracts a crowd; and the scene is really a gay one — but for all the men. To be sure, there are frequent dances, which I have heard called 'respectable,' but as long as so many members of the demimonde, who are very numerous and very showy here, patronize them, many honest women will hesitate to attend."[66]

While Clara Brown and the other respectable Easterners may have been put off by the demimonde, other residents found the saloon life downright respectable. Wyatt Earp had always been as much a gambler as a lawman, and gamblers enjoyed a respect above that accorded some other classes. The *Arizona Star* editorialized: "The profession of gamblers is as honorable as the members of any stock-exchange in the world—and braver. Their word is as good as their bond."[67] In the West, this was not a job that came with an apology, and Wyatt Earp always took pride in his position as a gambling professional. Nearly forty-five years later, when asked what he did in Tombstone other than wear a badge, he answered, "Well, I dealt awhile in pasteboard and ivory," his way of saying he ran a faro bank.[68] Earp and the majority of his frontier neighbors considered this a legitimate enterprise.

The Oriental's gambling room provided an atmosphere unequaled in the wilds of Arizona, and after its doors opened other gambling parlors noticed a falloff in business. According to Stuart Lake, John Tyler, Doc Holliday's old adversary, had been hired by a rival gambling operator to make trouble at the Oriental to try to keep patrons away. Earp offered some confirmation when he said in 1896: "Then the proprietors of 'the Oriental,' the biggest gambling-house in town, offered to take me into partnership. One of them—his name was Rickabaugh and he was a San Francisco man—was unpopular, and a coterie of the tough gamblers were trying to run the firm out of town."[69]

Owner Jim Vizina rented the Oriental's bar and restaurant to Milt Joyce, with the gambling room going to a small group of San Francisco gamblers headed by Lou Rickabaugh and including William Crownover Parker Jr., a 19-year-old whose wealthy father financed the investment. Also in the partnership was Bill Harris from Dodge City. They agreed to sell Earp a quarter interest— probably at a greatly reduced price—for his presence as an enforcer. Tyler showed up to cause problems shortly after Earp joined the partnership. Tyler purchased $100 worth of chips and sat in at Rickabaugh's faro table. The basic idea of the game is to place a bet on any of the thirteen ranks of cards on the layout. Two cards are drawn, one called the winner and the other the loser. Stakes are paid to those who hit the proper card. Tyler put his money on the queen, and Lake described what followed:

"Deal 'em, you big so-and-so," he challenged, "and if the queen loses, I'll blow that stack into your bank!"

Rickabaugh filled the dealer's slot to overflowing and a shot that scattered the stack of chips would send the forty-five caliber slug tearing through his body. Lou looked the gunman in the eye and made a turn. The queen did not show.

Johnny Tyler screamed with pain. A muscular thumb and forefinger was hoisting him from his seat by an ear-lobe. If he had an idea of gunplay, he abandoned it when he saw who had him.

"I didn't know you had an interest in this place," Tyler exclaimed.

"I have," Wyatt Earp assured him, "and you can tell your friends it's the fighting interest."

Using the ear as a lever, Wyatt propelled Tyler to the door. With a shove and a boot he sent the gunman sprawling into Allen Street. As he turned back into the Oriental, Wyatt saw Tyler's followers lined up at the bar, hands in the air, and looking into Doc Holliday's nickel-plated six-gun.

"Much obliged, Doc," Wyatt said. "Herd 'em outside with their friend."[70]

There is no confirmation that any such incident happened. It was not the type of event that would have been reported in the newspapers—sore ears did not make big news in Tombstone. And Lake often blew up little stories into major confrontations. But after Earp became a part owner in the gambling operation, trouble quieted down at the Oriental. Newspaper stories later refer to Tyler sitting in on big poker games at other gambling dens, but the attempt to stop business at the Oriental seemed to end with one act by Earp. The grand gambling salon would become a tough place for intimidators as Bat Masterson and Luke Short moved down from Dodge to work as dealers and provide two more competent gunhands. With Short, Masterson, and the Earps cruising the area, the Oriental would be the wrong place to cause trouble. A gambler named Charlie Storms found that out on February 25 when he drunkenly engaged in a heated argument with Short. Just as they drew their guns, Masterson jumped between them to prevent bloodshed. Bat then took Storms back to his room at the San Jose House and returned to try to calm Short, but Storms returned and started to draw. Short beat him.[71] Parsons recorded the details:

> Quite peaceable times lately, but today the monotony was broken by the shooting of Charles Storms by Luke Short on corner of Oriental. Shots—the first two were so deliberate I didn't think anything much was out of the way, but the next shot I seized hat and ran out into the street just in time to see Storms die, shot through the heart.
>
> Both gamblers, L.S. running game at Oriental. Trouble brewing during night and morning, and S. was probable aggressor though very drunk. He was game to the last and after being shot through the heart, by a desperate effort (steadying revolver with both hands) fired four shots in all, I believe. Doc Goodfellow brought bullet into my room and showed it to me—45 calibre and slightly flattened; also showed a bloody handkerchief, part of which was carried into wound by pistol.
>
> Short, very unconcerned after shooting—probably a case of kill or be killed. Played Abbott in chess tonight. Forgot to say that the faro games went right on as though nothing had happened after body was carried to Storms' room at the San Jose House.

Storms died in his room. All Bat Masterson's efforts to prevent a killing between two of his friends had failed, and a gambler lost the draw and his life. Masterson's testimony led to Short's acquittal as the court ruled self-defense.

All through January and into February, Wyatt Earp dealt faro and waited for Behan to deliver on his promise to name him undersheriff for the new county. Up in the territorial capital of Prescott, the representatives squabbled and argued over the details of carving up Pima. *Nugget* editor Harry M. Woods led the effort to form a new county, drawing the ire of his old friends from Tucson, who accused him of selling out the people who elected him to the legislative assembly. The main issue in conflict was that Pima had built a significant debt, and Tucson officials wanted the rich mining districts in the south to help pay. Finally they compromised: the new county would assume part of the debt, and on February 2, 1881, Tombstone became the seat of a new county rich in mining prospects and bustling with recent arrivals. It was to be named after famed Apache leader Cachise, but something went wrong.

"Cochise County—the right name is Cachise, but in the bill passed by the Legislature creating it, the spelling was done with an o, and it has to remain so," explained Richard Rule, who served as secretary to the legislature before coming to Tombstone to work at the *Nugget*.[72]

The *Epitaph* did not like it better one way than another. "It is immaterial whether it be spelled with an 'o' or an 'a,' either way is bad enough. Why the name of such a villainous enemy of our race should have been attached to our county is beyond comprehension."[73] Even the county stationery said Cachise, and the *Epitaph* ran Cachise in its masthead. Accuracy bowed to usage, however, and it has stayed Cochise County ever since.

The new county was ripe with political plums, and jobs would be filled by the governor to last until the November general election of '82. Territorial governors were appointed, not elected, and the Republican administration of President Rutherford B. Hayes had given the job to John C. Fremont, who led California's fight for independence and served as the Republicans' first presidential candidate in 1856. The old Pathfinder, as Fremont was called, had slowed with age, but he still had a few tricks left in what looked to be a big-time battle for jobs in the new county. Fremont made the appointments, but they had to be approved by the dominantly Democratic legislative council, the upper house of the territorial legislature. As Behan had told Earp, his political friends in Prescott could virtually assure him the appointment as sheriff of Cochise. Cockily, the Democrats believed they could control all appointments in the new county, and they sent a slate of candidates to the governor and demanded their appointment. Fremont responded by nominating six Republicans and five Democrats, including Behan.

The council quickly approved Behan and rejected three of the Republicans, including Lyttleton Price for district attorney. Fremont compromised and replaced a Republican nominee for supervisor with Democrat Milt Joyce, which gave the Democrats control of the county board. He then nominated Al T. Jones, another Democrat, for recorder.[74] However, the council adjourned without approving a district attorney, and Fremont arbitrarily appointed Price, a move that could not be countered by the Democrats because the session had ended. This led to months of conflict before Price would officially hold office. A Republican district attorney would be a powerful voice in county politics as well as an important party presence. Price criticized the Democratic legislators for their greed and vested interests. In a letter to the Republican *Epitaph*, he accused a few of the Democrats of creating the county with the intention of taking the best jobs for themselves, only to learn that U.S. laws forbade so blatant an abuse of power. "It is no secret that certain of the honorable gentlemen were to share in the emoluments of various offices, neither is it any secret that certain of the honorable gentlemen are now taking their division of the spoils while others are languishing under disappointment. The governor conceded to them most of the appointments, and they maligned and insulted him for not getting the rest."[75]

One of the men left yearning for power was Harry M. Woods, who had risked his Tucson friendships to push through the bill forming the new county and undoubtedly expected to profit from his actions. Woods would have been a logical candidate for county treasurer, but federal rules prohibited him from a chance to collect what he and his associates considered their just rewards.

The council approved Johnny Behan's appointment as sheriff of Cochise County on February 10 to a chorus of support from the press, with the exception of the *Epitaph*, which had boosted Thomas Sorin for the job. Wyatt Earp never received any serious consideration. The Republican Prescott Miner even supported Behan and wrote: "He has the stamina and courage to execute any order given him, and we predict that the Epitaph staff, now so terribly sorry, will have occasion to change their opinion of the gentleman before the close of his official term of office."[76] Many opinions would change indeed by the time Behan would leave office.

Behan quickly traveled to Prescott after the appointment. Whether he met with Woods then or the decision came later, he would soon agree to give Woods the job of undersheriff, where Woods could help collect taxes until the elections in 1882. Behan's promise to the politically naive Wyatt Earp could be forgotten. This was politics, and politics took priority over promises. Woods needed a government job, and his political friends were the same political friends who made sure Johnny would get the plum post of tax collector and sheriff. Pragmatic politics dictated only one maneuver—give Harry Woods the job of undersheriff and leave Wyatt Earp to fend for himself. Behan already had his profit from the deal—Earp had not actively sought the office to complicate the situation. Now the only problem left was to explain the change to Wyatt Earp. This, according to both Earp and Behan, the new sheriff never did.

LOVE STRUCK JOHNNY BEHAN. With a lucrative new job as sheriff and tax collector, Johnny bowed to passion. He went to San Francisco to woo the woman who, he said, would become his bride, the lovely daughter of a Jewish family, a young woman blessed and burdened with a spirit of adventure and a lust for excitement. Josephine Sarah Marcus met Johnny on her first trip to the frontier, late in 1879. Light opera had become a favorite in America, and Gilbert and Sullivan's *H.M.S. Pinafore*, the rousing tale of British seafarers, quickly became the most popular play in the land. Josephine Marcus, called Sadie by family and friends, longed to become an actress.

Sadie Marcus would often say she ran away from her rich San Francisco family for the excitement of a fling in show business, but the Marcuses were not rich. Hyman "Henry" Marcus worked as a baker, and the family lived in lower-middle-class neighborhoods while Josephine grew up. Her parents originally came from Germany to New York, then west to California in 1869 by sailing around the Horn, circling the lower tip of South America. No records of Josephine's birth have been discovered, and even her year of birth is uncertain, although it is most generally believed to be 1861 in New York.[77]

Sadie Marcus, with her friend Dora Hirsch, studied dance in San Francisco when an opportunity arose. George N. Pring and his wife were promoting a *Pinafore* tour of Arizona and brought a musical company by rail to end of the train line in Casa Grande, about sixty miles north of Tucson. On October 4, the women of the troupe refused to make the stage trip to Tucson, and the Prings found themselves loaded with dates and obligations but no *Pinafore* singers. Mrs. Pring returned hurriedly to San Francisco to recruit another troupe and struck it lucky: the acclaimed actress Pauline Markham had just finished an engagement at the Bella Union and agreed to join Pring on the Arizona tour. Markham had to quickly find singers to back her act and, apparently, Sadie and Dora were chosen.

Sadie would later tell writers Mabel Earp Cason and Vinnolia Earp Ackerman that she and Dora were "two giddy, stage-struck girls setting out in the world with very little equipment except their looks." By Sadie's account, the two girls sailed to Santa Barbara to join the troupe and later wound up on a stagecoach in San Bernardino. By her story, the coach rolled across the miles of desert toward Tucson when suddenly a band of riders joined the players, a group of scouts under the command of well-known scout Al Sieber. The performers were told that Apaches had jumped the San Carlos reservation, and the scouts would provide an escort. At one point Apaches were sighted over a distant hill, and Sieber's patrol rode out to drive them off. While Sieber's scouts hunted the Apaches, the coach passengers took refuge at a ranch, sleeping on the floor for about ten nights. "Even to this day the whole experience recurs to my memory as a bad dream and I remember little of its details," Sadie said a half-century later. "I can remember shedding many tears in out-of-the-way corners for I thought constantly of my mother and how great must be her grief and worry over me." Sadie said that one of Sieber's scouts, Johnny Behan, drew particular attention. "He was young and darkly handsome, with merry black eyes and an engaging smile, and my heart was stirred by his attentions as would the heart of any girl have been under such romantic circumstances. The affair was at least a diversion in my homesickness, though I cannot say that I was in love with him. I was in a state of too great confusion to allow of any such deep feeling." Sadie told her biographers that she returned home without ever appearing in a performance.

The entire story was fanciful, and it could not have happened as she told it. Markham's troupe passed through Los Angeles by train on October 20 with two other women in the cast—May Bell and Belle Howitt, apparently stage names for Sadie and Dora. They arrived in Tucson on October 25 in the early morning hours, about the expected time for such a trek, with no ten-day stop to wait out Apaches. Sadie apparently edited her story in later years to avoid any taint that would be associated with performing on a frontier stage.

The Prings' Hayne Operatic Company began holding open auditions for local talent to fill the cast in late October, then opened *Pinafore* shows in early November with May Bell (apparently Sadie) in the role of cousin Hebe and Belle Howitt (apparently Dora) playing Little Buttercup. However, Pring proved far from astute as a financial manager, and the *Pinafore* ran adrift. With the company in chaos, Markham dumped the Prings and reorganized her own English Opera

Company to finish the engagement in Tucson and continue on to other Arizona towns. The troupe proceeded to Tombstone for a one-week run, beginning December 1, 1879, about the same time the Earp families pulled in their wagons. The cast apparently still included Sadie Marcus, and no one could imagine that this performer in an eight-actor cast would emerge as a powerful influence on the future of Tombstone as she flitted between and flirted with two of the village's key political players. That would be months ahead. For now, she was simply a dancer in a performance that charmed Arizona.[78]

The troupe continued on through Arizona and broke up early in 1880 when Markham married in Prescott and briefly abandoned the stage. She would later move to New York and act in major productions. There is no record of Sadie's adventures along the way, but apparently she met a stage-door Johnny named Behan, who became charmed by the young dancer. Sadie said she returned to San Francisco where she contracted St. Vitus' dance, a nerve disease. Shortly after she recovered, Johnny came to call. "He had thought of me ever since we had met, he said, and wanted me to become his wife. I had thought often of him, too, but I was not at all sure that I cared enough for him to marry him and so he returned to Arizona."

Ida "Kitty" Jones, the wife of Tombstone attorney Harry Jones, visited San Francisco and stopped by to see Sadie. Jones carried a message from Behan, another marriage proposal. "Life was dull for me in San Francisco. In spite of my sad experience a few years ago the call to adventure still stirred my blood," Sadie said. "Kitty was alive with enthusiasm over her new home in the busy town with its color and activity. When Kitty left San Francisco, I was not with her—but I joined her in Los Angeles. I thought I was in love. How can any one love another whom he knew so little as I knew Johnny Behan?"

Again young Sadie left without her parents' knowledge, this time expecting the journey to end with a ring on her finger. By her account, she settled in with Harry and Kitty Jones and kept house for Behan and Albert, his ten-year-old son from a prior marriage, while awaiting the wedding. It is more likely she shared a residence with Johnny and functioned in town as Mrs. Behan. Stage records show a Mrs. Behan leaving town, and postal records show a money order sent by Josephine Behan.

Sadie said that she became depressed by Johnny's wandering ways and wrote home to explain the situation. Her father responded immediately, urging her to return home and enclosing $300 for her passage. Sadie stayed true to Johnny, however. When Behan found out about the money, she said, he talked her into using it to build a house, which would hasten their marriage. Sadie said she also sold a diamond ring she owned to help finance the little cabin on Safford and Sixth Streets she was to share with Johnny. The house actually was listed in Behan's name. The engagement broke off when Behan began running around with a married woman, and Sadie angrily had to find other pursuits.

Sadie Marcus was the type of woman who could draw men's attention. With ample breasts and a slender body, dark hair, an attractive face, and a laugh that sounded like the tinkling of champagne glasses, Behan's love interest certainly must have attracted notice around the male-dominated, female-hungry mining town. But Stuart Lake and Tombstone old-timers would recall another detail of

Josephine Marcus's early residence in Arizona. According to the old tales, the lovely Sadie did a turn as a prostitute.

Lake would repeat the story as fact, though he left little written record. He did write to an editor at Houghton Mifflin referring to Sadie as "the belle of the honky tonks, the prettiest dame in three hundred or so of her kind."[79] Old Tombstone residents would accept as gospel that she had whored in Tombstone. No real proof remains to establish whether Sadie Marcus entered the world of prostitution, though it would not be hard to imagine the destitute young woman being forced into the trade after the breakup with her fiancé. If indeed she did take a whirl at prostitution, it is doubtful she worked the brothels or cribs. More likely, she served as the frontier equivalent of a high-priced call girl, entertaining a very select clientele without offering her special services to the rougher elements. She would spend the rest of her days trying to cover the truth of her life in Tombstone, telling vague, inaccurate stories that leave her real activities open to question.

All that can be known with certainty is that by April she was signing herself as Josephine Behan, and several months later, probably in July, she separated from Behan and maintained a separate residence in town. As that summer of 1881 progressed, she would make the acquaintance of another ambitious young man, and the young woman with the adventurous spirit would find herself in the middle of a conflict that was about to spin out of control.

CURLEY BILL'S PERSONAL RIOT through Tombstone territory awakened the boomers to a new and very real threat. Robberies and murders had become commonplace in the more remote areas. Lone travelers were in constant danger, and livestock was being stolen. By late 1880, the character of the area was changing. With much of the nation in a financial downslide, the thought of escaping to the frontier became appealing to more and more of the greenhorn city types. They came knowing of the dangers of the Apaches and snakes; they did not expect or easily accept the presence of a group of backcountry toughs endangering travel and even their very lives. The early boomers had more or less accepted the cowboys. The cowboys did make excellent Indian fighters, and their presence helped dissuade Apache bands from raiding towns and ranches. They also spent their money freely and provided a supply of cheap beef. But tolerance began running thin with more and more robberies, and gradually even the term *cowboy* became a slur. "The cowboy is a name which has ceased in this Territory to be a term applied to cattle herders," the *Tucson Citizen* wrote. "The term is applied to thieves, robbers, cut-throats and the lawless class of the community generally. Anyone who attempts to defend Arizona cowboys by restricting the term to its literal meaning of herder simply makes an ass of himself. When a man follows as a legitimate occupation the tending of cattle or other stock he is called a herder and not a cowboy."[80]

Curley Bill's binge led to calls for cowboy blood, as did a murder in November of 1880 when Tombstone businessman Jerry Ackerson, a friend of the cowboys, was found dead in the backcountry. On February 25, 1881, the situation became increasingly serious with the first stage holdup in newly formed Cochise

County. Bandits stopped the coach about five miles out of town and stripped passengers of $135 before letting it continue. The holdup men were never caught nor identified.[81] Off to the south, Mexican ranchers began protesting strongly against the gringo rustlers coming down to steal their cows and raid their towns.

Apart from the real danger that cowboys presented, they were becoming just plain irritating. In Willcox, cowboys congregated to show off their marksmanship by shooting the heels off boots as people passed by or shooting to snuff out candles or cut the ashes from cigars.[82] A visitor from Washington showed up in the little town of San Simon and encountered a few cowboys in the saloon. One cowboy, probably Jim Wallace, pulled his gun and ordered the mining investor to dance. The investor responded with a show worthy of Eddie Foy. After finishing his steps, he invited his admirers for a drink, then slipped away to borrow a six-shooter. He turned to the dance-master and said, "Now you dance a while, damn you." The cowboy gracefully complied, according to a *Citizen* story.[83] Another cowboy wanted a serenade on a train and forced passenger George L. Upshur into full voice. Upshur sang as the cowboys chanted, "Open your mouth wider when you sing." Then Upshur went to the sleeping car and remained out of sight for the rest of the trip.[84] The *Arizona Star*, Tucson's Democratic paper, led the outcry against this new breed of banditti with a bold editorial in February:

> The depredations of the cow-boys are becoming so frequent and of such magnitude that no time should be lost in adopting measures which will insure either their total extermination or their departure from the Territory. Not less than two hundred of these marauding thieves infest the southeast section of Arizona. The stock industry is to-day paralyzed all through the section they roam. Not hundreds but thousands of cattle have been made away with by them during the last eight months. These bands of thieves go armed to the teeth and show up in all directions, take in small settlements, and cause terror wherever they make their appearance. They are worse than the Apache and should be treated as such. They are law-breakers of the most flagrant character. If they are allowed to carry on their trade of robbery they will become so strong that it will require a large force and much treasure to suppress a gang of outlaws who are depopulating the rich grazing lands of Arizona. Let prompt action be taken. Let the public consider them outlaws, depredating upon the rights and properties of the people, and wherever found let them be shot down like the Apache. Let our Mexican neighbors understand that our people are determined to rid them and Arizona of these outlaws and that they will be protected in following them across the line into our borders, and treating them in a summary manner, and thus we will save a repetition of the Rio Grande trouble. The cow-boys are outlaws, their hand is against the law-abiding people of the Territory; let them be dealt with accordingly.[85]

Many of the raids north of the border came against an Arizonan of Mexican ancestry named Jose M. Elias, who owned a large ranch on the San Pedro River near the border. Thieves stole eight valuable horses from Elias in October of 1880, then returned in January to steal nine more horses and four mules. Elias dispatched four men to chase the cowboys, and after a shooting skirmish recovered part of the herd. The thieves returned on January 30 to steal thirty cows, then again in April for another theft. While Elias became the prime target of the raiders, cowboys also struck against Anglo ranchers in the area.[86]

By early 1881, the border raids began to threaten relations with Mexico as robberies on the roads threatened commerce. Governor Fremont wanted action, immediate action, before the situation escalated and the growing bands of thugs took power over the county. In late February, Fremont sent a special message to the territorial legislature deploring cowboy actions and requesting a state militia to ride the backcountry, "looking to breaking up these bands, and the preservation and maintenance of peace along the frontier between the two countries."[87] The *Star* pushed for even stronger action:

> The question of how the cow-boys are to be dealt with is assuming more importance every day. The organization of a volunteer company of one hundred men to hunt them down or drive them out of the Territory, must evidently end with failures, from the fact that the outlaws are too strong for such a small force, and in a pitched fight would undoubtedly come out victorious, which would result in making matters tenfold worse than at present. We must either have a strong force for the work or not attempt it [at] all. It has been suggested that two companies of United States cavalry be sent out in the section where the outlaws camp, and stay with them, and whenever the cow-boys move to move with them; or in frontier language, "stay with them," until they will be forced to leave the Territory or fight for their ground. The business could thus be brought to an issue, or at least they could be prevented from committing their depredations. This plan, taken in conjunction with the establishment of a military camp in the scourged section, would undoubtedly meet the exigency, while the scheme of sending out volunteers would most probably prove fruitless.[88]

The *Arizona Star* emerged as the most aggressive opponent of the cowboys, calling for blood without mercy. Editor and publisher Louis C. Hughes never hesitated to take a strong stance, nor did he hesitate to change his position when political exigencies demanded. In the early months of 1881, Democrat Hughes and the *Star* stood firmly behind the idea to eliminate the cowboys by any means possible, and the Republican governor agreed wholeheartedly. But Fremont could not convince the Democrats in the legislature. His militia plan died quickly. The politicians in Prescott did not want to spend the territorial budget on a militia while the U.S. Army had a force in the area sufficient to chase cowboys. One legislator wrote, "The undersigned thinks the raids of the cowboys less detrimental to the territory than would be the proposed raid on our treasury."[89] The politicos could not be convinced that the army could not legally take over the duties of local law enforcement unless the president declared martial law, but Arizona politicians were never too quick in understanding how the government actually worked. The Arizona officials succeeded in saving a few dollars for the territorial treasury and left Curley Bill and the boys to do their damage in the backcountry. It was a political blunder that would cost the territory dearly, both in lives and stature.

When the legislature failed to act, the local ranchers began discussing the problem. The short-lived and aptly named *Tombstone Gossip* newspaper reported rumors that the Stock Association of Southern Arizona was considering taking a role in breaking up the rustlers unless the law took control. Any action by the cattle associations could never be confirmed, but it would later be rumored that several contributed to a $1,000 reward for Curley Bill, a dubious action since Bill had never been convicted of a crime.[90]

In the early months of 1881 the cowboys were still mostly a nameless, faceless group of backcountry ruffians. Curley Bill drew a notch of attention for killing Marshal White, and Pony Deal's name had been circulated around as a badman, though no one yet knew he was actually the escaped Texas outlaw Charles Ray, a native of Illinois. The cowboys were just a bunch of "thems."

By the early weeks of 1881, the Earps already knew that the biggest problems would come not just from the trail-riding toughs, but from the crooked ranchers who acted as sponsors for criminality, purchasing stolen cattle and providing sanctuary for the thieves. At times these ranchers would even join in on raids into Mexico and assist in the stealing and killing that occurred. The McLaury brothers and the Clanton family had already shown their alignment, though few citizens in Tombstone could distinguish them from the honest ranchers who owned neighboring spreads. As the *Star* continued its calls to eradicate the cowboys in a burst of blood, it is likely that Wyatt Earp waited patiently for Johnny Behan to name his new undersheriff. Something else would intervene before the announcement came.

MURDER AND
MADNESS

BOB PAUL AND BUD PHILPOTT sat side by side on the box—the driver's seat—of the stagecoach as it passed through the little town of Contention on the night of March 15, 1881. Paul still awaited the final decision on his appeal of the contested election against Shibell, and he continued in his job as a Wells, Fargo shotgun messenger. At 6-foot-4, Paul was a giant in a time when 6-footers were rare. He had served as sheriff of Calaveras County in California before moving on to Arizona, and he owned a reputation for honor and courage. Eli Philpott, always called Bud, came to Arizona from Calistoga, California; he was a top stage driver, a skilled and respected position.

Paul and Philpott were making the evening run from Tombstone to Benson, "a God-forsaken place, made up—aside from the station and a warehouse—of a few corrals and uninviting shanties."[1] Near Drew's Station, two miles from Contention, a man stepped onto the road and yelled, "Hold."

"By God, I hold for nobody," Paul responded, aiming his double-barreled shotgun as several more men stepped into the road. Blasts went off, almost simultaneously, one striking Philpott. He fell forward, between the two horses, and the stage lurched forward. The newspaper accounts tell the story of Paul answering the shots and wounding one outlaw, then fishing down to recover the reins and bring the horses under control a mile down the road. Paul discovered that passenger Peter Roerig had been badly wounded, then drove rapidly to Benson to send off telegrams describing the incident. When Paul returned to the scene, he found Philpott dead in the road. Roerig, too, would soon die from his wounds.[2] An unusual discovery was made at the crime scene—three masks made of rope, twisted into ringlets, plus a rope beard.

"A most terrible affair last evening," Parsons wrote in his diary. "Men and horses were flying about in different directions, and I soon ascertained the cause. A large posse started in pursuit. $26,000 specie* reported on stage. Bob Paul went as shotgun messenger and emptied both barrels of his gun at the

---

*The equivalent of about 100 pounds of gold coin.

robbers, probably wounding one. 'I hold for no one,' he said and let drive. Some 20 shots fired. Close call for Paul."

Sheriff Behan quickly assembled a posse to ride out of town in pursuit. Parsons, John Clum, and others remained in reserve if a call came, watching the streets to report on any nefarious characters or strange doings that might be of importance later. Deputy U.S. Marshal Virgil Earp said later that twenty-five or thirty men offered their services, but Behan told them all he wanted was the Earp boys and Bob Paul, who met the posse at the site of the robbery. Bat Masterson and Marshall Williams, the Wells, Fargo agent, joined the posse at Earp's behest. "We agreed to go and stay in pursuit as long as he [Behan] thought it best to follow them," Virgil Earp said.[3]

The posse arrived at a deserted cabin and found the floor strewn with old dime novels, sensational tales of adventure. Wyatt Earp picked up the books one by one, then tossed each aside until he found one that had been torn apart, with the last part missing. Earp put the book in his saddlebag and carried it along for the ride, according to the account by writer Forrestine Hooker. For three days the posse tracked the robbers, following the trail to a ranch owned by Len Redfield, believed by the Earps to be sympathetic to the outlaw cowboys. The Earps spotted a man trying to hide from them, and Morgan Earp made the capture. The man identified himself as Luther King. Wyatt took him to Behan and admonished the sheriff not to allow King to talk with either Len Redfield or his brother Hank, who had joined the group. Wyatt stepped aside to confer with Bob Paul on the next step and returned to find the Redfields chatting with King, despite Earp's instructions to Behan that this should not be allowed. Hank Redfield left immediately, and Wyatt went to work on King, who confessed to being at the attempted stage robbery.

King admitted to holding the horses while Billy Leonard, Jimmy Crane, and Harry Head did the actual shooting. King told where the outlaws had camped, but Hank Redfield had already galloped out, presumably to deliver a warning. The posse split up, with Paul, Masterson, Marshall Williams, and the Earps in pursuit of the robbers.

"Behan went back to Tombstone with King, and we followed the rest for six days longer before we could get to a place to telegraph for advice,"[4] Virgil Earp said. They found freshly extinguished campfires and signs of life. By Hooker's version, they also found pages from the cheap novel at the campsites, a sign that these campers were the same men who had holed up at the cabin planning the robbery. Behan arrived in town with Luther King on March 21 and placed the prisoner in custody.

Virgil telegraphed to Behan to bring fresh horses to replace the mounts worn down from nine days' work. When Virgil went to the meeting place with Behan, the new sheriff had not delivered. There were no fresh horses to carry the weary posse. Virgil said, "That night, Bob Paul's horse laid down and died. Wyatt's and Masterson's horses were so used up they were left at the ranch and the boys had to foot it in eighteen miles to Tombstone."[5]

Wyatt Earp and Masterson walked back to town while Virgil, Morgan, and Paul, with a new horse, continued in pursuit of the cowboys, who had gained ground after picking up fresh mounts at Redfields'. Perhaps not until Wyatt returned did he learn that Behan had made his appointment of a new under-sheriff—Woods. He had broken his deal with Earp, and Wyatt would not receive the high-paying job he had expected. For the moment, he was too occupied with the stagecoach killings to worry about a broken promise. With the rest of the posse still out chasing the robbers, Wyatt monitored incoming telegrams and watched over local affairs. Wells, Fargo detective Jim Hume arrived in town and posted a $300 reward on each of the would-be robbers.

"Wyatt told him [Hume] there were about seventy-five cowboys in town who would try to release King," Virgil said. "Hume got Wyatt to go with him to the Sheriff's office to notify them, and they asked as a favor of the Under Sheriff to put King in irons. He promised to do so, and fifteen minutes afterward King escaped, going on a horse that was tied back of the Sheriff's office."[6]

On March 28, King simply took off, leaving a string of questions behind. Angrily Parsons wrote in his diary: "King, the stage robber, escaped tonight early from H. Woods who had been previously notified of an attempt at release to be made. Some of our officials should be hanged. They're a bad lot."

The Nugget account said King quietly stepped out the back door while attorney Harry Jones drew up a bill of sale for the horse King had sold to John Dunbar, Behan's partner in the Dexter Corral. The Nugget speculated that a confederate had waited outside with a horse for the time the prisoner could make his escape. The Nugget pleaded for understanding, saying a guard had watched King since he was brought into town, and he took flight in the single unguarded moment.[7] Such paltry excuses did not sit well with the residents of southern Arizona.

The escape caused an outcry that echoed throughout Arizona. The Tucson Citizen editorialized: "A most flagrant dereliction of duty in a public officer is manifest in the manner in which Lew King, the cowboy . . . escaped from Under Sheriff Woods. Utterly disregarding the information that an escape was premeditated, the prisoner was given every opportunity to get away if not with official connivance, at least by a most simple ruse." The Citizen also said, "The escape was the result of inexcusable and culpable negligence on the part of the officer in charge, as he had been notified of the intended escape of King."[8]

Back on the trail of the thieves, Behan, Breakenridge, Ed Gorman, and Buckskin Frank Leslie joined Virgil Earp, Morgan Earp, and Paul on March 24, and the posses went on, sometimes apart, sometimes together. Virgil Earp learned that the suspects owned a ranch near Cloverdale, New Mexico, and sought directions. As Virgil told the story to the Epitaph, he and his posse were directed to a ranch fifty miles to the southwest in Grant County, where they found only deserted buildings. Despite having no food or water, they pushed forward, hunting for a ranch. After two hungry days they were virtually lost and had to stop their hunt to search for water. They found none. With both men and mounts starving and thirsty, Virgil's horse played out after seventeen days under a saddle. Morgan Earp loaded Virgil's gear on his own horse and the two Earps were forced to walk on, driving the horses ahead of them.

That night, almost exhausted, the party reached a spring. Sitting down to discuss their situation, they decided that Behan, Leslie, and Breakenridge would start back to Berlow and Pierce's ranch, a hundred miles distant, for food and water, leaving the others to follow as best they could. When Behan's group reached the ranch, they immediately dispatched men with provisions and water for Paul and the Earps. They had been four days in that almost trackless desert, and the only morsel of food that had passed their lips was a quail that one of the posse had shot.[9]

The party reached Galeyville but could not secure fresh horses to resume the chase and returned to Tombstone. The *Star* added an editorial note praising the posse riders for the unsuccessful effort: "The persistent pursuit of the murderers of poor 'Budd' is a credit to each individual member of the party, and will pass into our frontier annals—more especially to Bob Paul and the Earp boys, who followed the trail from the night of the murder—as a record of which all and each of them may well feel proud."[10] The bedraggled Earp party returned with no prisoners and growing rancor for Behan, who had failed to bring fresh horses, and his undersheriff, who had allowed King's escape.

By the time Virgil Earp returned to town from his long posse ride, Tombstone had paid its last respects to Bud Philpott. The town threw a fund-raiser, a musical show that earned $330 for the driver's widow, back in Calistoga. Wells, Fargo paid for a decorative casket for Philpott. "It was an act of generosity highly commendable, and is an exception to the rule that 'corporations have no souls,'" the *Tucson Citizen* wrote. The driver's body was shipped home, and Tombstone grieved its loss.[11]

The deaths of Roerig and Philpott had greater meaning to the community. For all the latter-day tales of the frontier, wanton murder was a rarity. Killing to settle a dispute was one thing, but killing just for the sake of killing was something altogether different. Even bandits seemed to live by a code of honor which prevented slaying except in self-defense. These murders shocked the West Coast, and the *San Francisco Exchange* gave voice to the anger:

The dispatches state that there is great excitement in Tombstone over the late attack on the Benson stage . . . and it is but natural there should be. That the crime was committed not by the ordinary road agents who generally hesitate to shoot, but by cowboys, the most reckless class of outlaws in that wild country, there is scarcely any doubt. The dispatches also state that a Vigilance Committee has been formed with a view of ridding the community of this desperate element, and we hope it is true. The cowboy is infinitely worse than the ordinary robber, who generally spares life if he can get money, in that he is utterly reckless of human life. He cares even less for it than money. He glories in being regarded a terror. He rarely cares to steal anything but cattle, but in the company of human beings his revolver is ever brandished, and on the slightest pretext, or fancied pretext, he sends a bullet into a victim's heart with as little compunction as he would kill a dog. He is worse than the Indians, in that he associates with whites and performs his reckless deeds amid peaceful surroundings. There should be no hesitation in driving this element out of Arizona, and it should be done at once. Cowboys should be declared outlaws. They should not be permitted to enter Tombstone or any of the mining districts in that section. They should be hunted down the same as hostile Indians, and, if necessary, the military should take the matter in hand. There is neither justice or sense in allowing a community to be terrorized by these white savages, and we hope that the Tombstone

Vigilance Committee will act promptly and do their work effectively. It will not be hard work; the rope for a few ringleaders, and the rest of the cowards will thereafter give the place a wide berth.[12]

San Francisco investors took great interest in the events in Tombstone, and stage robberies like this one could dissuade the big-money boys from opening their wallets. Business survived through the shipment of goods—if the robbers closed down the commerce, Tombstone would be closed as well, spelling disaster for the local residents and the San Francisco backers.

The whole Philpott incident proved a blot on Tombstone, an embarrassment to the little mining district with the big expectations. Wells, Fargo's Jim Hume reflected darkly on the town in a letter back home to his fiancée, Lida Munson, "Tombstone has a population of six thousand—five thousand of them are bad—one thousand of them known outlaws. I don't want much of Tombstone."[13]

The killing of Philpott brought to the surface the animosity against the cowboys that had been growing over the months. What had been accepted back in 1880 was no longer tolerated in 1881. Philpott's killing embittered the law-abiding citizens of Tombstone and started a public outcry to protect the community.

The events of March and early April would have other consequences. Behan's failure to replace mounts and his general incompetence on the posse furthered the split between the Earps and Johnny Behan. Moreover, the sheriff angered the Earps by refusing to pay them. As Virgil Earp told it, "Behan brought in a bill against the county for $796.84. We supposed it was to pay expenses for the whole party, but he rendered it as a private account. I went before the Supervisors and they said Behan must vouch for us. This he refused to do, saying he had not deputized us. Everybody but myself and brothers were paid, and we did not get a cent until Wells-Fargo found it out and paid us for our time."

The incident also strengthened the bad feeling between the Earps and the cowboys, friends of the accused robbers Leonard, Head, King, and Crane, according to Virgil: "From that time on our troubles commenced, and the cowboys plotted to kill us. They met at Charleston and took an oath over blood drawn from the arm of John Ring [sic], the leader, that they would kill us."[14] While there is no other known record of an April blood oath from the arm of John Ringo, it was not long before blood did flow in the streets of Tombstone.

Boyish-looking undersheriff Harry Woods, 33, came to his new job with an unusual resume. The blond native of Alabama had worked as a reporter for the *Tucson Record* long enough to make numerous friendships that would carry over into the future. After the *Record* folded, he moved to Tombstone in June of 1880 and became editor of the *Nugget* in late July when the paper went from a weekly to a daily. His political friendships in Tucson served him well when he ran for the legislative assembly; he drew many votes in the Tucson precinct. He was innovative, once jumping out a window to prevent the legislators from having a quorum to vote on a bill he opposed. But Harry Woods drew the wrath of Tucson for his support of the Cochise County bill and his failure to vote with Tucson assemblymen on other issues.[15]

Nine months after he came to town as a journalist, he added the title of undersheriff to editor and legislator. Woods and Behan made an odd couple.

Both were politicians far more than peace officers, and neither had any real experience fighting criminals. Woods suffered with "inflammatory rheumatism," arthritis, which occasionally forced him out of action. Behan, arriving in Tombstone on September 14, 1880, immediately joined the volunteer fire department, a politically prudent move. He never failed to shake a hand nor did he miss a political opportunity. Harry Woods was clever, and he brought a flair to the *Nugget* that enlivened the once dreary paper that had been started by Artemus Fay in October of 1879. Fay had remained as owner and publisher, with Woods handling most of the work. The paper had been tacitly Democratic, but the moderate Fay prevented it from becoming overly partisan.

In mid-March of '81, shortly after the Benson stage robbery, Harry M. Woods & Co. purchased the *Tombstone Nugget* from founder Fay to give a stronger voice in the community to Behan and the Democrats. Prescott politician Hugo Richards provided the backing for Woods's purchase, and Richards was charged with funding the newspaper to boost his political career. Such a motive was common practice in the purchase of newspapers.

Frontier journalism was rife with political partisanship; reporting and analysis were often highly biased. Newspapers had a great impact on the beliefs of the frontier populace. They were both a lifeline to the outside world and a barometer of public opinion. Editorials influenced how the citizenry would view major issues. Just about everyone who could read scanned a newspaper, and the literacy rate on the frontier was probably higher than it is more than a century later.

Newspapers had another important function as well. By 1881, both the *Epitaph* and the *Nugget* had daily and weekly editions, with the weeklies usually providing a summary of news highlights. Big investors around the country often subscribed to the weekly editions to keep up on important events in the mining town. The investors were really not too eager to read that their capital was in jeopardy in some wild territory teeming with outlaws. Constant stories of criminal doings could scare off investors with cash to open new mines or businesses and make the county prosper. Consequently the *Nugget* took to downplaying the dangers around the county, making the cowboys seem playful rogues rather than true desperadoes. The law-and-order-loving *Epitaph* took the opposite tack, sensationalizing cowboy depredations and calling for strict law enforcement to make the district safe to lure greater investment.

Richard Rule, a talented young journalist and the clerk of the territorial legislature, showed up in Tombstone on March 23, 1881, and a week later became the top reporter and local editor on the staff of the *Nugget*. Rule brought quality to the *Nugget* in contrast to the amateurish *Epitaph*, with consistently better writing and story development. Editorially, the *Nugget* always supported Behan and the emerging Democratic county government under saloonkeeper Milt Joyce, while the *Epitaph* espoused the Republican side and accused the county leaders of skimming taxes. County officials kept a percentage of the tax money, not an unusual practice on the frontier. The *Epitaph* labeled Joyce and his allies as the "Ten Per Cent Ring," a clever epithet that seemed to suggest thievery.

San Diego Union correspondent Clara Brown expressed the town's dislike of the plan: "Much dissatisfaction is manifested at the high rate of taxation decreed by the County Supervisors—$2.83 on $100—and at their course in allowing the

Sheriff 10 per cent for collecting it, a percentage whose exorbitance is without a precedent. Add to this a large city tax, and the people will find a heavy burden upon their shoulders, which they will not enjoy carrying for the aggrandizement of a few officials."[16]

Also in the competition between the two newspapers were lucrative advertising contracts with both the city and the county. The incumbent power determined which paper to advertise in, and these revenues could make the difference between large profits for the newspaper and running at a deficit. Almost from the start, the county voted Democratic and the city went Republican, with Tombstone's advertising going to the *Epitaph* and Cochise County's to the *Nugget*. *Epitaph* editor John Clum supported the Earps and railed against Behan and his friends.

Clum never hesitated to point out that his adversary Harry Woods was holding down the job of undersheriff at the same time he was running a newspaper, in effect holding two full-time jobs and never giving adequate time to his duties as a law officer. In addition, Woods and Behan always gave precedence to the lucrative duties of tax collecting, turning the sheriff's office into a dubious enterprise. Behan appointed a full crew of deputies, including tough Dave Neagle, who would serve as his crime fighter, plus Lance Perkins, Billy Breakenridge, and Frank Stilwell, who would patrol Charleston. This proved a less than distinguished cast of officers to try and battle crime against a continuing flow of no-accounts drifting into Cochise County. At the same time that Governor Fremont was trying to raise funds for a militia to fight crime in Cochise County, Behan built a sheriff's office more dedicated to collecting taxes than dealing with trouble. Such a department might be satisfactory in a law-abiding region, but crime-riddled Cochise County demanded tough enforcement.

The Earps could only sit and watch, apparently never quite understanding the back-room politics and deals that made such an inefficient operation possible. Tucson papers wailed about the problems down in Cochise and townsfolk complained, yet Johnny Behan was still riding high. The next election would come in November of 1882, and Wyatt Earp knew he would have to increase his popularity in Cochise County if he was to win the job of sheriff away from Behan. The Luther King fiasco, the broken promise to Earp about the under-sheriff's job, and Behan's refusal to pay the Earps had already built enmity between the two camps, and Wyatt came up with a plan to enhance his position as a lawman. It would be a most foolish and ill-advised decision.

THE 10-PERCENT COLLECTION FEE made the sheriff's job of Cochise County potentially one of the most lucrative civic positions in the territory. With the county growing constantly, mines, railroads, and sundry new businesses could be expected to tithe substantial sums, enough to make the sheriff a rich man. The sheriff could make two or possibly three thousand dollars a month, big money for a time when a working cowhand made a dollar a day plus board, and a Tombstone cabin rented for about $15 a month. Wyatt Earp wanted the job enough to come up with a trick to bring Philpott's murderers to justice, an accomplishment that would certainly raise his stock with the townspeople.

The Earps came to understand that Ike Clanton had become a leader among the cowboys, who often spent time at the Clanton and McLaury ranches. Wyatt said he met with Ike Clanton, Frank McLaury, and a cowboy named Joe Hill behind the Oriental Saloon to make an offer. The stage robbers Leonard, Head, and Crane had rewards of $1,200 each on their heads. Wyatt thought the large sum might tempt Ike Clanton and Frank McLaury to give them up. Earp later testified: "I told them what I wanted. I told them I wanted the glory of capturing Leonard, Head and Crane, and if I could do it, it would help me make the race for Sheriff in the next election. I told them if they would put me on the track of Leonard, Head and Crane, and tell me where those men were hid, I would give them all the reward and would never let anyone know where I got the information."[17]

Ike Clanton had a motivation other than the reward for wanting the robbers out of the way. He had run his cattle onto a ranch owned by Leonard near Cloverdale, New Mexico, probably assuming Leonard would not return. Virgil Earp said that Clanton pulled him aside and told him, "As soon as I heard of his robbing the stage I rounded up my cattle over on the San Pedro and drove them over and jumped his ranch, and shortly after you boys give up the chase, who should come riding up but Leonard, Head and Crane, and by God they have been stopping there ever since and it looks to me as if they are going to stay. They have already told me I would either have to buy the ranch or get off it. I told them that I supposed after they'd done what they had they wouldn't dare stay in the country, and I suppose you'd rather your friends would get your ranch than anybody else, but if you are going to stay in the country I will either get off or buy the ranch. . . . Now you can see why I want these men either captured or killed, but I had rather they would be killed."

Virgil said he responded, "There are three of them and three of you, why don't you capture or kill them and get the reward?"

"Jesus Christ. If we did that we wouldn't last as long as a snowball in hell," Clanton responded, according to Virgil. "The rest of the gang would think that we killed them for the reward and they would kill us. . . . We have agreed with Wyatt to bring them to a certain spot where you boys can capture them. . . . Now, I want to caution you never to give us away or say a word outside of this or the party we took along."[18]

According to Wyatt Earp, "Clanton said that Leonard, Head and Crane would make a fight, that they would never be taken alive; that I must first find out if the reward would be paid for the capture of the robbers dead or alive. I then went to Marshall Williams, the agent of Wells, Fargo in this town and at my request he telegraphed to the agent—or superintendent—of Wells, Fargo at San Francisco to find out if the reward would be paid for the robbers dead or alive. He received, in June, 1881, a telegram, which he showed me promising the reward would be paid dead or alive."[19]

According to Earp's version, Clanton and Hill insisted on seeing the telegram. When it was produced, they agreed to the deal and said Hill would go to Eureka, New Mexico, to lure the robbers back to Arizona, near the McLaury ranch about thirty miles from Tombstone. Clanton and McLaury would tell the robbers a paymaster would be going from Tombstone to Bisbee to pay off the miners, and they wanted them to come and take it. Hill then gave Virgil Earp his watch and chain and between two and three hundred dollars for safekeeping.

Ike Clanton told a different version, insisting he had never agreed to the deal. He said he had been approached alone by Earp, who feared he and Holliday would be implicated in the holdup. According to Clanton, the meeting took place at the Eagle Brewing Company, across the street from the Oriental, and Earp offered $6,000 to Clanton to turn over the robbers. "He then told me he would put me on a scheme to make $6,000. I asked him then what it was. He told me he would not tell me unless I agreed to do it, or if I would not agree to do it to promise him on the honor of a gentleman that I would never mention our conversation to any one else. I then asked him what it was. He told me it was a legitimate transaction. He then made me promise him a second time I would never mention any more. He told me he wanted me to help him put up a job to kill Leonard, Crane and Head. He said there was between $4,000 and $5,000 reward for them. He said he would make the balance of the $6,000 out of his own pocket. I then asked him why he was so anxious to capture these fellows. He said his business was such that he could not afford to capture them. He would either have to kill them or else leave the country. He said that he and his brother Morg had piped off to William Leonard and Doc Holliday the money that was going off on the stage, and that he could not afford to capture them; that he would have to kill them or else leave the country, for they were stopping around the country so damned long that he was afraid some of them would be caught and would squeal on him. I left town; never talked to Wyatt Earp anymore about it."[20]

While Ike swore he never made the deal, an admission of being party to such a plot with the law would have meant a death sentence from the cowboys. By the Earps' version, Ike had entered into an arrangement to turn over the robbers for cash. Joe Hill thought he knew just where to find the three robbers. He arrived one day too late and found two corpses instead. The *Epitaph* ran a letter, dated June 12, from an anonymous correspondent across the New Mexico line:

Well, about the shooting scrape. This is their [the cowboys] headquarters. Ike Haslett and his brother Bill have a ranch in the Animas Valley, the best one in it, and old man Gray, of Tombstone fame, has one on each side of it that he bought from Curley Bill and his gang and he wanted the one belonging to the Haslett boys, so some of the cowboys were going to run the H. boys out of the country or kill them. On Friday last [June 10th] Bill Leonard and three more cowboys or "rustlers," as they call them, came to camp to a store about one-quarter of a mile from the mine. . . . Well the rustlers went in there and got drunk and said they were coming up to the mine to kill the Haslett boys, so some fellow came up and told Ike, which put him on the lookout.

Yesterday I went down to the store, getting there at noon, so I went in and ate my dinner. Bill Leonard and the others were at the table with their six-shooters alongside their plates and their rifles lying in their laps, and a fellow outside guarding. I tell you it looked tough. Well, Bill said he was going to shoot the Haslett boys on sight, and we looked for them last night, but they did not come, so Ike thought that the best thing that he could do was to catch them himself, so this morning at day break he went to the store and laid in wait for them.

Back of the store is a corral and Ike and his brother got in there. The fence is about three and a-half feet high. Bill Leonard and the one they call Harry the "Kid" [Head] had to come down the road past the corral, so when they got within fifty yards Ike and his brother Bill jumped up, and opened fire on them. The "Kid" was on foot and Leonard on horseback. Ike let drive and got Leonard just below the heart, when he dropped to one side of his horse, when Bill thought that he would get away so he plugged the horse and he fell. The "Kid" pulled his gun when Ike pulled on him and told him to stop, but he was going to pull when Bill Haslett gave it to him in the abdomen, and he started to run when both Bill and Ike commenced to pop it with him. They put six balls in him. When they picked Leonard up he breathed his last breath. "Kid" is still alive, but they think he will die soon. Bill Leonard said last night that he wished somebody would shoot him through the heart and put him out of misery, as he had two big holes in his belly that he got the time he tried to rob the stage at Tombstone. He was put out of sight at sundown this evening.[21]

The Haslett brothers, the killers of Leonard and Head, never had time to collect their reward. Wells, Fargo reports indicated they were waylaid and killed, presumably by Jim Crane, the last member of the stage-robbing trio, and other friends of Leonard and Head. Nellie Pender lived nearby and wrote her friend Frances Jackson that fifteen or twenty cowboys stormed into West Mc-Fadden's saloon to assault the Hasletts and an immigrant named Sigman Biertzhoff, known as Joe. Nellie and Jim Pender were sitting on their porch when they heard the shots.

I counted eight, but they say there were more. My husband started to run, but I caught hold of him and held him back until I heard them mount their horses and ride away like the wind. I ran and put out the light, and then we started down. . . . When my husband got to the saloon he said he never saw such a dreadful sight. The place was just running with blood. Bill Haslett was shot six times in his bowels, and Ike was shot through his head and his left hand was shot to pieces. The boy Joe was shot six times through his stomach and once through his ankle. He suffered the worst of any of them. They were all conscious to the last. The Haslett boys made out a will leaving everything to their father and sister in Kansas. The German boy's people live in California—he had nothing, not even enough to pay his debts in camp, but the company gave them all as good a funeral as could be had in this country. It was a sorrowful sight to see those three coffins followed by all the men moving slowly through the camp.[22]

Wells, Fargo officials would believe Crane took a hand in the killing. Many cowboys would be associated with the raid, though none could be proven to have participated. The brutal murders had a more significant implication: Residents of Cochise County and southwest New Mexico were put on alert that the cowboys could become killers when challenged. For the first time, the cowboys were riding as a gang with the appearance of organization, seeking vengeance and killing. They now appeared as a fighting force, capable of storming a town or mounting an attack on the law. The anonymous letter to the *Epitaph* telling of the Hasletts killing the robbers, followed by Nellie Pender's chilling letter to her friend, undercut any sense of safety in Cochise County. By public perception, the cowboys were riding as an army; attack could be imminent.

While the shots were being fired in New Mexico, something else went wrong with Earp's scheme. Wells, Fargo agent Marshall Williams suspected from the telegram that Wyatt had a plan. While quite drunk, Williams approached Clanton and intimated he knew of the plot. According to Earp, an angry Clanton accused Earp of loudmouthing the secret, and Wyatt responded: "I've told him nothing. He handled those telegrams and may have seen me talking to you, but everything else is surmise on his part. I have told no one our plans."[23] But Ike no longer trusted the Earps, and he feared the deal had leaked out, a leak that could prove fatal.

While Wyatt tried to mollify the Clantons, Virgil acquired another badge. On June 6, city marshal Ben Sippy took a two-week leave of absence, and Virgil received the temporary appointment as city marshal. Rumors circulated that Sippy had made off with $200 of city funds and a load of unpaid debts. The *Nugget* noted: "One of the late Marshal Sippy's creditors has a large picture of him hanging in his office, and underneath the inscription: "Though lost to sight, to memory dear. Two hundred dollars worth."[24]

Despite Mayor Clum's early support, Sippy had endured an unpleasant tenure as marshal. In May, the city council reprimanded Sippy for his action in the release of some prisoners, and he had previously been absent without leave for a short period. Sippy never returned to Arizona, and Virgil kept the badges of both city marshal and deputy U.S. marshal.[25] Wyatt often served as his deputy as he tried to position himself to run for sheriff, and many of the U.S. marshal duties fell to Wyatt while Virgil was tied up with town business. Newspaper reports identified Wyatt as a deputy U.S. marshal during the autumn of 1881, and he actively pursued federal criminals. The brothers Earp, Wyatt would say later, developed a string of informants among the cowboys to keep them current with outlaw activities.

The Earps were gaining esteem in the community, along with personal wealth and some local power as lawmen, when something went very wrong. Apparently after a fight with Doc, Big-Nose Kate got drunk and swore out a warrant implicating him in the stage robbery and the killing of Philpott. On July 5, Holliday was arrested by Behan, with part of his bail being provided by Wyatt Earp. Kate got herself arrested the next day for drunk and disorderly behavior. As the *Nugget* phrased it: "Miss Kate Elder sought 'surcease of sorrow' in the flowing bowl." She was fined $12.50 and released. A day later Kate faced further charges for making threats against life, although whom she threatened is unknown. After spending a night in jail, she was discharged on a writ of habeas corpus. The *Nugget* wrote: "Such is the result of a warrant sworn out by an enraged and intoxicated woman."

Kate made her complaint against Holliday at a time when the district attorney's office was in chaos. Lyttleton Price and John Miller had been contesting the position since Governor Fremont made the audacious move to appoint Republican Price. The board of supervisors had refused Price's appointment and installed Democrat Miller, who appointed Deputy James Bennett Southard to handle the day-to-day operation. The situation had become so absurd that at one point both Southard and Price appeared in court to prosecute the same case. Price had charge of Holliday's case and conducted an investigation. It did not take long. When the D.A.'s report came to Judge Wells Spicer, it said he had "examined all the witnesses summoned for the prosecution and from their statements he was satisfied that there was not the slightest evidence to show the guilt of the defendant; and not even amount to a suspicion of the guilt of the defendant." The D.A. requested the complaint be withdrawn, and it was dismissed. The *Nugget* commented: "Thus ended what at the time was supposed to be an important case."[26]

While the court completely disregarded Kate's claims, the charge would be enough to begin gossip in a community where Holliday had already made more than his share of enemies ready to believe the worst of him. Doc had been a friend of Billy Leonard, jeweler turned stage robber, and Wyatt Earp would write that Holliday had visited Leonard's shack two miles out of Tombstone on the day of the holdup but had returned to town before the robbery, apparently the impetus to give Kate some grounds for her accusation.[27] Kate's comments marked the beginning of a rumor campaign that would long taint the memory of the Earps in Arizona history. Pioneer James Hancock later said, "Nearly all the old-timers believed it was Williams who tipped off the Earps as to shipments. . . . I have heard it stated that the money was not put in the box, but was held out in the office and the stage holdup pulled off as a blind. They were afraid that if the outlaws got the box they would pull out for Mexico and leave the Earp crowd to make the best of it. A smooth scheme—the money could be kept in the office and the Earps stay in town."[28] This absurd rumor began after the attempt on the Benson stage and obviously had no basis in fact. The strongbox was not stolen, and no money was missing. The shipment arrived safely when Paul pulled up in Benson. Over the next few months someone in the rustler camp created such a remarkable campaign of misinformation that it is likely many cowboys themselves believed Doc Holliday and the Earps had some role in the holdup.

John Pleasant Gray ran into Leonard, Head, and Crane on the range before they split up, and Crane told him a most unusual story. The outlaw said Paul drove the stage and Philpott held the shotgun, and the whole robbery had been planned by the Earps. Morgan Earp was to serve as shotgun messenger and had tipped the robbers that the strongbox would hold $20,000, according to Crane's story. However, Paul took over as messenger at the last minute and fouled up the plans. According to Gray, Crane said the Earps made a big show of hunting the robbers but never had any intention of finding them.

It defies logic that the cowboys expected Morgan Earp to be sitting on the box as part of the robbery plot. The bandits shot immediately at dark silhouettes, and killing Morgan would have stirred the wrath of the Earps, who were supposedly part of the scheme. This would have been a particularly dumb move, even for the most foolish cowboys, and even more absurd if Holliday had done the shooting as the cowboys claimed.

The story of Paul taking the reins from Philpott became public for the first time in August shortly after Crane's death, when an unidentified informant gave details of the robbery to the *Nugget*:

> To many it has always seemed a mystery that the parties mentioned should have killed Philpot [*sic*] and spared Bob Paul, Wells, Fargo & Co.'s messenger. According to Crane, however, when the ambushed robbers fired at Philpot, they thought it was

Paul, as the two had swapped places, Paul acting as driver, and poor Bud as messenger. They meant to kill Paul, thinking that his death would result in the stoppage of the stage, and the easy plunder of W.F. & Co.'s box and the passengers. The change from messenger to driver, so Crane says, was made somewhere between the change station and the place of ambush. This he claimed to know, as he was the party detailed to watch for the stage, and signal it to his comrades. Why the change was made will probably never be known until the great judgment. No one knowing Bob Paul will attribute it to fear or the possible consequences; his character for bravery is too well established to admit of question. Suffice it that poor Philpot now sleeps peacefully under the daisies, and the intended victim Paul, still lives, sheriff of Pima county, and dreaded terror to the class of whom his intended murderers formed a part.[29]

This informant may well have been John Pleasant Gray. By the cowboy account, Paul had taken the seat on the right-hand side of the box, while Philpott sat to the left in the spot occupied by the shotgun messenger. Ike Clanton would repeat the story under oath in November, after more killing. Other than the statements of Gray and Clanton, there is little reason to suspect that Paul and Philpott made the fateful decision to change seats. Both Wyatt and Virgil Earp emphasized in later interviews that Philpott had been the driver. Both Earps rode with Paul, and he must have told them the story. All newspaper accounts at the time give Philpott as the driver and tell of shotgun messenger Paul reaching for the reins as the horses ran away.

It is unlikely any such switch occurred. Paul ranked as a diligent and highly competent shotgun messenger, and he would not have given up his job of protecting the Wells, Fargo box except under the most extreme emergency. The stage had just passed through Contention, and an ailing driver would have been cause to stop, not to continue. All stories agree Paul fired almost immediately upon the command to halt, something he could not have done had he been driving the stage. This attempted robbery occurred only three weeks after another stage holdup, and Paul would have been extremely cautious. The story of the seating switch continued to circulate, the only substantiation coming from the cowboy camp. While it seemed to be given little credence by newspapers at the time, later generations would pick it up and repeat the gossip as gospel.

The story also became the basis for the belief that the robbery had been more than just a gold-grab. A rumor circulated that the holdup had really been an assassination attempt on Paul, still awaiting the final decision in the Pima County sheriff's election. Months later James Reilly, the judge arrested by Wyatt Earp, would write to the *Nugget* charging the entire affair had been a plot to kill Paul. Reilly's claim was repeated for decades.[30] This, too, defies logic. Most of the cowboys operated in newly formed Cochise County, not Pima, and eliminating Paul would have served no purpose and risked a hanging. Had the goal been to kill Paul, an ambush in an alley would have been more efficient. This was one of the more far-fetched of the frontier conspiracy theories.

Tombstone must have been a little less pleasant for the Earps once the rumors of Holliday's involvement became public. Luke Short and Bat Masterson had already returned to Kansas, Bat going back after receiving a telegram that his brother Jim was in serious trouble. After Wyatt's ill-advised reward deal, the rift between the Earps and the Clantons had grown wider. Already the Mc-Laurys disliked the Earps because they associated them with Lieutenant Hurst's accusation of stealing the army mules, and now the Clanton family had their own little dispute with the Earps. It all happened in a strange setting of civility, where opposing sides would drink, gamble, and talk together before arguing, sometimes violently.

There were other problems in Tombstone during mid-1881. Late in the afternoon of June 22, a worker at the Arcade Saloon dropped a cigarette into a whiskey barrel and set off a fire that burned four substantial blocks of the small town, including the Oriental Saloon, and caused an estimated quarter-million dollars in damage. Tombstone had no fire engine, and the volunteers battled to stop the blaze, tearing down burning buildings and throwing water in all directions. The conflagration burned the most valuable blocks of the town, from Fifth to Seventh and from Fremont through Toughnut Streets. Ironically, Mayor Clum returned home the evening of the fire, from a trip east to purchase a fire engine and two hose carriages.[31]

Diarist George Parsons distinguished himself in the blaze, leaping on a burning verandah to try to prevent the fire from spreading into the building. The verandah fell, and a board shattered part of his face. Wyatt Earp probably also contributed his share of heroism, although the documentation is slim. Sadie Earp would later say that Wyatt rescued an invalid woman from the flames. While there is no substantiation, such deeds are often lost in the turmoil of a fire.[32]

Marshal Virgil Earp drew the praise of the *Epitaph:* "He put on a large force of special police to protect life and property."[33] According to Fred Dodge, the city marshal stepped in to stop lot-jumpers who were trying to take control of property. Dodge wrote:

The next morning after the fire, Lot jumpers were much in Evidence and were squatted on many good business lots. The titles to all Tombstone lots were in dispute and were waiting the result in the Courts. The men who had lost all they had in the business that they were carrying on, had over night lost possession of the lot—the lot jumpers were now in possession. It looked to all of us that the man who was in possession when the fire wiped him out Should be put in possession and when the Courts adjusted the Controvverses over the title, the occupant would then have to abide by the Court decision. Virgil Earp and Wyatt Earp talked with Several of the leading business men and the head ones of the Safety Committee. And the above was the Consensus of opinion—

So Virgil Earp Selected the Posse of which I was one. We Started on Allen Street—Many of these Lot Jumpers were supposed to be Gun Men and some of them were sure enough Gun Men—We proceeded up one side of Allen Street and Come down on the other side. On all lots that there was a Lot jumper on, we took him off and put back the man who had been on the lot before the fire. Fremont Street had not had the Damage that Allen Street had, and by the time we were through with Allen Street, the Lot jumpers on Fremont Street were quitting the lots on the Street. It was a fair and just proceeding.

On the upper End of Allen and on 6th Street to 7th, there were Many Women of the Sporting Class that had their Houses and the best of these lots had a jumper on the lot. They put up little round Tents and the jumper was going to sleep in his

Tent. That Night, there was a selected number of men on Horseback and when the night was far enough Advanced and all was as quiet as it was at anytime, these Horsemen rode arround and just dropped a Lasso Rope over a Tentpole and then on a Gallop, they jerked the tent free from its holding and left the Lot jumper lying there. There was also another Smaller Committee that started the Cry, "Lot jumper, you *Git*," and they did. The Names of these men who done the riding and roping, and the Committee who started the Cry of "Git" were not at the time given out and will *not* be given out now.[34]

Optimism survived the fire, and Clara Brown told of Tombstone's rapid renovation: "The ruins uptown present a disheartening spectacle, but many of the people so suddenly burned out appear not to *feel* disheartened," Brown reported. "Buildings are going up as rapidly as possible, and most of them will be superior to the ones destroyed, being made of adobe instead of wood."[35]

Tombstone showed signs of new growth. In July the city council tried to induce a phone company to bring those newfangled telephones into town, and in August a water company began laying pipes. The townsmen also expected the railroad line would be extended into Tombstone.

Another rumor ran through Tombstone. It would only be a matter of time before Harry Woods would resign as undersheriff to devote full time to running the *Nugget*. The *Star* printed the rumor, and the *Epitaph* called for him to give up the public position. The job of undersheriff was designed as a full-time occupation. Other civic officials—the mayor and members of the town council—were to be businessmen working for the public good. Mayor/editor John Clum saw a distinct difference between his role and that of undersheriff/editor Woods, whose duties at the *Nugget* could only interfere with his position as No. 2 lawman in a county that demanded efficient law enforcement. Woods held a very partisan interest in supporting the Ten Per Cent Ring, since he took home a share of the profits. With Behan and Woods in the two top positions of the office, the Cochise County sheriff's department had, essentially, two politicians and no top-gun enforcers to protect the county. It was a formula for disaster in an area that would soon be identified as the most crime-riddled in the country. Deputy Dave Neagle earned praise for his work, though at 5-foot-8 he did not present an imposing figure. Another deputy seemed questionable from the outset—Frank Stilwell had been arraigned on murder charges a year earlier, which were later dropped. But Stilwell came from a well-known family, an important consideration in those times. He was the brother of Comanche Jack Stilwell, a heralded Indian fighter and later a lawman. From the start, the Behan–Woods sheriff's office seemed overmatched by the outlaw bands that stalked the county. The *Arizona Star*, the most outspoken foe of the criminal element, called for a solution by editorializing: "The common enemy to all of our law-abiding citizens and to our Mexican neighbors must be wiped out, root and branch. They should be hunted down like reptiles, and made to answer the penalty of their crimes, without the law's delay. If the business is not settled soon, it will cost the government much treasure and many lives to redeem lost time."[36]

And standing between the encroaching lawlessness and the increasingly frightened citizens of Cochise County was Sheriff Johnny Behan and his little force. It was like trying to hold off a hurricane with a sheet of tissue paper.

ALMOST FROM THE TIME THE COWBOYS FIRST ARRIVED in southern Arizona, they hit hard against the Mexicans, with raids against the ranchers in the state of Sonora and attacks on Mexican traders coming north to buy goods in Tucson and Tombstone. By early 1881 more and more drifters had moved into Cochise County to prey on travelers. Rustling had increased on both sides of the border, and general rowdiness had grown tiresome for both Mexicans and Americans.

By the early spring, Mexican ranchers were on the alert for raiding parties coming south. With pressure mounting, Galeyville butcher Alfred McAllister and George Turner, identified as "well-known cowboys," obtained the contract to furnish beef to Fort Bowie in the Chiricahua Mountains. Turner, McAllister, and two others went into Sonora to acquire stock. On May 13, a band of rustlers ran off between four hundred and five hundred head from the ranch of Jose Juan Vasquez, about three miles from Fronteras. Vasquez and his vaqueros rode off in pursuit and found Turner and his three friends camped for the night with a herd of cattle. Vasquez's men surrounded the Americans and demanded their surrender. When the Americans responded with a volley of gunshots, the Mexicans returned fire, killing three of the group and wounding the fourth. Vasquez approached the wounded man and offered to take him to his ranch. The American instead fired his revolver and killed Vasquez. The Mexicans quickly gunned down the American. The *Nugget* said that along with Turner and McAllister, two men identified only as Oliver and Garcia were killed. By one account, a body search revealed that Turner and McAllister still carried the funds they had brought to Mexico to purchase the cattle, which was considered proof that they had not paid for the herd they drove.[37]

The Turner massacre stirred emotions on both sides of the border. The *Nugget* printed rumors that American cowboys would band together to "clean out" Fronteras and avenge the killing. Military observers saw a horde of cowboys apparently preparing for battle. The Mexicans anticipated a frontal attack from the north, and Sonora Governor Luis Torres posted a force of two hundred men, cavalry and infantry, at the border under the command of Commandant Filipe Neri to try to keep the cowboys out of Mexico. Torres also began a letter-writing campaign to John Fremont before the governor left on an extended trip, then to Acting Governor John J. Gosper in Prescott, seeking help in stopping the cowboy raiders. But the governors were hamstrung by the laws, which left control to the local sheriff; and by the legislature, which refused to provide funds for any other intervention. Major General Orlando Willcox, head of the Arizona forces, secretly wired U.S. army headquarters in San Francisco to receive authorization to intervene. General J. C. Kelton, adjutant general of the Division of the Pacific, refused the request as illegal and ordered Willcox to leave cowboy herding to the civil authorities.[38]

Smuggling had become a big business in northern Mexico in the late '70s. The Mexican government increased taxes on alcohol and tobacco to the point where a good profit could be made smuggling across the border. Mexican smugglers went north to Tucson or Tombstone loaded with diamonds and gold and silver coins and bullion, made their purchases of alcohol and tobacco, and returned to Sonora to sell their goods well below the government's tax-added price. The cowboys found easy pickings in the northern-bound smugglers, loaded with treasure. There is no record of how many pack trains were robbed or how much booty taken since both the robbers and victims were operating illegally. The cowboys apparently satisfied themselves with theft rather than murder, at least until one group of Mexicans decided to fight back.

In late July, a rancher named Bob Clark came into Tombstone and told of encountering a pack train of about thirty mules in disarray, with their packs overturned and no one in charge as the animals bounded through Skeleton Canyon, part of the smuggling route to Mexico. Clark surmised rustlers had attacked the train and killed the owners.[39] This would be the first indication of a raid that would shock citizens on both sides of the border. On the morning of July 27, a band of cowboys estimated at fifty in strength attacked a group of Mexican traders, robbing them of $2,500 in coin and silver bullion, plus another estimated $1,500 in mescal, merchandise, and livestock. Four Mexican bodies were left scattered on the canyon rocks. Joseph Bowyer, manager of the Texas Consolidated Mining and Smelting Company in Galeyville, listened to the cowboy raiders tell of their attack. "One of the cow-boys in relating to me the circumstances said that it was the damndest lot of truck he ever saw; he showed me a piece of bullion, I should judge it looked half gold. Upon my telling him that trouble would likely arise from this, he replied that it was a smuggling train and they would not dare say much."[40]

But the Mexican smugglers did complain. On the evening of the attack several from the party showed up at the door of Commandant Neri, who quickly transmitted details to Governor Torres and other Mexican officials. The four men killed became a cause célèbre in Mexico. Dead were Miguel Tarazona, Joaquin Montano, Jose Samaniego, and Reinaldo Samaniego, murdered by what Torres called "Texan Cow-boys." Mexican consul Vicente Morales protested angrily to Acting Governor Gosper: "I take the liberty of requesting Yr. Exc. to use all the means at your command in order to effect the extermination of those who lay waste whole districts of my country, murder my countrymen and rob them when they come to contribute to the commerce of this Territory."[41]

Torres wrote to Gosper demanding retribution, and rumors passed through southern Arizona of impending Mexican retaliation. "The citizens . . . and troops are after the cowboys and are disposed to take summary vengeance if they overtake them," the *Tucson Citizen* reported.[42] No names were mentioned in either the official documents or the newspapers, but Curley Bill and John Ringo were the usual suspects for any such raids.

The cowboys struck again about a week later, this time far closer to home, just a few miles outside Charleston. The August 13 *Epitaph*, under the headline "The Murdering Cowboys," told of a pack train of three Mexican soldiers who were returning from buying supplies in Tombstone with merchandise and about a thousand dollars in gold and silver:

> When this latter party got above Hereford, and about half way to Ochoaville, they were set upon by a party of five cow-boys, who fired mortally wounding one of the Mexicans and killing one of the horses. They took a rifle and one package of goods and it is supposed killed the one who had the money, as he had not up to last evening

been seen or heard from since the encounter. It is said that the Mexican who escaped recognized one of the bandits having seen him in Tombstone the day before.

Grown bold with the deeds of crime they have committed between here and Deming, and their merciless murders at Fronteras, these outlaws, having no fears of the civil authorities, have taken up the San Pedro valley as their head-quarters, knowing that there is a large travel between Benson, Contention, Tombstone, Charleston and Bisbee, besides the Mexican travel from Sonora to these points. It will be seen from the foregoing that they have made a good beginning and unless immediate steps are taken by the citizens to rid the county of these outlaws there will be no more protections to life and property between Benson and the Sonora line than there has been in the San Simon and eastward for the last year. When the civil authorities are insufficient or unwilling to protect a community the people are justified in taking the law into their own hands and ridding themselves of the dangerous characters who make murder and robbery their business. It remains to be seen how much longer such damnable acts as Fronteras massacre and the San Pedro murders shall go unpunished.[43]

The cowboys had antagonized the government of Mexico, and protests were flowing from Hermosillo to Prescott. Curley Bill and his friends were moving from the class of local toughs to criminals of international repute. The rustling ring had grown nasty, with a series of crimes that enraged the public. In June, unnamed cowboys assailed five members of the friendly Maricopa Indian tribe, forcing one to the ground and killing him in cold blood.[44] Robberies became commonplace on the roadways outside Tombstone, beyond Marshal Virgil Earp's jurisdiction, and rumors trickled in of even worse deeds, real and imagined.

Before the summer of '81, the cowboys had been mostly a nameless lot roving the hinterland. Gradually they received a degree of notoriety. Curley Bill had already drawn attention for killing Marshal White, and his dubious fame would grow now. John Ringo, "Billy the Kid" Claiborne, and even Ike Clanton would emerge as outlaws of note, men whose reputations were being reported across the West.

Ike Clanton stirred up a little ruckus late on the night of June 7 when he traded punches with "Little Dan" Burns. The two parted, with Clanton "expressing his determination to change the nature of the fight as soon as they met," the *Nugget* reported. The next morning, Ike saw Burns in front of the Wells, Fargo office on Allen Street, and they both reached for their guns. Before either man could draw, Virgil Earp and Constable Hugh Haggerty broke up the action, possibly saving Ike from Little Dan's bullet.[45]

Even Clanton's less than fastidious personal habits drew attention. "He was a despicable character and he ate like a pig," early Tombstone resident Ethel Macia said, repeating a family story to historian and author Jack Burrows. Before the summer of '81, most townsmen had apparently identified Ike as a rancher; but as his transgressions mounted it grew clear that Ike kept friends with the cowboy troublemakers and had become a hell-raiser himself.

More troublemakers gained recognition, sometimes based more on perception than reality. John Ringo left his own trail of tales. A quiet, often drunk cowboy, he came to Arizona with a reputation for trouble. He would gradually be built into one of the most remarkable myths of the West—a Latin-spewing intellectual, former college professor turned bad and deadly. Billy Breakenridge provided the description that would echo through the years:

> Ringo was a mysterious man. He had a college education, but was reserved and morose. He drank heavily as if to drown his troubles; he was a perfect gentleman when sober, but inclined to be quarrelsome when drinking. He was a good shot and afraid of nothing, and had great authority with the rustling element. Although he was the leader on their trips to Mexico after cattle and in their raids against the smugglers, he generally kept by himself after they returned to Galeyville. He read a great deal and had a small collection of standard books in his cabin.[46]

In reality, Ringo was a grade-school dropout who probably kept his mouth closed while others manufactured his reputation. The 6-foot-3 Ringo did seem to own a persona and bearing, and he had the ability to inspire fear and respect. "Every Tombstoner of his time I've met has recalled his FORCE," author Eugene Cunningham wrote. "We have all met that type—good and bad men whose personality came out at others. Not whom he *had* shot but whom he might shoot, seems to me is the question men asked."[47]

The recollections of Ringo's acquaintances proved even more unusual. Emma Muir, who grew up in Shakespeare, recalled that the polite, apparently well-educated outlaw often visited the ranch of Jim Hughes and made a special friend of 11-year-old Mary Hughes. Muir wrote: "Whenever Mary, scanning the country from the watchtower, saw him coming she put on her prettiest dress and combed her glossy, black hair. John Ringo, when he spoke to her, made her feel like a great lady. He had read many books, and he told her of what he read, and this made Mary want to learn how to read. So he taught her English from the family Bible, and Spanish from a book he had picked up in Tombstone. He taught her how to write, and she took enormous pride in copying his beautiful Spencerian chirography."[48] Such is the odd legacy of John Ringo, the outlaw who may have stopped a few times to read with a little girl, then rode off to raid and plunder.

While Ringo may have shown a gentle side at times, he was a dangerous man indeed. As a child, the Indiana native was nearby when a shotgun accidentally went off, killing his father during the wagon train trip west, and John grew up with his widowed mother in San Jose, California. He went to Texas to fight in the so-called Hoodoo War, a territorial battle. He left Texas for Arizona with at least one murder on his hands. His activities in Arizona will never be certain—rustlers did not keep records. He stole cattle, almost certainly participated in the raids and murders against the Mexicans, and may well have taken a hand in a stage robbery. His record of tangles with the law is skimpy, notably a drunken incident shortly after the Fronteras raid.

Nugget editor Richard Rule said, "One night when Ringo was a little too tight he took a hand in a poker game with two others and got beat. He didn't say much then, but went out quietly. In a little while he came back with a six-shooter in each hand, pointed them at the players and remarked that they might beat him at poker, but there was one little game where he could hold even with them. He then told them they could go, and needn't be particular about counting the money on the table, as he would take care of that. They left in a hurry, and he helped himself to the money."[49] The *Nugget* ran the story of the poker game on August 11, between the raids on Fronteras and the murder of the Mexican soldiers on the San Pedro. Presumably, Ringo had blood money to push across the table. The *Nugget* report said Ringo and cowboy Dave Estes took around $500 from the poker game, then stole a horse from former deputy sheriff Newt Babcock on the way out of town.[50] According to Joseph Bowyer, Estes was brought to trial, but charges were dismissed for lack of evidence.

Ringo had also been involved in a shooting in December of 1879, when the outlaw offered a man named Louis Hancock a drink of whiskey. Hancock refused, saying he preferred beer. According to the *Arizona Daily Star,* "Ringo struck him over the head with his pistol and then fired, the ball taking effect in the lower . . . left ear . . . and the fleshy part of the neck; half an inch more . . . would have killed him."[51] When the case came before the grand jury, Ringo wrote to Sheriff Shibell, explaining that he could not attend because of some unknown incident with a gun:

> I write this letter to let you know why I can not appear—I got shot through the foot and it is impossible for me to travel for awhile.
>
> If you get any papers for me, and will let me know, I will attend to them at once as I wish to live here. I do not wish to put you to any unnecessary trouble, nor do I wish to bring extra trouble on myself. Please let the Dist-Atty know why I do not appear, for I am very anxious that there is know [*sic*] forfeiture taken on the Bond.[52]

While Ringo's record is sketchy, he certainly engaged in numerous nefarious activities. He just didn't get caught. Bowyer wrote, "A notorious cow-boy known as John R. offers to sell all the mutton the town can consume at the rate of $1.00 per head. No secrecy is observed in this kind of transactions."

Even 21-year-old Billy Claiborne's reputation reached the big cities. He was often confused with New Mexico's "Billy the Kid," Henry Antrim, alias William Bonney. Cowboy pal Tom Thornton tried to clear up the confusion in the *Examiner:* "You paper men have got them confounded. Young Billy worked for me in my hotel. He waits on tables and is a quiet, inoffensive fellow, if let alone; but he will shoot a man that tries to impose on him. He is out on the range south of Tucson to get out of the way of the officers who want him for his last shooting scrape. He is still alive and likely to cause somebody trouble if they bother him."[53]

Thornton's comments came shortly after Claiborne's indictment for killing James Hickey in Charleston after Hickey reportedly alluded to him as a homosexual. One of the Earp brothers may have been involved in Claiborne's arrest.[54] Claiborne also ran into trouble for horse stealing, but the victim chose not to prosecute the case after the horses were returned. Bowyer said he knew the reason: "The same person told me afterward that if he prosecuted the boy the other cow-boys would steal every head of stock he had which he being a poor man, could not afford to stand."

Perhaps the most despicable of the cowboys was a miscreant named Sandy King, who reputedly stopped an old man in the backcountry and made him dismount from his horse. When the man said, "It's pretty rough to leave an old man afoot like this," King drew his pistol and responded, "You damned old scoundrel, I'll give you something to remember me by," and grazed his head with a bullet. King later went into a store in Lordsburg, New Mexico, and ordered goods. When the shopkeeper asked to whom he should charge the merchandise, King put his hand on his pistol and said, "To this." The storekeeper responded by drawing his own gun and grazing King's neck with his shot.[55]

Gradually, during the summer of '81, more and more drifters would be identified as cowboys. Newspaper accounts called Zwing Hunt a rustler, although he was not charged. He and his pal Arthur Boucher, alias Billy Grounds, were among the friends of Curley Bill. Charles Ewing, Lewis McGinnis, and Milt Hicks would all be charged with rustling, but rustlers were hard to convict. The grand jury lamented that citizens were afraid to come forward and testify for fear of their own safety.

As more no-accounts drifted into southeastern Arizona, townspeople and ranchers alike began running short on patience. The cowboys' value as Apache fighters became insignificant compared to their troublemaking tendencies, prompting Bowyer to write to Gosper: "The cow-boys frequently visit our town and after saluting us with an indiscriminate discharge of firearms, and after indulging in a few drinks at the saloons, practice shooting at the lamps, bottles, glasses, etc. Sometimes going to the length of shooting the cigar out of one's mouth; this of course produces a nervous feeling among the visitors especially. The situation at this writing is not materially changed from the above. The cowboys as a class are not over brave, though there are some among them who have gone through so much difficulty that they have become desperate and will take desperate chances."[56]

San Francisco papers raged against the cowboys and the "good" citizens who protected them. The *Stock Report* editorialized: "What is to be expected when half the law officers of the border districts are their allies and when one-third of the so-called business men are their allies and protectors? The stolen cattle are harbored by ranchers, the cowboys have their own butchers in every place and the proceeds of the robberies of ranches and teams are bought without question by half the 'merchants' of Southern Arizona. The Territory is honeycombed with corruption and the life and property of no man are safe unless he himself is a ruffian or thief."[57] The paper did not identify which officers were thought to be in league with the cowboys, leaving the question open to speculation among San Francisco readers.

Depredations became rampant in the summer of '81. Another stage robbery, on August 17, stunned the county. The stage stopped at Benson and unloaded several bars of silver bullion on the platform at the station. The messenger began loading them inside the building, leaving several on the platform. The robber slipped up and stole one of the 150-pound bars, valued at $2,000, and escaped before the messenger stepped out to continue loading. Consistently the *Epitaph* railed against the cowboys and called for a committee of vigilance: "Desperate diseases require heroic treatment."

Even the most polite sorts in Cochise County dropped their refinement and hoped for emphatic action against the criminal element. Parsons wrote in his diary: "Two men probably killed at Charleston for robbery and I'm glad of it. Time a lesson was taught the cowboys."[58]

One big lesson came on August 13 when gunfire sounded at the U.S.–Mexican border marker. Old Man Clanton and six others brought a herd north into Guadalupe Canyon, a wide trail running through Sonora and into Arizona about a hundred miles east of Tombstone. With a steep mountain on one side and a rocky hill on the other, the trail led to a large flat about a hundred yards north of the border. Mexican troops were required to stop at the border marker, placing Clanton and his helpers beyond the range of retribution. Shortly after midnight a new arrival joined the party. Jim Crane, the long-sought-after stage robber, made his appearance.

Billy Lang and Charles Snow awoke during the night to hear the cattle stirring and suspected a bear. Harry Ernshaw awoke a few minutes later and sent Snow to get a gun and search for the animal. He had taken only a few steps when the shooting started. Snow, Lang, Clanton, Crane, and Dixie Lee "Dick" Gray were killed, the latter three still in their sleeping rolls. William Byers, with an arm wound, and Ernshaw escaped, Ernshaw grazed on the nose by a bullet as he ran.

"When they first fired and killed Charley Snow I thought the boys were firing at a bear," Byers told the *Nugget*. "[I] jumped out of my blankets, and as I got up the boys around me were shot. As soon as I saw what was up I looked for my rifle, and not seeing it I grabbed my revolver, and seeing them shooting at us from all sides, started to run, but had not gone forty feet when I was shot across my body, but I didn't fall, and in a few more steps was hit in my arm, knocked the pistol out of my hand and I fell down."

Ernshaw ran past, and Byers lay down and played dead. "When I saw the Mexicans begin stripping the bodies, I took off what clothes I had, even my finger ring, and lay stretched out with my face down, and as I was all bloody from my wounds, I thought they would pass me by, thinking I was dead, and had already been stripped. I was not mistaken, for they never touched me, but as one fellow passed me on horseback he fired several shots at me, one grazing the side of my head, and the others striking my side, throwing the dirt over me. But I kept perfectly still and he rode on."[59]

An unidentified American coming north from Sonora told a grisly story of the events that preceded the massacre. He said that a few days before the killings in the canyon, about twenty-five cowboys raided into northern Sonora and gathered all the loose stock they could find before starting home. The Mexicans quickly organized a posse to chase the raiders. When they caught up, bullets began flying through the air, and eight Mexicans lay dead as the rest retreated to report to their military leaders. Commandant Neri immediately dispatched Captain Carrillo and a force of Mexican regulars to Guadalupe Canyon, the most likely spot for the rustlers to cross. While the Mexican government never officially acknowledged the attack, there is little doubt Carrillo and his force ambushed Clanton on American territory in the belief that his party had been guilty of raiding and killing.[60]

It is likely the Clanton group was a mixture of rustlers and honest cattlemen. Ernshaw ran a milk ranch, and Dick Gray was the son of Mike Gray, proprietor of the Town Site Company. John Pleasant Gray, Mike's son and Dick's brother, would later say his 19-year-old brother was simply riding to town with the cowboys. Parsons saw this as little excuse when he wrote in his diary, "This killing business by the Mexicans, in my mind, was perfectly justifiable as it was in retaliation for killing of several of them and their robbery by cowboys recently, this same Crane being one of the number. Am glad they killed him. As for the others, if not guilty of cattle stealing, they had no business to be found in such bad company." Crane's death ended any chance of a deal between Ike Clanton and the Earps, and left Ike at the Earp's mercy not to tell of their discussions.

The killing sent Tombstone into a frenzy. The *San Francisco Examiner* reported that Mike Gray and Lang's father raised a party to avenge the murders, and the Clanton brothers put together a troop of two hundred, "and as desperate a gang could not be imagined. . . . They will carry the war into Mexico. Great apprehension is felt for the Americans in Sonora, as it will more than likely be a war of retaliation. We are hourly expecting a collision as the Mexican troops are in force on the line and will repel the invaders. . . . lawlessness seems to be the order of the day. Serious international complications will arise unless immediate steps are taken to put a stop to the movement on foreign soil, and blood will flow like water before another week rolls round."[61]

Clara Brown decried the actions of this private army and feared it would bring war with Mexico. "While no one upholds the recent massacre, those who think dispassionately about the matter realize that the Mexicans were not the first to inaugurate the present unhappy state of affairs along the border. They have suffered greatly from the depredations of those outlaws who, under the guise of 'cowboys,' infest this country and pursue the evil tenor of their ways with no attempt at interference on the part of those whose duty it is to suppress crime. The Mexicans have lost a great deal of stock, and some of their countrymen have been murdered. They are about to establish three forts near the line and will take further measures to prevent raiding. This Government should not be backward in the performance of an equal duty."[62]

The *Nugget* did not find a war with Mexico such a bad idea. In an August 20 editorial, the paper said the war seemed inevitable and noted the advantages of conquering the country and annexing its northern states for mining and development. The *Epitaph* lambasted Harry Woods and the *Nugget* for their anti-Mexican views and needled Woods for his failings as undersheriff:

> Our hot-headed under Sheriff, who but a day or two since was crying for the blood of the "Greasers" and their territory, provided it did not require any exertion on the part of the gentleman whose duty it is to enforce the laws and collect the taxes, has cooled down considerably, and now wants the responsibility shifted on the shoulders of somebody else. There is altogether too much good feeling between the Sheriff's office and the outlaws infesting this county, as evidenced by the "escape" of King, who was supposed to be implicated in the attempted stage robbery and murder of Budd Philpott. By the way, the true inwardness of that mysterious affair has never been given the public. Will our legislative editorial Under Sheriff rise and explain?[63]

Tombstone's unauthorized militia turned out to be nothing more than a burial party organized by Mike Gray to take care of the remains of his son and the others, and then to round up the remaining cattle. The Clanton brothers' threats never seemed to pan out, either. But the rumors had served to stir up much excitement, and on August 19, Mexican General Adolfo Dominguez, the adjutant to General Jose Otero, commander of the troops on the border, arrived in Tombstone to try and quiet the commotion. "Our people have been great sufferers," Dominguez said. "We have lost many citizens killed and much property stolen. We are therefore taking active steps to protect our citizens and repel raiders. There are 200 regulars besides the militia on the line, and three forts and supply camps are to be established at once. Every precaution will be taken to protect both our own citizens and such Americans as are engaged in legitimate industry within our lines."

Dominguez came to Arizona to purchase supplies for the new forts and to try to act diplomatically to quiet the furor that could lead to war. He called for a joint U.S.–Mexican effort to launch attacks against the cowboys, saying: "We can only drive out these thieves and murderers by united action. We are not only willing, but very anxious that united action should exist. The American raids did much damage in our country, and affairs have been gradually growing more and more desperate. It is estimated that within the last month more than ten citizens have been killed and upward of $30,000 worth of property taken. We do not believe that this disposition to raid is general among citizens of this section. We think that the American officials and a great majority of the citizens deprecate these acts of lawlessness, and believing this we have courage to hope that by united effort the outlaws may be suppressed and an early adjustment of difficulties effected."[64]

As the summer progressed, the troops under Commandant Neri took control of the situation in Sonora, and the rustling raids into Mexico ceased. The citizens on both sides of the border paid a price. Americans were not allowed to enter Sonora without a pass from Governor Torres or Neri, and Mexicans lived in apprehension of a cowboy raid coming at any time. Back in Cochise County, the mounting bands of rustlers found themselves without the easy pickings across the border and intensified their activities on the American side. By early autumn, newspaper reports appeared of horse or cattle stealing in the remote regions of Cochise County. In September, the wagon trade carrying lumber into Tombstone from the mountains ceased when "men owning teams suitable for hauling lumber positively refuse to take any more chances outside of the city limits so long as the present state of insecurity for stock exists." Businesses were forced to order lumber from California while the cowboys halted virtually all trade on the roadways. The *Nugget* angrily editorialized, "The scarcity of hemp and rope factories is a serious drawback to all new and unsettled countries," a veiled call for hangings to rid the county of the criminals who strangled commerce.[65]

Through most of the events, Fremont was virtually a governor in absentia. He went East to check his business investments and try to convince Congress to intercede in the mounting border crises. In a New York newspaper interview he lambasted the territorial legislature for refusing his militia plan. He then tried to recruit support for a measure that would allow use of the military to quell the border troubles.[66] Fremont drew Acting Governor Gosper's ire for prolonging his stay in the East during the time of crises, and for failing to take action. Both the Democratic and Republican press railed against the governor's long absence and called for a replacement. The citizenry picked up the cry, and even cowboy pal Tom Thornton scoffed at the old Pathfinder when he said: "Governor Fremont, who, by the way, is a terrible old governmental fraud, has never paid any attention to Arizona affairs, and Gosper, who acts [as] Governor, is afraid to interfere with these men."[67] Oddly, almost nobody in Arizona seemed to remember that only a few months earlier, it was Fremont who foresaw the severity of the problem and tried to provide a solution before it got out of control.

Dominguez and the cooler heads in the Southwest prevailed, and the border war never erupted. During much of the latter half of 1881 the U.S. government was paralyzed after President James Garfield was shot on July 2 and lingered until September 19. While he lay close to death for two months, newspapers gave daily updates on his condition, and no government action was taken on the Arizona question. By the time Chester A. Arthur, the vice president, took the presidency, Arizonans faced the more immediate fear of a war with the Apaches, and that took precedence over a border battle with Mexico.

Everybody's pal Johnny Behan was no longer in favor with the Earps by the late summer of 1881. The forgotten promise of appointing Wyatt as under-sheriff, followed by the dubious events on the posse and his refusal to pay the Earps for their services, had caused a definite rift. As 1881 progressed, it grew more and more obvious that Behan was overmatched by his position. Some were hinting that he might even be in league with the outlaws. He had done little to quell the cattle thieving through Cochise County, and on his watch the outlaws had grown into a greater threat. The *Epitaph* grew derisive of the sheriff's office, while Woods's *Nugget* continued to defend Behan's honor.

The lovely Sadie Marcus, the one-time actress who represented herself as Behan's wife, exacerbated the sheriff's problems in late July when she returned from a trip to find Johnny keeping company with a married woman. Sadie did not take kindly to her "husband's" courting another woman, and she left the sheriff. What she did for the the next few months has remained a mystery. At some point in the months of August and September, Sadie Marcus and Wyatt Earp began a friendship that would eventually blossom into romance. By unconfirmed stories, Wyatt began squiring her around town on occasion, enough to cause suspicion but not enough to cause a public scandal.[68] Wyatt and Mattie were still living as man and wife, and if Wyatt became serious about Sadie at this time, no evidence remains. Stuart Lake wrote to his editor at Houghton Mifflin that Wyatt "fell for Sadie and Sadie for him. There apparently is some doubt with those who were their intimates as to which did the 'propositioning' but the first thing Johnny Behan knew, Wyatt had his girl."[69] Lake may have exaggerated the extent of the relationship, but enough happened between Earp and Marcus to further aggravate the situation with the sheriff, who was facing public scorn in the *Epitaph* and private humiliation at losing his "wife."

Much of Tombstone continued to buy Behan's glad-handing friendliness. Sociable, always ready with a joke, and continually puffing up his achievements, he was easy to accept as one of the good guys. Behan was good company, the type of man who would always brighten a dinner party as long as he didn't bed the host's wife. *San Francisco Examiner* correspondent Ridgely Tilden wrote of the sheriff: "John H. Behan, the present Sheriff of Cochise county, has proved himself an able and efficient officer, and will beyond a doubt be elected to succeed himself. He is a Democrat of the Jeffersonian school, being honest, efficient and capable."[70] But others grew to distrust the cordial sheriff. Clum attacked him constantly in *Epitaph* editorials, and letters to various papers kept insinuating he was in league with the cowboys.[71]

The Earps, particularly Wyatt, were less open, not as friendly as genial Johnny. Western writer Eugene Cunningham, a friend of Billy Breakenridge, gave the deputy sheriff's opinion of the Earp family: "He thoroughly disliked them. They got on his nerves, strutting like they did because they had Wyatt behind them."[72]

Whether Breakenridge and Behan liked it or not, the four blond-haired Earp brothers became part of the fabric of Tombstone, with Jim tending bar, Wyatt and Virgil in law enforcement, and Morgan riding shotgun, filling in as a deputy, and doing whatever else caught his fancy. *Examiner* correspondent Tilden described the family: "Jimmy, as he is familiarly called, is one of the jolliest, best-natured men that ever the sun shone on. In truth he was a general favorite. Bacchus would occasionally get the better of him, but Jimmy never hunted fights, and if he accidentally found one would, as soon as sober, fix things up. Virgil was of different texture. Marshal of Tombstone for months, he kept the town as quiet as a cemetery. Poor Morgan was as brave and reckless a man as ever put foot in stirrup or pulled the trigger on a 45. Wyatt, who never drank, was as cool as the icebergs in Alaska, brave and determined as any man on earth, and General of the whole outfit."[73]

Tough guy Wyatt shunned hard liquor for ice cream, stopping almost daily for a cold scoop at a little parlor on Fourth Street. Still, the Earps never quite fit in with the best element of town. They were saloonkeepers and gamblers, not mining engineers or merchants. Virgil applied for membership in the Masonic lodge and was refused. Tombstone's upper class respected the Earps and needed them. They did not necessarily want to be lodge brothers with them.

Reporter Tilden was not so cordial toward Doc Holliday, whose friendship with the Earps seemed to puzzle Tombstone. "Now comes Doc Holliday, as quarrelsome a man as God ever allowed to live on earth. A Georgian, well bred and well-educated, he happened in Kansas some years ago. Saving Wyatt Earp's life in Dodge City, Kansas, he earned his gratitude, and notwithstanding his many bad breaks since, has always found a friend in Wyatt."[74]

Holliday seemed to lead contrary lives in Tombstone, antagonizing much of the community with his downright orneriness yet winning some sort of acceptance with the Earps. Holliday had a quirky sense of humor and a love of practical jokes. When a stranger entered Tombstone wearing a derby hat, Holliday followed him through the streets ringing a dinner bell.[75] He was prematurely gray at the age of 30, possibly due to his chronic tuberculosis. But the hot, dry Arizona climate seemed to agree with him; the coughing fits became rare and his fragile body seemed to grow stronger.

As troubled as the situation in Tombstone seemed when September began, it would only grow worse as the month progressed. Pony Deal and Sherman

McMasters had been the primary suspects in a stage robbery in Globe in February, and Pima County sheriff Bob Paul had been seeking them for months. On September 9, he captured Deal and wired to Virgil Earp in Tombstone. Virgil responded that McMasters was in town and asked Paul if he wanted an arrest made. As Virgil awaited the reply, John Ringo rode into town with his horse in a lather and joined McMasters. For more than two hours, Virgil awaited word whether to arrest McMasters, keeping an eye on Ringo all the time. But a snag developed, according to the *Epitaph*. Paul sent his wire authorizing an arrest to Wells, Fargo agent Marshall Williams, who was not in his office. The telegraph operator delivered it to the office without telling Virgil of the contents. Sam Clayton, the agent sitting in for Williams, eventually opened it and went out searching for Virgil, but found him minutes after McMasters had left, bound in the direction of the O.K. Corral.

Unarmed, Virgil had to borrow a pistol from a friend of Clayton's, then deputized brother Jim Earp to join him in the search. They checked several saloons, then headed for the O.K. Corral to notify the proprietor not to let McMasters take his horse. As they reached the corral, a man came loping out on McMasters's horse. Virgil ordered the rider to halt, but he kept riding. Virgil fired a shot into the air, and the rider spun around and asked if the marshal wanted him. It was not McMasters but a stranger, and Virgil allowed him to ride on. Virgil ran after him on foot and stopped him again, taking the horse, according to the *Epitaph*. Just as Earp got in the saddle, McMasters leaped from a bunch of bushes about a hundred feet away and dashed for a fence. Virgil ordered him to halt, but McMasters kept running. Virgil unloaded his six-shooter, then rode around the fence in pursuit to find McMasters had made good his escape. Behan finally arrived to help with the hunt, too late to catch the escaping fugitive. The *Epitaph* lamented: "Had Sheriff Paul telegraphed direct to the Marshal, McMasters would now have been in custody and safely reposing in the County Jail."[76] McMasters went on foot to the Contention mine, where the hostler, a black man named Jim Smith, apparently helped him steal two horses. McMasters then rode off, eluding Behan's pursuit.

As with just about everything in Tombstone, there would be more to the story. According to Wyatt Earp's statements in 1925, he employed McMasters as an informer. Most likely, Wyatt had lured McMasters away from the rustlers, and Virgil's pursuit was primarily a ruse to convince Ringo and the rest that McMasters remained a wanted man. It is very possible that the hostler Jim Smith was also part of Earp's chain of informants. Smith, a tough Civil War veteran, became a noted Tombstone character in his own right for backing down Frank Leslie with a shotgun. Smith could have been an important operative since he would have drawn little notice among the rustler crowd. They would not have expected a black man to serve as one of the Earps' sources of information.

While Virgil handled his duties in town, Wyatt rode away on other business. The night before the McMasters chase, the stage from Tombstone to Bisbee pulled through the Mule Mountains a few miles north of the Mexican border, passing through the small mining town of Hereford. Just beyond, town driver Levi McDaniels heard a voice call "Hold on," and two men stepped out with bandannas covering their faces. The two robbers took the mail sack, a Wells,

Fargo box with $2,500—there was no shotgun messenger—and then lined up the passengers and collected their valuables. The robber carrying a shotgun climbed up to McDaniels's seat, said, "Maybe you have got some sugar," and went through the driver's pockets. He returned to the ground and took a gold watch and $600 cash from two passengers. The robbers then allowed the stage to proceed.

The holdup happened at about ten on the night of September 8, but word did not reach Tombstone until 9:30 the next morning when two messengers rode into town and reported to Wells, Fargo agent Williams. Within a few hours, the *Epitaph* reported, Deputy Sheriff Breakenridge and Wyatt and Morgan Earp were on the trail. Williams, Dodge, and another deputy, Dave Neagle, were to join the posse later. According to the *Nugget*, Wyatt wore the badge of a U.S. deputy marshal during the search.[77] The trail could be easily followed because one of the robbers had used an unshod horse, unusual in the rocky backcountry.

The posse had one real clue: "One of the robbers was or appeared to be of a jocose turn of mind and in the use of many cant phrases which were known to be familiar sayings of Stilwell," the *Tucson Citizen* said.[78] Most notable was the use of the word "sugar" for money, a term common in the Frank Stilwell vernacular. Dodge said the posse split, with Breakenridge and Neagle following one trail and he and the Earps taking another. Wyatt and Dodge were experienced trackers, and as they followed the trail, they came across something out of place, a boot heel that matched the tracks they had seen around the site of the stagecoach robbery. According to Dodge, "Wyatt and I were both off from our horses when we found the boot heel while we were trailing the robbers in the Mule mountains. When we got to Bisbee we were satisfied as to the man who had done the job and Wyatt went to question the shoemaker and I slipped down to where Frank Stilwell and Pete Spence hung out."

Pete Spencer, usually referred to as Spence, lived with his young Mexican wife on the corner of First and Fremont in Tombstone, across the street from Virgil Earp. He was reputedly a dangerous man, with some allegiance to the cowboys. No one knew at the time that his real name was Elliott Larkin Ferguson, and he was a Texas outlaw on the run.

"There I found that Frank Stilwell had one new boot heel," Dodge continued. "Wyatt found out from the shoemaker that he had put a new heel on Frank Stilwell's boot. We arrested Frank Stilwell and [later] Pete Spence. On our way in to Tombstone Stilwell and Spence both swore they would get Wyatt, Morg and myself for this arrest."[79] Shoemaker R. P. Dever would later testify he had removed Stilwell's narrow heels and replaced them with others much broader.[80]

The posse brought Stilwell and Spence back to Tombstone, where they appeared before Justice of the Peace Wells Spicer in a preliminary hearing and were granted bail of $2,000 each, with Billy Allen, Ike Clanton, and C. H. "Ham" Light paying part of the bail. Spence and Stilwell were quickly discharged by Spicer on insufficient evidence when alibi witnesses assured the court that the two accused robbers were elsewhere when the stage was stopped. Dodge and the Earps were convinced they had the right men, whether the courts thought so or not, and Stilwell and Spence would later be arrested on federal charges for the stage robbery.

FROM THE FIRST DAY THE BOOMERS POURED INTO TOMBSTONE, one fear had stood above all others. The Mexicans, the rattlesnakes, and the cowboys were dangers they knew. Most frightening of all, though, was the danger they rarely saw. Somewhere, off in the hills, Tombstone townsmen envisioned hordes of Apaches just waiting for their chance to attack. Nearly every day newspaper stories detailed a battle at some remote post, where the Apaches would murder some settler for simply building a home on native land. While nearly all the reports were false, most of the miners and cowboys feared they would be next. Tombstone formed a militia in September and waited in readiness.

Finally the call came late on the night of October 4. A friend dropped in on Parsons to tell him that soldiers and Apaches were fighting in Dragoon Pass, north of Tombstone. The battle could only mean the beginning of the war. Parsons wrote: "The Indian scare spread through town, although . . . I slept tranquilly through it last night. Being on the edge of town, I did not hear whistles blowing and the general commotion, and was surprised at the excitement existing this a.m. and all last night. Armed squads went out and reconnoitered and it seems that after their fight, the Indians started for my mountains, the Huachucas, but the noise drove them back."

The whistles from the Vizina and Tough Nut mines, used to signal emergencies, awakened the rest of the town, and it was learned that Geronimo and Cachise's son Natchez had led a band of Apaches who had jumped the San Carlos reservation. The Apaches appeared headed for Cachise's old stronghold, a natural fortess in the Dragoon Mountains.

Mayor Clum, who had earlier served as agent at the San Carlos, Sheriff Johnny Behan, and Marshal Virgil Earp led a forty-man militia to ride into the hills to fend off Apache attack. Parsons, just two years removed from his bank job, volunteered to become an Indian fighter, carrying a rifle and a cartridge belt. Behan was chosen captain and Virgil Earp the first lieutenant for the so-called Tombstone Rangers. Wyatt Earp rode as a trooper. John Pittman Rankin, a black man, served as cook and trooper for the expedition. The band rode out of town toward a ranch owned by Edwin B. Frink.

Parsons recorded the journey, telling of passing deserted hay ranches, with food left on the tables when the inhabitants made quick exits. Heavy rains came to soak the troops and wash away tracks. "Some [posse members] slunk away and gave it up," Parsons wrote. "Clum and I were left some distance behind; in fact, many of us had hard work to get along, the ground was so soft and boggy, horses going in nearly up to their knees at times. Didn't feel entirely comfortable, sometimes away behind so, as the thought of possibly being taken in entered my mind, but after dark awhile, we reached our destination, or rather appointed place for rest, and crowded the room after picketing horses from the storm. About ten o'clock that day, the Indians attacked Frink's Ranch and stole a good part of his stock, and he claimed to know just where they were, saying he could put us right onto them. He was positive of their being in force about 20 miles from his place in a pass in the Swisshelm Mountains, southern end of Chiricahuas.

"We dried as much as possible, cleaned guns and saw they were in good working order, made some coffee into which one fellow's shoe fell, but coffee couldn't be wasted, and laid all over one another to catch some sleep, an unsuccessful matter," Parsons recorded. "Some of us looked out for horses, rounding them up once in awhile, as Indians might stampede them. Our sleeping postures were beautiful. I crawled under table and had to twist legs around one table leg to let M.W. [Marshall Williams] recline, and we were in all manner of shapes all over the little room . . . finally about 3 A.M. the call to horse was given, and we left single file with Frink as guide, following a trail by light of the moon which was full and shed a ghastly light over the line of determined men riding over that vast prairie, as it seemed to be, through the long, wet grass and across the soggy country. Providence favors the Indians, the boys said, as they crossed dry shod, and we floundered in mud part of the distance; but Providence was on our side, I think."

By the next morning, October 6, a little of the fervor had dampened among the remaining militia members who had not deserted. Parsons succinctly analyzed the mess: "I deemed it foolishness for our small party to attempt a fight, but of course being in for it now, I determined to stand by them to the last man. . . . Well, at last in the bright morning, we reached the mountain pass but found no Indians. Scouted thoroughly but, with the exception [of] some pretty fresh, scattering trails, there were no signs and none of a large force, such as we had expected to find. After a feed for man and beast, we recrossed the Sulphur Springs Valley to [McLaury's ranch] under a hot sun and over a boggy valley, leaving Frink behind, who shortly came in on a run with several head of his stock. It seems that a while after we left him and while he was hunting up some stock, the Indians opened fire on him, but he escaped unhurt; so, the red devils saw us all the time, and we didn't see them."

The Earps and Behan had put aside their differences to join together and chase Apaches, to prevent an attack on the town and settlers. The Earps may have resented Behan, and Behan may have hated the thought of his Sadie flirting with Wyatt Earp, but saving the city took precedence. At the McLaury ranch, something strange happened.

"At McL's was Arizona's most famous outlaw at the present time, 'Curly Bill,' with two followers," Parsons wrote. "He killed one of our former Marshals, and to show how we do things in Arizona, I will say that our present Marshal [Virgil Earp] and said 'Curly Bill' shook each other warmly by the hand and hobnobbed together some time, when said 'Curly Bill' mounted his horse and with his two satellites rode off, first though stealing a pair of spurs belonging to one of our party, as they couldn't be found after their departure. 'Curly Bill' was polite and considerate enough though to sharply wheel his horse to one side of my bridle, which I had accidentally dropped. He's not a bad-looking man, but looks very determined. . . . It was amusing to me to see with what marked deference his two young followers acted towards their chief, and how they regarded us, affecting a devil-may-care, braggadocio sort of manner."

Parsons noticed something else that he would not reveal until half a century later in a letter to Stuart Lake: "The best of feeling did not exist between Wyatt Earp and Curly Bill and their recognition of each other was very hasty and at some distance. Virgil Earp at that time was on better terms with Curly Bill and he and I walked up to him and had a chat, while the others rested and took things easy for a little while. It was a rather tense situation. It, however, did not last very long as Curly Bill and his two pals went off."[81]

By the time the party reached McLaury's the threat of an Indian war was subsiding, and several militia members returned to Tombstone. Parsons had a curiosity to satisfy. He camped with the soldiers and wrote: "Soldier encampment was a pretty sight. . . . I viewed [the Apache] Scouts with much interest with Clum, who found some he knew at San Carlos when he was agent and [they] were delighted to see him. Their confab was quite extended in Indian talk, Apache. . . . One company or two of Negro or Buffalo Soldiers, as the Indians call them, are in this command. They deride them, the hostiles I mean, do. They fought well though in Dragoon Pass."

The Buffalo Soldiers would gradually earn the respect of much of the frontier, and this battle helped build their reputation. The October 27 *Nugget* headlined, "And the colored troops fought nobly."

The next day Clum passed on what he had been told by the Apache scouts. The marauders numbered only about one hundred and were not nearly as imposing as the townspeople feared, Parsons realized: "Clum contended last night that the Indians were driven off of San Carlos by bayonets, and forced into this thing and it certainly looks like it. The coal lands there are valuable and the S.R.R [Southern Pacific Railroad] wants them. . . . It looks like a put-up job."

The *San Francisco Stock Report* saw the same scenario: "The Indians have been deliberately goaded into hostility in order that their property may be seized. Some officers of the army are in the plot."[82]

Another Tombstoner had a different explanation, telling the *Stock Report*: "Contractors in Arizona had been trying for years to get up an Apache war, and the outbreak was the final result of their efforts. With the contractors were associated the cow-boys who supply the contract beef. This beef represents stolen cattle. The cow-boys steal cattle and sell the beef at low rates to certain contractors, and the latter compete with the cattle-raisers. The cow-boys and contractors and a few storekeepers put up the job for the war, but did not make a complete success of it. The war ceased rather abruptly and two or three big business men went into insolvency."[83]

Whether the cowboys or the railroad prompted the brief Apache war, it became apparent that even Indian attacks had become a tool of the business interests. Both the beef contractors and the railroad would benefit from such an outbreak, and it is likely that all were pushing for conflict. Lost lives—Apache, black, and white—would be of little consequence to the businessmen.

Clum's little party returned safely to Tombstone, never sighting an Apache or firing a shot in anger. The entire Apache threat may have been more a fear than a reality. The army dispatched General J. C. Kelton, adjutant general of the Department of the Pacific, to investigate, and he returned to San Francisco to tell the *Examiner:* "The Apache war, as it is called, has been much exaggerated. There really has not been a war, and I am tempted to assert that never before has eighty or one hundred men created as much noise and excitement and given so much trouble as have those eighty Chiricahuas, who have just sought refuge in Mexico. There has never been, nor has there been any likelihood of any general outbreak among the Arizona Indians."

Kelton's report appeared on the *Examiner*'s front page on October 27, 1881. Back on page three of the same issue was another dispatch from Tombstone about an event that would long be remembered.

While the Earps were chasing Apaches, Cochise County experienced its fifth stage robbery in eight months, a dubious distinction indeed. On October 8, five highwaymen tried to stop a stage near Charleston, only to have the driver jump from his seat and flee. The abandoned team took flight and raced down the road before crashing. The robbers pursued and found the shattered coach with eleven shaken passengers. At gunpoint, they emptied the passengers' pockets and made off with about $800, then returned $5 to each passenger for expenses.[84] Five days later, Wyatt and Virgil Earp arrested Frank Stilwell and Pete Spence for the robbery, further antagonizing the cowboy crowd.

The McLaurys and Clantons held a grudge. According to Wyatt, they had long been friends of Stilwell and Spence, and they blamed the Earps for the arrest. Frank McLaury even said that he would never speak to Spence again because he had been arrested by the Earps. After Wyatt and Morgan took the two suspects into custody, Ike Clanton and Frank McLaury took offense, pulling Morgan into the street in front of the Alhambra saloon where John Ringo, Joe and Milt Hicks, and Ike Clanton began shouting at him for chasing the hold-up men. According to Wyatt, Frank McLaury said to Morgan, "If you ever come after me, you will never take me." Morgan replied that if he ever had occasion to go after him, he would arrest him. Frank McLaury then said to Morgan, "I have threatened you boys' lives, and a few days ago had taken it back, but since this arrest, it now goes." Morgan walked off without responding.[85]

The Earps were never good at taking humiliation, and having a favorite brother embarrassed in public would have been maddening to Wyatt and Virgil. They were not on the scene to take action, and Morgan's report would have festered in their minds through the coming weeks.

BETWEEN CHASING APACHES AND AVOIDING COWBOYS, the citizens of Tombstone enjoyed the good life of the frontier. Diarist Parsons delighted in visiting one of the town's ice cream parlors nearly every night. Oysters, shipped in ice, were an often-enjoyed delicacy, and traveling performers showed up to entertain the audience of miners, merchants, and cowboys at Schieffelin Hall. Many of the businessmen, transplants from San Francisco, New York, or Boston, expected a higher level of sophistication than bawdy houses and cheap entertainment.

Tombstone had changed dramatically in just a year. A more educated element began moving into town, providing a burgeoning intelligentsia capable of arguing Washington politics or debating the merits of classic literature. Sol Israel ran a successful newsstand, stocking selections of books as well as newspapers from around the West. He would soon have competition from a young bookseller named Aleck Robertson, who would later become one of the most respected publishers in the West. Robertson brought his bride, Jennie, to Tombstone.

"All sorts and conditions of men were going there—wild natures and others of the best in the race and culture," Jennie Robertson told her granddaughter, Cynthia Pridmore. "Some were writers, artists, professional men, lawyers and physicians. These were noticeably in the ascent, not daunted by a lack of water which was delivered in buckets at five cents a gallon. . . . The people who came to this frontier in the early '80s making homes and carrying on their businesses and professions were, as a rule, fine families from the east, south and west with high courage, ability and talents."[86]

The presence of an intelligentsia distinguished Tombstone from most other mining communities, which were made up largely of rougher elements. Tombstone emerged during a national recession, when even the more educated and cultured were migrating in search of opportunity. These were people unfamiliar with the recklessness of frontier life, more demanding of order and the vestiges of civilization. Where old-line frontiersmen might have been willing to accept a few shoot-'em-ups in the streets, the new breed of sojourner could never tolerate such madness. In its first year of existence, Cochise County grew with an oddly contrasting mix of new arrivals, dangerous drifters in the backcountry and people of education and refinement in the towns. Wanted criminals rubbed shoulders with legitimate businessmen as both sought wealth in the promising mining district.

They also sought entertainment. The rougher crowd was drawn to dancing women and bawdy displays, while the more refined enjoyed other diversions. *Pinafore* shows, repertory companies, and even a few Shakespeareans visited the half-dozen Tombstone stages, with Schieffelin Hall the most prominent. The little town also had amateur performing groups and a glee club.

"Music was of a high class," Jennie Robertson said. "There was much in private entertainment; the usual affairs to raise money for churches. One great event was the Martha Washington Tea Party, given in Schieffelin Hall. A minuet was danced as part of the entertainment. Colonial costumes were ordered from San Francisco for the men taking part. The ladies were adding watteaus and panniers of whatever material there was to be found to the evening gowns and some very handsome laces were seen. Hair was powdered and all details of a minuet of 20 parties carried out."

This was the remarkable contrast of Tombstone. Inside the halls, the good citizens danced the minuet in citified elegance. Down the road in Charleston, the rustlers plotted dangerous deeds while chewing down tough steaks and gulping whiskey. In town, they had more refined tastes. Parsons often went for a chop at a restaurant with a Chinese owner and chef, and Tombstone boasted fine dining. The Rockaway Oyster House, the Russ House, and the Grand Hotel offered gourmet dinners. Miss Nellie Cashman operated the Russ House, providing for the city's more discerning appetites at 50 cents a meal. For Thanksgiving in 1881, the Russ House menu included salmon, corned beef, ham, veal cutlets à la jardinière, fillet with beout sauce aux huîtres, ox tongue à la subeis, and an assortment of pies, cakes, and puddings.

The misplaced Brahmins and brokers could satisfy most of their appetites for food, drink, and pleasure. Among the 375 or so businesses were 47 saloons, and drinks were available in perhaps another dozen locations. Saloons even offered cold beer, a rarity on the frontier where ice was always in short supply. The finest whiskeys were shipped from San Francisco, and good cigars were always available. Baseball, the growing national passion, had become a local staple as early as 1881, and both Tombstone and Charleston fielded town teams that played on holidays.

The town was almost devoid of the elderly. The population was made up mostly of men and women ranging in age from their mid-20s through their 40s. There were children—enough for a school—and the *Epitaph* raged against young boys being allowed in saloons, "watching the gaming and listening to the vulgar talk and profanity that so often occurs around the bars and gaming tables. . . . There ought to be a law enacted entailing heavy pecuniary penalties upon the head of a family whose boys, under the age of eighteen, shall be found in any saloon, dance house or house of ill fame."[87]

Prostitutes' cribs still lined a block on Allen Street, and the San Jose House had its string of high-class women to entertain wealthier customers. Most of the principal saloons were also on Allen, and most had gambling rooms attached, filled with men intently making their wagers at keno, faro, or poker. The town boasted three major hotels; the Grand catered to transient travelers, while Brown's and the Cosmopolitan served more as rooming houses. By October of '81, Italian immigrants had arrived to open fruit markets, selling produce brought from Los Angeles. Just a year earlier, an apple would have been considered a delicacy. Several laundries opened, run by Chinese owners; about 150 Cornishmen worked the mines, which operated 24 hours a day. Brothels, bars, and gambling dens now shared the streets with fine restaurants and fairly elegant hotels. Well-made Eastern clothing could be purchased in the stores. By autumn of 1881, civilizing influences had hit town with force, bringing some trappings of city life and an air of refinement to at least a few locations.

It was nearly a wonderful life. As the elite and working classes gathered, they shared a fear for survival from cowboy attacks and from Apache raids. Growing also was the realization that the lawmen were so busy battling each other they didn't always have time to battle the wrongdoers. Parsons received an invitation to a series of secret meetings in January and left only a cryptic record: "Town unsafe; some decisive steps should be taken."

Two forces formed in town, the first the out-in-the-open Tombstone Rangers, an on-call band ready to ride out against Apache attacks. In whispers, most of the town knew of the second group, the one Parsons barely even discussed in his diary. They called it the Citizens Safety Committee. History gives them another name: vigilantes.

"It is said that the committee is very strong and they propose to put an end to the nefarious business," the *Tucson Journal* reported. "No doubt if they carry their designs into execution there will be warm work for them, as this class of men are accustomed to danger and will not submit without a desperate struggle. It seems to us that the civil authorities of our sister county of Cochise ought to be able to enforce order and arrest criminals without necessity of resorting to mob law. It is better to suffer a temporary wrong than to bring measures outside the pale of all law and good government. It is true the provocation at times would seem to justify any action that will rid a section of the depredations of bad men, but mob law invariably causes suffering and loss to the innocent along with the guilty. It is better that ten bad men should escape than that one innocent person be sacrificed."

The men who invested their money in Tombstone could not agree less. The *San Francisco Exchange* of October 8, 1881, carried the *Journal* story and responded: "The civil authorities, however, have shown themselves powerless to cope with those law-defying scoundrels. They are not able to enforce order and arrest criminals, and therefore the stranglers have become a necessity to that portion of Arizona Territory. Two or three prompt executions and the cowboy will become as meek as the product of the animal from which he takes his name. He is a bad canderon [blot] on Arizona, and nothing but the heroic treatment will eradicate him."

It was this principle that would be debated in courtrooms and across gun barrels for the next year in Arizona and throughout the West. American justice believed in the concept of innocent until proven guilty and cherished the rights of the accused. In Tombstone, the rights of the accused did not matter nearly as much as the survival of the victims when much of the townsfolk saw themselves as potential victims.

Cochise County's law-and-order advocates had grown sick of Behan's inaction. Parsons, the diminutive former bank teller, Mayor Clum, and many other top citizens vowed to back up the law if the lawless made their move to take over Tombstone. They swore in each member of the committee at a secret ceremony in which the inductee wore a black gown and mask, then kissed his six-shooter to complete the initiation.[88] The vigilantes were the worst-kept secret in town. By September, even the *Nugget* would make brief mention of the committee, and Frank McLaury did not like the idea. He stopped Virgil Earp in the street to ask him about it.

"I understand you are raising a vigilance committee to hang us boys," McLaury said, according to Virgil, who responded, "You boys?"

"Yes, the McLaurys and Clantons and Hicks and Ringo and in fact all of us cowboys," McLaury said.

"Frank, you remember the time that Curley Bill killed Fred White? Who guarded him that night, and run him to Tucson the next morning to keep the vigilance committee from hanging him?"

"You boys," McLaury replied, according to Virgil.

"Who saved Johnny-Behind-the-Deuce from being hung?"

"You boys."

"Now do you believe we belong to it?"

"I can't help but believe the man that told me," McLaury replied. Virgil asked who that man was.

"Johnny Behan. I'll tell you, it makes no difference what I do, I will never surrender my arms to you. I had rather die a-fighting than to be strangled."[89]

Virgil Earp would tell the story in November, when McLaury would not be alive to respond. The mere formation of a vigilance committee proved a threat to the lawless element of Cochise County. By the late summer of 1881, the legal principles of due process under law seemed far less important than simply preserving order.

With Commandant Felipe Neri and his troops on the Mexican border, Mexican targets became far more risky and the cowboys hit harder against the big

American ranchers, such as the likes of T. W. Ayles, Charles Veil, and Henry Hooker. Hooker's extensive Sierra Bonita spread was the largest in the area. The Cattlegrowers Association apparently even put an illegal $1,000 bounty on Curley Bill's head.[90] The rustlers still had their friends among the small ranchers, the butchers, and the saloon owners who profited from their deeds, but they were making more enemies than friends.

The problem in Arizona was twofold. The cowboys held some degree of power by building at least a loose political alliance with Behan and other Democratic leaders, as shown by the voter fraud in the Paul–Shibell election and Ringo serving as a county delegate. More complicated, however, was that no one really quite understood whether or not the cowboys were organized or knew who served as their real leaders. At various times, Old Man Clanton, George Turner, Ike Clanton, John Ringo, and Curley Bill were all identified as the leaders. Wells, Fargo officials said in March of 1882 that the cowboys were a gang of about seventy-five under the leadership of Ike Clanton.[91] At about the same time, Virgil Earp told the *Examiner* that there had been about two hundred cowboys, but about fifty had been killed, and they were under Ringo's leadership. Thornton, the Galeyville hotel manager and friend of Curley Bill, probably had the best understanding of the group when he said: "The cowboys have no chief, nor do they run in gangs, as is generally supposed. Curly Bill . . . has no gang, and since his last partner shot him . . . Bill don't take well to partners. No, sir, the 'cowboys' don't herd together in droves, but come and go about their own personal business wherever they desire to go."[92]

Acting Governor John Gosper even came to Tombstone for a firsthand evaluation. He spoke with Virgil Earp and Behan in September and filed a startling report to the secretary of state. It read in part:

> In Galeyville, San Simon and other points isolated from large places, the cow-boy element at times very fully predominates, and the officers of the law are at times either unable or unwilling to control this class of out-laws, sometimes being governed by *fear*, at other times by a hope of *reward*. At Tombstone . . . I conferred with the Sheriff . . . upon the subject of breaking up these bands of out-laws, and I am sorry to say he gave me but little hope of being able in his department to cope with the power of the cow-boys. He represented to me that the Deputy U.S. Marshal, resident of Tombstone, and the city Marshal for the same, and those who aided him (the Deputy Marshal) seemed unwilling to heartily co-operate with him (the Sheriff) in capturing and bringing to justice these out-laws.
>
> In conversation with Deputy U.S. Marshal, Mr. Earp, I found precisely the same spirit of complaint existing against Mr. Behan (the Sheriff) and his deputies.
>
> And back of this unfortunate fact—rivalry between the civil authorities, or an unwillingness to work together in full accord in keeping the peace—I found the two daily newspapers published in the city taking sides with the Deputy Marshal [Virgil Earp] and Sheriff [Behan] respectively; each paper backing its civil clique and condemning the other. And still back of all this, the unfortunate fact that *many* of the *very best law-abiding* peace loving citizens have no confidence in the *willingness* of the *civil officers* to pursue and bring to justice that element of out-lawry so largely disturbing the sense of security, and so often committing highway robbery and smaller thefts.

The opinion in Tombstone and elsewhere in that part of the Territory is quite prevalent that the civil officers are quite largely in league with the leaders of this disturbing and dangerous element.

In the light of the few facts above given connected with the greatly unsettled state of affairs (and I have only touched the border) one of two results is sure to follow in our time. The cow-boys will come to control and "run" that part of our Territory with terror and destruction, and probably cause serious complications with our sister Republic Mexico, with which we are now in fullest peace; or the law-abiding citizens of that county will be compelled to organize vigilante committees to protect their persons and property. I am secretly informed that a movement of that kind is now on foot in that county.

The greatest difficulty now in the way, perhaps of enforcing the law and bringing to justice these reckless spirits is the inability or indisposition of the civil officers of that particular county to do their duty.

Something must be done, and that right early, or very grave results will follow. It is an open disgrace to the very name of American liberty and the peace and security of her citizens, that such a state of affairs should exist . . . as is cursing certain portions of this frontier county.[93]

The situation had grown in dimension, and from all directions lawlessness became rampant. The *Nugget* on October 24 would editorialize strongly in favor of capital punishment, condemn the citizenry that opposed it, and demand stricter gun laws. "The arming of oneself in a peaceful community, as every well organized community is supposed to be, and walking about like a moving arsenal, is highly ridiculous and, as events demonstrate, exceedingly dangerous. Boys and men of all ages and conditions are armed, and at the first flash of anger the pistol is drawn and somebody shot down." Copies of the newspaper would probably still be sitting in a few barrooms two days later when the McLaury brothers rode into Tombstone.

To compound the problem, most residents had trouble distinguishing the lawless from the lawful. Frank Stilwell, a deputy sheriff, seemed an unlikely candidate for a stage robber. Behan spun stories, told jokes, and charmed just about everyone in town. The McLaury brothers were well-liked, and most townsmen believed they were honest ranchers just making a living on the frontier. Weeks later, *Examiner* correspondent Ridgely Tilden still could not believe that seemingly honest ranchers were dangerous men. He wrote: "The McLowerys [*sic*] and Clantons were never, in any sense of the word, 'rustlers.' "[94]

Further complicating the problem were the persistent rumors that Holliday and perhaps even the Earps had been involved in stage robberies. In addition, a newspaper story tied Morgan Earp to a con game in Benson, most likely an inaccurate report but enough to further tarnish the Earps' reputation.[95] Tombstone had fallen into one grand state of confusion, and most of the townsmen just wanted to avoid problems and get on with their own business.

A MARCH TO DESTINY

IKE CLANTON HAD SPENT FIVE MONTHS living in terror. The Earps possessed a weapon potentially more dangerous to Clanton than any pistol—they knew his secret; they knew that Ike and Frank McLaury had negotiated to turn over stage robbers Leonard, Head, and Crane for a reward. The Earps knew that Ike's life would be in jeopardy if word ever got back to Curley Bill and the most dangerous outlaws. Clanton and McLaury grew angry and came to Virgil Earp. "They said they could not live in this country an hour if Leonard's friends learned that they had plotted against him," Virgil told the *San Francisco Examiner.*[1]

Fear continued to fester in Ike Clanton and the McLaurys as the summer moved into fall. Through July, August, September, and early October, word had not leaked out about the failed secret deal, but, by the Earp version, Ike always feared that one of the Earps would slip: Wyatt perhaps could confirm it to Marshall Williams or Morgan might tell their pal Holliday.

At about 5 P.M. on October 24, Sheriff Behan's jailer, Billy Soule, went uptown on business, leaving assistant Charles Mason in charge of the prisoners, including Jim Sharp, Charles "Yank" Thompson, and Milt Hicks. Sharp was awaiting trial for killing a Mexican in Charleston, Thompson had 80 days left on a 150-day sentence for grand larceny, and Hicks was charged with rustling. A few moments later a boy delivered dinners for the prisoners, who had an appetite only for freedom. Mason unlocked the cell and Sharp stood near the door as the boy entered. Sharp turned quickly, catching Mason by the coat and pulling him into the cell. "We have been in here for some time. Come in and try it yourself a while," Sharp said as he pitched Mason in. Hicks darted out and ran for freedom while Thompson and Sharp began pushing the door against Mason's arm. Jerry Barton, another prisoner, stepped from inside the cell to push against the door and prevent Mason's arm from being broken. Mason threw a padlock at Thompson, hitting him on the cheek and drawing blood, before the prisoners locked the cell and raced out. Mason called frantically for help and finally drew the attention of a Chinese neighbor, who retrieved Soule.

Quickly, Behan, Deputy Breakenridge, Frank Leslie, Morgan Earp, Wyatt Earp, and city marshal Virgil Earp were in the saddle to chase the escapees, only to be turned back by darkness. At eleven that night, Behan outfitted a posse with Virgil Earp and sheriff's deputies Dave Neagle and Breakenridge to visit

113

the outlying ranches. They found no trace of the escapees. Behan and Virgil returned to town, while Neagle and Breakenridge continued the search.[2] With the
public already jarred by stage robberies and problems with the Apaches and the
cowboys, the escape of three dangerous criminals exacerbated a tense situation.
Between dances, sing-alongs, and fancy dinners, the new breed of Tombstoner
had grown to believe that criminals could rarely be captured and even more
rarely held for justice.

Shortly after Virgil returned from the night search and went to sleep, Ike
and Tom McLaury rode into town, still fretting that the Earps might reveal their
past deal. Fifteen years later Wyatt would say, "Clanton was terrified at the
thought of any third person knowing our bargain."[3] Marshall Williams had
made his drunken guess months earlier, and now Ike and Tom feared that the
Earps had told Holliday, a one-time friend of Leonard who had at least a speaking acquaintance with the more notorious outlaws. Wyatt continued to deny that
any of the Earps had revealed the deal, and finally he dispatched Morgan to
Tucson to bring Doc Holliday back to Tombstone, apparently to satisfy Ike that
no one had been blabbing.

Morgan found Doc playing faro at the San Augustin Feast and Fair in Tucson's Levin's Park. Big-Nose Kate was behind Doc when Morgan arrived, and
later wrote: "Morgan Earp came to the park, tapped Doc on the shoulder &
said, Doc, we want you in Tombstone tomorrow, better go up this evening. Neither of them wanted me to go with them, Doc wanted to take me back to the hotel. I insisted on going back with them."[4]

Holliday returned on Saturday night, October 22, and Earp said he asked
the dentist if he knew anything about Ike's accusation. Holliday said he did not.
The next Tuesday night, Holliday found Ike in the lunchroom of the Alhambra
Saloon and told him "he was a damned liar if he said so," according to Earp.
Holliday continued to berate Clanton for several minutes.

Wyatt sat at the counter munching on lunch while Morgan chatted up the
bartender. Wyatt called to Morgan, who served as Virgil's special deputy, and
told him to go stop the quarrel: "You're an officer—you should do something
about that." Morgan climbed over the lunch counter and entered the room,
snagging Doc by the arm and leading him into the street with Ike following behind. Wyatt finished eating and stepped through the door to hear them still arguing outside.

Virgil arrived to quell the conflict by threatening to arrest them if they
didn't stop quarreling, Wyatt said later. The combatants separated, with Morgan
returning home, Ike going off to the Grand Hotel, Virgil going across the street
to the Occidental, and Holliday heading to the Oriental. Wyatt said he walked
into the Eagle Brewery, where he had a faro game going that he had not closed.
He remained in the Eagle for a few minutes and walked into the street, where he
met Ike. "He asked me if I would take a walk with him, he wanted to have a talk
with me. I told him I would if he did not go too far, that I was waiting for my
game in the Brewery to close, as I had to take care of the money. We walked
about halfway down the side of the brewery building on Fifth Street and
stopped.

"He told me when Holliday approached him in the lunch room that he was not fixed just right. He said that in the morning he would have a man-for-man, that this fighting talk had been going on for a long time, and he guessed it was about time to fetch it to a close. I told him I would fight no one if I could get away from it, because there was no money in it. He walked off and left me, saying, 'I will be ready for all of you in the morning.' I walked over to the Oriental. He come in, followed me in rather, and took a drink, having his six-shooter on and playing fight and saying, 'You must not think I won't be after you all in the morning.' He said he would like to make a fight with Holliday now. I told him Holliday did not want to fight, but only to satisfy him that this talk had not been made. About that time the man that is dealing my game closed it and brought the money to me. I locked it in the safe and started home. I met Holliday on the street between the Oriental and Alhambra. Myself and Holliday walked down Allen Street, he going to his room and I to my house, going to bed."[5]

Ike Clanton portrayed himself more innocently in his version: "As near as I can remember it was about 1 o'clock in the morning. I went in there to get a lunch. While sitting down at the table, Doc Holliday came in and commenced cursing me and said I had been using his name; that I was, 'A son-of-a-bitch of a cowboy,' and to get my gun out and get to work. I told him I had no gun. He said I was a damn liar and had threatened the Earps. I told him I had not, to bring whoever said so to me and I would convince him that I had not. He told me again to pull out my gun and if there is any grit in me, to go to fighting. All the time he was talking, he had his hand on his pistol in his bosom, I mean he had his hand in his bosom, and I believed on a pistol. I looked behind me and I saw Morg Earp with his feet over the lunch counter. He also had his hand in his bosom, looking at me. I then got up and went out on the sidewalk. Doc Holliday said, as I walked out, 'You son-of-a-bitch, you ain't heeled,* go heel yourself.' Just at that time Morgan Earp stepped up and said, 'Yes, you son-of-a-bitch, you can have all the fight you want now.' I thanked him and told him I did not want any of it. I am not heeled. Virgil Earp stood then about fifteen feet from me down the sidewalk. Just about this time Wyatt Earp came up. Wyatt did not say anything. Morgan Earp told me if I was not heeled, when I came back on the street to be heeled. I walked off and asked Morg Earp not to shoot me in the back."[6]

Ike left drunk and mad. The Earps were clearly riled, an aftereffect, they said, of the threats made earlier against Morgan. About a half hour later Ike found his way into the Occidental Saloon. What followed was one of the most improbable events in what was to be an incredible day as Ike settled in for an all-night poker game with Virgil Earp, Tom McLaury, John Behan, and an unknown player. A few hours before they would meet under distinctly different circumstances, Virgil Earp tossed aces and eights at Tom McLaury, who had already threatened his life, and at boisterous Ike Clanton. In Tombstone, during those early morning hours of October 26, civility would serve as a prelude to death.

---

*Armed for combat.

VIRGIL EARP HAD ENOUGH POKER, and he headed for home around 7 A.M. Ike had a going-away message for Virgil to deliver to Doc Holliday: "The damned son of a bitch has got to fight," Virgil recalled the statement.

"Ike, I am an officer, and I don't want to hear you talking that way at all," Virgil said he responded. "I am going down home now, to go to bed, and I don't want you to raise any disturbance when I am in bed."

Virgil said he had just taken a few steps when he heard Ike call, "You won't carry the message?" Virgil said of course he would not, and Ike yelled, "You may have to fight before you know it." Virgil ignored him and went to bed. He would not have long to rest.

Ike kept drinking and fuming. A little after 8 A.M. he ran into Ned Boyle, a bartender at the Oriental and a friend of the Earps. Seeing Ike's pistol clearly exposed, Boyle covered it with Ike's coat. Boyle kept telling Ike to go to bed. Ike insisted he would not. Boyle recalled Ike's eerie threat: "He said that as soon as the Earps and Doc Holliday showed themselves on the street, the ball would open, and that they would have to fight." Boyle went to Wyatt Earp's house to deliver the ominous message.[7] Wyatt stayed in bed. They had all heard Ike talk before, and Ike's talk usually did not lead to much.

Ike kept up his dawn patrol with a stop at Julius Kelly's Wine Room, where he talked with a man named Joe Stump, telling him of the previous night's problems. Kelly overheard the conversation and asked what trouble Ike had been having. "He said that the Earp crowd and Doc Holliday had insulted him . . . when he was not heeled; that he had now heeled himself, and that they had to fight on sight," Kelly said.[8]

Ike's tour of the saloons started a flow of rumors. Deputy Marshal Andy Bronk heard the talk and awakened Virgil Earp, telling him, "There is likely to be hell." Like Wyatt, Virgil remained in bed.

Ike continued his meander through Tombstone's saloons, stopping at Hafford's Corner and telling owner Roderick F. Hafford that he was searching for Holliday or the Earps, and they had agreed to meet him before noon. Hafford recalled Ike saying, "It is five minutes past 12 now," as he pulled out his watch. Hafford looked at the clock and said, "It is 10 minutes past, and you had better go home. There will be nothing of it." A few minutes later Ike left the bar.[9]

Drunk and boisterous, Ike Clanton went from saloon to saloon, pleading his case at the bar. His threats had aroused the village, creating a furor and building the anticipation of confrontation. Tombstone settled in for a showdown, even before the Earps were out of bed. Ike kept walking and talking. He showed up at Camillus Fly's boarding house, where Holliday kept a room. Big-Nose Kate awakened to find Mary Fly, Camillus's wife, at the door. She told Kate, "Ike Clanton was here looking for you and had a rifle with him." Kate quickly woke up Doc to say that Ike Clanton had been seeking him out. "If God will let me live to get my clothes on, he shall see me," Holliday said as he got out of bed.[10]

Wyatt arose and picked up his coat for protection against the unseasonably cold wind. He went to the Oriental Saloon, where attorney Harry Jones told him that Ike was armed with a Winchester and a pistol and "hunting you boys."

Mayor Clum, who had not heard the rumors, saw Ike at the corner of Fourth and Fremont and innocently greeted Clanton with "Hello, Ike, any new war?" Clum learned shortly that a war would soon occur.[11]

About noon, Virgil Earp stepped into the chilly afternoon and came up behind Clanton, with a six-shooter jammed in his pants and a Winchester rifle in his hand. Virgil said he grabbed the rifle with his left hand. As Ike started to draw his pistol, Virgil crashed his six-shooter into Ike's head, knocking him to his knees, then relieved him of his pistol. Virgil recalled, "I asked him if he was hunting for me. He said he was, and if he had seen me a second sooner he would have killed me. I arrested Ike for carrying firearms, I believe was the charge, inside the city limits."[12]

Ike had a different version, saying Virgil and Morgan Earp had approached him from behind, struck him on the side of the head, and knocked him against a wall. "Morgan Earp cocked his pistol and stuck it at me, towards me. Virg Earp took my arms, six-shooter and Winchester. I did not know or see that they were about there; I did not know who struck me until I fell against the house, then they pulled me along and said 'You damned son-of-a-bitch, we'll take you up here to Judge Wallace's office.'"[13]

The Earps hauled Clanton to the recorder's court, where he took a seat on a bench and dabbed at his bloodied head with a handkerchief. Virgil left to search for Judge Albert O. Wallace while special deputy Morgan held Clanton's Winchester and six-shooter as he leaned against the wall. The two were heatedly discussing the incident when Wyatt Earp walked in, followed by Rezin J. Campbell, clerk of the Cochise County board of supervisors.

Wyatt looked toward Ike and said, "You damn dirty cowthief. You have been threatening our lives, and I know it. I think I would be justified in shooting you down any place I would meet you. But if you are anxious to make a fight, I will go anywhere on earth to make a fight with you—even over to San Simon, among your own crowd."[14]

"Fight is my racket, and all I want is four feet of ground," Clanton defiantly responded, according to Campbell. The clerk then heard Clanton say, "If you fellows had been a second later, I would have furnished a Coroner's Inquest for this town."

Morgan Earp, holding the guns, taunted Ike, offering to pay the fine if Ike would make his fight. "I'll fight you anywhere or any way," Ike said he replied. Morgan offered a weapon, but Ike did not fight. Ike said he didn't like the odds. Deputy Sheriff Dave Campbell shoved Ike back in his chair. The confrontation sent the courtroom into a frenzy as spectators dived to the floor or scurried for the doorway.

Wyatt Earp said the months of tension caught up to him in that little courtroom. "I was tired of being threatened by Ike Clanton and his gang. I believed from what he said to me and others, and from their movements, that they intended to assassinate me the first chance they had, and I thought that if I had to fight for my life with them, I had better make them face me in an open fight."

Judge Wallace finally showed up and fined Clanton $25 plus $2.50 in court costs. Virgil asked Clanton where he wanted his arms, then left them for him at the Grand Hotel. At about 1 P.M., the small gathering left the courtroom, and Wyatt encountered Tom McLaury, who had come by to check on Ike.

"Are you heeled?" two witnesses heard Wyatt say. McLaury reportedly said he had never done anything against the Earps and was a friend of Wyatt's. But, "If you want to make a fight, I'll make a fight with you anywhere."

"All right, make a fight," one witness heard Earp say before he slapped McLaury with his left hand, then slammed his pistol against McLaury's head with his right, sending a blood stream across the cowboy's face. Butcher Apolinar Bauer, a friend of McLaury's, said Earp struck "two, three or maybe four" blows with the pistol. Other witnesses said only one.

"I could kill the son-of-a-bitch," Earp said, according to Bauer, then McLaury "opened his eyes up large and trembled all over." Earp left the dazed McLaury and headed to Hafford's Corner to buy a cigar. At about this time Frank McLaury and Billy Clanton rode into town and headed to the Grand Hotel for a drink. Doc Holliday, master of the unexpected, greeted the two cowboys by politely inquiring, "How are you?" Disarming and dashing, Holliday had a distinct flair.

Ike needed medical attention, and Billy Claiborne, the friend of the Clantons, helped him to Dr. Charles Gillingham's office. At the Grand, Billy Clanton and Frank McLaury ordered drinks for themselves and rancher Edwin Frink. Billy Allen walked in. The cowboys invited Allen to join them, but he pulled Frank McLaury to one side and told him that Wyatt had pistol-whipped his brother. Frank looked surprised and said, "What did he hit Tom for?" Allen did not know. Frank McLaury said, "I will get the boys out of town. We won't drink," Allen recalled. Frank McLaury and Billy Clanton left, walking toward the O.K. Corral.[15]

Claiborne returned from helping Ike and ran into Billy Clanton and Frank McLaury. "Billy [Clanton] asked me where was Ike. He said, 'I want to get him to go out home.' He said he did not come here to fight anyone, 'and no one didn't want to fight me.'" Frank McLaury and 19-year-old Billy Clanton seemed more interested in preventing a battle than in fighting one.[16]

Ike Clanton's threats had clearly riled the Earps, and Wyatt became tense and alert. The rumors flooded Tombstone, and it is likely that at every stop Wyatt made, he heard another call to arms. When men hear the sound of death pounding in their ears, they assume every action or innuendo by their foes to have some hidden meaning.

Billy Clanton and the McLaurys visited Spangenberg's Gun Shop, loading up on ammunition. Wyatt moved closer for a better look as Billy Clanton and Frank McLaury shoved cartridges into their gunbelts in what appeared to be a show of force. Frank McLaury's horse strayed up on the sidewalk and stuck his head into the door of the gunshop. Wyatt Earp provided a little bravado by walking into the lions' den. He took the bit and started leading the horse back into the street. The McLaurys and Billy Clanton charged to the door. Billy Clanton placed his hand on his pistol and Frank McLaury took the bridle. Earp said, "You will have to get this horse off the sidewalk." Frank McLaury guided his horse back into the street as Ike Clanton walked up and joined the party in the

gunshop. Wyatt watched through the window and saw the cowboys again loading their cartridge belts.[17]

Ike tried to purchase a pistol from shop owner George Spangenberg but, according to Ike, "The gentleman who owns the gunshop remarked that my head
was bleeding, that I had been in trouble and he would not let me have it. My
physical condition was such that . . . I was sick and bleeding," from the blow he
had received from Virgil Earp.

With trouble brewing, Virgil stopped by the Wells, Fargo office to pick up
the shotgun he left there in case of emergencies. The marshal began heading out
when saloon owner Bob Hatch rushed up and said, "For God's sake, hurry
down there to the gun shop, for they are all there, and Wyatt is all alone. They
are liable to kill him before you get there."[18]

The cowboys left the shop. Tom McLaury stopped at Everhardy's Butcher
Shop on Allen Street before joining his friends at Dexter's Livery and Feed Stables, co-owned by Johnny Behan and John Dunbar, where they picked up Billy
Clanton's horse, then strolled across the street to the O.K. Corral. Doc Holliday
joined the Earps at the corner of Fourth and Allen streets. Several townsmen
came by, prodding the Earps. Mining man Ruben F. Coleman told Virgil, "They
mean trouble. They have just gone from Dunbar's Corral into the O.K. Corral,
all armed, and I think you had better go disarm them."[19]

Sheriff Johnny Behan had slept late. Then he went for a leisurely shave at
Barron's Barber Shop at about 1:30 in the afternoon. "Someone in the shop said
there was liable to be trouble between Clanton and the Earps," Behan said.
"There was considerable said about it in the shop and I asked the barber to
hurry up and get through, as I intended to go out and disarm and arrest the parties." Behan, more a tax collector than a lawman, himself faced a most difficult
situation. His two top enforcement deputies, Breakenridge and Neagle, were off
chasing escapees. Behan had no deputies to call in to stop the fight.

Behan said he left the barber shop and crossed to Hafford's Corner, where
Virgil was standing. He asked about all the excitement, and Virgil responded
that there were "a lot of sons-of-bitches in town looking for a fight." Behan said
he told Virgil he should disarm the crowd, but Virgil said he would not; that he
would give them a chance to make a fight. Behan said he then told Virgil: "It is
your duty as a peace officer to disarm them rather than encourage the fight."[20]
Then, the sheriff said, he was going down to disarm the cowboys.

Johnny always came out the hero in his own stories. Virgil Earp told a far
different version of what occurred when he and Behan stepped into Hafford's
Corner Saloon to talk. "I called on Johnny Behan, who refused to go with me, to
go to help disarm these parties. He said if he went along with me, then there
would be a fight sure; that they would not give up their arms to me. He said,
'They won't hurt me, and I will go down alone and see if I can't disarm them.' I
told him that was all I wanted them to do; to lay off their arms while they were
in town."[21]

Ike had been seen earlier near the telegraph office, and a rumor passed
through town that he had sent a telegram, possibly recruiting help from his
brother Fin, Ringo, or other members of the cowboy contingent. Rumors flowed

fast on this day when the citizenry expected the yield would be greater in lead than in silver.

William Murray, a stock and mining broker, came up to Virgil in Hafford's Saloon and offered help. "I know you are going to have trouble, and we have men and arms ready and willing to assist you. Twenty-five armed men can be had at a minute's notice," Virgil Earp recalled Murray saying. "I told him, as long as they stayed in the O.K. Corral, where at the time they were, I would not go down to disarm them; that if they came on the street, I would disarm them. He said, 'You can count on me if there is any danger.' "[22]

The McLaurys and the Clantons paused in front of the O.K. Corral, angrily talking among themselves. Just within hearing distance was H. F. Sills, an engineer on temporary layoff from the Atchison, Topeka, and Santa Fe Railroad; he had arrived in Tombstone only the day before. He was standing on the street when he overheard a conversation: "I saw four or five men standing in front of the O.K. Corral . . . talking of some trouble they had with Virgil Earp, and they made threats at the time, that on meeting him they would kill him on sight. Some one of the party spoke up at the time and said that they would kill the whole party of Earps when they met them." Sills knew none of the participants and asked a man on the street about Earp. When told that Virgil Earp was the city marshal, Sills took action. He found Virgil near Hafford's and pulled him aside to pass on the threats.

John L. Fonck, a tough former Los Angeles police captain, stopped Virgil. "The cowboys are making threats against you. If you want any help, I can furnish 10 men," Virgil recalled Fonck's words. The marshal declined and said he would not bother them if they were in the corral, getting their horses to leave town. If they went onto the street, he would take away their guns as the city ordinance required.

"Why," Fonck responded, "they are all down on Fremont Street now."[23]

Virgil Earp turned to Holliday, who was wearing his long gray coat against the chilly October wind, and to his brothers. Virgil handed his shotgun to Holliday to hide under his long coat so as not to draw attention. Holliday gave his walking stick to the marshal as they began a walk through the streets of Tombstone.

The cowboys separated. The McLaury brothers went through the rear entrance of the O.K. Corral to the Union Market on Fremont Street. The two Billys, Clanton and Claiborne, passed through the open corral and entered the rear of a vacant lot next to the two buildings that made up Fly's Photo Gallery and rooming house. Ike, who had his team of horses and wagon at another corral, apparently walked onto Fremont Street and turned left, toward the vacant lot where he would meet his brother and Claiborne. Wesley Fuller, known as West, a hard-drinking 20-year-old gambler, saw the Earps begin their march and started off to warn his cowboy friends. Instead the young gambler with a big hangover tarried with Mattie Webb, the madam of a brothel near the corral.

Behan met Frank McLaury outside the butcher shop at about Fourth and Fremont. Johnny said he told McLaury to give him his weapon, only to have Frank say he had no plans to cause trouble and insisted the Earps be disarmed before he would surrender his guns. Behan saw Claiborne and the Clantons down the street and ushered the McLaurys toward the vacant lot next to Fly's boardinghouse. Johnny said he quickly patted Ike for weapons and found none. Tom McLaury opened his coat and proclaimed he was unarmed. The series of exchanges took nearly twenty minutes while the Earps and the townsmen waited tensely for the sheriff to complete his mission. After Behan finished his talk, he ordered the Clantons and the McLaurys to wait and told them he was going to disarm the other party—the city marshal, his brothers, and Holliday coming down the street.[24]

Stride by stride, the march continued. The Earps and Holliday walked a block down Fourth Street, then turned left on Fremont, past the post office and toward Bauer's butcher shop. Behan, still talking to the cowboys, stood at the front of the vacant lot and saw the Earps approach. Turning to the Clantons and McLaurys, Behan said, "Wait here. I see them coming down. I will go up and stop them." Ruben Coleman, standing nearby, said he heard one of the cowboys call out, "You need not be afraid, Johnny, we are not going to have any trouble."

The Earps and Holliday marched past the Papago Cash Store, then across the rear entrance to the O.K. Corral, about ninety feet from the vacant lot. Behan came forward.

"Gentlemen, I am sheriff of this county, and I am not going to allow any trouble, if I can help it," Behan said were his words to the Earps. They just brushed past, and he followed from behind, calling for them to stop. Wyatt Earp recalled Behan's words as, "For God's sake, don't go down there or you will get murdered."

"I am going to disarm them," Virgil replied. There was then some misunderstanding. The Earps thought Behan responded with, "I have disarmed them all." Behan said his words were "I was there for the purpose of arresting and disarming them."[25]

Virgil Earp carried the walking stick in his left hand with his right on the pistol jammed into his pants, but when he took Behan's comment to mean the cowboys had already been disarmed, he switched hands, placing the walking stick in his right. He also shoved his gun to his left hip.

The butcher at the Union Market had just finished cutting a piece of meat when Martha King heard someone yell "there they come." She stepped to the door to see the Earps pass. The town had been waiting for trouble, and it would come to pass this afternoon.[26]

The wind kept blowing open Holliday's long gray coat. "I knew it was a gun because his overcoat flew back and I saw it," King testified. Her dinner meat sat on the counter as she stood by the door and watched the four men walk past. "What frightened me and made me run back, I heard him [one of the Earps] say, 'Let them have it.' And Doc Holliday said, 'All right,'" King said. She could not identify what preceded the "let-them-have-it" remark, words that may have changed the perception of the comment.[27] "Then I thought I would run, and ran towards the back of the shop, but before I reached the middle of the shop, I heard shots; I don't know how many." King and most of the other witnesses were stunned by what occurred so quickly.

The Clantons, the McLaurys, and Billy Claiborne stood talking at the front of a 15-foot-wide vacant lot when the Earps arrived. West Fuller approached from the other side of the lot, and Behan and Billy Allen trailed the Earps. Behan moved toward the door of Fly's rooming house. Fuller ducked and moved back. Claiborne stepped aside, and the Clantons and McLaurys slipped deeper into the vacant lot, standing at a slant between Fly's and a house owned by W. A. Harwood. Much to the Earps' surprise, the cowboys had not been disarmed. According to Virgil Earp, Billy Clanton and Frank McLaury had their hands on their six-shooters while Tom McLaury reached for a rifle in a scabbard on a horse's saddle.

"Boys, throw up your hands, I want your guns," Virgil Earp yelled. He lifted the walking stick in the air with his right hand, his shooting hand. He said Billy Clanton and Frank McLaury reached for their six-shooters, and he heard the *click click* of the guns being cocked, probably as they were being pulled from their holsters, and saw Ike Clanton throw his hand into the opening of his shirt.

"Hold, I don't want that," Virgil said, throwing both hands in the air. Virgil said Billy Clanton lifted his cocked six-shooter and two shots exploded at nearly the same time, one from Billy and one from Wyatt. Virgil changed the cane to his left hand and drew his gun with his right, "and went to shooting; it was general then, and everybody went to fighting."[28]

The cowboys told a much different version—that both shots came from the Earp side. All agreed that the first two shots erupted virtually at once, almost with the same sound. By the Earp version, Clanton missed while Wyatt took aim at Frank McLaury, the most dangerous gunman of the bunch, and drilled him in the stomach. Frank McLaury staggered but returned to the fight. The two shots sounded almost in harmony, then came a momentary pause. Tom McLaury failed to get the Winchester from the saddle scabbard as the horse jumped, startled by the shots.

The gunfight came in bursts, snippets and spurts so rapid that witnesses and participants never agreed on an order of events. Gunfire exploded in the cold afternoon air; cowboys struggled to control their twisting, bounding horses. It was a scene of disarray, where impressions were left frozen in time.

After the two shots and the pause, the rest of the fight took perhaps twenty seconds. Early in the shooting, a bullet passed through Billy Claiborne's pants leg as he stood near Behan, by Fly's doorway. Behan grabbed the Kid and shoved him inside.

Doc Holliday lifted the shotgun from under his gray coat and stalked Tom McLaury behind the horse. Holliday closed in, then fired, sending a charge that hit Tom under the right armpit and left him staggering into the street.

In the strangest moment of the affair, Ike Clanton lurched forward and grabbed one of Wyatt Earp's arms. Wyatt saw Clanton had no gun and shoved him aside as he coolly told him, "The fight has commenced. Go to fighting or get away." Ike Clanton took flight, racing through the Fly house, into a vacant lot, through Kellogg's saloon, and finished his sprint two blocks away on Toughnut Street, where he was later arrested.

The volleys continued. Virgil took a shot through the calf, most likely from the wounded Frank McLaury, and dropped to the ground. A bullet, probably Morgan's, crashed into Billy Clanton's chest, then another into his wrist, then a shot hit his stomach. Young Billy switched gun hands, then leaned back against

Harwood's house and slowly crumpled to the ground. He continued firing, with his pistol balanced against his knee, as he sat in the dirt.

Morgan stumbled and fell, yelling, "I am hit," then rose again to return to the fight before stumbling, probably on the dirt mound dug for the new water pipes. Holliday threw away his shotgun and drew his nickel-plated revolver.

From the alley to the east of Fly's Photo Gallery, a sound rang out, possibly shots or an errant bullet glancing off a piece of metal. Wyatt Earp would forever think a gunman—Behan, Ike Clanton, Billy Allen, or Claiborne—had fired from hiding.[29]

Badly wounded, Frank McLaury tried to use a horse for cover as he pushed the animal toward Fremont Street. He ran into the street, holding the animal's reins, then shot at Morgan. McLaury's horse broke away and ran, leaving Frank to squat in the street in exhaustion. Holliday pursued. Frank stood and lifted his pistol to take aim, saying, "I've got you now."

"Blaze away. You're a daisy if you have," Doc replied, according to the *Nugget* account. Others would recall Holliday's response as, "You're a good one if you have." McLaury shot Holliday through the pistol pocket, grazing his hip. "I'm shot right through," Doc yelled.[30]

Frank McLaury, shot in the stomach, staggered across the street. Morgan Earp and Doc both fired at Frank. Morgan's shot crashed through the right side of McLaury's head. Doc's charge penetrated McLaury's chest. Frank still seemed to be showing some signs of movement, and Doc Holliday ran up screaming, "The son-of-a-bitch has shot me, and I mean to kill him."[31]

Under the haze of white gunsmoke that covered Fremont Street, Tom McLaury had collapsed at the corner of Third and Fremont, and lay dying at the base of a telegraph pole. Billy Clanton tried desperately to reload his pistol as the shots subsided. Photographer Fly came from his rooming house to grab Clanton's pistol. The bloody fight had ended, and the Earps took stock.

Virgil had been shot cleanly through the calf and Holliday just grazed. Morgan's wound proved far more severe. The bullet entered through one shoulder, chipped a vertebra, and passed out through the other shoulder.[32] Frank McLaury, Tom McLaury, and Billy Clanton were obviously dying. Ike Clanton, the instigator, was the sole cowboy survivor. Wyatt Earp emerged unscathed.

The fight lasted less than thirty seconds. Estimates were that about thirty shots exploded into the air. Justice had gone awry in that little vacant lot of a frontier boomtown, and townspeople struggled to comprehend what had happened and why blood had settled into the Arizona dust.

"The inmates of every house in town were greatly startled by the sudden report of fire arms, about 3 P.M., discharged with such lightening-like rapidity that it could only be compared to the explosion of a bunch of fire-crackers," Clara Brown wrote.[33] The fight erupted so quickly that not even the participants were quite certain exactly what had just happened.

MOMENTS AFTER THE FIRING CEASED, loud whistles from the steam hoisting works sounded through town, a signal to townsmen who made up a vigilante force whose existence had previously only been rumored in Tombstone. Most in town did not know what had happened, and Clara Brown described the frenzy: "'The Cowboys!' cried some, thinking that a party of those desperadoes were 'taking the town.' 'The Indians!' cried a few of the most excitable. . . . In the midst of this, when the scene upon the streets was one of intense excitement, the whistle again sounded, and directly well armed citizens appeared from all quarters, prepared for any emergency. This revealed what was not before *generally* known, the existence of a 'Vigilance Committee,' composed of law abiding citizens who organized with the determination of upholding right and combatting wrong, and who agreed upon a signal of action from the mines. Their services were not needed, however, on this occasion, as no further trouble ensued."[34]

As the armed vigilantes congregated in the streets, Harry Woods and West Fuller helped carry Billy Clanton into a nearby house. Clanton was "wonderful with vitality," the *Nugget* would write. "He was game to the last, never uttering a word of complaint, and just before breathing his last he said, 'Good-bye, boys; go away and let me die." Fuller would recall Clanton asking him to examine his wounds—near the left nipple and in the belly—then saying, "Get a doctor and give me something to sleep."[35]

Carpenter Thomas Keefe told of a less noble departure by Billy Clanton, "halloing so with pain . . . that I sent for a doctor to inject morphine in him. . . . The doctor [William Millar] arrived, and I helped him inject morphine into him, alongside the wound. He was turning and twisting, and kicking in every manner, with the pain. He said, 'They have murdered me. I have been murdered. Chase the crowd away from the door and give me air.' The last words [Billy Clanton] said before he died were, 'Drive the crowd away.'"[36]

Frank McLaury died in the street before he could be moved. Tom McLaury was carried into the house and braced against a pillow on the carpeted floor, near Billy Clanton. His clothes were loosened, and he died without speaking. Coroner Henry M. Matthews arrived a few minutes later to examine the bodies. On Tom McLaury he found a dozen buckshot wounds from a shotgun, a cluster he could lay his palm over, and a significant amount of money—$2,943.45 in cash, checks, and certificates of deposit. Most important, the coroner did not discover either a gun or cartridges on the body.[37]

Wells, Fargo secret agent Fred Dodge showed up moments after the shooting to help the Earps. "Wyatt was cool and collected as usual, and was quietly giving directions for the removal of Morg and Virg to their home," Dodge wrote. "I helped them all that I could and when they were fixed as comfortable as possible, Wyatt and I started up town. When about opposite to the Sheriff's office, Johnny Behan come across the street and said to Wyatt, 'I will have to arrest you.'

"Wyatt looked at him for two or three seconds and then Wyatt told him— more forcibly than I had ever heard Wyatt talk before—that any decent officer could arrest him. But that Johnny Behan or any of his kind must not try it."

Ruben Coleman recalled the exact words as, "I won't be arrested. You deceived me, Johnny, you told me they were not armed. I won't be arrested, but I am here to answer what I have done. I am not going to leave town."

Theater manager William Cuddy said city official Sylvester B. Comstock entered the conversation. "There is no hurry in arresting this man. He done just right in killing them, and the people will uphold them."

"You bet we did right," Earp responded to Behan, according to Cuddy. "We had to do it. And you threw us, Johnny. You told us they were disarmed."[38]

Ike Clanton was finally found and arrested on Toughnut Street. Fin Clanton arrived in Tombstone that evening and placed himself under sheriff's guard. He stopped by the morgue to see Billy's body, then spent the night visiting Ike in jail, with an extra ten deputies placed on guard to protect the prisoner.

On the evening of the 26th, after one of the bloodiest gun battles in the history of the frontier, the injured Earps were resting at home when Johnny Behan came to call. Also present were James Earp, three of the four Earp wives, another man, probably Sherman McMasters, and Winfield Scott Williams, who would soon be appointed deputy district attorney. The events of that evening would be recalled far differently in the weeks to come. The sheriff later said he received an angry reception at the little cabin. Behan said he told Earp he did not want to argue, he was just there to do his duty. According to Behan, they discussed the gunfight, then Virgil accused him of trying to get the vigilantes to hang Holliday and the Earps. Behan denied the charge. This little conversation would take on greater meaning as the weeks passed.

Contrary to any notion that the vigilantes wanted to hang the Earps, most of them cheered the action, as if Doc and the Earps had exterminated rodents from their houses. Clum editorialized in the *Epitaph* the next day: "The feeling among the best class of our citizens is that the Marshal was entirely justified in his efforts to disarm these men, and that being fired upon they had to defend themselves, which they did most bravely. So long as our peace officers make effort to preserve the peace and put down highway robbery—which the Earp brothers have done, having engaged in the pursuit and capture, where capture have been made of every gang of stage robbers in the county—they will have the support of all good citizens. If the present lesson is not sufficient to teach the cow-boy element that they cannot come into the streets of Tombstone, in broad daylight, armed with six-shooters and Henry rifles to hunt down their victims, then the citizens will most assuredly take such steps to preserve the peace as will be forever a bar to further raids."

The *San Francisco Exchange*, a business paper read by moneyed investors, immediately heralded the killings as a major step forward for the mining town.

> The people of Tombstone have reason to congratulate themselves that they have not only courageous Marshals but Marshals who are dead shots. That performance yesterday, wherein three cowboys were left dead on the field and one lodged in jail, is among the happiest events Tombstone has witnessed, and especially so as it was attended with so little injury to the law vindicators.
>
> Marshal Earp and his assistants deserve well of their fellow citizens, and we hope the Tombstoners appreciate the fact. The cowboy class are the most despicable beings on the face of the earth. They are a terror to decent people and a disgrace to even frontier civilization. . . . Southeastern Arizona with its rich mines, varied resources, and increasing civilization and prosperity, should rise up if need be and drive every wretch of them beyond the border.[39]

The Earps were held up as heroes, from Arizona to the Pacific Coast. Immediately after the fight, they heard little other than congratulations from the press and their peers. Parsons recorded his thoughts on the fight by writing: "A bad time yesterday when Wyatt, Virgil and Morgan Earp with Doc Holliday had a street fight. . . . Desperate men and a desperate encounter. Bad blood has been brewing for some time, and I was not surprised at the outbreak. It is only a wonder it has not happened before. A raid is feared upon the town by the cowboys, and measures have been taken to protect life and property. The 'Stranglers' were out in force and showed sand. . . . Had to laugh at some of the nervousness. It has been a bad scare, and worst is not yet over, some think." Parsons would prove remarkably correct. The worst, indeed, was yet to come.

The bodies of Billy Clanton, Tom McLaury, and Frank McLaury were loaded onto wagons and carried to a cabin behind Dunbar's Stable on Fifth Street for examination by Coroner Henry M. Matthews. The corpses then went for another ride, moving on to Ritter and Ream, City Undertakers, in preparation for the ceremonies that would follow. Almost a portent of what would soon happen, the three bodies in coffins were propped behind the window in the undertaker's parlor under a large sign, "MURDERED IN THE STREETS OF TOMBSTONE." The Earps' reign as heroes would pass quickly.

Almost forty-eight hours after the shooting, the business class of Tombstone was stunned by the turnout for the funeral. Under the headline "An Imposing Funeral," the *Nugget* wrote: "While it was not entirely expected, the funeral of Billy Clanton and Thomas and Frank McLowry [*sic*] yesterday was the largest ever witnessed in Tombstone. The bodies of the three men, neatly and tastefully dressed, were placed in handsome caskets with heavy silver trimmings. Upon each was a plate bearing the name, age, birthplace and date of the death of each." Tombstone's brass band led the procession, playing a "solemn and touching march for the dead." Billy Clanton's body rested in a single hearse, followed by another carrying the remains of the McLaury brothers. Ike and Fin Clanton rode in the wagon following the caskets. Then came about three hundred on foot, twenty-two carriages and buggies, a four-horse stage, and a line of horsemen. Onlookers packed the sidewalks for nearly four blocks. The procession stretched two blocks long, the *Nugget* reported, as the party marched off to the graveyard. The McLaurys were buried together in one grave, with Billy Clanton nearby.

Surprised by the size of the procession, Clara Brown wrote: "A stranger viewing the funeral cortege, which was the largest ever seen in Tombstone, would have thought that some person esteemed by the entire camp was being conveyed to his final resting place. . . . No one could witness this sight without realizing the solemnity of the occasion, and desiring proper regard to be observed for the dead; but such a public manifestation of sympathy from so large a portion of the residents of the camp seemed reprehensible when it is remembered that the deceased were nothing more or less than thieves."[40]

Death often became a show in late nineteenth-century America, with spectators joining in the mourning. Certainly, not all the three hundred or so who tramped to the graveyard were friends and admirers of the Clantons, but the procession proved imposing, larger even than the funeral parade for Marshal Fred White a year earlier. Almost immediately a sense of remorse set in among the residents of Tombstone, including some of the people who had been calling for the mass murder of cowboys just a few days earlier. Clara Brown assessed the conflicting reactions:

The divided state of society in Tombstone is illustrated by this funeral. While there are many people of the highest order sojourning here, whose business is honorable and whose voices are always heard on the side of law and order, there yet remains a large element of unscrupulous personages, some outwardly regardless of restraining influences, and others (more than one would suspect) secretly in sympathy with the "cowboys," acting in collusion with them. Even the officers of the law have not escaped the stigma of shielding these outlaws, some of them being believed to have accepted bribes to insure their silence. One must not judge the whole by a part, but it is undeniable that Cochise county started out upon its career hampered by a set of officials which might be improved; and doubtless will at the next election.

Opinion is pretty fairly divided as to the justification of the killing. You may meet one man who will support the Earps, and declare that no other course was possible to save their own lives, and the next man is just as likely to assert that there was no occasion whatever for bloodshed, and that this will be "a warm place" for the Earps hereafter.[41]

The mighty turnout for the funeral did not go without notice in San Francisco, where businessmen wanted a Tombstone district safe for investment. The *Exchange* sarcastically wrote: "Having laid out three cowboys in their gore and rid themselves of about as worthless specimens of manhood as civilization could boast, the people of Tombstone evidently resolved, like Buck Fanshaw, that as a tribute to their 'land' they would give the victims a 'first-class sendoff to the grave.'" The reference was to the Mark Twain story "Buck Fanshaw's Funeral."[42]

A collective case of the jitters engulfed Tombstone: As Parsons said, townsmen feared retaliation from the cowboys and were caught in the passion of the moment. They also knew that such events would be bad for business. The story circulated that during the gunfight a potential investor from the East had simply been passing through the streets when a bullet cut through his pants. He left town on the morning stage, with the comment that the town was too warm for timid capital.[43] Nobody in Tombstone much liked the idea of losing a potential cash flow. Clara Brown added, "He left for home on the next train, and will probably convey the impression that the notorious camp is a den of cut throats, when in reality, a man had not been shot for many months prior to this tragedy."[44]

The news went out around the nation, distorted and mangled through the magic of telegraph wires. In San Diego, one report credited the "Carp brothers" with pulling the triggers, in Yuma a "Billy Clinton" took the bullet, and back in Nashua, New Hampshire, the locals were told the whole thing happened in "Madstone." And much would be mad in Tombstone for weeks to come.

Immediately after the shooting, newspaper reports showed little doubt the cowboys had at least prompted the fight. The *Nugget*, without attribution, wrote that Frank McLaury "made a motion to draw his revolver, when Wyatt Earp pulled his and shot him, the ball striking the right side of his abdomen." The *Epitaph* provided a more conclusive story, quoting Ruben F. Coleman, the mining man, who claimed to be an eyewitness from beginning to end. Coleman said that as soon as Virgil commanded the cowboys to give up their arms, "There was some reply made by Frank McLaury, but at the same moment there were two shots fired simultaneously by Doc Holliday and Frank McLaury." If the cowboys had even motioned toward their guns, there would be little question of the Earps' justification. There seemed little question, at least for a few days.

The coroners' inquest began on October 28 with a surprise. Sheriff Johnny Behan told the eight-man panel that Billy Clanton had yelled out, "Don't shoot me, I don't want to fight." Behan continued by saying that Tom McLaury had screamed, "I have got nothing," and threw open his coat to show he was un-armed as the shooting began. The sheriff was satisfied that Tom McLaury was unarmed. Behan was saying, in effect, that his political rivals, the Earps, had committed murder. For the first time, Tombstone grew aware there may have been more to this than law enforcement against thieves and rustlers.

Ike Clanton testified that his party had been on their way out of town, sim-ply stopping for a couple of essential errands before following the Earps' dictum to depart. He said when the Earps arrived at the vacant lot, "Frank McLaury and Billy Clanton threw up [their hands]; Tom McLaury threw open his coat and said he had nothing; they said you sons of bitches came here to make a fight. At the same instant Doc Holliday and Morgan Earp shot. . . . All of us threw up our hands, except Tom McLaury, who threw open his coat saying he had nothing."[45] Ike said the Earps opened fire while the innocents were standing with their arms in the air.

Interestingly, Ike Clanton also said that he had had trouble previously with the Earps, an apparent reference to the deal gone awry to turn over Leonard, Head, and Crane. "There was nothing between the Earps and the boys that were killed. The Earps and myself had a transaction which made them down on me; they don't like me."[46] Billy Claiborne supported Ike's statements, agreeing that the three men had their hands in the air and saying Morgan Earp and Doc Hol-liday fired the first shots. The Earps and Holliday were not called to testify in the coroner's hearing, apparently because they could be implicated in murder charges.

Coleman, the *Epitaph*'s star interviewee, told a different story. He no longer claimed to have seen the initial blasts. "I thought I was too close, and as I turned around I heard two shots, then the firing became general." But Coleman contin-ued to embroider the story, prompting the *Nugget* to editorialize, "One never re-alizes what a great blessing memory is, or the wonderful power it is capable of, or the extent and acuteness of eyesight, until they read the testimony given at a coroners inquest, then the illustration would be sublime, were it not so often ridiculous. At the inquest yesterday one witness said on some points, and they were of particular importance, his 'mind was cloudy,' but it was so remarkably clear as to other details, that no doubt our readers will join with us in forgiving him this unfortunate and certainly unexpected omission of memory." The *Nugget* chided Coleman for knowing that Holliday had been grazed either on the hip or on his scabbard. "This when the ball didn't hit his hip, and he had no scabbard on, but in this case good eyesight saw through Holliday's heavy ulster and saw the ball strike the hip that was fartherest from him." Coleman, the eyewitness, had not proven a good witness at all.[47]

Patrick Henry Fellehy provided the biggest shock of the second day when he testified he had seen the beginning of the meeting between Behan and Virgil Earp and overheard Virgil say, "Those men have made their threats. I will not arrest them but will kill them on sight." This remarkable statement virtually accused the Earps of committing premeditated murder. Strange as it seemed, Behan had not recalled the crucial statement a day earlier in his testimony.

Nine men who testified on October 28 and 29 told of seeing the Earps pistol-whip Ike Clanton and Tom McLaury; they portrayed the Earps as provoking a fight, then sending off the first shots against two unarmed men and two others with their arms in the air. There were conflicts in the testimony, but even Behan supported the view that the Earps had unnecessarily killed three men.

When Coroner Henry M. Matthews made his report, the conclusion was simple. "William Clanton, Frank and Thomas McLaury, came to their deaths in the town of Tombstone on October 26, 1881, from the effects of pistol and gunshot wounds inflicted by Virgil Earp, Morgan Earp, Wyatt Earp and one—Holliday, commonly called 'Doc' Holliday."

No determination was made whether the marshal had acted in the line of duty or whether the Earps should be brought up on charges. Yet enough controversy arose that the city council unceremoniously suspended Virgil as police chief on October 29 pending investigation of the shooting, and ordered that Jim Flynn serve in his place.

On October 30, the *Nugget* sarcastically responded to the coroner's decision under the headline "Glad to Know": "The people of this community are deeply indebted to the twelve [actually eight] intelligent men who composed the coroners jury for the valuable information that the three persons who were killed last Wednesday were shot. Some thirty or forty shots were fired, and the whole affair was witnessed by probably a dozen people, and we have a faint recollection of hearing someone say the dead men were shot, but people are liable to be mistaken and the verdict reassures us. We might have thought they had been struck by lightning or stung to death by hornets."

The next day, diarist Parsons, an avowed law-and-order sort, ran into Wyatt Earp at the Cosmopolitan Hotel. "[Wyatt] took me in to see Virgil. He's getting along well. Morgan too. Looks bad for them all thus far." Parsons, again, proved prescient.

"I THINK WE CAN HANG THEM"

J UST DAYS AFTER NEWSPAPERS throughout the West had celebrated their heroism, Ike Clanton filed murder charges against the Earps and Holliday, and they went from acclaimed to accused. Oddly, Behan did not make the charge himself, which would have carried far more weight than the claims of a cowboy troublemaker. Morgan and Virgil, still recovering, were not served. Wyatt and Holliday were brought before Justice of the Peace Wells Spicer, who "denied bail as a matter of right, but upon a showing of facts by affidavits, bail was granted and fixed at the sum of $10,000 each."[1]

The money came quickly, far more than Wyatt Earp needed to post bail. Wells, Fargo secret agent Fred Dodge contributed $500, James Earp threw in $2,500, and Wyatt Earp contributed $7,000 to the $14,500 that eight men raised for Holliday. Wyatt himself drew a grand total of $27,000 from ten contributors. The largest contribution, $10,000, came from Tom Fitch, the attorney who would stand for the defense when Wyatt Earp went before the court. Spicer's duty was to determine whether sufficient evidence existed to bring the Earps and Holliday before the grand jury on murder charges. This was a preliminary hearing, not a murder trial. For the next month, Tombstone became engrossed in the court battle, complete with dramatic testimony, surprise witnesses, and strange interruptions. Tom Fitch, for the defense, proved very able in the role.

Fitch, 43, had an interesting background. He had worked as a newspaper reporter in Wisconsin, California, and Nevada and served in the California legislature. He had been a delegate to the Nevada statehood convention, had made friends with Mark Twain, and was elected to Congress. In the 1870s Fitch moved to Utah and managed criminal and civil litigation for the Mormon Church, then went to San Francisco before winding up in Arizona in 1877, where he served in the territorial legislature. He was an accomplished orator and had delivered the town's Fourth of July address. Also on the defense team was T. J. Drum, representing Holliday, and the firm of Howard & Street.

Fitch, with his political prestige and courtroom polish, faced off against able opponents. District Attorney Lyttleton Price served as prosecuting attorney in an unusual situation. He had only officially taken over the office weeks earlier, after the prolonged confusion over his appointment. Clum and other Republicans had been strong in their support of Marshal Virgil Earp and his "deputies," and Republican Price risked infuriating his own political supporters with a controversial case that it was his duty to prosecute. The *Los Angeles Herald* said unnamed friends of the deceased had raised $10,000 to help run the prosecution, which led to the addition of several lawyers, most notably Ben Goodrich, a native Texan and former Confederate officer who neither drank nor gambled and who had already built a reputation by defending several cowboys. The firms of Colby & Smith; Smith, Earll, Campbell & Robinson; and J. M. Murphy filled out the prosecution team.

A decision by Virgil Earp, still the U.S. deputy marshal, on the first day of November drew much scorn from his townsmen. He telegraphed General Orlando Willcox at Fort Huachuca to send a company of cavalry to Tombstone to protect the town from a cowboy invasion. Willcox referred the matter to Acting Governor Gosper and ordered the cavalry into readiness to move if the order came. Gosper said the order could come only from the president. Tombstone supervisor Milt Joyce, visiting Prescott, wired Behan to learn if a threat of trouble existed. "No trouble, everything peaceable," Behan responded, and no troops were sent. The *Nugget* lampooned the Earps for this call for martial law.[2]

When the hearing before Judge Wells Spicer finally began, Billy Allen and then Behan were the first to take the stand for the prosecution on November 1 and 2, 1881, telling of how the Earps had not saved the town from outlaws, but instead had committed murder.

Allen testified that after meeting with Billy Clanton and Tom McLaury in the saloon, he followed the Earps on their march down Fremont Street to face off against the cowboys. Allen said he heard someone from the Earp party yell, "You sons of bitches, you have been looking for a fight" at the same time that Virgil threw up his hands. Allen described what followed: "Tom McLaury threw his coat open and said, 'I ain't got no arms.' He caught hold of the lapels of his coat and threw it open. William Clanton said, 'I do not want to fight' and held his hands out in front of him. He had nothing in his hands when he held them in this position," Allen said, showing the motion. "I did not notice what Frank McLaury did. I did not notice him or Ike. Just as William Clanton said, 'I do not want to fight,' and Tom McLaury threw open his coat and said, 'I ain't got no arms,' the firing commenced by the Earp party."[3]

Allen testified he believed Holliday fired the first shot and that the second blast also came from the Earp party, while Billy Clanton had his hands in the air. The defense dug into Allen, trying to damage his credibility. They asked about an indictment in Colorado for larceny, which the court refused to allow, and Allen left the stand.

Behan came to tell his story on November 2, explaining how he had attempted to prevent the gunfight by trying to stop the Earps, only to have them brush past him. He said he heard one of the Earps, he thought Wyatt, yell, "You sons of bitches," and another say, "Throw up your hands."

"I saw a nickel-plated pistol pointed at one of the Clanton party—I think Billy Clanton—my impression at the time was that Holliday had the nickel-plated pistol. I will not say for certain that Holliday had it," Behan said. "These pistols I speak of were in the hands of the Earp party. When the order was given 'Throw up your hands,' I heard Billy Clanton say, 'Don't shoot me, I don't want to fight.' Tom McLaury at the same time threw open his coat and said, 'I have nothing' or 'I am not armed.' . . . I can't tell the position of Billy Clanton's hands at the time he said, 'I don't want to fight.' My attention was directed just at that moment to the nickel-plated pistol, the nickel-plated pistol was the first to fire, and another followed instantly. These two shots were not from the same pistol. The nickel-plated pistol was fired by the second man from the right. The second shot came from the third man from the right. The fight became general. Two or three shots were fired very rapidly after the first shot, by whom I do not know. The first two shots were fired by the Earp party. I could not say by whom." Behan said he thought the next three shots also came from the Earps, and he believed the nickel-plated pistol went off immediately when Virgil yelled for the cowboys to throw up their hands. The sheriff never said he was certain Doc Holliday had started the gunfight, but he left a strong implication that the drunken, dangerous dentist began firing while Virgil tried to make the arrest.[4]

In the midst of Behan's testimony, a few side dramas became part of the main show. The defense had tried to keep details of the trial from being reported in the newspapers. "This is made necessary from the fact that there is great excitement here, but it is hoped no further trouble will occur," the *San Francisco Morning Call* reported on November 2. "Friends of the deceased are determined to prosecute the case to the bitter end in the courts. It will be a long and tedious case, and if it goes to the District Court, a change of venue will have to be taken and the case tried elsewhere as so much feeling is manifest on both sides here." Gag order or no gag order, the industrious *Nugget* ran a detailed story from the first day of the hearing, much to the dismay of the defense. Fitch relented and asked Spicer to remove the order, "as it appeared impossible to curtail the enterprise of the press."[5] Spicer removed the order in time for Behan's testimony to appear in both papers.

The echo of Behan's testimony was heard throughout the West. The Earps, hailed in many newspapers as heroes, were suddenly being portrayed as murderers by a respected and well-liked sheriff whose word should be believed. The *Arizona Star* took the lead in editorializing against the Earps, thundering on November 3:

It now appears, after the smoke of the Tombstone bloody street affray has passed away, that but one side of the tale had been told. It is claimed by many that the killing of the McLowrys [*sic*] and Clanton was cold blooded and premeditated murder with little or no justification.

It appears the parties who did the killing were hostile in feeling to those who fell before the bullet, and that threats had been made, and when the shooting occurred the boys who were killed were preparing to leave Tombstone; two of them were unarmed and that they showed no disposition whatever to quarrel or create a public disturbance. If this be so, then those who committed the tragedy, under the color of the law, should be classed as public offenders and as such be punished to the fullest extent of the law. It makes no matter what the character of the parties killed, they were entitled to protection. As long as no offense or an attempt at breaking the law was made, there was no warrant for officers of the law committing a breach of the peace. . . . It is to be hoped that every means within the power of man will be used to reach the bottom of the whole affair, and if the Marshal's posse were doing their duty, let them not only be set free but commended. But if under color of authority, they wreaked their vengeance on these victims, as set forth, then let the law claim its due, no matter what the consequences.[6]

The same *Star* that had been editorializing for months that the army should be turned loose on a murderous crusade against the cowboys now called for a complete investigation of cowboy killings. Once the blood flows, the tough talk withers.

The controversy continued to grow. A letter from Tombstone dated November 1 appeared in the *Star* accusing the papers of making "patriots out of murderers, and the voiceless tongues of the murdered boys cannot deny the libel which brands them as thieves, ruffians and rowmakers."

True they dealt in and handled cattle instead of handling cards. They may have bought stolen cattle, and under their reputations were able to dispose of the same publicly in our markets.

Even admit that these boys were thieves that it was their occupation to steal cattle, yet this fact does not justify, and cannot justify in the light of recent public sentiment, the foul murder which our papers seem to commend. Admit the worst that can be said of these boys as proven facts, and they stand in Angel robes of innocence as compared with the cut-throat who shot Tom McLowry [*sic*] with buckshot while he was protesting that he was unarmed.[7]

Johnny Behan's words began to turn public opinion against the Earps. The sheriff's testimony portrayed a far different gunfight than had been first reported in the local papers, and the letter-writers waxed poetic about the poor boys who never deserved to die. A gun battle takes on a far different connotation in ink than in lead.

Behan returned to the stand for two days of cross-examination and redirect, entrenching his position. He said he had thoroughly examined Ike Clanton and was certain he had no weapon, and that he was convinced Tom McLaury was unarmed, although his search was not so complete. "I was satisfied that Ike Clanton and Tom McLaury had no arms," he said.[8]

The defense tried hard to shake the nickel-plated-pistol story. The lawyers asked, if Holliday had the shotgun, where did the pistol come from? Behan did not know, he just stuck to his version. If Behan wanted to discredit the Earps, Holliday made a much more vulnerable target than the city marshal or Wyatt. The prosecution's key witnesses — Allen, Claiborne, Behan, and Ike Clanton — would all make it appear that Holliday had been first to pull the trigger with his nickel-plated pistol, though none could explain how he could have been holding the shotgun at the same time.

Lawyers Fitch and Drum attempted to break the sheriff's testimony, asking Behan if he and Allen had met to compare testimony, or whether Behan had promised to contribute to the fund to pay the prosecution attorneys. Behan coolly denied both charges. The sheriff also denied he had told one of the Flys he was the only witness to the shooting. He said the McLaurys and Billy Clanton were not troublemakers, and that Ike's problems were not all that serious.

In his testimony, Behan made a statement that seemed trivial at the time, but nearly three weeks later would become one of the turning points of the hearing. He told his version of the post-shootout visit to Virgil Earp's home: "I went down that evening and when I got in the house, Virgil Earp said, 'You better go slow, Behan, and not push this matter too far.' I told him I did not come there to have any words—that I intended to do my duty as an officer. Then he said he heard I tried to get the vigilance committee to hang them. I told him I did nothing of the kind, that I never called for them. He said about the same thing that Wyatt Earp did, about me deceiving them or throwing them off. This is when I explained to him about stopping him and telling them to stop. In the conversation he told me he was my friend. I told him I had always been his friend. That seemed to settle the matter about the vigilance committee. I suppose I told him that I heard him say, 'Throw up your hands.' I never told him I heard McLaury say anything or that I saw him draw a pistol. I never said that they did right."[9]

Behan reconstructed the failed agreement that would have made Wyatt Earp undersheriff. By Behan's version, the deal fell apart because of that December ride to Charleston when Earp intimidated the Clantons into returning his stolen racehorse. Behan said Ike Clanton had told him the situation came near a war. Behan never explained why this would have any impact on making Earp undersheriff, though the implication was that Earp had interfered with delivery of a subpoena. Nor did Behan allude to the backroom deal that put him in office or the likely deal that landed Harry Woods the job as undersheriff. Ironically, it was District Attorney Lyttleton Price who had exposed the questionable deals in a letter to the *Epitaph*.

When Behan left the stand, the advantage definitely rested with the prosecution. Newspapers picked up the change in sentiment, and the *San Francisco Examiner* reported on November 7: "The trial of the Earps and Doc Holliday for the killing of the cowboys is progressing slowly. . . . Public feeling, which at first was for the Earps and Holliday, seems to have taken a turn, and now nearly all the people of Tombstone condemn the murderers."

The *Arizona Star* wrote: "The killing of the McLowrys [*sic*] and Clanton at Tombstone seems more dastardly day by day as the evidence is brought before the public. What justifiable excuse can be raised to explain the killing is hard to surmise. It is to be hoped, however, for the sake of the good reputation of our neighbor that the absence of malice and premeditation upon the part of the slayers may at least be established."[10]

On the night of November 3, before Behan had finished his testimony, the stage arrived carrying a most important passenger. William R. McLaury, a lawyer from Fort Worth, came to look into the death of his brothers. He was immediately admitted as associate counsel for the prosecution and spent three weeks sitting in the same courtroom as Wyatt Earp and Doc Holliday. Iowa-reared Will McLaury was considered a "radical" Republican in Texas, a term used in the post–Civil War era to indicate supporters of the Union's reconstruction programs. In heavily Democratic Texas, he struggled financially before gaining acceptance by going into partnership with former Confederate officer S. P. Greene. McLaury came to Tombstone on a vendetta. His dead brothers "were very dear to me, and would have walked through fire for me," he wrote back to brother-in-law David D. Appelgate in Iowa. McLaury spent his days in court and his evenings in the saloons, winning support among the townsmen and defaming the Earps. He bought into the whole cowboy story of his brothers being shamelessly murdered and stood drinks to the bar loungers who regaled him with tales about what fine fellows Tom and Frank McLaury were. "I find that with the exception of about thirty or forty men here whose business is gambling and stealing among whom are the Earp brothers and one J. H. Holliday, my brothers were universally esteemed as Honorable, Peaceable, and Brave citizens never having been charged nor suspected of having committed any offense," he wrote to Appelgate.[11]

McLaury arrived as a brother in grief. Many townsmen sympathized with him and appreciated his buying them drinks. He wrote that $1,600 had been stolen from Tom's body, and that his two brothers had sold their cattle and had been packing up to leave the area before the fight. There is no confirmation of this, and not even the dead brothers' friends made the assertion. "I can only say it was as cold-blooded and foul a murder as has been recorded," McLaury wrote to Greene. "My brothers had no quarrel nor interest in any quarrel with these men."[12]

Will McLaury was a man wronged, and he came to Tombstone to preserve the family honor. "This thing has a tendency to arouse all the devil there is in me — it will not bring my brothers back to prosecute these men but I regard it as my duty to myself and family to see that these brutes do not go unwhipped of justice," he wrote to his law partner, Greene. ". . . I think I can hang them."[13]

Will McLaury joined the prosecution for the examination of Martha King and Thomas Keefe, minor witnesses who helped set the scene. West Fuller took the stand on Monday, November 7, giving his profession as jeweler. He added to and supported the story already told by Behan and Allen:

"Billy Clanton threw up his hands and said, 'Don't shoot me, I don't want to fight.' At the same time the shooting commenced. . . . The Earp party fired the first shot; two shots were fired right away; they were almost together; I think they were both pistol shots. Both parties then commenced firing rapidly. . . . When Billy Clanton first drew his pistol, about six or seven shots had been fired by the Earps and Holliday. Billy Clanton was shot through the right wrist. At the time I saw Frank McLaury draw his pistol, his appearance and his action indicated he was shot. He was staggering and dizzy." Fuller said Morgan Earp and Holliday fired the first two shots, though he could not tell if Holliday fired a pistol or a shotgun.

The defense tried to shake Fuller. They asked if he had been talking to a woman named Mattie Webb when the shooting started, suggesting he had not actually seen the battle begin. Fuller answered simply, "No, I was not." Fuller admitted he had been "drinking considerable" the night before the gunfight, but he had not been imbibing on the fatal day. The most questionable admission came on the final defense queries. First Fuller stated his feelings toward Holliday. "We have always been good friends, and are so now." The defense then asked: "Did you not, on November 5, 1881, at about 5 o'clock P.M. in front of the Oriental Saloon, in Tombstone, say to or in the presence of Wyatt Earp, that you knew nothing in your testimony that would hurt the Earps, but that you intended to 'cinch Holliday,' or words of like import or effect?" Fuller answered, "I told Wyatt Earp that I thought Holliday was the cause of the fight. I don't say positively I might have used words, 'I mean to cinch Holliday,' but I don't think I did."[14]

Fuller's testimony injured the Earps' case. Prosecution attorneys moved that Wyatt Earp and Doc Holliday be remanded to jail without bail, saying the evidence appeared conclusive. The defense argued that bail had already been granted, so the freedom of Wyatt Earp and Doc Holliday could not be denied until evidence was completed. Spicer ruled he had jurisdiction at all times to decide on bail, "according as the evidence showed the guilt or innocence of the offenses charged . . . Judge Spicer being convinced that the evidence already adduced was sufficient to hold them on the charge of murder," the *San Francisco Chronicle* reported on November 8. The jailing and reports made clear that the prosecution had already produced enough evidence to force the Earps and Holliday to stand trial for murder.

Fitch and his team received a writ of habeas corpus from the probate court and appeared before Judge John Henry Lucas. After legal argument, their petition was denied. Sheriff Johnny Behan took Wyatt Earp and Holliday to his jail.

Will McLaury wrote that he played the key role in getting the Earps jailed. He said Wyatt and Doc came into the room heavily armed, and the district attorney "was completely cowed" by the sight. He said Price had promised to jail the Earps, but the fearful prosecuting attorneys did not want to risk the defendants' wrath. McLaury went ahead with the motion. "I did not think they . . . would make a move and did not fear them. The fact is I only hoped they would as I . . . thought I could kill them both before they could get a start." Once he made his motion, he wrote, "they were quiet as lambs, only looking a little scared."[15] "Instead of making a fight when I made the motion, these men sat and trembled and whenever I go near them I can see it makes them nervous—I think we can hang them. I shall do my duty to that end."[16] Earp and Holliday were in jail, "but . . . this don't bring back my dead brothers. . . . Last night, after it was known the murderers were in jail, the hotel was a perfect jam until nearly morning, everybody wanted to see me and shake my hand.[17] They nearly shook my hands off. Witnesses were there plenty."[18]

Putting Wyatt and Doc in jail meant more to McLaury than mere revenge. He wrote that prosecution witnesses had reason to be frightened because the defendants still walked the streets heavily armed. "We fear some of our most important witnesses will be killed by the friends of these brutes. There is [*sic*] two Earp brothers who were not engaged in the murder."[19] McLaury also noticed what had become obvious—and he had been part of the process. Many Tombstone townsmen had turned on the Earps, believing the prosecution story of murdered innocents with their hands in the air. The same citizens who once cried out for law and order didn't much like the sight of a bloody killing in the street with murky undertones. McLaury said as much when he wrote to Appelgate: "I had little support from the people when I came here. I now have the whole camp with the exception of a few gamblers."[20]

Holding Wyatt and Doc in custody posed an immediate problem. Behan feared Earp supporters would try to break the now-defamed hero out of jail, and he took appropriate action. "By the direction of Sheriff Behan, Under Sheriff Woods placed a strong guard around the jail to prevent any attempt being made by either side to interfere with the officers of the law," the *Chronicle* reported. "To-night the town is quiet and no trouble is anticipated, as the citizens are determined that the law shall take its course and justice be done both the living and the dead. Virgil Earp, City Marshal, and his brother, Morgan Earp, who were engaged in the shooting, are still confined to their rooms from the effects of wounds received during the fight, but are reported to be slowly recovering. It is not known when they will be brought into court to stand trial." Acting Governor Gosper would later write that the guardians around the jail were not there by direction of Behan—they were members of the committee of safety watching closely to prevent cowboys from breaking in to kill Earp and Holliday.[21]

The prosecution case grew stronger when Billy Claiborne took the stand and said the two Clantons had their hands in the air and Tom McLaury was opening his coat to show he was unarmed when the shooting started. "About six or eight shots were fired rapidly by the Earp party, counting the first two shots. Billy Clanton, while lying on the ground, jerked his six-shooter and sitting up fired across his knee," Claiborne testified. He remained consistent in cross-examination and repeated that the Earp party fired the first six shots, saying Holliday fired first and Morgan Earp second.

The defense tried to shake him, asking him about the killing of James Hickey, of which he had been accused, but the question was ruled inadmissible. The defense asked whether he was out of sight in Fly's boardinghouse at the time the shooting began; he insisted he remained long enough to hear the first sixteen or eighteen shots. Again the defense suggested he had coordinated stories with Behan, and Claiborne flatly denied such a claim. The defense asked how he happened to be called Billy the Kid, and Claiborne said it was simply because he was so young when he started riding with the cattle herds, with no claim to emulating another Billy in New Mexico. The Kid came off as the innocent. The prosecution held the hot hand this first week of November, and Will McLaury's hope of a hanging seemed a step closer.

By the time Ike Clanton stepped to the witness stand on November 9, the prosecution had already built an impressive case. Fuller, Allen, Claiborne, and Behan had testified that Tom McLaury was unarmed, that Billy Clanton had his hands in the air, and that neither of the McLaurys was a troublemaker. They portrayed Ike Clanton and Tom McLaury as being unjustly bullied and beaten by the vengeful Earps on the day of the gunfight. With Wyatt and Doc in jail, there were those who feared that Behan might allow a kidnapping. However, Behan was far too wise for that sort of ploy. He had the chance to dispose of the Earps by legal means. Unless someone quickly rode to the rescue, Wyatt Earp might end his life in the noose of a hangman's rope.

The man who did the most to save Earp was none other than Ike Clanton, who stepped to the witness stand and presented a tale so contradictory, so permeated with evasions and fabrications, that his credibility was virtually nil.

Ike held up fine during the direct examination, repeating the story of the abuses he had suffered from Holliday and the Earps the night before the battle and the next day in court when Morgan Earp offered him his gun and asked where he wanted to fight. Ike reiterated that Holliday and Morgan Earp had fired the first two shots, with the next barrage coming from the Earp party, Virgil then Wyatt, before the cowboys had time to draw their weapons.

Clanton told a heroic story of trying to push Wyatt out of the fight. "He shoved his pistol against my belly, and said 'Throw up your hands,' and said, 'You son of a bitch, you can have a fight.' I turned on my heel and took Wyatt Earp a hold of his hand and pistol with my left hand and grabbed him around the shoulder with my right hand and held him for a few seconds. While I was holding him he shot. I pushed him around the photograph gallery door [actually Fly's boardinghouse] and jumped into the photograph gallery door. I went right on through the hall and out the back way. I then went on across Allen Street and into the dance hall on that street. As I was leaving and as I jumped into the door of the photograph gallery, I heard one or two bullets pass right by my head. As I passed through an opening on my way from the gallery I heard another bullet pass me."[22]

He testified he was simply on his way to retrieve his team so he could peaceably leave town, unarmed and inoffensive. The final question from the prosecution had been simple: Had you, at the time you state that Doc Holliday charged you with having threatened the Earps, ever in fact threatened the Earps or Doc Holliday? "No sir," Ike answered. "I had never threatened any of the Earps nor Holliday."

When he stepped down on November 10, he gave all appearances of innocence; seemingly the grieving brother wronged by spiteful killers. Cross-examination was delayed a day at the request of the defense; then Ike had his own problem, asking to be excused for a day because of "neuralgia of the head," the *Nugget* reported. Period medical books describe the condition as a severe pain in the front of the head, near the eyes. The common neuralgia treatment in the 1880s was a solution of cocaine and water. Although no medical records survive to tell if Ike Clanton was actually coked up when he returned to the stand, during the next two days he displayed overweening confidence and seemed to glory in his own perceived brilliance. By the time he left the stand, his attorneys were probably the ones with the headache.

After a few set-up questions, the defense attorneys asked Ike if he knew Neil Boyle, the saloonkeeper at the Oriental. No, Ike did not know a Neil Boyle, but he did know the saloonkeeper at the Oriental by another name, and he did not remember visiting the bar at 6 A.M. on the day of the shooting, nor did he remember making any remarks that might be considered threats against the Earps.

Had Ike been in Kelly's saloon at about 10 A.M. before the gunfight? "I was."

Didn't Ike say in the presence of Kelly and Joseph Stump something to the effect that "the Earp crowd and Holliday insulted me the night before when I was unarmed. I have fixed or heeled myself now, and they have got to fight on sight"? the defense asked.

"I remember that there was very near that language used in Kelly's saloon. I think it was about the hour of 10 A.M.," Ike responded, admitting he had indeed threatened the Earps on the day of the shootout.[23]

The defense then delved into the deal between Clanton and the Earps to deliver stage robbers Leonard, Head, and Crane to the law. Clanton said he had discussed it once with Wyatt Earp and had promised never to mention it again. He said he did not accept Earp's offer.

Then Clanton came up with a most interesting version of the story: "I asked him why he was so anxious to capture these fellows. He said his business was such that he couldn't afford to capture them, that he would have to kill them or else leave the country, that he and his brother Morg had piped off to Doc Holliday and William Leonard the money that was going off on the stage. They [the robbers] were stopping around the country so damned long that he was afraid some of them would be caught and squeal on him. I then told him I would see him again before I left town. I never talked to Wyatt Earp any more about it." Ike used the colorful colloquialism "piped off" to mean the Earps had stolen the money and transferred it to Holliday before the stage left town.

Clanton's statement would become the fulcrum of anti-Earp debate for a century. Could Wyatt Earp have been so foolish as to actually tell Ike Clanton he was involved in the stage robbery? Could Ike have been clever enough to make up the story on his own? Could Wyatt have purposely deceived Clanton to make him think the Earps were in league with the cowboys? And the biggest difficulty with the story is that no money was actually missing from the stage. Ike's courtroom testimony would divide Tombstone in 1881 and remain controversial for generations.

Defense attorneys frantically tried to catch Clanton. They asked if Wyatt Earp had not called him into the yard behind the Oriental Saloon and told him of the plan to catch the robbers so Wyatt could have the glory to enhance his run for sheriff, while Clanton and his friends would receive the cash reward.

"I never had no conversation with him in regard to that, in the back yard of the Oriental," Ike responded. "I never had no conversation with him in company with Virgil Earp, Frank McLaury and Joseph Hill. I never heard him say anything about running for sheriff. I never heard him say he wanted to catch them."

Ike constantly denied he had agreed to any deal with the Earps, although during the coroner's inquest a few days earlier he had said: "They don't like me; we once had a transaction, myself and the Earps."

The defense kept pounding away at Clanton, asking about the deal, asking about the purported telegram from Wells, Fargo saying they would indeed pay for the robbers, dead or alive. They even presented Clanton with a copy of the missive. Clanton steadfastly denied ever seeing such a telegram or being involved with such a plan. Then the defense brought up another telegram: Hadn't Ike wired to his brothers, Fin and Billy, in Charleston to come with help? Ike denied it. With that, testimony ended on Saturday afternoon, and Ike Clanton was allowed to go home and rest his aching head.

Clanton returned to the witness stand Monday morning and was greeted by a series of questions about the gun battle. "When you took hold of Wyatt Earp's arm at some stage of the shooting, did he not say to you, 'This fight has commenced and you must either fight or get away'?" the attorneys asked.

"He did not make any such remark. The only thing he said was 'Throw up your hands,' and cocked his pistol and stuck it at my belly," Clanton responded. He said no shots had been fired when Wyatt took aim at him, and that he grabbed Wyatt and pushed him around the building after about four or five blasts. By Ike's latest story, Wyatt could not have fired any shots in the first fusillade, while earlier he claimed Wyatt had fired.

The defense teased Clanton, asking, "How many head of cattle have you secured by legitimate means?" Clanton said he and the McLaurys had been partners on seven hundred head, all of which he had acquired honestly, by raising or by purchasing.

Then defense returned to the Boyle issue, and this time they got the barkeep's name right. "Do you know a Ned Boyle, who is bartender at the Oriental?"

"Yes, sir," Clanton answered.

Defense asked if Clanton recalled saying to Boyle, "As soon as the Earps show themselves on the street, they had to fight." And was Ike holding a pistol when he made this comment?

"I don't remember talking to Ned Boyle about it. I think I saw him that morning. I did not make the remark stated. I don't think I said that the Earps had to fight, for the reason that there were three of them that I never had an unpleasant word with in my life. I don't remember having a pistol in my hands."[24] Boyle would have a much different recollection when he finally came to the stand two weeks later.

In redirect questioning by the prosecution, Ike told the remarkable story of how Doc Holliday, too, had confided in him his greatest secret. "Doc Holliday asked me if I had seen William Leonard and his party. I told him I had seen them the day before, and they told me to tell Doc Holliday that they were going to the San Jose mountains. He then asked me if I had had a talk with them. I told him, 'only for a moment or two.' He told me that he would see me later in the evening. This was in front of the Cosmopolitan Hotel. Later I met him at Jim Vogan's place and after talking with him awhile, he asked me if Leonard had told me how he [Holliday] came to kill Bud Philpott. I told him that Leonard had told me nothing about it. He [Holliday] told me that Bob Paul, the messenger, had the lines and Bud Philpott had the shotgun, and Philpott made a fight and got left. About that time someone came along and the conversation ended. I told Doc Holliday not to take me into his confidence, that I did not wish to know any more about it. Doc Holliday told me he was there at the killing of Bud Philpott. He told me that he shot Philpott through the heart."

Ike turned to the court and said, "Scratch that out and put it down just as Doc Holliday said." Then he resumed: "He said he saw 'Bud Philpott, the damn son of a bitch tumble off the cart.' That is the last conversation that I ever had with Holliday in connection with the affair. He has often told me to tell Leonard, Head, and Crane if I saw them, that he was all right."

Without being questioned, Ike gave his version of his conversation with Wyatt Earp, saying he had been promised $6,000 for helping capture Leonard, Head, and Crane, then telling of a meeting with Morgan: "The next morning after my conversation with Wyatt Earp I met Morg Earp in the Alhambra Saloon. He asked me what conclusion I had come to in regard to my conversation with Wyatt. I told him I would let him know before I left town. He approached me again in the same place, about four or five days after this. We had considerable talk about it then at that time, but I only remember that he told me that 10 or 12 days before Bud Philpott was killed that he had piped off $1,400 to Doc Holliday and Bill Leonard, and that Wyatt Earp had given away a number of thousand dollars, I think $29,000, the day Bud Philpott was killed—which sum was going off on the train that night. We talked a while longer, but I don't remember what was said, only I told him I was not going to have anything to do with it. I meant I would have nothing to do helping to capture Crane, Leonard, and Head." Ike quickly corrected himself from "capture" to "kill." The defense asked that the change be noted, and Judge Spicer agreed before Ike continued.[25]

"Virg Earp told me to tell Billy Leonard at one time not to think he was trying to catch him when they were running him, and he told me to tell Billy that he had thrown Paul and the posse that was after him off his track at the time they left Helms' ranch, at the foot of the Dragoon Mountains, and that he had taken them on to a trail that went down into New Mexico, and that he had done all he could for him, and he wanted Billy Leonard to get Head and Crane out of the country, for he was afraid that one of them might be captured and get all his friends into trouble."

When asked why he had kept this stunning information a secret, Ike valiantly replied, "I made a solemn promise to them never to tell. I would not have told had I not been put on the stand. I found out from Wyatt Earp's conversation that he was offering money to get men killed that were his confederates for fear that Leonard, Crane and Head would get captured and tell on him. I knew after Leonard and Head were killed that some of them would murder me for what they had told me."[26]

Ike Clanton left the stand that Monday afternoon portraying himself as the man who, unarmed, bravely tried to tackle Wyatt Earp and honorably kept his promise to the villains who killed his brother. It was, simply, too much for Judge Spicer to believe.

Apparently after leaving the witness stand on Monday, Ike and Behan jointly took out a $500 loan. While the reasons for such a strange action are subject to speculation, it seems plausible that an immediate cash influx was needed to fund the prosecution. In this whole unlikely series of events, one of the strangest occurences is that the county sheriff would help Ike Clanton secure a loan.[27]

Ike returned to the stand Tuesday morning to face Fitch and Drum and a few unsettling questions. Ike swore he had never told the secret before stepping on the stand, but, the defense asked, didn't he confide it to the prosecution attorneys?

"I did communicate it to my counsel before yesterday noon, but not until I was put on the stand as a witness here; I have never told it to any other person," Ike replied.

But, the defense queried, hadn't he told the same story to county recorder Al Jones and his deputy three days earlier?

"I did," Ike answered, making his vow of silence no longer seem so solemn.

And had Leonard, Head, or Crane ever said Holliday was part of the stage robbery?

"Bill Leonard afterward told me that if Doc Holliday had not been there and drunk, that Philpott would not have been killed."

The defense pressed on, inducing Clanton to detail his meetings with Holliday and Wyatt, Virgil, and Morgan Earp to discuss their roles in the stage robbery. Then, in a flight of sarcasm, the defense asked, "Did not Marshall Williams, the agent of the Express company at Tombstone, state to you . . . that he was personally concerned in the attempted stage robbery and the murder of Philpott?"

Spicer sustained the quick objection, but the sarcasm continued.

"Did not James Earp, a brother of Virgil, Morgan, and Wyatt, also confess to you that he was [a] murderer and stage robber?"

Objection sustained. But the defense had made its point: Why, on earth, would all the Earps have chosen to take Ike Clanton into their confidence on an issue so sensitive when they knew he could become their personal hangman? The Earps—all the Earps, not just the impetuous Morgan—must be absolute fools to do such a thing. Either that, or Ike Clanton had just told a series of lies so enormous that nothing he said could be believed. The prosecution case that seemed so sure after the seemingly credible testimony of Behan unraveled with Ike on the stand.

Years later, Fitch would confirm this when he told Colorado journalist E. D. Cowen: "The witnesses for the prosecution were the best witnesses for the defense."[28]

Before Ike Clanton took the stand, the prosecution had presented enough testimony to have the Earps and Holliday bound over for trial. When Clanton walked off Tuesday afternoon, the entire prosecution case had become suspect. The man who had provoked the fight, then run away, had undermined the effort to hang Wyatt Earp.

The defense still had a difficult decision ahead—whether to parade witnesses at this preliminary hearing or wait to give the whole show at a court trial. In Tombstone's tense atmosphere, this was not so simple a choice as it seemed. Both sides apparently feared their witnesses could be murdered if they came to testify, and for the defense to put on a complete case would amount to giving the cowboys a hit list if Clanton and his cronies were so inclined.

Fitch and his associates determined to try their case before Spicer, an attempt to prevent the Earps and Holliday from facing the uncertainties of appearing before an Arizona jury. The first man on the stand would be Wyatt Earp, following an unusual plan set out by his attorneys. Earp answered a few preliminary questions—his name, age, length of stay in Tombstone—then gave his occupation as saloonkeeper. He began reading from a long prepared statement, a surprise to the prosecution.

The objections began, with Price and associates charging misuse of a statute. Arizona's territorial laws allowed a defendant in a preliminary hearing to make a statement in his behalf without facing cross-examination. The prosecution said this skirted the intent of the statute, contending the law meant an oral statement, not a carefully prepared statement read before the court.

Spicer ruled that the statute "was very broad, and under it he felt that the accused could make any statement he pleased whether previously prepared or not," the *Nugget* reported. Earp then read from the manuscript, and he would not face cross-examination from prosecution attorneys.[29]

Wyatt Earp outlined a history of confrontations between the law and the Clantons and McLaurys. He told of the army mule theft that led to the McLaurys' earliest threats against the Earps. He spoke of the ill-fated deal to enlist Ike Clanton's and Frank McLaury's help in catching the stage robbers, a plan he said leaked out only because the drunken Marshall Williams sent the telegram and then guessed at Clanton's and McLaury's involvement. Ike Clanton and Frank McLaury believed the Earps had given them away. He said the animosity grew after the arrests of Spencer and Stilwell for stage robbery.

"The McLaurys and Clantons have always been friends of Stilwell and Spencer, and they laid the whole blame for their arrest on us, though the fact is we only went as a sheriff's posse," Earp told the court. "After we got in town with Spencer and Stilwell, Ike Clanton and Frank McLaury came in. Frank McLaury took Morgan Earp into the street in front of the Alhambra, where John Ringo, Ike Clanton and the two Hicks boys were also standing by, when Frank McLaury commenced to abuse Morgan Earp for going after Spencer and Stilwell. Frank McLaury said he would never speak to Spencer again for being arrested by us. He said to Morgan: 'If you ever come after me, you will never take me.' Morgan replied if he ever had the occasion to go after him, he would arrest him. Frank McLaury then said to Morgan, 'I have threatened you boys' lives, and a few days ago had taken it back, but since this arrest it now goes.' Morgan made no reply and walked off."

Wyatt Earp continued to relate a trail of misdeeds by the men he had faced across the barrel of a gun. The McLaurys, the Clantons, Joe Hill, and Ringo had threatened to kill the Earps, he said. Marshall Williams and a half-dozen others had told him of the death threats.[30] "I knew all those men were desperate and dangerous men, that they were connected with outlaws, cattle thieves, robbers and murderers," Wyatt Earp said. "I knew of the McLaurys stealing six government mules and also cattle, and when owners [*sic*] went after them — finding his stock on the McLaury boys' ranch — that he was driven off, and told that if he ever said anything about it they would kill him, and he has kept his mouth shut until several days ago for fear of being killed. . . . I heard of Ringo shooting a man down in cold blood near Camp Thomas. I was satisfied Frank and Tom McLaury killed and robbed Mexicans in Skeleton Canyon two or three months ago, and I naturally kept my eyes open, and I did not intend that any of the gang should get the drop on me if I could help it."

He told his version of what had happened the night before the shootout when Holliday and Clanton quarreled at the Alhambra, with Morgan Earp escorting Holliday from the saloon. According to Wyatt's testimony, Ike Clanton was wearing his six-shooter when he followed him to the Oriental and said, "You must not think I won't be after you all in the morning." Clanton wanted to fight Holliday immediately, but Earp said Holliday wanted no fight. Wyatt left and walked Holliday, "who was pretty tight," to Fly's boardinghouse, next to the lot that would soon become the site of the gun battle.[31]

Earp told his version of the events of the next day; of Ike's threats in Judge Wallace's court a few hours before the gunfight, and of the confrontation with Tom McLaury. By Earp's account, McLaury said, "If you want to make a fight, I will make a fight with you anywhere," before Wyatt slapped McLaury and drew his pistol. "I said, 'Jerk your gun and use it.' He made no reply and I hit him over the head with my six-shooter and walked away down to Hafford's Corner . . . and got a cigar," Earp said.

Wyatt told of meeting Behan on his march down Fremont Street. "I heard Behan say to Virgil, 'Earp, for God's sake don't go down there for you will get murdered.' Virgil replied, 'I am going to disarm them,' he being in the lead. When Morgan and I came up to Behan, he said 'I have disarmed them.' When he said this, I took my pistol which I had in my hand under my coat, and put it in my overcoat pocket."

Wyatt said the McLaurys and Billy Clanton were standing in a row against Harwood's house, with Ike Clanton, Billy Claiborne, and a man he did not know—probably West Fuller—in the middle of the lot. "I saw that Billy Clanton, Frank and Tom McLaury had their hands by their sides. Frank McLaury's and Billy Clanton's six-shooters were in plain sight. Virgil said, 'Throw up your hands, I have come to disarm you.' Billy Clanton and Frank McLaury commenced to draw their pistols. At the same time Tom McLaury threw his hand to his right hip, throwing his coat open like that." Wyatt displayed the motion.

"I had my pistol in my overcoat pocket, where I put it when Behan told us he had disarmed the other parties. When I saw Billy Clanton and Frank McLaury draw their pistols, I drew my pistol. Billy Clanton leveled his pistol on me, but I did not aim at him. I knew that Frank McLaury had the reputation of being a good shot and a dangerous man and I aimed at Frank McLaury. The first two shots which were fired were fired by Billy Clanton and myself, he shooting at me and I at Frank McLaury. I do not know which shot was fired first, we fired almost together. The fight then became general.

"After about four shots were fired, Ike Clanton ran up and grabbed my left arm. I could see no weapon in his hand, and thought at the time he had none, and so I said to him, 'The fight has now commenced. Get to fighting or get away.' At the same time I pushed him off with my left hand. He started and ran down the side of the building and disappeared between the lodging house and the photograph gallery. . . . I never fired at Ike Clanton even after the shooting commenced because I thought he was unarmed."

Wyatt said he never drew his pistol until Billy Clanton and Frank McLaury reached for their guns, and his first shot hit Frank McLaury in the stomach, who staggered off after firing a shot at Wyatt.

As to the critical question of the hearing, "If Tom McLaury was unarmed I did not know it. I believe he was armed and fired two shots at our party before Holliday, who had a shotgun, fired at and killed him. If he was unarmed there was nothing in the circumstances or in what had been communicated to me, or in his acts or threats, that would have led me even to suspect his being unarmed."

And, almost ominously, Wyatt Earp explained his motivation on the day the bullets flew: "I believed then, and believe now, from the acts I have stated and the threats I have related and other threats communicated to me by different persons, as having been made by Tom McLaury, Frank McLaury and Ike Clanton, that these men last named had formed a conspiracy to murder my brothers,

Morgan and Virgil, Doc Holliday and myself. I believe I would have been legally and morally justifiable in shooting any of them on sight, but I did not do so, nor attempt to do so. I sought no advantage when I went, as deputy marshal, to help to disarm them and arrest them. I went as a part of my duty and under the directions of my brothers, the marshals. I did not intend to fight unless it became necessary in self-defense or in the rightful performance of official duty. When Billy Clanton and Frank McLaury drew their pistols, I knew it was a fight for life, and I drew and fired in defense of my own life and the lives of my brothers and Doc Holliday."

Before leaving the stand, Wyatt refuted the charge of his involvement in the stage robbery. "The testimony of Isaac Clanton that I ever said to him that I had anything to do with any stage robbery or giving any information of money going on the stage or any improper communication whatever in any criminal enterprise is a tissue of lies from beginning to end."

He also answered Behan's remarks about the broken deal that was to have made Earp undersheriff of Cochise County: "Sheriff Behan made me an offer . . . that if I would withdraw and not try to get appointed sheriff of Cochise County, that we would hire a clerk and divide the profits. I done so, and he never said another word to me afterward in regard to it." As to Behan's story of not giving Earp the job because of his December conflict with the Clantons in Charleston, Earp said: "The reasons given by him here for not complying with his contract are false."

In a show of support, he presented signed statements from Dodge City and Wichita vouching for his competence: "That during his whole stay here he occupied a place of high social position and was regarded and looked upon as a high-minded, honorable citizen; that as marshal of our city he was ever vigilant and in the discharge of his duties, and while kind and courteous to all he was brave, unflinching, and on all occasions proved himself the right man in the right place," read the notarized statement from Dodge. "Hearing that he is now under arrest, charged with complicity in the killing of those men termed 'Cow Boys,' from our knowledge of him we do not believe that he would wantonly take the life of his fellow man, and that if he was implicated, he only took life in the discharge of his sacred trust to the people, and earnestly appeal to the citizens of Tombstone, Arizona, to use all means to secure him a fair and impartial trial, fully confident that when tried he will be fully vindicated and exonerated of any crime."[32]

Among the forty-nine signers was R. M. Wright, Wyatt's former Dodge adversary and the man he would later say tried to have him murdered. Also signing was Sheriff George Hinkle, with whom he would clash years later.

The Wichita document also praised Earp, calling him "a good and efficient officer, . . . well known for his honesty and integrity," and stating "that his character while here was of the best, and that no fault was ever found with him as an officer or as a man." Notary Charles Hatton added a note: "I hereby certify that I knew personally Wyatt S. Earp during his residence in the city of Wichita. That I served four years as city attorney of said city and have known personally all of the officers of said city for the past ten years. I take great pleasure in saying that Wyatt S. Earp was one of the most efficient officers that Wichita ever had and I can safely testify that Mr. Earp is in every sense reliable and a trustworthy gentleman."[33]

Wyatt Earp left the stand defending his honor and that of his brothers. He had refuted Clanton's charges, and he had cast doubt on the testimony of Behan, Claiborne, Allen, and Fuller and taken the blame for igniting the fight with what may have been the first shot. By his version the cowboys were reaching for their guns, not holding their hands in the air; and he never had reason to believe Tom McLaury faced the Earps unarmed. Wyatt's strong statement provided a powerful beginning to the defense case.

Over the next two weeks, Fitch and his team gradually tore apart the prosecution's case. Saloonkeeper Bob Hatch had been walking down the street with Deputy Sheriff Billy Soule when the Earps walked past Behan. Hatch saw the gunfight, and he said he saw Morgan Earp fall before he saw him in the act of shooting.

Will McLaury wrote his sister, Margaret Appelgate, that evening, telling her the defense had expected better from Hatch. "One of their principal witnesses has been on the stand today and they feel bad his evidence is much stronger for us than it is for them. I think the scoundrel feared to act out his role, and I am of the opinion that his fears are not wholly groundless. I do not think that by perjury these men shall escape." Will McLaury believed his case secure. "I think their only hope is in escape and should they escape from jail, their bones will bleach in the mountains. . . . I find a large number of my Texas friends here who are ready and willing to stand by me and with winchesters if necessary. The only thing now is to keep my friends quiet—their [*sic*] came near being a general killing here last night which had it not been prevented would have closed my business here. I am trying to punish these men through the courts of the country first. If that fails—then we *may* submit."[34]

His language had been stronger in an earlier letter to David Appelgate: "I think the men will be punished according to law—and in the event they escape by any trick or otherwise there will be more 'Press Dispatches.' "[35]

McLaury did not seem to be getting the full support of his family as he sat in the courtroom staring down Wyatt Earp. Apparently Margaret assailed him for leaving his two young children back in Texas while he went to Arizona. "I do not like your letter," Will McLaury responded. "It does not suit my mind or temper. My children will be provided for and I don't think a father would be any great advantage to them who would leave it to god to punish men who had murdered their uncles. . . . had I died these brothers . . . would have loved and cared for my babies. Now when these men are dead by one means or another and the friends who aided them are dead all of which may occur soon then I will go home."[36] As McLaury sorted through his personal problems, the defense case slowly came together.

Ned Boyle followed Hatch, but Price objected, saying Ike Clanton's threats were irrelevant and immaterial. The lawyers spent most of that Friday, November 18, wrangling over the issue, with the prosecution quoting the law that mere threats to kill or do great bodily harm are never admissible unless there is a doubt raised by the evidence as to which party commenced the affray, or when there is some evidence that the party making the threat by some sort of demonstration at the time of the killing led the defendant then and there to believe the party making such threats was about to put it into execution.

Fitch brought out the law books, saying that such evidence was admissible since it would shed light on the intent of the party committing the homicide and illustrate the motives of the party accused of murder. The wrangling continued until late in the afternoon, when Spicer sustained the prosecution objection and kept Boyle from telling his story. If the decision stood, it could mean disaster for the defense.[37]

A day later, court reconvened in Virgil Earp's room at the Cosmopolitan Hotel, and the city marshal told his version of a fight he swore he tried to avoid. Virgil said that Wyatt and Morgan were both deputies, Morgan as a special and Wyatt both as a special and as the U.S. deputy marshal.[38] Virgil said he had asked Holliday to come along and help. He gave his version of the events leading up to the gunfire, then laid out what he considered treachery from Behan. "He threw up both hands like this and said, 'For God's sake, don't go there or they will murder you.'

"I said, 'Johnny, I am going down to disarm them.' By this time I had passed him a step and heard him say, 'I have disarmed them all.' When he said that, I had a walking stick in my left hand and my right hand was on my six-shooter in my waist pants, and when he said he had disarmed them, I shoved it clean round to my left hip and changed my walking stick to my right hand. As soon as Behan had left them I moved in between the two buildings out of sight of them. We could not see them, all we could see was about half a horse."

Virgil said the walk continued until they saw the cowboys. "They were all standing in a row. Billy Clanton and Frank McLaury had their hands on their six-shooters. I don't know hardly how Ike Clanton was standing, but I don't think he had his hands in any attitude where I supposed he had a gun. Tom McLaury had his hand on a Winchester rifle on a horse. As soon as I saw them I said, 'Boys, throw up your hands. I want your guns, or arms.' With that Frank McLaury and Billy Clanton drew their six-shooters and commenced to cock them—click, click. Ike threw his hands into his breast this way," Virgil showed the motion as he spoke.

"At that I said, throwing up both hands, with the cane in my right hand . . . 'Hold, I don't want that.' As I said that, Billy Clanton threw his six-shooter down full cocked. I was standing to the left of my part, and he was standing to the right of Tom and Frank McLaury. He was not aiming at me, but his pistol was kind of past me—two shots went off right together—Billy Clanton's was one of them. At that time I changed my cane to my left hand and went to shooting. It was general then, and everybody went to fighting. At the crack of the first two pistols, the horse jumped to one side, and Tom McLaury failed to get the Winchester. He threw his hands back this way," Virgil showed the motion, "he followed the movement of the horse around, making him a kind of breastwork, and fired once, if not twice, over the horse's back."[39]

Virgil left the guns blazing as the court broke for lunch. The marshal was excused to rest his sore leg, and the afternoon concluded with city clerk Seward Breck Chapin coming to the stand to read city ordinances directing the chief of police to arrest anyone engaged in brawling in the streets or carrying a gun without a permit in the city limits. The prosecution objected to the city ordinances being introduced, saying they were immaterial. Spicer deferred a decision, and the long hearing adjourned for two days of rest.

Virgil continued his testimony on Tuesday morning, finishing the story of the series of threats against Holliday and the Earps that fateful morning before the fight and telling of previous encounters with the Clantons and the McLaurys. He remained firm under cross-examination, stating he believed Wyatt Earp and Billy Clanton fired the first shots, and that he had never previously met H. F. Sills, the mysterious train engineer who happened to be standing outside the O.K. Corral.

Virgil Earp's testimony had gone far to focus in on the question of who really provoked the fight and who started the actual shooting. The prosecution's key points were weakened, and the testimony of the prosecution witnesses became suspect.

Sills spent the afternoon on the witness stand telling of standing in front of the O.K. Corral and hearing one of the cowboys say they would kill the whole party of the Earps when they met them. He said he then told the marshal and watched the action. His story backed up that of the Earps, saying he saw Virgil raise his cane and Wyatt and Billy Clanton pull off the first shots, then held firm when the prosecution began its cross-examination.

Sills came off as the perfect witness, a stranger to all concerned who just happened to be in town from Las Vegas, New Mexico, after a temporary layoff from the Atchison, Topeka, and Santa Fe Railroad. Since he had no allegiance to either side, he was impartial, with no motive for lying. He was almost too good to be true, at least in the eyes of the prosecution. Price and his associates dug into Sills's story when court resumed Wednesday morning, asking him to recount trivial details of his life. The detailed cross-examination was designed to shake his credibility and try to link him to the Earps, either in the past or, perhaps, as a witness who had been hired to lie on the stand. Never for a minute did Sills waiver, even describing the horses pulling the wagon on which he first rode into town. The prosecution finished by asking if he had a nickname at the railroad. "Curley," he responded. But Curley Sills was no Curley Bill.

In supporting the Earps' story, Sills's account succeeded in absolutely shaking the credibility of the cowboys' version. Now, certainly, there appeared a serious question as to the cowboy testimony that the Earps had fired upon men with their arms in the air. Sills's testimony made relevant the issue of what prompted the gunfight, and now Spicer would allow the testimony regarding the threats that came earlier on the day of the shooting. It was a staggering defeat for the prosecution.

Saloonkeeper Julius Kelly followed Sills to the stand, and Spicer allowed testimony about Clanton's threats. "Ike Clanton and Joe Stump came in and called for drinks," Kelly said. "At the time I was waiting upon some other customers, when I heard Clanton telling Stump of some trouble he had had the night previous. I asked Clanton what trouble he had been having. He said that the Earp crowd and Doc Holliday had insulted him the night before, when he was not heeled; that he had now heeled himself and that they had to fight on sight. I cautioned him against having any trouble, as I believed the other side would also fight if it came to the point, or words to that effect."[40]

Ned Boyle, the bartender at the Oriental, followed, and the prosecution again objected that Ike's threats were irrelevant since he was not part of the actual gunfight. The prosecution charged that such threats would matter only if they came from Billy Clanton or the McLaurys. Spicer overruled the objection, and the defense now had a wide-open road to make Ike Clanton the incendiary of the shootout.

Ike's pattern of threats became clear as Boyle told his story: "After I went off watch at 8 o'clock in the morning, I saw Ike Clanton in front of the telegraph office in this town. His pistol was in sight, and I covered it with his coat and advised him to go to bed. He insisted that he wouldn't go to bed; that as soon as the Earps and Doc Holliday showed themselves on the street the ball would open, and that they would have to fight." Boyle said that the Clantons and the McLaurys had reputations as courageous men and experts with firearms, "the finest in the country."

The prosecution asked whether Boyle knew any of the deceased to have been troublemakers. He said he did not. But his testimony on Ike's threats had already done the damage.

Rezin J. Campbell, clerk of the board of supervisors, came next and told of the skirmish in Wallace's courtroom and Ike's comment to Morgan Earp: "If you fellows had been a second later I would have furnished a coroner's inquest for the town." Campbell also told of the dead men's reputations for courage and accuracy with guns as the defense built the sense of danger the Earps had faced.[41]

Every prosecution objection that day had been overruled, and the defense had clearly established serious doubts in the prosecution case. Spicer reconsidered the motion for bail, and respected mine operators E. B. Gage and James Vizina stepped in to add their names to the list providing the bail of $20,000 each. After sixteen nights under Behan's guard, Holliday and Wyatt Earp left jail in time for Thanksgiving; they had four days off from the hearing, part of which Wyatt spent sick in bed.

When court resumed November 28, Fitch and friends entered the hearing room with some startling testimony. Army surgeon J. B. W. Gardner testified he thought Tom McLaury was armed. "[I] saw no pistol but supposed at the time on seeing the right hand pocket of his pants extending outwards that he had got his pistol." Gardner said he told hotelkeeper Albert Bilicke "that I was sorry to see Tom McLaury had gotten his pistol."

Then came perhaps the biggest surprise of the trial. Winfield Scott Williams, Price's recently appointed assistant district attorney, virtually called Sheriff Behan a liar for what he reported of the conversation with Virgil Earp on the night of the shooting. "Virgil Earp was lying in bed," Williams testified. "Sheriff Behan came in and sat down on the edge of the bed at the foot. I sat down on a sofa at the head of the bed and facing the sheriff. Sheriff Behan said, speaking to Virgil Earp with reference to the affray which had taken place a few moments before, 'I went down to the corral to disarm them, and I could not,' or 'They would not,' I don't know which expression was used."[42]

According to Williams, Behan said, "I then met you and your party and spoke to you. You did not answer. I heard you say, 'Boys, throw up your hands, I have come to disarm you.' One of the McLaury boys said, 'We will,' and the shooting then commenced." Williams added, "That is as I remember it."

The defense question had included whether Williams had heard Behan say he had seen one of the McLaurys draw a pistol after the words, "We will," and Williams said that had been his understanding. The new assistant D.A.'s testimony proved a direct contradiction to what Behan had said more than three weeks earlier, when he stated, "I never told him I heard McLaury say anything or that I saw him draw a pistol."

Williams also reported Behan's remark "I am your friend, you did perfectly right." Behan had testified that he only said he and Virgil were friends, nothing about applauding their actions. An outside witness, with no discernible reason to lie, had stood before the court and stated that he heard the sheriff acknowledge that the cowboys had drawn first. An assistant district attorney had virtually called Johnny Behan a liar from the witness stand. Now even the sheriff's testimony had to be held in doubt. A shadow had fallen on the most credible of the prosecution witnesses, and Price's case slowly disintegrated.

Cosmopolitan hotelkeeper Albert Bilicke came next and said Tom McLaury's appearance had changed between the time he entered Everhardy's butcher shop, and the time he walked out. "When he went into the butcher shop his right-hand pants pocket was flat, seemingly nothing in it. When he came out his pants pocket protruded as if there was a revolver therein."

Testimony about bulging pants stirred the prosecution. Why would Bilicke be watching McLaury's pants so closely?

Bilicke answered easily: "Every good citizen in this city was watching all these cowboys very closely on the day the affray occurred, and as he was walking down the street my attention was called to this McLaury by a friend and so it happened that we watched him very closely."

Sarcasm spilled from the prosecution: "Did you know every good citizen in Tombstone, or did you on that day?"

"I know not all of them but a great many," Bilicke responded, unruffled.

"Do you know what the opinions of all good citizens of Tombstone were on the day by conversation or conversations with them about watching Thomas McLaury in this city, and if so, tell us who they were," the prosecution continued sarcastically. The question was withdrawn without answer.[43]

Dressmaker Addie Borland, a single woman in her mid-30s, lived across the street from the scene of the shooting and came to the stand with some confusing testimony. She said she watched the Earp party walk up to the cowboys and saw Doc Holliday push a pistol into the chest of one of the men, then step back. Was the gun nickel-plated? No, she said, dark bronze. She did not know who fired first, and she had not seen the cowboys raise their hands.

Borland's testimony muddied the issue. The cowboys had all testified Doc started the shooting with his nickel-plated pistol, while the defense insisted he carried the shotgun to the scene, fired on Tom McLaury only after the shooting began, then discarded the shotgun before drawing his six-shooter. Holliday, with his frail 135-pound frame, would have been unlikely to be wielding a pistol in one hand and a shotgun in the other like some fantasy gunslinger from a pulp novel. Most likely Borland had seen only the barrel of the short shotgun protruding from under Holliday's coat and had mistaken it for a pistol.

Since the first volley was pistol shots, the defense was trying to show that Holliday could not have set off the fight. Now Borland appeared with another version. She did help the Earps somewhat by saying she did not see the cowboys raise their hands, but her testimony left more questions than it answered. During the noon break, Spicer did one of the oddest things of the hearing. He visited Borland at her home, then took it upon himself to recall her for the afternoon session. When court resumed, Spicer stunned the room. He believed Borland knew more than she had stated, and he brought her back to the stand to answer his questions. The prosecution protested mightily at having a witness returned without solicitation from either side. Spicer overruled the objection and questioned Borland on his own.

The judge asked if she had seen the cowboys with their hands in the air, or if they were firing back at the Earps.

"I did not see anyone hold up their hands," Borland replied. "They all seemed to be firing in general on both sides. They were firing on both sides at each other. I mean by this, at the time the firing commenced."

The prosecution attacked, asking first about the firing, then querying her about Spicer's actions at her home.

"He asked me one or two questions in regard to seeing the difficulty, and if I saw any men hold up their hands, and if they had thrown up their hands whether I would have seen it, and I told him I thought I would have seen it," Borland answered.

The dressmaker's most important comment came at the end: Had the cowboys been standing with arms upraised, she would have seen it, she believed. She did not think she could have missed such a sight, and her statement contrasted with the remarks of Claiborne, Clanton, and Fuller.[44]

When Borland stepped down, John Lucas, a former Los Angeles farmer turned lawyer and probate court judge in Tombstone, finished the defense case by saying he rushed from his office in time to see Billy Clanton continue to fire through the fight. This undercut prosecution testimony that Billy had gone down early in the fight.

The defense rested. Two weeks after the Earps seemed certain to face trial, the hearing had turned strongly in their direction. Price, McLaury, and their team had little ammunition left to fire. On Tuesday morning they made their final attempt, calling butcher Ernest Storm, who worked at the meat market Tom McLaury had visited. Storm said: "I saw Tom McLaury going into my shop about two or three o'clock in the afternoon. [He] stayed there about four or five minutes and went out. [I] did not see any arms on his person. He did not get any in there that I saw."

Price submitted the case without argument, and Spicer was left to make a decision.

SPICER WRESTLED WITH HIS STATEMENT OVERNIGHT, although the decision had already become apparent to everyone involved. During the last few days of the hearing he had consistently ruled in favor of the defense and even brought a witness back to the stand to strengthen the defense case. When he returned to the courtroom at 2 P.M. on that final day of November, he came with a long, reasoned statement that will stand as one of the most revealing legal analyses ever made on the course of frontier justice. Spicer said he considered only the facts that were conceded by both sides or were established by a preponderance of testimony, which ruled out the disputed issues of the cowboys having their arms uplifted and of Doc Holliday's purported stage-robbing background.

The judge read on, explaining the decision that would come at the end of the statement. Spicer believed Clanton had been making his threats, and it was indeed Virgil Earp's job to disarm anyone violating the city ordinance by carrying weaponry on the streets. It was proper to arrest and disarm Ike Clanton, though the cowboy may have been treated roughly. "Whether this blow was necessary or not is not material here to determine," Spicer said.

He did not condone all of Virgil Earp's decisions, citing the background of animosity between the McLaurys and Wyatt Earp: "Virgil Earp, as chief of police, by subsequently calling upon Wyatt Earp and J. H. Holliday to assist him in arresting and disarming the Clantons and McLaurys, committed an injudicious and censurable act, and although in this he acted incautiously and without proper circumspection, yet we consider the condition of affairs incident to a frontier country, the lawlessness and disregard for human life, the existence of a law-defying element in our midst, the fear and feeling of insecurity that has existed, the supposed prevalence of bad, desperate and reckless men who have been a terror to the country and keep away capital and enterprise, and considering the many threats that have been made against the Earps, I can attach no criminality to his unwise act. In fact, as the result plainly proves, he needed the assistance and support of staunch and true friends upon whose courage, coolness and fidelity he could depend in case of an emergency."

As to the McLaurys' and the Clantons' actions moving through town: "With what purpose they crossed through to Fremont Street will probably never be known. It is claimed by the prosecution that their purpose was to leave town. It is asserted by the defendants that their purpose was to make an attack upon them, or, at least, to feloniously resist any attempt to arrest or disarm them that might be made by the Chief of Police and his assistants. Whatever their purpose may have been, it is clear to my mind, that Virgil Earp, the Chief of Police, honestly believed, and from information of threats that day given him, his belief was reasonable, that their true purpose was, if not to attempt the death of himself and his brothers, at least to resist with force and arms any attempt on his part to perform his duty as a peace officer by arresting and disarming them. . . .

"Was it for Virgil Earp, as Chief of Police, to abandon his clear duty as an officer because his performance was likely to be fraught with danger? Or was it not his duty that as such officer, he owed to the peaceable and law-abiding citizens of the city, who looked to him to preserve peace and order and their protection and security, to at once call to his aid sufficient assistance and proceed to arrest and disarm these men? There can be but one answer to these questions, and that answer is such as will divert the subsequent approach of the defendants toward the deceased of all presumption of malice or illegality. When, therefore, the defendants, regularly or specially appointed officers, marched down Fremont Street to the scene of the subsequent homicide, they were going where it was their right and duty to go. They were doing what it was their right and duty to do. And they were armed, as it was their right and duty to be armed when approaching men whom they believed to be armed and contemplating resistance. The legal character of homicide must, therefore, be determined by what occurred at the time, and not by the precedent facts. To constitute a crime of murder there must be proven, not only the killing, but the felonious intent. In this case, the corpus delicti, or fact of killing, is in fact admitted, as will be clearly proven. The felonious intent is as much a part to be proven as the corpus delicti, and in looking over this mass of testimony for evidence upon this point I find that it is anything but clear.

"Witnesses of credibility testify that each of the deceased, or at least two of them, yielded to a demand to surrender. Other witnesses of equal credulity testify that William Clanton and Frank McLaury met the demand to surrender by drawing their pistols, and that the discharge of fire arms from both sides was almost instantaneous. There's a dispute as to whether Thomas McLaury was armed at all, except with a Winchester rifle that was on the horse beside him. I will not consider this question, because it is not of controlling importance. Certain it is, that the Clantons and McLaurys had among them at least two six-shooters in their hands and two Winchester rifles on their horses; therefore, if Thomas McLaury was one of a party who were thus armed and were making felonious resistance to an arrest, and in the melee that followed was shot, the fact of his being unarmed, if it be a fact, could not of itself criminate the defendants, if they were not otherwise criminal. It is beyond doubt that William Clanton and Frank McLaury were armed and made such quick and effective use of their arms as to seriously wound Morgan and Virgil Earp.

"In determining the important question of whether the deceased offered to surrender before resisting I must give as much weight to the testimony of persons unacquainted with the deceased or the defendants, as to the testimony of persons who were companions and acquaintances, if not partisans, of the deceased. And I am of the opinion that those who observed the conflict from a short distance and from points of observation that gave them a good view of the scene, to say the least, were quite as likely to be accurate in their observation as those mingled up in or fleeing from the melee. Witnesses for the prosecution state unequivocally that William Clanton fell or was shot in the first fire, and Claiborne says he was shot when the pistol was only about a foot from his belly. Yet it is clear that there were no powder burns or marks on his clothes and Judge Lucas says he saw him fire or in the act of firing several times before he was shot, and he thinks two shots afterward.

"Addie Borland, who saw distinctly the approach of the Earps and the beginning of the affray from a point across the street where she could correctly observe all their movements, says she cannot tell which fired first—that the firing commenced at once, from both sides upon the approach of the Earps, and that no hands were held up; that she could have seen them if there had been. Sills asserts that the firing was almost simultaneous, he cannot tell which side fired first.

"Considering all the testimony together, I am of the opinion that the weight of evidence sustains and corroborates the testimony of Wyatt Earp and Virgil

Earp, that their demand for a surrender was met by William Clanton and Frank McLaury drawing, or making motions to draw their pistols. Upon this hypothesis my duty is clear. The defendants were officers charted with the duty of arresting and disarming brave and determined men who were experts in the use of firearms, as quick as thought and as certain as death, and who had previously declared their intentions not to be arrested nor disarmed. Under the statutes as well as the common law, they had a right to repel force by force."

Spicer said the angle of Billy Clanton's wrist wound was "such as could not have been received with his hands thrown up." And Tom McLaury's wound was not the sort that would have come with him holding his lapels. "These circumstances being indubital facts throw great doubt upon the correctness of the statement of witnesses to the contrary."

He flatly disbelieved Ike Clanton. "The testimony of Isaac Clanton that this tragedy was the result of a scheme on the part of the Earps to assassinate him, and thereby bury in oblivion the confessions the Earps had made to him about piping away the shipment of coin by Wells, Fargo & Co. falls short of being sound theory because of the great fact most prominent in the matter, to-wit: that Isaac Clanton was not injured at all, and could have been killed first and easiest. If he was the object of the attack he would have been first to fall, but as it was, he was known, or believed to be unarmed and was suffered, and so Wyatt Earp testifies, told to go away, and was not harmed."

Spicer even used Behan's testimony against the cowboys, an interesting twist in the case. Frank McLaury's refusal to give up his arms to the sheriff unless the chief of police was also disarmed showed a reasonable intent of violence, the justice rationalized.

"In view of the past history of the country and the generally believed existence at the time [of] desperate, reckless and lawless men in our midst banded together for mutual support, and living by felonious and predatory pursuits regarding neither life or property in their career, and at this time for men to parade the streets armed with repeating rifles and six-shooters, and demand that the Chief of Police of the city and his assistants should be disarmed is a proposition both monstrous and startling. This was said by one of the deceased only a few minutes before the arrival of the Earps."

Since Billy Clanton and the McLaurys chose to fight back, "It does not appear to have been a wanton slaughter of unresisting and unarmed innocents, who were yielding graceful submission to the officers of the law, or surrendering to, or fleeing from their assailants, but armed and defiant men accepting the wager of battle and succumbing only in death."

Much of the prosecution case had been based on the Earps' eagerness to fight, their intent to murder. Spicer brushed it aside. "I cannot believe this theory, and cannot resist the firm conviction that the Earps acted wisely, discreetly and prudentially to secure their own self-preservation. They saw at once the dire necessity of giving the first shot to save themselves from certain death. They acted; their shots were effective, and this alone saved all the Earp party from being slain. In view of all these facts and circumstances of the case, considering the threats made, the character and position of the parties, and the tragical results accomplished in manner and form as they were with all surrounding influences bearing upon the res gestae of the affair, I cannot resist the conclusion that the defendants were fully justified in committing these homicides—that it was a necessary act done in the discharge of an official duty.

"The evidence taken before me in this case would not, in my judgment, warrant a conviction of the defendants by a trial jury of any offense whatever. I do not believe that any trial jury that could be got together in this Territory would, on all the evidence taken before me, with the rules of law applicable thereto given them by the court find the defendants guilty of any offense."

He invited the Cochise County grand jury to reevaluate his decision, but everyone knew that was unlikely. The preliminary hearing had ended. Wyatt Earp and Holliday left without being bound over for a murder trial.

The Earps had won their day in court, but they had lost in a higher tribunal—the court of public opinion. Spicer's decision freed the Earps, left the townsmen to ponder the issues, and caused a continuing puzzle for historians. The prosecution case had portrayed cold-blooded murder: the Earps firing upon a party of men, two unarmed and three with their hands in the air. Back on November 7 guilt seemed clear enough to send Wyatt Earp to Johnny Behan's jail, where he would fear for his life suspecting the sheriff and his deputies would happily hand him over to any cowboy lynch mob that trotted into town.

Several of the prosecution's key points were left unanswered by the defense, such as Ike Clanton's charge that Holliday and the Earps had been involved in laundering money after the stage robberies and whether or not Ike Clanton had sent a telegram to summon other cowboys to fight an expected battle. Instead of clearing the Earps' reputation, the defense had left only a muddy field from which lies and innuendo would be remembered long after the decision.

While Fitch and friends left no explanation, the probable reason for such seeming oversights is that this was only a preliminary hearing, and the defense had no desire to expose all its weapons so the wily prosecution attorneys would know how to prepare for the big trial. The defense did little to undermine Ike Clanton—he fumbled mostly by himself. Had Fitch brought out the simple point that no money was missing from the stage after the robbery, where Ike accused the Earps of stealing the loot before ever putting the strongbox on the stage, Clanton would have much time to figure out some answer. Better to put him in front of a jury, then make him appear the fool. And by not producing Ike's telegram to Charleston summoning help, if such a telegram existed, the prosecution would have to stew over how to respond, not knowing whether their planning would be a waste of effort. Fitch could have been waving a red herring, a distraction, or he could have been holding back evidence that would have made Ike Clanton appear even more foolish when he told his story to a jury.

It is likely that Fitch had no expectation of having the case resolved at the preliminary hearing until Clanton stepped on the stand and presented his bizarre story. The meeting of defense attorneys on the night of November 12 can only be imagined, with the team debating whether to parade witnesses before Spicer or let the case rest and take the best shot before a jury. It was a dicey question—too much testimony would expose the defense case, too little would leave the Earps indicted and under Behan's guard for about another month.

Fitch made a tough call and won. No one in that tiny wooden courtroom in a dusty mining town could ever imagine that the fine points of the case would be debated for a century. Fitch secured the Earps' release, and that was his job. He could never have considered the impact his defense would have on subsequent history.

More puzzling was the prosecution case. Will McLaury, Price, and their pals did not summon two witnesses who might have provided key testimony. Charles Hamilton "Ham" Light, who testified at the inquest that Tom McLaury had been the first to go down, was never called by the prosecution. But Light had a history of allegiance to the cowboys. He had been among the men who posted bail for Pete Spence after the stage robbery arrest, and his pro-cowboy bias could quickly have been exposed by the defense team.

The most interesting absence is that of Patrick Henry Fellehy, who told the inquest panel that he had overheard Virgil Earp say he would not arrest the cowboys but would kill them on sight. Fellehy's testimony would have established premeditation and would have greatly enhanced the prosecution's case. Most likely the lawyers considered Fellehy's recollection faulty—not even Behan made the claim that Virgil Earp had planned murder, and Behan said everything he could to undermine the Earps. Had Virgil Earp made such a comment, Behan would have repeated it. Fellehy's declaration becomes particularly important because the Spicer hearing elicited no statement indicating premeditation by the Earps. The only other evidence of premeditation came in Martha King's report of overhearing the snatch of conversation, "Let them have it," from one of the Earps. King did not hear what words preceded this comment—the speaker could have said, "If they go for their guns, let them have it," which would change the meaning of the comment. Without the Fellehy statement, and with the King statement apparently only part of a conversation, there is no indication of premeditated murder.

That Fitch did put Sills on the stand probably indicates the itinerant engineer was no hired defense stooge. Had he actually been a false witness, the prosecution would have had time to break his story before the case came to trial, and Fitch would not have been likely to take such a gamble.

Spicer became the focus of bias charges that lingered for generations. Earp bashers would charge him with everything from being intermarried in Wyatt's family to being a business associate. While Spicer definitely leaned toward the Republican law-and-order crowd, his rulings seem to conform with standard territorial law, and he followed proper procedure. Perhaps the greatest issue was his allowing Earp to read a prepared statement. The prosecution argued that such a statement should be virtually an ad lib. But Arizona's territorial law allowed such testimony in a preliminary hearing and did not differentiate between a prepared reading and off-the-cuff remarks. Territorial law also said such a statement could be read without the witness facing cross-examination. This was an accepted point of Arizona jurisprudence and never questioned by the prosecution. Spicer clearly ruled within the bounds of the law, even if the law itself would not survive modern scrutiny.

The most untidy part of the Earps' preliminary hearing was that it failed to resolve the issue clearly enough to exonerate the Earps in the minds of the

Tombstone townspeople or to history. The thought of unarmed and surrendering cowboys being shot down in the streets made a much greater impression on the town's collective psyche than did the Earps' defense of marshals simply doing their duty to disarm the rowdy element. Shock value always has longer shelf life than tedious detail.

The McLaurys and Billy Clanton probably never really appreciated the severity of the situation in Tombstone that cold October day. They may well have simply been finishing their business before leaving town, and Billy appears to have been trying to mollify his hot-headed, drunken brother and get him out of town before trouble began. Large-scale shootouts in the streets almost never happened, even on the frontier, and even the more sensible of the group—Billy Clanton and Tom McLaury—could not have expected such a gunfight, if indeed they planned to leave town. Their rifles were still in their scabbards, and they were obviously unprepared for confrontation. The Earps had every reason to expect an attack after Ike's threats, then finding the cowboys congregated near Doc Holliday's rooming house and armed after the Earps understood Behan to say he had disarmed them.

Spicer did not condone the Earps' action. He criticized Virgil Earp for his choice of deputies. The head-bashing Earps may well have been far too zealous in their treatment of Ike Clanton and Tom McLaury. And they may have been injudicious in asking Holliday to join the fight. But when Wyatt, Virgil, Morgan, and Doc walked up Fremont Street to that vacant lot, their minds were acutely aware, primed by Ike Clanton's threats. They knew they were facing skilled gunmen, and they had to be prepared for action.

When the marshal's posse walked up the street, they found not just the Clantons and the McLaurys, but also Billy the Kid Claiborne, with sharpshooter West Fuller, Behan, and Billy Allen nearby. They were in the vacant lot next to Holliday's rooming house, where Clanton had earlier made threats against the dentist. Rumors of Ike's telegram for help floated through town. The Earps could have been facing eight men, with Fin Clanton and a dozen more riding into town at any minute. Never could they imagine that bold Billy Claiborne would break and run, or that Ike would make his dash. The Earps drew their pistols expecting far more opposition than they received.

The key points of the prosecution case rested on whether the Clantons and the McLaurys had their hands in the air, whether Tom McLaury was unarmed, and whether Holliday fired the first shot.

As to the alleged surrender, seemingly impartial witnesses said there were no hands in the air. Even Behan never claimed to have seen the Clantons or McLaurys raise their hands. Perhaps the most condemning statement appeared in the *Tombstone Nugget* the day after the fight:

> Sheriff Behan appeared on the scene and told Marshal Earp that if he disarmed his posse . . . he would go down to the O.K. Corral, where Ike and Billy Clanton and Frank and Tom McLowry [*sic*] were and disarm them. The Marshal did not desire to do this until assured that there was no danger of an attack from the other party. The Sheriff went to the corral and told the cowboys that they must put their arms away and not have any trouble. Ike Clanton and Tom McLowry said they were not armed, and Frank McLowry said he would not lay his aside. In the meantime, the Marshal

had concluded to go and, if possible, end the matter by disarming them, and as he and his posse came down Fremont Street towards the corral, the Sheriff stepped out and said: "Hold up boys, don't go down there or there will be trouble; I have been down there to disarm them." But they passed on, and when within a few feet of them the Marshal said to the Clantons and McLowrys: "Throw up your hands boys, I intend to disarm you."

As he spoke Frank McLowry made a motion to draw his revolver, when Wyatt Earp pulled and shot him, the ball striking on the right side of his abdomen. At the same time Doc Holliday shot Tom McLowry in his right side, using a short shotgun.[45]

Since *Nugget* editor and publisher Harry Woods served as Behan's under-sheriff, he probably interviewed Behan for the story, before the sheriff likely made little twists that could result in hanging the Earps and eliminating his political and romantic rival. The story indicates Frank McLaury made the move to draw. He may well have hesitated for just a moment, long enough for the quick-acting Wyatt to draw and shoot in unison with Billy Clanton.

And the *Nugget* story says Behan's words were "I have been down there to disarm them," a statement that is accurate but misleading. Behan had tried, unsuccessfully, to disarm the cowboys, and his report to the Earps would have served to confuse the situation and lead to the later bitter exchanges between Behan and the Earps.[46]

The absence of Tom McLaury's weaponry proved more damning. The defense showed that his loose-fitting blouse could well have hidden a gun, but no gun was ever found. Spicer chose to disregard the issue.[47]

Years later, Wyatt would say West Fuller's father told him that young Wesley had taken Tom McLaury's pistol after the fight.[48] Perhaps the most important indication that Tom McLaury had been armed came from Mrs. J. C. Collier, whose family had been visiting her brother-in-law, Boston Mill foreman John Collier. She traveled to Kansas City shortly after the fight and waited two months to tell her story of witnessing the fight from a half-block away at the corner of Fourth and Fremont.

[The Earps and Holliday] approached the cowboys and told them to hold up their hands. The cowboys opened fire on them, and you never saw such shooting as followed. Three of the five cowboys were killed and two of the officers seriously wounded. One of the cowboys after he had been shot three times raised himself on his elbow and shot one of the officers and fell back dead. Another used his horse as a barricade and shot under his neck.[49]

Mrs. Collier left town before telling her story, possibly unaware that her testimony would have provided critically important evidence; or possibly fearing the retribution of the cowboys. The statement of a cowboy firing from behind his horse could have referred to either Tom or Frank McLaury, and would have been clarified in court. Had she made the same statements under oath, it would have resolved many historical questions. Instead it is just another newspaper story.

As to the cowboy claim that Holliday fired the first shot with his nickel-plated revolver, even pro-Earp writers have accepted the possibility that the hot-headed dentist, not Wyatt Earp and Billy Clanton, shot first. However, it seems unlikely that the frail Holliday would have been holding the pistol in one hand and the shotgun in the other. Holliday certainly could not have controlled the shotgun's mule-kick with one arm. To have fired the first shot, Holliday would have had to perform a quick pistol-shotgun shuffle in the midst of a gunfight. This seems both unlikely and foolish.

The most likely scenario remains the way Wyatt and Virgil Earp told the story: that Billy Clanton and Wyatt fired at almost the same time, with the barrage following seconds later. The fight almost certainly erupted more out of happenstance than through plan or premeditation. Nerves had grown raw on both sides, and Behan's misstatement led the Earps to be surprised when they arrived at the lot to find Billy Clanton and Frank McLaury still wearing their guns. When Frank McLaury moved his hand toward his six-shooter, Wyatt Earp anticipated a draw and pulled his own gun. The cowboys were clearly unprepared to fight at that point, and Virgil Earp raised the cane and tried to prevent gunfire. Both sides feared firing too late would be far worse than firing too soon.

Ike Clanton may actually have saved Wyatt Earp's life with his strange grab at Wyatt. Had Ike not blocked Wyatt from the guns of Billy Clanton and Frank McLaury, Wyatt would have been the logical target for their fire. Ike then came through again for the Earps with his unbelievable story on the witness stand at a time when the Earps seemed almost certain to go to trial. No matter what Ike attempted, it always seemed to backfire.

Wyatt left no record of how the gunfight personally affected him or his brothers. They were never completely certain who shot whom, and figuring out the fatal bullets is guesswork without certainty. Most likely, Morgan's shot killed Frank McLaury; Holliday's shotgun killed Tom McLaury; and Morgan and Virgil got hits on Billy Clanton. By hitting Frank McLaury in the stomach, Wyatt fired the single most important shot, disabling the most dangerous cowboy on the lot. However, he did not fire a killing shot. It did not really matter. After seven years, off and on, as a lawman in Kansas and Tombstone, Wyatt Earp had fought a standup gunfight.[50] He had found a way to avoid killing the Dodge City troublemakers and the Tombstone toughs, but once the shooting began, there was to be no escape.

NEWS OF SPICER'S DECISION stirred the dusty town, with rumors of injustice and pending cowboy vengeance. Rumors live a life of their own, and all this talk of the Earps' involvement in the stagecoach robberies just would not die. It is a trait of human nature that many people believe the "inside story" over the facts, whether or not there is basis for the inside story.

Most Tombstone residents had been far too involved in their own pursuit of profits to take sides in the incomprehensible feud between sheriff and marshal. The dour Earps were never popular public figures, and Behan had always been one of the best-liked men in town. That Wyatt stole Behan's girlfriend could have only worked to discredit the Earps. Most townsmen knew the dead McLaurys only as ranchers before the fight and knew nothing of their links to the rustlers.

Most important, the Earps' actions had put Tombstone in jeopardy of cowboy retribution—they had not solved the problem, they had exacerbated it. From the perspective of many Tombstone residents, the Earps had shot the wrong men and needlessly threatened the town with attack. Gang war nearly broke out the night of Spicer's decision. Mrs. J. C. Collier said the cowboys planned a hit on the Oriental Saloon, where Wyatt ran the gambling concession.

"The night before we left, the cowboys had organized a raid on the saloon," Collier told the *Kansas City Star.* "Fifteen or twenty cowboys heavily armed were in the saloon. Just on the edge of town were almost thirty more and others were scattered around town ready to jump into the fight at the signal. A fire broke out and so rustled them that they gave it up for that time. You see we became intimately acquainted with a gentleman who boarded at the same hotel that we did and was in sympathy with the cowboys, and acquainted with all their plans. He told us about this raid being in contemplation and said that this was the second time they had been prepared to make a raid, and were thwarted by a fire breaking out and calling all the people out on the streets. He said, 'You're going away, and I don't mind telling you this.' "[51]

The cowboys had not made much trouble in town during the previous year, while Virgil and his brothers wore badges. The Earps' not so gentle buffaloings helped convince the cowboys they should find their fun in Charleston or Galeyville, rather than look into the cold blue eyes of the Earp brothers. But the townsfolk knew the shooting and Spicer's decision could combine to end the sense of tranquillity, especially with Virgil still hobbling and Morgan slow to recover. They could all be dancing in the nude before Curley Bill's six-shooters, or they might never dance again.

"There being two strong parties in the camp, of course this verdict is satisfactory to but one of them," Clara Brown wrote of the Spicer decision. "The other accepts it with a very bad grace, and a smouldering fire exists, which is liable to burst forth at some unexpected moment. If the Earps were not men of great courage, they would hardly dare remain in Tombstone."[52]

Tombstone was a town on the edge, and many citizens blamed the Earps for placing the citizenry in danger. They had not killed Curley Bill or Ringo or even Ike Clanton, just a 19-year-old boy and two brothers with no public reputation as troublemakers. Instead of the police protecting Tombstone's safety, the Earps had placed the city in jeopardy. The saloon talk turned the gunfight into undeserved death, and the blame fell to Holliday. "Doc Holliday is responsible for all the killing, etc., in connection with what is known as the Earp-Clanton imbroglio in Arizona," Ridgely Tilden wrote in the *Examiner.* "He kicked up the fight and Wyatt Earp and his brothers 'stood in' with him, on the score of gratitude. Every one in Tombstone conversant with the circumstances deprecates the killing of the McLaurys and Clanton."[53]

Gossip proved more dangerous than the drunken plans of the cowboys to attack the Oriental. Many Tombstoners believed the stories connecting Holliday and the Earps to the stage robberies and piping off gold that had never been stolen. Had the case gone to a full trial, the absurd tale would have been extinguished, but the uncertainties from the preliminary hearing worked against the Earps, with citizens ready to believe the worst.

It is a classically American story: The town complains about crime, the police overreact, and the citizenry turns against the law enforcers. It has been played out time and again in U.S. history, and the pattern keeps repeating.

While Justice Wells Spicer's decision may not have surprised the many townsmen who closely followed the case, it came as a blow to Behan and his supporters. Not only had the Earps been turned loose, with Virgil still holding his commission as U.S. marshal, but the sheriff had been publicly embarrassed for being caught in an apparent lie under oath when Williams testified that he heard Behan admit that one of the McLaurys had gone for his gun.[54] The only remaining hope for the anti-Earp faction was that the grand jury would investigate the gunfight. On the day of Spicer's decision, the *Nugget* leveled a blast that would echo through town. After noting the decision was not a surprise, the *Nugget* wrote:

> While it is true that in some instances the evidence was conflicting, the mass of testimony adduced by the prosecution has created a general desire that all the circumstances leading up and connected with the affair be thoroughly investigated. . . . As it has appeared from day to day in the columns of the local press the testimony has been eagerly scanned and commented upon and a decided revolution took place, many who at first upheld the Earp party becoming the most earnest in expressing a desire for a full examination.
>
> The remarkable document which appears in another column [Spicer's decision] purports to be the reasons which actuated the judge in his final action. But the suspicion of reasons of more substantial nature are openly expressed upon the streets, and in the eyes of many the justice does not stand like Caesar's wife, "Not only virtuous but above suspicion."
>
> The affair will probably be investigated by the Grand Jury, now in session, but from the confessed and known bias of a number of its members, it is not probable that an indictment will be found.[55]

The Earp brothers might have been free to continue their overbearing ways in the streets of Tombstone, but they carried a taint as possible robbers — even murderers — in the eyes of many of their townsmen. As ridiculous as Ike Clanton's testimony appeared in the courtroom, it provided enough innuendos to keep the gossip churning through the county and cast suspicion on the Earps. The Spicer hearing left many in Tombstone unsatisfied, a meal that does not quell the appetite.

Will McLaury stayed in town, waiting for the grand jury to determine whether it would take up the case. His wait was in vain. On December 16 the grand jury determined not to reverse Spicer's decision. The Earps would not be held for trial.

On the day he was released, December 1, Wyatt Earp registered to vote in Cochise County, a necessity since previous Pima County registration had to be updated. It would begin a most unsettling month for the family that came to Tombstone to find their fortune. Virgil and Allie, along with Morgan, moved into the Cosmopolitan Hotel, where Virgil and Morgan would be in a safer location to recover from their wounds. The hotel provided greater protection from a cowboy raid than the row of cabins where, apparently, Mattie and Jim's family remained most of the time. Wyatt seemed to move around from the hotel, to the family dwellings, to Fred Dodge's cabin.

The situation had been difficult for the entire Earp family. Back at the clan's San Bernardino County home in the newly demarcated town of Colton, a drunken Nicholas Earp began yelling "vile epithets" at lawyer Byron Waters, in a bank. The argument moved outside, with the elder Earp apparently following Waters down the street screaming. Waters finally knocked Nick down, and the city marshal arrived to lead the old man away. There is no record on what antagonized Nick Earp, but he certainly would have been sensitive to just about any remark about his sons.[56]

Something else had changed while Wyatt and Doc sat in Behan's jail during the hearing. Big-Nose Kate left town under very peculiar circumstances. Kate would later write that John Ringo had twice visited her room at Fly's boardinghouse, where she remained alone hoping for Doc's release. She said Ringo advised her to return to Globe. "He said the Clantons were watching for Doc to come to the room and intended to get him there," Kate wrote. When she told Ringo that she had no money, he gave her $50 to return to her home in Globe.

Remarkable as it seems, Doc Holliday's occasional wife kept company with an outlaw leader while her husband sat in a jail cell facing a trial that could lead to his execution. Almost poetically, Kate described Ringo as "a fine man anyway you took him. Physically, intellectually, morally. . . . His attitude toward all women was gentlemanly. He must have been a gentleman born. Sometimes I noticed something wistful about him, as if his thoughts were far away on something sad. He would say, 'Oh, well,' and sigh. Then he would smile, but his smiles were always sad. There was something in his life that only he, himself, knew about."[57]

Neither Earp nor Holliday mentioned Kate's friendship with Ringo in later interviews, but one can only imagine that Holliday did not take it kindly. The dentist and Ringo would emerge as intense enemies during the next few weeks, and there may well have been a personal grudge between the two because of Ringo's visits with Kate. How far that friendship developed can only be imagined.

Another development took place while the hearing mesmerized Tombstone. Off in Shakespeare, New Mexico, the citizens had taken it upon themselves to lynch two rustlers on November 9—Sandy King and "Russian Bill" Tettenborn. The *Epitaph* warned that such a hanging could scare a few cowboys out of New Mexico and direct them toward Cochise County.

Virgil, still incapacitated from his wounds and suspended by the city council, had been replaced by Jim Flynn as town marshal after the shootout, and Flynn sought election on his own in January. Mayor Clum and most of the vigilantes continued to support the Earps as the town divided into factions, but the ever-present, usually unspoken, threat of pending violence hung over Tombstone. Everyone knew that between oysters and ice cream socials, bullets could fly at any time.

TOMBSTONE
IN TERROR

T HE COWBOYS KEPT ONE SPECIAL ROOM at the Grand Hotel, with the shutters always closed except for one slat, which had been removed. Ringo, Milt Hicks, and others remained inside the room, keeping watch on the street. In early December, the story circulated that a man had entered the room to find one of the cowboys aiming his Winchester down at the street.

"What in the hell are you doing there?" the newcomer asked.

"I'm going to shoot that damned son of a bitch Rickabaugh," the gunman answered. Lou Rickabaugh, Wyatt Earp's partner at the Oriental, walked down the street, unaware of impending danger.

"Don't do that. He has never injured us. He has only spent his money for his friends the Earps, and that is what either you or I would do for our friends," the newcomer said.[1]

The *Epitaph* reported the story of the shuttered room weeks later, but that tale and others had swept through Tombstone earlier, leaving the pro-Earp faction feeling tense and targeted. Clum would later write: "It was rumored about town that several residents of Tombstone had been 'marked for death' by the rustler-clan, and I was assured that my name was written well up toward the head of their grim list, which besides myself included the Earp brothers, Doc Holliday, Judge Spicer, Tom Fitch, Marshall Williams and one or two others whose names I do not now recall. And in order that we might more fully realize the certainty of our fate, it was whispered that the Death List had been prepared with most spectacular and dramatic ceremonials enacted at midnight within the recesses of a deep canyon, during which the names of the elect had been written in blood drawn from the veins of a murderer. Not one of those whose names appeared on this blood red Death List would be permitted to escape from Tombstone alive. We did not believe all we heard. Nevertheless, we realized that the situation was extremely serious."[2]

In fact, the situation was so serious that Mayor Clum telegraphed to Acting Governor Gosper requesting guns to arm the Citizens Safety Committee. Gosper forwarded the message to President Chester A. Arthur and asked for repeal of the Posse Comitatus Act, saying that the release of the Earps "enrages cow-boys—new dangers apprehended. Give us use of the military and we will give you peace at the borders."[3]

Clum had business out of town, and it was a good time to leave. He wrote: "As for myself, I felt that if a fight should occur within the city, the rustler-clan would not overlook an opportunity to rub me out, but I did not believe— desperate as I knew them to be—that they would deliberately plan to murder me. I was mistaken. I did not then realize that their fight with the police on the streets of Tombstone was destined to go down in history as the first, last and only fight the rustlers would make in open daylight; that henceforth these desperado- outlaws would operate only as cowardly midnight assassins—and that the Fates would single me out as the first of their intended victims."

Shortly before the mayor mounted the stage on the evening of December 14 for a trip back East, he spoke with *Epitaph* business manager Oscar Thornton. "I told Mr. Thornton, of the *Epitaph* staff, that my greatest probable danger was that, if the rustlers knew I was going, they would pull off a sham stage-robbery, during which they would make it convenient to properly perforate my anatomy with a few spare bullets, and thus definitely blot me out of the picture."[4]

John P. Clum, mayor, editor, and postmaster, had already reached the peak of paranoia when he boarded the stage to the train depot in Benson with four other passengers. Clum took the middle seat, fearing he might have to make a quick exit. Jimmy Harrington drove the six-horse team, followed by an empty bullion wagon driven by Dick Wright, always called "Whistling Dick." The little party passed through Malcolm's Station, a lone dwelling and water stop four miles outside Tombstone.[5] The stage rolled into a gully and Harrington heard the cry "Hold," followed almost immediately by a volley of shots into the team of horses. The panicked team bolted and ran past the robbers.

"The four men with me dropped to the floor of the coach the instant the shooting began, and they called to me to do the same or I would be shot," Clum said. "But I had other plans. I had two six-shooters, and I was thinking fast how I might be able to use them to the best advantage if we were commanded to halt a second time."

Clum said he stepped out the door of the careening coach, with one foot on the step so he could jump off if the need arose. The stage bounced about a half- mile past the point of the gunshots, when Harrington pulled the coach to a stop. Whistling Dick had been shot through the leg, and one of the horses had been badly wounded and would have to be left behind. The two lead horses were cut from their harnesses, and the stage prepared to proceed.

"I stepped about fifty paces into the darkness to look and listen for sight or sound of horsemen," Clum wrote. "As I looked at the coach with its side-lights I realized that my presence in the coach only jeopardized the other passengers and that I was in a much better situation with my feet on the ground. Very promptly I decided to walk."

The four men inside the coach assumed Clum to be riding atop the stage or with Whistling Dick in the wagon, so his absence was not discovered until the stage pulled into Contention. News that Clum was missing was wired back to Tombstone, where Sheriff Behan and Charles Reppy, Clum's partner in the *Epi-*

taph, mounted a search party. They rode out and found two pools of blood and the carcass of a horse, but no Clum.

Rather than returning the five miles to Tombstone, Clum set off on a twenty-mile hike toward Benson. On that dark night he found himself walking through fields filled with mining pits, where one misstep could mean a fall to death. Clum later told a daring tale of his meander through the mines before arriving at the Grand Central Quartz Mill. The mine superintendent there relayed the message to Tombstone to tell of Clum's safety, then the mayor borrowed a horse and rode off. He said he rode through a camp of sleeping rustlers, who never stirred, and on to Benson.

"There has never been the least doubt in my mind that those rustlers intended to assassinate me in the darkness. They had declared that I should not leave Tombstone alive," Clum wrote. "In the gulch near where the attack was made was ample evidence that horses had been picketed there on several occasions, indicating that these would-be executioners had been anticipating my departure for about a week; that each evening all but one of the conspirators assembled at this rendezvous half an hour before the coach was due to pass that point; that one of the gang remained in the city to watch my movements, and that when this spy saw me enter the coach on the night of December 14th, he went quietly to his horse on the outskirts of the city, and then raced to the gulch and informed his pals that their intended victim was rapidly approaching the trap they had set for him."

Clum pointed out that the stage carried no valuables, and the absence of a shotgun messenger indicated there was nothing aboard worth stealing. His political foes scoffed at such a crazy idea as assassinating Clum, and made fun of the disappearing mayor. On December 16, the *Nugget* wrote: "At this writing, 2 A.M., several hours have elapsed, no tidings have been received from him. The prevailing opinion is he is still running."

The shaken Clum finally mounted the train for the trip East, where he encountered Thomas Gardiner, a founder of the *Los Angeles Times,* who wrote back to his paper: "The Hon. John P. Clum jumped the train I was on, looking paler than ever before. He had been shot at the night previous and was the worst scared man I have ever seen for some time. In passing Deming [N.M., a cowboy hangout] he crawled under a seat, tramp fashion, to keep the cowboys from raising his hair in case they happened to pass through the cars."[6]

Seward Chapin, sitting in for Clum at the post office, sent a message to Clum, balancing black humor with a warning of pending danger:

> Dear Johnny,
> Enclosed find copy of newspaper with letter to Spicer. You may get one when you get back.
> All is quiet and it rains, but there is another storm brewing, more than rain and hail. When it commences, look out for blood [written in red ink].
> Had a fine old hunt for you the night you left. Why didn't you get shot so we could find your remains or get some satisfaction out of our hunt?[7]

The *Nugget*'s frivolous line about Clum's flight enraged Reppy, who ran the *Epitaph* in Clum's absence. The *Epitaph* responded by saying:

Whether the affair was a brutal attempt at assassination or a bungling effort to rob the stage, the passengers and drivers had a narrow escape from death amidst the whistling bullets, and it is hardly presumable that the most ignorant Hottentot or brutal Apache would be so callous and unjust in the meagre light of yesterday morning's news, as to attempt to ridicule any person who was upon the coach. This was reserved for yesterday morning's Nugget, and when this is said the utmost dregs of possibility have been reached.[8]

In the same edition, the *Epitaph* ardently editorialized against the cowboys and said there could be no doubt the stage attack had been a plot to kill Clum, calling the assault "the greatest outrage ever perpetuated upon the traveling public of Arizona and is an event calculated to do more harm to the business interests of Tombstone than all other causes operating against us put together." The paper condemned the rumored death threats against the Earps, Spicer, Fitch, and Williams and railed for military intervention to quiet a situation that had grown outrageous: "The killings and attempted killings heretofore recorded in Tombstone and the surrounding country have been the outgrowth of drunkenness, wrongs or fancied wrongs, suffered at the hands of one or the other parties to the difficulties. This last has neither the one nor the other to plead in extenuation of the crime. As affairs now stand, there seems to be no remedy for our evils other than for the general government to step in and declare military law, and to keep a sufficient force here to maintain peace and order. It is evident the civil authorities are unable to put down the lawless element that surrounds us. The remedy is one that we exceedingly dislike to see applied, but where all other remedies fail we must accept the only remaining one, for life and property must be made as safe in Tombstone as elsewhere in the Union, or else all good men will abandon the place."

A day later, a letter in the *Epitaph* signed "A Citizen" made the stage robbery seem even more likely to have been an assassination attempt:

> The fact of firing about fifteen shots into the stage and the exclamation which two of the passengers heard them make of "Be sure to get the old bald-headed son of a b——," explains it all! They were assassins seeking to murder our mayor, and to do so even willing to murder a stage load of passengers. If there could be any doubt of their intent, it would be at once removed by knowing of the previous threats made by the gang to murder, not only the Earps but also Clum, Spicer, Williams, Fitch and Rickabaugh.

The letter-writer's interpretation was never verified by an independent witness, but it was enough to convince most of the purported members of the hit list that a bloodbath could be coming any day, and even walking the streets could lead to death. The Earps and the citizens who supported them believed that the cowboys' intent was murder. Fitch would be the lone dissenter, writing the *Epitaph* to say he had received no such letter; he then quickly changed his residence to Tucson.

The *Nugget* scoffed at the skittish citizenry, running letters stating that Clum had panicked when the bullets started flying and that he would be a wasted target for assassination because his term expired in three weeks anyway. The *Nugget* said that Clum's trip to Washington was to seek reappointment as Indian agent at the San Carlos reservation, and that the mayor flattered himself by thinking that any outlaw would think him worthy of assassination. But in the divided, uneasy community of Tombstone, no explanation could satisfy a citizenry that feared for its safety.

The attempted stage holdup incited another ugly happening. A day after the shots sounded, supervisor Milt Joyce stood in the Oriental Saloon talking with Virgil Earp. According to the *Nugget* account, "Joyce laughingly remarked to Earp that he had been expecting something of the sort ever since they [the Earps and Holliday] had been liberated from jail." This was an indirect accusation that the Earps were involved in the stage robberies. What followed was another confrontation that would further divide the Earps from the county political leadership. According to the *Nugget*, Virgil took offense and slapped Joyce in the face. Several heavily armed Earp partisans rushed forward, and Joyce took his leave with the words, "Your favorite method is to shoot a man in the back, but if you murder me you will be compelled to shoot me in the front." The *Nugget* praised Joyce for remaining calm, saying "his coolness and good judgment undoubtedly saved Tombstone from the disgrace of another bloody tragedy, all who are cognizant of the peculiar characteristics of the Earp party will readily admit."[9]

Something else happened in that December confrontation, and details are subject to question. Nearly a half-century later, Billy Breakenridge would recount that Joyce carried two six-guns into a saloon the following day. Confronting the Earps and Holliday, he asked if they wanted to fight as much as they did the day before. Joyce called the Earps bastards and said he was ready to fight, only to be stopped when Johnny Behan grabbed him from behind and arrested him. The *Epitaph* offers some confirmation, stating that Behan arrested Joyce for disturbing the peace, and the supervisor received a $15 fine. "Up to this time, Joice [*sic*] and Behan were close friends, but from this time Joice was very bitter toward him," Breakenridge wrote.[10]

In an already edgy town, a physical confrontation between the chairman of the board of supervisors and the suspended town marshal could only serve to further frazzle the nerves of the community.

THE *EPITAPH* AND THE *NUGGET,* with offices across the street from each other on Fremont, had never been good neighbors. The attack on Clum's stage set off a full-scale war between the two newspapers, with two San Francisco papers, the *Exchange* and the *Stock Report,* throwing in a few licks and reprimands. The *Exchange,* an afternoon business paper, covered Tombstone extensively for the moneyed interests in the big city. Copies, with puckish comments, analysis, and reports from correspondents, usually arrived in Arizona a day or two late. With its constant barbs at the cowboys, the *Exchange* did much to create the image of wild Tombstone in the minds of the West's movers and shakers. The smaller-circulation *Stock Report* sent off its weekly editions to Tombstone, also laced with attacks on the cowboy crowd.

After the *Nugget* gave its elaborate description of the funeral for the McLaurys and Billy Clanton, the *Exchange* lambasted the Tombstone paper, saying, "A

cow-boy met the natural fate of all cow-boys in Camp Rice yesterday, being riddled with bullets. The Tombstone Nugget should send down a special reporter
to weep over the remains. That journal is now recognized in Arizona Territory
as the great obituary organ of all slaughtered cow-boys."[11] The *Report* got even
nastier the week after the imposing funeral:

> Drooling and driveling over the three murderous young thieves who were executed
> in such an inexpensive and timely manner in Tombstone, the other day the Nugget
> remarks:
> "No unkind remarks were made by anyone, but a feeling of unusual sorrow
> seemed to prevail at the sad occurrence. Of the McLowery brothers we could learn
> nothing of their previous history before coming to Arizona. . . . They did not bear the
> reputation of being of a quarrelsome disposition, but were known as fighting men, in
> a quiet and orderly manner when in Tombstone."
> Was ever more cowardly trash penned by an editor? We don't believe what he
> says. We believe the citizens of Tombstone said the ruffians were served just right
> and were glad they were out of the way. The Nugget man himself could give no ex-
> planation of his latter sentence except that it was meant to please the surviving mem-
> bers of the gang the McLowerys belonged to. The Nugget ought to change its name
> to the Cowboy—The Tombstone Daily Cowboy.[12]

In three separate stories, the *Report* lambasted the *Nugget* for praising the grit
of the cowboys. "If we are to gush over the courage of murderers and desperadoes when they resist arrest, why not eulogize the skill of burglars, the alertness
of sneak thieves, the boldness of garroters, and the enterprise of incendiaries. To
read such stuff as this—it is from the *Nugget*—is enough to make the healthiest
feel sick. . . . We depend on the *Epitaph* to neutralize the effect of the Daily Cowboy's affection for Tombstone's ruffian population."

The Republican *Epitaph* delighted in the title "Daily Cowboy" and constantly pulled it up to joust the Democratic *Nugget* and its proprietor, Harry
Woods, the undersheriff who had allowed Luther King to escape after the
Philpott killing. Woods and editor Richard Rule responded with jibes against
the "Daily Strangler," a reference to the *Epitaph*'s boosting of the vigilantes in the
Citizens Safety Committee. Daily taunts passed back and forth, with the situation growing increasingly mean after the gunfight, then becoming decidedly
nasty after the attack on Clum's stage. With an election coming in early January,
the two Tombstone papers were playing for high stakes. Whoever controlled the
city government determined where lucrative advertising funds would be placed.
Under Clum's administration, the *Epitaph* received the city ads, while the *Nugget*
received most of the advertising in Democratic Cochise County. The papers
were playing for more than just civic pride when they battled each other.

Reading the papers a century later, it becomes evident each was devoted
more to furthering its own agenda than to reporting the news. The *Epitaph* rel-
ished every report of cowboy outrages in the county. The *Nugget* jousted with the
mayor's administration and ran numerous cracks about baldness, an obvious reference to Clum's state of pate. Because the Republican paper emphasized crime
reports, the *Nugget* charged the *Epitaph* with irresponsibility, saying such tidbits
would only serve to scare investors away from Tombstone.

Other players moved on the scene briefly in 1881. The *Tombstone Union* and the aptly named *Evening Gossip* both appeared during the year, and in December, ex-judge James Reilly—the same Reilly arrested by Wyatt Earp a year earlier—started the *Tribune* and used it as a forum to back his ardently Democratic views. Tombstone's *Tribune* also died a quick death. The *Nugget* and the *Epitaph* would be the major papers during the few months when Tombstone would shoot its way to national attention.

Newspapers were the lifeblood of a frontier town, chronicling events for the citizenry. Both the *Epitaph* and the *Nugget* had daily and weekly editions, with the weeklies usually mailed out to investors around the country to summarize local events and herald investment prospects. Local papers played a big role in molding public opinion and electing candidates.

The *Epitaph* gave Tombstone a legacy it could never escape in 1880 when it picked up an exchange from the *Harshaw Bullion* that said: "Tombstoners have a man for breakfast occasionally. They lock up the dead man in jail; the murderer has better accommodations."[13] With those few words, spread across the West, Tombstone became the town that had a "man for breakfast every morning." The comment referred to the citizenry awakening to find a dead body left over from the night before. The comment was inaccurate—most of the murders occurred out in the wilds of Cochise County, not within the bounds of Tombstone. But for the gentle sojourners who had landed in Tombstone, the violence was far more than they had ever expected. While the man-for-breakfast slogan had been applied to other towns before, latter-day writers would embrace the title and make it part of the Tombstone legacy. Inadvertently, the *Epitaph* had forever colored the image of Tombstone.

The *Nugget* unintentionally gave Tombstone another nickname. In July of 1881, a miner wrote to the paper and told of his friends who had come to Arizona seeking their fortune. Instead they wound up washing dishes or working at other menial jobs. Most people who came to Tombstone found a "Hell Dorado" rather than the fabulous riches of the legendary El Dorado, the miner wrote.[14]

That turbulent December of 1881 began with the Spicer decision and ended with bullets flying through the night air. In between came the attack on Clum's stage and a fierce political campaign that the papers believed would determine the future of Tombstone. Both papers were embarrassed early in the month when a letter from Acting Governor Gosper to U.S. Secretary of State James Blaine became public. Gosper wrote of the problems in the territory and said, as quoted in the *Epitaph*, "And back of this . . . I found two daily newspapers published in the city [Tombstone] taking sides with the deputy marshal and the sheriff, respectively. Each paper backing its civil clique and berating the other."[15]

An angry response sounded from Reppy, sitting in for Clum. "So far as the Epitaph is concerned, that is not true. With whatever feeling there has existed between the city and county officers we have never sympathized nor taken sides. It is true that the Epitaph has criticized the conduct of the sheriff's office, as it also has given it good words upon occasions. . . . If we have criticized the Sheriff's office unfavorably, it has been because there were ample grounds for so doing."

As the days of December passed, Tombstone grew even more tense. On December 15, the *Nugget* reported rumors that leaders of the anti-Earp faction had been threatened, but "a Nugget reporter investigated the matter, and found no such notifications had been received by the parties mentioned, although there is no doubt but threats have been freely indulged in by certain members of the self-appointed committee."

The *Epitaph* took seriously the threats against Spicer, Clum, and the Earps, but disbelieved the seriousness of threats against Behan and supervisor Milt Joyce. Spicer responded to his hate mail with humor, joking that he would like to meet the anonymous writer. "I think he would be an amiable companion — when sober." In his December 15 letter to the *Epitaph*, Spicer said he did not believe the Clantons were involved in the threats — "The real evil exists within the limits of our city." But the judge stated his position in an emotional and courageous reply:

> I am well aware that all this hostility to me is on account of my decision in the Earp case, and for that decision I have been reviled and slandered beyond measure, and that every vile epithet that a foul mouth could utter has been spoken of me, principal among which has been that of corruption and bribery. It is but just to myself that I should here assert that neither directly nor indirectly was I even approached in the interest of the defendants, nor have I ever received a favor of any kind from them. Not so the prosecution — in the interest of that side even my friends have been interviewed with the hope of influencing me with money, and hence all this talk by them and those who echo their slanders about corruption. And here, too, I wish to publicly proclaim every one who says that I was any manner improperly influenced is a base and willful liar.
>
> There is a rabble in our city who would like to be thugs, if they had courage; would [be] proud to be called cow-boys, if people would give them that distinction; but as they can be neither, they do the best they can to show how vile they are, and slander, abuse and threaten everybody they dare to. Of all such I say, that whenever they are denouncing me they are lying from a low, wicked and villainous heart; and that when they threaten me they do so because they are low-bred, arrant cowards, and know that "fight is not my racket" — if it was they would not dare to do it.
>
> In conclusion, I will say that I will be here just where they can find me should they want me, and that myself and others who have been threatened will be here long after all the foul and cowardly liars and slanderers have ceased to infest our city.
>
> History teaches us that in all contests between law and order on one side and lawlessness on the other, that the former invariably prevails. So it will be here, and that too very soon.

Angry over the dangerous state of affairs, the citizenry sought scapegoats. Many townsmen blamed the Earps for exacerbating the situation. The pro-Earp faction fell squarely against Behan and Woods. The San Francisco papers had branded the *Nugget* as "The Cowboy Organ," and the *Epitaph* did everything it could to make the nickname stick. And like-minded readers did their part, as in a December 17 letter to the *Epitaph* over the signature "A Citizen":

> The Nugget may think it is funny, and they are so cunning when they write their witty articles making merry over the pastimes and sports of their pretty pets — such as breaking up religious services and making the preacher dance at the mouth of their revolvers, insinuating improper motives to those who oppose them, and becoming exceedingly hilarious over a race for life made by our mayor to escape being assassinated by them. . . . The constant repetition of outrages by this gang of despera-

does known as cow-boys is driving capital, capitalists and enterprise out of the country, and for a journal published in our midst to treat these outrages with levity is an insult to the entire community.

Up in the big city, the *Exchange* took notice of how its favorite little mining camp had spun out of control. "Tombstone seems to be in a nice condition of disorder," the paper wrote on December 20. "The cowboys rule the town, and the Sheriff claims that he is powerless to keep that formidable nuisance within bounds. Of course the saloonkeepers take sides with the cowboys, for the latter, contrary to the custom of other classes of desperadoes, pay for their liquor, and spend twenty dollars where the law abiding citizen will spend one. There is . . . honor but there is certainly no peace of mind in being Mayor of Tombstone, as Mr. Clum discovered when the stage in which he was seated was riddled with bullets, all aimed with the design of leaving the Tombstone municipalities without a head. Yet there are soldiers enough in the territory to enforce order unless the people have made up their minds to let the cowboys run things to suit themselves."

As to the *Nugget*'s displeasure with the *Exchange*'s barbs, the big-city journal responded with a cute twist of words:

The Tombstone Nugget objects to the Daily Exchange calling it the "cowboy obituary organ," and says: "The cause of the alleged witticism arose from the fact that we published a full account of the funeral of Billy Clanton, Frank and Tom McLowry, which we consider was just and proper."

Thanks, esteemed contemporary, we are glad you have at last become convinced that the relegation of the Messrs. Clanton and McLowry to another world where there is probably no whisky to drink, no greasers to shoot and no stock to steal was the correct thing to do under the circumstances.[16]

As Christmas approached, the *Nugget* kept up its attacks on the Earps. "It is reported that the Earps have received intelligence of a lively mining camp in San Bernadino [*sic*] county, California, and that they contemplate making it the scene of their future operations," the *Nugget* commented on December 23. "Should the report prove true, it would be rather rough on the aforesaid mining camp in San Bernadino county."

On the same day, chief-of-police candidate Jim Flynn took out an ad in the *Nugget* to proclaim his independence from any of Tombstone's factions. Flynn had been Virgil Earp's deputy and was closely associated with the Earps, a fact he knew could prove a detriment in his upcoming election against Deputy Sheriff Dave Neagle.

Former judge Reilly, in a letter to the *Nugget*, made the strongest anti-Earp attack. He decried the effort to organize the vigilantes, called the attempt on Clum a sham, and implied that the Earp-Clanton gunfight had been premeditated assassination. "Holliday and the Earps have no fear (and to judge them by their acts neither have they any conscience, character or respect for the laws or the rights of their neighbors)."

Reilly said the vigilantes believe:

it is necessary not only to tolerate but encourage and sustain them in defying law, order and public opinion, and in shooting or driving away all who refuse to surrender their convictions, their liberties and their manhood at their dictation. For proof, is it, or is it not true, that the Earps and Holliday, while undergoing examination, threatened that when they get out they would make those men who called the killing of the McLowrys a murder, "take it all back," and that since they got out they have gone around town armed, abusing and picking quarrels with men of that opinion and have threatened many persons, telling them they had better leave.

If this be true, it clearly demonstrates the following propositions:

First, that the Earps and Holliday are not good men, and do not themselves believe that they were justified in that homicide, for if good men are unfortunate enough to be compelled to kill, they regret it; they are sorrowful, modest, and ask only to be allowed to live down the prejudice excited against them, but good conduct and submission to the laws. They do not, but by threats, assaults and braggadocio, attempt to bulldoze a whole community into giving countenance to their acts.

Second, that these men place no value on their own lives, have no conscience or respect for law or public opinion, and are therefore, reckless of and dangerous to the lives of others.

Third, that their supporters are foolish enough in their eagerness to suppress imaginary assassins and to correct evils at most, only temporary, and incident to all countries alike, and capable of redress by the ordinary methods—ballot box and jury box—to incur the danger of encouraging and assisting real assassinations."

Reilly said the attempt on Clum's life probably originated in "that thug's den, where they keep their implements of terrors," apparently a reference to the Oriental Saloon. He went on to intimate the Earps were somehow connected in the holdups. "I purposely avoid all comment on stage robberies, because my convictions on that subject . . . are a result of large frontier experience. . . . I am convinced that seven of every ten of the stage robberies committed in Arizona for the last fifteen years have been put up and engineered by the trusted agents of the post-office, of Wells, Fargo & Co.'s agents and agents of the stage companies. And Tombstone has been no exception to the rule. . . . And no men, or body of men, shall by force or threats, prevent me from expressing my convictions on this or other public subjects when or where I think proper."[17]

Such a passionate call from a former judge could not be easily dismissed in a terrorized town trying to understand its problems. Reilly was no Ike Clanton making a feeble defense of his misdeeds; this call came from a lawyer wearing the mantle of authority, even if Wyatt Earp had arrested him months earlier and publicly embarrassed him with a petition calling for his resignation.

Ned Boyle, the bartender at the Oriental who helped contradict Ike Clanton's testimony, responded to Reilly with equal passion:

The people of Tombstone have had the pleasure of reading another essay from the pen of that philanthropic expounder of justice, James Reilly; and as the old saying is, a burnt child dreads the fire, he takes the occasion to attack men that he never spoke to, and don't know this day when he meets them in the streets, but calling their place of business a den of thugs. These gentlemen happened to be associated in business with one of the Earp brothers and old Vox Populi Vox Dei Reilly takes occasion, for the benefit of a lot of office seekers and bunko sharps, to champion their cause, and throws his billingsgate on the Earp brothers and Holliday. But, considering the source it comes from, they treat it with contempt. . . . Reilly was charged when he lived in Yuma with being connected in a stage robbery and the taking of

Wells-Fargo's box, he likely knows what he is talking about when he says, "Mr. Editor, I purposely avoid all comments on stage robberies." You old fox! Well you may avoid blowing that good Samaritan breath of yours on a spark, as it may kindle into a blaze to your detriment, but the tax-paying citizens of this town and county will remember your assault on Mayor Clum for trying to save his life from a band of murdering cow-boys. You speak like a hired blackmailer who is paid to assail any and everybody who is opposed to that class of outlaws. As to the Earps you have so much to say about, I shall speak only of one of them, Wyatt Earp; he is one of the partners of the firm I am working for, and a more liberal and kind-hearted man I never met. As to my working in a dive, or in your language a thug's den, let me say you have not the manliness about you to meet one of the Earps face to face and speak your piece like a man, but you are like many others in this camp who talk behind their backs; but, as they don't want to get into any newspaper talks with the likes of you, and as the case suits me, I denounce you as a lying mountebank when you call the place I work in a thug's den. I throw down the gauntlet to you, and then I will show you who James Reilly is.[18]

With Reilly's help, the *Nugget* succeeded in making the Earps seem a liability to Tombstone, and the repeated attacks were unnerving to the family. "We have two weekly and two daily papers," Louisa Houston Earp, Morgan's common-law wife, wrote to her sister. "The *Epitaph* is our friend and the *Nugget* our bitterest enemy. As you will see by the *Epitaph*. I would not send the *Nugget*, it has so many falsehoods in it, you would almost feel like doubting the other paper."[19]

As December came to an end, the factions hardened. On one side were the Earps, Clum, and a belief in vigilante justice and strict law enforcement to rid Tombstone of a serious threat from a thought-to-be large, organized gang of desperadoes. On the other side were Behan, Woods, and Reilly, defending the sheriff's office and due process of the courts while advocating that the evils of vigilantism and brutal enforcement outweighed short-term gains in safety; that vigilante killing of a few men was too high a price to pay for protection from the overrated cowboys. And, of course, both sides had a significant amount of self-interest in determining who governed and received the plum appointments.

The streets of Tombstone daily grew more dangerous for the Earps. Members of the family would tell a strange story about someone in women's clothing who came to the door of one of their cabins, but left suddenly when Jim answered. Wyatt would come to believe it was a man dressed as a woman, ready to shoot should he answer. The family gradually packed up and moved into the seeming safety of the Cosmopolitan Hotel, across the street from the cowboy's favorite hotel, the Grand.

Sadie Marcus, the dancer turned love interest to both Behan and Wyatt Earp, apparently remained in Tombstone for some time after her breakup with Behan, gradually growing friendlier with Wyatt. Neither Sadie nor Wyatt left a record of what happened between them during those months, and the enigmatic Sadie did everything she could in later years to protect her secrets. During the autumn and winter of 1881, she and Wyatt apparently formed enough of a friendship to draw the ire of Sheriff Behan and the attention of Mattie and the rest of the Earp women.

With the gunfight controversy surrounding him, Wyatt had little chance of winning an election for sheriff in '82. He had been Behan's most likely opponent, but the *Nugget* had picked him apart so cleanly that he had barely a dream of mounting a campaign, although he still planned to run. Virgil, hobbled by his leg wound, wisely chose not to enter the race for chief of police, and the only law job that would remain for the Earps would be Virgil's post as U.S. marshal, with Wyatt serving as his deputy. Wyatt kept busy running his faro game, and the brothers invested in mining properties, water claims, and the like.

In late December, Tombstone celebrated the opening of a new theater that would later be called the Bird Cage Variety Theatre, a dandy little stage that hosted bawdy performers to the delight of miners and cowboys.

The Earps could only hope for a happier new year in 1882, even though the threat of danger still hung over Tombstone. With most of the family sequestered at the Cosmopolitan, there seemed a degree of safety until a young clerk at the Grand, Jack Altman, noticed the unusual visits of cowboys Pony Deal, Curley Bill, Ike Clanton, Ringo, and several others to the room they kept at the Grand, the same room from which the intended attack on Rickabaugh nearly took place. Altman also discovered that a slat had been removed from the room's window shutters, giving a good view of the Earps' room across the street at the Cosmopolitan. The Earps would be an easy target, when the assailants found the opportunity. Altman slipped across the street to warn the Earps of impending danger.[20] Even forewarned, the Earps were not prepared. Such tips had become commonplace, Virgil recalled: "When Morgan and I got well, reports came in daily that we would be assassinated at the first opportunity."[21]

Three nights after Christmas, at about 11:30 P.M., Virgil Earp headed back toward the Cosmopolitan. "I stepped out of the Oriental Saloon to go to the hotel, when three double-barreled shotguns were turned loose on me from about sixty feet off," Virgil said.

The blasts came from between charred boards of a burned-out building across the street. As Virgil fell into the street, several men dashed out of the building, ran down Fifth, and disappeared into the darkness.

"Cries of 'There they go,' 'Head them off' were heard," Parsons wrote in his journal. "But the cowardly, apathetic guardians of the peace were not inclined to risk themselves, and the other brave men all more or less armed did nothing."

Three men raced down Toughnut Street, then into a gulch behind town. The blasts knocked Virgil into Fifth Street, with streams of buckshot passing through a window at the Eagle Brewery. The *Epitaph* said: "It is simply a miracle that Mr. Earp was not instantly killed, as in the darkness, with the simple aid of a bit of lighted paper the marks of nineteen shots were found on the east side of the Eagle Brewery and in the awning posts."[22]

Virgil pulled himself to his feet and staggered into the Oriental to find Wyatt. The marshal was helped to his room and two doctors were summoned. Virgil's left arm took most of the assault, with a longitudinal fracture between the shoulder and elbow. He was also hit from the rear, left of the spinal column, but that shot missed all vital organs.

Parsons delivered medical supplies to the hotel room and found a most unpleasant scene: "Hotel well guarded, so much so that I had hard trouble to get to Earp's room. He [Virgil] was easy. Told him I was sorry for him. 'It's Hell, isn't it!' said he."

Virgil's wife, Allie, was distraught. "Never mind, I've got one arm left to hug you with," Virgil told her, as Parsons recorded.

The next morning crowds assembled outside the Eagle Brewery to view the damage and speculate on who the perpetrators were. Parsons guessed that Ike, Curley Bill, and Will McLaury were the guilty parties. "Bad state of affairs here. Something will have to be done," Parsons wrote.

Up in the hotel room, the doctors conferred on a major decision. They had to decide whether to take the arm off completely or to try more surgery. They removed 5 1/2 inches of splintered bone from Virgil Earp's upper arm. One report said chances were four in five that Virgil Earp would die from his wounds.

The *Epitaph* reflected the terror in Tombstone, writing, "This further proves that there is a band of assassins in our midst. . . . The question naturally arises, who will be the next subject? And a further question, how long will our people stand for this sort of thing? It is no fault of these damned assassins that several persons were not killed in their dastardly attempt to murder a United States officer last night; for there were many people in the Eagle Brewery, over the heads of whom the passing shots flew on their course. A few inches lower and there would have been corpses prostrate upon the floor in place of frightened people wondering what had happened to cause this bombardment."[23]

Will McLaury, whom Parsons had suspected of pulling a trigger, had left town two days earlier to return to Fort Worth and was quickly dropped from the list of suspects. Many years later he would again become a suspect when a letter appeared hinting that he may have paid for the assassination attempts on the Earps. Lawyer McLaury wrote to his father in Iowa saying of his dealings in Tombstone: "My experience out there has been very unfortunate—as to my health and badly injured me as to money matters—and none of the results have been satisfactory—the only result is the death of Morgan and crippling of Virgil Earp." While not conclusive, it seems possible that the surviving McLaury brother instigated and funded the cowboys' retribution campaign.[24]

Wyatt had no trouble identifying suspects. "Virgil saw Stilwell go into the vacant building just as he was coming out of the Oriental," he wrote to Lake. "We found Ike Clanton's hat, that he dropped in getting away from the rear end of the building."[25]

Ike, ever the master of mess-up, apparently lost his hat with his name in it as he ran from the burned-out building. Ike Clanton had that remarkable facility to make a muddle of just about everything he undertook, then emerge as a survivor blaming everyone else. No matter what Ike tried, he just couldn't get it right.

The next afternoon Wyatt wired U.S. Marshal Crawley Dake in Phoenix:

> Virgil was shot by concealed assassins last night. His wounds are fatal. Telegraph me appointment with power to appoint deputies. Local authorities are doing nothing. The lives of other citizens are threatened.
>
> WYATT EARP

Dake responded immediately, telegraphing Wyatt Earp the appointment as Deputy U.S. Marshal, with the authority to select his own deputies. Virgil and Leslie Blackburn continued to hold commissions as deputy marshals, but Wyatt Earp had the badge and the power behind it. Now he could challenge the assassins with federal authority behind him. That would have to wait, however, as he remained quietly in Tombstone for ten days watching over Virgil and his family.[26]

With Virgil Earp crippled and the family in chaos, the *Nugget* made the Earps the issue of the political race. In the late nineteenth century, local campaigns were usually short, lasting three weeks or a month, with all the excitement packed into a few days. In Tombstone in January 1882, the politicos, led by the two politician-editors, battled for political prizes. The Earps had been forced out of politics by gunfire and public sentiment. As Allie nursed Virgil in their room at the Cosmopolitan, the *Nugget* went at the Earps.

January began with another letter from Reilly to the *Nugget*, railing against the *Epitaph* and its pro-Earp bias, calling Clum's paper "a traitor to its supporters."

> The Epitaph has devoted all its power . . . to give to the world the opinion that none but fighting officers could preserve the peace and none but fighting citizens could live in peace in Tombstone, and for this purpose it has continually praised the Earps, and called their gambling or worse quarrells [*sic*], "brave deeds in the interest of law and order," took their texts from them or from the boyish fears of Mr. Marshall Williams or men equally blind. It has sent telegrams all over the country giving its distorted views of occurrences in Tombstone, and then gathered up the publications, the result of its own falsehoods, and published them here in Tombstone with a view to justify its course.

The *Epitaph* belonged to the new Associated Press, which received news stories from around the country, then condensed them and sent them out to member papers. Both Tombstone papers received AP dispatches, but most of the news from Tombstone came directly from the *Epitaph*. Reilly's charge was not totally accurate, because such papers as the *San Francisco Exchange* and *San Diego Union* had correspondents in Tombstone, and the *Exchange* received reports from both the *Nugget* and the *Epitaph*.

Reilly's letter went on to charge that Philpott's murder was "the result of a well-concocted scheme, put up by the men who knew all about Wells, Fargo & Company's business, to rob the stage and kill Robert Paul, whose known honesty, energy and bravery was dangerous to the clique that hoped by a monopoly of gambling, stage robbing and dead-fall keeping to control the politics and business of Tombstone."

Reilly accepted the *Epitaph*'s condemnations of the county government but added, "If the Epitaph had with as much zeal and vigor attacked the malfeasance of United States Deputy Marshal Earp, Deputy Sheriff Earp and City Marshal Earp, when they carried in their pockets half a dozen warrants against their friends with whom they were gambling and drinking without arresting them . . . then the McLowrys would be alive today; the last act of the drama would have not occurred; Holliday and the Earps whatever their propensities might be, would never have dared to gratify these propensities under the cloak of official duty; and Tombstone would not to-day be the unwilling asylum of four or more men whose lives must be a burden to them and who cannot hope to live in it except by continuous bloodshed."[27]

Amid election passions, the *Tucson Journal* provided rumors that a band of New Mexico cowboys were riding into Arizona to make it their base after the people of Shakespeare showed they meant to drive away the outlaws by hanging two rustlers, Sandy King and Russian Bill. The *Tucson Star* heard and reported a different but equally dangerous scenario. "It is rumored, on good authority, that the cow-boys are disposing of all their stock and ranches in Arizona with a view of emigrating elsewhere." The paper concluded, "If this is true, there is liable to be still warmer times in Tombstone than yet experienced."[28]

Up in San Francisco, the *Stock Report* called for the citizens of Tombstone to take action and stop the cowboys quickly and with finality:

> Hitherto, cowboyism has been considered a good joke in Tombstone. Men who personally are law-abiding citizens and holding good positions in the community would argue that the cowboys were a benefit to the town, as they circulated money and another element that gives the cowboys a strong backing is composed of men who reap the profits of the cattle raids. It is a poor argument that ill-gotten money expended recklessly by thieves, gamblers and murderers makes a town prosperous. It creates a state of society that in the long run will cost the taxpayers more than was ever realized by the circulation of the cowboys' spoils.
>
> When an attempt is made to assassinate the Mayor of the town and a United States Deputy Marshal is assassinated in the public street, it is time for respectable citizens to take the law into their own hands, if the officers are powerless to enforce the laws. Vigilance Committees have often proven salutary in such case, and this seems to be one of the cases in which a Vigilance Committee and a few hangings would be justifiable.[29]

The *Epitaph*, with Clum still in Washington, battled hard to make the election political rather than an attack on the Earps. The paper emphasized the "Ten Per Cent Ring," which skimmed 10 percent of the tax money to reward civic officials. Reilly, a candidate for city recorder, became the focus of many attacks, although he was not part of the *Nugget*-endorsed People's Independent Party ticket. In the mayoral race, the *Epitaph* supported lumberyard owner Lewis W. Blinn over John Carr, who received the heavy endorsement of the *Nugget* and the People's Independent Party. Behan's respected deputy Dave Neagle had the *Nugget* endorsement for marshal over Flynn, who never succeeded in distancing himself from the Earps. It would be one of the grand oddities in politically confused Tombstone that the *Nugget* would support Carr, a Republican who appeared neutral on the Earp issue, while the *Epitaph* supported pro-Earp Democrats Blinn and Flynn in an election where party membership became of little importance.

"If the Ten-per-cent Ring get control of the city government as it already has that of the county, there will be no other way for a man to live in this community except to join the ring or the rustlers," the *Epitaph* editorialized. "The fact that the Daily Cow-boy and the Ten-per-cent Ring are advocating the claims of John Carr for mayor and Dave Neagle for city marshal is a sufficient reason why all citizens who would have the city government conducted differently from that of the county should vote against them."[30]

The *Nugget* came up with the charge that if Flynn won, "he will shortly after the election resign his position, and thereupon the new Mayor, should it be Mr. Blinn . . . will proceed to fill the vacancy. . . . The statement is made that an agreement has been entered into to this effect, and further that one of the Earps has been mutually agreed upon as the appointee. We have the utmost confidence in the reliability of our informant . . . and there is little doubt that a vote for Flynn is equivalent to a vote for a new lease of power for the Earps, and the citizens of Tombstone know full well what that implies."[31]

On election day, January 3, the *Nugget* ran the squib, "Doc Holliday and the Earps are solid for Blinn and Flynn. So is the Daily Strangler." Another squib said, "Jim Flynn is a good fellow and has many friends in Tombstone, but he is a victim of disreputable associations. Handicapped as he is by the support of the Stranglers' organ and the gang of thugs who follow in its wake, his chances of election are now conceded as hopeless." But most important, the Nugget ran the damning, "The election will to-day decide whether Tombstone is to be dominated for another year by the Earps and their strikers. Every vote against the People's Independent Ticket is a vote in favor of the Earps. Miners, business men and all others having the welfare of our city at heart should remember this."

Everything the *Nugget* said seemed to be remembered as the miners and merchants of Tombstone trooped to the polls. The election proved a triumph for the *Nugget* and the anti-Earp faction, with Carr winning the mayoral race, 830–298 over Blinn. Neagle carried the marshal's race, 590–434, and People's Independent candidates won three of the four city council seats and the treasurer's post. Reilly lost in a close election for city recorder.

"Exeunt Earps!" the *Nugget* headlined in bold type. The paper called it, "A triumph of the people over the Stranglers. The honest masses of people were jubilant at the complete discomfiture of the open and insidious enemies of the prosperity of our city, and the Stranglers' organ . . . no doubt many votes were cast for the People's ticket through sheer disgust at the ruinous and wanton course pursued by the Stranglers' organ."

The *Nugget* also ran an erroneous exchange from the *Las Vegas Optic* saying, "Wyatt Earp, a former Las Vegas slumgullion, got his stomach full of buckshot at Tombstone three or four days ago, and has been planted for worm feed. He was previously a policeman at Dodge City under Bat Masterson and had something to do with Fort Worth, Texas, before coming to Las Vegas." While the *Nugget* obviously knew the falsity of the rumor, printing the story would help to discredit the Earps.

Even up in the territorial capital, the voting made big news. The *Prescott Democrat* took the opportunity to offer its own repudiation of the Earps.

> The election in Tombstone we consider a decided victory for law and order, and we feel almost certain that the disturbing elements which have been so great a drawback to its advancement, will hereafter take a back seat. The fact that men of such insignificance, socially, morally and mentally, as the Earps have been given so much prominence, shows a very unhealthy, not to say unnatural, state of feeling in the bonanza camp. Those distinguished swash bucklers honored Prescott with their presence some two years ago, and the odor of their unsavory reputation still taints the nostrils of our citizens. They came here from Kansas with an evil name, which seemed to be their only stock in trade. . . . We hear it stated that they championed assiduously the defeated ticket in the late election; if so, it is a good thing for the peace, progress and security of the people of Tombstone that the ticket was defeated. When

desperadoes attempt to dictate to respectable people, it is time they were squelched, and there is no more effectual way of doing it than by the ballot.[32]

The *Epitaph* barely covered the election results and editorialized, "The election is happily past, and the electors are again free to pursue their daily vocations without recurrence to the subject as to who shall govern us for the next two years. The result is not just what we should have been pleased to see, and not what we labored for, but recognizing the fundamental principles upon which our government is based—that the majority shall rule—we acquiesce in the result without a murmur, and have only the kindliest feelings and best wishes for the officers elect, and will support them in every effort for the promotion of the public good."

A day later, the *Epitaph* said its Citizen's Party ticket "did not fare so badly after all, securing as it did the election of five good men." This was a rather remarkable statement, since the ticket's only important win was Judge Albert O. Wallace for city recorder.

The Earps could not have paid more than passing attention to the campaign. Up in their rooms at the Cosmopolitan, the family held a vigil around Virgil. While Virgil battled for life, business continued in the streets outside. Saloons ran day and night, faro tables remained in perpetual motion, and the election kept just about everyone's attention.

Harry Woods and his *Nugget* seemed to have had everything their way. By all appearances they were rid of the Earps in town politics, and their candidates had just emerged with a grand victory. The paper editorialized: "After the People's Independent candidates shall have assumed the offices . . . it is quite possible that there will not be so many walking arsenals perambulating our streets." A day after the election, the Nugget made a promise to the people:

> There need be no fears of turbulence or violence on the part of the lawless elements of Tombstone in the future. Our Mayor-elect is a man of considerable adipose tissue and he will suppress 'em. He will set down on 'em, as he did on one Mr. Blinn yesterday.

The *Nugget*'s promise would be unrealistic. The turbulence in Tombstone had only just begun.

HAD JIM HUME NEVER LIVED IN THE WEST, the Westerns would have had to create him. Hume perfectly fit the image of a frontier hero: smart, brave, canny, and building a glorious reputation. As Wells, Fargo's chief special officer he had spent more than a decade running down stage robbers in California and Nevada, and usually received the proper degree of respect from the press for his achievements. Wells, Fargo was not amused when its No.1 hero was held up to ridicule.

Hume was two weeks shy of his 55th birthday on January 7, 1882, when he settled down for a pleasant little Sunday-night stage ride from Benson to Tombstone along with eight other passengers and the driver, Jack Sheldon. Stage robberies had become commonplace in Cochise County, and only a few hours earlier $6,500 had been stolen from another stagecoach. But this stage carried no Wells, Fargo box, and no shotgun messenger sat next to the driver.

As the stage rolled on between Contention and Tombstone at about one o'clock Sunday morning, two men stepped out of the shadows and ordered the driver to halt and get off the stage. The robbers passed among the passengers, taking about $1,500. Most notably, they took two fancy pistols and $75 from Hume, a serious humiliation for the man in charge of keeping stage robbers away from Wells, Fargo treasure.

Hume visited the *Epitaph* office to detail the holdup and said he and most of the other passengers had fallen asleep when the stage pulled to a stop. "Before he was sufficiently awakened to take in the situation the driver was holding the leaders and the outside passenger was standing near the wheelers," the *Epitaph* story said. The shapes of the driver and passenger in the moonlight made it appear they belonged to the robber party, leading to the conclusion that there were four in on the heist instead of two, according to Hume's story in the *Epitaph*. "One of the robbers held a shotgun at the window on the inside passengers and forbade any one of them to stir on pain of instant death. Mr. Hume says that to attempt to use his revolvers under the circumstances—and being under the impression there were four robbers—would inevitably involve a sacrifice of the lives of several of the passengers, and as there was none of his employers' treasure on board, he considered he would be acting the part of wisdom to refrain from violent measures."

The bandits, disguised with black cloth masks, were disappointed at the absence of a treasure box, then proceeded to quickly fleece the passengers, missing a good deal of the money. The *Epitaph* said the robbers "though firm in their demands, were polite in their language and were evidently no novices at the business."[33]

Wells, Fargo took the unusual measure of offering a $300 reward, although none of its funds had been stolen. The mighty express company did not like the idea of having its top star disgraced, and it could not have enjoyed the situation the next morning when the *San Francisco Exchange* ran the story under the headline, "An Inefficient Officer," then lampooned Hume in another item:

> Tombstone must be a delightful place to live. The decent citizen if he remains in town is almost certain to be shot down in the streets by cowboys, and if he attempts to leave he is sure to be robbed in the stage. Between the two the life of the average Tombstoner must be a burden. By the way, it does not occur to us that Detective Hume, of Wells, Fargo & Co., distinguished himself greatly last night when he allowed a brace of highwaymen to relieve him of a pair of big revolvers. A man of Hume's reputation and supposed 'sand,' armed to the teeth as he was, should have been able to take care of two highwaymen.[34]

According to Fred Dodge, secret agent for Wells, Fargo, Hume did more than just turn over his guns while the robbers were doing their deed—he kept up a string of banter while they were fleecing the passengers, doing a good enough job to keep them entertained while he got a read on their speech and physical characteristics. When Hume reached Tombstone, he saw Dodge and asked him to summon Wyatt Earp. Dodge recalled: "I sent for Wyatt at once, and Jim Hume called me into the back room where Wyatt soon joined us, and Hume gave such an accurate description of the robbers . . . such as height, build and voice and other details, that I could almost have named the men. . . . And they always held out at Charleston."

The rustlers kept a hangout at Jeptha B. Ayers's saloon in Charleston, and Dodge would reveal years later that Ayers was one of his paid informants. Dodge and Earp told Hume of the likelihood of finding the robbers there, then cautioned him to stay away. Wyatt and Morgan left Virgil's bedside to make the chase, along with Fred Dodge and another deputy. They first checked an area in the foothills of the Huachucas where the suspects kept cabins, then moved on to Charleston.

Much to Dodge's surprise, he saw a familiar form when the posse reached Charleston: "As we dismounted, we saw Hume in the saloon leaning with his back against the bar, and as we entered I saw two of the men who were in the robbery, one on each side of Hume. Hume gave us no salutation, only to say, 'we were just about to have a drink when you speeding gentlemen rode up. Will you join us?' Which we did. This was not the safest place in the world for us to be in, and we took our places at the bar that were the most advantageous to us in case anything started. I took a schooner of beer and when Ayers was waiting on me, he was joking me about drinking slop etc.—and in the meantime managed to indicate to me with his eyes the two men that were in the robbery."[35]

When Dodge had a chance to talk with Hume, he learned that Hume had come to Charleston on his own. While he was convinced that two men standing nearby had been guilty of the robbery, he said that there was not sufficient evidence to arrest them. Dodge did not name the robbers, although he knew who they were. The *Epitaph* would later identify the prime suspect as Alex Arnold, a lesser light among the cowboy crowd. The robbers had taken more than cash; they stole Hume's dignity.

Another robbery, 34 hours earlier, hit Wells, Fargo in an equally sensitive area, because the company had to make up any losses caused by the bandits. On the night of January 6 at about three o'clock in the morning, three men stepped onto the deserted road from Hereford to Bisbee, near the Clanton ranch, and fired a volley of shots at the moving coach. Shotgun messenger Charley Bartholomew and a passenger jumped off, and the stage circled onto a back road toward Hereford, Bartholomew told the *Nugget*. After an exchange of shots, Bartholomew and the passenger ran back and again mounted the coach, which raced on with Bartholomew firing shots at the pursuers. The robbers finally maneuvered around the stage and stopped it from the front; they then ordered that the strongbox be thrown down. They broke the box open, took the $6,500 and Bartholomew's shotgun, then threatened driver W. S. Waite, saying that if he ever leaked their identity he would be killed. He kept their secret, but the *Los Angeles Times* would later identify the prime candidate as "a desperate character named Ringo, who is suspected of being one of the party who lately robbed the stage near Bisbee. He is one of the ringleaders of the cowboys." No other record has been found linking Ringo to the robbery.[36]

The two weekend robberies gave further evidence that the Earps' shootout on Fremont Street had done nothing to end the crime wave in Cochise County.

In fact, the situation had only grown worse. More and more no-accounts seemed to be drifting into Cochise County at a time when traditional crime had become less profitable. The Mexican army had built three outposts and increased border patrols, limiting the cowboys' access to all that good Sonoran beef. In addition, the Clanton-McLaury fencing operation was in disarray after the gunfight. It is likely that smuggling diminished because of the obvious outlaw dangers and the Mexican patrols. The cowboy-criminals needed new targets, and everyone in Cochise County became a potential victim. Crime problems were only getting worse, and many of the residents blamed the Earps for stirring up the cowboys and setting off the crime wave. Rumors became rampant that the family had played some obscure role in the robberies.

Wells, Fargo never believed any such misinformation. Back in San Francisco, Wells, Fargo management was flat-out mad. Their shipments would have to be delivered or they would be required to replace the losses. Wells, Fargo did not like losing shipments, and it did not like paying rewards. Shortly after the robberies, rumors began circulating that Wells, Fargo planned to remove operations from Tombstone, a move that would have crippled commerce in southern Arizona. The company carried virtually all shipments of bullion and cash to and from southern Arizona and insured against loss or theft. If Wells, Fargo pulled out, the mine operators would have been left to try and transport their own payrolls through dangerous backroads or hope that another company would assume the risk.[37]

While Hume denied the rumor of a pullout from Tombstone, he did say the company planned to remove routes through Bisbee and Benson, "the risks being greater than the profits." That was troubling news in itself. Wells, Fargo had in the past employed the tactic of starting rumors of withdrawing offices to spur the local citizenry to demand better law enforcement.[38] In this case, rumors and the reality of a Bisbee pullout were enough for some Tombstoners to join the call for action. A correspondent to the *Los Angeles Times* bemoaned the impending loss of Wells, Fargo and called for the federal government to use troops to scour the country for criminals and protect the roads.[39] However, such martial law tactics were not unanimously desired. Other factions in Tombstone believed that the whole notion was overblown and civilian authorities could do just fine at guarding the county.

Dake's appointment of Wyatt Earp as his new deputy did not meet with acclamation in the territory. The *Prescott Democrat* denounced the decision: "We join with other Territorial papers in calling the attention of Marshal Dake to the impropriety, to say the least, of appointing one of the Earps to the position of Deputy United States Marshal. If he knew the facts, we are satisfied that a decent regard for public opinion would restrain him from placing such character in so responsible an office."[40]

The Earp controversy had already spread through Arizona and would continue to build. The Democratic press had accepted Harry Woods's analysis of the situation and would print exchanges from the *Nugget*, probably unaware of the odd machinations in Tombstone, where the undersheriff served as editor amid intense political and personal rivalry. Troubled Tombstone grew even more confused. Many prominent townspeople lived in fear of every step, with any shadow in a dark alley providing the imagined potential for instant death.

Billy Breakenridge, Behan's deputy, recounted a rainy night when he patrolled the streets and walked into a gun barrel, which was placed against his breast. Frank Stilwell carried the gun and told the deputy he had heard that a "certain party" had been boasting that he would kill Stilwell that night, but Stilwell would do the killing if he spotted the other party first. Breakenridge told Stilwell that he was already in too much trouble and should head home immediately. As Stilwell left, Breakenridge saw Doc Holliday on his way home, the possible target of another assassination plan. "It flashed through my mind that I had inadvertently saved Doc Holliday's life that night," Breakenridge said.

Back in the Cosmopolitan, Virgil gradually grew stronger, although reports of his impending death kept appearing into mid-January. Deputy Marshal Wyatt Earp found himself out of the saloon business when Milt Joyce, head of the board of supervisors and the Earps' adversary, resumed control of the Oriental Saloon from Lou Rickabaugh. Wyatt sold off his gambling concession.[41] A new advertisement for the Oriental appeared in the *Nugget*, proclaiming: "Again in the field — M. E. Joyce. Having again assumed the proprietorship of this well known and popular establishment, will in the future as the past, keep only the finest brands of Wines, Liquors and Cigars to be obtained. . . . All games conducted in an honest and gentlemanly way."

Wyatt Earp's primary focus became serving as deputy U.S. marshal. His priorities would be to find the men who shot his brother and to make certain they did not pull their triggers again against Earps or Clum or any of the other townspeople who had supported them. Breakenridge said that after the shooting of Virgil, "the Earp party consisted of five to eight men, and they were always together heavily armed. Wyatt Earp as deputy United States marshal, asserted that they were a posse under him, and that they were looking for mail robbers." This would be typical of Wyatt Earp, the same strategy he had used in Kansas. He would not avoid a fight, but he sure wanted the odds in his favor if it came.

By mid-January, the threat of further trouble forced the entire Earp family into quarters at the Cosmopolitan, with the cowboys keeping rooms across the street in the Grand. *Nugget* editor Richard Rule said: "Their apartments were perfect armories, and it was impossible to tell when shooting would begin. Miners and other workmen were very cautious about going into saloons at night, fearing that any moment would bring a fight and they were as likely as not to be shot."[42]

With most of Tombstone already alarmed, on January 17 Doc Holliday made matters worse. Holliday engaged in something of a face-off with Ringo on the streets of town. As with many of the Tombstone stories, this one has been retold and reinvented to the point of uncertainty. It is likely that Ringo and Holliday met and began snarling at each other, then placed their hands on their guns, both ready to draw. Parsons saw most of the rest and wrote: "Ringo and Doc Holliday came nearly having it with pistols. . . . Bad time expected with the cowboy leader and DH. I passed both not knowing what was up. One with hand in breast pocket and the other probably ready. Earps just beyond. Crowded street and looked like another battle. Police vigilant for once, and both disarmed."

Officer Jim Flynn grabbed Ringo from behind while Wyatt came over and hustled Doc away before either could act on their impulses. Police court records show that Ringo, Holliday, and Earp were all charged with carrying concealed weapons on January 17. The charge against Wyatt was dismissed because he was a U.S. marshal, while Holliday and Ringo were fined $32 each.[43] Whether the incident was prompted by Big-Nose Kate's friendship with Ringo can only be surmised. This face-off between two of the most feared shootists in town could only serve to exacerbate the already tense situation.

Clara Brown wrote: "While there is much to encourage the settlers in this new country, there is also an element of lawlessness, an insecurity of life and property, an open disregard of the proper authorities, which has greatly retarded the advancement of the place. It has occasioned much annoyance and loss among men who have invested their little all in Arizona's resources, not to speak of the lives that have fallen a sacrifice to a set of unprincipled beings who are above working for an honest living. Worse and worse the evil has grown, until now the state of affairs in this camp is far worse than in the early days of its settlement."[44]

The situation would grow even more unsettled in the weeks after the Holliday-Ringo confrontation, with Tombstone's factions angrily debating the issues. The safety-first citizens screamed for action against the cowboys, while the *Nugget* and the Behan supporters insisted the situation was exaggerated; that due process and the frontier version of civil liberties mattered far more than sinking to the depths of vigilantism.

Amid the confusion, Deputy U.S. Marshal Wyatt Earp went on the offensive. Riding out of Tombstone with Morgan, Doc Holliday, and five others on January 23, a Monday, he carried warrants for the two surviving Clantons, Ike and Fin, and Pony Deal. Townsfolk lined the sidewalks, speculating on their intentions. Each of the horsemen carried a shotgun, a Winchester rifle, and two pistols, plus at least a hundred rounds of ammunition. A boy rode into Tombstone that evening with a worrisome story, according to the *Nugget:* "He met the Earp party fifteen miles from town, riding hard in the direction of the [Helms] ranch. About one and one half miles behind the Earps was a company of from fifteen to twenty cowboys, all heavily armed, riding furiously in pursuit, with every probability in favor of their soon coming up with the foremost party. If the boy's statements are true, and there seems no reason to doubt them, a bloody combat will surely be the result. The cowboys, in addition to their well-known fighting proclivities, are in this instance animated by a thirst for revenge, and the Earp party is composed of desperate men who will fight each to the death."[45] The prediction never came true, and there was no January battle. But the dramatic story served to further shake up the town.

Meanwhile, John Ringo was in town for a review of his bond on two separate counts of robbery. Judge Stilwell determined that the bond was insufficient, and that Ringo should be jailed. After the Earp party left town on Monday, Ringo rode out, too. Breakenridge would later say that Ringo's lawyer had reported the bond had been approved, and Ringo believed he was free to leave. Apparently the bond had been posted, but not accepted or verified by the court. Jim Earp stepped in and arranged for the warrant for Ringo's arrest. The Earp party had no warrants for Ringo, and another posse, twenty-one men under the command of John Henry Jackson, rode out before sunrise Wednesday to join the pursuit for Ringo. "There's something the matter now, sure," a bystander remarked to Clara Brown.

Parsons helped find horses for John Jackson's large band, then returned to the comfort of his diary to express a little hope: "At last the national government is taking a hand in the matter of our trouble, and by private information I know that no money or trouble will be spared to cower the lawless element. Our salvation I think is near at hand. It looks like business now when the United States marshal Dake takes a hand under special orders." Dake had visited San Francisco and raised $3,000 from Wells, Fargo to fund the posse.

The *Nugget* provided a different view. "The ostensible object of the movement is the capture of stage robbers and other malefactors, but there are many in this community who believe the gratification of private malice will be the first consideration with the leaders of the party."[46] The *Nugget* and many members of the community believed that there was no place for personal revenge in law enforcement.

Jackson's posse reached Charleston at daybreak and headed for the Occidental Hotel for breakfast, where Jackson ran into Ike Clanton. Jackson told Ike that he had come to arrest Ringo, and several cowboys muttered in the background that nobody would be arrested unless they wanted to be. The possemen saw the barrels of several rifles pointed over the adobe walls behind Clanton and his friends. Doing the talking for the cowboy band, Ike said that Ringo had always acted the gentleman toward him, and he would see what could be done. After talking to Ringo, Ike assured Jackson that Ringo would return with the posse to Tombstone. Almost immediately, attorney Ben Goodrich came on the scene and pulled Ringo aside for a little talk. Clanton then told Jackson that Ringo had slipped away, but was on his way to Tombstone. Ringo arrived within ninety minutes and turned himself in to the sheriff's office, where he would be under Behan's guard.[47] After Jackson's posse returned to Tombstone, yet another posse entered the field, this one led by Charley Bartholomew, the shotgun messenger who had been held up three weeks earlier. With three posses riding the backcountry, the *Nugget* noted, "The large number of armed men leaving town the past few days has completely exhausted the supply of rifle scabbards usually kept by Patton, the harness-maker."[48]

Mayor Carr, elected on the anti-Earp ticket, surprised his backers by issuing a statement to both papers asking citizens not to interfere with the work of the marshal's brigade and vouching for the legitimacy of the warrants Earp carried against Deal and the Clantons. Although the mayor endorsed it, the *Nugget* railed against Earp's posse, "The cause of the intense local feeling that exists here is that a large majority of our citizens believe that the recent killing in our streets was a murder in reality, but done under the cover of a city marshal's authority. To again place such power, in a slightly different form, in the hands of the perpetrators of the former act is an outrage upon the public that could only be committed by a stupid or vicious magistrate. If the blood of either party is again spilled within our county borders, this judicial authority . . . is forever stained and burdened with the moral guilt, if not the actual."[49] The *Nugget* further said, "It should be stated, however, that the 30 extra deputies who left here on the night in question had been more than ordinarily successful in their quest of the 'flowing bowl,' as a consequence the majority of them were chuck full of courage, which might account for their self confidence." The paper portrayed a drunken, ragtag posse under the leadership of murderers, out for the purpose of quick killing, not law enforcement. The story ran under the provocative headline "A PESTIFEROUS POSSE."

The *Epitaph* struck back, saying the posse "consisted of hard-working miners and others who have volunteered to assist in the carrying out of the law." It intimated that members included workers from the ranch of Henry Clay Hooker, who had been raided heavily by rustlers in recent months.[50]

While the papers debated the issue in town, Wyatt Earp had work ahead. He planned a quiet entry into Charleston on a chilly Wednesday evening. Hoping to draw out the cowboys, he and Sherm McMasters rode across the Charleston bridge, while the rest of the band waited, sequestered in reserve. But no cowboys showed up, much to the surprise of the Earps. They could only speculate later that two passersby had seen the large posse and informed the rustlers.[51] Before reaching the village, they encountered Ben Maynard, a troublemaking pal of the cowboys, and took his guns. The Earp posse forced Maynard at gunpoint to lead them through Charleston, using him as a human shield as they moved through town, knocking on doors of buildings where the cowboys might be hiding. They repeatedly told him that if shots were fired, he would "not last as long as a snowball in hell."

After awakening the entire town, the posse determined that there were no cowboys in Charleston that night.[52] There were no Clantons, no Ringo, no Pony Deal. The only find, apparently, was a Mexican stockherder who carried a rifle that belonged to Pete Spence, which the posse confiscated. They set Maynard free and continued the search.

Deputy Sheriff S. H. Sperry also ran into the posse, according to the *Nugget*. Sperry was stopped on the road to Charleston and encircled by the members, who began berating him with such epithets as "cattle thieving son-of-a-bitch" before asking his business and allowing him to depart.

Sheriff Behan remained in Tombstone while the posses rode through the county he was charged to protect. According to the *Nugget*, he received a telegram on Thursday saying, "Doc Holliday, the Earps and about forty or fifty more of the filth of Tombstone, are here armed with Winchester rifles and revolvers, and patrolling our streets, as we believe for no good purpose. Last night and to-day they have been stopping good peaceable citizens on all the roads leading to our town, nearly paralyzing the business of our place. We know of no authority under which they are acting. Some of them, we have reason to believe, are thieves, robbers and murderers. Please come here and take them where they belong." At least that's what the *Nugget* reported. Telegrams were charged by the word, and a missive that wordy would have been costly. Whether a true dispatch from Charleston or a hoax by either Behan or Harry Woods, the message helped fan the outrage against the Earps.

The *Nugget* also ran an interview with Mayor Carr saying he thought the marshal's actions in sending the posse were uncalled for. "He has no doubt that the Sheriff of the county is abundantly able and willing to deal with the lawless element. . . . He is most emphatic in the statement that in 30 years experience on the Pacific coast, he has never known a more quiet and law-abiding community than are Tombstone and Cochise county." According to the story, Carr further suggested that the reason for the posse might just be to cover the use of the several thousand dollars used to fund it. This was the same mayor who only days earlier had endorsed the posse.

The war of editorials between the *Nugget* and the *Epitaph* grew more intense as the posses were in the field. With Clum still absent, Reppy and the *Epitaph* leveled their most vicious attacks on Behan and the *Nugget*, filled with phrases in bold capital letters. Reppy assailed the *Nugget* for editorializing against the Earp and Jackson posses, with remarks that were "surely calculated to arouse a sympathy with the STUPIDLY VICIOUS element of this community. . . . And whence comes the authority for the doctrine that persons charged with crime shall have the extreme courtesy extended to them of selecting those mild ministers of the law who shall approach them gently as a sucking dove, and fairly coo them into jail?"[53] Against Behan, the *Epitaph* said the sheriff held "bench warrants, unexecuted, in his hands against men charged with crime, who frequently parade our streets in the most unconcerned manner."[54]

The *Nugget* responded by denying the charges against Behan and writing, "Is it such a monstrous dogma that 'every man is to be believed innocent until proven guilty?' If this doctrine . . . is true, is it not then better to 'fairly coo them into jail' than to go forth red-handed and shoot down men with up-thrown arms? . . . The Earps have had their examination and were acquitted of criminal intent, and we say, let the matter drop. So, too, let the cowboys accused of crime have their trial, and let all abide by the result."[55]

As Tombstone awaited the posse with excitement, Charleston continued under siege. The Earps spent Thursday patrolling the hills outside town and did not return that night. Charley Bartholomew remained in town with fifteen men. In town that night between 10 and 11 P.M. a "perfect pandemonium" broke out, according to a writer to the *Epitaph*, when a bonfire was lit in the middle of the main street and rifle and pistol shots were fired incessantly. It seems the cowboy sympathizers were trying to intimidate Bartholomew's posse into leaving town, a move that worked when the posse slipped away in the night undetected. Wyatt Earp returned the next morning and took his posse to breakfast before departing for a trip down the river to chase the Clantons.

Earp's posse spent Friday, Saturday, and Sunday Clanton-hunting through the back country of Cochise County. Jackson again mysteriously left Tombstone and joined up with Bartholomew. The combined posse somehow picked up Pete Spence as a trail guide and found the quarry that had eluded the Earps. At about 2:30 Monday morning, Fin and Ike Clanton gave themselves up to the Jackson-Bartholomew posse. According to the *Nugget*, they had repeatedly offered to surrender to anyone who would provide them protection from the Earps, and the offer came from Bartholomew and Jackson.

Their return drew attention in Tombstone. "It is hoped that this inauguration of the war of extirpation will be attended with success, and that the ball will be kept vigorously rolling until the bane of the county is satisfactorily disposed of," Clara Brown wrote.[56]

While the Clantons were being brought back to Tombstone, another arrest warrant went out, this time for a member of the Earp party. Dave Neagle, serving as both city marshal and deputy sheriff, rode out and arrested Sherm Mc-Masters on charges of horse stealing. McMasters was still wanted on charges of stealing two horses from the Contention Mining Company after he had eluded Virgil Earp, and before McMasters had made public his affiliation as an Earp ally and informant. Neagle located the entire Earp party near the camp of Pick 'Em Up a couple of miles from Tombstone and, with no resistance, marched McMasters back to town as the Earps, Doc Holliday, and the rest of the party followed closely behind.

George Parsons packed up his outfit Monday morning and rode off to inspect mining claims. He passed by the Earp party outside Charleston, then rode into the little town. "Charleston looked almost like a deserted village, and as though having undergone a state of siege," he recorded in his diary.

The courts were busy that Monday. McMasters was booked and released on $1,000 bail. The case would be continued but never tried. The Clantons' hearing proved far more dramatic. Defense attorneys Goodrich and Alexander Campbell went into Judge William Stilwell's court fuming. They had been lied to, and they didn't like it. A few days earlier Goodrich had approached the judge and told him the Clantons did not want to surrender to the Earps for fear they would be killed. Stilwell responded with a most unexpected decision: he appointed Jackson—just back from catching Ringo—to form another posse and chase the Clantons. This was a direct repudiation of Johnny Behan, who as sheriff should have had the legal authority to lead the chase. When Goodrich protested that Behan should lead the posse because Jackson did not hold an official law enforcement position, Stilwell intimated that Jackson carried an appointment as a U.S. deputy marshal, satisfying Goodrich that Jackson held at least a comparable position to Wyatt Earp and would have the right to hold prisoners. After the Clantons returned to town, Goodrich learned that Stilwell had misled him—Jackson held no federal appointment. When the case reached court that Monday, Goodrich assailed the judge for giving Jackson the right to carry warrants with no legal authority. Goodrich argued mightily against Stilwell's judgment, saying that the Earps could have taken the Clantons from the Jackson party at any time because Wyatt did have a badge. Stilwell's decision, Goodrich said, could have led to murder.

Judge Stilwell disagreed vehemently. He said that Jackson's posse had been an attempt to prevent any such murder. It was, in fact, a remarkable undertaking for the court to assemble and assure the fees for such a second posse. "I endeavored if the accused desired to come in and have a hearing, to take such steps that would conduct them into town in such security and safety that no one would doubt; that I have done so no one need any proof. As to the legality of the party deputized to do so, I will not pass on until I have considered it somewhat." Goodrich had asked that all charges be dropped because of the uncertain legal status of Jackson's posse, but withdrew the request after the long confrontation with the judge. He would have the Clantons ready to answer charges.

By then, Ike and Fin had already had a surprise of their own. They had come to town believing they were facing a hearing for robbery of the mails.

When they arrived, they learned the accusation was for something quite different—the attempted assassination of Marshal Virgil Earp.

"The offense is a grave one," prosecutor William Herring told the court. "The party alleged to have been assailed by these parties is lying dangerously ill—so dangerous that death may ensue. It may become necessary for a process of a higher nature than this to be issued against them."

Herring asked for a bail of $5,000 each. Stilwell instead accepted a bail of $1,500 each, and the bonds were met immediately. The Clanton boys could only wait and wonder if their preliminary hearing would be on a murder charge.

The previous week had been difficult for the Earps, with Wyatt and Morgan leading their assault on Charleston and Virgil lying close to death back in Tombstone. While Wyatt rode on patrol, Marshal Dake called a meeting in Tombstone to select a new deputy for Cochise County, as it had become apparent Virgil could not continue with his duties. Mayor Carr held a meeting of Tombstone Republicans to discuss the issue. City Councilman Jim Nash spoke out. A moderate who was not affiliated with either side, Nash said that the U.S. deputy marshals should not be men with private wrongs to avenge, and the appointee should not be a member of either faction.

Carr appointed a five-man committee to recommend the new candidate for marshal, and an open citizens' meeting was held the next night for further discussion. According to the *Epitaph*, the discussion ended with a big joke—troublemaker Ben Maynard, the cowboys' friend, received the endorsement for the marshal's job.

"The nomination was seconded by the Hon. Judge Murphy, who in the light of twenty years' acquaintance, eulogized Mr. Maynard as a whole-souled, noble, courageous man, equally as good as the president, and a gentleman who would represent the solid views of the solid men of the camp," the *Epitaph* wrote of the tongue-in-cheek statements, a pointed barb at the *Nugget*'s laudatory report from Maynard a week earlier after he served as a human shield for the Earps. The citizens voted to endorse Maynard as the next marshal and left laughing.

The next morning, the joking ended. Wyatt Earp, a man who rarely laughed in the best of times, had taken all the public criticism very seriously, and he did not like the idea of his town turning against him when he perceived that he was serving as its protector. All he received for his efforts was constant harping and criticism. Enough was enough. If the citizenry wanted him out, he would leave. On the morning of February 2, the *Epitaph* ran a startling letter signed by Wyatt S. Earp and Virgil W. Earp under the headline: "DRAW YOUR OWN INFERENCE/ Resignation of Virgil W. Earp and Wyatt S. Earp as Deputy Marshals":

> Major C. P. Dake, United States Marshal, Grand Hotel, Tombstone—Dear Sir: In exercising our official functions as deputy United States marshals in this territory, we have endeavored always unflinchingly to perform the duties intrusted to us. These duties have been exacting and perilous in their character, having to be performed in a community where turbulence and violence could almost any moment be organized to thwart and resist the enforcement of the processes of the court issued to bring criminals to justice. And while we have a deep sense of obligation to many of

the citizens for their hearty cooperation in aiding us to suppress lawlessness, and their faith in our honesty of purpose, we realize that notwithstanding our best efforts and judgment in everything which we have been required to perform, there has arisen so much harsh criticism in relation to our operations, and such a persistent effort having been made to misrepresent and misinterpret our acts, we are led to the conclusion that, in order to convince the public that it is our sincere purpose to promote the public welfare, independent of any personal emolument or advantages to ourselves, it is our duty to place our resignations as deputy United States marshals in your hands, which we now do, thanking you for your continued courtesy and confidence in our integrity, and shall remain subject to your orders in the performance of any duties which may be assigned to us, only until our successors are appointed.

The *Epitaph* commented, "The document is a manly and generous one, and should meet with impartial criticism from the public. The position of deputy marshal on the frontier is no sinecure. An officer who honestly tries to do his duty encounters many perils that the public know not of, and raises within the breasts of criminals that desire for their death that comes from fear of the gallows and imprisonment. It would be much out of place for a public journal, under the attendant circumstances, to endeavor to create public opinion upon these resignations, as to prejudge a case at court. It is sufficient that the matter is before the United States Marshal, who has had ample opportunity to investigate the condition of affairs, and who will give the subject that deliberate and careful consideration that comes of experience in official life."[57]

Dake refused Wyatt Earp's resignation and also gave John Henry Jackson an appointment as U.S. deputy marshal, a move that met with high praise from the *Epitaph*.[58] Wyatt Earp kept his badge, a decision that did not meet with unanimous glee in a Tombstone weary of conflict. Democratic newspapers in the territory began calling for Dake to accept Wyatt's resignation and wondering why he had not. Dake never made his reasons clear, but he remained a supporter of Wyatt Earp. Whether Wyatt had vengeance in his heart or public protection as his goal, he was the man Dake wanted serving as a U.S. marshal in Tombstone.

On the same day he resigned, Earp apparently tried to end the feud that had engulfed and endangered Tombstone. According to the February 2 *Nugget*, Wyatt sent a message to Ike Clanton that "he wished to interview with him with a view of reconciling their differences and obliterating the animosity that now exists between them. Mr. Clanton most emphatically declined to hold any communication whatever with Earp." Ike had other plans, and peace was not on his agenda.

Even in the midst of continuing danger, the townsfolk still enjoyed a little fun. There were snowball fights, football in the streets, and top performers visiting the local theaters. But not everyone had a good time in the early weeks of February. Johnny Behan, the friendliest man in town, learned he no longer had quite as many friends as he thought.

Judge Stilwell's validation of Jackson's posse had been a direct repudiation of Sheriff Behan. The sheriff had jurisdiction to round up anyone accused of a shooting in Cochise County, and legally Behan should have been the man to do it. Had the charges actually been robbing the mails, a federal crime, the posse should have been under a U.S. deputy marshal. Judge Stilwell's appointment of a civilian was a slap in the face of the glad-handing sheriff.

This was only the beginning. Johnny Behan would be knocked around quite often by the courts and the press in late January and early February. When a man identified as J. Gardner was shot and killed near San Simon, the coroner's jury issued subpoenas for two saloonkeepers. Behan and his deputies failed to deliver the summonses, and the members of the coroner's jury said in their report that they could not reach a conclusion because the sheriff "has been derelict in his duties."[59]

Shortly after the Clantons left Judge Stilwell's court from their preliminary hearing on January 31, Behan came in to face charges of perjury. Sylvester B. Comstock, a local merchant, claimed Behan had falsified records and charged the county twice for the same $365 bill. Behan's lawyer, James B. Southard, first asked that the hearing be shifted to another court, stating that Judge Stilwell had shown prior prejudice against the defendant, "by having ignored the sheriff of the county in placing warrants for arrest of suspected persons in the hands of those not authorized or deputized by the sheriff to serve the same." Judge Stilwell disclaimed all prejudice, and, according to the *Nugget*, said "A magistrate who, having bias or prejudice in any cause, would sit upon the same would be guilty of prostituting his position." Stilwell refused the change of venue request and heard the case. The decision came quickly. Southard showed that Richard Rule, the *Nugget* editor and clerk of the board of supervisors, was not legally empowered to administer the oath that must be taken before an official discusses his accounts, as had been the custom since Cochise County began business. Because the bills were not processed under a legal structure, Southard argued that the case should be dismissed. The surprise argument caught the prosecution off guard, and Southard's statement could not be refuted. Judge Stilwell dismissed the case, and Behan went free on the technicality.

The decision set off a passionate war of editorials, with the *Epitaph* questioning Behan's actions in office and the *Nugget* defending the sheriff's every move. Under a headline "Sheriff Behan Arrested on Trumped Up Charge and Honorably Discharged," the *Nugget* wrote: "The detestable cliques who for the past three months have scrupled at nothing in the endeavor to foment disorder and oppression to the constituted authorities of this city and county yesterday indulged in what they doubtless fondly imagined would prove a coup d'état in their favor." The full column, which also included the story on the Clantons' surrender, appeared under the all-capitals headline "THE GENTLEMEN WIN."[60]

The *Epitaph* wrote, "One thing is manifest to our citizens, that where a county official fails to execute the public trust reposed in him, there will not be lacking the courage to assail such want of fidelity. The handwriting on the wall should be an admonition that every lawful means will be adopted to protect the public treasury . . . while the sheriff walks out of court a free man on account of this technicality, the next attempt is not likely to meet with similar success. He is not legally guilty of the crime charged, but the public will undoubtedly await his explanation of the double charges referred to in the complaint."[61]

Three days before the hearing, the *Epitaph* had exploded its bitterest attack on Behan in an editorial defending the Earp-Jackson expedition against Cochise

County's wild bunch. The commentary in the most purple of prose said Behan held warrants "in his hands against men charged with crime, who frequently parade our streets in the most unconcerned manner," and chastised the sheriff for never having solved any of the stage robberies or major crimes in the county.

Dake and Judge Stilwell had publicly slighted the sheriff by ignoring him in the formation of the posse. A month later he would be publicly lambasted in the *National Police Gazette*, a publication that circulated around the nation and had several hundred issues delivered weekly to Sol Israel's Union News Depot in the lobby of the Tombstone post office, and more sent a few blocks down to Aleck Robertson's bookstore.

The *Gazette* interviewed Wells, Fargo chief detective Jim Hume, who was not kind to Johnny Behan:

> Even the sheriff of the county, the detective says, is in with the cowboys and has got to be or his life would not be worth a farthing. The robbers are picked desperadoes, excellent horsemen and dead shots from Colorado and Texas. There are five brothers . . . who have sworn vengeance on the outlaws. One of these is the chief of police of Tombstone, who is now confined to his house suffering from gunshot wounds inflicted by his sworn enemies.[62]

The most eloquent indictment against Behan came not from the rantings of the *Epitaph*, but from the delicate hand of the woman who came to Tombstone expecting to write dispatches about sewing circles and community theater. Clara Brown hinted that certain officials might be "influenced by bribes or intimidated by threats so that they do not enforce the law as invested in them against violators of the peace." She continued:

> Unfortunately for the camp, there has not been a unanimity of feeling and action among the officials. Opinion is more equally divided among the people than an outside observer would deem credible. It can hardly be otherwise when the two leading daily papers, each with a large circulation and commanding a corresponding influence, take diametrically opposite views of the same subject, one being known as the "cow-boy" organ, and the other as the "stranglers."
>
> One would suppose that all peaceable, honest men would denounce and oppose the outlaws, for they are virtually such, but a large proportion of otherwise good citizens waste a surprising amount of sympathy on them, in the face of evidence against them which ought to be thoroughly convicting. . . .
>
> With this state of public and private sentiment, the work of cleansing Cochise county of the nuisance becomes particularly difficult. If an effort is made by one side to bring to justice some transgressor, or ferret out some sort of crime, emissaries of the other party prostrate the movement by giving secret information to those in jeopardy, and otherwise assisting them to evade the law.
>
> The case is complicated because one cannot tell who is a 'cowboy'—their supporters deserve no better name. . . .
>
> It has been reported, and quite generally believed for some time past, that Doc Holliday and the Earps, who were concerned in the homicide last autumn, would leave town if they dared to, but every high way was watched by men anxious to avenge their murdered comrades. These parties a week ago demonstrated the falsity of the rumors of their cowardice by setting out with a posse commissioned with the arrest of certain criminals in the county, a dangerous undertaking and far more so

for them than for others. They were followed the same day by two parties belonging to the disturbing element, and a bloody time was anticipated. One side expresses indignation at "murderers" being allowed to "hunt down better men than they are," and the other retorts that these men are U.S. Deputy Marshals and who else should do the work? Certainly it would be no easy matter to find other men who would jeopardize their lives, and exercise the requisite bravery in "bearding the lion in his den."[63]

Clara Brown, the finest writer to settle in Tombstone, did not need fiery adjectives or loud screeds in ink to condemn the sheriff. She made her point by commending the Earps while intimating that the cowboys paid bribes to public officials.

Before Behan even had a chance to shrug off public controversy over his court case, something else went wrong in his life. Undersheriff and editor Harry Woods simply became Undersheriff Harry Woods. The *Nugget*, owned by Prescott politico Hugo Richards, was sold on February 3, and Woods was replaced as editor. No ownership details were made public, but the *Nugget* ran a story on the change and vowed to report without partiality toward the town's different factions. Woods's name disappeared from the top of the paper, replaced simply by "Richard Rule Editor." The *Nugget* remained Democratic, pro-Behan, and anti-Earp, but the tirades against the Earps disappeared, replaced by more measured editorials against vigilantism. Behan still had a supporter in the *Nugget*, but he no longer had an unquestioning newspaper voice.

Tombstone must still have been abuzz over the Earps' resignation when Ike Clanton came to Judge Stilwell's court on February 2. He must have walked in a most optimistic man, anticipating acquittal and expecting his adversaries to lose their legal authority. Two days earlier, according to the *Nugget*, Pony Deal and Fin Clanton had faced the court on charges of assault with intent to kill Virgil Earp, but had been discharged from custody, "no evidence being adduced to warrant their being held to answer."

When the case began against Ike, the prosecution called James W. Bennett, who testified that immediately after the shooting he found a hat, identified as belonging to Ike Clanton, in the partially burned building from which Virgil was shot. Sherm McMasters then came on the stand to testify that three days after the assassination attempt, he had overheard someone ask Clanton about the shooting. Ike replied he "would have to go back and do the job over."

Then the defense began its parade, bringing seven witnesses, including constable George McKelvey and Jeptha B. Ayers, to the stand to testify that Ike had been in Charleston when Virgil Earp's arm was blasted into fragments. Ike said he lost his hat before the shooting and couldn't imagine how it wound up on the scene. Stilwell questioned the witnesses, then ruled the evidence inconclusive. Ike and Fin Clanton went free, "having been honorably acquitted of the charges against them," the *Nugget* said.[64]

Whether Ike actually pulled a trigger is uncertain. He could have lost his hat while scouting ambush locations, then remained behind in Charleston while others did the actual shooting. Outlaw Johnny Barnes would later tell Fred Dodge that he had fired the shot that crippled Virgil, with Pony Deal at his side. No witnesses could or would identify Ike as one of the men running from the scene. The hat was only circumstantial evidence, not enough to send a man to jail. The Earps and their supporters would continue to believe that Ike had been in the building with the other assassins.

Wyatt Earp later said that Judge Stilwell told him, "Wyatt, you'll never clean up this crowd this way; next time you'd better leave your prisoners out in the brush where alibis don't count." These would be important words to a man who had spent so much of his life avoiding killing.[65]

The trial of Ike Clanton made very clear to the Earps and their supporters that there would be little chance of ever getting a conviction against the cowboys. Any case would be met with a flood of witnesses to provide an alibi, and nothing but absolute proof would give any chance of conviction.[66] In those days before fingerprinting and forensics, the only way to convict a cowboy would be to catch him committing a crime. The law-and-order advocates in Tombstone must have been most disheartened to see a smiling Ike Clanton walk out of court.

"If by chance one or more of these robbers are arrested they have innumerable friends through whom they always do prove an alibi," a letter-writer wrote to the *Tucson Citizen*. "Hence they obtain their liberty regardless of what may be the evidence against them. I venture to assert that a conviction of one of these festive cowboys will never be obtained in Cachise county so long as the present state of affairs exists. I have conversed with many of the leading citizens of Tombstone, and they with one accord assert that the industries of the county are paralyzed through the lawlessness existing there."[67]

Ironically, when Ike's alibi witnesses took the stand to clear their friend, they may well have been signing death warrants against a few other cowboys. But Ike had other thoughts. After one big victory, he was ready for another. He went before Justice of the Peace J. B. Smith in Contention on February 9 and again filed charges against the Earps and Doc Holliday for the murder of Billy Clanton and the McLaurys. Smith issued the standard order, "To Any Sheriff, Constable, Marshal or Policeman in the Territory of Arizona, Greetings." He then commanded the officers "to arrest the above named Wyatt Earp, Morgan Earp, Virgil Earp and J. H. Holliday and bring them forthwith before me at my office on Main Street in the Village of Contention in the County of Cochise, Territory of Arizona."[68]

With Tom Fitch away on business, the Earps retained William Herring, a member of the Citizens Safety Committee. Ike hired J. S. Robinson and brothers Ben and Briggs Goodrich to handle the prosecution, a move that was technically legal because Robinson and Ben Goodrich had helped prosecute the original case. Behan took Wyatt, Morgan, and Doc Holliday into custody while Virgil again remained behind at the Cosmopolitan recovering from his wounds. Herring quickly filed for a writ of habeas corpus on February 11, asserting they were "illegally restrained of their liberty by John Behan, sheriff of the County of Cochise" on the order of Smith, "an alleged justice of the peace."

Of course, the legal situation grew complex. With no district court judge present to consider the writ of habeas corpus, the duty should have fallen to T. J. Drum, the county commissioner. But Drum was automatically disqualified because he had represented Holliday back at the Spicer hearing. So the defendants applied to Judge Lucas, arguing on two grounds: that the charge had already been examined and rejected by both Spicer and the grand jury, and that Smith did not possess the legal authority to order an arrest.

The *Epitaph* railed against the new charges. "If it is a fact that this warrant has been allowed to issue without new evidence to warrant it, the code of rights that protects all alike has been violently infringed. Cleared by a lengthy examination before a magistrate and then by a grand jury, it is only in the province of another grand jury to take up the case, unless new evidence is brought forward before the issuance of a warrant. These are cold facts, and not contingent turkey."[69] The Earps had not been subjected to trial, so they could be indicted again should new evidence arise. The burden would be on the prosecution to provide that new evidence during the new hearing.

Amid the wrangling, the prosecution asked Lucas to disqualify himself because he had been a witness in the Spicer hearing back in November. Lucas determined that he should make the decision, although "it would be a pleasant task to avoid hearing the question," Lucas said at the February 13 hearing. The main argument centered on whether Smith had the authority to hold the hearing, since he had never been elected. But Ben Goodrich showed a recent act of the legislature that made appointments such as Smith's legal. Lucas determined that the Contention justice of the peace did indeed have the right to make the call for another hearing. As to the charge that the case had already been decided, Lucas said that was beyond his jurisdiction.

Ike Clanton expected his greatest triumph in this hearing. In a letter dated February 14, he wrote Guadalupe Canyon massacre survivor Billy Byers in Leavenworth, Kansas, "I have got the Earps all in Jail, and am not going to unhitch. I have got them on the hip and am going to throw them good."[70]

By again bringing the killings to court, Ike forced the Earps to take action. First, Wyatt and Mattie, listed as husband and wife, mortgaged their Tombstone home for $365, agreeing to pay 2 percent interest per month.[71] This could well have been to meet legal fees necessitated by the heavy demands of court time Wyatt had been facing.

Wyatt's friends then got together to consider the situation. Herring, Wyatt, and his allies were convinced that this February 14 hearing in Contention was a ruse to put the Earps onto the unprotected roadway, with just Behan serving as guard, so that any ambush would kill Wyatt and put the matter beyond the reach of the courts.[72] Behan asked Wyatt to surrender his arms for the ride, but Earp flatly refused and Behan did not persist. Much to Behan's surprise, twelve citizens rode up armed with Winchesters to escort Holliday and the Earps to Contention. Herring arrived in his buggy, with his 16-year-old daughter on one side and a Winchester on the other.

Parsons recorded the incident: "Earps were taken to Contention to be tried for the killing of Clanton. Quite a posse went out. Many of Earps' friends accompanied, armed to the teeth. They came back later in the day, the good people below beseeching them to leave and try the case here."

They arrived at Contention for the noon hearing and walked into the courtroom fully armed. Herring reportedly opened with the words: "Your honor, we come here for law, but we will fight—if we have to."[73] Herring followed with his argument against the unnecessary trip from the county seat. Smith remanded them back to Tombstone, where the Contention justice of the peace would hold a hearing in a Tombstone courtroom.

The proceeding began at ten the next morning in Tombstone, and Herring asked for the papers by which the Earps and Holliday were being held so they could fully examine the charges. Smith had left the paperwork back in Contention, and Herring demanded an immediate discharge. Smith refused, adjourning the case until the next morning. Herring quickly filed a second motion of habeas corpus with Judge Lucas, charging that the justice of the peace had failed to show them the warrants and had not ordered them bound over. Herring called Smith as a witness, and his testimony confirmed his judicial ineptness. On the technicality, the Earps were released. The prosecution immediately filed a new warrant for murder charges, issued by Justice Smith, but Lucas quickly dismissed it, writing in his decision: "The evidence (depositions) of the various witnesses is now in the possession of the District Court, and another examination would simply duplicate it, and when they have been discharged by one magistrate, and a failure to indict by one grand jury, it would seem to be unwise to enter into an examination anew at this time." He added that new evidence should be submitted before a second hearing would be called. Because the November hearing before Spicer was not a trial, Clanton and his pals had the right to continue pushing for prosecution; this technically was not double jeopardy. But they would have to come up with some new evidence of murder before the case could be considered in any courtroom outside Contention.

The decision did not sit well with Clanton, who had been so optimistic just a day earlier. Parsons expressed the fears of the community in his little diary when he wrote: "A bad time is expected again in town at any time—Earps on one side of the street with their friends, and Ike Clanton and Ringo with theirs on the other side, watching each other. Blood will surely come. Hope no innocents will be killed."

Two days after being released by Judge Lucas, U.S. Deputy Marshal Wyatt Earp was in the saddle again, leading a posse toward the Mexican border in search of outlaws. Along with brother Morgan, Holliday, McMasters, and two or three others, Wyatt began another mysterious chase. The *Nugget* account said it was believed that he was searching for Pony Deal, who had been named by Bartholomew as a robber of the Bisbee stage, along with Al Tiebot [or Thibolet] and Charles Haws. But Deal and associates were supposedly jailed in Texas awaiting extradition. Wyatt Earp's second posse proved as unsuccessful as the first, and the Earps returned to town with no robbers and just a bill for costs.

Arizona's plight drew increased national attention. Acting Governor Gosper had gone to Congress in December to make a call for action. He detailed the depredations of the cowboys and said he feared that they would lead to serious problems with Mexico. Gosper called for federal intervention in Arizona's problems. Interior Secretary Samuel J. Kirkwood said that certain sheriffs were intimidated by or desired to curry favor with the outlaws, and he called for a law to allow territorial governors to suspend sheriffs.[74]

President Chester A. Arthur responded by asking Congress in December for an amendment to the Posse Comitatus Act so the army could intervene in the border raids, but Congress did not respond. The situation continued to worsen. On February 2, Arthur forwarded letters from Gosper and the secretary of state on lawlessness in Arizona to Congress in hopes of reviving the Posse Comitatus Act. Gosper had been actively campaigning for the governor's job Fremont had vacated a month earlier, but the appointment did not come. On February 6, Arthur appointed Frederick A. Tritle, a mining man and territorial booster, to the job of governor.

Gosper's letter to Congress became public on February 9, and an excerpt from it ran on the Associated Press and was picked up by both Tombstone papers, under vastly different headlines. "THE COW-BOY CURSE: The Attention of Congress Called to It," the *Epitaph* headlined. The *Nugget* ran, "GOSPER'S GUSH: Remarkable Statements Emanating From Arizona's Late Acting Governor." The letter asked that the Posse Comitatus Act be amended to allow civil authorities to enlist the army's help to protect the territory, and said that local law enforcement officials were unable to deal with the problem.

Gosper managed to offend most of Tombstone's citizenry with his letter. "The people of Tombstone and Cochise county, in their mad career after money, have grossly neglected local self-government until the lazy and lawless element of society have undertaken to prey upon the more industrious and honorable classes for their subsistence and gains. The cowboys are not always white, some are Mexicans, but Americans direct and control the lawless element."

Only an excerpt from the letter appeared in the Associated Press report, but nine days later the *Nugget* published Gosper's full commentary, an indictment of the activities in Cochise County. The acting governor said civil officers ignored crimes and neglected their duties "for hope and sake of gain." Gosper said the law-abiding citizens "are very generally of the opinion that the officers of the law are themselves in league with the cowboy element to obtain legal gain." He wrote of the difficulties between the Earps and Behan and said, "the rivalry . . . having extended into a strife to secure influence and aid from all quarters, has led them and the particular friends of each to sins of commission and omission, greatly at the cost of peace and property." Gosper also attacked the *Nugget* and the *Epitaph*, saying they had selfishly taken sides to gain patronage and printing contracts. He criticized ranchers who bought stolen cattle from the rustlers and merchants who happily catered to the free-spending cowboys: "under the guise of respectability and the pretense of observing the laws, [they] keep up a secret partnership with the robbers and profit by their lawlessness. This class is quite as difficult to handle as the extreme criminal class."[75]

In early February, Congress requested the President to enter discussions with Mexico to try to formulate an agreement of cooperation with the Mexican government to improve enforcement and extradition procedures between the two countries.

Rampant confusion continued in Tombstone. Marshall Williams, the trusted and respected Wells, Fargo agent, fell quickly into disrepute when it was discovered he had altered the books. Williams, who also ran a cigar and stationery shop from the Wells, Fargo office, left town on the afternoon of February 3, apparently taking a prostitute along. "Marshall Williams . . . has skinned out of Tombstone and, it is said, hied toward the Orient . . . and had a sport with him," the *Arizona Star* reported. "Wonder if the resignation of the Earps did not have something to do with his sudden departure."[76] The details of his debt were reported differently, ranging from $8,000 to $30,000, with a couple of thousand pilfered from Wells, Fargo accounts. The final accounting showed Williams left behind only $4,000 in debts, but this would still serve as an embarrassment for his one-time friends. Dodge would later write in a letter to Stuart Lake, "Marshall Williams did do some tipping off," meaning he informed stage robbers about company shipments. This could never be proven, but could explain the many rumors about an inside informant playing a role in the robberies.

As for the Earps, details of their home life are difficult to sort. Virgil and Allie remained sequestered at the Cosmopolitan. Jim, Mattie, and the clan probably spent most of their time in the hotel, although surviving records do not indicate they checked in until late March. Louisa Houston Earp wrote to her sister on January 31: "Ever since our trouble we have stayed at the Cosmopolitan Hotel and it is very disagreeable to be so unsettled."[77] Virgil slowly recovered from his wounds, growing stronger each day. In February, Morgan sent Louisa to the Earp family home in Colton, California, a safer location to wait out the danger.

At some point after the gunfight, in late '81 or early '82, Sadie Marcus returned to her family in San Francisco. It is obvious that Wyatt and Sadie could not have spent much time together in January and February, when he alternated between sitting in Behan's jail and riding on posses. It is highly probable that Behan continued to pursue her. He traveled to San Francisco on March 10, presumably to visit his one-time fiancée, and returned alone.[78] Sadie had already served to add fire to the feud between Behan and the Earps.

As for the rest of Tombstone, the situation seemed to be settling down and returning to normal. Wells, Fargo had not followed up on its threat to pull out, although it did close its office in Bisbee, and business as usual settled about the dusty mining camp. The city had a brief Apache scare and rumors of a smallpox outbreak, but they turned out to be minor problems. The *Nugget* joked, "It is said that people who are much among cattle never have the smallpox. We'll bet Curly Bill is never pockmarked."

By the end of February, Wyatt, Morgan, and Warren Earp were on constant patrol through southern Arizona. Apparently Warren had moved back and forth between Colton and Tombstone, and he had had little previous involvement in Arizona activities. The *Prescott Miner*, in a dispatch carried by the *Nugget*, said Dake had authorized the formation of posses to patrol the Mexican border and try to capture outlaws, and added that Dake had organized the posse on his own responsibility, trusting Congress for reimbursement. The *Nugget* added its own commentary: "One of the peculiarities of Major Dake is, that he says one thing and does another. When the posse referred to, consisting of the Earp party, left this place for the Mexican border he telegraphed to certain parties in this place that he knew nothing of their movements, but supposed they desired to serve some old warrants, and further, that John H. Jackson was his deputy at this place. When he was here some time ago, he made many promises to reform in his management of this portion of the Territory, none of which he has fulfilled;

but then it requires something more than the average man to make a good and efficient United States Deputy Marshal, especially on the frontier."[79]

On the same page, the *Nugget* picked up an illogical item from the *Prescott Democrat* saying, "We are informed by Marshal Dake that the resignation of the Earps, as Deputy United States Marshals, has not yet been accepted, owing to the fact that their accounts have not yet been straightened up. As soon as that is done, they will step out." In all likelihood, Dake meant Wyatt would step down to run for sheriff in the next election.

With the posses on patrol, Tombstone enjoyed its interlude of tranquillity, and the town's skittish residents hoped for peace. Clara Brown sent a comforting message back to San Diego: "The turbulent condition of affairs which was prevailing at the time of my last letter has been for some time subdued, though exactly in what manner I cannot say, as the movements of the posses sent from here almost daily at that time were secret. The presence of United States Marshal Dake on the field of action is undoubtedly the principal cause of so speedy a change for the better, and Judge Stilwell of the District Court is commended for the part he has played in the secret drama. There being a lull in cowboy criminality (which we hope is something more than temporary), and the Indians apparently having left the Dragoons, Tombstone people have been obliged to look to other causes of excitement."[80] They would not have long to look. The furor that had embraced Tombstone for five months only served as preliminary to the events that would forever create a legacy of blood in Cochise County.

WHEN THE W. H. LINGARD THEATRE COMPANY came to town for a one-night showing of *Stolen Kisses*, Morg Earp did not want to miss a good show just because Wyatt urged caution after a few of his fidgety friends thought the troubles might heat up again. Two and a half months had passed since Virgil had been shot, and Tombstone had been quiet for nearly three weeks, a long period by Cochise County standards. It was a Saturday night, March 18, and Morg wanted a little fun.

Wyatt thought something was amiss on Friday night, and he approached Briggs Goodrich, Ben's brother and law partner, who maintained a cordial relationship with the Earps, despite representing many cowboys in their court cases.

"I think they were after us last night. Do you know anything about it?" Wyatt asked Goodrich. The attorney said he did not.

"Do you think we are in any danger?" Wyatt asked.

Goodrich looked back at the marshal and told him he was liable to get it in the neck at any time.

"I don't notice anybody particularly in town now—any of the crowd," Wyatt said.

"I think I see some strangers here that I think are after you," Goodrich responded. "By the way, John Ringo wanted me to say to you, that if any fight came up between you all that he wanted you to understand that he would have nothing to do with it; that he was going to take care of himself, and everybody else could do the same." The message came through clearly: Ringo knew trouble was coming. He either chose not to be part of it, this time, or he wanted to set up an alibi should he be implicated.

A few minutes later, Goodrich had a conversation with Frank Stilwell, who told Goodrich, "There are some boys in town who will toe the mark, and what bothers me is the Earps will think I am in with it, as they don't like me. What would you advise me to do?"[81] The lawyer told him to keep off the street at night and make himself visible so he could prove an alibi for all times if the action started. Then Goodrich offered to tell the Earps that Stilwell would not be a party to any action against them, the same as he had done for Ringo. Stilwell refused; he said he would rather die than let them know he cared a damn what they thought.

Goodrich saw men with guns walking the streets as he made his way to the theater. He ran into Morg and Doc Holliday and told them: "I saw some fellows with guns. You fellows will catch it if you don't watch out."

The attorney knew that Wyatt had been sufficiently warned, enough so he could look after the safety of his family. Good-timing Morgan had other plans and would not miss a big show on the stormy, windy night. Wyatt returned to the Cosmopolitan and began to undress, according to his story in the Hooker manuscript. He had already scouted the town and seen Florentino Cruz and Hank Swilling, two known troublemakers and foes of the Earps. Goodrich had given him warning, and several businessmen had tipped various Earp allies that something was about to happen. Dan Tipton would later testify they had been "warned to look out, as some of them would catch it that night."

Wyatt Earp pulled on his boots and went back to catch Morgan as he came out of the theater to try to convince him to return to the hotel. Morgan insisted on one game over at Bob Hatch's poolroom before retiring, and Wyatt relented. Along with Tipton and Sherm McMasters, they went to the little poolroom in Campbell and Hatch's saloon and took seats as Morgan played it out with Hatch, a duel of two expert players.[82]

About ten minutes before 11, Morgan walked around the table to line up a shot, leaving his back to the glass door at the rear of the room, the bottom half ground glass and the upper half clear. With the lights on inside, anyone standing in the alley could easily see through the glass and spot the figures inside.

Morgan leaned over the table to make the shot, and suddenly a blast crashed through the glass, knocking him against the table. The bullet passed through Morg's body and lodged in the leg of bystander George A. B. Berry. Almost immediately another shot crunched through and hit the wall just over Wyatt's head. The poolroom partisans dived for cover, knocking over chairs and hunting for safety. Morgan Earp slowly slid off the table and collapsed in a pool of blood.

By the time Hatch and McMasters could run into the alley, the assassins had fled, leaving no clues. McMasters, Tipton, and Wyatt lifted Morgan and moved him to the lounge of an adjoining cardroom. "The death scene is said to have been very affecting," Clara Brown wrote back to San Diego. "The man was surrounded by his brothers and their wives, whose grief was intense. He whispered some words to Wyatt, which have not been given to the public, but spoke aloud only once when his companions endeavored to raise him to his feet: 'Don't, boys, don't,' he said. 'I can't stand it. I have played my last game of pool.'"[83]

Morgan rested in the cardroom.The bullet entered just to the left of the spinal column, passed through a kidney, and came out the loin. Three doctors watched as Morgan clung to life for nearly an hour. "Each breath came with a gasp and a struggle as his heart yielded drop after drop of his life blood," the *Nugget* reported. By midnight, Morgan Earp, 30, the family favorite, had died.

"At the front door of the saloon stood a hound raised by the brothers who with the instinct peculiar to animals seemed to know that his master had been struck down, and despite entreaties remained whining and moaning," reported the *Nugget*. "And when the body was taken to the hotel, no sadder heart followed than that of the faithful dog."

Morgan's last whispered words were the subject of much speculation and many stories. By one source, Morgan said, "Do you know who did it?" and Wyatt responded, "Yes, and I'll get them."

"That's all I ask," Morgan whispered. "But Wyatt, be careful."

Two months later, Wyatt would say: "I promised my brother to get even, and I've kept my word so far. When they shot him he said the only thing he regretted was that he wouldn't have a chance to get even. I told him I'd attend to it for him."[84]

Promise made. But no promises were really necessary. The cowboys had twice attacked from hiding, maiming Virgil and murdering Morgan. The court system had failed in the Clanton trial, and Wyatt knew that as long as assassins had friends to swear their alibis, malefactors would be free to continue doing their evil deeds. It would take stronger measures than just bringing a criminal before a judge. By his way of thinking, Wyatt Earp would have to become a justice unto himself to avenge Morgan's death and, perhaps, to ensure the survival of the townspeople who had supported his cause.

Wyatt Earp in about 1869, a young man beginning a life of adventure. (Charles W. Dearborn Collection/Courtesy C. Lee Simmons)

Virgil Earp as a young man, about the time he left to fight in the Civil War. (Charles W. Dearborn Collection/Courtesy C. Lee Simmons)

Nicholas and Virginia Earp, parents of Jim, Virgil, Wyatt, Morgan, and Warren Earp. Newton Earp was Nicholas's son by a previous marriage. (C. Lee Simmons Collection)

Ben Thompson in 1879. Whether Wyatt Earp disarmed the dangerous Thompson is one of the lingering mysteries of the frontier. (Robert G. McCubbin Collection)

Wyatt Earp and Bat Masterson in Dodge City, where Wyatt served as assistant marshal and Bat as Ford County sheriff. They would combine to help form a most effective frontier law enforcement unit. (Courtesy Arizona Historical Society/Tucson [76636])

E. (Larry) DEGER
—1883—

Larry Deger served as city marshal when Wyatt Earp came to Dodge City, and would later emerge as an opponent of Earp and his associates. (William Secrest Collection)

PHOTOGRAPHED FROM DODGE CITY TIMES, ISSUE OF JUNE 8, 1878

DENTISTRY.

J. H. Holliday, Dentist, very respectfully offers his professional services to the citizens of Dodge City and surrounding country during the summer. Office at room No. 24, Dodge House. Where satisfaction is not given money will be refunded.

Doc Holliday offered refunds if his dental customers were not satisfied. (William Secrest Collection)

Clay Allison had to recover from a broken leg in about 1870, but he had no trouble walking the streets of Dodge City in his search for Wyatt Earp. (West of the Pecos Museum)

Saloon owner Milt Joyce served on the Tombstone board of supervisors and became an enemy of the Earps after ugly quarrels with Doc Holliday and Virgil Earp. (The Chafin Collection)

Bob Paul won the disputed election for sheriff of Pima County and rode with the Earps in the pursuit of stage robbers. (The Chafin Collection)

Tom McLaury quarreled with Wyatt Earp before he joined his brother Frank and the Clanton brothers at the O.K. Corral. (Courtesy of the New-York Historical Society, New York City)

Robert Findley "Frank" McLaury threatened Virgil Earp after being accused of rustling army mules. (Courtesy of the New-York Historical Society, New York City)

Diarist George Parsons left his job as a bank clerk in San Francisco to seek his riches in Tombstone, and found himself in the midst of a crime spree. His diary provides a daily record of incidents and emotions during the dangerous days of Arizona. (The Chafin Collection)

Joseph Isaac "Ike" Clanton talked big and ran fast on October 26, 1881. (Courtesy of the New-York Historical Society, New York City)

Doc Holliday in Prescott, shortly before he came to Tombstone to join his friend Wyatt Earp. (Craig A. Fouts Collection)

Don't post, but place in the hands of discreet and reliable persons only.

$3,600 00 REWARD.

ARREST THE MURDERERS!

About 9 o'clock Tuesday evening, March 15, 1881, the stage bound from Tombstone to Benson was attacked by three men armed with Winchester rifles, at a point about two miles west from Drew's stage station, and Budd Philpot, the driver, and Peter Roerig, a passenger, shot and killed.

The attack was no doubt made for the purpose of robbery. The Territory and Wells, Fargo & Co. have a liberal standing reward for the arrest and conviction of persons robbing or attempting to rob the Express. In addition, the Governor and Wells, Fargo & Co. have each offered $300 for the arrest and conviction of each of the murderers of Philpot and Roerig, so that the rewards now offered amount to $1,200 or $1,400 each.

It is believed that the attempted robbery and murders were committed by Bill Leonard, Jim Crain and Harry Head, described as follows:

BILL LEONARD.

American; about 30 years old; about 5 feet, 8 or 9 inches high; weight, 120 ℔s.; long, dark, curly hair, when cared for hanging in ringlets down to shoulders; small, dark, boyish mustache, otherwise almost beardless; teeth very white and regular; dark eyes; small, sharp and very effeminate features; rather weak voice; left arm full of scars caused by injecting morphine; is subject to rheumatism; chews tobacco incessantly; speaks good Spanish; good shot with rifle and pistol; a jeweler by trade; is known in Silver City, Otero and Los Vegas, N. M.

JAMES CRAIN.

American; about 27 years old; about 5 feet, 11 inches high; weight, 175 or 180 ℔s.; light complexion; light, sandy hair; light eyes; has worn light mustache; full, round face, and florid, healthy appearance; talks and laughs at same time; talks slow and hesitating; illiterate; cattle driver or cow-boy.

HARRY HEAD.

About 18 or 20 years old; 5 feet, 4 or 5 inches high, weight, 120 ℔s.; chunky and well built; dark complexion; dark hair and eyes; rather dandyish; almost beardless; small foot and hand; good rider, and handy with rifle and pistol.

All mounted, and well armed with rifles and pistols, and the last trace of them they were going toward San Simon Valley.

If arrested, immediately inform Sheriff Behan and the undersigned by telegraph at Tombstone, A. T.

R. H. PAUL,
Special Officer of W., F. & Co.

Tombstone, A. T., March 23, 1881.

The wanted poster for stage coach robbers Bill Leonard, Harry Head, and Jimmy Crane, who eluded capture by the law only to die violent deaths in other battles.

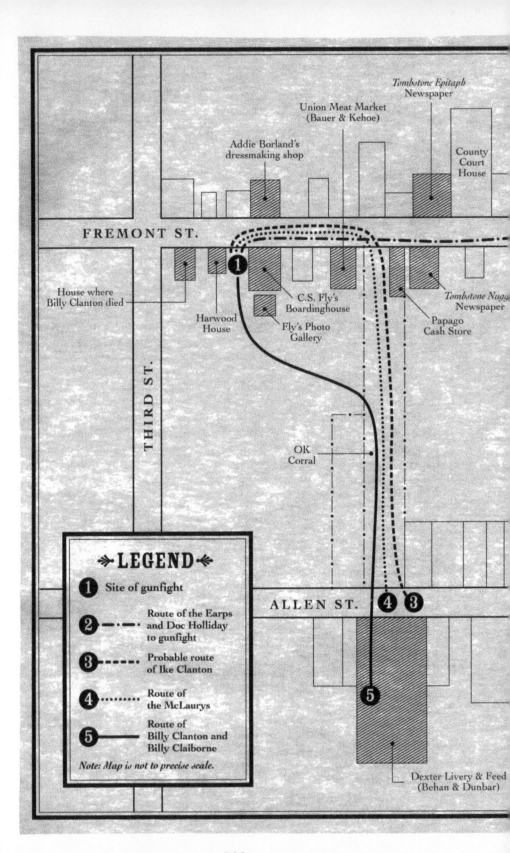

Tombstone Epitaph
Newspaper

Union Meat Market
(Bauer & Kehoe)

Addie Borland's
dressmaking shop

County
Court
House

FREMONT ST.

House where
Billy Clanton died

C.S. Fly's
Boardinghouse

Harwood
House

Fly's Photo
Gallery

Tombstone Nugg
Newspaper

Papago
Cash Store

THIRD ST.

OK
Corral

LEGEND

1 Site of gunfight

2 Route of the Earps
and Doc Holliday
to gunfight

3 Probable route
of Ike Clanton

4 Route of
the McLaurys

5 Route of
Billy Clanton and
Billy Claiborne

Note: Map is not to precise scale.

ALLEN ST.

Dexter Livery & Feed
(Behan & Dunbar)

210

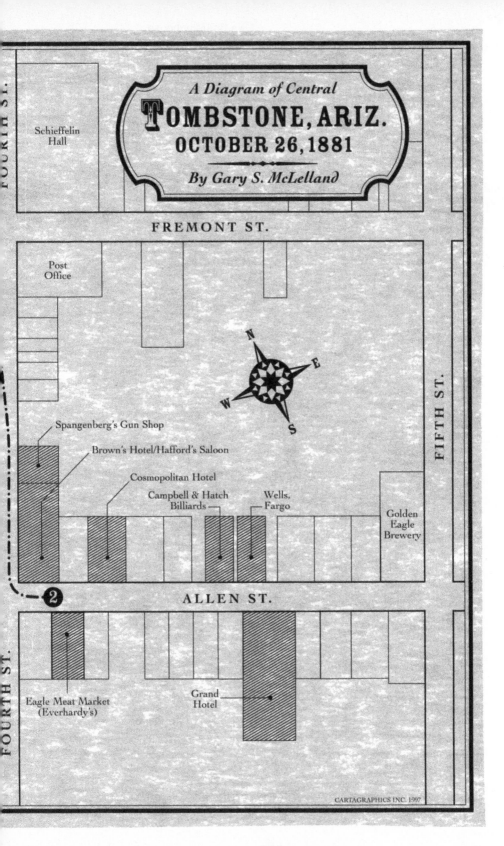

Fly Photo Gallery

Fly's Boardinghouse

Grand Hotel

Toughnut Street

Nellie Cashman's

Tombstone Looking North
Late 1881 or early 1882
All photos are from Fly originals.

McLelland Collection

A sixteen-mule team pulls out of Tombstone in late 1881 or '82. The three-story building at right is the Grand Hotel on Allen Street, where the outlaws placed a lookout to watch the activities of the Earps and their allies. The site of the gunfight was in about the center of the picture, behind the large white building. (Gary S. McLelland Collection)

Gird Block

Golden Eagle

Schieffelin Hall

Grand Hotel

Nellie Cashman's

Fire House

Tombstone Looking North
Late 1881 or early 1882

McLelland Collection

Schieffelin Hall, in center at top, stands above the other buildings in Tombstone in this picture taken in late 1881 or early 1882. The Grand Hotel is the two-story building at left. (Gary S. McLelland Collection)

212

Newman H. "Old Man" Clanton (above) was killed by Mexicans after bringing a herd
of cattle across the border. The photo was sent to massacre survivor Billy Byers, and
on the reverse (below) is written: "Mr. Clanton Killed on Aug. 13-81 by Mexicans with
4 other Americans in Guadalupe Canon New Mexico. Tomb Stone A.T. Sept. 13, 1881.
Compliments of Ike and Fin Clanton." (Robert G. McCubbin Collection)

Billy Byers (above left) played dead and survived the attack by Mexicans at Guadalupe Canyon. Billy Lang (above right) was killed in the first barrage while three of his cohorts were murdered in their sleeping rolls. (Robert J. McCubbin Collection)

Cochise County sheriff John Behan, whose friendly, outgoing personality made him a quick favorite in Tombstone, emerged as the political and romantic rival of Wyatt Earp. (Courtesy Arizona Historical Society/Tucson [27243])

Celia "Mattie" Earp, who lived as Wyatt's wife in Tombstone before Earp made the decision to pursue the affections of *Pinafore* dancer Josephine "Sadie" Marcus. (Courtesy Arizona Historical Society/Tucson [24245])

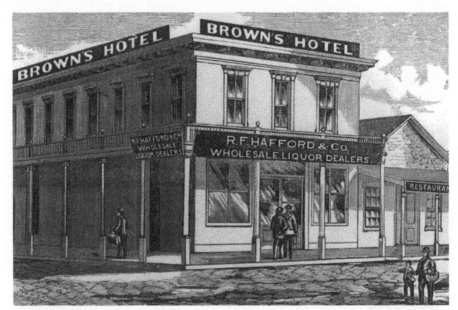

Hafford's Corner Saloon, located in Brown's Hotel, where the Earps congregated before they began their march to the gunfight against the Clantons and the McLaurys. (The Chafin Collection)

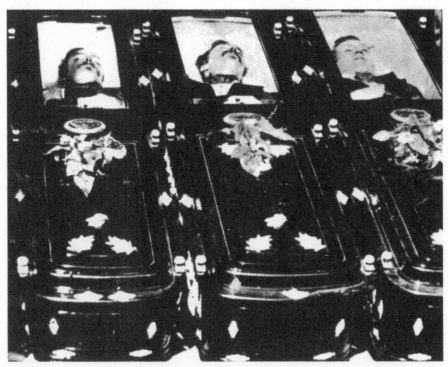

Tom McLaury, Frank McLaury, and Billy Clanton in their caskets after the gunfight. (Courtesy Arizona Historical Society/Tucson [17483])

215

Wells Spicer, justice of the peace in Tombstone, presided over the preliminary hearing to determine whether the Earps and Doc Holliday would go free or face a trial that could result in their executions. (The Chafin Collection)

Thomas Fitch put together the strategy that led to the Earps and Doc Holliday being freed after the Spicer hearing. (Gary L. Roberts Collection)

Epitaph editor and Tombstone mayor John Clum became the stongest voice of support for Wyatt Earp during his adventures in Arizona. (The Chafin Collection)

COL. JOHN P. CLUM.

Richard Rule came to the *Nugget* as city editor and later became editor. His anti-Earp editorials helped shape public opinion against Wyatt and his brothers. (The Chafin Collection)

Outlaw John Ringo faced off against Doc Holliday in the streets of Tombstone. (Courtesy Jack Burrows)

Morgan Earp marched with his brothers and Doc Holliday to the vacant lot on Fremont Street and drew blood. (Courtesy Arizona Historical Society/Tucson [49661])

Texas Jack Vermillion, as he appeared during the Civil War, joined Wyatt Earp for his vendetta against the cowboys who threatened Tombstone. (Courtesy John P. Vermillion)

Sam Purdy became editor of the *Epitaph* shortly after the Earps left the territory, and his writings would long confuse the issues in Tombstone. (Courtesy Arizona Historical Society/Tucson [49661])

Bat Masterson in Colorado, about the time he helped Doc Holliday avoid the extradition to Arizona that Doc believed would be his death warrant. (Craig A. Fouts Collection)

The Dodge City Peace Commission, one of the most famous pictures in frontier history. Standing, from left, W. H. Harris, Luke Short, Bat Masterson, and W. F. Petillon. Seated, from left, Charlie Bassett, Wyatt Earp, Frank McLain, and Neal Brown. (Craig A. Fouts Collection)

Wyatt Earp about 1887, while he was running saloons and dealing in real estate in San Diego. (Craig A. Fouts Collection)

Believed to be Doc Holliday's last photo, taken in Glenwood Springs in 1887, shortly before the dentist died of tuberculosis. (Craig A. Fouts Collection)

ON THE ROAD TO ARIZONA!

The *San Francisco Call* spoofed Wyatt Earp and *San Francisco Examiner* publisher William Randolph Hearst in the aftermath of the Sharkey–Fitzsimmons fight. The booklet dangling from Earp's neck is entitled: "Bloody Wyatt's Adventures/With a thrilling chapter on 10,000 fouls/Published by the Examiner."

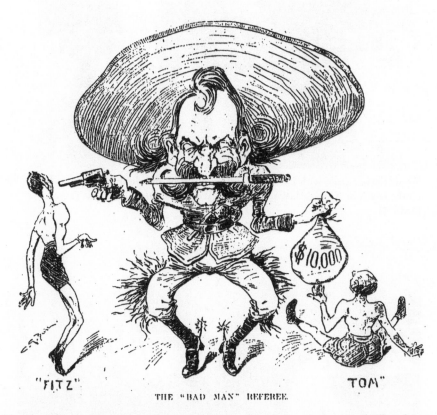

"FITZ"

THE "BAD MAN" REFEREE.

"TOM"

The *New York Herald* produced this demeaning cartoon during the hearing held to determine whether the Sharkey–Fitzsimmons fight had been fixed.

Wyatt Earp, center, with Ed Englestadt on his right and John Clum at his left on the beach in Nome, Alaska. (Courtesy Arizona Historical Society/Tucson [28167])

An aging Wyatt Earp looks across the Colorado River in 1925. He was by now a Western legend who could never escape his past. (Courtesy Arizona Historical Society/Tucson [76616])

Josephine "Sadie" Earp in about 1921. As a young woman, she was the beauty who was engaged to Johnny Behan. She wound up sharing her life with Wyatt Earp. (Robert G. McCubbin Collection)

VENDETTA

T HE NEWS REACHED COLTON in the flash of a telegraph key. Louisa Earp, Morgan's beautiful wife, fell to the floor and sobbed as the family gathered around her. She had returned to the safety of the family home in California, away from the dangers of Tombstone.

The Earps knew there was reason to worry. Those two shots through a poolroom window were a declaration of war between the cowboy criminals and the Earps, and Wyatt and his younger brother Warren were the only Earps left to fight. Ike Clanton had gone free, although it appeared he had been guilty of Virgil's shooting, at least in planning the ambush. Every criminal, it seemed, had pals ready to swear an alibi; conviction could come only if a shooter were found with a smoking gun in his hand standing over a body.

On Sunday, his 34th birthday, Wyatt made arrangements to send Morg's casket home to Colton. The funeral cortege left the Cosmopolitan shortly after noon, with the fire bell solemnly ringing "Earth to earth, dust to dust," the *Epitaph* reported. The procession moved to the train station in Benson, and left James to escort the coffin. Wyatt returned to Tombstone and went to Virgil's bedside. "Now, Virgil, I want you to go home. I am going to try to get those men who killed Morgan, and I can't look after you and them too. So you go home."[1] Wyatt had a bloody agenda ahead, and he could not leave his crippled brother and his wife in town at the mercy of robbers and killers. With an entourage, he took Virgil and Allie to the train station at Contention, where they received a warning.

"We were notified by persons in Tucson that Ike Clanton, Frank Stilwell, Billy Miller and another cowboy were watching every train coming through to kill me," Virgil told the *San Francisco Examiner* two months later. "They all had shotguns tied under their overcoats. Wyatt, Warren, Doc Holliday, John Johnson and Sherman McMasters concluded to see me through at Tucson." In the darkness of night, the Earps provided an easy target through the lighted windows of the train as it pulled into the Tucson depot.

"Almost the first men we met on the platform there were Stilwell and his friends, all armed to the teeth," Virgil continued. "They fell back into the crowd as soon as they saw I had an escort, and the boys took me to the hotel to supper. They put me on the train and I have not seen any of them since. While waiting for the train to move out a passenger notified me that some men were lying on a flat car near the engine. Just then the train moved out and immediately the firing commenced."

Apparently Wyatt saw Frank Stilwell and another man he believed to be Ike Clanton lying prone on a flatcar, shotguns in hand. Wyatt left the train from the opposite side and slipped around to the platform, where in the dim glimmer of gaslights he saw the reflections of two gun barrels aimed toward the lighted window with Virgil and Allie clearly visible inside. As Wyatt approached, the two men turned and ran, with Wyatt chasing after. One of the sprinters fell behind, allowing the marshal to catch up.[2]

"I ran straight for Stilwell. It was he who killed my brother," Wyatt Earp said. "What a coward he was. He couldn't shoot when I came near him. He stood there helpless and trembling for his life. As I rushed upon him he put out his hands and clutched at my shotgun. I let go both barrels, and he tumbled down dead and mangled at my feet. I started for Clanton then, but he escaped behind a moving train of cars. When the train had passed I could not find him."[3]

With one shotgun blast in a train yard, the once judicious and temperate lawman had turned killer. By Wyatt Earp's own admission, he shot a man begging for his life. The cowtown marshal who took pride in avoiding bloodshed had become what he once despised: a life-taker. He had crossed his own boundaries of decency, and he seemed to do so with a sense of pride.

Ike, again, made a running exit instead of facing the vengeance of a gun barrel. Wyatt would believe that Hank Swilling had also been at the scene, somewhere in the shadows. Earp's band rode off for Tombstone while Virgil and Allie made their lonely train ride to California. As the train pulled from the station, Wyatt apparently ran up and signaled to Virgil through the window, mouthing the words, "One for Morgan." Tiny Allie Earp strapped Virgil's big six-shooter around her waist and stayed within easy reach of Virgil's right arm so he could draw the gun if another attacker approached. The former marshal was too badly injured to wear his own gun.[4]

The next morning, workers found Stilwell's body filled with bullets and shotgun wounds. One ball passed from one armpit to another, piercing the lungs. Another penetrated the upper left arm, and another hit the right leg. A close-range shotgun blast went through the abdomen, liver, and stomach, and another chewed into the left leg.

"The expression of pain or fear on the face would seem to indicate that the man was aware of his danger, which he sought to avert with his left hand, as it was burnt and blackened with powder," the *Tucson Citizen* wrote.

Saloonkeeper George Hand got a glimpse of the body. "Frank Stillwell was shot all over, the worst shot-up man that I ever saw," he wrote in his diary.[5]

The brutal killing did not sit well with most Tucson residents. The Democratic *Arizona Daily Star* headlined, "A DARK DEED, Murder in Cold Blood of a Supposed Innocent Man—The Shadow of Tombstone's Bloody Feud Reaches Tucson." The *Nugget*'s headline was even more provocative: "Cowardly and Brutal Assassination of Frank Stilwell—His body filled with Bullets and Buckshot."

Ike Clanton sat down for a rare interview with the *Star* and said that Stilwell had been subpoenaed to appear before the district court and had arrived in Tucson on Sunday. Federal charges were still pending against Stilwell for stage robbery. Ike said he had been seated under the verandah of the hotel when Stilwell approached and asked him to join him on a trip downtown, because the Earps intended to kill him. Clanton said he first refused to go, then joined Frank on a short walk around the hotel. Then they separated, and Ike returned to the hotel. According to the *Star* report, the Earps and their friends emerged from the train, and soon several shots were fired in rapid succession, with a loud scream following the first shot. The engineer sat in his engine about two hundred yards from the incident, but the lights of the locomotive prevented him from seeing the killing. Several railroad hands approached the scene but were warned back by the shooters. The *Star* further said that Stilwell had an alibi for the time when Morgan was shot, a little detail that would later prove false. But the idea that Stilwell had an alibi had been planted in the public's mind.

Ike told the *Star* he heard the shooting, then armed himself and started back for the depot. He ran into several people and asked them the cause of the shooting. He was told they were celebrating the illumination of the city by new gaslights. Ike then went to bed, despite Stilwell's disappearance, audible gunshots, and the knowledge that the Earps had been on the train.[6] As with the Spicer hearing, Ike's story seemed implausible.

The inevitable coroner's inquest provided little detail on the shooting. A baggage checker named David Gibson testified that a newsboy had told him, "I guess there will be hell here tonight. The Earps and Holliday were aboard and were going to stop here as they had told him that the man who killed Morgan Earp was in Tucson."

Deputy U.S. Marshal J. W. Evans saw Doc step off the train with two shotguns, check them at the railroad office, then instruct a shorter man—probably McMasters—to reclaim the guns shortly before the shooting. Witnesses testified as to who they thought had guns and who did not; several saw muzzle flashes at a distance. James Miller, the fireman on the departing locomotive, provided the only important detail, saying he noticed a man running along the track, followed by four armed men. Miller heard "five or six shots fired in rapid succession" and saw one man in the act of shooting. As the train pulled out, he could see the other three men as well, all with guns in their hands.

W. J. Dougherty, who resided near the tracks, recalled the shooting differently. "I heard one shot and saw a flash, then in about half a minute heard another followed in quick succession by two more."[7] As the closest earwitness, Dougherty's story makes it likely that Wyatt shot first before other members of the band fired more slugs into Stilwell's body.

The inquest resulted in a warrant against Wyatt and Warren Earp, Doc Holliday, Sherman McMasters, and Jack Johnson for the murder of Frank Stilwell. Fueled by the coverage in the *Star* and the *Nugget,* many in southern Arizona were repelled by what appeared to be cold-blooded murder; the Earps and their supporters would stand by their conviction that Stilwell's attempt to assassinate Virgil and the killing of Morgan justified their action.

"One thing is certain," Virgil Earp said, "if I had been without an escort they would have killed me. I had to be lifted in and out of the car. I had not been out of bed before for nearly three months."[8]

The issue that had divided Tombstone would now divide all of Arizona and become a prime topic throughout the West. The proponents of due process would decry these U.S. marshals taking the law into their own hands, serving as juries and executioners without benefit of trial. The advocates of order at any cost would delight in the demise of another villain.

"A quick vengeance and a bad character sent to Hell where he will be the chief attraction until a few more accompany him," Parsons wrote in his journal.

The *Arizona Star* eloquently expounded the other view:

The sad condition of affairs which has existed in Tombstone during the last six months, in which several human beings have been hurried into eternity, is assuming a magnitude which calls upon all good citizens to stand abreast and put it down at any cost.

The assassination of Morgan Earp last Saturday night at Tombstone was a foul crime . . . but was the natural outgrowth of the cowardly assassination of William Clanton and the McLowery [*sic*] brothers by the Earps and Holliday, under the guise of official authority. Both crimes were equally heinous and the perpetrators should have been made to pay the severest penalty of the law.

But worse than all this was the deep-dyed assassination of Frank Stillwell [*sic*] at the depot last Monday night, when without any provocation a band of four or five slayers pursued a lonely man in the dark and without a word of warning murdered him in cold blood and then hied to their stamping grounds as unconcerned as though they had been out on a hunting expedition, or like so many blood thirsty Apaches rejoice over their crime.

The *Star* stood firm in its belief that in a nation of laws, due process must be followed; that Stilwell deserved his day in court. The paper noted that Stilwell had never been convicted of a crime, that murder and stage-robbing charges had been dropped against him; it failed to mention that a charge remained against him. The editorial then lashed against the Earps: "They are a roving band; their path is strewn with blood . . . wherever they halt in a settlement stage robberies follow and human life ceases to be sacred."[9]

While this inquest captured the attention of Tucson, another stunned Tombstone. On Tuesday, Marietta Spence, Pete Spence's wife of eight months, faced the coroner's inquest on the killing of Morgan Earp with a remarkable story to tell. The Spences lived across the street from Wyatt and Mattie, and Marietta Spence certainly had some knowledge of the Earps. She said Spence met with Stilwell, Indian Charlie, and a German named Freeze.

"Both Charlie and Stilwell were armed with pistols and carbines when they returned to the house Saturday night," Marietta Spence said. "The conversation between Spence and Stilwell and the others was carried on in a low tone. They appeared to be talking some secret. When they came in, I got out of bed to receive them and noticed they were excited. Why, I don't know. Stilwell came in the house about an hour before Spence and the other two."

The marriage of Pete and his Mexican wife had been marked by turmoil and beatings. The next morning, Marietta Spence said, more threats and abuse began: "On Sunday morning Spence told me to get breakfast about 6 o'clock, which I did—after we had a quarrel, during which he struck me and my mother, and during which he threatened to shoot me, when my mother told him he would have to shoot her, too. His expression was, that if I said a word about something I knew about he would kill me; that he was going to Sonora and would leave my dead body behind him. Spence didn't tell me so, but I knew he killed Morgan Earp; I think he did it, because he arrived at the house all of a tremble, and both the others who came with him. Spence's teeth were chattering when he came in. I asked if he wanted something to eat, and he said he did not. Myself and my mother heard the shots, and it was a little after when Stilwell and Indian Charlie came in, and from one half to three quarters of an hour after Spence and the other two men came. I think that Spence and the other two men, although they might have arrived during the night, had left their horses outside of town, and, after the shooting, had gone and got them. I judged they had been doing wrong from the condition, white and trembling, in which they arrived."

She also told of seeing an incident four days earlier, when Spence had been talking to an Indian, probably Charlie or Hank Swilling, as Morgan Earp walked past. "Spence nudged the Indian and said, 'That's him, that's him.' The Indian then started down the street, so as to get a good look at him."[10]

Marietta's mother, Francisca Castro, testified and backed up her daughter's story. Castro had filed assault charges against her son-in-law. Attorney Briggs Goodrich told of his meetings with Frank Stilwell, Ringo, and Wyatt Earp before the shooting. The testimony portrayed a trembling, teeth-chattering Pete Spence, who had some involvement in the murder, even if he had not held the gun. From Marietta's statements, it appeared Stilwell, too, had been part of the plot. The coroner's jury held that Spence, Stilwell, "John Doe" Freeze, Indian Charlie, and another man were the prime suspects in Morgan's assassination. Spence quickly turned himself in for the safety of Behan's jail. He kept a gun for protection should the Earps ride back to town and come looking for him.[11]

Stilwell's participation in the killing would become subject to question because, as the *Star* reported, he had been seen in Tucson early in the morning after Morgan's murder, a ride on horseback of about seventy miles. While it would have been difficult to make such time, he could have done so with a fast horse or by catching a train. John Pleasant Gray and others would later say that a small, fleet horse carried Stilwell on his night ride.

Deputy Sheriff William Bell captured Swilling in Charleston, after Hank engaged in a bloodless gunfight in a saloon over a disputed rifle. Swilling received a sentence of twenty days in jail for the affray.[12] The *Epitaph* would confuse the story and erroneously report that Swilling was Indian Charlie, but Charlie had chosen another sanctuary.

John Doe Freeze was almost immediately identified as Frederick Bode, a native of Germany who had listed his occupation as teamster, his age as 31, and his residence as Charleston in the 1880 census. Marietta Spence said that the man had been working as a teamster for the Acostas, who did hauling for Pete Spence's wood camp. The Freeze name probably came from the German pronunciation of Frederich—Freed-uh-reek—or he could have carried the nick-name Fritz. The case against Spence, Bode, and the others for murdering Morgan Earp came up for trial on April 2 and ended quietly. According to the *Epitaph*, the prosecution called Mrs. Spence to the stand, and the defense immediately objected. The prosecution dropped the case. Bode also was discharged. The paper did not give the reason for the objection. It can only be assumed the defense invoked the statute that wives could not then testify against their husbands. By that time, Wyatt Earp had made his own determination as to who had killed Morgan, and the cast of characters would be slightly different from the one described by Marietta Spence.

The *Star* and the *Nugget* kept railing against the injustice to Stilwell, but the Earps believed that Virgil survived his train trip only because they prevented Frank Stilwell from carrying out his execution plans. Through his years as a lawman, gambler, and buffalo hunter, Wyatt Earp had never been one to take human lives wantonly. Even after the shooting of Virgil, Wyatt Earp had not sought bloody vengeance. He had never been the vigilante—he had been the man who stood between the vigilantes and their form of justice. Now he believed he had no choice. After the Clanton trial and Morgan's murder, Wyatt Earp had come to believe that there was no solution other than to strike first, to become the victor before he became the victim.[13]

Wyatt Earp and his friends returned from Tucson to Tombstone Monday evening and settled into the Cosmopolitan Hotel. Pima County justice of the peace Charles Meyer wired Tombstone to say that the Earps were wanted in Tucson for the killing of Stilwell, and Behan should arrest the Earps. But the manager of the telegraph office, a friend of the Earps, showed the message to Wyatt before passing it on to Behan; he agreed to hold it as the Earp posse prepared to leave town again. Behan did not receive the telegram until 8 P.M., just as Wyatt's posse was getting ready to leave.

Billy Breakenridge said that Behan told him he had to arrest the Earps, and the sheriff wanted deputies Breakenridge and Dave Neagle to fetch their shotguns and return to back him up. Breakenridge said: "We had not gone a block on our way after our weapons when [the Earps] came out of the hotel. Behan met them on the sidewalk as they were getting on their horses and tried to arrest them. . . . They drew their guns on them and said they had seen him once too often and rode out of town as fast as they could go." The *Nugget* told the same story, with all members of the party pointing six-shooters at Behan.[14]

In a much different version, the *Epitaph* reported the Earp possemen had not raised their guns but were carrying rifles in the normal manner. "As Wyatt advanced to the front and approached Sheriff Behan, the sheriff said to him, 'Wyatt, I want to see you.' Wyatt replied, 'You can't see me; you have seen me once too often,' or words to that effect. He passed out into the street and turned around and said, 'I will see [Pima County sheriff] Paul,' and then the party passed on down the street."

They went to the stable, mounted their horses, and left town. Clara Brown repeated the *Epitaph* version, then debunked the sheriff's statement. "Behan claims they resisted arrest, but the bystanders claim this was all that passed, and nothing was said about an arrest. He also asserts that every one of the party drew their guns on him, which is denied by the spectators. All were heavily armed, but no motion was made."

Behan's credibility was further damaged, and with it went the last shred of respect he retained among the law-and-order types in Tombstone. "Bad muss this," Parsons wrote in his journal. "Sheriff is awake now that one of his friends is killed. Couldn't do anything before. Things are very rotten in that office. Fine reputation we're getting abroad."

Even the *Nugget* took a little jab at the sheriff.

> The action of sheriff Behan in attempting the arrest before completing his preparations to enforce it, if necessary, was strongly censured last night by many of our citizens. The Sheriff certainly has as good cause as any in this community to know the desperate character of the men with whom he had to deal, and it is possible he was a little hasty or over confident in the authority vested in him.[15]

Because Behan had neither presented a warrant nor said he was placing the party under arrest, it was not resisting arrest, and the little band rode out of Tombstone and into the national spotlight.

The murder of Morgan Earp had passed almost unnoticed outside Tombstone, but the Stilwell killing drew attention throughout the nation. One of the main reasons was timing. Morgan was killed late on a Saturday night, after most newspapers had closed their Sunday editions and editors had stopped checking wire reports. Stilwell's body was found in the early-morning hours, in time to make Monday's afternoon editions with follow-ups on Tuesday. Parsons, Clara Brown, and other Tombstone law-and-order sorts would believe that the wrong killing had become the focus, but the Stilwell story still drew more attention and clearly affected the public perception of the Earps.

With the discovery of Stilwell's body, newspapers labeled Wyatt Earp's actions a vendetta. It quickly became *the* Vendetta, capitalized; a major story in California papers, which were devoting much column space to Earp's activities. The Fremont Street gunfight had been barely a blip in the newsprint of the West, but headlines of "The Arizona Vendetta" became commonplace in the San Francisco dailies. Earp, as a deputy U.S. marshal, had the jurisdiction to chase criminals for whom he carried a warrant. He also had the right to appoint possemen, and it can be assumed that Holliday and the rest were duly sworn in, though no confirmation exists.

Life went on in Tombstone. A new ice cream store opened on Fourth Street, and the singing societies held their meetings. Mattie and Bessie Earp prepared to leave town on Friday morning. For the first time since December of 1879, there would be no family members to watch over the business interests that had made the Earps major property owners in Tombstone.

"Mrs. James Earp and Mrs. Wyatt Earp left to-day for Colton, California, the residence of their husbands' parents," the *Epitaph* wrote on March 24. "These ladies have the sympathy of all who know them, and for that matter the entire community. Their trials for the last six months have been of the most severe nature." When the train passed through Tucson, a deputy sheriff had heard rumors that the Earp party was aboard and quickly rode into the station to search for Wyatt and Warren, only to find the two women.[16] In Colton, James and his father, Nicholas, awaited a telegram requesting their appearance in Arizona. Up in Sacramento, Newton, the eldest of the Earp brothers, also began packing his belongings should the call to arms arrive. Newton was the son of Nick's first wife, and he also had a background in law enforcement.[17]

Wyatt had all the help he needed with his band of questionable repute. Warren Earp was a tough fighter. Texas Jack Vermillion, whose long hair flowed down his back, had been a carpenter before joining Earp's posse, and was considered fearless and a crack shot. Holliday had been disparaged throughout the Southwest, and both McMasters and heavy-set Jack Johnson—called Turkey Creek Jack—had once ridden with the rustlers, McMasters being accused of stage robbery and horse stealing. Earp would explain later that they had long worked as Earp informants among the rustlers, providing information.

"Well, I had this Johnson with me and the thing was getting pretty warm between me and the rustlers and Johnson had joined my party, and he had been identified with this other party for a while and they got on to him," Earp said in a 1925 deposition. "I was using Johnson at that time the same as [today's police] would use a stool pigeon, but we didn't call them stool pigeons in those days. I was letting him get information for me. They had got on to him, of course it was a little dangerous for a man like that to go out alone."[18]

Earp identified this Johnson as John Blount, who apparently took on the undercover assignment in an effort to get Earp and Wells, Fargo to support the release of his brother, Alan Blount, from territorial prison, which happened shortly before the killing of Morgan. According to Earp, John Blount had been a bookkeeper in Missouri and was well educated before going under the alias of Johnson in Arizona.[19] McMasters, from Illinois, also had an unusual background, though few particulars are known. He spoke fluent Spanish, and his acquaintances believed him well educated.

Angry over the public rebuff from Wyatt Earp in front of the Cosmopolitan Hotel, Behan acted quickly, raising a posse of twelve men to pursue the Earps through Cochise County on the Tucson murder charge. He departed on Friday for a most unusual adventure.

Parsons seemed surprised as he wrote in his diary: "Excitement again this morning. Sheriff went out with a posse supposably [*sic*] to arrest the Earp party, but they will never do it. The cowboy element is backing him strongly, John Ringo being one of the [Behan deputies]. There is a prospect of a bad time, and there are about three men who deserve to get it in the back of the neck. Terrible thing, this, for our town, but the sooner it is all over with the better."

Behan's posse became one of the true oddities of the bizarre Arizona conflict. Backed by deputies Ringo, Fin Clanton, and other members of the cowboy-outlaw crowd, the sheriff rode out to pursue the U.S. marshal's band of Wyatt and Warren Earp, with troublemaker Doc Holliday, suspected thief Sherm McMasters, and the other shady characters. It is no wonder many Arizonans would view the situation as one band of crooks against another.

Deputy Breakenridge, who did not accompany the posse, defended Behan's unusual selection of deputies. "He took those men knowing that the Earp party would resist arrest, and, on account of the feud between them, he believed the cowboys would stay and fight."[20]

Behan defended himself to the *Nugget*. "He urges that the desperate character of the men for whom he had warrants, and the nature of the country in which
they sought refuge, demanded that the pursuing party should be composed of
men equally inured to the hardships of mountain life—men who are at home in
the saddle, and of whose fighting qualifications there is no doubt. Of such men
the posse was supposed to be composed. If necessary to capture criminals, we
deem it would be right to employ Indian scouts and trailers, for 'the law must be
supreme.' To some this may not seem just, but it is reasonable."[21]

Pima County sheriff Bob Paul rode down from Tucson to meet Behan's
posse before it returned to Tombstone. "As I had had no sleep since leaving Tucson I went to sleep in the express office and told Behan where I could be found,"
Paul wrote later. "He agreed to call me if he heard where the Earps were, as I
wished to go with him. . . . I had a horse engaged to go with Behan and he
agreed to call me if he started out again, but he did not do it and I returned to
Tucson."[22] Without Paul, Behan would be under no constraint to return the
Earps alive.

Before Behan could find the Earps, the Earps found their first suspect. The
little band rode into Pete Spence's wood camp in the South Pass of the Dragoon
Mountains in the late-morning hours of Wednesday, March 22. According to the
Hooker manuscript, the camp had been used as a rendezvous for rustlers, where
stolen cattle would be driven to have their brands changed with running irons.
Wyatt Earp and his band rode up to ask a group of mostly Mexicans for directions. The Earp party then approached Theodore Judah, an American among
the workers, to try to locate Spence. But Spence was still in town, sitting safely
in Behan's jail beyond reach of the Earps. Wyatt kept asking questions as he
tried to locate Hank Swilling. When he finished the questioning, Earp led his
party toward the Tombstone road.

From the distance another Mexican worker saw the band and realized it
was coming after him. The Earp party went off the road and rode up the hill in
pursuit of Florentino Cruz, called Indian Charlie by his cowboy pals, who they
believed had been a lookout at the killing of Morgan. Simon Acosta, another
worker, said he saw the Earp party start firing on Charlie. Through a translator,
Acosta said: "I immediately ran up the hill and saw them shooting at Florentino.
I did not see Florentino fall; I saw them following up the hill and firing at him. I
did not pay attention to the number of shots fired. They stayed on the top of the
hill awhile, dismounted, and soon after went off. . . . When I saw Florentino, he
was running away. The pursuing party spread out, some on each side, and others immediately following."

Epimania Vegas added, "I saw the man that was shot running and jumping
from side to side. I saw him fall."

Wyatt Earp never spoke much about this killing, avoiding the subject in
newspaper interviews. In later years he spoke with three biographers, and the
story was written differently each time. One version says Florentino ran away,
then turned with gun drawn to receive a barrage of shots from Earp and his
pals; another says Wyatt approached Florentino and extracted a confession from
him that he had been in the group that killed Morgan, along with Hank Swilling, Curley Bill, Ringo, and Stilwell, and that he had been paid $25 to help. By

this version, Earp then challenged him to a one-on-one shootout, giving Florentino a chance to save his life. While such a shootout is probably a fabrication, there is a distinct possibility that Earp did talk with Cruz before leaving him dead in the Dragoons. Earp would later write to author Walter Noble Burns, "I am satisfied that Spence had nothing to do with the assassination of Morgan, although he was against us." Earp named Ringo, Curley Bill, Swilling, Stilwell, and Cruz as the murderers, information that could have come from Florentino Cruz before he received the barrage of bullets. Four shots struck Cruz, probably more than Wyatt Earp would have fired in a face-to-face shootout.[23]

The Earp band had finished its business. "They then came down the hill very leisurely to the road and returned in the direction of the camp," Judah testified at the coroner's inquest. "They proceeded but a short distance and turned around again. They then went along the road until it makes a sharp turn, and kept in the same direction, easterly, passing into the hills."[24]

The second killing of the Arizona Vendetta further stirred the passions of the population, with Parsons commenting: "More killing by the Earp party. Hope they'll keep it up."

The *Arizona Star* railed against the bloodshed, continuing to trumpet the need for due process over justice dealt from the barrel of a revolver. "As the hours roll on, the condition of affairs is growing into a war, and the banditti appear to be ignoring law and common decency, and have taken to the mountains as highwaymen, murdering whoever their fancy may lead them to believe are their enemies. They are heaping crime upon crime and lawlessness upon outrage."[25]

As further incitement, the *Star* ran a letter from mine owner J. S. Browder praising Cruz, his former employee. "I know the man Florentino Cruz. . . . We always found Cruz to be a harmless and inoffensive man." Browder further condemned punishment without observing the legal technicalities. "I very much question whether law abiding people sanction the kind of justice which is administered from the muzzle of guns in the hands of Doc Holliday and the Earp party."[26]

Florentino may have seemed harmless to Browder, but he had been arrested late in 1880 on charges of horse stealing, and Earp would forever believe that there was no question that Cruz was indeed Indian Charlie, the lookout who watched while the triggermen killed Morgan. No matter the justification, however, Wyatt Earp had stepped beyond the law.

All this talk of vendetta grew a little too strong for even the most ardent boosters of vigilantism. The *San Francisco Exchange* hoped for a bloody end to the whole affair:

> The Earp vendetta still booms. The latest dispatch from the seat of war tells of another murder by the Earp party—a Mexican named Florentine, whom the Earps suspected of being concerned in Morgan's murder. The Sheriff has enlisted the cowboys under his banner, and he himself evidently has no stomach for the job. Still the outlook is hopeful for the people of the Territory. When the cowboys and the Earps meet a sanguinary conflict is inevitable. It may fortunately happen that the slaughter on both sides will leave but a few survivors, and a big funeral, with the Earps and cowboys to furnish the remains, would be the lifting of a great weight from the minds of the citizens of Tombstone.[27]

Across the West, newspapers gave daily reports of Wyatt Earp's Vendetta, and it held fascination for a nation that romanticized its tough law enforcers. Many Americans could identify with a man avenging the death of a brother killed by assassins, and the image emerged of Wyatt Earp as a noble but rogue officer. The image would continue to grow for more than a century.

Even as this noble image grew among some elements of the populace, press reports continued to criticize the rogue lawman. Back in San Francisco, top officials of Wells, Fargo & Co. made a most uncharacteristic move. The usually circumspect executives sat down for an interview with the *Examiner* to provide unqualified backing for Wyatt Earp, once a loyal and trusted employee.

The officials were not identified, but it is likely that Jim Hume sat in for the little talk. They described the cowboys as a gang of about seventy-five, "some of whom own ranches and are engaged in the legitimate raising of cattle. Others of them are cattle thieves, and for a change will occasionally rob a stage. The gang are under the leadership of Ike Clanton, and they have a large number of adherents in Tombstone, through whose countenance they are able to terrorize the town. In fact, it is stated that a leading official stands in with them whenever occasion arises." The reference, of course, was to Behan.

"The majority of the best citizens of Tombstone, however, are in favor of the Earps, who have incurred the enmity of the cowboys simply because they refused to allow them to have their own way when they came to town on a protracted spree, Virgil Earp being Marshal of the place. Wyatt Earp is represented to be the brains of the Earp confederacy, now consisting of James, Virgil, Wyatt and Warren, Morgan having been killed."

The executives said it was untrue that Wyatt was a professional gambler, then cited the petitions from Dodge City and Wichita to support his character.

"From the above it will be seen that up to the time that Wyatt Earp was engaged in the fight which resulted in the death of Billy Clanton, Tom McLowry and Frank McLowry, he bore an excellent reputation, and the statement that he and his brothers were ever concerned in any of the stage robberies is pronounced by the officials of Wells, Fargo to be absolutely untrue. Doc Holliday, although a man of dissipated habits and a gambler, has never been a thief and was never in any way connected with the attempted stage robbery when Philpot [*sic*], the stage driver, was killed. For three-quarters of an hour after the stage passed the Wells, two and a half miles from Tombstone, he was seen at the latter place, so drunk that he was helped upon his horse, and the robbery occurred thirteen miles from Tombstone, so it was utterly impossible for him to be there.

"Neither did he form a part of agent Williams' and detective Paul's posse afterward. The statement that he was present on the occasion of that robbery was put forth by the cowboys and their friends to throw further discredit upon the Earp brothers and their friends."

The officials continued to detail incident by incident, pointing out that they had never telegraphed Wyatt about the reward for Crane, Leonard, and Head being "Dead or Alive"; such rewards are paid if the suspect is killed in the course of an arrest attempt. (They did not mention that the wire supposedly had gone to Marshall Williams.) They referred to the *Nugget* as "The Cowboy Organ," and decried the impact of the gang on southern Arizona.

"These men have complete control of certain parts of the Territory, especially Tombstone and Cochise county, where one of the newspapers of the town, leased by a Deputy Sheriff until recently, was published in their interest."

The officials detailed recent events, climaxing with Earp's repudiation of Behan in the streets of Tombstone. "Wyatt Earp has said that he would never surrender to Sheriff Behan, because he believed that if he was once in his power without arms, the Sheriff would allow the cowboys in the jail to murder him. Which party will come out victorious in the conflict it is difficult to tell, but that there will be more bloody work in Arizona from the well-known desperate tangle of the contending parties, there can be no doubt."[28]

For Wells, Fargo to come out with such an unqualified statement of support was unusual for the conservative company. It was certainly in response to newspaper editorials throughout the West condemning Wyatt Earp for becoming a law unto himself. Some element of public relations may have entered into the decision to present such a resounding show of support, but the company had little to gain by taking sides against an incumbent sheriff charged with protecting their shipments. Wells, Fargo definitely took a stand in voicing complete support for Deputy U.S. Marshal Wyatt S. Earp.

Bob Paul apparently returned to Tombstone and refused to join Behan's cowboy band. Parsons, on March 23, seemed to have inside knowledge of the situation when he wrote: "Paul is here but will not take a hand. He is a true, brave man himself, and will not join the murderous posse here. If the truth were known, he would be glad to see the Earp party get away with all these murderous outfits. . . . Behan will get it yet." Paul returned to Tucson and said he did not pursue the Earps because the members of Behan's posse were mostly hostile to them, "and that a meeting meant bloodshed without any possibility of arrest." Paul said he expected the Earps to ride into Tombstone and surrender.

Behan sought any means of striking at the Earps. On Thursday night he arrested Earp allies Dan Tipton and Charlie Smith for resisting a law officer and conspiracy. Bail was raised immediately, paid by Hatch and several others. A day later the two men were discharged because of a flaw in the arrest warrant.

Behan quickly took to the saddle again, riding out with his posse. Yet they could not find Wyatt. Behan's actions grew suspect to some. Parsons wrote: "Mileage still counting up for our rascally Sheriff. He organizes posses, goes to within a mile of his prey and then returns. He's a good one." Behan and his posse were making a big dent in the budgets of Pima and Cochise counties.

WITH INDIAN CHARLIE DEAD, the Earps began their ride back toward Tombstone. Still awaiting trial on the shooting of Morgan, Pete Spence sat in jail, armed and fearing retribution. The townsfolk were in a furor, hearing rumors that the Earp posse would ride in to kill Spence and hoping that there would not be some wild shootout on their streets.

Reports told of two sheriffs' posses in pursuit of the Earps, one led by Behan and the other made up of Charleston cowboys, deputized for the chase. The Charleston posse rode into Contention on the 24th, and saloonkeeper George Hand recorded the incident in his diary: "The cowboys, 20 or more, have been prowling around all the morning. They are well mounted, well armed and seem intent on biz. They are in search for the Earp party who took break- fast two miles above here this morning."[29] Curley Bill, the most notorious outlaw in the territory, led the posse and apparently represented himself as having been deputized by the sheriff—the *Nugget* identified him as a deputy. Although Behan would later deny that he had authorized Curley Bill to form his own posse, Behan had virtually given all the cowboys in the country a license to hunt Earps by deputizing the likes of Ringo and Fin Clanton.

Wyatt needed money for his posse. He had the friends to deliver quick cash. Charlie Smith, freshly out of jail, met the Earp party outside Tombstone and Wyatt sent him back to town with a message to mine operator E. B. Gage asking for a thousand-dollar loan. Earp wanted it delivered the next day at a waterhole in the Whetstone Mountains known as Iron Springs.[30] However, Smith made the mistake of stopping at the Alhambra to buy a bottle of whiskey, and Deputy Dave Neagle detained him again. Two other men were assigned to carry the cash to the little watering hole. Tony Kraker and Dick Wright—Whistling Dick—made the trip to Iron Springs on Friday morning, March 24, while the Earps were coming from another direction.

The Earp party rode on to Iron Springs, leaving Warren behind to watch for a messenger with money. On that hot spring day, Wyatt loosened his car- tridge belt and let it sag down at the side. The party rode toward the little mud- hole of Iron Springs and began to descend a sloping trail. When the waterhole came into sight, the riders found a surprise.

"As we got near the place I had a presentiment that something was wrong, and unlimbered my shotgun," Earp said. "Sure enough, nine cowboys sprang up from the bank where the spring was and began firing at us." One of them was Curley Bill. A bullet hit Vermillion's horse and the animal fell atop Texas Jack's leg.

Earp leaped off his horse and threw the bridle over his arm. "I expected Holliday and my companions to do the same thing and make a fight," he said. "I was surprised when I looked around to see them disappearing in a cloud of dust as fast as their horses could carry them. My horse reared and tugged at the bri- dle in such a wild fashion that I could not regain the saddle. I reckoned that my time had come. But if I was to die, I proposed that Curley Bill at least should die with me."

The rustler fired rapidly with his shotgun, tearing into the skirts of Earp's long coat. Earp brought his own shotgun to his shoulder and pointed directly at Curley Bill's heart, then fired both barrels. "His chest was torn open by the big charge of buckshot. He yelled like a demon as he went down," Earp said.[31]

This became one of the great images of the Earp legend—Wyatt leaping off his horse with gunfire blasting around him, his friends retreating, and bullets tearing through his clothes.

With his shotgun empty, Earp reached for the rifle in the scabbard on his saddle as the outlaws fired from the thicket. The firing so frightened his horse that it reared repeatedly, keeping the Winchester beyond Earp's reach. Earp reached for his six-shooter, only to find the cartridge belt had slipped down around his thighs, and the guns had worked their way to his back. He pulled a pistol and fired into the thicket of cottonwoods, wounding outlaw Johnny Barnes. Wyatt then tried to mount his horse.

"When I tried to get astride I found that [the belt] had fallen down over my thighs, keeping my legs together," Earp said. "I was perched up there, trying to pull my belt higher with one hand."

It became a strange, almost comical, sight as Wyatt tried to balance in one stirrup as the horse twisted. He grasped the saddle with one hand and tugged his cartridge belt with the other, his nose almost against the horn. His peculiar gyrations would have made Earp a most difficult target to hit. One of the rustlers' bullets knocked the saddle horn loose, striking between Earp's hand and nose, and he nearly fell off the horse. Another bullet hit the heel of his boot with such force he believed he had been shot. Finally, he pulled up the cartridge belt and mounted the horse. With bullets flying around him, he stopped long enough to pick up Vermillion, then galloped back to join his party.

Earp said his left foot and leg went numb, and he rode back believing he had been shot in his heel. It was not until he pulled off his boot that he realized he had not been touched by a bullet. "When I got to the ground, I found that the skirts of my coat, which had been held out at my sides by my leather holsters, had been riddled into shreds." When Earp rode up, Holliday grabbed him gently by the arm and said, "You must be shot all to pieces." The party was stunned to find he was untouched. Holliday wanted to mount a charge against the cowboys. Earp said he had had enough. "If you fellows are hungry for a fight you can go on and get your fill," he said and turned his horse in the other direction.

"Our escape was miraculous," Holliday said.[32] "The shots cut our clothes and saddles and killed one horse, but did not hit us. I think we would have been all killed if God Almighty wasn't on our side."

Wright and Kraker, carrying Wyatt's loan money, rode up to Iron Springs but failed to find Warren. Instead, they discovered several cowboys in the camp where they expected to find the Earps. The outlaws pointed their guns at the pair, and Kraker yelled, "What are you doing here, you lop-eared Missourian?" in his Austrian accent. Wright whistled up a phony story about hunting for lost mules, then they joined the rustlers for a meal and rode out without revealing they were carrying funds for Wyatt Earp's posse.[33] At the outlaw camp, Kraker and Wright learned the amazing story of the shotgun duel between Wyatt and Curley Bill. Without yet delivering the thousand dollars to Earp, they returned to Tombstone and met with a *Nugget* reporter who printed an account of the battle from an unnamed source almost exactly as Earp would tell it in coming years.[34]

Word of the gunfight filtered quickly back to Tombstone, with details reported inaccurately. The *Epitaph* placed the battle at Burleigh Springs, miles away from the actual site, apparently in an attempt to cloak the real location of the Earp band. The *Nugget* printed a report that Wyatt Earp had been killed or badly wounded.

Parsons heard his news from other sources and wrote: "Rumors of battle and four of Earp party killed received this a.m. Discredited. I got strictly private news though later that 'Curly Bill' has been killed at last by the Earp party, and none of the latter hurt. Sheriff Behan has turned all of the cowboys loose against the Earps and, with this lawless element, is trying to do his worst. I am heartily glad at this repulse, and hope the killing is not stopped with the cutthroat named. Feeling is growing here against the ring, sheriff, etc., and it would not surprise me to know of a necktie party some fine morning. Things seem to be coming to this pass. Then let it come. The time is ripe and rotten ripe for change."

The "Battle of Burleigh" drew headlines throughout the West, with newspapers from San Francisco to San Diego printing one set of false rumors one day, another the next. The *Epitaph* had the first report of the event, with this description of the Earp charge into the cowboy fusillade: "Like a thunderbolt from the hand of Jove, the six desperate men charged up on their assailants like the light brigade at Balaklava and, within easy reach, returned the fire, under which one man went down never to rise again. The remaining eight fled to the brush and regained their horses, when they rode away toward Charleston as if the King of Terrors was at their heels in hot pursuit." The report, mixed images and all, went out on the Associated Press wires and received wide play through the country. Some papers condemned Wyatt's direct but questionable style. Others celebrated it.[35]

"So Curly Bill has at last been gathered in," the *San Francisco Exchange* wrote. "Arizona tourists will miss the cheerful presence of Bill when they stop over night at Tombstone or Tucson. His merry pranks were the talk of the town and the newspapers. His playful exhibition of his skill with the pistol never failed to delight those communities which the peripatetic William favored with his presence. . . . This makes the fourth [actually third] the Earp party has scored to the cowboys' one. We are beginning to doubt the courage and invincibility of that much-talked-of class, and are willing to give long odds on the murderous superiority of the Earp crowd."[36]

After the fight, the cowboy survivors quickly took away Curley Bill's body and buried it, probably at the nearby Patterson ranch.[37] They then began a campaign of misinformation that denied the outlaw leader's death. This could have been done to prevent the Earp band from collecting a rumored $1,000 bounty placed on Curley Bill's head by Henry Clay Hooker and other members of the Cattlegrowers Association, or to keep Wyatt Earp from receiving public acclaim for shotgunning the toughest and most desperate villain in Cochise County. The cowboys and the *Nugget* would consistently deny Curley Bill's death, reporting he had actually been miles away from Iron Springs at the time. They also said he used the rumor of his murder as an opportunity to move to Texas or Colorado for a new start on a clean life.

In reality, there is little doubt that Earp actually killed Curley Bill. Outlaw Johnny Barnes, wounded at the scene, would confirm it to Fred Dodge. Wyatt Earp repeatedly told the same story, and both Doc Holliday and Warren Earp were quoted in newspaper interviews repeating Earp's story. And while several Curley Bill sightings were made around the West—he got around then nearly as much as Elvis does now—none could be confirmed beyond what one old-timer told another. For the outlaw to disappear and leave Earp claiming the kill simply does not make sense.

After the gunfight, Wyatt and his band remained in the hills on Friday night, then came to the outskirts of Tombstone long enough for a Saturday-

evening meal. Parsons made note of the strange sounds: "Some long and continued firing right by the house Saturday evening, so that the whistling bullets
were heard, is now accounted for. It was signalling going on between the Earps'
friends and themselves undoubtedly. I went out several times to see what was
up. Discovered nothing." According to one report, some of the cowboys left Iron
Springs and stole four mules from a Mexican near Calabasas then robbed two
Chinese restaurateurs of $200 and their clothes before sending the cooks on a
naked scamper as the cowboys fired their guns.[38]

Cochise County was distracted by another murder on Saturday, when Mar-
tin Ruter Peel took a bullet from two masked men at the Tombstone Milling and
Mining Co. office near Charleston. Behan, busy with his Earp chase, left Billy
Breakenridge to deal with the killing of Judge Bryant L. Peel's son.

Newly appointed Territorial Governor Frederick A. Tritle arrived in Tombstone on Monday, and enjoyed a fine reception in the midst of the Arizona War.
Tritle discussed the situation with local officials and stayed overnight with Mil-
ton Clapp, a member of the Citizens Safety Committee. Tritle had been a former
partner of William Murray, who had offered Virgil Earp a vigilante force on the
day of the gunfight in Tombstone and was clearly aligned with Clum's law-and-
order faction. After Tritle left town, the *Tucson Citizen* reported on his observations:

> He found matters in a very chaotic condition. There is a general feeling of insecurity,
> owing to the evident powerlessness or unwillingness of the civil authorities to afford
> protection to life and property. The condition of affairs is insurrectionary and
> processes of law cannot be served without violence. A virtual reign of terror exists,
> which makes peaceable, law-abiding citizens unwilling to serve as posse and stifles a
> free expression of opinion upon the tragic occurrences of the past few weeks.
>
> Tritle took action, raising a posse to help deputy U.S. Marshal Jackson, re-
> cently appointed to the post. He also urged Tombstone citizens to set up their own
> defense fund to pay special deputies, then wired President Arthur to explain, "the ut-
> ter failure of the civil authority and the anarchy prevailing; the international trouble
> likely to grow out of this cattle thieving along the border, the fact that business is
> paralyzed and the fairest valleys in the Territory are kept from occupation by the
> presence of the cowboys."[39]

By this time, Wyatt Earp was not drawing too fine a point on the legalities
of his actions. And while he would forever maintain he was functioning as a
deputy marshal, hunting stage robbers and holding a warrant for Curley Bill, no
evidence of such remains. Wyatt Earp was making his own law.

Charlie Smith joined the little group outside Tombstone. The addition of
Smith brought the total of Earp's posse to six, with the two Earps, Holliday,
Texas Jack, and Turkey Creek Jack. The band left the Tombstone area and
rode into the Dragoons, where they boarded a westbound passenger train and
searched the cars, apparently expecting to find a friendly messenger delivering
money to them.[40] They continued on to a ranch owned by brothers Jim and
Hugh Percy, where they hoped to find a meal and a place to sleep, but the Percy
brothers obviously feared cowboy retribution if Wyatt Earp were found on the
premises.

"We're for you boys, all right, but if certain people knew you had stayed here, they'd give us the worst of it," one of the brothers said. The Earps would learn later that two of Behan's deputies, Barney Riggs and Frank Hereford, were hiding in the barn during the visit.[41]

Earp's party napped, then rode on to the Hooker ranch for a little rest in a place that would offer sanctuary. Hit hard by rustler raids, Hooker supported Earp and sided with him against Behan. More important, Hooker was not intimidated by the threats of a cowboy gang coming to his Sierra Bonita Ranch. The Earp horses had grown fatigued from the long rides, and men and beasts needed time to rest.

Back in Tombstone, Deputy Sheriff Breakenridge, left behind by Behan to run the office with two other deputies, learned that two wanted outlaws, Zwing Hunt and Arthur Boucher, alias Billy Grounds and nicknamed "Curley Bill's Kid," were staying at the Chandler Milk Ranch eight miles outside town. The *Epitaph* described the two as "notorious hard cases, the worst of the types of cowboy rustlers," and some suspected they had killed Peel.[42] Breakenridge had warrants for their arrest on other charges, and he led his citizen posse to the dairy, ready for a fight. In the ensuing shootout, Deputy John Gillespie was killed, and deputies Edward Allen and Jack Young were wounded. Hunt and Grounds were badly wounded. Tombstone townsfolk again began fearing a cowboy vengeance raid.

"Calky times, very," Parsons wrote. "14 murders and assassinations in ten days. More than one a day. A hanging bee anticipated tonight, but not carried out. Cowboy raid on town expected tonight. Things quiet thus far. The two cowboys shot, Hunt and Grounds, were taken first to undertakers and kept awhile, but not dying quick enough, were removed to hospital. A regular epidemic of murder is upon us. What and when the end will be, God only knows."

The end came quickly for Grounds. Hunt recovered sufficiently from his injuries to escape Behan's custody, as many did, when his uncle walked him out of the unguarded hospital.

Martin Peel's murder a few days earlier would officially be listed as unsolved, and the dead man's father, Judge Bryant L. Peel, made an emotional call to the people of Cochise County to put down the lawlessness:

> *To the People of Tombstone:* Perhaps I am not in a condition to express a clear, deliberate opinion, but I would say to the good citizens of Cochise county there is one of three things you have to do. There is a class of cut-throats among you and you can never convict them in court. You must combine and protect yourselves and wipe them out or you must give up the country to them, or you will be murdered one at a time, as my son has been.[43]

Peel's grief-stricken cry crystallized the fear and feeling of the terrified town.

WYATT EARP TRADED HIS FATIGUED HORSES for fresh mounts at Hooker's Sierra Bonita and languished over a long meal happily free of trail dust. Earp said he took his first drink of hard liquor in Arizona while he waited at the ranch. Off in the distance a brown cloud indicated that several riders were headed for the ranch, and both Earp and Hooker knew who was coming. Behan had left Tombstone Monday morning. One of his deputies had visited the Percy ranch earlier and discovered Earp's destination. Behan rode off toward Hooker's, and a confrontation seemed imminent. Earp decided to choose the battle site and led his band to a bluff a few miles from the ranch. There he waited, expecting the conflict to come at any moment.

What followed would be reported very differently by Hooker's side and by Harry Woods in his comments to his old pals at the *Nugget*. By the *Nugget* version, Hooker refused to provide any information. He said he didn't know where the Earps were and wouldn't tell even if he did, concluding with "Damn the officers and damn the law." Hooker provided food but refused to supply horses. After breakfast, Behan and Woods went to Fort Grant, ten miles distant, with the intention of hiring government scouts to trail the Earps. However, the commander informed Behan that he had discharged the Apache scouts a few days earlier. Behan and Woods were unable to find the Earps' trail, so they rode off on another search, then returned to Hooker's, where Henry Hooker informed them that the Earp party had been better armed and would have their way with Behan's posse. According to Woods, Behan again bravely went off searching for the Earps, without finding a trace. The report concluded with an editorial comment: "Under-sheriff Woods speaks in the highest terms of the treatment of the posse by the citizens of both Cochise and Graham counties; with the single exception already noted, Mr. H. C. Hooker of the Sierra Bonita ranch, a man whom from the large property interest he has in the country, would naturally be supposed to be in favor of upholding the constituted authorities and the preservation of law and order."[44]

Not surprisingly, Hooker and his ranch hands told a very different version. This time, Behan and Woods don't quite come out as noble heroes bravely searching for the cowering Earps. According to the Hooker version, Earp and his little band rode into the Sierra Bonita and were given food, fresh horses, and hospitality. After a meal, despite Hooker's invitation to make the fight at the ranch, Wyatt chose to make his defense elsewhere—the other location would provide a better battle site and would not involve Hooker in the affair. On the evening of March 27, they rode out and set up on the little bluff about three miles from the ranch, an ideal spot to await Behan because they could see riders approaching from all directions.

A Hooker ranch hand told the *Epitaph* that "the next morning the sheriff and his posse rode up to the house of Mr. Hooker and DEMANDED refreshments for themselves and beasts which was freely granted to them. . . . Sheriff Behan asked Mr. Hooker if he knew the whereabouts of the Earp party. Mr. Hooker replied that he did not know and that if he did he would not tell him. Sheriff Behan then said, 'You must be upholding murderers and outlaws then.'

"'No sir, I am not. I know the Earps and I know you and I know they have always treated me like gentlemen; damn such laws and damn you and damn your posse. They are a set of horse thieves and outlaws,'" Hooker said, and told Behan he should be ashamed to be in such company.

One of Behan's posse members took offense and said, "Damn the son of a bitch, he knows where they are and let us make him tell."

Hooker was not armed, and Billy Whelen, the ranch foreman, stepped up beside his boss with a Winchester in his hand and said, "You can't come here into a gentleman's yard and call him a son of a bitch. Now you skin it back. Skin it back. If you are looking for a fight and come here to talk that way, you can get it before you find the Earps. You can get it right here."

Hooker turned to Behan and said, "These are a pretty set of fellows you have got with you; a set of horse thieves and cut-throats."

Behan and Woods responded quickly. "They are not our associates, they are only here on this occasion with us."

"Well, if they are not your associates I will set an extra table for you and set them by themselves," Hooker responded. He fed the posse, with Behan and Woods at one table and Clanton and the rest at another. After breakfast, Behan went to the stable and told Whelen, "Don't say anything about this," and pulled a diamond stud from his shirt to present to the foreman. "Take this. It cost a hundred dollars, but don't say anything about what occurred here."

Behan then told Hooker, "If I can catch the Earp party it will help me at the next election."

By the Hooker version, Behan then went to Fort Grant, where he tried to acquire Indian scouts to track the Earps. However, Colonel James Biddle was not accommodating. "Hooker said he didn't know and would not tell you if he did? Hooker said that, did he? Well if he did, you can't get any scouts here."

At some point, Hooker pinpointed the location of the Earp party for Behan and told the sheriff he would not need scouts now to find Wyatt Earp. Behan ate, then rode off in another direction. Henry Hooker said that Behan's posse was "willing to ride any direction in Arizona except where [the Earps] were waiting for them. They came back here the next day, but didn't stay long. Behan said he was going back to Tombstone as expenses of the trip were running pretty high, and he had a bill against the county for thirteen thousand dollars for ten days riding after [the Earps]. He didn't stay very long after I told him what I thought about that expense bill."[45]

Out on the hill three miles away, Wyatt Earp and his friends watched the clouds of dust coming in and out of the Hooker ranch, never heading off to the direction where they waited. Finally a big cloud indicated that Behan and the full posse had left the ranch, and Earp and his little group returned to the Sierra Bonita to hear the story of Behan's farcical and expensive romp through the Arizona outback.

Wyatt's band rested several days at the ranch. According to the Hooker version, he offered to pay Earp the $1,000 reward for the killing of Curley Bill, which had been put up by the Cattlegrowers Association. Earp refused, saying, "I don't want any reward for carrying out my promise to Morgan. If the Cattlegrowers Association feel they owe me anything, let them pay you for the horses you have given us."

While Earp relaxed at the Sierra Bonita, Dan Tipton arrived at the ranch with the $1,000 from Gage, the same money Kraker and Wright had carried into Curley Bill's camp, and Lou Cooley brought an extra $1,000 from Wells, Fargo.[46] Cooley had worked as stage driver in Tombstone and had friends in Wells, Fargo management.

While the Earps rested, one of the band wrote a letter to the *Epitaph*. The *Star* would disparage it as a fraud, but the details appear so accurate that it is almost certainly from the posse. The letter was written in response to Woods's account in the *Nugget*. A century later, one can only imagine Wyatt, Texas Jack, and the rest of the group sitting around Hooker's ranch house and helping one of their more educated members—it has all the wit and puckishness of Holliday—prepare the letter that would be their parting statement to the citizens of Arizona.

In Camp, April 4, 1882

Editor Epitaph:—In reply to the article in the Nugget of March 31, relating to the Earp party and some of the citizens of Graham and Cochise counties, I would like to give you the facts in this case during our trip in Cochise and Graham counties. Leaving Tombstone Saturday evening, March 25, we went into camp six miles north of town. Next morning we were overtaken by three prospectors on the road from Tombstone to Winchester district, who asked us to partake of a frugal meal, which we ate with relish, after which we traveled in company with them on the main road to Summit station where we had dinner and awaited the arrival of the passenger train from the west expecting a friendly messenger.

From here we continued our journey on the wagon road to Henderson's ranch where we had refreshments for ourselves and horses. Here we were informed that a gentlemanly deputy sheriff of Cochise county, Mr. Frank Hereford (for whom we have the greatest respect as a gentleman and officer) was at the ranch at the time of our arrival and departure, and have since learned the reason for not presenting himself, was fears for his safety, which we assure him were groundless. Leaving this ranch we went into camp on good grass one mile north. At seven next morning, we saddled and went north to Mr. H. C. Hooker's ranch, in Graham county, where we met Mr. Hooker, and asked for refreshments for ourselves and stock, which he kindly granted us with the same hospitality that was tendered us by the ranchers of Cochise county.

As regards to Mr. Hooker outfitting us with supplies and fresh horses, as mentioned in the Nugget, it is false and without foundation, as we are riding the same horses we left Tombstone on, with the exception of Texas Jack's horse, which was killed in the fight with Curly Bill and posse, which we replaced by hiring a horse on the San Pedro river. In relation to the reward offered by the Stock Association, which the *Nugget* claims Mr. Hooker paid to Wyatt Earp for the killing of Curly Bill, it is also false, as no reward has been asked for or tendered.

Leaving Hooker's ranch on the evening of that day, we journeyed north to within five miles of Eureka Springs. There we camped with a freighter and was cheerfully furnished the best his camp afforded. Next morning, not being in a hurry to break camp, our stay was long enough to notice the movements of Sheriff Behan and his posse of honest ranchers, with whom, had they possessed the trailing abilities of the average Arizona ranchman, we might have had trouble, which we are not seeking. Neither are we avoiding these honest ranchers as we thoroughly understand their designs.

At Cottonwood we remained overnight, and here picked up the trail of the lost Charlie Ross, "and a hot one." We are confident that our trailing abilities will soon enable us to turn over to the "gentlemen" the fruit of our efforts, so they may not again return to Tombstone empty-handed. Yours respectfully,

One of Them[47]

One of Them's letter obviously protected Hooker and the Percy brothers and confused a few details to prevent cowboy revenge. It was designed to show that the little band had been well received during the ride and to lampoon Behan's posse, which the *Nugget* had called "honest ranchmen" and "honest farmers" in earlier stories. It also indicated that the Earps had plans of continuing the search, to what degree is uncertain. In 1896 Wyatt himself said that there were some other skirmishes, and by many accounts a number of rustlers left for Mexico, California, or other less dangerous sites. It is not likely that any of the skirmishes led to killing, although Warren Earp may have taken a leg wound during the Vendetta ride.

The possemen reclaimed their original horses, now rested, at the Sierra Bonita and remained close to the Hooker ranch. Wyatt Earp told one visitor that if the sheriff of Cochise County wanted him, he could always find him at his camp.[48] Apparently in mid-April the Earp band entered Fort Grant to do a little business. Henry Morgan was in the fort's store when Wyatt came in seeking a notary public. Morgan said Earp deeded his property to his sister, then dropped the documents into the mail.[49] The Earp posse then met with Colonel James Biddle, according to Hildreth Halliwell, repeating a story she said she heard from Wyatt. At the meeting, Biddle said, "Wyatt, I'm going to have to hold you here. They're looking for you and there are warrants out for your arrest. We're going to have to hold you. But come in and have something to eat first." The Earps ate dinner while expecting arrest. Biddle called for an orderly and told him to prepare fresh mounts and leave them at a certain gate. A short time later, Biddle rose and excused himself. Earp and the others finished dinner and rode out on the rested horses.[50]

Rumors of Earp's location were noted almost daily in the newspapers, and resident wits at the *San Francisco Exchange* began to spoof the whole situation:

> It was rumored that the Earp brothers would arrive in Oakland and the Light Cavalry was immediately put under arms. That gallant and well-trained body resolved that if the two Earps came to Oakland and showed the least disposition to attack them, every man would bite the dust before those redoubtable bandits were allowed to run the town.
>
> Fortunately the men were mistaken for the Earps proved to be the Earl brothers, on their way to this city. The joyful news spread like wildfire, and the meeting between the calvarymen and their wives was affecting in the extreme. Many of those gentler creatures, when they learned that this fine company had been turned out to meet the two Earp brothers, set to work preparing lint and bandages, and arranging cots for the wounded. Happily, there was no necessity for this forethought. Everything is quiet in Oakland now.[51]

The *Nugget* and the *Epitaph* debated the truth of Curley Bill's death, with the *Nugget* offering a $1,000 reward for proof that the outlaw had become a corpse. The *Epitaph* followed with a reward of $2,000, to be paid to any worthy charity, if Curley Bill would appear at the paper's office.[52] Neither a live body nor a dead one ever showed up in Tombstone. The reports of Curley Bill's survival came from questionable sources, and he never again appeared in public although there were no warrants for his arrest.

Public opinion would continue to shift against the Earps. The *Star* received a letter from Jacob Stilwell of Douglas County, Kansas, mournfully seeking information on his dead nephew, Frank. Jack Stilwell, Frank's brother, who had fought heroically at Beecher's Island, came to Tombstone in mid-April and found enough supporters to convince him that his brother had been shot down by thugs. Arizona learned that even stage robbers like Frank Stilwell have loving families, and the sympathy for Jack, who was grieving for a brother he believed murdered, further added to the public outrage against the Earps.

By the time Jack Stilwell—along with Ringo, Ike Clanton, Pete Spence, and a posse of about thirty—began scouring the hills for Wyatt Earp, the band had made preparations to leave. With the $2,000 from Gage and Wells, Fargo, Earp and his compatriots rode through Fort Grant, then arrived in Silver City, New Mexico, on April 15. They slept in a private home to avoid registering at a hotel, then took breakfast the next morning at the Broadway restaurant. When they placed their horses in the Elephant corral and the proprietor asked their names, one answered John Smith and another said Bill Snooks. This drew the attention of the stable owner and led to an investigation that confirmed their identity. They sold their horses, then took the stage to Deming, then the train to Albuquerque.[53]

The Earp seven, with Dan Tipton joining the original six, arrived in Albuquerque, where Wyatt Earp made a surprising move. He went to the offices of the two local newspapers and offered an interview in exchange for a promise that the papers not report his movements until he secured safe refuge. A month later, the *Evening Review* wrote:

> He stated that they had come to Albuquerque to escape persecution while awaiting the result of an effort being made by Governor Tritle to secure their pardon from the president; that they were then being sought for by their foes, and that they would not give themselves up to the Arizona officers without resistance. . . . The party remained in Albuquerque for a week or more, their identity being well known to fifty people or more. . . . During their stay here, "Doc" Holliday and Wyatt Earp quarreled, and when Albuquerque was left the party disbanded, Holliday going with Tipton. . . . The party, while in Albuquerque, deported themselves very sensibly, performing no acts of rowdyism, and this way gained not a few friends for their side of the fight.[54]

From Albuquerque, the group caught a train that would take them to Colorado. The Vendetta that had enthralled newspaper readers of the West had ended. The flow of blood would quickly be replaced by a flood of ink.

LAW VERSUS ORDER

BEFORE WYATT LEFT FOR COLORADO, the press led a vendetta of its own against him, the deputy U.S. marshal who had become the most controversial figure in the West. Tucson's *Star* joined the *Nugget* in outspoken opposition to the Earps and their friends, vilifying Wyatt for his method of enforcement and questioning his motives.

The Republican papers—the *Tucson Citizen* and the *Epitaph*—continued to support Earp and rail against the cowboys. All the papers decried lawlessness; they just couldn't agree on whether the cowboys or the Earps were the more dangerous. Outside Arizona, in the cities of California, the focus became equally obscured as papers bewailed the bands of desperadoes trying to kill one another, with the rich mining prospects of Arizona becoming the ultimate victim. The *Los Angeles Herald* wrote:

> We know nothing of the inner history of this Earp Vendetta, nor do we care a whit about how the quarrel started. The one patent, glaring fact is that the progress and development of a great territory are being made subordinate to the personal quarrels of a set of people one side or the other of whom must contain a terrible set of blackguards and murderers. The law should be supreme in Arizona as elsewhere. Every man who is going about with arms in his hands, whether he belongs to the Earps or the cowboys, should be made to lay them down, and to submit his case to the arbitrament of a jury of his peers, even if it should require the whole power of the Federal government and the whole force of the people of Arizona! If there is no other way to bring this result about, we commend to the people of that territory the beneficent example of the famous San Francisco Vigilantes. Anything is better than downright anarchy.[1]

The Vendetta crystallized the doctrines of party politics in Arizona and throughout the West. Earp's supporters, mostly Republicans, placed greatest importance on keeping order and maintaining public safety. Earp's critics, usually Democrats, called for a nation of laws, where all must play by the same rules, and the rights of the accused must be protected from maverick marshals who make their own standards to enforce justice. The debate no longer centered on law and order, but became one of law versus order. The arguments reached extremes in Arizona in 1882, and Wyatt Earp became the center of a debate that would grow to national importance. Law versus order was the issue, and Wyatt

Earp became the example. Tucson's *Star* summarized the Democratic viewpoint by editorializing:

> One of the worst features of the present state of outlawry which is being carried on . . . is that they are Deputy United States Marshals sworn to protect and sustain the laws of the country. Instead of this, they have, and are continuing to take the law into their own hands. . . . What a comment on the United States government, that a band of so-called officials with a high hand rove over the country murdering human beings out of a spirit of revenge. This red-handed assassination will not do. No matter how much the friends of the Earps may sympathize in their loss, there is another side to the question. The community have some rights which must be respected. The world at large are not supposed to stand and behold this high handed violation of the law and not denounce it, for in striking at law, it is an assault upon every citizen in the country. If they can kill one citizen in defiance of the law, they can do so with every citizen. The question is, law or no law: which shall prevail? The people say the former must.[2]

The Earps had their defenders, who made equally articulate arguments on the need to preserve order so that laws can thrive. This is one of humankind's oldest questions and has long inspired debate in many civilized societies.

The saga of Wyatt Earp in Tombstone is engaging on several different levels. First, and most important, is the overriding issue of law versus order, with the Earps defending public safety over legal principle. This is the question of how a just man responds to an unjust society, and it is a question that has continued long after the gunfire ceased in the Arizona backcountry. While vengeance certainly served as a motivation for Wyatt Earp, he believed that he had little choice but to kill, not to capture, the men who maimed one of his brothers and murdered another because the courts could not effectively deal with the outlaws.

Second is the question of malfeasance of duty on both sides, with Clum and the Earp supporters maintaining that Johnny Behan profited from the cowboys' cattle rustling and siphoned off public funds. Woods and the *Nugget* tried desperately to link the Earps to the stage robberies.

Third is the private feud between the Earps and Behan, with its string of broken promises and treachery, and a romantic triangle while both the sheriff and the deputy U.S. marshal were wooing the lovely Sadie Marcus.

The Behan–Earp feud certainly existed, beginning probably in February of 1881 when Behan reneged on his promise to appoint Wyatt as his undersheriff. It escalated after the Benson stage robbery when Behan refused to pay the Earps for their posse service, then intensified in August or September when Wyatt and Sadie began keeping company. Morgan Earp had verbally sniped at Behan on several occasions, and the two sides developed a strong distaste for each other. The Earps and their supporters would always believe that everyone's pal Johnny Behan was the ultimate political crook.

The level of Behan's chicanery can never be known with any certainty. It does appear that he avoided pursuing the rustlers who pilfered Mexican beef and sold it to the McLaury brothers and others for resale to Tombstone butchers. Whether he actually received bribes or just tax revenue and promises of political support cannot be known. He may simply have seen the cowboys and their supporters as good taxpayers, or he may have had a more active involvement. Behan's term as sheriff proved notably unspectacular, with a series of jailbreaks and few convictions, leading to Hume's remarkable statement in the *Police Gazette* that "even the sheriff of the county is in with the cowboys, and has to be or his life would not be worth a farthing." And Doc Holliday would say in May, "John Behan, sheriff of Cochise County, is one of the gang and a deadly enemy of mine, who would give any money to have me killed. It is almost certain that he instigated the assassination of Morgan Earp."[3] A letter-writer to the *Citizen* said of the sheriff, "There is no hope for any honest man to get justice here against these scoundrels, so long as Behan is in office, for he is in with them and I have no doubt divides the spoils with them. The Earps are the only men these cutthroats are afraid of, hence, their great anxiety to get them out of the way. Behan knows that if they return here and are set at liberty, he and his gang will have to leave here."[4]

In 1930, after Clum reminisced in a little magazine story, retired Wells, Fargo secret agent Fred Dodge wrote to his old friend, "I note that you have been quite generous in your reference to Johnny Behan. One knows, who can read between the lines that there has been much left unsaid."[5] And much of it must stay unsaid. Behan wisely kept no records of his political indiscretions, although his bankbooks indicate he earned $40,000 for one year in office, an extraordinary amount for public service in those days.[6] It does seem most likely that Behan fed generously at the public trough and made his highest priority personal gain rather than civic duty.

As to the Earps' involvement in stage robberies, it seems impossible. For Wells, Fargo to make a stunning defense of Wyatt Earp virtually ends any question of his involvement in robbing their stages. It seems far more likely that some clever rustler or associate—perhaps Ringo, perhaps Behan—understood the value of gossip and planted stories that would muddy the reputations of the Earps.

There are no easy answers to century-old questions, but if Hume, Clum, Dodge, George Parsons, Clara Brown, and others of stature are to be believed, the Earps earnestly attempted to keep the peace, with a style many others found too brutal to accept. Frontier towns were tough and demanded tough marshals, Earp and his supporters believed. Wyatt Earp and his ride against the cowboys had brought into question a cherished American principle by asking: How can a nation of laws survive when the laws fail to work?

The issue reappears every time rampant lawlessness makes the streets unsafe and interferes with business. It is a question that is central to the democratic experience. History has generally shown that when law supersedes order, crime and violence become epidemic; when order supersedes law, the enforcers overstep the boundaries of their duties. Tombstone provides a remarkable microcosm of an issue that is at the heart of social thought.

Earp became a vigilante, a marshal, and an outlaw all at the same time. He enforced beyond his authority; he punished without due process. The oddity of the Earp story is that he had always spurned vigilante methods until forced into a situation where he believed he had no other choice. After the killing of Fred

White, and again in the Johnny-Behind-the-Deuce affair, he had turned back vigilantes. When he perceived the courts as impotent, the anti-vigilante became the ultimate vigilante justice. As such, the Earp saga is not a defense of vigilantism; it is an acceptance of such actions only under the most dire necessity. Wyatt Earp cannot be defended, but he can be understood.

IN HIGHLY CHARGED SOUTHERN ARIZONA, the Earps became hot politics. The Democratic *Star* and Republican *Citizen* in Tucson made the Earps' activities into top-drawer political controversy. More at issue, however, was the bill Behan submitted to Pima County, a whopping $2,593.65, to pay for Ringo and the cowboys to ramble around the Arizona backcountry avoiding the Earps.[7]

The newspaper bickering went on continuously for two months as the Democratic press stood stoutly for law, and the Republicans advocated order. The very life of Wyatt Earp became a political issue to be used in the next territorial election. "The rope that hangs the Earps will strangle the Republican party," the *Star* dropped into a column on May 21. On May 25, the *Star* further said, "The Republican issue in Arizona is the vindication of the Earps. They are the father, son and holy ghost of the Republican party in the Territory."

When the *Citizen* wrote, "The cowboys used to make quiet, law-abiding people get up and dance under the gentle pressure of drawn revolvers," the *Star* answered, "In this, however, they differed from the Earp crowd, who killed law abiding people, instead of making them dance. As between dancing and death, public sentiment will rather incline to the method of the cowboy."

False Wyatt sightings came regularly in Arizona. He was ubiquitous in his absence. Further rumors of his death appeared in print several times. Wyatt far outlived the rumors.

The *Nugget* and the *Epitaph* kept up their usual hectoring through most of April, until a little notice showed up in the April 24 *Nugget* announcing that it had purchased the *Epitaph*. It also took over the *Epitaph*'s rights to provide Associated Press dispatches. Richard Rule had railed at length about Clum's pro-Earp dispatches affecting the national perspective on both Tombstone and the Earp issue. Now the Democrats had control, but it was too late to change the pro-Earp stories that had filled the nation's papers.

The sale of the *Epitaph* by co-owners Clum and Reppy left Tombstone without a Republican voice in the aftermath of the town's greatest controversy. Before he left, Clum zealously attacked Sam Purdy, the ardent Democrat who would come from Yuma to edit the *Epitaph*. In his Yuma writings, Purdy denigrated the Earps with relish, picking up the Democratic stories and editorializing with glee against the marshals' defiance of the law. Purdy took control on May 1, promising balanced and fair coverage without loyalty to political cliques. What followed was most unusual. From the outset, Purdy railed passionately against the Earps. All this came under the same *Epitaph* banner that had served as the Earps' primary voice of support, and it totally confused much of the citizenry. Purdy, who had not been near Tombstone during the controversial period, became the great anti-Earp voice in the aftermath of the Arizona War, writing editorials against the Earps in the same paper that had defended them.

It is not hard to see from whence Purdy drew his information. Four years earlier he had been a partner in the *Yuma Expositer* with James Reilly—the same Judge Reilly who feuded with Wyatt Earp for years. Reilly almost certainly provided Sam Purdy with the anti-Earp view of stage robberies and thuggery. Purdy ate it up and spit it out in ink. He forever confused the Earp story. Many new arrivals in Tombstone would receive the gospel according to Sam Purdy, which regurgitated the Clanton–cowboy line about the Earps' involvement in crime. Purdy made the Earps appear as crime bosses and the cowboys as victims. The new editor came in with the avowed purpose of promoting business in Cochise County, and of playing down the dangerous reputation of Tombstone. The *Epitaph* had become more a public relations sheet than a newspaper.

The *Tucson Citizen* stood alone as Arizona's only major supporter of the Earps when the war of words reached a crescendo. The *Nugget* would continue to publish for another month, with Richard Rule uncharacteristically becoming something of a spokesman for moderation. But only one real voice remained in Tombstone, and that was distinctly Democratic with no sympathy for Wyatt Earp.

After Wyatt's departure for Colorado, the situation in Arizona gradually calmed. By the end of April, *Star* columnist O'Brien Moore visited Tombstone and dispatched a report beginning, "I am now more than a week in Tombstone and haven't, so far, seen a single killing. If I should make this statement in an Eastern newspaper I would immediately be dubbed a liar of a high order of genius. But such is the real state of affairs, without gloss or glamor. There hasn't even been a street fight, a knock down or a game of fists." Moore used his pen to lash out at the Earps. "The Republicans are in a terrible state of demoralization owing to the Earp imbroglio, a good portion of the party being still firm adherents of the outlaws. These may be called the 'swallow tails.' . . . There is hardly a doubt that the best feelings of the people are in unison with the county government regarding the Earps."

Outside Arizona, the situation remained a focus of national attention. The raids against Mexico had nearly set off an international incident, and the outlawry outraged the wealthy mining operators, who counted on southern Arizona to create the next boom that would boost the economy. President Chester A. Arthur responded by formally denouncing the lawless elements of the territory. In response to a request from Governor Tritle, Arthur ordered the military to intercede in enforcing the laws of the United States against the cowboys of Cochise County:

> It has been made to appear satisfactorily to me . . . that, in consequence of the lawful combination of evil-disposed persons who are banded together to oppose and obstruct the execution of the laws, it has become impracticable to enforce, by the ordinary course of judicial proceedings, the laws of the United States within that Territory, and that the laws of the United States therein have been forcibly opposed, and the execution thereof forcibly resisted; and whereas the laws of the United States require whenever it may be necessary in the judgment of the President, to use military forces for the purpose of enforcing the faithful execution of the laws of the United States, he shall forthwith by proclamation, command such insurgents to disperse and retire peaceably to their respective abodes within a limited time. Now, therefore, I,

Chester A. Arthur, President of the United States, do hereby admonish all good citizens of the United States and especially of the Territory of Arizona against siding, countenancing, abetting or taking part in any such unlawful proceedings; and I do hereby warn all persons engaged in or connection with said obstruction of the laws to disperse and retire peaceably to their respective abodes on or before noon of the 5th day of May.[8]

Amazing as it seems, the President of the United States had ordered the cowboys to disperse and quit riding the countryside, staging naked dances, robbing stagecoaches, and pilfering cattle. The cowboys were most surprised by the order to disperse because they had no idea they had ever been organized. This is a crucial point in understanding the cowboy outlaws of Arizona. President Arthur, Wells, Fargo, and the Earps would refer to the cowboys as an organized outlaw group. Cowboy friend Tom Thornton said that they were generally a group of outcasts who had wound up in the territory, committing crimes and causing general chaos. Most of the anti-Earp group tended to believe that there was no real organization, although Curley Bill, Ringo, and Ike Clanton were held in some respect. In likelihood, it was a loose-knit collection of gangs, generally on friendly terms, who could join together to rustle Mexican cattle or attack a smuggling caravan. Individual cowboys often moved from one gang to another. By most modern definitions, this is organized crime. In 1882, the notion seemed outrageous; in addition, many Arizona Democrats did not appreciate Washington's involvement in territorial problems.

The *Star* blamed the state of lawlessness on renegade deputy marshals "who used their commission as warrants for rapine and murder. To wait until these criminals had fled and then declare their innocent victims lawless, is an outrage upon the intelligence and an insult to the dignity of the people."[9] In Tombstone, Sam Purdy began turning the outrage in a little different direction.

"Great indignation is felt here regarding the President's proclamation," the Associated Press report from Tombstone said. The new Democratic owners of the *Epitaph* also controlled AP reports from the city. "A mass meeting will be held here . . . to denounce the Presidential interference. The meeting will be addressed by prominent members of all parties. A like meeting will be held in Charleston."

Sam Purdy's first contribution to the Tombstone scene would be to promote these two meetings, with citizens speaking out against President Arthur's interference in territory business. However, the meetings did not quite draw the support expected. "As announced the cowboys and their political friends held an indignation meeting last night," the *Arizona Gazette* in Phoenix reported. "The meeting was a complete fizzle and its action in no way represents the sentiments of the respectable portion of this community. Resolutions denouncing the President and Governor were introduced and when the vote was taken the noes had it six to one, but Judge Robinson declared it carried. The meeting then dispersed. It was a complete farce." The *Nugget* lampooned: "The meeting fell flat as a cold mashed potato, and the Governor still lives and the President is reported well."[10]

The *Epitaph* sent out a report saying, "Cochise County is in as peaceful a state as any other section of the country. There is no outlawry, no outrages, no resistance offered to the exception of the law. Tombstone is as peaceful a city as there is in the Union. It has a perfect police system and efficient officers. Public opinion is unanimous in calling the President's action an outrage." The *San Francisco Exchange* responded with sarcasm. "It is gratifying to know at last that Cochise county is 'in as peaceful a state as any section of the country.' What have become of all the cowboys there? Are they out chasing the Earps or out fighting Indians? And where are those other gentlemen who shoot holes through people's hats, knock cigars out of their mouths, and cut telegraph wires with bullets? And how about the stables and corrals of the honest yeomanry of Cochise county—are they not still locked at night? And it used to be a pleasing custom in Cochise county to enter a ball room, strip the ladies stark, and with revolvers pointed at their heads, make them dance. It is pleasant to hear that these pastimes no longer exist in Cochise county, but we believe they do all the same."[11]

The Republican *San Diego Union* zealously supported the presidential proclamation and denounced the Democratic press for its defense of outlawry. The *Star* struck back by calling the paper "a small edition . . . published by a small man in a small town on the Pacific coast. . . . The editor lives in the sagebrush and combs his hair with a splinter." And that was only the beginning. In the course of a long editorial, the *Star* accused the Earps of being "gamblers, murderers and robbers," and accused the Republicans of fostering lawlessness. The editorial climaxed with: "The outlaws who made Cochise county a hell were not the cowboys, but federal officials supported and maintained in their lawlessness by the Republican party. Peace and order came back to the county when these outlaws, red with murder and dripping with the blood of innocent people, fled the country."[12]

It is little wonder the Earp affair became a morass of confusion when it was twisted from a question of public safety to the major political issue in Arizona. Nobody liked killing, and few savored the thought of the police killing anyone they believed a criminal. That notion would change for some when they were personally touched by the deeds of the desperadoes.

The *Epitaph* railed against Arthur's proclamation, with no opposing voice in the press. It was left for the public to respond. The most articulate answer came in another letter to the editor from Bryant L. Peel, whose freshly buried son still burdened his heart. On May 9, two days before the indignation meeting, he wrote to the *Nugget*:

> The Epitaph has repeatedly assailed the Governor for his proclamation, and threatens to get up an indignation meeting and denounce his acts. I have read these editorials until I am disgusted. I know the object of such articles. It is to cover the deficiencies of a set of county officials in Cochise county. The most outrageous crimes have been committed by the wholesale, and not an arrest made nor an attempt made to arrest. Farmers at their homes, engineers in their offices, teamsters on the road and miners in their camp, had been murdered in cold blood, and our county officials took no pains to ferret out the perpetrators of these crimes. These things caused the best citizens of Tombstone to appeal to the Governor for relief. I was one of that number. The Governor had two classes of advisors when he came here. One advised him to call out 100 militia and head them and take this class of outlaws as a class, and shoot them wherever found, which I think is the only way to deal with fiends. A more conservative class advised him to call on the Government for aid. He took the

advice of the latter, and asked the president for $150,000 and permission to remove the inefficient officers.

The President asked Congress for permission to use the military to aid the civil authorities—a thing that nobody asked for, nor no one wanted. But that was not the fault of Governor Tritle, nor shall he be blamed for it. All that Governor Tritle said is true, and we stand ready to prove it to the world. Let the Epitaph get up its indignation meeting, and give the names of those who are chagrined. We want to know them and we want the world to know them; and when his meeting is over we will have a meeting of the law-abiding citizens to endorse all the Governor said. We were assured that henceforth the Epitaph would be published in the interest of truth and Democracy. We have been deceived. A ring runs and controls the paper. Democracy has nothing to do with it and shall not be contaminated by it. I am a Democrat, and Democracy shall not be responsible for anything a ring or clique does.

Wyatt Earp and the Citizens Safety Committee still had their friends, Democrat and Republican. Legal principles do little to console a grieving father.

WYATT EARP'S FAME HAD PRECEDED HIM when the train pulled into Gunnison, Colorado, in late April of 1882. The Earps and their friends were still in the contradictory situation of being both lawmen and fugitives when they made camp outside Trinidad, Colorado, where Wyatt's old friend Bat Masterson had taken over as city marshal.

Wyatt and Doc had their falling out in Albuquerque, but still remained on fairly good terms. "We had a little misunderstanding, but it didn't amount to much," Holliday told the *Denver Republican*. The *Albuquerque Review* reported that while the Earp party stopped in Albuquerque, Holliday "became intoxicated and indiscreet in his remarks, which offended Wyatt and caused the party to break up. Holliday went with Tipton."[13]

The little group probably stayed a few days in Trinidad, with McMasters and Turkey Creek Jack taking off in other directions. "Messrs Wyatt and Warren Earp are still with us," the *Trinidad News* reported on May 5. "Their brothers [*sic*] went south Wednesday morning. Again the *News* takes great pleasure in saying they are all 'way up' boys—gentlemen of the first water."[14]

Doc Holliday left the Earps and went on to Pueblo and then Denver. Wyatt, Warren, and Texas Jack set up camp on the outskirts of Gunnison in early May. They remained quiet at first, rarely coming into town for supplies. Eventually, Wyatt took over a faro game at a local saloon.

In Pueblo, according to Doc Holliday, a Perry Mallen spoke to him at Tom Kemp's variety theater and played up to the volatile dentist to gain his confidence. Mallen said Doc had once saved his life, and he wanted to return the favor. Stilwell was chasing Doc, trying to kill him, and he wanted to give Doc the warning. A few days later, Doc and a few friends went to Denver for the horse races at the local fairgrounds. While walking down the streets on Monday evening, May 15, Mallen stepped from the darkness and brandished two six-shooters in Holliday's face.

"Doc Holliday, I have you now," Mallen said. Accompanied by Arapahoe County sheriff's deputies Barney Cutler and Charles Linton, Mallen marched

Holliday to the sheriff's office, followed shortly by a reporter for the *Denver Tribune*. Mallen claimed to be a deputy sheriff from Los Angeles and provided telegrams ordering Holliday's arrest on the killings of Stilwell, Billy Clanton, Curley Bill, and an unnamed railroad conductor. When Holliday entered the police station, he demanded to know why he had been arrested. Mallen, a heavy man with a short-cropped reddish mustache, aimed a revolver at Holliday.

Holliday looked at the gun and said, "Oh, you can drop that. Nobody is going to try to get away from you. I have no weapons."

Mallen kept his pistol pointed and spoke angrily. Holliday maintained his calm, with "that coolness which knows that it is his only salvation, for he evidently feared that Mallen might kill him at any moment," according to the *Tribune* report. A rough-looking crowd then filed into the police station, and the reporter expected a lynching. Mallen started a heated exchange as Deputy Linton frantically telephoned for a hack to take Holliday to jail.

"No, you won't get away from me again," Mallen said, still holding the pistol. "You killed my partner, you blood-thirsty coward, and I would have taken you in Pueblo if the men I had with me had stood by me."

"I did not come here to be abused," Holliday said.

The toughs spilled into the sheriff's office, and Holliday asked to make a statement.

"This is not a court or jury," Linton said.

"But I want to set myself right," Holliday responded. "Is it customary in this country to deny a citizen the right of speech? Is it right? Is it justice?"

With no answer from the deputies, Holliday turned to speak to the little group that had streamed into the office. "I can show who that man is. I can prove that he is not the sheriff, and, in fact, no officer of Cochise County. I can show you his reason for bringing me here. I can show . . ." Mallen and the officers cut him off. The hack arrived to take him to jail, and the *Tribune* reporter rode along.

Mallen claimed that seven years earlier Holliday had killed Harry White, Mallen's partner, and that Mallen had been following him at his own expense for revenge. Mallen said Holliday had also been involved in numerous other crimes.

Bat Masterson showed up at the jail and vouched for Holliday, telling the *Tribune* reporter that Doc was a responsible man and a deputy United States marshal. The *Tribune* speculated that Mallen was "a cowboy playing detective," perhaps none other than "Sim"—actually Fin—Clanton. The court ordered Holliday held in jail to await what would be yet another judicial and journalistic battle surrounding the Earps and their affairs.[15]

Bat Masterson acted quickly, wiring the city marshal in Pueblo for a warrant to arrest Holliday, which would change the jurisdiction. Masterson had the Pueblo authorities swear out a complaint. In 1907 Bat wrote: "The charge . . . made against Holliday at this time was nothing more than a subterfuge on my part to prevent him from being taken out of the state by the Arizona authorities."

The warrant charged Holliday with running a confidence game in which a victim was relieved of $150. Pueblo marshal Henry Jameson presented the warrant and asked to immediately take the prisoner. Arapahoe County sheriff

Michael Spangler did not bite, saying he would hold the prisoner until officers arrived from Arizona.[16] At that point again a crowd identified as "gamblers, bunko, and confidence men" gathered outside the office, and Spangler took Jameson by the arm and ushered him out the door and into the crowd.

"Here, you get out of here—and damned quick, too," Spangler said, then turned to the crowd. "I don't want any monkey acting, and all of you men who have no business here will get out in quick order."

Excitement swirled in Denver as the city tried to grasp the role Holliday had played in the wild doings in Arizona. In the wake of the arrest, the *Denver Republican* wrote, "Doc Holliday, the prisoner, is one of the most noted desperadoes of the West. In comparison, Billy the Kid or any other of the many Western desperadoes who have recently met their fate, fade into insignificance. The murders committed by him are counted by the scores and his other crimes are legion. For years he has roamed the West, gaining his living by gambling, robbery and murder. In the Southwest, his name is a terror."

The *Rocky Mountain News* ran an interview with a former Arizona resident stating the conflict had been a battle between the bunco-steerers and the cowboys, and that Virgil Earp had been shot for participating in a bunco scheme. "The better class of citizens, including the business men and the moneyed men have preferred the 'bunko' men to the cowboys, because the latter have been accustomed to come into the cities, get drunk, get into fights and inaugurate hades generally. The bunko-steerers are there as everywhere, a peaceable, quiet class of people who outside of the bad habits of lying and stealing, would make quite respectable Sunday-school superintendents."[17] There was never a shortage of wild stories surrounding Arizona affairs.

Masterson wisely responded with a public relations campaign, polishing Doc's image and smearing Mallen's. Masterson told the *Republican*, "I tell you that all this talk is wrong about Holliday. I know him well. He is a dentist and a good one. He . . . was with me in Dodge, where he was known as an enemy of the lawless element."[18] The press battle lines were quickly drawn. The very Democratic *Rocky Mountain News*, building on past reports from Tucson's *Arizona Star,* vilified Holliday. The *Denver Republican,* as Republican as its name, sided with Holliday. The *Tribune* and the *Pueblo Chieftain* also championed the dentist. It was the same old press–political war, moved from the desert to the mountains.

The *News* glorified Mallen for his heroic capture of Holliday, but Masterson cleverly chose to defame the defective detective. The *Republican* wrote, "Masterson . . . claims that Mallen is a fraud and a friend of the cowboys, whose only object is to get Holladay [*sic*] back in order that he might be killed." Masterson confronted Mallen at the sheriff's office and told him that Holliday could not have killed a man in Park City, Utah, because Doc had never even visited Utah. Mallen finally admitted that he could be mistaken.

Mallen responded to Bat's press campaign by writing a letter to the *News*, saying that Behan had offered a $500 reward to anyone who captured Holliday, and that the Cochise sheriff had given him the authority. Mallen also denied reports of his previous involvement in a swindle.[19]

While Masterson was trying to keep Holliday in Colorado, another battle began back in Arizona. Both Behan and Pima County sheriff Bob Paul, the longtime friend of the Earps, sought the right to deliver Holliday's extradition papers to Denver, with more at stake than a good time in the big city. The Earps and their friends sincerely believed that they would have no chance of surviving in Behan's custody.

A *Republican* reporter asked Holliday if he expected trouble back in Arizona. The doctor paused for a moment and gazed earnestly out of the window, into the rain. "If I am taken back to Arizona, that is the last of Holliday. We hunted the rustlers, and they all hate us. John Behan, Sheriff of Cochise County, is one of the gang and a deadly enemy of mine who would give any amount of money to have me killed. . . . Should he get me in his power, my life would not be worth much."[20]

The *News* also visited Holliday in jail and described him as "a delicate, gentlemanly-looking man, slightly built and with prematurely gray hair. He wears a heavy sandy moustache. He seems to have at all times a nervous frightened manner, as if he felt some one was pursuing him."[21]

Behan received a telegram from Denver saying that not only Holliday but Wyatt and Warren Earp were also in custody. Behan sought a requisition to make the trip to Colorado and applied to Governor Tritle for the proper papers. Before completing the procedure, two Pima County supervisors interceded with the acting Pima County district attorney, who expressed outrage that Behan would seek the right to chase men wanted in their county. Behan had already billed Pima almost $2,600 for his cowboy posse, and the supervisors did not want to give him another crack at their treasury. According to Tritle, when he finally received the papers they were made out for Bob Paul, not Behan. The papers did not have the proper seal, however, so Sheriff Paul was to make the trip with the corrected papers to be forwarded later. To further confuse the situation, Paul received a telegram from Gunnison telling him that the Earps were there, not in Denver.

The *Epitaph* called it an outrage that Behan would not be sent to Colorado after preparing the case and offering a reward from his own pocket for the capture of the Earps and Holliday. Again the *Star* spoke out:

> The impression shared by many that Sheriff Paul will not bring the Earps to Tucson but will permit them to escape in transit, the *Star* considers an injurious suspicion which is not justified by the high reputation of the officer. Neither does it believe that the requisition was entrusted to him by the Governor for that purpose. Sheriff Paul will undoubtedly bring the Earps back to Tucson and they will receive here a fair and impartial trial. Hence there is every prospect of these notorious criminals soon being lodged within the walls of the Pima county jail, notwithstanding the efforts of Sheriff Behan, of Cochise county, to get his hands upon them.[22]

The *Star* and the *Citizen* agreed that Paul should make the trip—this was Pima County business. The *Citizen* made the point clearly: "It would have simply been an outrage upon this county for the Governor to have issued the requisition to the Sheriff of Cochise county, upon a warrant issued in this, and have allowed that officer to have proceeded to Denver with a carte blanche against this county for expenses, a county to the people of which he owes no responsibility."

Paul arrived in Denver on Friday, May 19, and talked with a *News* reporter two days later. The story said he spoke reluctantly, reticent about discussing

Holliday or the Stilwell killing. When asked whether Holliday was involved with the Earp gang, Paul was quoted with a most uncharacteristic remark:

> He was, and in fact, was one of the leaders. The so-called Earpp [*sic*] gang, or faction if you please, was composed entirely of gamblers who preyed upon the cowboys, and at the same time in order to keep up a show of having a legitimate calling was organized into a sort of vigilance committee, and some of those including Holliday, had United States Marshal's commissions.

Later in the interview he was asked the sentiment in Arizona. Paul reportedly responded:

> That, sir, is a difficult thing to answer. The feeling is, however, very strong, especially among the more respectable citizens who have been terrorized for years by the cowboys and the Earp gang and justice will no doubt be meted out to Holliday and his partners.[23]

Those two statements have been taken by historians to indicate that Paul turned against Wyatt Earp after the Vendetta. However, Paul also spoke briefly with the *Tribune*, and the reporter wrote: "Sheriff Paul, while he is not willing to talk, is evidently in favor of Holliday and the Earps. The fight was a factional and political one. The cowboys, who represent the worst element of Arizona, were Democrats to a man. Holliday and the Earps represented the Republican element of Tombstone and the best class of citizens."[24] The Democratic *News* and Republican *Tribune* presented very different interpretations of Paul's sentiments. Paul had been a solid Earp supporter during the Tombstone affairs, and he would defend the Earps again in 1898 with a letter to the *Tucson Citizen*. Most likely, the *Tribune* account more accurately reflects Paul's thinking, while the *News* either misquoted the sheriff or confused the story.

Back in Arizona, the anti-Earp faction had grown angry with the sheriff's slow return, and the *Star* voiced the complaint:

> It looks as if Sheriff Paul, who was apparently so anxious to go after the Earps, will return with only one of the criminals. That is probably the reason why he was selected to go. If Behan, of Cochise county, had been commissioned for the enterprise the result might possibly have been different. The Star admitted frankly Paul's right to go after the outlaws if he desired to. The crime upon which the requisition was based was committed in this county and as an officer of this county was the proper person to execute it. But this concession is based on the presumption that Paul had the intention and the courage to perform his duty. His return with only Holliday in custody will be simply an outrage upon public decency.[25]

While Arizona simmered, rumors circulated through the territories. The *Albuquerque Review* wrote that the cowboys had left Tombstone, apparently to prepare an ambush for Paul when he tried to return with Holliday. "They have threatened that Holliday will never again enter Tombstone alive," the paper reported.[26]

The sheriff of Pima County settled in to wait for the extradition hearing, scheduled on May 30. Late in the evening of the 29th, Masterson arranged to meet with Colorado governor Frederick Pitkin and enlisted the aid of the *Tribune*'s Capitol reporter, E. D. Cowen, who said Masterson came to the paper's office and asked for help. Cowen said: "He submitted proof of the criminal design upon Holliday's life. Late as the hour was, I called upon Pitkin and he agreed to order a public hearing of the requisition. The true motive of the arrest was sufficiently proved out of the mouth of [Paul]."[27] If Cowen, an eyewitness and top journalist, was accurate, Paul confirmed Masterson's story and helped prevent Holliday's return to Arizona.

Pitkin denied extradition on two grounds. The first was faulty legal terminology in the drawing up of the extradition papers; the second was the warrant for Doc that Bat had fabricated in Pueblo, which meant that Colorado had priority on any charge against Holliday. Paul returned to Arizona empty-handed to face the political assault that would surely follow.

A *Star* reporter waited with the sheriff's wife, Mary, to meet the train on the evening of Friday, June 2. Paul explained to the reporter that the proper papers had been delayed, and the judge refused to grant an extension. Paul then made an appointment for a meeting with the governor to discuss extradition.

"After examining the papers he said another charge had been made against Holliday at Pueblo, that of swindling a man in a confidence game out of $150," Paul said. "He also said that he had been informed by prominent citizens of Denver that if Holliday was placed in my custody he would be murdered by cowboys before reaching Tucson."

Paul said he assured Governor Pitkin that he had made every attempt to make the trip safe, with men stationed at Willcox, Bowie, and Deming to telegraph any indication of a possible cowboy attack. Paul said he even offered to take Holliday back by way of San Francisco to throw the cowboys off the trail. Pitkin then examined the papers. Finding they were signed only by the court clerk, not by Governor Tritle, Pitkin declared the paperwork defective and allowed Holliday to be arrested by the Pueblo authorities. Paul followed the dentist to Pueblo and sat in on the preliminary hearing, where Doc was freed on $300 bail. Paul said that he was unable to pursue the Earps because he had to stay in Denver to watch over Holliday.

"When I arrived in Denver I received a telegram that Wyatt Earp was there [in Gunnison] sick, and that the rest of the gang could be had any time. I at once bought a ticket for that town but was influenced to remain in Denver and look out for Holliday. I however wrote to the Sheriff at Gunnison asking further particulars and he telegraphed that Wyatt and Warren Earp had just left in a wagon but could be captured if I had the necessary papers ready. I hadn't the requisition and hence could do nothing."

Paul said he had heard that McMasters and Turkey Creek Jack had taken off for the Texas Panhandle. He also reported that Holliday had said he intended to return to Pima County for trial when court opened. "He does not deny or acknowledge the killing of Stilwell," Paul said. "He however states that when his party were at the depot in this city some of them were standing on the rear platform of the train. Two men approached. One he was sure was Stilwell, and the other it was presumed was Ike Clanton. The latter leveled their guns at the Earp party, when he and his friends dodged into the cars, procured guns and jumping from the train started down the track after the other two. At this point Holliday stopped the story and would not say what occurred afterwards."

The great Earp extradition debacle had ended, with Doc Holliday on perpetual parole in Colorado. Bob Paul never made the trip to Gunnison to meet with Wyatt and Warren, and Tritle did not pursue any further attempt to bring the marshals back to face the courts. The Earp affair had ended in reality, but would live on as a political issue in Arizona, with the *Star* constantly digging at the Republicans for their inaction:

> Sheriff Paul's return to Arizona without the prisoners he ostensibly went to secure really creates no surprise. It was not expected he would bring them. It was not believed that those who commissioned him to do so intended that he should discharge his duty. The Republican officials could not afford to have the Earps or any of their crowd returned for trial; and of course the papers were defective. It was the easiest way out of the difficulty. Of course the Governor would not intentionally sign defective papers. Of course not. But being a lawyer he might have detected the defect if he had scrutinized them closely. So he omitted to scrutinize them. . . . We only know that the law has been cheated, and the Republican party of this Territory saved from a very embarrassing predicament. That is the length and breadth of the whole transaction.[28]

While the *Tucson Citizen* defended the Earps' actions, the *Star* continued to insinuate that the Earps had indeed been party to the crime wave in Cochise County by saying:

> The Star has contended that the lawlessness in this Territory was the outgrowth of the Earp dynasty; that it began with their advent in the Territory and ended with their departure. This is so self evident a truth that even the Citizen has not had the hardihood to deny it. The Star has only treated the political aspect of the Earp difficulty and has not sought to prejudge their personal responsibility for individual crimes.[29]

In San Francisco, Virgil Earp would bemoan that his family had become a political issue. "The press dispatches that have been sent here have been very unfair to us and have been made to conform to a plan to carry these fights into politics this season. . . . I am sorry to see the thing taken into politics as a personal measure, because the true aspect of the trouble will be lost and new enmities are likely to be created."[30]

With remarkable clarity, Virgil Earp predicted a debate that would continue for years to come. The facts had already become secondary to the political storm that blew through the territory. Arizona would never agree on Wyatt Earp. To some, he would stand as the noble hero who made the Territory safe for commerce, enforcing the law when the courts could not. To others, he would be the ultimate vision of evil, perhaps even the mastermind of stage robberies. These conflicting legacies would haunt Wyatt Earp through the rest of his life. Even in his later years, Earp never really understood why he remained so controversial. In his eyes, he had just done what needed to be done. The courts could not convict a cowboy; Morgan's murderers could not be allowed to roam free, not just for vengeance but because they could return to kill Clum, Spicer, E. B. Gage, or the legion of others who still spoke out for the Earps. Wyatt Earp never recognized that in five months in Tombstone his actions had ingnited an issue that would continue to be debated for years to come — law versus order, the right of

self-preservation over adherence to legal structure. It is one of the most basic elements of any system of laws, and a debate that reemerges when the Curley
Bills, Capones, and Crips of the world persevere beyond control of the court
system.

THE EARPS WERE DONE IN TOMBSTONE. Their friends knew it, Behan knew it.
Everyone seemed to know it except the Earps.

The family had amassed large land holdings; one section of land had even
taken on the name "the Earp addition." They had mining claims they hoped
would turn into silver strikes and real estate that would grow in value as the
town expanded, bringing them the riches that were sure to follow. Gunnison was
simply a way station, a stopping point before returning to Arizona.

"I shall stay here for a while," Earp told a reporter for the *Gunnison News-
Democrat* in early June. "My lawyers will have a petition for a pardon drawn
up. Everybody in Tombstone knows that we did nothing but our duty. Anyway,
I'd do it over again under like circumstances, and all the best people there will
sign the petition. Governor Pitkin knows the facts pretty well and will sign it
too. We look for a pardon in a few weeks, and when it comes I'll go back; but if
no pardon is made I'll go back in the fall anyway and stand trial. I'd go now, but
I know we would have no show; they'd shoot us in the back as they did my
brother. . . .

"I'm going to run for sheriff this fall. Behan knows he can't get it again, and
that's what makes him so hot towards me. I heard the gang is breaking up and a
good many are going to other parts of the country. I hold out my place, but we
have some mining property back there yet. Doc Holliday is in Pueblo now, and
he may come over here."[31]

Doc joined Wyatt in Gunnison in mid-June, after Pitkin refused extradition, and remained at the camp for a couple of weeks. The rift between Earp and
Holliday was minor enough not to have impaired their friendship. Gunnison police officer Judd Riley recalled the camp as quiet and prepared for conflict: "The
bunch was well heeled and went armed. Earp was a fine looking man, tall with
drooping mustache that curled at the ends. He was quiet in manner and never
created a bit of trouble here, in fact, he told us boys on the police force we could
call on him if we needed help at any time. He was a dead shot, I guess. [He] always wore two guns high up under his arms, but he never used them here. Doc
Holliday was the only one of the gang that seemed to drink much, and the
minute he got hilarious, the others promptly took him in charge and he just disappeared."[32]

Back in Los Angeles, Jim Earp told the *Times* he and his brothers had too
much property in Tombstone to leave; they would fight it to the bitter end.[33]

While Wyatt and Warren waited in Gunnison, Virgil made the trip to San
Francisco to have top surgeons examine his battered left arm. An *Examiner* re-
porter met him near Oakland for the first of two extensive interviews detailing
Arizona affairs. He described the former marshal:

> Virgil Earp is not a ruffian in appearance. He was found in the sleeping car smoking
> a cigar. His face, voice and manner were prepossessing. He is close to six feet in

height, of medium build, chestnut hair, sandy mustache, light eyebrows, quiet, blue eyes and frank expression. He wore a wide-brimmed slate-colored slouch hat, pants of a brown and white stripe, and a blue diagonal coat and vest, both the latter with bullet holes in them, bearing testimony of a recent fight when he was shot in the back, the bullet coming out at the front of the vest. His left arm was carried in a sling, also a memento of his last fight, when he received a bullet in his arm, since causing the loss of about six inches of bone which crippled him for life.[34]

Virgil acknowledged that his brother's band had been responsible for the Stilwell killing and said that Stilwell had confessed before his death and named his co-conspirators. More likely it was Indian Charlie who did the talking. Virgil said Wyatt would return to Tucson in the fall. "The Court in Tombstone does not sit again for six months yet, and they didn't want to lie in jail all that time waiting for trial, but when the Court sits again they will give themselves up, and, with fair play, will be acquitted."

The *Star* picked up these comments, leading to a scoffing response from the very Democratic *Epitaph*. "Without any desire to irritate Mr. Earp, we nevertheless cannot help expressing astonishment that a man with two pounds of buckshot in his stomach, four bullets in his heart and his head mutilated by lead beyond recognition, could have had either time or inclination to make any statement whatever." And for the Earp's planned return to Tombstone: "Extremely doubtful."

Wyatt Earp's national fame had begun the day Frank Stilwell died at the depot, and grew with every killing of the Vendetta. In wire releases and exchanges he was both glorified and vilified, and much of the nation had closely followed his every move through the local papers. Papers in Silver City and Albuquerque reported his advance toward Colorado. In Gunnison, it was big news when a reporter cornered Wyatt and Warren for an extensive interview.

A Gunnison local pointed out the brothers and called Warren by his nickname, "the Tiger." Warren walked with a limp, the aftereffects of a gunshot wound, the paper said. A local businessman told the paper: "The Tiger is a good one. He's a square man, but he will fight when necessary, and you just ought to see him turn himself loose. He'll just grab his two six-shooters and shut his eyes and wade in. He's a holy terror when he gets started. Wyatt is the general of the party, but the Tiger is generally on hand when there's any fighting to be done. . . . The boys are not outlaws by any means and they have lots of good, influential friends. Why, the Governor of Arizona would do anything he could for them, and the best people of Tombstone are on their side. The other crowd are a gang of cattle and horse thieves, stage robbers and cut-throats generally. They call them the 'Rustlers,' and the only people in Tombstone who stand in with them are the butchers and livery men, who buy cattle and horses cheap, and a few of the whisky men. Sheriff Behan sides with them, too. On the Earps' side are the Governor, Sheriff Paul . . . all the court officers, mining men, and nine out of ten of the respectable people of Tombstone."

Warren Earp told the basic story of the Vendetta to the reporter. He then added perspective by saying the family regretted having returned to law enforcement: "If we had left the offices alone we could have made a barrel of money. Wyatt had the finest saloon and gambling house in Tombstone. The bar alone cost him three thousand dollars, and he was doing a rattling business. But the citizens prevailed upon him to take the office of deputy sheriff and United States marshal. He used to be [assistant] marshal of Dodge City, Kansas, and anybody from there will tell you what kind of a marshal he made."[35]

Virgil also clearly stated the demands of law enforcement in Tombstone: "An officer doing his duty must rely almost entirely upon his own conscience for encouragement. The sympathy of the respectable parties of the community may be with him, but it is not openly expressed."[36]

Wyatt may have best explained the frustrations of law enforcement some fourteen years later when he told the *Examiner* of the life of a shotgun messenger for Wells, Fargo. His frustration riding shotgun mirrors his life as a lawman in Tombstone: "That is part of the cursedness of a shotgun messenger's life—the loneliness of it. He is like a sheep dog, feared by the flock and hated by the wolves. On the stage, he is a necessary evil. Passengers and driver alike regard him with aversion. Without him and his pestilential box their lives would be 90 per cent safer and they know it. The bad men, the rustlers—the stage robbers actual and potential—hate him. They hate him because he is a guardian of property, because he stands between them and their desires, because they will have to kill him before they can get their hands into the coveted box."

The statement refers to strongbox guards, not lawmen, and the ambitious ghostwriter probably juiced up the wording. But the statement well represents Wyatt and Virgil's role in Tombstone—sheep dogs feared by the flock and hated by the wolves.

Wyatt and Warren waited for several months, quietly camped outside Gunnison, but the expected pardon never came—the Earps were too hot a political issue. It grew evident that Wyatt and Warren would not return to Tombstone. Their interests in mining property were sold off for taxes, and the stake the family had amassed eroded. Three cowboys had lost their lives in the Vendetta, and Johnny Barnes would later die of his wounds, but Wyatt Earp emerged a big loser, too—in the death of Morgan and the crippling of Virgil, and financially as well.

What Wyatt Earp won was a fame that would grow through his life and even more after his death. He had been the only gunman unharmed in the Fremont Street gunfight, then he had single-handedly fought Curley Bill, killed the outlaw but remained standing, his clothing in tatters and no bullets in his body. He had never felt a bullet in his life, something that would lend him an absurd aura of supernatural power as the stories were told around the West.

Virgil had remained under medical supervision in San Francisco. He ran into some foolish trouble when he was arrested for running an illegal faro game at a sleazy spot on Morton Street. Police Sergeant Thomas W. Bethell broke in the door at 15 Morton and climbed to the second story, where Virgil, his left arm in a sling, ran the game. Virgil, another dealer, and thirty-eight gamblers were arrested in a series of raids on the night of August 2. The two dealers paid bail of $200 each, which became the fine for their infraction when they failed to appear for the hearing. Apparently Virgil continued dealing, because a month later the *San Francisco Report* cryptically ran the editorial comment: "Are all the faro games still closed up or has Earp been permitted to join the ring? How is it?" Members of "the ring" apparently paid the expected bribe money to prevent police from breaking up their games.[37]

Sometime late in 1882, Wyatt and Warren left Colorado and joined Virgil in San Francisco to share a residence on Pine Street, in a neighborhood filled with rooming houses.[38] During the final months of 1882 Wyatt Earp rekindled the romance between him and Sadie Marcus, the lovely dancer who had once been Johnny Behan's fiancée. While Mattie Earp remained in Colton awaiting her husband's return, Wyatt enjoyed the big city with Behan's former flame. By now, even Wyatt Earp realized there could be no future for him in Tombstone, no sheriff's badge or big mining claims. As he sat in his rooms he faced one of the most difficult decisions of his life: whether to return to Colton and join Mattie or submit to the charms of Sadie Marcus, with her bountiful breasts and the ability to bring laughter to a man who rarely laughed. Wyatt Earp chose Sadie, and she became his companion for the next forty-six years as they drifted across the West. When Wyatt and Sadie left San Francisco early in 1883, they were probably looking for a life far quieter than what they had lived in Tombstone. They could not know that Tombstone would never be left behind them.

Doc Holliday had barely been released from jail when Perry Mallen, the bogus detective, suddenly became the focus of a major controversy in Colorado. It seems that Holliday's captor never really had any legitimate credentials as a police officer, either in Los Angeles or in Arizona, and turned his time in Denver into a bunco scheme. The *Denver Republican* delighted in his downfall:

> For a genuine romance of crime with detectives, bloody avengers, bulldogs and dark lanterns thrown in, the country has never produced anything half as good as the Doc Holladay [*sic*] case. It has been written up so much of late that the Republican would not impose another article on the subject were it not for several facts which have come out of late. These facts round off the hideous tale with a burst of laughter and turns what was nearly a tragedy into a roaring farce. The villain of the first act [Holliday] becomes the hero in the second, and the avenger and detective in one, the man [Mallen] who has devoted his life to his dead comrade, and has been shot so often that he has trouble in retaining his food, proves to be a petty swindler.

The *Republican* reprinted a correspondent's bizarre story from the *Cincinnati Enquirer*, painting Holliday as one of the most evil men in creation—"fearing neither God nor man, he became a devil incarnate and truly his horned godfather had no cause to feel ashamed of his namesake," with a list of killings that approached fifty, according to Mallen. The correspondent further credited the detective with "one of the most important captures the world ever saw, and one that will cause a fervent 'Thank God' to arise from the lips of all in this Southwestern country."[39]

The editors at the *Republican* could hardly keep from guffawing in print when they called Mallen "the famous man from nowhere" who falsely claimed to be an officer from Los Angeles. It seems that after the Holliday arrest, Mallen pulled a little con job on a Denver man named Julius Schweigardt. Mallen filled Schweigardt with wonderful tales of heroism from his life as a detective, then arrested Doc Holliday to provide a flourish to the stories. Mallen then let Schweigardt in on the scheme: he knew the whereabouts of a terrible murderer living in Kansas City who carried a reward of $1,500. All Schweigardt had to do was pay the expenses, and he could be a partner in the glory and reward. Schweigardt eagerly handed over $310 to fund the trip, and joined Mallen on the journey to Kansas City. Mallen disappeared with the cash, leaving the sucker to bemoan his loss.

Almost from the beginning, the strangest set of characters seemed to fill the periphery of the Wyatt Earp saga. From the absurd Ike Clanton to the bombastic Mallen, weird personalities were always in the background.

By mid-July, one of the most unusual characters of Tombstone was gone. Sullen, brooding, mysterious John Ringo died in the mountains from a single bullet through his brain. The coroner's jury called it suicide, but rumors swirled through Cochise County blaming just about every man who owned a gun. Years later, some even thought Wyatt returned to claim another victim in his Vendetta, but it is most unlikely that Wyatt Earp returned to kill John Ringo.[40]

Another fire swept through Tombstone in late May, burning much of the business district and destroying the three major hotels, the Grand, the Cosmopolitan, and Brown's. Also lost was the Golden Eagle Brewery; a saloon called the Crystal Palace would be built on the site. The *Nugget* office was completely destroyed by the flames and the paper would never publish again. It had become redundant anyway, since the owners had purchased the *Epitaph* and both papers spoke with the same voice.

Tombstone continued, with Marshal Neagle's police department cracking down on Chinese opium dens and hauling the smokers into court. The cowboy criminals, depleted by the loss of their leaders, grew tamer as time passed. There were still robberies on the roadways and occasional shootings, but organized cattle rustling diminished, and stage robberies became a rarity instead of a regularity.[41]

The Town Site land dispute continued. Most merchants either capitulated or won court cases proving their claims; the issue was not settled until 1886, when the Territorial Supreme Court ruled against James S. Clark and invalidated the claims of the Town Site Company. By that time, Tombstone was in decline, the Earps were long gone, and many of the cowboys were dead or had fled. Clark continued to have problems. In September of 1885, an angry Tombstoner placed dynamite in Clark's stove. When his wife, Lydia, lit the stove, it exploded in her face, causing damage and serious injury, but not death.

Behan again was hauled into court on malfeasance charges but released quickly by Judge Stilwell when the charges did not stick. He faced another indignity in September when he sought renomination, only to face a rebuff from Cochise County Democrats. Behan fired Billy Breakenridge in August;[42] a month later the former deputy challenged him for the sheriff's nomination. Harry Woods had nominated Behan at the county convention, but Behan finished dead last among six candidates on the first ballot. The voting continued for ballot after ballot, with Behan never making a significant showing. Finally, after six ballots, Breakenridge withdrew his name, Woods withdrew his nomination of Behan, and Larkin Carr edged Mike Gray for the right to run for sheriff.[43] The stoutly Democratic *Epitaph* supported Carr and said on September 30 that if Republican Jerome L. Ward were elected sheriff, "it is reported Wyatt Earp will be the undersheriff and the ghost of Zwink [*sic*] Hunt a deputy." Ward won easily.

After losing office, Behan held various political jobs, running into trouble at times for abusing his finances. He became warden at Yuma Prison, prompting Clum, Parsons, and the other pro-Earpers to suggest that Behan was on the wrong side of the bars. Ever the womanizer, Behan in 1886 apparently engaged in a torrid affair with Bert Dunbar, the wife of his former livery stable partner John Dunbar. She wrote passionate love letters to "My Darling Brown Eyed Boy," telling "how I love you," and hoping that he wasn't feeling restrained because of his friendship for her husband.[44]

Marshal Crawley Dake came under investigation in 1885 for missing federal funds that had been assigned to finance his campaign against the cowboys. He said he could not show receipts because of Wyatt Earp's disappearance. Earp was found easily by the investigators and said he had received only a small part of the money appropriated. While the situation appeared suspicious, charges were not filed because it appeared unlikely any money could be recovered. During the investigation, one agent contacted Johnny Behan. "He informed me that he himself had done more to quiet the disturbance than anyone else, and that he regarded the whole affair as a fight between two lawless factions," investigator Leigh Chambers reported.[45] Johnny Behan could make himself the hero as well as anyone.

After Wyatt Earp left Tombstone, Sam Purdy kept the *Epitaph* faithfully Democratic, jabbing the Earps with regularity, attacking the *Tucson Citizen*, and praising the local police and sheriff. He left a legacy of falsehoods that would confuse several generations to come. Not everyone liked Sam Purdy. His partner, Patrick Hamilton, left the *Epitaph* and went off to start the competing *Tombstone Independent*. Purdy and Hamilton grew so antagonistic that they challenged each other to a duel. They met across the border in Sonora. They could not agree on the weapons, however, and the duel fizzled, with Hamilton calling Purdy a coward.[46] In early October Purdy was gone—back to Yuma—and Richard Rule again took over as editor of the *Epitaph*.

Billy the Kid Claiborne, who had run away from the Fremont Street gunfight, could not run away from Buckskin Frank Leslie. At seven on the morning of November 14, Leslie stood talking to friends at the Oriental Saloon when Claiborne pushed through and began insulting Buckskin Frank. Leslie led the young cowboy outside and continued the row before returning to the saloon. Claiborne was outside on the street with his rifle, and Leslie was told the Kid was waiting. Buckskin Frank rolled a cigarette, jammed it between his lips, and lit it before he picked up his pistol and walked into the street. Claiborne fired once and missed. Leslie fired and hit.[47]

"Frank Leslie . . . shot and killed the notorious Kid Claiborne this a.m., at 7:30, making as pretty a center shot on the Kid as one could wish to," Parsons wrote in his journal. "The Kid threatened and laid for him near the Oriental with a Winchester, but Frank got the drop on him, being quick as lightning and used to killing men, and the Kid has gone to hell. I say so because, if such a place exists and is for bad men, he is there, as he was a notoriously bad egg and has innocent blood on his hand. I state facts. Frank has done the county a service. . . . Frank didn't lose the light on his cigarette during the encounter. Wonderfully cool man."

Tombstone's mine production fell off over the years. Water slowly began seeping into the mines, a minor problem at first. In 1886, a fire burned the pump shaft at the Grand Central, and sinking silver prices made it impractical to rebuild. Parsons pulled out in '87. Tombstone remained the county seat for five decades, the main reason for its survival. Most of the mining operators left before Parsons, and the boom had busted. For a few years at least, Tombstone would become a quiet little town with a noisy reputation.

Ike Clanton got himself shot and killed in 1887 by a detective named J. V. Brighton, hired by Graham and Apache counties to chase outlaws. According to Brighton's story, Clanton pal Lee Renfro took over a ranch belonging to Isaac N. Ellinger. Ellinger went to the Clanton ranch and met up with Renfro, who shot and killed him. Brighton tracked down Renfro and killed him when he reached for his six-shooter. Ike had also run into trouble, collecting several felony indictments, and was dodging the law. Some weeks after killing Renfro, Brighton found Ike. This time, he could not run. Brighton said that at the sight of the officers Clanton pulled his Winchester from its scabbard and tried to gallop off. They ordered him to halt, but his answer was to bring his Winchester to his shoulder. Before he could fire, Brighton shot and the rustler fell dead on the trail.[48]

Fin Clanton was convicted of cattle rustling and went to the territorial prison at Yuma, the hellhole of the Southwest. Lark Ferguson, alias Pete Spence, also wound up there. Spence's tale is particularly unusual, because he began by enforcing the law in Georgetown, New Mexico. The *Silver City Enterprise* called him "one of the best peace officers in the West." However, the constable ran into trouble for rustling and spent most of the '90s in prison stripes. He later married Fin Clanton's widow and lived under the name Peter Ferguson until his death in 1914.

Perhaps the strangest change came in the connotation of the word "cowboy." In the 1880s it had been synonomous with criminal, lowlife, and villain; by the early '90s, however, the word had become a romantic title for so-called knights on horseback, with not the slightest taint of the pejorative. Cowboys would continue to be romanticized through the decades, the previous connotation lost to history.

By the 1890s, most of the mining sojourners left Cochise County to the ranchers. The old friends of the McLaurys and Clantons would continue the political tales of Wyatt Earp's villainy. Earp's supporters would settle in different areas, throughout California and back to the East, and continue lauding his heroism. It created a strange schism, with Earp receiving praise throughout the country while being vilified at the scene of the crimes. Wyatt Earp would never escape the debate, no matter where he wandered.

WYATT AND SADIE RETURNED TO COLORADO and settled in Gunnison, where Wyatt continued to run a faro bank, when the call came for him to leave. Luke Short, Wyatt's old friend from Dodge City and early on in Tombstone, had run into trouble back in Dodge. Short had returned to Kansas in April of 1881 to manage the gambling concession at the Long Branch Saloon for Bill Harris and

Chalkley Beeson. In February of 1883, Beeson sold his interest to Short. The Long Branch sat on Front Street amid a line of saloons and gambling houses, between George Hoover's retail and wholesale liquor store and the Alamo Saloon, owned and operated by Dodge City mayor Ab Webster, who had recently purchased the bar. Native Texan Short had developed quite a following with the Texas trail hands, taking business from his saloonkeeper neighbors. Webster did not take the loss of revenue gracefully.

With the city elections coming up, the old Dodge City Gang, headed by former mayor Jim "Dog" Kelly, selected Harris, Short's partner, to top the ticket. A few days later, the opposition group led by Webster chose former marshal Larry Deger as candidate for mayor with the promise of political reform. Deger, the former marshal and son of German immigrants, could be counted on to deliver the German vote and make reforms without hurting his sponsor, Webster. In this movement, the reforms would be made selectively. After a bitter campaign, Deger won easily, 214 to 143.

Within a month, the new mayor and the city council enacted laws against vagrancy and prostitution, with fines of $5 to $100 for keeping a brothel or working in one, plus fines of $10 to $100 for "loitering, loafing or wandering," with the stipulation that brothel keepers and gambling operators were subject to arrest. On April 28, two days before the ordinances went into effect, city clerk Lou Hartman, who wore the badge of a special policeman, and city marshal Jack Bridges went to the Long Branch and arrested three women, euphemistically called singers, charging them with prostitution.

Such moves were not unusual. Gambling had long been illegal in Dodge, and the fines collected were looked upon virtually as taxes. The city took its share, and the games went on. The new antiprostitution laws were just another tax ploy, Short believed. Nearly all the saloons allowed shady ladies to entertain the drovers, and the new fines would be the cost of doing business. A few hours after the arrest, Short received some unsettling news: No women had been arrested at the neighboring saloons. He went next door to Webster's Alamo, where several women were present, some perched on patrons' laps.

"Luke then smelt a mouse," Bat Masterson wrote in 1907. "All the time Luke was trying to get his employees out of the calaboose, the music in the mayor's place was in full swing. This, as can well be imagined, did not tend to help matters in the least."[49]

The angry Short strapped on his six-shooter and marched toward the city jail, where the girls from the Long Branch waited. Hartman, the clerk and cop, standing on the plank sidewalk near the jail, recognized Short. The frightened Hartman drew, fired, and missed. The shot splattered the dust behind the oncoming gambler. Hartman turned to run as Short returned fire, the bullet whizzing past Hartman's ear as he tripped and fell to the sidewalk.

Thinking that he had killed the city clerk, Short returned to the Long Branch, loaded his shotgun, and barricaded the door. He refused arrest through the night until it was explained to Short that he had not killed Hartman, and that if he surrendered he could go to police court and plead guilty to disturbing the peace, a charge that would amount to only a small fine. Short agreed and put down his guns. As he stepped out the door unarmed, two officers moved beside him and marched him to jail, where he was locked up on charges of assault. He was released on $2,000 bond, then rearrested the next day with saloonmen and gamblers W. H. Bennett, Doc Neil, Johnson Gallagher, and L. A. Hyatt. When they asked about the charges against them, they were told that they were undesirables. Webster was getting rid of the competition.

"The annual revolutionary spirit was again exhibited on our streets again yesterday," the *Ford County Globe* wrote. "Wars and rumors of war was the outcry all along the line."[50]

Short and his partner Harris tried desperately to take legal action, but were denied access to counsel. Deger, Webster, and a band of men took the gamblers from jail and marched them to the depot where they could choose their trains out of Dodge. Short picked East, and departed for Kansas City. The Long Branch was far too lucrative an investment for Short to simply abandon, and he quickly telegrammed for Masterson to return from Colorado.

"I was in Denver at the time, and he wired me to come to Kansas City at once, which I did," Masterson wrote in 1907. "We talked the matter over when we met and concluded to go up to Topeka and place the matter before the Governor. The next day we did so. The Governor denounced the conduct of the Dodge City authorities, but said that he could do nothing as the local authorities at Dodge had informed him that they were amply able to preserve the peace and did not desire to have state interference."

Short filed a petition with Governor George Glick requesting protection for his return to Dodge. W. F. Petillon, court clerk for Ford County, was called to the capital and attested to the truth of Short's charges, and Glick wired Sheriff George Hinkle for a report on the problem. Hinkle responded that no problems existed:

> Mr. L. E. Deger our mayor has compelled several persons to leave the city for refusing to comply with the ordinances. No mob exists nor is there any reason to fear any violence as I am amply able to preserve the peace. I showed your message to Mr. Deger who requests me to say that the act of compelling the parties to leave the city was simply to avoid difficulty and disorders. Everything is quiet here as in the capital of the state and should I find myself unable to preserve the present quiet will unhesitatingly ask your assistance.

Hinkle's message proved unsatisfactory to an angered governor. Glick responded quickly with a long letter on May 12 displaying his intense interest in the situation. It read in part:

> I am glad to be assured by you that you are able to preserve the peace in Dodge City, and of your county. The accounts of the way things have been going there are simply monstrous, and it requires that the disgrace that is being brought upon Dodge City, and the State of Kansas, by the conduct that is represented to have occurred there, should be wiped out. Your dispatch to me presents an extraordinary state of affairs, one that is outrageous upon its face. You tell me that the mayor has ordinances. Such a statement as that if true, simply shows that the mayor is unfit for his place, that he does not do his duty, and instead of occupying the position of peace maker, the man whose duty is to see that the ordinances are enforced by legal process in the courts starts out to head a mob to drive people away from their homes and their business. . . . It is represented to me by affidavits, and by statements, that the best

men in Dodge City have been threatened with assassination, and with being driven away from their homes, if they raised their voices against the conduct of this mob. Now if this is true, it is your duty to call to your assistance a respectable number of people, sufficient to enforce the law, and protect every man in Dodge City, without any reference to who he is, or what his business is, and if he is charged with crime, or the violation of law, to see that he has a fair trial before a proper tribunal, and that the sentence of the law is executed by you or by the authorities, according to the command of the court.[51]

Glick continued at length to lay out the charges he had heard and to instruct Hinkle that his duty was to protect all citizens from government gone amuck. The governor called on Hinkle to form a citizens' committee to defend the law and offered arms and ammunition. If Hinkle could not do his job, then a train of militia would be on the way to do it for him. According to Short, Governor George Glick advised him to return to Dodge. He was not foolish enough to go alone, and Masterson returned to Colorado to recruit an old friend to join them. That friend, of course, was Wyatt Earp.

Hinkle and the governor continued to heat up the telegraph wires between Dodge and Topeka, with Hinkle and Deger seemingly oblivious to the threat posed by the governor. They were even less aware of the more serious threat that would be arriving in the next few days. The May 15 *Kansas City Journal* reported Masterson's return, saying he preceded by twenty-four hours "a few other unpleasant gentlemen who are on their way to the tea party at Dodge. One of them is Wyatt Earp, the famous marshal of Dodge, another is Joe Lowe, otherwise known as 'Rowdy Joe;' and still another is 'Shotgun' Collins; but worse than all is another ex-citizen and officer of Dodge, the famous Doc Holliday." The *Journal* called Doc a "famous 'killer.' Among the desperate men of the West, he is looked upon with the respect born of awe, for he has killed in single combat no less than eight desperadoes." As for Wyatt, "Wyatt Earp is equally famous in the cheerful business of depopulating the country. He has killed within our personal knowledge six men, and he is popularly accredited with relegating to the dust no less than ten of his fellow men."

Rumors of the members of the band reached the absurd, with "Black Jack Bill," "Cold Chuck Johnny," "Dynamite Sam," "Dirty Sock Jack," and numerous other sobriqueted sharpshooters expected to join the raid on Dodge. Just about every great nickname in the West, short of Buffalo Bob the puppeteer, was rumored to be in the gang. Holliday, of course, remained behind in Colorado. The legion of dangerous nicknames posed a mighty threat, more implied than actual, to the safety of Dodge.

Hearing the news of the gathering storm, Sheriff Hinkle frantically wired Topeka. "Are parties coming with Short for the purpose of making trouble? Answer quick." Glick's answer has been lost, but Short said the governor refused to send the militia and advised Hinkle to form his own posse.[52] Hinkle, with a posse, met the trains and found no Short, and no notorious band. Short and Masterson were in Topeka, meeting with Glick at the time. The governor sent Attorney General Thomas Moonlight to Dodge City to investigate.

When the real force came together in the Kansas town of Caldwell, it did not include Doc, Rowdy Joe, or the many other members of the society of sobriquets. Instead, it was made up of former Kansas lawmen Frank McLain, Charlie Bassett, Neal Brown, and a few other dangerous characters. "It was decided that if a fight was all that would satisfy the mayor of Dodge—a fight he would have," Masterson wrote. Bat said the strategy was for Wyatt to arrive in Dodge first, while several other members of the band would gradually filter into town to be prepared for action should the need arise.

As Earp told the story, his train arrived in Dodge at 10 A.M., and he marched up Front Street followed by an armed posse of Johnny Millsap, Shotgun Collins, Texas Jack Vermillion, and Johnny Green, called "Crooked-Mouth" because a bullet had passed through his cheek, distorting the appearance of his mouth. When the district attorney approached, he said, "My God, Wyatt, who are these people you've got with you?"[53]

Earp responded calmly, "Oh, they're just some bushwackers I've brought over from Colorado to straighten you people out." Earp said he met Ab Webster a few yards down the street. Earp's little party filed into Short's saloon, where they were all sworn in as deputies by constable "Prairie Dog" Dave Morrow, a Short supporter. The badges legitimized the Earp party carrying guns.

Webster and Deger quickly convened a meeting of the town council and asked Wyatt his intentions. Earp said, "I told them that I wanted Luke Short and Bat Masterson to return to Dodge at their pleasure. I added that if this were accomplished peacefully I would be so much better pleased, but that if necessary I was prepared to fight for my demands." The council offered a compromise—they would allow Short to return for ten days to complete his business. Masterson could not enter town. Earp simply walked out of the room without responding.

Again the council summoned Earp, and he assured them there would be no compromise—Masterson and Short must be permitted to live in Dodge as long as they desired, provided they obeyed the laws. Earp then wired Short to meet him in Kingsley, Kansas, thirty miles from Dodge. The two decided to return together and agreed that if the fighting started, it would be Deger's men who initiated the action. Earp and Short carried shotguns as they jumped off the train before it reached the platform, expecting to catch their attackers by surprise if a posse awaited their arrival. They met no opposition. They looked around town and found no force ready to fight on Short's return, so Earp wired for Masterson to join them the next day.

Bat arrived the following morning. A deputy sheriff asked Bat for his shotgun, which he would not surrender. Wyatt joined Masterson, and after great difficulty convinced him to join him for a walk to shake hands with his old adversary Webster, and probably Deger as well. There would be no battle. Earp had used tact, as well as the intimation of force, to avoid battle between the two sides, both of which considered Wyatt something of a friend. Hinkle and other Webster supporters had signed the petition for Wyatt's release in Tombstone just nineteen months earlier.[54]

The so-called Dodge City War, filled with bluster, bluff, and braggadocio, but fortunately free of bullets, had ended. Masterson wrote a tongue-in-cheek note to the *Kansas State Journal* on June 9:

I arrived here yesterday and was met at the train by a delegation of friends who escorted me without molestation to the business house of Harris & Short. I think the inflammatory reports published about Dodge City and its inhabitants have been greatly exaggerated and if at any time they did "don the war paint," it was completely washed off before I reached here. I never met a more gracious lot of people in my life. They all seemed favorably disposed, and hailed the return of Short and his friends with exultant joy. I have been unable as yet to find a single individual who participated with the crowd that forced him to leave here at first. I have conversed with a great many and they are unanimous in their expression of love for Short, both as a man and a good citizen. They say that he is gentlemanly, courteous and unostentatious—"in fact a perfect ladies' man." Wyatt Earp, Charley Bassett, McClain and others too numerous to mention were among the late arrivals, and are making the Long Branch saloon their headquarters. All the gambling is closed in obedience to the proclamation issued by the mayor, but how long it will remain so I am unable to say at present. Not long I hope. The closing of this "legitimate" calling has caused a general depression in business of every description, and I am under the impression that the more liberal and thinking class will prevail upon the mayor to rescind the proclamation in a day or two.

The antiprostitution proclamation had this time been enforced against all parties. It soon was voted out, and Short was back in business. Wyatt, Bat, and Luke met with the council and Short received several concessions. In the second week of June, Wyatt and his friends visited a Dodge City photographer for one of the most famous pictures of frontier history. Eight men, most holding cigars, gazed into the camera at the Conkling Studio. Along with Wyatt, Short, and Masterson were Bill Harris, Petillon the clerk, Frank McLain, Charlie Bassett, and Neal Brown. Six weeks later this picture ran in the *National Police Gazette*, labeled the "Dodge City Peace Commission," surrounded by a story detailing the events. "All the members of the commission, whose portraits we publish in a group, are frontiersmen of tried capacity," the *Gazette* wrote. Earp said later that "Crooked-Mouth Green and my other henchmen did not figure in this group as they felt sensitive about submitting their physiognomies to the fierce light of frontier history."[55]

The size and makeup of the real band commanded by Earp and Masterson remains a mystery. Certainly Bassett, Brown, and McLain were there. Collins, Millsap, Texas Jack, and Green also were on the scene but chose not to be photographed, Earp said. As for the rest—Dynamite Sam, Dirty Sock Jack, and the other so-called dangerous bushwackers—they may have been waiting outside town or just have been the creations of rumor to help convince the townsmen of the futility of a fight against Earp and the others. Few would want to go toe to toe with Dirty Sock Jack. These unknown dangerous characters may even have been inventions of the press. In any case, the Dodge City War ended peacefully. Luke Short happily went back to running his gambling house, with the "singers" making their own kind of music. Wyatt Earp would be listening to another song, chasing the disappearing frontier.

Wyatt Earp left Kansas behind for the life of a sport and sometime celebrity. With Sadie at his side, he spent much of the next decade running saloons and gambling concessions and investing in mines in Colorado and Idaho, with stops in various boomtowns. He would spend far more of his life as a saloonman and a gambler than he had as a lawman. Earp would bring to the card tables the same knack for handling people that carried him through the tough Kansas cowtowns. Bat Masterson would recall one such incident that probably occurred in late 1882 or early '83, while Earp was still in Colorado.

As Masterson told the story, a gambler named Ike Morris, with a reputation as a bad man with a gun, ran a game in Gunnison and decided he would pay a call on Earp's game while Wyatt was away from his gambling house. Morris put a roll of bills on one of the cards and told the dealer to turn the card. The dealer made his turn and won the bet, then deposited the bankroll in the drawer. Morris noisily claimed he had been cheated and demanded his money be returned. The dealer would not comply and advised Morris to wait for Wyatt's return. When Wyatt came back, Morris informed him of the dispute and asked for a refund. Wyatt asked him to wait and went into conference with the dealer, who assured him the bets had all been fair.

By this time a rumor had circulated through town that Earp and Morris would likely have a set-to, and a crowd gathered in anticipation. In a surprise move, Wyatt told Morris the dealer had admitted cheating him, and Wyatt would like to return the money but could not. Wyatt said, "You are looked upon in this part of the country as a bad man, and if I was to give you back your money you would say as soon as I left town, that you made me do it, and for that reason I will keep the money."

Earp caught Morris completely off guard, and Morris had no idea how to respond. Wyatt had not accused the gambler of lying, which would have forced a fight; he simply left Morris in a position where he could not find a way to resolve the problem. Morris said no more about the matter and invited Wyatt to join him for a cigar. A few days later Morris left Gunnison.

Masterson praised Earp's unusual handling of the situation: "The course pursued by Earp on this occasion was undoubtedly the proper one—in fact, the only one . . . [that would] preserve his reputation and self-respect. It would not have been necessary for him to have killed Morris in order to have sustained his reputation, and very likely that was the very last thing he had in mind at the time, for he was not one of those human tigers who delighted in shedding blood just for the fun of the thing. He never, at any time in his career, resorted to the pistol excepting in cases where such a course was absolutely necessary. Wyatt could scrap with his fists, and had often taken all the fight out of bad men, as they were called, with no other weapon than those provided by Nature." Masterson was referring to Earp's fists.[56]

The Gunnison incident says much about the unusual way Earp handled his affairs. It was the verbal equivalent of the slap in the face to Tom McLaury on the streets of Tombstone—so unexpected that the adversary did not know how to respond. A credo of the best early-day frontier lawmen was to use the element of surprise as the primary weapon, before your fist or six-shooter, and Earp was a master at this. Had he denied cheating Morris, the gambler would have branded Wyatt a liar throughout the camp. Earp instead confused the situation by creating such a bizarre turn of events that Morris could not figure out an answer. It was the same type of ploy he and Masterson used with their rumored army of ghost sobriquets during the Luke Short affair, and a style Earp employed most of his life. He was always more an innovator and a scrapper than a gunfighter; the guns came only when fists, talk, and courts had failed.

Wyatt and Sadie continued their wanderings through the West, usually turning cards or trying to hit the ultimate jackpot with a mining venture. The Earps were boomers, following the next big strike, hoping their fortunes would come in a mining camp where selling whiskey, dealing cards, and dabbling in claims could yield big returns.

Early in 1884, Wyatt arrived in northern Idaho with Sadie and his brother Jim for the short-lived Coeur d'Alene rush. The Earps landed in the snowy little town of Eagle City, a flat spot where a small creek ran into Eagle Gulch. Newly thrown-up tents and freshly hewn log cabins filled quickly with miners who arrived almost daily. The Earps purchased a round circus tent, 45 feet high and 50 feet in diameter, for $2,250 and started a dance hall. Later, they opened the White Elephant Saloon, which an advertisement in the *Coeur d'Alene Weekly* called "The largest and finest saloon in the Coeur d'Alenes."

It had almost become a pattern in Earp's life that he came to town to make a fortune but instead would find himself in the middle of trouble. In Idaho, it happened again.

A. J. Pritchard discovered gold in the Coeur d'Alene region in the fall of 1882 and set about filing claims to tie up much of the land. This was always a touchy situation in mining boomtowns: local courts had to determine just how many claims one miner could file. Local mining law also dictated it illegal to file by proxy for someone living outside the region, which Pritchard had done. The Earps, along with partners Danny Ferguson, John Hardy, Jack Enright, and Alfred Holman, formed their own land syndicate and set about locating claims and challenging Pritchard's right to tie up extensive holdings. Wyatt and his associates wound up as regular defendants in the Eagle City courts, battling claim-jumping charges and arguing miners' rights.

Pritchard sued and won on a mining lot he claimed the Earps jumped. William S. Payne sued Earp and associates over possession of some town land in Eagle, alleging that two men armed with revolvers had forcibly taken possession of the land. Payne received a $25 judgment, which the judge trebled, and regained possession of the land. Oddly, Payne showed up in another legal suit siding with Wyatt. The Earps also won a suit for a mining claim they had allegedly jumped. Wyatt Earp was listed as locator on four mines—the Consolidated Grizzly Bear, the Dividend, the Dead Scratch, and the Golden Gate, while Jim located the Jesse Jay.

Between running a saloon, bringing legal actions, and locating claims, Wyatt Earp took another job. The exiled U.S. marshal became deputy sheriff of Kootenai County. The new mining territory was on land claimed by both Shoshone and Kootenai counties, and the legislature had not yet determined the proper authority. Shoshone County stationed both the sheriff and a deputy in Eagle City, while Kootenai was represented only by part-time deputy Earp.[57]

A lot in the tiny downtown of Eagle City became the site of gunplay. Property rights in the area were determined by who made a legitimate claim to a parcel, then made improvements. Enright, Payne, Ferguson, and Holman, but not

Earp, claimed to have legally purchased the lot from a Philip Wyman, who had built foundations on the front of the property. William Buzzard said that he bought the same lot from Sam Black, and he erected his own cabin. To further confuse the situation, Enright claimed Buzzard's cabin was not on the same lot and that the holdings were separate properties.

In March, Buzzard hauled logs on the site to begin construction of a hotel, and Enright protested. Both declared they would hold their land in any way necessary. On March 29, Buzzard pointed a Winchester in Enright's face and ordered him off the property. Enright said he would return. He did, and he was not alone. Enright, Payne, Holman, and Ferguson marched up the main street of Eagle City, carrying Winchesters, revolvers, and shotguns, making a show of force. Buzzard and three associates readied their weaponry for the arrival as spectators scampered out of the way. Buzzard stepped onto the log foundation and fired two quick shots, then ducked down as bullets began flying in all directions.

About fifty shots were fired in rapid succession, according to a newspaper report. Enright's party began to advance as the besieged fought back for about ten minutes before retreating into the cabin in the rear of the property. Buzzard, the last to enter the cabin, had two bullets pass through the crown of his hat. A bullet closely missed Enright's face as he continued his advance into the gunfire from Buzzard's cabin.

With bullets flying in both directions, Wyatt and Jim Earp stepped into the middle of the fray. The report said they took a prominent role as peacemakers, and "with characteristic coolness, they stood where the bullets from both parties flew about them, joked with the participants upon their poor marksmanship, and although they pronounced the affair a fine picture, used their best endeavors to stop the shooting." Shoshone County deputy sheriff W. F. Hunt arrived to order both sides to stop shooting. Hunt entered the cabin and disarmed Buzzard's band, and the Earps ordered Enright and his shooters to put up their guns. With the shooting finished, Enright and Buzzard met and smoked together, complimenting each other on their courage. The only casualty was an onlooker who took a shot through the fleshy part of his leg. [58]

The papers of the day referred to Earp as a peacemaker, not a warrior. A little more than a decade later, when Earp found himself in a bigger mess, a reporter hunted up Buzzard and quoted him as saying that Wyatt was the brains of a lot-jumping and real-estate fraud scheme; that he sat in his saloon while his henchmen went out and did the dirty work. Buzzard's version of events would gain the attention of the West and again tarnish Earp's reputation.[59]

Problems in the mining camp continued. On June 19, Danny Ferguson, a 23-year-old Nebraska native and Earp's partner in the land syndicate, found himself in serious trouble for, by his version, playing good Samaritan. Thomas Steele, the son of an Omaha doctor, went drinking with a prostitute who drank beyond her limit. She dropped down in the muddy street and announced that she planned to spend the night there, prompting Steele to slap her on the face several times. According to Ferguson, he came out of Johnny Donnoly's saloon and saw the battering. Another bystander told Steele not to hurt the woman, and Steele jumped to his feet and mistakenly confronted Ferguson.

Ferguson said that Steele approached within six feet of him when he heard the familiar clicks of a Colt six-shooter. Ferguson stepped back at the sound and Steele stepped up and slapped him across the nose and said, "Now what have you got to do with this?"

"Nothing," Ferguson answered, "only I wouldn't hurt a wo- . . ."

Ferguson did not complete the sentence when Steele knocked a gun against his left temple. The pistol discharged, tearing off some flesh and hair. The blow knocked Ferguson backward so hard against a tent wall that he bounced off, drawing his gun and firing. Two shots went off instantaneously. Ferguson missed; Steele's return shot zinged next to Danny's face and grazed his ear. Ferguson fired again into the night, directly at the spot where Steele's gun had flashed. Ferguson ducked his head below the haze of gunsmoke and saw nothing. Then he heard footsteps running down the sidewalk and muttered, "Is it possible I missed him?"

From not far away a weakened voice called, asking for a doctor. Steele, mortally wounded, had fallen between two pine trees, out of sight. Ferguson went to see Deputy Sheriff Wyatt Earp standing in his long underclothes at the door of his cabin. Ferguson recalled the conversation.

"Those pistol shots sounded like there was a fight up the street," Earp said.

"Yes, I had one," Ferguson answered.

"Did you win it?"

"Yes."

"Well, wait until I get my clothes on, and I'll go up and look over the battleground."

Earp left Ferguson in his cabin and went up to confer with the Shoshone County sheriff. Steele had died moments after Ferguson's departure. Earp told the sheriff that Ferguson would not surrender until the coroner's inquest the next morning. When he returned to his cabin Earp asked Ferguson, "Now what are you going to do, ride or stay?"

"Stick," Ferguson answered, then returned to his cabin.

The coroner's jury did not recommend charges against Ferguson, but the grand jury was to meet in July, and charges could then be brought against him for Steele's murder. Ferguson went south to the Wood River area.

"Wyatt Earp's loyalty to a friend now enters into the story," Ferguson wrote. Ferguson said that the grand jury would convene in a few weeks, and Wyatt expected his friend to be indicted. Earp went to the telegraph office and asked the operator, named Toplitz, if anyone had contacted Ferguson to warn him of impending trouble.

"No, and if they do we will indict them," Toplitz responded, according to Ferguson. Wyatt tried to grab the operator, but he ducked under Earp's arm and darted outside. Knowing he could not catch him, Earp fired a rock past Toplitz's head, causing him to trip and fall. Wyatt grabbed him around the neck and dragged him back to the office to send a telegram warning Ferguson of the approaching danger. "Now send that telegram or I'll beat you to death," Wyatt said, according to Ferguson. Toplitz sent the telegram, giving Ferguson warning that he could expect to be indicted. Ferguson skipped out before the indictment was completed. He would live out his life under the name of Danny Miller.[60]

Earp apparently played no role in another gun battle a few weeks later. Enright, who had eluded Buzzard's bullets, could not survive his next quarrel. On
July 2, Enright argued with Henry Bernard, manager of the *Eagle City Pioneer*.
"You have been trying to make me suck the hind teat, and I will make you suck
the bung hole," Enright shouted in the newspaper office. As the shouting continued Bernard grabbed a gun and fired. Enright took a bullet in the ribs and
died.[61]

The Coeur d'Alene gold rush petered out quickly, and many of the hard-
fought claims that were the subject of court challenges for the Earps were sold
at taxes. Again, the Earps came up losers.

The Earps were in El Paso in '85. Wyatt was in the gambling room of the
Gem Saloon on April 14th when Will Rayner and Buck Linn quarreled with
dealer Robert Cahill and cowboy R. B. Rennick in a confrontation that began
with a disagreement on a faro bet and erupted into gunfire. Cahill and Rennick
killed Rayner and Linn. Earp apparently had no involvement other than to testify at the inquest.

He moved on to Aspen in May and entered into partnership with H. C.
Hughes in the Fashion Saloon. In October Arizona deputy U.S. marshal E. M.
Mills showed up and recruited Wyatt Earp to help him arrest stage robber
James Crothers. Mills and Earp simply walked up to Crothers, tapped him on
the shoulder, and said, "I want you." Crothers went to jail, and Mills went to
Earp's saloon to smoke cigars and talk.[62]

While the event itself proved uneventful—no shootouts or shotgun duels—
it shows that Earp remained in high esteem among at least some Arizona lawmen. Mills chose Earp as his backup, something he would not have done had the
marshal's office believed the canards circulated by Sam Purdy and Behan's
friends.

Probably in late 1885 or in '86, Wyatt and Sadie stopped at the Windsor
Hotel in Denver. Sadie Earp recalled sitting in the lobby when a familiar form
appeared:

> There, coming toward us, was Doc Holliday, a thinner, more delicate-appearing Doc
> Holliday even than he had been in Tombstone.
>   I have never seen a man exhibit more pleasure at meeting a mere friend than did
> Doc. He had heard that Wyatt was in town, he said, and had immediately looked
> him up. They sat down at a little distance from us and talked at some length, though
> poor Doc's almost continuous coughing made it difficult for him to say anything.
> Wyatt repeated their conversation to me later.
>   Doc told Wyatt how ill he had been, scarcely able to be out of bed much of the
> time.
>   "When I heard you were in Denver, Wyatt, I wanted to see you once more," he
> said, "for I can't last much longer. You can see that."
>   Wyatt was touched. He remembered how Doc had once saved his life . . . in
> Dodge City. . . . My husband has been criticized even by his friends, for being asso-
> ciated with a man who had such a reputation as Doc Holliday's. But who, with a
> shred of appreciation, could have done otherwise? Besides my husband always
> maintained that the greater part of the crimes that were attributed to Doc were but
> fictions created by the woman with whom he lived at times when she was seeking so-

lace in liquor for the wounds to her pride inflicted during one of their violent disputes. . . .

Wyatt's sense of loyalty and gratitude was such that the world had been all against Doc, he should have stood by him out of appreciation for saving his life.

"Isn't it strange," Wyatt remarked to Doc that day in Denver, "that if it were not for you, I wouldn't be alive today, yet you must go first."

Doc came over and chatted with us for a few minutes, then he and Wyatt walked away, Doc on visibly unsteady legs.

My husband was deeply affected by this parting from the man who, like an ailing child, had clung to him as though to derive strength from him. There were tears in Wyatt's eyes when at last they took leave of each other. Doc threw his arm across Wyatt's shoulder.

"Good-bye old friend," he said. "It will be a long time before we meet again."

He turned and walked away as fast as his feeble strength would permit. Only a short time after this we heard that he had died.[63]

Doc Holliday died on November 8, 1887 in Glenwood Springs, Colorado.

Dead at the age of 36, Doc would constantly be reborn in the legend and mythology of the American West. He was intelligent, educated, and always a caliber or two above most of the men around him, both with his mind and with his six-shooter. He was hated by some, but he was totally loyal to Wyatt Earp at the time Wyatt most needed a friend. Dr. John Henry Holliday may have written his own epitaph shortly before his death. A reporter asked if he had ever been troubled by his conscience. "No," Doc replied. "I coughed that up with my lungs long ago."[64]

As the years passed, Wyatt Earp gradually grew into a true Western sport, adroit in a card game and always ready to bet the horses. At different times he managed racing stables, handling details for the racehorse owners. He and Sadie kept traveling, never settling too long in one spot until they landed in San Diego in 1886 for a stay that would last nearly four years.

The Earps hit San Diego during a land boom, where a great influx of population led to rising property values. Wyatt bought property and leased concessions for three gambling halls in the burgeoning seaside town and generally had a pleasant time. He refereed prize fights, judged horse races, and occasionally did a little bounty hunting on the side. According to Sadie, they joined Bat Masterson on a trip to Ensenada to reclaim a prisoner. The Earps left San Diego briefly to join in the 1889 boom in Arizona's Harqua Hala Valley, where Wyatt set up a saloon. The boom ended before anyone could make much of a profit.

The legend of Wyatt Earp had barely begun. Early in 1887, an article from the *Police Gazette* went into national distribution retelling the story of Wyatt Earp and the Arizona War. The details were simply a remembrance. The opening paragraph was the stuff that makes legends:

Wyatt S. Earp is one of the most famous Western characters living. Probably no man has a wider spread reputation throughout the Western territories than Wyatt S. Earp, of the famous Earp Brothers, who created such a sensation a few years since at Tombstone, Arizona, by completely exterminating a whole band of out-lawed cutthroats who had sought safe refuge in Arizona's mountain ranges.[65]

There is no indication Wyatt Earp was seeking the limelight. The story reads as if one of his friends had recalled the events for an interviewer, providing first-hand details without any personal insights. Such stories would reappear period-ically over the next two decades, recalling the wild times on the frontier. Earp would variously be named hero or villain.

Mattie Earp continued to use the name she acquired in common-law mar-riage. She had returned to Colton with Bessie after Morgan's assassination, and it seems almost certain that the family had expected to reunite in Tombstone once Wyatt's troubles blew over. Mattie waited for a telegram that never ar-rived. She went to Globe, Arizona, and became a prostitute, possibly her trade before hooking up with Wyatt. Mattie seems to have been servicing impecu-nious old men, probably with little financial return. At the end of June in 1888, she told her friend S. E. Damon that she was going to "make away with herself as she was tired of life." She had been drinking heavily for three months, and the slide had been difficult. On July 3, 1888, Celia Ann Blaylock Earp, always called Mattie, took an overdose of laudanum, a popular painkiller of the time. It was almost certainly suicide, and both Wyatt and Sadie would forever have an embarrassing secret to hide.[66]

A FIGHT FOR HONOR

WYATT S. EARP, CAPITALIST. A fine way for a frontier sport to list his occupation in the San Francisco city directory. The lure of the big city had called to the Earps, partly because Sadie wanted to be closer to her family and partly because of Wyatt's new job, managing horses for a stable in Santa Rosa, north of San Francisco.

In the 1890s, when Wyatt brought Sadie back to her childhood home, San Francisco reigned as the great city of the West. The city pulsed through the '90s, serving as residence to many of the great characters of the time. Wyatt cultivated friendships with *Examiner* publisher William Randolph Hearst, whose father had known Wyatt in Tombstone, and with millionaire Lucky Baldwin and a legion of other prominent people. Here Wyatt Earp could be just another big fish in a giant pond. But even here, Tombstone remained a fresh memory. In 1891, the *San Francisco Chronicle* ran a retrospective on the Earp–Clanton feud in Arizona, retelling the basic story. One Sunday the *Chronicle* even ran a dramatic though impossible full-page account of the killing of John Ringo, saying that it was done by an angry neighbor seeking vengeance. Even a decade after the Arizona War, its events were being revisited in print.

For the most part, the newspapers were interested in current events, allowing an aging legend to slip into the background. San Francisco papers had much to write about. The headlines were filled with breaking news of immigration problems and unrest on the mysterious Caribbean isle of Haiti, while inside the papers were advertisements for clinics treating cocaine addicts.

Earp would later call San Francisco his favorite city and indicate that this was probably the happiest period of his life. He had some money; Sadie's sister Henrietta, called Hattie, had married prosperous chocolate maker Henry Lehnhardt, and the family was flush. Something else happened in San Francisco: Wyatt Earp started changing, hanging with a moneyed crowd and keeping up appearances. Earp had always been a gambler, never a drinker. During his years in Tombstone he rarely indulged in more than an occasional glass of beer or wine. After a few years by the Bay, however, he had started taking his liquor with the sporting crowd, stopping for drinks after the races and eating often at the Pup Rotisserie on Stockton Street or at the Cafe Zinkand.

281

There are few known details and many old stories of Wyatt Earp in San Francisco. Perhaps the most tantalizing began in the parlor of the St. Francis Hotel when Zeb Kendall, a speculator in horses and mining stocks, met with the old lawman. Earp had traded in his revolvers and marshal's star for a black business suit, but he still had a passion for gambling. Kendall told Earp that he had sworn to his wife that he would never bet on horses again. After several drinks they agreed that the best place to take such an oath was at the racetrack, so they set off together. When they returned four days later, Kendall's wife was waiting for him in their room. Before he could say a word, she seized his briefcase and threw it out the window.

"Wait, ma," he yelled. "There's eighty-five thousand dollars in that thing that I won!"

"I beat the elevators getting downstairs," Belle Kendall recalled. "The dispatch case was still bouncing when I got there. And do you know—there really was eighty-five thousand dollars in it."[1]

Even in his new life, he remained the same old Wyatt Earp—a man not to be trifled with. In April of 1893, Earp confided in a bookie named Billy Roeder that his harness horse Lottie Mills had been running particularly well, and Roeder bet up the odds, meaning Earp had to bet two dollars to win just one. After Lottie Mills won, Roeder came by and snickered at Earp, who warned the bookie that he should leave before Earp took action. Roeder laughed and threw another insult. Earp responded by slapping Roeder in the face, then spinning him around and kicking him in his backside. Angering Earp was never a good practice.[2]

Earp traveled, racing horses at various tracks through the West, and even journeyed to the 1893 World's Fair in Chicago, with a stop in Denver to visit old friends. The *Denver Republican* reported: "His hair, which was once as yellow as gold, is beginning to be stranded with white. A heavy, tawny mustache shades his firm mouth and sweeps below his square, strong chin. He wore, while here, a neat gray tailor-made suit, immaculate linen and fashionable neckwear. With a derby hat and a pair of tan shoes he was a figure to catch a lady's eye and to make the companions of his old, wild days at Tombstone and Dodge, who died with their boots on and their jeans pants tucked down them, turn in their graves."[3]

Wyatt and Sadie lived at several San Francisco addresses, occasionally sharing a home with her parents, Henry and Sophia Marcus. They always seemed solvent, occasionally seeming to border on prosperous. Wyatt took pride in wearing custom-made clothing. Despite a lingering taint from his days in Arizona, he made a point of cultivating friendships with the right people. During the San Francisco years, Wyatt variously listed his profession in the city directories as capitalist, sporting, and horseman. He spent much of his time at the Ingleside track and at the Oakland track across the bay, but apparently in 1894 he found time to do some work for the railroad. In a story that cannot be substantiated, he worked for Southern Pacific as a guard on a train carrying a payroll through dangerous country, in which the train might be stopped by strikers or outlaws before the money could be delivered to pay the strikebreakers. Sadie Earp said that she begged Wyatt not to take the job. He responded: "There's practically no danger at all. I have been in tighter places than this will be hundreds of times." Sadie still fretted and said, "I know, but you never can tell. This might be the time they'll get you. You belong to me now, and I don't want anything to happen to you." Earp returned without incident.[4]

His main concern was racing. Some wins, some losses. Never enough to hit big. According to Sadie, their racing colors were navy-blue polka dots on a white background, and for every win Wyatt would give her jewelry. "Sometimes our fortunes were up, sometimes they were down, but there was always Wyatt with me and nothing mattered a great deal to me so long as I had him," she said. Something else began to matter to Sadie. In an unusually candid statement, she said she started betting regularly at the track, "with more fresh-handedness than wisdom." She borrowed money from Lucky Baldwin, giving him a piece of jewelry she had received from Wyatt and expecting to retrieve them with her winnings. Instead, Wyatt paid off her debts until he ran out of patience.

"You're not a smart gambler," Wyatt told her, as Sadie recalled. "And you have no business risking money that way. Now after this I'm not going to redeem any more of your jewelry." Wyatt told Baldwin to stop lending her money and said he would no longer retrieve her jewelry. Sadie said the experience awakened her and forced her to use better judgment in her bets.[5] In actuality, the problem had only just begun. Wyatt Earp, a professional gambler, was not the only or the biggest gambler in his household.

In the summer of 1896, Earp agreed with a friend, *Examiner* editor Andrew Lawrence, to prepare a memoir with the help of a ghostwriter, probably star reporter Robert Chambers. They conducted long interviews for a three-part series that began appearing in the *Examiner* in August, beginning with a dose of dramatic prose that certainly was not Earp's style:

> It may be that the trail of blood will seem to lie too thickly over the pages that I write. If I had it in me to invent a tale I would fain lighten the crimson stain so that it would glow no deeper than demure pink. But half a lifetime on the frontier attunes a man's hand to the six-shooter rather than the pen, and it is lucky that I am asked only for facts, for more than facts I could not give.

While Chambers pumped up the prose, the stories present Wyatt Earp's personal account of the events in Arizona and Kansas, and they were told only fourteen years after he rode out of Arizona amid controversy. A few days after the series began, the *Examiner* complemented it with an editorial:

> The eruption of genuine bad men in San Francisco during the past few days adds a contemporary interest to the true tales of the frontier which Wyatt Earp is writing for "The Sunday Examiner." You may know your Bret Harte and your Dan Quinn [Alfred Henry Lewis] from beginning to end, but you will never know the frontier until you have read Wyatt Earp.
>
> Why, there is nothing in fiction to compare with the cold record of this man's experience. His mind is simply saturated with the vivid colors that bedaub the life of the plains and the mining camp, and he has the gift to bestow those colors upon the canvas so that people who live in cities and never heard the cracking of six shooters may know the life for what it really was. Just consider the wealth of literary material that has soaked into the great peace-officer's consciousness, now to be squeezed out again for the entertainment of "Sunday Examiner" readers. As a boy he crossed

the plains with a caravan and learned to use a rifle on the Indians who infested the trail. Later he drove a Wyoming stage through territory devastated by the Sioux. Since then he has lived in every mining camp of importance; has trailed nearly every desperado of prominence in the country—and killed many of them—has been a shotgun messenger, Deputy United States Marshal, proprietor of a gambling house, miner and man hunter, has known the most renowned gamblers, bandits, gun-fighters and bad men in the country, and has the reputation of being the bravest fighter, squarest gambler, best friend and worst enemy ever known on the frontier.[6]

The legend of Wyatt Earp grew with its own retelling, and the Earp story caught the imagination of a city angered by the reemergence of ruffians. The stories helped make Wyatt a celebrity of sorts in the biggest city west of the Mississippi.

At the time, Earp was only a distant party to an ink war between the *Examiner* and the *San Francisco Call*, a smaller-circulation paper owned by the powerful Spreckels family and operated by Charles Shortridge. Shortridge had been sued for libel, and the *Examiner* took every opportunity to embarrass him in print, with both words and cartoon caricatures. The *Call* responded with sundry attacks on the Examiner. None of this could have seemed particularly important to Earp, at least not until early December, when he again wound up in the middle of a newspaper war.

Shortly after the *Examiner* stories appeared, sport came into focus in San Francisco. Since the bare-knuckled days, boxing had been banned. But the police and courts began ignoring the laws as the new Marquis of Queensberry rules made fighting more civil. In the old days, the fighters went to secret barges on the Bay to slug it out barehanded, gouging and kicking as much as punching. Now the sweet science seemed more refined, with the boxers donning gloves and hitting only above the waist. And now, San Francisco was set to hold its most heralded prizefight ever under the new rules.

Cornwall native Bob Fitzsimmons and sailor Tom Sharkey were to meet for the heavyweight championship of the world at Mechanics' Pavilion on December 3, 1896, perhaps the most important sporting event to be held on the West Coast in the nineteenth century.

It was not quite everything a world championship fight should be, mainly because of a taint on Fitzsimmons's claim to the title. San Francisco native Jim Corbett had won the title in 1892, stopping the aging John L. Sullivan. But Corbett grew more involved in theater than the ring, and he refused to defend his title. He finally renounced it and announced his retirement from the sport, suggesting that Peter Maher and Steve O'Donnel fight for the crown. On November 11, 1895, Maher stopped O'Donnel in only 63 seconds of the first round, much to the dismay of Corbett, who had backed O'Donnel. Corbett entered the ring and told Maher, "I give you the title." Maher refused to accept it unless Corbett would fight him, and Corbett stormed out of the ring in disgust.

Unlike Corbett, Maher kept fighting. He agreed to meet Fitzsimmons on February 21, 1896, near Langtry, Texas, under the auspices of Judge Roy Bean, one of the West's true eccentrics. Fitzsimmons struck fast, knocking out Maher in 95 seconds to claim the much-disputed title. Corbett still would not fight. He disliked Fitzsimmons and had ignored him in naming the two men he thought should battle for his crown. Fitzsimmons owned a title that hardly seemed legitimate, and sports across the nation labeled him "the great pretender." Fitzsimmons did not hesitate to defend his pretension, and scheduled the fight against Irish native Tom Sharkey, who had come to the United States as a boy and later enlisted in the Navy.

San Francisco settled into the excitement, with four major newspapers billing the event as a world championship and spending much of November scrutinizing the daily training routines of the two fighters. But behind the hype, a problem festered: the two sides could not agree on a referee. All the usual names were suggested, then dismissed. Finally, the sponsoring National Athletic Club had to step in and make a decision. They chose "the bravest fighter, squarest gambler, best friend and worst enemy ever known on the frontier." The call went out for Wyatt Earp to step into another fight.

As with just about every fight of that era, weird rumors floated through the streets. The morning before the fight, a strange note arrived at the offices of the *San Francisco Bulletin:*

> Editor Bulletin: The opinion prevails, and belief in its truth is growing, that the police have been instructed to protect the interests of their official superior, Moses Gunst, who wagers on Fitz, by stopping before the final round the mill between Sharkey and Fitzsimmons, contingent upon the apparency of Sharkey winning. FAIR SPORT.

Police Commissioner Moses Gunst blustered and denied betting the fight. "I don't believe in ten-round set-tos," he said. "Five times out of six the end is unsatisfactory. But this is not to the point. I couldn't stop the fight if I wished. San Francisco is not like New York, where the commissioners have the say. There Mr. [Theodore] Roosevelt can stand up and call a halt any time he sees fit." Moses Gunst stood accused, and he had no desire to see his reputation tarnished.[7]

Wyatt Earp went to meet a friend at Lucky Baldwin's hotel a little after noon on Wednesday, December 2. Earp had a horse racing at the Ingleside track, and the friend wanted some inside information. James Groom and James Gibbs of the National Athletic Club, sponsors of the night's big fight, spotted Earp in the room and called him aside.

Earp would later say Groom and Gibbs explained to him that the fighters could not agree on a referee and asked if he would step in to officiate. Earp said he refused—he already had refereed all the fights he wanted to. But the sponsors told him what an honor it would be for him to officiate in such a major event. Earp said he considered it for a while and said, "I don't know but what it will be a little bit tony to referee a fight of this kind. I think the two best men in the world are coming together now, and probably it will be a little bit of tony to referee a fight of this kind." With that he accepted.[8]

It would be among the worst decisions of Wyatt Earp's life. He had refereed at least thirty fights in the San Diego–Tijuana area and earned a pretty fair reputation as an official. But nothing could prepare him for walking into the heavyweight championship ring for the biggest fight of the year, using the Marquis of Queensberry rules. Earp had not refereed since arriving in San Francisco, more than five years earlier, and most likely he had never officiated a fight under the new rules. The *Bulletin* called Earp "a man with a reputation for bravery, but inexperienced in ring tactics."

The fight fans packed Mechanics' Pavilion that night, a diverse crowd estimated at ten thousand, which included the elite of San Francisco and all the usual sports. For the first time, women were allowed to attend a major fight. Chinese fans "were sitting in common brotherhood with the whites. That may be called a step in the direction of social equality—and they all yelled just the same."[9] Tightly packed bleachers rose to frame the ring, with the down-front $10 boxes holding millionaires, supreme court judges, politicians, a few wealthy Chinese, and several heavily veiled women. Up higher, in the $2 and $3 seats of the galleries, the crowd was packed together so tightly that even breathing became difficult. The hastily constructed boxes were of half-painted pine with narrow aisles that filled with vendors hawking programs, candy, popcorn, and soda; and with helmeted police officers trudging through to show a presence.[10]

The card began with five preliminaries, including one featuring a young lightweight named Harry Woods. Just the name must have aroused a few memories for Wyatt Earp. Fitzsimmons entered the ring at 10:10 on that Wednesday night, followed shortly by Tom Sharkey. Billy Jordan, the master of ceremonies, stepped into the ring and called for Wyatt Earp. Moments after entering the ring, Fitzsimmons's manager Martin Julian jumped in and spoke to Danny Lynch, Sharkey's manager. Their discussion could be heard only at ringside. A *Bulletin* reporter listened in on the exchange and reported that Julian said he had heard enough around town to convince him the referee had been fixed, so Julian objected to Earp's officiating. Lynch stubbornly refused to allow a change and insisted the rules be followed. The National Club had the right to select a referee, and the decision had been made. Julian responded by saying, "Take anybody in the house, we don't care whom; but spare us from Earp." Lynch continued to refuse any change, and at last Fitzsimmons rose, lifting one arm over his head and shouted: "I'll do as I've always done before. I give in."

According to Gibbs, Earp stepped over and asked to be excused from officiating, but Gibbs asked him to stand his ground and referee the fight. Earp agreed. With that settled, at least reluctantly, police captain Charles W. Wittman apparently noticed an unsightly bulge in the referee's pocket.

"Have you got a gun?" Wittman asked, according to the *Examiner* report.

"Yep," Earp responded.

"You'd better let me have it."

"All right."

Examiner writer Edward H. Hamilton called the disarming of Earp "an 'event' of the evening," and added, "So, for the first time in the history of the prize-ring in California it was necessary to disarm the referee." The event apparently happened quite quickly and quietly, because few seemed to notice, and the *Bulletin* did not report it. The *Call*, however, latched onto the incident in a big way, saying Earp "showed the 'yellow dog' in him by going into the ring with a Colt's Navy revolver in his pocket, indicating that he feared trouble over the decision that he would give if opportunity offered. When Captain Wittman saw it pushing out of his coattails he demanded the gun, and it was only after repeated orders from the big police officer that Earp gave up his weapon on which he depends for a living." What seemed an unusual though unimportant occurrence at the time grew to become one of the stranger events of the Earp legacy: a pistol-packing gunfighter carrying the frontier into civilized San Francisco.

With Earp disarmed, the fight began. Fitzsimmons, a lean 172-pounder standing a quarter-inch under six feet, seemed to take early advantage of Sharkey, who carried the same weight and stood three and a half inches shorter. The *Bulletin* described Fitzsimmons as always holding the edge:

> Fitzsimmons played with the sailor from start to finish. Sharkey fouled him frequently, but the Cornishman never lost his temper. Once in a while his beady little eyes would light up with a peculiar glitter, once in a while he showed his teeth. But he fought on with great judgment though he did show a little surprise at the clever way Sharkey ducked to avoid his swings. Sharkey countered well, too, more than once, and Fitz got it, strictly, in the neck.
>
> The gong saved Sharkey twice. But he stayed the six and seven rounds required to win a host of bets, and was deservedly cheered for his performance. The people were willing to have it go at that; let Sharkey get the credit for staying his rounds, and now let Fitz knock him out and have done with it, a thing which appeared to come to pass in the very next round. Sharkey was badly punished, and being driven to the ropes, was sent reeling by a vicious uppercut. It looked as though no coup de grace were necessary. But it is to be presumed that Fitz was anxious to make assurance doubly sure, and the result was a blow which the referee declared a foul.[11]

In the eighth round, Fitzsimmons went into a flurry, punching Sharkey about the face and body. The taller Fitzsimmons continued the battering, launching a heavy blow toward the gut. Sharkey fell. According to the *Examiner*, Sharkey then put his hand down to his groin and began making grimaces and groans as Sharkey's top trainer and cornerman Danny Needham rushed into the ring, claiming the sailor had been fouled. Fitzsimmons just laughed at Sharkey's antics, grinning in his corner as Sharkey turned on his side and writhed while the police entered the ring.

Quietly Wyatt Earp walked over to Sharkey's corner and told his seconds that their man had won the fight. Sharkey's staff lifted him into a chair, where he sat with his head sunk on his chest, seeming to take no interest in Earp's decision. Needham stepped to the center of the ring and began waving a towel over his head to signify that Sharkey had indeed been named the winner. The stunned Julian ran over to Earp as Wyatt bent down to pass through the ropes. Wyatt informed him of the decision, and Fitzsimmons grew excited. He tried to make a speech but could not be heard in the uproar of the crowd. Spectators jumped out of the rickety wooden bleachers and charged the ring, trying to learn exactly what had occurred. Gradually word passed through the pavilion that Sharkey had been awarded the victory and the $10,000 purse, a surprising finish to a fight where the winner was carried from the ring.[12]

Wyatt Earp, lawman turned referee, called the foul for a low blow into the center of the groin and awarded the fight and the championship to Sharkey. Such a decision is solely the responsibility of the referee, who has no one to ask for help. Earp made the decision in a split second, just as he had against Billy Clanton and Curley Bill. And there were no second chances in the ring. The scene was so convincing that *Examiner* boxing writer W. W. Naughton wrote that Sharkey "was making grimaces and placing his hand on his groin. And if he were not in agony all I can say is that he must be a consummate actor and must have rehearsed that particular scene many a time and often."

Fitzsimmons and manager Julian ranted, accusing the sanctioning National Athletic Club and Earp of fraud. Fitz appeared fresh and absolutely uninjured as he spoke at length to the papers. He said he was robbed by the decision and that he had been warned by several people earlier in the day that Earp was part of a plot to "fix" the fight. He had accepted Earp, however, because he did not want to tarnish his reputation as champion—"If I had refused to fight, the whole country would have said that I was afraid to meet the man who nearly put Corbett out." He ended by saying: "No pugilist can get a square deal from the thieves who handle fighting in this city and it is a safe bet that the last big fight San Francisco will ever see was pulled off to-night."[13]

Sharkey rested about half an hour in the dressing room, weakly shaking hands with a reporter and saying, "I'd have licked him if he hadn't hit me that way." When asked about his condition, he said he felt "awful bad." He said he was certain of winning the fight and was growing stronger and more confident as Fitzsimmons wore down. "I am certain that Fitzsimmons fouled me deliberately. He did it to save himself from defeat. It was getting plain to him that I was growing in strength, while he was going down hill, so to speak, and rather than be knocked out, he thought he would lose on a foul. Had he not delivered that nasty blow which crippled me, I would certainly have finished him in that round. . . . I was for a moment paralyzed when I received that blow, and was wholly unable to protect myself. I felt myself sinking to the floor, and I was doubled up in such a way, that I could not guard myself from the last upper-cut which he sent in—I suppose as a finisher. I am sorry that the question of supremacy was not settled on its merits, rather than in this way."[14]

Then something very odd happened. Dr. Daniel D. Lustig, the official medical examiner for the National Athletic Club, and four other physicians came to call on Sharkey and were refused admission to his room. Lustig protested at length, to no avail, and the doctor charged with determining the severity and legitimacy of the injury was barred from seeing the prize patient. It was a deliberate act—or a mistake—that would make Fitzsimmons's claims seem far more plausible.

After about half an hour in the dressing room, the seconds lifted Sharkey onto a stretcher to carry him to the Windsor Hotel, followed by a string of reporters. Dr. Benjamin Lee was called to attend the fighter, an unusual choice because he was not one of the club doctors. Lee immediately certified the injury and said, "Mr. Sharkey is without doubt in great pain from the result of a blow in the region of the groin. He is badly swollen and may have to remain in bed two or three days."

Reporters frantically scrambled around the pavilion, putting together stories that would try to clarify the bizarre turn of events. Hearst's *Examiner* devoted six heavily illustrated pages to the contest, viewing it from all angles and interviewing just about anyone with an opinion. The *Examiner* printed fifty-four spectator statements, with twenty-eight saying no foul had been committed, seventeen viewing a foul, and nine saying they could not clearly see and were uncertain. Of course, this probably reflected their bets more than their vision, and most boxing fouls are not clearly seen by much of the crowd.

Earp was quoted at length in both the *Chronicle* and the *Examiner*, describing the fight and defending his position. According to the *Examiner*, he said:

> When I decided this contest in favor of Sharkey I did so because I believed Fitzsimmons had deliberately fouled him, and under the rules the sailor was entitled to the decision. I would have been willing to allow half-fouls—that is, fouls that might be considered partly accidental—to pass by with only a reprimand, but in such a case as this I could only do my duty.
>
> Julian approached me before the contest, and said he had heard stories to the effect that I favored Sharkey. We talked a few moments and he went away, apparently satisfied that everything was on the square. Any talk to the effect that I was influenced in any way to decide wrongly against Fitzsimmons is rubbish. I saw Sharkey but once before in my life, and that was when he boxed with Corbett. I had no reason to favor him. If I had allowed my feelings to govern me, my decision would have been the other way.
>
> I am a pretty close observer, and under most conditions I think I am cool. I went into the ring as referee to give a square decision and, so far as my conscience speaks, I have done so. It made no difference to me who won; the victory should be to the best man. . . . I feel that I did what was right and honorable and feeling so I care nothing for the opinion of anybody. I saw the foul blow struck as plainly as I see you, and that is all there is to the story. . . . No man until now has ever questioned my honor. I have been in many places and in peculiar situations, but no one ever said, until to-night, that I was guilty of a dishonorable act. And I will repeat that I decided in all fairness and with a judgment that was as true as my eyesight. I saw the foul blow.[15]

In the *Chronicle* interview, Earp said he had been introduced to Fitzsimmons by Masterson, "the best friend I have on earth. If I had any leanings they would have been toward Fitzsimmons, for I know that Bat Masterson, who is in Denver tonight, had every dollar he could raise on Fitzsimmons."

The next morning the papers screamed the decision around San Francisco. The *Call*, making no pretense of fair coverage, headlined, "FITZSIMMONS WAS ROBBED," then followed with dropheads of "REFEREE EARP GAVE A RAW DECISION" and "The Cornishman Was Warned Against Accepting the Ex Faro Dealing Sharp."

It was rumored locally that *Call* editor Shortridge had bet heavily on Fitzsimmons, and his loss, combined with the simmering feud against the *Examiner*, gave Shortridge an outlet to attack both Earp and the rival paper. The *Call* would long continue the attack with vindictive bias. The furor continued in San Francisco on Thursday morning when a *Bulletin* reporter called on Sharkey at the Windsor Hotel and filed his report in time for the afternoon editions:

> No one who saw the doughty sailor rolling on the platform gasping with agony, could doubt that he was badly hurt in some tender spot. And all doubts on this point are forever set at rest by Sharkey's condition this morning.
>
> Tom Sharkey passed a sleepless night. It was almost noon to-day before he shut his eyes for a slumber. Dr. Benjamin Lee, who was called in immediately after

the fight, remained at his bedside all night and administered to his injury. About 10 o'clock this morning Dr. Rottanzi and Dr. Ragan called at the Windsor and examined the disabled pugilist. There is no gainsaying the fact but what Sharkey is horribly crippled. There was an immense swelling in his groin about 5 o'clock. Then it perhaps reached a climax. By means of leeches and hot applications the swelling was reduced almost one-half. Hot cloths were continuously applied for twelve hours; the leeches were not used until daybreak. Accompanying the swollenness there is, of course, more or less inflammation, but this was nearly allayed before Sharkey went to sleep.

Sharkey displayed his bruised groin, and the *Bulletin* wrote, "People who saw the fight and who entertain doubts about the Cornishman striking below the belt should visit the sailor's room and make a personal examination. Should they do so they will be convinced that there was a foul blow struck by none other than Mr. Robert Fitzsimmons. . . . The old maxim that 'the best test of the pudding is the eating' might in Sharkey's case be worded, 'the best proof that he was foully hit is the seeing.'" Unfortunately, Sharkey chose not to stand atop Lotta's Fountain and display his bruised and swollen scrotum. Even if it would not have stopped public debate, it certainly would have provided another dandy San Francisco story for the ages.

The *Bulletin* reporter remained in the room when Wyatt Earp came to call and reported the scene:

> He stayed a few seconds. The swollen groin satisfied Mr. Earp that he did not err in giving the prize to Sharkey. "It was the most deliberate foul I ever saw struck," said the referee. "Fitz hit him squarely below the belt. I can understand how many could not see where the blow landed. It was an upswoop, which to many not near the ring looked as if Fitzsimmons struck him in the stomach, when in reality it was clear below the belt. Of course Fitz was the favorite in the betting, and he carried more money. You know how it is at the racetrack when they tip over a favorite well played. Won't a roar go up to the clouds especially if the judges disqualify the favorite for fouling?"

The roar had only begun. Once again, Wyatt Earp would find himself in the middle of a tempest of press attention that would be carried across the nation on telegraph wires, with debates on both coasts as to whether Earp threw the fight. New York sports took the news badly, raging en masse that the fight had been thrown or the call had been blown. Sharkey received challenges from around the country, including one from Jim Corbett, the real owner of the title, and another from John L. Sullivan, the aging former champ.

On Thursday Dr. Lustig further exacerbated the issue with an angry letter to the *Examiner* outlining the events that followed the fight, when he and a team of physicians were not let into Sharkey's room. Lustig said he was not allowed to examine the patient until late the next afternoon when Groom asked him to check Sharkey's condition. Lustig and several other doctors performed full examinations and met in another room for consultation. They agreed there was swelling and discoloration in the groin, but did not give a cause. Lustig said Dr. D. F. Ragan had told him the swelling had increased in the fourteen hours since he had first seen it, and Lustig said dramatically: "in my judgment had it been due to a blow such as he complains of having received I think the swelling and discoloration would be far greater than it is at present. . . . I am unable to understand why, if Sharkey was suffering such severe pains as were attributed to him, none of the physicians at the Pavilion were called upon to attend him or even permitted to see him."

Lustig hinted the disabling blow may have been committed after the fight, when Sharkey's associates realized there was no choice other than to really injure their fighter. Lustig certainly appeared slighted by the Sharkey group, and he struck out against them.

An *Examiner* reporter tracked down police commissioner Gunst, who owned a chain of cigar shops and was a political appointee with no law enforcement background. Gunst had told Fitzsimmons of the fix rumors before the fight, and he showed his anger in the interview: "Fitzsimmons was robbed by an unjust decision and honest sport in this city has been struck a blow from which it will not recover for a long time. The decision of Earp was deliberate robbery, and I have reason to believe that I was rightly informed when I was told before the fight that the referee had been 'fixed,' and that the fight would be given to Sharkey. I expected such a decision much earlier in the contest. I am not at liberty to tell my informant's name, but he is thoroughly reliable and, as events proved, quite as well informed. I was sitting in the Baldwin restaurant shortly after 6 o'clock when my friend approached me and asked me if I had bet anything on the fight. I told him that I had not. . . . My friend surprised me and I asked him why he had asked such a question. He replied that the fight had been 'fixed,' and that a 'crooked' decision would be given in Sharkey's favor. This information was given positively without rumor or insinuation."[16]

With a police commissioner and the National Athletic Club physician questioning the result, the accusation of a fix now seemed far more plausible than it had twenty-four hours earlier when Fitzsimmons and his dapper trainer were doing most of the ranting. Something had definitely started to stink in San Francisco, and Wyatt Earp stood directly in the middle.

SADIE EARP SAID SHE DID NOT LEARN until late on the day of the fight that Wyatt would be the third man in the ring, and that night she waited at home for Wyatt to return. "When at last Wyatt did come home, I knew at once something was seriously wrong. He seemed tired and depressed," she wrote.[17] Wyatt explained the events of the fight, and how he had been carrying a gun to protect against robbery. Sadie asked why her husband had not removed the gun, and she recalled that Wyatt answered, "I am certainly sorry I didn't, but I was so excited about having to referee the fight that I forgot it was there. Wearing it all day I don't feel the weight of it and am no more conscious of its being there than of my coat or my vest. I wouldn't have had it happen for anything. Even though it was an accident it will be hard to convince some people that it was, in view of the way the decision went. . . . I am sorry I was ever drawn into it, but I did what I knew was right and I'm not sorry about my decision, It's all I could do."

Wyatt Earp had more trouble Thursday, as the aftermath of toting a gun into the prize ring. Earp left for the race track early in the morning, apparently unaware that he was supposed to appear in court on charges of carrying a concealed weapon, and officers were alerted to watch for him. That evening, Captain Wittman sent officer Frank W. Riley to the Pup Rotisserie on Stockton Street, where Earp was known to take his meals. At about 7 P.M., the former U.S. marshal walked in to have dinner.

"You are wanted at police headquarters," Riley said, according to the *Examiner*.

"All right," Earp replied. The two boarded a streetcar and were soon at headquarters.

"I have been looking for you all day, and had begun to think that I would not be able to find you," Wittman said.

"Very sorry to have troubled you," Earp responded. "I may as well confess that I went to the Ingleside track early this morning for the purpose of avoiding persons that might desire to discuss last night's fight. I am now, however, entirely at your service."

"You will have to answer to a charge of carrying concealed weapons," Wittman said.

"Very well. What is the bail?"

"Fifty dollars."

"I did not expect to be arrested or I would have surrendered myself," Earp said, according to the *Call*.

"I would have arrested you at the fight, but fearing trouble I concluded to wait until today," Wittman said.

"You did not think I would run away?" Earp asked.

"I knew where to get you," Wittman answered, smiling. "You could not have avoided us very long."[18]

Earp attended to the procedures before returning downtown. The next morning, Wyatt Earp and attorney Frank Kelly walked into police court to face charges of carrying a concealed weapon and obtained a continuance before sitting down for a conversation with a *Bulletin* reporter.

A quiet, determined-looking man is Wyatt Earp. Not the fierce desperado that many unjust rumors have pointed out, by any means. He looks peaceable enough, even kindly, though he has a steel blue eye that is the outward and visible sign of the inward and spiritual temperament of a man not to be trifled with. Tall, and of an athletic, agile build, he looks like a man who has been in training all his life. He is courteous, too. During his conversation with the Bulletin representative his hand did not wander once toward his hip pocket.

"I am asking for a continuance of this matter," he said, because I have not yet decided what I shall do. I want time to think it over.

"You see, I make no pretense that I did not have a gun. I had it all right, just here," slapping that hip pocket. "It was foolish of me to have it, of course. But I gave it up when called upon. It happened in this way. I am out at the races all day, and when the last race is run I have to cross over from the stables to the cars after everybody has gone, and I do not reach home sometimes until 8 or 9 o'clock. I never know whom I am going to meet, so I deem it right to protect myself.

"Now on the night of the fight I got in very late from the races, much later than I expected, and had to go straight out to Mechanics' Pavilion. If I had any place to leave my gun I'd have put it away, but I hadn't; so I just clambered up into the ring with it on. It was foolish of me, of course.

"But there is another consideration which makes me uncertain as to whether I should plead guilty and take my fine or whether I should demand a hearing. I'll decide by Tuesday. This is a new experience to me. I was never arrested like this before."

Earp was most unwilling to talk about the fight. "I've said enough, and have been reported to have said more than I have. My attorney, Mr. [Frank] Kelly, advises me that the less I say the better. So I'll await results."[19]

Earp returned to court to plead not guilty, then went to trial on December 10. Wittman took the stand and produced the Colt, "fully a foot long," according to the *Bulletin*. Earp again said he needed the gun for protection because of late dealings at the track, adding that released convicts all over the West had vowed to have his life on sight and he was not inclined to die a martyr at their hands, the *Bulletin* said. When Earp said that recent robberies had shown the need for protection, Judge Low remarked that there was greater danger of losing money at the track. According to the report, everyone laughed except Wyatt. Jesse Hardesty, formerly a district attorney in Arizona, appeared as a character witness and said many rustlers in the Tombstone area had vowed to shoot Wyatt if they ever saw him again.[20] Low ruled that Earp had committed a "technical violation" of the ordinance against concealed weapons and fined Earp $50, or 25 days in jail. Earp paid with the $50 he had already put up for bail, and the incident ended. But the uproar over the fight had been growing all during the week that Wyatt Earp struggled with his legal problems.

The very character of Wyatt Earp became subject to passionate debate in the saloons and sporting halls of San Francisco. Earp clearly disliked the situation and apparently was ready to fight to protect his honor. By one account, he confronted Frank McLaughlin, chairman of the state's Republican Committee, and asked him to explain why he had called Earp's decision unsavory. Onlookers expected an encounter, but Earp's friends pulled him away before a fight broke out.[21]

Julian and Fitzsimmons, through their attorneys, filed a formal complaint the morning after the fight against Sharkey, the National Athletic Club, and others supposedly involved in the alleged fix, but did not name Earp. A restraining order was granted, preventing Sharkey from collecting the $10,000 prize. And the newspapers continued their clamor. The *Call* carried the cudgel of rabid anti-Earpism, with the *Chronicle* and the *Bulletin* trying to establish balance, and the *Examiner* reporting in depth as it attacked the *Call*.

Manager Julian stood as the most outspoken Earp critic. He told the *Bulletin* he had heard Earp was looking for him. "He ought to have little trouble [finding] me. Everybody knows where I am stopping. Mr. Earp may be an expert with a gun, but there are others."[22]

Julian and the *Call* continued anti-Earp diatribes as both sides prepared for a hearing. Probably the most inflammatory accusation concerned a telegram trainer Danny Needham was alleged to have sent to an Eastern sport on December 2 supposedly saying: "Place all your money on Sharkey. Will explain further." Needham denied ever sending such a telegram. The ever inquisitive *Bulletin* sent a reporter to the Postal Telegraph Company, where manager L. W. Storror confirmed the trainer's comment. Storror told the *Bulletin:* "We sent no

such dispatch. The printed dispatch is a fake upon the face for there is no destination mentioned. We are not in the habit of sending messages without having
the destination stated expressly in the 'head.'"[23]

The prehearing hype almost matched the publicity engendered by the fight
itself. From Arizona to Idaho and on to San Francisco, Wyatt Earp had been involved in dealings that earned him strong supporters and equally bitter enemies,
where right and wrong would be matters of judgment rather than certainty. The
hearing in a San Francisco courtroom ostensibly concerned whether Sharkey or
Fitzsimmons should receive the $10,000 check, but the real issue on trial was the
honesty and character of Wyatt Earp.

For the next week, the upcoming hearing became the local circus as the *Call*
and the *Examiner* engaged in a war of invectives. The *Call* took the attack, lam-
basting Earp and the *Examiner* with stories and cartoons. Earp appeared as a
slouchy old man with a sombrero, pistol, and drooping mustache. *Examiner* editor Andy Lawrence became simply "Long Green," alluding to his alleged involvement in journalistic blackmail, and the paper unrelentingly blasted Hearst
at every turn. The real victim became Wyatt Earp. The *Call* dug for every ugly
old story it could find about Earp, and there were many.

The *Examiner* ran a concise excerpt from the August series, telling of Earp's
adventures in Arizona, and the *Call* responded with an interview of Charles H.
Hopkins, described by the paper as a veteran newspaper man from St. Louis
who claimed to know the Earps in Arizona while he was a mining reporter:

> There were five of the Earps—Virgil, Wyatt, Warren, Julian, and Jessie, their sister.
> All the boys were excellent types of frontier bad men. All this talk about Wyatt
> Earp being a brave man on the square makes me tired. He was brave enough in a
> certain way, but there is good reason to doubt if he ever possessed that kind of brav-
> ery that will make a man dash into a burning building and save a woman's life. As to
> being on the square—well, he was as square as a circle. The Earps were the leaders
> of a gang of gentlemen that operated in Cochise County, and an opposition gang was
> led by John Behan. Wyatt Earp was City Marshal of Tombstone and Behan was
> Sheriff of Cochise County. Both men hated each other.
> Doc Holliday, who has grown famous as the Wells-Fargo shotgun messenger,
> was a member of the Earp crowd. Everybody has read about how Holliday stopped
> stage-robbing in Arizona. Well, he did stop it to a certain extent—that is to say, no-
> body could rob a stage who was Holliday's enemy. The Earps stood in with Holliday
> and his crowd of Wells-Fargo messengers, and every time we would hear of a stage
> that carried a lot of money or bullion being held up Wyatt Earp would collect a
> posse of his gang and start out to run the robbers down. If they could manage to
> catch any of the "rustlers" of the opposition crowd they would hang them without
> ceremony, come back to the town and explain how they tracked the road agents
> down.
> Many incidents led a good many people to think that Earp was not so game as
> he might be; so one night a job was put up to test him. Just about dusk a crowd of
> men got on the flat roof of an adobe building, commenced firing at a great rate and
> threw a dummy figure of a man over into the street. Earp was at the town pump,
> about 100 feet away, and saw it all. It looked like a case of real trouble, requiring the
> interference of the Marshal, but Earp disappeared and was not seen around his
> usual haunts until things had quieted down. After this, Earp's nerve shrank in the es-

timation of the inhabitants of Cochise County, and the suspicion that the gang was implicated in most of the stage robberies led to a decision that the town could get along without them.

Early in 1883 Jake Schieffelin, the man who founded and named Tombstone, determined to run the Earps out of the country. He secured the co-operation of the best citizens in the town and county, including Charles Reppy, editor of the Epitaph; Jim Sorin, a big mine-owner, and Jim Clum, the Postmaster.

A posse was organized under the leadership of Sheriff Behan. I went along to write up the funeral. At the time the Earps and their crowd were camped about three-quarters of a mile from Tombstone. The intention of the Sheriff's posse was to surround the camp and fill the Earps and their followers with lead. Somehow the Earps got wind of the design about an hour before the posse started for their camp. When the posse arrived the birds had flown. They started for Benson, the nearest railroad point, and made the distance of twenty-six miles in an hour and a half. At Benson they were concealed by Big Ed Burns, who had been formerly City Marshal of Leadville and who was afterward hanged in California, until a train came along. They made their escape and never showed up in that part of the country again. Warren Earp had been killed by a rustler before this enforced emigration. Afterward Julian Earp was killed in Colorado by Ike Clanton, chief of the rustlers. Clanton had married Jessie Earp, but this only added fire to the bitter feud. Clanton was killed two years later by Wyatt Earp. This was the last appearance of the Earps in the Middle West. The two survivors, Wyatt and Virgil, emigrated to the coast, where they have been ever since."[24]

"Distinguished journalist" Hopkins sure could spin a story when accuracy didn't get in the way. Charles H. Hopkins shows up in Tombstone records for the first time in June of '81 when he was arrested by an Earp deputy on a drunk-and-disorderly charge. He listed his occupation as a teamster in October of '82 when he registered to vote. Hopkins was mostly hot air, but his story would often re-emerge to confuse the actual events that had occurred in Arizona.

Relentlessly, the *Call* continued its Earp bashing. A correspondent dug up Bill Buzzard, Earp's old enemy from the Coeur d'Alene country, who told a very odd story of the events in Eagle City. Buzzard said Earp was the head of a gang of lot-jumpers who plotted the assault on his cabin. According to the report, Buzzard said: "Of course, I don't know if Earp shot at me, or, if he did, how many times, but I do know that he engineered the scheme and was in the gang. Earp was considered a bad and unscrupulous man. He was not particularly brave in gun plays, but he was always considered 'out for the dough.'" The reporter said he interviewed several early miners from the Coeur d'Alenes, and none had anything good to say about Earp. "He was generally regarded as a bad man at that time, and in that camp," the story said.[25]

Buzzard's purported view of the events in Idaho certainly differed from the newspaper accounts of twelve years earlier hailing Earp as a peacemaker. The *Call* had succeeded in finding Earp's worst enemy in Idaho, who presented a most distorted version of the truth.

Repeatedly the *Call* referred to Earp as *Examiner* editor Lawrence's bodyguard, a charge Earp waited more than a decade to refute in a letter to Bat Masterson, then a New York sportswriter. When journalist Bob Edgren repeated the bodyguard story, Earp wrote: "He may have seen me talking with Mr. Law-rence, the managing editor, as I frequently called upon him. . . . When Edgren says that I ever acted as a bodyguard for a newspaper man in Frisco or else-where, he stated a deliberate falsehood."[26]

Another *Call* item told of Earp supposedly failing to meet a debt in Stock-ton. Apparently, he had stood as security to an attorney in the case of three con-fidence men who received a sentence for swindling a farmer out of $2,000. When the jailed con men did not pay their lawyer fees, the debt fell to Earp, who was slow to reach in his wallet and eventually had two horses impounded. Earp had done a favor for his nefarious cronies, and he had to pay the price. Other *Call* stories detailed various exploits of "Desperado Wyatt Earp." One said he fixed a horse race, another accused him of serving as referee in a fight in Utah in which George A. Morrison had unknowingly been given a dose of the medica-tion belladonna, which made him ill and caused him to lose the fight. The *Call* even demeaned Earp in doggerel, running a silly poem under a woodcut cartoon of the open-mouthed ex-marshal yelling "Foul."

Wyatt Earp, the man who looked down a shotgun at Curley Bill and stared into Billy Clanton's pistol, had become a subject of ridicule in the pages of a San Francisco newspaper. The *Call* impugned Earp's character in a way that would long tarnish his reputation.

BOB FITZSIMMONS SHOWED UP for the first day of the hearing wearing a silk-lined overcoat and a top hat. Sharkey remained in bed, and Wyatt Earp's ab-sence was noted, since he had been subpoenaed to testify. A warrant was issued for his arrest, and the hearing proceeded. Manager Lynch and Groom and Gibbs of the National Club testified in a relatively uneventful day. The most in-teresting events seemed to happen outside the courtroom. The *Chronicle* re-ported, "Even jockeys are beginning to shun Wyatt Earp, for fear they will be suspected of connection with an erratic referee. Earp asked Patsy Freeman to ride a horse for him at Ingleside yesterday, but the jockey refused. He afterward said that he made his refusal on account of suspicion cast on Earp because of his decision in the Sharkey–Fitzsimmons contest."[27]

The relative sedateness of the scene changed before court resumed on Tues-day, December 8. Before the session, Martin Julian promised to prove beyond a reasonable doubt that a gigantic conspiracy existed to rob Fitzsimmons of the prize money and his share of the championship. A *Bulletin* reporter witnessed an exchange between Julian and Groom. Julian said: "I am going to show Need-ham, Lynch and Earp up in such a light that if they have a spark of manhood in them they will fly the country and seek parts unknown. If ever there were three men caught with goods on them they are the people. I have positive, indis-putable proof that they concocted the fraud and the National Club is not clear of it, either." Julian then charged that Gibbs had known of the plot and confessed his guilt to Groom.

"I have nothing to confess," Groom answered. "I don't know what you mean by your insinuations. My record is absolutely clean."

"No matter; you know very well what I allude to," Julian said, then refused to clarify his statement.[28]

Earp took the stand after the confrontation and answered a reprimand from Judge Gottlob C. Groezinger for failing to appear at the previous session.

"Well, your honor. I must apologize humbly for my neglect. You see, when the officer served me, I was very busy with some telegrams at the Baldwin. I thoughtlessly put the subpoena in my pocket, thinking that I would attend to it later, and then clean forgot all about it. I am very sorry."

"It is a very peculiar thing that you should forget the service of a subpoena," Groezinger said.

"That is so, your honor, but really, I was so much engaged in talking about the fight, that the whole matter was driven out of my head. I can assure you that I did not mean any disrespect. Why, I have been an officer for twenty years myself, and know what a serious thing it is to disobey the order of the court. I beg your pardon, your honor, I'm sure."

Groezinger ended the problem quickly by accepting the apology and ordering testimony to proceed.[29] Earp said he had accompanied Lynch to two banks in an attempt to cash the check for the $10,000 winnings, and they had been informed that payment had been stopped. Earp further claimed poverty, saying the horses that were run in his name were leased from Mrs. Orcher of Santa Rosa. According to the *Chronicle*, "The announcement of his absolute poverty seemed to affect him greatly, and as he made the statement, his voice sunk to a whisper and he leaned his head in a melancholy manner on the four-carat diamond that adorned his little finger." Court adjourned with Julian's promises and threats still unfulfilled. As for Earp's claim of poverty, he was a gambler, and his fortunes rose and fell like those of any gambler.

When the hearing resumed Wednesday morning, Judge Austin A. Sanderson had taken over the case from Groezinger. When Julian was late arriving, Danny Lynch told reporters he was certain the whole threat had been "a bluff from beginning to end." By 10 A.M. the courtroom crowd, described as "sports, pugs, rounders with a goodly sprinkling from San Francisco Lodge of the Independent Order of Sons of Rest" began stamping their feet and showing impatience. With a grand flourish Julian's attorney, Henry I. Kowalsky, entered the room, followed by Fitzsimmons, Julian, and several others, among them Australian trainer Billy Smith.

Calmly and in a clear voice, Smith told of taking walks with Sharkey three weeks before the fight when Sharkey said he had repeatedly vetoed all possible referees. Smith said the referee question was finally settled by Lynch, who said he planned to object to every name proposed so that the choice would fall on the National Athletic Club. The club would then appoint "the kind of man we want," and pay him $2,500 for awarding the fight to Sharkey on a foul. "He told me they had the referee that they wanted, and he would suit—Referee Earp, the racehorse man—and that he was to [win] on a foul in the first round, and Referee Earp was to give him the decision—give Sharkey the decision. . . . He said the first time that Fitzsimmons was to hit him in the body Needham was to jump in and claim a foul."

After Julian's ringside objections to Earp, Wyatt ordered Sharkey to humor Fitz by taking off his wrist bandages. Smith said he overheard Earp say, "It will be all right, anyway." Smith said he could not see the blow that dropped Sharkey, but saw Lynch climb into the ring and overheard him say to Sharkey, "Put your hand on your groin and pretend to be in great pain." To which Sharkey replied, "All right." Sharkey was then taken to the dressing room where Lynch kept watch while George Allen did something to him, Smith did not know what. Smith said he stayed with Sharkey until Monday after the fight. When strangers called, Sharkey would be in great pain, but when alone with his trainer Sharkey would prance around the room and smoke cigars.

Smith also told an unusual story of Earp's visit to Sharkey's room the morning after the fight. "I was sitting on a trunk. He . . . looked at me and said, 'Sharkey, how do you feel?' I said, 'I am not Sharkey. There is Sharkey in bed over there.' He said, 'You look a little bit like Sharkey; I thought it was he.' "[30] The lawman turned sport seemed to be having trouble keeping the faces straight during his hazy days in San Francisco.

On Thursday morning, George Allen, who served with Needham and Smith as trainers to Sharkey, took the stand to corroborate Smith's story. Another husky-voiced Australian, Allen said he helped Smith prepare Sharkey and looked after the fighter when Smith had other business. Allen said when he saw Sharkey knocked down, he jumped into the ring to wave a towel over his head. "Then Danny Needham jumped in and they pulled me down. A policeman interfered, too."

He said his job was to watch every blow in the fight, and he never saw Fitz strike a foul blow, and Sharkey showed no sign of injury in the dressing room after the fight. He said the boxer did not complain in the dressing room, but screamed in pain when he was carried out, before the crowd. The Australian told how Sharkey's camp had underpaid him for his services; how he had to argue for $150.

According to the *Examiner*, Wyatt Earp responded quickly to Smith's story. "Smith's allegations to the effect that I entered into any kind of a conspiracy with Mr. Lynch, Sharkey or anybody else are positively untrue, and absurd on their face. I did not agree to give the decision in favor of Sharkey on a foul in the first or any other round as he says. I have always been honorable in my dealings, and defy anybody to prove otherwise. When I accepted the National Club's offer to referee the recent contest the only promise I made was that I would decide the match on its merits. I was offered no money by Lynch or anybody else to give an unfair decision. I would not have listened to a proposition of that kind to begin with, and everybody who knows me will not doubt my word."

Lynch threatened to prosecute Smith for perjury; Groom defended his honor and said if a fix had indeed happened, it must have come after Earp was selected, not before.

Sharkey's Australian trainers, Allen and Smith, testified that their boxer had appeared uninjured in the groin when he left the ring, and Smith stated that Lynch had instructed Sharkey to grab his groin. The double testimony certainly cast aspersions on Sharkey and upon the fight itself, and seemed to show that Sharkey and Lynch had tried to pull a fast one, claiming foul to see if Earp would agree. But it should be remembered that trainers of the day had unsavory reputations. They were an underpaid lot who survived on the generosity of the fighters. Allen said he was dissatisfied with the payment received from Sharkey's camp, and Smith said he had not yet been paid. It would not be impossible, or even unlikely, that Julian had bribed the two men to testify. And it would be equally possible that they had independently chosen to sell their story to get a cut of the purse when it became obvious no more money would be coming from Sharkey. Prizefighting seemed to attract a disreputable coterie.

Something else troubled Earp during the legal proceedings—no one seemed able to pronounce his name properly. The *Chronicle* reported his ire.

> Wyatt Earp is indignant about the manner in which the various parties to the present case are meddling up the correct pronunciation of his name. The words themselves have a tongue-tying sound about them that may account for the trouble, and it is certain that every attorney and witness who has spoken in public so far has a novel notion of his own about the right way to handle them. The bailiff calls "Wah Yah," Colonel Kowalsky addresses the referee as "Wat Yirrup," while Witness Smith mentions him as "White Hurp." General Barnes with no regard whatsoever for the gentleman's feelings invariably refers to him as "Wart Up." Judge Sanderson, believing discretion to be the better part of valor, says something like this:
> "Now, witness, where did you first see—er, this—er, this man who officiated at the fight?"
> And his pronunciation is by far the best of the lot.[31]

This had not been a good week for old Wart Up. The former marshal now in the hazy, boozy world of San Francisco sporting circles had missed two court dates, been fined for carrying a gun, admitted to poverty, and was said to have misidentified Sharkey in his hotel room. Wyatt Earp, the man who shunned whiskey for ice cream in Tombstone, now seemed in a continuing state of confusion. As the trial recessed for the weekend, the 48-year-old Earp did not cut a dashing figure.

The *Call* took advantage of the weekend recess to escalate the barrage against Earp and the *Examiner,* running a story by Alfred Henry Lewis that first appeared in Hearst's *New York Journal.* Lewis called Earp, "Grim, game and deadly. He never took water, but he doesn't kill as he used to. Age has cooled his blood. Many wounds have brought caution. Moreover, the communities he honors with his presence won't stand those gayeties which marked Wyatt Earp's earlier career. As a result, he has not taken a scalp in many years. His business just now should be that of a blackleg gambler—crooked as a dog's hind leg. If there are any honest hairs in his head, they have not grown since he left Arizona. He is exactly the sort of man to referee a prize fight, if a steal is meditated, and a job is put up to make the wrong man win. Wyatt Earp has all the nerve and honesty to turn the trick. The mere name of Wyatt Earp shows that Fitzsimmons was against a hard game."[32] Ironically, just seven years later Lewis would write a biography of Bat Masterson, and his opinion of Earp would change dramatically.

Court began Monday morning, with Sharkey in attendance for the first time. Julian's attorney, Kowalsky, called Dr. Daniel Lustig to the stand to describe how he was not allowed to see Sharkey after the fight. Kowalsky then asked his big question: "Could those injuries have been caused by artificial means?"

"Yes, sir."

"By the injection of fluid?"

"Yes."

"What fluid?"

"Any acidulated water."

Lustig said that as far as could be judged, the groin was not injured. Such an injury would have caused greater swelling, accompanied by discoloration. He said he would have expected to find the injury in worse condition had it come from a blow by Fitzsimmons.[33]

Fitzsimmons followed the doctor and insisted there had been no foul. "I have never made a mistake of that kind yet," he said. "If I had been in a dazed or groggy condition, it might have been possible for me to have made a mistake. But I was as cool then as I am now. Sharkey was not fouled at all. I have been through an experience of that kind, and know just how an injured man acts." Fitzsimmons said he had been hit in the most tender of locations by a cricket ball, and he knew what would happen.

Julian followed and told of a meeting with Riley Grannan and Moses Gunst in which he was told, "Don't you under any circumstances stand for Wyatt Earp to referee that fight." According to Julian, Grannan had overheard Earp in conversation with horseman Joe Harvey. Harvey said, "It's all right then." And Earp responded, "You rely on me." After that, a number of sure-thing-only gamblers put down big bets on Sharkey.

Sharkey, Needham, and Earp all took the stand on Tuesday, denying that any plot existed. Earp's comments proved particularly unusual: The *Chronicle* headlined it "Peculiar testimony of the referee," while the ever-partisan *Call* headlined: "WYATT EARP EXPOSES EXAMINER'S FAKE METHODS; Swears He Never Gave Any of Long Green's Young Men the Statements Printed as From Him." The *Chronicle* presented a less than flattering picture of the one-time marshal:

> Wyatt Earp was in court all afternoon looking, as far as outward appearances go, less like a bad man [than] about anybody else present. His testimony was startling in some particulars. He swore more than once that Sharkey had never fouled Fitzsimmons, that the sailor had never caught his opponent by the legs, that Fitzsimmons was fouling all the time throughout the fight, and that Martin Julian never made any announcement of any kind in the ring on the night of the fight about the referee being "fixed"; all of which evidence astounded nobody more than [Earp's attorney] General [William H. L.] Barnes himself.[34]

Earp's confused, repetitive comments took up most of the afternoon. He had trouble remembering Gibbs's name, calling him Hibbs or Dibbs, and said he had never spoken to reporters or given a signed statement to newspapers. Of course, the *Call* leaped on the issue to denounce the statements run in the *Examiner*.

Earp described the fight and forcefully denied any conspiracy to help Sharkey. He said Julian's statements of his involvement were false: "I will say now that what he testified to, the other day, was a pack of falsehoods in every respect."

Kowalsky, Julian's attorney, quickly moved to strike the statement. Earp spoke up before a ruling could be made, saying "I am on the stand now, and have got my right hand up, and I say it is a pack of falsehoods."

Judge Sanderson told Earp to just answer the questions, and he responded quickly, "I am not like him, going around and shutting people's mouths."

"Mr. Earp, I instruct you to only answer the questions," Sanderson said before Kowalsky continued his cross-examination. Earp denied all allegations of favoritism and bristled when the attorney asked why he had separated the fighters by pushing Sharkey in the breast and placing his fingers in Fitzsimmons's eye.

"I never did it," Earp said. "I emphatically say I did not do it on any occasion—and I don't believe Fitzsimmons will say that I did it."

Earp left the stand sounding confused about details while maintaining his innocence. Fifteen years earlier he had been a vision of clarity in Tombstone courtrooms; now he struggled and stumbled through cross-examination. Testimony ended after a couple of minor witnesses, and a decision was left to Judge Sanderson.[35]

The crowd returned to court on Thursday, December 17, for the expected climax of the hearing, with a judge determining the quality of Wyatt Earp's honor. The expectation never met the reality. Sharkey's attorneys moved to dissolve the injunction, arguing that the case was unworthy, nothing more than an argument over the purse of a prize fight. The Fitzsimmons team repeated its massive conspiracy theory, then submitted the case to Sanderson. His ruling followed strictly technical grounds.

Prizefights were still illegal—technically illegal—in San Francisco. And the judge took it to be so: "In my opinion, under the statute standing as it does now, they can no more legalize a fight in this city than they can legalize a duel," Sanderson said. "And this is simply an instance to disobey the law. There is no doubt in my opinion . . . that these men were fighting, must have been fighting if this complaint is true. For, if they were boxing they were fighting. They were committing an offense against the law; and it is elementary law, and no lawyer will challenge it, that no court, either of law or equity will take cognizance of a suit of this character the moment it is challenged. . . . I understand that these exhibitions are given; and they are given because the people and the police wink at them. But no court will recognize any such proceeding. And there is no doubt in my mind that this injunction should be dissolved and it would have been dissolved if the motion had been made immediately upon the heels of issuing it, as the court in fact expected. The order to dissolve the injunction will be granted."[36]

Sanderson's ruling provided no vindication for Earp, Sharkey, or the National Club. Sharkey could cash his $10,000 check. Earp would be free to hang out around the race track again. As to guilt, innocence, or culpability, Sanderson made no ruling.

Debates would continue through the saloons and beer halls of the city, most centering on the direct question of whether Earp took the bribe and fixed the

fight. The question can never be satisfactorily answered, but there are three possibilities:

- Fitzsimmons actually fouled Tom Sharkey, and Earp made the correct
  ruling.
- Earp took a bribe and fixed the fight.
- Sharkey pretended to be fouled, doing so convincingly enough to fool
  Wyatt Earp and a good portion of the crowd.

It is certainly not impossible that a blow by Fitzsimmons caught Sharkey in
the tender region. Sharkey fought from a crouch, and could well have risen after
Fitzsimmons's shot to the head, which preceded the blow that Sharkey claimed
landed too low. The most damning evidence against this came from Dr. Lustig,
who said that the injury appeared more likely concocted than actual. While
Sharkey may have been legitimately injured, the circumstances surrounding the
post-fight dressing room scene make the legitimacy of Sharkey's injury highly
suspect.

Author Eugene Cunningham met Sharkey around 1915 and asked about
the incident. "Tom looked down at his feet and up at the ceiling and seemed honestly embarrassed," Cunningham told Robert Mullin. "Finally, he muttered
something about there being 'more to it than folks knew about' and 'no use talking about it.'"[37]

As to the great conspiracy theory, that seems far-fetched. A conspiracy to
deliver Wyatt Earp as referee would have had to involve at least one of the
Gibbs–Groom combination, probably both, along with Earp, Lynch, Sharkey,
and probably several others. Keeping this legion silent before the fight would
have been difficult; preventing them from talking in later years would have been
impossible. The only evidence of such a conspiracy comes from hearsay among
the sporting crowd, a circle where rumors travel faster than comets. In addition,
had Earp been paid to throw the fight, this would have been an awfully poor
way to do so. Waiting until the eighth round left him open to the risk that
Fitzsimmons would finish Sharkey with an unquestionably clean blow.

What seems most plausible is that Sharkey, Lynch, and Needham simply
duped Wyatt Earp. Earp had refereed about thirty fights, probably all bare-
knuckle affairs, before the Marquis of Queensberry rules became the accepted
code. Referees of the time were instructed to follow the rules and never allow
the freewheeling fighting that had accompanied the old bare-knuckle brawls.

Manager Lynch's wrangling over an official could well have been devised to
rule out competent and experienced referees, forcing the National Club to come
up with a man lacking the experience with the Queensberry rules to properly
recognize a foul. Wyatt Earp fit the description perfectly, with his past reputation for honesty and current status as both a local character and an oft-confused
saloon denizen and sport. If trainer Smith is to be believed, Lynch quickly re-
minded Sharkey to grab his groin and scream foul, an acting job that fully convinced the *Bulletin* reporter as well as Wyatt Earp. This would also square with
the strange post-fight scene, in which Dr. Lustig was refused admission in favor
of the dubious Dr. Lee. And it would have allowed Sharkey a chance to see if he
could win the fight on his own merits before lowering himself to cheating.

Charles Fernald wrote of riding on a steamer to Alaska with Earp. "He claimed that there was a lot of money bet on this fight, and he told me that to make the foul stick, somebody injected iodine into Sharkey's groin. I always understood Wyatt Earp was on the square in his decision, but he did not know about this iodine business until sometime afterwards."[38]

Had Earp not called the foul with Sharkey rolling around in the ring, the referee would have faced an outcry from Sharkey's bettors nearly equal to the one he faced from Fitzsimmons's backers. And he would have been accused of incompetence or conspiracy by the Sharkey forces. In the early days of the Marquis of Queensberry rules, it was one of the great downfalls of boxing that such a decision rested simply with the official in the ring. In this case the official — Wyatt Earp — lacked the experience and qualifications to make such a determination.

Devil or dupe, Earp's reputation in San Francisco had been seriously damaged by the decision. He had become a local joke for the wags of San Francisco. From bar to beer hall, they laughed and told stories about the famous lawman, the kind of stories that ridicule a reputation. San Francisco had become, for him, a city filled with scorn.

It was left for his friends to defend him throughout the West. Diarist George Parsons, now in Los Angeles, attended a party and heard carping about the fight. "Wyatt Earp disliked because of awarding Fitzsimmons Sharkey exhibitions or physical culture symposium to latter on a claimed foul. Wyatt was always straight in Tombstone. Tracked Apaches with the Earps. Good man as men went there."[39]

And Bat Masterson ran into a little tussle of his own in Denver while defending the honor of Wyatt Earp. Felix O'Neill, a Colorado politician and regular sports gambler, lost heavily on the fight. He publicly denounced the whole affair as a swindle, and the word got back to Masterson.

The *Bulletin* wrote: "Bat Masterson is known from the Golden Gate across the Rockies, and his record in Arizona shows him to be a man who has a fancy for backing up his opinion. And it also happened that Bat Masterson had followed the example of O'Neill and had wagered large sums on the Cornishman's end of the fight."

Masterson and O'Neill met in a saloon, "and in a few minutes from the start Felix O'Neill had all sails set and was bowling along at a high rate of speed in his denunciation of Yurrip. It was high time that prize-fighting was stopped in San Francisco if such men were to be permitted to act as referees; men like Earp should be driven out of the community, and so forth. Who was this man, anyhow? A scoundrel, a thief, a bully, everything that was bad." Masterson listened quietly before replying that he knew Wyatt Earp and strongly believed in his old friend. O'Neill yelled across the saloon, "I say he's a thief. You read the papers. Did you hear of such a . . ."

"Stop." Masterson cut him off. "You are all wrong. I was with this man Wyatt Earp in Arizona, Tombstone, Arizona. I know his character. He was my friend there. In all America there is not a fairer, squarer, straighter man than Wyatt Earp. He's game as a pebble, too, and no game man is a cheat. Now, O'Neill, you've got to take back all you said about Earp just now."

"Take it back," O'Neill roared.

"That's what's the matter," Masterson said coolly.

"I'll see you damned first," O'Neill yelled.

"Now, O'Neill, be sensible. You lost your money; I lost mine. But we both lost fairly and squarely. If there was any job Earp wasn't in it, you bet."

"I say he was. I say he's a . . ."

And Masterson quickly ended this argument with his fists. O'Neill was left, "laid up for repairs," getting by far the worst of this fight, which had no referee.[40]

The aftermath of the fight left her husband greatly disturbed, Sadie said:

> The falsehoods that were printed in some of the newspapers about him and the unjust accusations against him hurt Wyatt more deeply than anything that ever happened to him during my life with him, with the exception of his mother's death and that of his father and his brother, Warren [in 1900]. He was not a man to show emotion by tears but I knew him so well that I could read the extent of his mental pain. Even the articles praising his fairness, his courage and sincerity that other newspapers, both in San Francisco and the rest of the country, published in his defense, could not wipe out the sting of these attacks. They were so viciously untruthful and unfair. . . .
>
> It had left Wyatt weary and dispirited, sick with longing to get away again to unsettled country and to be wrapped in its quiet and obscurity.[41]

Wyatt Earp had always been a proud man—proud of his ability to avoid trouble and proud of his ability to handle trouble when it could not be avoided. The ridicule he faced after the fight scarred him inside. He had twice in his life become a victim of press attacks. Now he would keep his mouth shut for nearly three decades.

Before Earp moved on from northern California, he would suffer one more humiliation. Fitzsimmons and Corbett finally settled on a date for what would really be a title fight—March 17, 1897, in Carson City, Nevada. Bat Masterson was to supervise a squad of special ringside police and probably recruited Earp as a member of the force, although that cannot be confirmed. Whether as an officer or not, Earp attended the fight, and his decision in San Francisco three months earlier was not forgotten. Earp made an effort to visit Fitzsimmons, which came as a surprise to just about everyone. According to the *Examiner,* a New York newspaperman brought a wagon loaded with guests to Fitzsimmons's house. Among the guests was Wyatt Earp, and Fitz still carried a grudge. The journalist hailed the fighter and Fitzsimmons nodded, then noticed Earp and turned his back on the wagon and walked away. Fitzsimmons avoided the problem, but his wife said she had no regard for a man who, after having deeply wronged her husband, sought to make his acquaintance—and as for the newspaperman, whose act of bringing Earp out there had the appearance of an intentional affront, she could only say that she "regretted that an important newspaper was represented by such a one."

The unhappy Fitzsimmons told the *Examiner:* "That fellow evidently brought Earp out here to insult me. Of course, the roads are open to people—but people are not taking any pleasure drives out here on a cold and snowy day like this, and if they did not intend to go to my place, they would not have been out in that direction. At any rate, for a man to speak to me, when he is in company with Wyatt Earp, is a little more than I care to stand. I suppose this person, being employed by a newspaper, thinks he can insult me as he pleases. Possibly it is true, for I don't see any means of redress. I believe Earp deliberately wronged me, and shared the profits of the wrongdoing, and I don't want to have any dealings with him whatever."[42]

The fight came off the next day, and Fitzsimmons refused the customary prefight handshake. In the fourteenth round, Corbett saw the last of Fitzsimmons's hands, taking a knockout blow that ended the fight. As with most fights, the rumors of a fix had circulated before this one, too. Only it was Fitzsimmons who had been the expected fall guy.

"I trust I will be pardoned for dwelling a little on the general impression circulated by my enemies that I had been 'fixed' to lie down," Fitzsimmons said. "If the truth were known, and I see no reason why it should not be, I was offered $500,000 by a San Francisco combination to throw this fight and $250,000 by a New Yorker. I gave my answer to those overtures to-day." Fitzsimmons ended this fix rumor with a knockout of Corbett.[43]

A note of irony would be added five years later when Fitzsimmons returned to San Francisco to fight Jim Jeffries in July of 1902. The aging Fitz fought gamely until Jeffries floored him in the eighth round. The *Examiner* headlined "Fight a Fake," and charged that Fitz had taken a fall. This time the *Call* argued the fight was honest while the *Examiner* charged the fix. The charges and countercharges would sell many newspapers.

10

THE LAST
FRONTIERS

YATT AND SADIE SAW THE SHORES OF ALASKA for the first time in the fall of 1897 as they chased another gold rush. His first two years there, Wyatt managed saloons and ran gambling concessions. He then went into partnership with Charlie Hoxie in the Dexter Saloon in Nome, Alaska's most prominent boomtown. He was a celebrity again, a man with a reputation as he handed out beer to the thirsty miners. At the end of the 1899 mining season, the *Nome Gold Digger* wrote: "Wyatt Earp, who was a Deputy U.S. Marshal in Arizona at one time, and who is a celebrated personage in nearly all the mining camps of the country, left on the steamer *Cleveland* for San Francisco."[1] The *San Francisco Examiner* noted Earp's apparent success on November 13, 1899, by reporting, "He is making money perhaps faster than he ever made it before and he told his friends that if business runs with him next summer as it did after his arrival in the camp . . . he will be able to retire with all the money he desires."

Hildreth Halliwell, Allie Earp's relative, said the family always believed a house of ill repute operated above the Dexter, although family stories vary as to Wyatt and Sadie's involvement. Peggy Greenberg, Sadie's niece, recalled a story that Sadie became angry when she learned of a whorehouse above one of Wyatt's saloons.[2] In her unpublished manuscript, Sadie made a point of denying that the rooms were used as a brothel.[3]

The first three years were relatively quiet for the Earps in Alaska. In the winter, when the mines were unworkable, they would spend time in San Francisco or Seattle. They welcomed the new century in San Francisco, with Wyatt renewing acquaintances with some of his old sporting friends. According to the *Call,* on April 28, 1900, he wandered into the Peerless saloon, where he ran into sport and brawler Tom Mulqueen:

> Wyatt Earp, gun-fighter and all around bad man was knocked down and out late Saturday night by Tom Mulqueen, the well-known racehorse man. The trouble . . . was precipitated by Earp. Both men had been drinking at the bar, when Earp brought up the subject of a recent scandal at the Tanforan track. He made several disparaging remarks about a jockey who is on very friendly terms with Mulqueen.

When called down he became belligerently indignant and threatened to wipe the floor with the horse owner. Instantly Mulqueen grabbed him and after throwing him against the bar landed a blow on the gunfighter's face, knocking him out.

John Farley, the proprietor of the saloon, fearing serious trouble between the two men, managed to induce Mulqueen to leave the place. Earp, after recovering from the effects of the blow, was also led from the saloon and placed aboard a passing street car. Earp was not armed at the time, having left his trusted "gun" with a friend shortly before the occurrence.

Mulqueen was around as usual yesterday but refused to discuss the affair. . . .

Earp first came into prominence in the city when he officiated as referee in the fight between Fitzsimmons and Sharkey several years ago and gave the decision to the sailor on an alleged foul after he had been knocked out, a decision that created general dissatisfaction.[4]

The tale was picked up and ran in papers throughout the West. Surprisingly, the story is not mentioned in other San Francisco papers. But there is no record of Earp's denying this story, as he did with the many false rumors that circulated. When papers picked up a far-fetched tale about Earp being knocked out by a midget mountie in Dawson, Yukon Territory, Earp squawked and accurately said that the incident had never happened and that he had never even visited Dawson. The incident in San Francisco only served as the beginning of what would be a most eventful summer.

He returned to Alaska soon after the Mulqueen affair. A brawl started on Front Street in Nome on June 29, when drunks Dan Kane and E. P. Lopez engaged in a tussle. Two deputy marshals arrested the men and started to march them toward the barracks that served as a jail. According to the *Nome Daily News*, several men, including Wyatt Earp and Nathan Marcus, Sadie's brother, came forward, apparently to interfere with the arrest.

Wyatt Earp was . . . taken into custody; he is charged with interfering with an officer while in the discharge of his duty. Kane is now confined in jail. Earp, upon reaching the barracks, asserted that his actions had been misconstrued and that he had interceded to assist the deputy marshal.[5]

Earp was released without charges. A few weeks later, he received some deeply troubling news. On July 6, a range foreman named Johnnie Boyett shot and killed 45-year-old Warren Earp in Willcox, Arizona. The early reports connected the killing to the previous problems between the Earp brothers and the cowboys, although it seems more likely that Warren had been taunting Boyett, who responded with lead. News took weeks to reach Alaska, and the *Arctic Weekly Sun* reported on August 5 that Wyatt "seems inclined to break the record and die a natural death."[6] Because it took so long to travel to Arizona Wyatt had no recourse but to remain in Alaska, making great profits at the Dexter, and leave Boyett to another justice.

Down in the States, Earp still had enough of a reputation to merit front-page coverage in the *New York Tribune*, even if the story strayed far from the truth. On July 15, 1900, the *Tribune* ran the headline, "Wyatt Earp Shot at Nome; The Arizona 'Bad Man' Not Quick Enough With His Gun." The report said Earp had been the terror of Nome "because of his reputation as a dead shot. He bullied every one, and he was particularly offensive" in his own saloon, the

Dexter. After Earp quarreled with a customer, Earp reached for a gun, but the customer drew more quickly and fired, wounding Earp in the arm. There is no other record of Earp taking a bullet in Nome, and it is extremely unlikely any such event ever took place. But there it was, on the front page of a New York newspaper.

The press was rarely kind to the marshal turned gambler. That summer of 1900 was a big season for Earp press coverage, most of it remarkably inaccurate. The *Seattle Post-Intelligencer* reported the "Death of Virgil Earp," confusing Virgil with Warren, then picked up the Charles Hopkins fable that had Wyatt's sister marrying Ike Clanton and Wyatt killing him. The *Chicago InterOcean* ran a bizarre Tombstone tale of a young Englishman who came to town and complained about the tamales in an eatery owned by one of the Earps' Chinese friends. Virgil grew angry and had the cook make the spiciest hot tamales imaginable, then forced the Englishman to eat them at gunpoint. The stories kept growing wilder and wilder, and the Earps' reputation continued to grow, fed not by facts but by fables.[7]

The Seattle story did include a note on Wyatt's winter stays in the area: "During his residence in Seattle, he was one of the most quiet citizens, but it is not of record that any bluff was put up against him that went uncalled. It is known that in an unostentatious manner he promptly and severely rebuked the few attempts made to hand him what is technically known as the 'con,' and his manner was always such as to instill a wholesome respect in the minds of his immediate associates."[8]

Wyatt probably never knew of his New York notoriety or the other strange tales, but he did know about Warren's death, and it must have had a major effect on him. On August 30 he sat down with two old friends from Tombstone for a long talk. Diarist George Parsons had come to Alaska on business and joined Earp and John Clum, there on post office duties. Parsons wrote: "John Clum . . . and I had an oldtimer with Wyatt Earp tonight at his place, a regular old Arizona time, and Wyatt unlimbered for several hours and seemed glad to talk to us who knew the past. It was a very memorable evening. He went home with us." The next day he added in his diary: "We had such a seance last night. That evening with Wyatt Earp would have been worth $1,000 or more to the newspapers."

On September 10 he again met with Parsons. "Wyatt Earp and I had a little confab today. This reputed badman from Arizona is straight and fearless I believe and is a good friend of mine and respects me and I him, even though he runs perhaps the biggest drinking and gambling places here. It's well to have such a friend here and let the thugs see it."

In brawling, bawdy Nome, trouble could come with the next patron through the door. Wyatt and his brother-in-law, Nathan Marcus, became involved in a major fight. On September 12, the *Daily News* reported their latest difficulty.

COMMISSIONER'S COURT: The Principals in a fracas which occurred in the Dexter Saloon, were arraigned before Commissioner Stevens this morning. The accused parties were Wyatt Earp, N. Marcus and Walter Summers. About 12 o'clock last night Patrolman Vanslow of the U.S.A. arrested Summers for disorderly conduct. The soldier, while performing this duty, was assaulted and beaten by Wyatt

Earp and N. Marcus. The latter is a porter in the Dexter Saloon. Assistance was rendered to the officer, and eventually the apprehension of Summers, Earp and Marcus was effected. Summers, at a trial this morning, established his innocence, and he was accordingly discharged. The cases against the other two prisoners were continued at 2 o'clock tomorrow afternoon, and in the meantime the defendants are at liberty upon cash bonds of $20 each.[9]

The disposition of the case is unknown, but Earp was back at the Dexter quickly.

Wyatt traveled with fast company in Nome. He met playwright Wilson Mizner, cattleman Charlie Welsh, and two novelists who would become famous, Rex Beach and a kid named Jack London. Beach wrote of the Nome rush in his book *The Spoilers*, which told of corrupt local officials making their fortune through trickery.

Earp also had a chance to do a favor for an old friend when Lucky Baldwin and David Unruh showed up to start a gambling house and bar. Baldwin could never come up with a satisfactory location, and he headed back to San Francisco, leaving Unruh to close the operation down. Much to Unruh's surprise, local officials slapped a claim for $2,500 against him and held the equipment, worth about $10,000.

Unruh said he went to Earp for advice, and Wyatt responded by getting two of his business friends to arrange the bond. Unruh took the bond to the marshal, who informed him that it was not valid and instead demanded $20,000 in gold dust. Unruh said, "I went back to Earp. He was mad. But he got together the $20,000 worth of gold and gave me a man to lug it to the marshal's office, where I got a receipt and the property was released. Then I sold the stuff for a profit of between fifty and sixty thousand dollars. Wyatt Earp refused a cent of pay for his accommodation. He said he was more than satisfied to put a crimp in the grafting of that crowd of crooks."[10]

Sadie also received some acclaim in Alaska that summer, leading a relief effort to raise funds for victims of a violent ocean storm that flooded parts of Nome. But these were not always good times for the couple. Wyatt would later complain to his friend Charlie Welsh that Sadie had gambled heavily on the boat trips to Alaska. Sadie would later say that Wyatt had affairs with other women. It is likely that there were separations and disruptions during the Alaska years.[11]

Wyatt and Sadie returned to Alaska for the last time in 1901. While it is unconfirmed, the family legend is that they left Alaska with $80,000, a virtual fortune in those times. It would be enough to stake them through various business ventures for the next few years.

While passing through southern California in 1901, Earp spoke briefly with a reporter for the *Los Angeles Express*:

Wyatt Earp, the well-known sporting authority, passed the day in Los Angeles with his wife. He has just returned from Nome, where he has mining properties sufficient to make him financially comfortable for the rest of his life. He states that the inland prospects at Nome are proving rich and that practical miners who apply themselves steadily are taking out good money.

Mr. Earp has not retired from the world of sport. He states that he intends to enjoy the roped arena and other characteristic sports for some time yet, although the criticism he received from the decision in the Sharkey–Fitzsimmons fight was unfair, he alleges.

"I easily can explain the attack of certain newspapers," said Mr. Earp. "I had been doing work for the Examiner for three months previous to the fight. At that time both the Call and Chronicle were bitterly fighting the Examiner, and when I refereed the mill, I was their chance to get back at their rival over me. However, a referee is always open to attacks of newspapers, friends of either fighter and to incompetent sporting editors who have exalted opinions of themselves."

Mr. and Mrs. Earp will continue their journey south tomorrow and will return to Nome the coming season.[12]

They did not return to the Alaska gold fields. Instead Wyatt and Sadie would follow the booms in Nevada for the next decade, often traveling back to join the Marcus and Lehnhardt families in San Francisco and Oakland or spending time in Los Angeles.

In 1902 the Earps moved to Tonopah, Nevada, where Wyatt and partner Al Martin ran a saloon called "The Northern," with "Wyatt Earp, Prop." on the sign over the false-front wooden building. He took out an ad in the local paper proclaiming: "A Gentleman's Resort, Lower Main St., Tonopah; Only the choicest wines, liquors and cigars are passed over the bar; Courteous Mixologists and kind treatment to all patrons When thirsty sample the goods at 'The Northern.'"

During the brief silver boom, Wyatt also served as a deputy U.S. marshal under Marshal J. F. Emmitt, a job that primarily meant serving summonses in federal court cases. John Hays Hammond, a famed mining engineer, hired Earp to lead a private police force to run off claim jumpers, and he gave Wyatt explicit instructions:

"You will not shoot except in self-defense," Hammond told Earp.

"O.K., but I must be the judge when the self-defense starts," Earp responded, leaving Hammond with little recourse but to agree. Earp had always acted in self-defense; it was just a matter of judgment when self-defense started.[13]

For unexplained reasons, Sadie spent much of this period back in Oakland with her family. If the stories of the old-timers are to be believed, the marriage continued to have rough periods, with occasional separations where one or the other would move out.[14]

Back in Los Angeles in 1903, the tale of Wyatt's being bashed by a midget mountie in Dawson appeared in the *Herald*. The story ran under the headline "The Taming of Wyatt Earp, Bad Man of Other Days," and told of the drunken Wyatt bullying the townsfolk in a gambling hall, then backing down when the mountie politely threatened him. Earp reacted angrily to the accusation by writing an articulate response, which the Los Angeles paper published:

Editor Herald: An article published in your Sunday edition entitled, "The Taming of Wyatt Earp, Bad Man of Other Days," does me an injustice. It relates an experience I was reported to have had in Dawson City in which I was said to have attempted to "shoot up the town" and to have been subdued by one of the Canadian Mounted Police.

The falsity of the article is shown by the fact that I never was within 1,000 miles of Dawson City.

I wish to say that neither I nor my brothers were ever "bad men," in the sense that term is used nor did we ever indulge in the practice of "shooting up" towns. We have been officers of the law and have had our experiences in preserving the law, but we are not, and never have been, professional bad men. In justice to me and my friends and relatives I would like to have you make this statement.

Wyatt Earp[15]

A day later, George Parsons wrote the *Herald* in Wyatt's behalf:

Editor Herald: As an old Tombstoner and one who knew the Earps in the stormy days of the early '80s, I wish, in simple justice to the family in general and Wyatt Earp in particular, to confirm his statement in yesterday's Herald that they were not "bad men" in the common acceptance of the term, but were ever ready to discharge their duty as officers of the law, and did it so effectively that they incurred the enmity of the rustlers and desperadoes congregated in that lively town and section of the country and were always on the side of law and order.

There was one exception. When their brother Morgan was assassinated, Virgil Earp shot and Wyatt Earp's life attempted, then they took the law into their own hands and did what most anyone would have done under the peculiar circumstances existing at the time, and what anyone reading the Virginian would consider their right to do.

I speak of a time I am familiar with for I lived in Tombstone during the entire stay of the Earps, chased Apaches with them, and have seen them, and particularly Wyatt Earp, defending and enforcing the law in the face of death. To call such men "bad men," when the better element was siding with and supporting them morally and financially, is to deal in terms misapplied; and I feel today as I felt in Nome, Alaska, where I saw Wyatt Earp, that if anybody was undeservedly ill-treated and particularly an old Tombstoner, he would find a champion in the same Wyatt Earp, who is older now but none the less gritty, I believe. I state this in justice to a much maligned man who, as a public character, was a benefit and a protection to the community he once lived in.

G. W. Parsons[16]

A few days later Parsons ran into his old friend on the streets of Los Angeles and returned home to write in the diary he still kept religiously: "Met Wyatt Earp, Arizona's 'bad man' according to the <u>Herald</u>'s ideas, and he thanked me for my defence of him. He has killed a few but they ought to have been killed and he did a good job. I may be yet called "Bad Man" myself because I knew him and chased Apaches with him and would have done more if occasion required."[17] Wyatt Earp still had his defenders, even if the old stories had already begun spinning beyond control.

Stories as far back as the Dodge City Peace Committee credited Earp, Masterson, and the rest with far more bloody deeds than they could have even imagined. Most Earp-tales refer to nebulous numbers of outlaws he blasted at different times. Reputations expanded through word of mouth, with stories growing as they passed along the way. In 1886, a Chicago reporter visiting Silverton, Colorado, ran into two self-proclaimed acquaintances of Doc Holliday who claimed to know of eleven killings he had committed. The reporter then found Holliday, who said that he had been blamed for numerous murders when he was not within five hundred miles of the gunfire. Holliday said: "When any of you fellows have been hunted from one end of the country to the other as I have been, you'll understand what a bad man's reputation is built on. I've had credit for more killings than I ever dreamed of. . . . The claim that I make is that some few of us pioneers are entitled to credit for what we have done. We have been the forerunners of government. As soon as law and order were established anywhere we never had any trouble. If it hadn't been for me and a few like me there never would have been any government in some of these towns. When I have done any shooting it has always been with this in view."[18]

IF A FEW OF THE OLD STORIES ARE TO BE BELIEVED, even age did not take the fight out of Wyatt Earp. Former police officer Arthur M. King said that he served as Earp's assistant on a series of special missions for the Los Angeles Police Department that were not strictly within the law. King said that he and Earp illegally chased fugitives into Mexico and brought them back to stand trial.

"In those days it used to take two years or more to get a wanted man extradited from Mexico, so there was a constant stream of criminals south of the border," King said. "Earp wanted someone to go over the border with him and bring a man back but without the benefit of formal extradition. I had been with the Los Angeles Police Department and was a good shot, so Earp offered [me] the job."

King said he and Earp usually disguised themselves as miners on these jobs. They had their sources of information and eventually they would find their man and bring him back for trial. "The Mexicans had our graves dug for us a number of times, but we managed to outsmart them. Earp was a very quiet fellow—a fine man, one of the coolest I've ever seen. He was afraid of nothing. When he'd get angry the corner of his right eye would twitch just a little. He loved to gamble, too. Faro, or Bucking the Tiger, was his choice. And he was a prospector at heart. He loved being around miners."

Wyatt's former helper did not paint a particularly attractive picture of the one-time marshal. King said they served as strikebreakers delivering beer to saloons when the regular workers refused to work. As in San Francisco a decade earlier, Earp took his liquor in large doses.

"He . . . was an artist at swearing, and he took to drinking pretty heavily when he reached fifty," King said. "You see, Earp never used to drink at all. The old days of Dodge, Ellsworth, and Wichita were far behind him and Earp was not too proud to work for $10 a day the same as any peace officer who wanted to eat."

King told how he and Earp halted a run on a bank with a little trick. In 1909, bank examiners checked Isaias W. Hellman's bank and revealed that more money had been loaned than remained in the vaults. Depositors stormed Hellman's office to pull their money. In the days before bank insurance, this could mean disaster. Earp told King that the mayor of Los Angeles had asked him to intercede to save the bank.

"I'd rather skin a wildcat or walk into a shooting than do a job like this," Wyatt said, according to King. "People nowadays get to thinking I'm a damned magician or something."

Hellman apparently expected Earp to intercede and bring order to the mob. But Earp had another idea. He took some empty money sacks from the bank and hired a big wagon and driver. Then, with King at his side, he rode to a nearby iron works and filled the sacks with iron slugs the size of $20 gold pieces. Earp and King rode shotgun as the heavy wagon rattled across the cobblestone and brick streets to the bank, where police were holding back the angry depositors.

"Pull in here, back those plugs up," Earp shouted to the driver, then stood and waved his hat to recruit police help. An officer came over and asked Earp what he had. "About a million dollars," Earp responded. "Now get these loco jugheads out of the way and tell your boys to pass the word that we've got a million dollars aboard and that any gent who thinks he can find a better bank to put his money into to go and find it. But he'd better be damned careful he don't get hit over the head and robbed while he's doing it."

Earp and King loaded the sacks onto the counter, in plain sight, long enough to assure the depositors of the bank's stability, then moved them into the vault. The run subsided, and Earp and King went for a drink. King recalled Wyatt's words as he lifted his glass: "I guess I'm growing old when I got to ride shotgun on a lot of bridge washers from an iron works just to convince a lot of damned fools."[19]

Earp apparently did have police connections. In October of 1910, he received a most unusual offer from LAPD commissioner Tom Lewis. George Parsons had been asked to lead a posse of thirty men, apparently without legal sanction, into the remote regions of San Bernardino County to dispossess parties holding disputed mining claims.

"Like old Arizona times again," Parsons jotted in his diary. "But my lame ankle prevented any action as this is an immediate case and I was selected as the best man to lead party and do the business. . . . Second choice for leader of expedition fell on Wyatt Earp, the old Arizona outlaw (so called) and mankiller, also old friend of mine and a square man if he did gamble and kill occasionally. Certainly this selection of me is a high compliment to my courage, fighting abilities and tact, and I appreciate all."[20]

With Parsons resting his aching ankle, 62-year-old Wyatt Earp led the posse into the desert to take control of a potash field near Searles Lake in northern San Bernardino County. The California Trona Company and Henry E. Lee & Associates both claimed legal ownership of the potash, which was used in explosives. Awaiting a decision in court could have taken years, while control of the potash fields meant quick profits with threats of war in Europe. Earp, along with Lee and Lou Rasor, served as leaders of the posse organized to defend the claim of Henry Lee & Associates. Earp ordered the men to lie in the sagebrush in preparation for a night battle, ready to open fire should Trona's force arrive and try to take control of the mining site. Far in the distance, headlights bobbed along the road leading toward the claim, and the leaders conferred, choosing Earp to parley with the Trona representatives. Earp went to sleep, knowing it would take the rest of the night for the Trona band to arrive.

Early the next morning, S. W. Austin, then federal receiver, and three armed men appeared in the camp, Rasor testified when the case came to trial. With his pistol pointed, Austin ordered the Earp party to leave. Earp snatched a rifle from one of Austin's deputies and calmly faced Austin's revolver, then discarded the captured gun.

"Wyatt grabbed that gun and threw it down in the dirt swearing with as much color as any pirate," Arthur King recalled. "He said he hadn't had his breakfast yet and didn't want no gun in his empty belly."

The Austin party made no further requests and both groups sat down for what must have been one nervous breakfast before Austin and his assistants left peaceably.

"It was the most nervy thing, Earp's act, that I ever saw," Rasor told the court.[21]

The case did not come to trial until 1916 and took nearly three months of court time. Although court observers expected Earp to testify, he was never called. Almost five months after the case ended, Judge H. T. Dewhirst ruled in favor of Trona and gave the company possession of the valuable fields just as the conflict in Europe was building into a full-scale world war.[22]

It would be Wyatt Earp's last known confrontation. The one-time lawman had become a hired tough to protect a corporation's property.

Wyatt and Sadie settled into a more tranquil lifestyle. In 1905 they had located what they would call their "Happy Days" mines near the Arizona–California border, close to a town that would later be named "Earp." The claim would never amount to much. The Earps would follow a peripatetic lifestyle the rest of their days, wintering at the claim as they tried to work the small mines, then summering in more comfortable climes, usually Los Angeles and occasionally Oakland, near Sadie's sister.

There are no records to certify that Sadie and Wyatt ever went through the formality of a marriage ceremony. Sadie would later tell relatives they had been married aboard Lucky Baldwin's yacht. Several times she gave the date as 1888—but the Earps were in San Diego then, apparently before the friendship with Baldwin even began. The census taker caught up with the Earps in 1910, when they were living in Los Angeles. Sadie gave her birthplace as New York and her birthdate as 1866—her birthday seemed to move up as the years passed, and she always kept it her secret. Once again they said they had been married in 1888.

There would always be stories that followed the Earps. But old stories do not build big houses or buy nice clothes. They invested in oil wells near Bakersfield, mining claims and other ventures that made some money, nothing big. The Alaska money gradually dwindled, and Wyatt S. Earp, Capitalist, could not find another boom. Earp had become an aging frontiersman when America ran out of frontiers.

BACK IN THE OLD DAYS, in both Dodge City and Tombstone, Wyatt Earp never seemed too bothered by con artists. It was one thing to take a man's money at gunpoint, and something else entirely to cleverly extract it from him by playing on his own greed. Many of the old frontiersmen saw such questionable activities as a good way to teach greenhorns the ways of the West. By this morality, robbing a stagecoach would be repugnantly wrong while playing a little confidence game fell within some range of acceptability.

Stuart Lake often told the story of Bat Masterson being pestered for his guns by New York collectors. Masterson then sent a kid scribe—sometimes a young reporter named Damon Runyon—to the pawn shop to buy an old gun, and the lawman emeritus would carve in his twenty-two notches and sell it to the happy collector. The tale may be fiction, but the likes of Earp and Masterson seemed to condone taking advantage of another man's gullibility.

Thirty years after Tombstone, Wyatt Earp was neither a moral giant nor a bright light of goodness. He certainly was not above separating a fool from his money when the opportunity arose, and in 1911 he would be caught and publicly embarrassed. Wyatt Earp, still a hero or a horror to opposing groups, found himself again trying to raise bail.

The Los Angeles newspapers told the story of a clever scheme to bilk Los Angeles real estate agent J. Y. Peterson out of $2,500. Three men attempted to lure Peterson into a room at the Auditorium Hotel for a rigged faro game. According to Peterson, he was to purchase $2,500 in chips, then leave when his pile reached $4,000, in a larcenous attempt to get money from the big San Francisco syndicate that backed the game. The three men told him that they were angry with the San Francisco group, which paid them only $10 a day for running a game that netted hundreds of dollars. Peterson was told that the "sharps" would prick the cards in the middle so they could see the cards underneath, then make sure he left a winner. Peterson went to a practice session, then informed police of the planned game on the evening of July 21, 1911. According to one report, Peterson did not bring the agreed-upon $2,500 when he arrived at the club rooms. He found only the three men and was told that he was early, but the others would arrive later. Peterson refused to accept the excuse and said that he would leave and return in an hour or so. When he opened the door, three L.A. police detectives walked in and placed the sharpers under arrest. All three were booked as suspected confidence men.[23]

When police took the accused bunco men to the station, they registered as E. Dunn, Walter Scott, and W. W. Stapp. It quickly became clear that Mr. W. W. Stapp had a better-known identity, that of Wyatt Berry Stapp Earp. According to the *Los Angeles Times* report, "Earp, who in addition to being known by the police as a professional gambler and all-around sharper, has made his headquarters here several years. He was a prominent figure here during the days when racing thrived."[24]

Two L.A. papers, the *Times* and the *Examiner,* placed the story on an inside page. The more sensationalistic *Los Angeles Herald* ran it at the top of the front page, under the headline, "Detectives Trap Wyatt Earp, 'Gun Man,' in Swindle." The *Herald* called Earp "the noted western 'gun man' and survivor of the famous Earp–Clanton feud" and laced into the old marshal: "Earp, who since race track gambling became a dead letter in California is alleged to have devoted his time to fleecing the unwary in card games here, conceived the plot, it is declared."

The day after the arrest, officials realized the police had erred. The officers had broken up the game before it began, before anyone had actually tried to bilk Peterson and before a card had even been tossed. Charges were reduced to conspiracy to violate the laws prohibiting gambling, a misdemeanor that would be heard in police court. Earp and Scott were quickly released on $500 bail. Dunn changed his identification to Harry Dean of Montana and remained jailed, unable to make bail.

The situation, of course, grew more complex. According to police records, Dean pleaded guilty to a battery connected with another charge, and the courts dropped the conspiracy charge. Dean received a six-month suspended sentence.[25] But Wyatt Earp and his attorney, Frank Dominguez, vowed to fight the accusation with a big-time defense that would include calling former governor Henry T. Gage and other prominent California pioneers as character witnesses. Earp told the *Los Angeles Examiner:* "I was told that a faro game was in operation in the hotel where Scott and Dean had apartments. I like faro and went to the hotel to play. I know absolutely nothing else of what transpired there as there was no game in sight when I entered."

Former Tombstoner T. C. Lovejoy wrote the *Examiner* to defend Earp's integrity. "I am and always have been an admirer of the Earp boys, braver men never lived. I was in Tombstone, Ariz., during all of their trouble with the Clanton gang of cowboys. As chief of police, Virgil Earp did good work, Wyatt Earp as United States marshal made Tombstone a quiet little burg from a 'shoot-your-eye-out town.' I am indeed sorry to see Earp in this trouble. I have always heard of Earp being a high bettor—the higher they stacked the chips the better he liked it—and I can't make myself believe Earp was looking for crooked work."[26]

The hearing proved anticlimactic. Earp and Scott appeared in the police court of Judge H. H. Rose on September 27. The city attorneys had expected a guilty plea from Scott, but he instead informed the court he had no intention of pleading guilty and demanded a jury trial. Earp repeated the claim that he had just visited the room by accident and no evidence had been secured against him. A disgusted Rose discharged both prisoners, and Earp's brush with the law ended as another misfire. As with the Spicer hearing in Tombstone and the Sharkey–Fitzsimmons case, there was freedom without exoneration.[27]

Coming to a conclusion about his role in the bunco is virtually impossible. His defenders have believed he simply tried to set up a game, unaware that Scott and Dean were trying to rig it. This is certainly possible. It is also possible that Earp, down on his luck, tried to find a pigeon. This would be one of those stories he would not tell in later years.

One thing is certain—above all else he considered himself a gambler, far more than a lawman. He had spent most of his years turning cards and running a faro layout, and only a few years wearing a badge. Even in his later years, he was proud of his gambling skills and enjoyed discussing them. He shied away from talking of Tombstone, almost to the end. But America had changed in the early twentieth century. The free-wheeling days of the frontier were over, and the nation embarked on a moral crusade in one of its periodic swings to bring higher standards to a country adrift in sin. With venereal disease reaching epidemic proportions, prostitution became illegal in all forty-six states. Although police tended to wink at a few upper-class houses in some areas, many of the former prostitutes elaborately hid their past.

In Los Angeles a few years later, Samantha Taylor, once madam of the exclusive San Jose House in Tombstone, would find religion and try every ruse to keep her past a secret. One of her former employees married a prominent dentist and worked equally hard to keep her past private.[28] In the wild days of Tombstone and other frontier posts, life as a prostitute or a gambler had bordered on acceptability with even something of a romantic tinge.

With gambling and prostitution illegal throughout the land, the crusade against sin peaked in 1919 with the passage of the Volstead Act—Prohibition—which made the sale of alcohol illegal across the United States. As morality changed around the Earps, Wyatt had trouble changing his morality. The aging ex-lawman kept working: driving wagons, digging in his mines, and doing other jobs. Hattie Lehnhardt, Sadie's sister, probably helped with expenses when stakes ran low. Wyatt had helped Hattie establish claim to an oil field near Bakersfield, and she may have had some undocumented agreement to pay her sister. Still, the meager income did not amount to much.

Always, Wyatt Earp's reputation followed him. The bizarre story from Charles Hopkins of Wyatt's sister Jessie marrying Ike Clanton would occasionally show up again in print. In the December 1919 *Saturday Evening Post*, Frederick R. Bechdolt rekindled the old Tombstone stories and confused them badly.

Forrestine Cooper Hooker already had a stake in the Wyatt Earp story. The daughter of Indian fighter General Charles Lawrence Cooper, she had married the son of Henry Hooker and lived with her husband and father-in-law on the Sierra Bonita Ranch during the early years of her marriage, before moving to Los Angeles. As a bright young writer, it was only natural that she would seek out Wyatt Earp to try to clear up one of the most confused and captivating stories of frontier history. At some point around 1920—the exact year is uncertain—Forrestine Hooker met with Earp to discuss his story. She also spoke with James Earp and used reminiscences from either her husband or her father-in-law to complete a manuscript detailing many of the events in Tombstone, with a definite predilection in Wyatt's favor. While many of Hooker's stories parallel the newspaper accounts very closely, but add significant details, the manuscript ends with a very strange story about Earp killing John Ringo as Wyatt left Arizona. Clearly, Earp did not kill Ringo on the retreat to Colorado. If Earp had any involvement whatsoever, which is highly unlikely, it would have been on a surreptitious return trip that would have made an even greater story, one Earp apparently never told.

Earp and Hooker had some disagreement over the manuscript, and Earp refused to allow publication. The document was eventually donated to the Southwest Museum in Los Angeles and remained uncatalogued for years until found by curator Richard Buchen and Earp researcher Jeff Morey. For reasons only he knew, this would not be the version of his story Earp wanted published.

AMERICA'S NEW BOOM CAME not from metals and minerals but from movies. It was only fitting that Wyatt Earp would find himself at least on the periphery of a burgeoning industry. Hollywood loved the West, and old frontiersmen of all stripes began drifting into southern California to work as extras on motion pictures. The sets were open to the public in those days of silent movies, and locals could wander into the Los Angeles hills to watch the actors. One afternoon in 1915, Wyatt Earp went for a little ride with author Jack London, an acquaintance from Alaska days. Director Raoul Walsh told the story in his autobiography:

> One day when I was taking it easy between studio shots, Buck Friedman came looking for me. "Two guys at the gate asking to see you. One says his name is London."
> "What's his first name?"
> "I didn't ask."
> "If it's Jack, bring them in."
> That was how I met Jack London and Wyatt Earp. London was getting on in years, but his seamed face was still as rugged as his stories, which had thrilled me when I was growing up. His books had been published in most countries of the world. The legendary Earp was tall and a little stooped, but I could still see him as the marshal of Tombstone. . . .
> I tried to draw both men out about their own doings. Neither wanted to talk about himself, but I did manage to get a few good details from Earp about the Clanton family and the famous shootout at the OK Corral. London reminisced about Klondike days and the circumstances that spurred him to write "The Call of the Wild."
> I was listening with both ears when Charlie Chaplin, sitting with friends at another table, got up and went into his waiter act. I called him over and he bowed to us with a napkin over one arm and produced an order pad. "Cut it out," I cautioned him, "or I'll tell [director Mack] Sennett you're breaking your contract."
> He quirked up one side of his mustache in a typical leer. When I introduced my guests, he viewed Earp with evident awe. "You're the bloke from Arizona, aren't you? Tamed the baddies, huh?" He looked at London and nodded. "I know you, too. You almost made me go to Alaska and dig for gold." He sat down and related some of his experiences "when I was a snot-nosed brat in Cheapside." I had a fine time just listening to them and later wished I had some way of recording their conversation.[29]

Earp made other friends around the sets, including the young extra and prop man Marion Morrison, who later took the name John Wayne, future director John Ford, who served Earp coffee on the sets, and actor Tom Mix. Wayne would later tell Hugh O'Brian that he based his image of the Western lawman on his conversations with Wyatt Earp.

But the best friend Wyatt Earp made in Hollywood was William S. Hart, a Shakespearean actor who became the biggest cowboy star of his time. In 1920, Earp and Hart began a correspondence that would last the remaining years of the former marshal's life. Wyatt congratulated Hart on his triumphs and sympathized with his struggles. Earp's friends would later say that Earp tried to teach Hart the fast draw, practicing with him for several hours and laughing heartily at Hart's fumblings. Hart dropped his gun so often that a blanket was spread on the floor for padding.[30] Hart paid tribute to Earp in a letter to the *New York Telegraph* under the headline "Bill Hart Introduces the Real—Not Reel—Hero":

> Now, I am just an actor—a mere player—seeking to reproduce the lives of those great gunmen who molded a new country for us to live in and enjoy peace and prosperity. And we have today in America two of these men with us in the flesh. . . . One is Wyatt Earp, the other is William B. (Bat) Masterson.
> To those few who have studied the history of the frontier days, these names are revered as none others. They are the last of the greatest band of gunfighters—

upholders of law and order—that ever lived. Wild Bill Hickok, Luke Short, Doc Holliday, Shotgun Collins, Ben Thompson, all have crossed the Big Divide but Bat Masterson and Wyatt Earp still live—and long may they do so!

Gentle-voiced and almost sad-faced, these men are today uncheered while I, the imitator, the portrayer, am accorded the affection of those millions who love the West. I appreciate from my heart of hearts all the honors bestowed upon me, and in my work I do my best to be worthy; but "lest we forget," don't let us pass up those real men—those real figures—who did so much for us in bygone days. . . .

Let us not forget these living Americans who, when they pass on, will be remembered by hundreds of generations. For no history of the West can be written without their wonderful deeds being recorded.[31]

Earp, who developed a sincere friendship with the actor, would soon ask Hart for one of the biggest favors of his life.

As Earp hobnobbed with the stars, two items appeared in 1922 that grated heavily on Wyatt's pride. He always believed he had done the right thing in Tombstone—that he had followed the only course possible in a wicked time when courts could not convict and the law failed to function. Others did not agree. Frederick Bechdolt, author of the 1919 *Saturday Evening Post* story on Earp, published his *When the West Was Young*, the ultimate blood-and-thunder western saga, telling the story of Wyatt Earp as it had never been told before. Of course, most of the facts were wrong and the Earps emerged as stage robbers.

More troubling was a story that appeared on March 12, in the Sunday edition of the *Los Angeles Times*, where Wyatt's friends and all his Hollywood pals could read it. Written by retired journalist John M. Scanland, the story told how Sheriff John Behan tried to rid the town of Earps, recounted far-fetched tales of the Tombstone events, and even said that Doc Holliday shot a man in Los Angeles. Even worse, Scanland wrote that Earp had died. The article so rankled Earp that he hunted down Scanland two years later and knocked on his door to tell the story from his point of view. A surprised Scanland, whom Earp described as an old man, apologized profusely. "He expressed regret over the incident and offered apologies and amends, and gave me a type-written retraction of the story which he very willingly signed," Earp wrote to Hart.

Wyatt's meager efforts to counteract his bad publicity did little to stop the flow. In the March 1925 issue of *Scribner's* magazine, John Hays Hammond, his old friend from Tonopah, dug up the absurd story of the midget mountie who supposedly humbled Earp in Dawson, an incident that never occurred. From Sam Purdy to Bechdolt and Scanland, the false stories combined to produce an embarrassing picture he could no longer tolerate. With his emotions clearly showing through the writing, Earp wrote Hammond: "Notoriety has been the bane of my life. I detest it, and I never have put forth any effort to check the tales that have been published in recent years, of the exploits in which my brothers and I are supposed to have been the principal participants. Not one of them is correct. My experiences as an officer of the law are incidents of history, but the modern writer does not seem willing to let it go at that. . . . What actually occurred at Tombstone is only a matter of weeks. My friends have urged that I make this known on printed sheet. Perhaps I shall; it will correct many mythic tales."[32]

After the *Scribner's* story appeared, Earp wrote to Hart to ask him for help in righting the wrongs he believed had been done to him:

> During the past few years, many wrong impressions of the early days of Tombstone and myself have been created by writers who are not informed correctly, and this has caused me a concern which I feel deeply.
>
> You know, I realize that I am not going to live to the age of Methuselah, and any wrong impression, I want made right before I go away. The screen could do all this, I know, with yourself as the master mind. Not that I want to obligate you because of our friendship but I know that I can come to you with this and other things and not feel hurt at anything you may wish to say. . . . This is something I can't write very well. I wonder whether I might come and talk the matter over with you?[33]

Hart probably responded during a personal discussion, suggesting Earp start by telling his story in the form of a book, which could be made into a motion picture script. It would be Earp's responsibility to find a biographer and tell his story properly.

The person he found was John Flood. Mining engineer John Flood first met Wyatt and Sadie in 1906, and began an on-and-off acquaintance that would last the remainder of the old gambler's life. An expert typist, Flood handled much of Earp's correspondence and helped with some personal duties. He became a friend of the Earps and some of their acquaintances, and he adored listening to their stories. Flood eagerly agreed to take on the project of writing Wyatt's biography. He would later tell of spending nights in a room filled with cigar smoke, listening to the old tales and jotting notes.

Earp's final decade was one of struggles. He hobnobbed with movie stars, then returned to a life of quiet poverty. The 1920s were not always kind to an aging legend. Wyatt and Sadie continued their pattern of wintering at the Happy Days copper mine and returning to L.A. during the summer, usually residing in low-cost rentals or staying with friends. There were no Social Security payments or pensions for retired gamblers/lawmen. The oilfields and mines never hit big. Hildreth Halliwell recalled: "Once in a while he'd find a little something, then there'd be months they wouldn't take anything out." The Happy Days mines did not guarantee all days would be happy.[34]

Earp, it seems, served as a deputy sheriff in a mostly ceremonial position in San Bernardino County in the early '20s; he apparently assisted in one arrest. According to an oft-told story, Constable James Wilson came to Calzona to arrest a reputed badman waving a gun in a local store and located Earp in the vicinity. Earp was to walk in the front door as Wilson waited at the back, expecting the holdup man to flee. Instead, Earp walked in, ordered the intruder to hand over the gun, and marched him outside for Wilson to arrest.[35]

Wyatt may still have had grit, but by the mid-'20s, his funds were running low and he also had kidney problems. The Earps were living in a shack near Vidal, in the present town of Earp, when Wyatt's friend from Alaska days, Charles C. Welsh, invited them to move into his top-floor apartment in Los Angeles, giving 9-year-old Christenne Welsh, Charlie's granddaughter, a summer she would never forget.

"Grandpa and Mr. Earp used to take me for a walk down to the fire station on Washington Boulevard, and we'd stop at Harry's Drug Store and have a chocolate ice cream soda," Major Christenne Welsh, a retired Women's Army Corps officer, said in 1994. "Mr. Earp was a very neat, neat man. I can always remember as sick as he was, as slow as he walked, because he was sick then, he was always straight as an arrow, and I used to just love to walk with them, my grandfather on one side and Mr. Earp on the other." The man who chose ice cream over whiskey in Tombstone now chose quiet walks with a little girl in his old age.

While Wyatt stayed home, Sadie was preoccupied with something else. "He was sickly, and she'd go off to San Bernardino on the [Big] Red Car and gamble, she played poker," Christenne Welsh recalled. "It was a hotel that had a poker game in the back room. My uncle worked for Baker Linen and he saw her several times when she'd go in and lose all her money and she'd have a round trip ticket and come home. She was a compulsive gambler."

Pat Welsh, Christenne's uncle, told her of seeing Sadie enter the private card room in the back of a San Bernardino hotel where an illegal game took place. "Uncle Pat said when he was selling the linen to the hotel, they'd see her coming and say, 'Well, we'll be able to more than eat today.' They'd take the money away from her. She didn't know how to play poker," Welsh said. "People say Wyatt was the compulsive gambler—he was a normal gambler, I imagine. She was the compulsive one."

Welsh and others understood that Sadie received an allowance from her sister, Hattie Lehnhardt, who had remained affluent even after her husband's suicide in 1912 and the sale of his chocolate shop. Grace Welsh Spolidoro, Charles Welsh's daughter, said in 1994: "The check would come on the first, she'd be nervous and she'd say, 'I'm going to go see my friends.' She'd take the check and we wouldn't see her until the check was gone. And then they'd be hungry."

Hattie Lehnhardt came to Los Angeles once or twice a year to visit her sister, but usually Sadie had ridden off on the Big Red Car, the train that ran through the Los Angeles area. "When she'd come to town my grandmother would say, 'Well, Mrs. Lehnhardt, you'll have to stay for tea,'" Christenne Welsh recalled. "She was a delightful lady—how Sadie came out of that, I'll never know."[36]

While the Welsh family maintained an affection for Wyatt, Sadie became an unwelcome burden. Spolidoro said, "She was tough. There was nothing soft about her. She never struck me as a lady, she was just *Sadie*. She gambled on anything, she liked to gamble. I think [Wyatt] got angry with her on her gambling, that was the one thing that used to bother him an awful lot. Wyatt called her 'Say-dee' when he got mad; he gave a certain tone in his voice: 'Say-dee shut up.'"

The Earps stayed at the Welsh home on and off through the '20s, though there was some friction. As much as the Welshes liked Wyatt, they were sick of Sadie. "She was stealing food out of the icebox," Christenne Welsh recalled. "My aunt would always count the eggs, and there would be three or four missing. She'd come in and say in her high voice, 'Have to fix a little something for

Wyatt.'" Wyatt Earp did what he could to maintain his pride. Charity came hard, even from friends. When the family offered him dinner, he always declined: "Don't do anything for me, Sadie will take care of me," he said.

"He'd say Sadie will fix my dinner, and the only thing she ever fixed was hot dogs," Spolidoro said. "Then my sister would say, 'Oh no, Wyatt, we have this.'" The family made certain the Earps remained fed.

It was in the little apartment above the Welsh home that John Flood began a series of interviews that he hoped would finally tell the truth about Wyatt Earp's life. Spolidoro recalled that Flood would visit almost every night. "They would sit up in his bedroom and talk, and Sadie would come up and interrupt and tell it the way she wanted, and Wyatt would get so upset because he wanted to tell the truth. How he got some of the truth out, I don't know, with her interfering. She wanted to make it that nothing bad would be said about him—that he gambled, she didn't want that. There was an argument all the time. He said, 'Sadie, get out.' He'd tell her to go downstairs, then when [Flood] would read back what he had written, she'd correct it. Then she'd get upset because she didn't like the way he treated her. If there is confusion, it is on her part."

It took Flood more than two years to piece together the book, and the finished product was indescribably awful. Flood's description of Earp's escape after killing Curley Bill is only one bad example:

> Crack! he was in a desperate plight; he felt in front, then at his side, and his hip. Gradually, his hand followed his belt around which had slipped down over one of his hips and he remembered now that in the long ride out, he had loosened his belt to relieve the strain, and the weapon was dangling at his back half way to the ground.
>
> Crack! another hornet let loose, and Earp commenced to pull and tug.
>
> Crack! Crack! "Don't let him get away fellows!" still the weapon was out of reach.
>
> Crack! Ah, he touched it with the tips of his fingers, closer, now he had it in his grasp. Crack! Crack! Crack! he started to return fire.
>
> Crack! Crack! Crack! they certainly were warming up.
>
> Crack! Crack! Crack! he was giving them shot for shot, and scattering this way and that, they ran for the willows.
>
> Once more his ammunition was gone and he reached for the horn of his saddle. Instantly, his horse was in the air; up and down, backwards and forwards he struggled, and then came the whine of the slugs.
>
> Crack! Crack! Crack! ing! ing! ing! "Some one get him!" "Put him over the jumps!"[37]

Even worse than the writing was Flood's badly jumbled story, taking sections from Earp and items from Sadie and possibly others to create a most confusing tale. He reworked the manuscript at least three times. In two versions, he has Earp killing Ringo on the way out of Arizona, just as in the Hooker manuscript, while in another there is no mention of such a killing. He variously changed structures, with one version in the form of a series of lectures by Earp and other efforts listed as a biography by Flood. All were long on useless description and short on details, accompanied with more cracks, pops, and bangs than were ever heard on the real frontier. And, obviously, Sadie did her part to add to the confusion.

Flood began promising a completed manuscript late in 1924, and Earp continually mentioned it in his letters to Hart, asking the actor to use it for a movie: "I am sure that if the story were exploited on the screen by you, it would do much toward setting me right before a public, which has always been fed up on lies about me."[38]

Finally, in February of 1926, Flood delivered his awful concoction. Hart sent the manuscript to the *Saturday Evening Post,* then to book publisher after publisher, always receiving the same answer. The most candid response came from Anne Johnston, an editor at Bobbs-Merrill in Indianapolis:

> I read the Wyatt Earp manuscript with interest—at least I began it with interest, for I am very keen about the history of the old West, but I must confess to you that I was deeply disappointed. The material itself does not strike me as so fascinating as the stories of Wild Bill and Billy the Kid and some of the rest, but it would show to far better advantage in a more skillfully done setting. The writing is stilted and florid and diffuse. It would be far more effective if it were simple, direct, straightforward. A lot of the stuff ought to be cut out altogether and the rest boiled down. Then there *might* be a story. Now one forgets what it's all about in impatience at the clutter of unimportant detail that impedes its pace, and the pompous matter of its telling.[39]

Hart sympathized with the flood of Flood rejections, writing to Earp, "I cannot figure what the devil is the matter with them. It may be some literary defect that they can see which is beyond our vision. However I am for hammering them until the hot place freezes over."[40]

Well before the hot place froze, a series of events happened to change the perceptions of all involved. In July of 1926 Chicago journalist Walter Noble Burns dropped in on the Earps in Los Angeles and asked about the possibility of writing Wyatt's biography. Earp declined, saying Flood was already on the job, and Burns came up with another idea—he would write Doc Holliday's story, clearing up the old myths and bringing out the true Holliday. Earp agreed to help and sent a wonderful eleven-page letter telling his version of many of the Holliday-related events. He also told of his frustration with the continuing series of stories which falsely portrayed his career:

> I am getting tired of it all, as there have been so many lies written about me in so many magazines in the last few years that it makes a man feel like fighting. I know you mean to do the right thing by me, but I would ask of you please to say as little as possible about me. And I am more than sorry Mr. Burns that I was not able to give you my life story. Have as yet done nothing with it, and I may have it all rewritten.[41]

Burns had already earned a degree of fame with the publication of his *The Saga of Billy the Kid.* He was a top-level Chicago journalist who had spent much of his time covering the early years of the gangster era. Now he was on the trail of gangsters in the old West, and he went after the story. Apparently with the best intentions of writing the Holliday book, Burns visited Tombstone, scoured newspaper files, and talked to old-timers. He was onto a good story, far too good to pass up. As the book evolved, Holliday developed into a side character and Earp, of course, became the leading player.

Before Burns's book reached publication, Hart and Flood realized that the insurmountable problem might be Flood's lack of ability, not Earp's story. As the rejections kept arriving, Hart suggested they meet to reevaluate the situation. Flood responded quickly that he would be willing to turn the book over to a more experienced writer and suggested Burns. "For an amateur writer, I surely got off to a poor start. Phew! didn't the publishers pen me to the queen's taste though! I was lucky to have those things fired at me in printers ink rather than hard, cold steel," Flood wrote to Hart.[42]

But Burns already had his book. He had visited Tombstone, pulled up the old records, and talked with the survivors. Not only did he not need Earp, Wyatt would have been a hindrance. Burns could tell his story without the hero worship that would be inherent in a biography.

Earp protested mightily, writing to the publisher, Doubleday, Page and Co., to try to stop the book. It was far too late. By December of 1927, Burns's *Tomb-stone* began hitting the bookstores. Earp grew increasingly angry. He was an old man, and there would be little to support Sadie when he could no longer work the mines. All that remained of real value was his life story. Now that was being taken away.

CELEBRITY HAD OFTEN FOLLOWED WYATT EARP. Wherever he went, someone recalled the old stories of Tombstone. In the years before movies and television, celebrity meant having your name appear in the papers for simply passing through town. Now, in the 1920s, Wyatt Earp still drew attention. On separate visits to the Bay Area in 1924 and 1926, newspaper reporters interviewed the former marshal, sympathetically telling his story.

"Terror of Evildoers Is Here; Alive Because He Was Quick With Trigger," the *Chronicle* headlined a 1924 story giving a brief overview of his adventures in the West:

> And it was the same old Wyatt Earp—though his hair has silvered—full of life, gay as ever, and with a gait as springy as that of a boy, who, as he puts it, is on hand "to give the old town the once-over."
>
> Despite his 77 years, and the rough times he has had while serving as United States Marshal, when the job was strictly a "straight shooting" proposition, Earp looks much the same as when he acted as the arbiter of that classic bout between Sharkey and Fitzsimmons.[43]

The stories credited him with cleaning up Wichita and Dodge City before moving on to protect Tombstone. Even after the barrage of bad press in the past, Wyatt seemed disinclined to do interviews. Both papers commented on how reluctant he was to discuss his exploits. C. H. Baily wrote in the *Bulletin:* "Earp helped a lot to make this great Western empire the place it is. You wouldn't think so, though, to hear him talk, because it's like pulling teeth to get any personal information out of him."[44]

Jack Armstrong, a young cattleman, recalled sitting in on a meeting with Earp and Bill Tilghman around 1920. Tilghman had come to Los Angeles to try to pump a movie, and met his old friend. After Earp left, Armstrong turned to Tilghman and said, "I sure did like that man Earp." Tilghman responded: "You would. He is the kind of man you would recognize and get along with, but you would hate him as much if you were outside the law. Wyatt is a good man to work with but a hard man to keep up with. His aspirations are of high standard, but his loyalty to mankind keeps him on the front line of trouble. He makes and enacts his own law and rule which I must admit beats all the written code we have or ever will have. Written law is made to serve a general purpose, to be broken, ignored or trifled with. No man can follow the written law with efficiency or safety to himself. I know, I've tried it. . . . Wyatt is a man that can forget his badge, make his own law and rule and enforce them in justice and fairness to all and defend himself at the same time both physically and socially with the legal factions."[45]

The Earps continued to winter at the mines, then find a spot at the coast for the summer. After the Welsh family moved to a smaller home, Wyatt and Sadie became regular summer customers at a little court of dingy one-room buildings on 17th Street in Los Angeles. Wyatt spent most of his days alone in the tiny house while Sadie took her trips. Christenne Welsh recalled the tiny apartment as one small room with a small kitchen sink and a stove in one corner, hidden behind a pull curtain. The tiny bathroom had a shower, basin, and toilet jammed closely together. The feel was that of a cheap motel. Always, Sadie searched for ways to raise funds.

"I think her two nieces sent her boxes of clothes," Hildreth Halliwell recalled. "They were beautiful clothes. And she used to sell them, to people she knew and people in the court. I know they had a hard time scratching out a living the last few years. It was hard for him. He lived a glorious life in his earlier days, then to have to come down to just sitting and living really off of Sadie's folks. It was a pretty bitter pill for him, and it made him a bitter man."[46]

Wyatt Earp grew quiet in his later years, generally declining to discuss the old days. Peggy Combs Greenberg, Sadie's niece, said: "He [Wyatt] was a very kind man . . . very generous to my family . . . very soft-spoken, a very gentle sort of man. You'd never think of him shooting anyone. But ah, he had to be gentle. Josie [Sadie] was a bit of a demon. Very suspicious of everyone. She was quite a character . . . a very strange woman."[47]

There were few amenities in the one-room apartment. The Welsh family moved within sight of the bungalows, and for a summer Christenne Welsh delivered Wyatt his lunch every day as he sat alone while Sadie played poker. Christenne recalled, "He was a very mannerly man. Even . . . [though I was just] a little girl, he always took his hat off when I came in."

From the porch of the small apartment he greeted Hollywood celebrities and writers coming to try to learn the real story of Tombstone. The publication of Burns's *Tombstone* brought the story back to America and christened Earp as "The Lion of Tombstone," partly for his blond hair and graceful, feline movements; partly for the courage he displayed. The book caught the public's attention and made Wyatt more of a celebrity without increasing his wealth or satisfactorily telling his version of the story.

Stuart Lake began writing to Wyatt Earp on Christmas Day in 1927, half a year after it had become painfully clear that Crack Crack, Zing Zing John Flood could not be the man to put Earp's story into words. Lake had a varied background, working for papers in New York shortly after the turn of the century, promoting a professional wrestling tour, serving as a press aide to Theodore Roosevelt during the Bull Moose campaign of 1912, then receiving a wound and being run over by a truck during the war. After a long recovery, he became a magazine writer, with credits in the top publications of the day. He would often say that he first conceived the idea of writing Earp's biography during his talks with Bat Masterson in New York, and that Masterson had told him many stories about his old friend. Lake eventually moved to San Diego and started tracking Earp. When he contacted Wyatt Earp, he was the right man in the right place at the right time.

Wyatt and Sadie began a series of meetings with Lake, starting in June of 1928. In all, Lake probably met personally with Earp about half a dozen times, though the author would later claim a much longer acquaintance. For the next six months they also exchanged letters in which Earp filled in details of his complex adventures. During the meetings, Lake carefully plumbed the old lawman's mind, bringing out some of the old stories and struggling to piece together very complicated details. It was, indeed, a task. Lake explained his travails in a 1941 letter to writer Burton Rascoe:

> As a matter of cold fact, Wyatt never "dictated" a word to me. I spent hours and days and weeks with him—and I wish you could see my notes! They consist entirely of the barest facts. First, I got from Wyatt what might be called a summary of his years, which I put down in chronological order. Then, I tackled this year-by-year, and finally month-by-month and day-by-day. In certain instances I worked on an hour-by-hour basis—in the case of the OK Corral fight, minute-by-minute. I was pumping, pumping, pumping, for names and incidents and sidelights; all of which Wyatt could supply but none of which he handed out in any sort of narrative form. It was question and answer, question and answer all the way through.
>
> Do not misconstrue this. Wyatt had an excellent background, was much better educated and read than most men of his time and place. He and I got on beautifully. He talked freely to me, that is answered my questions fully and freely, but it just wasn't in the nature of the man to speak at any length. He was delightfully laconic, or exasperatingly so.
>
> During all of the months in which I was talking with Wyatt, I was checking and re-checking against what he told me—with some other oldtimers, old newspapers and documents. From such explorations I'd come up with long-forgotten names and incidents which I'd employ to stimulate Wyatt's memory. So it went. . . . Mrs. Earp contributed nothing.[48]

Earp's health failed during the later months of 1928, as he and Lake continued their discussions and correspondence. Earp kept talking of a trip to the mines as soon as he felt well enough; the trip continued to be delayed. Lake corresponded with Earp's old acquaintances from Arizona, Kansas, and Alaska and worked hard on the details. Lake located several of Earp's old friends, including George Parsons and Fred Dodge, and put them back in touch with Earp during the last months.

Parsons spent an October afternoon in 1928 renewing acquaintances. "I was very pleased to see the physical condition and the mental condition also, of Wyatt Earp," the longtime diarist wrote to Lake. "He certainly has the same old charm that he had years ago. And certainly anybody who is a judge of human nature and human characteristics could not call him a 'bad man,' and certainly he proved to be quite the opposite in his maintenance of the law and order in the old days."[49]

As the project progressed, something unexpected occurred. Houghton Mifflin published the autobiography of Billy Breakenridge, Johnny Behan's old deputy in Tombstone. While Burns's work had been mostly flattering, Breakenridge sympathized with Behan and painted a far less heroic portrait of Earp.

The book angered Wyatt and maddened his friends. It had the air of authenticity that comes from first-person narratives, and a professional approach added by William MacLeod Raine, who did the writing. Raine made Breakenridge the hero of Tombstone, the man who delivered law to a lawless country. It sounded good, except to the folks who had actually survived Tombstone.

"Poor Billy is now 84 years of age and has only a little time left in which to enjoy his imaginary glory," Clum wrote to Fred Dodge.[50]

Perhaps most infuriating to Earp was Breakenridge's claim that Wyatt had worn a "steel vest"—a bulletproof vest—in the fight with Curley Bill, when he walked alone into the gunfire from the outlaws' camp and emerged without taking a bullet.

"I never wore a steel vest, and never had such a thing in my possession," Earp wrote to Lake. "Another one of his <u>damn</u> <u>lies</u>. I can't just understand him. As he has always of late years seemed friendly towards me . . . he is a sly fox of the worst kind, and naturally feels sore because I told Behan and his so-called brave men which were his deputies and Breakenridge being one of them. And when they came to arrest me, I just laughed at them and told them to just run away. And he holds that up against me. If there ever was a mean contemptible person he certainly is the man. . . . A man like him needs to be called down just by a <u>bad</u> <u>man</u> as he paints me to be and make him show what a lowdown coward he is. I am not through with him you may rest assured in that point."[51]

Earp took such exception to Breakenridge's book that he wrote ghostwriter Raine. According to Sadie, Raine responded that he had just taken Breakenridge's word for the story.

A bout with the flu sickened Lake through much of December 1928. By the time his health returned, Wyatt Earp had begun fading. The old marshal died on January 13, 1929, a victim of chronic cystitis, a prostate problem.

Lake wrote of the scene in a letter to Dodge, saying Wyatt had been optimistic to the end, planning another trip to the desert. He fell sick on the 12th, and Sadie called a doctor. Lake wrote that Sadie Earp, with a doctor and a nurse, stayed by Earp's bedside through the night. Wyatt awoke about five in the morning and asked for a glass of water, then went back to sleep. Sometime between seven and eight he said clearly, "Suppose, suppose." Sadie Earp leaned over and asked what Wyatt had said. He did not answer. A moment later he ceased breathing.[52]

Wyatt Earp, whose life had been scarred by controversies, died two months short of his 81st birthday in a cheap Los Angeles bungalow. The Lion of Tombstone left roaring at Breakenridge and Burns, uncertain whether his legacy would be that of hero or villain. He would have preferred not to be remembered at all. Wyatt Earp never really understood his own story. In life, he had been mostly a gambler, saloon man, and wanderer, always chasing a new opportunity. He was a man defined less by his character than by his courage. He had been reckless in his youth, but he seemed to find honor in the cowtowns. He had been honest and dependable, a standout among the unusual breed of frontier lawmen. He moved to Tombstone to make money, not to follow some higher calling. When the situation around him became desperate, he responded with unrelenting courage to avenge his brother's death and protect the lives of his townspeople. Through the years that he wandered the West, he could never really leave Tombstone behind. He was not a man of esteemed character or dedication to a noble cause. He was not a better man than those around him; he was a braver one.

LONG MAY HIS
STORY BE TOLD

ILL HART CAME TO HELP TOTE WYATT EARP'S CASKET. So did diarist Parsons and John Clum. Cowboy star Tom Mix attended the service. The *Los Angeles Times* headlined the story of the funeral: "Earp Buried By Old West; Pioneer Folk Gather at Rites of Peace Officer Whose Life Molded Frontier History." Even the *New York Times* ran his obituary, calling him a "Noted Gunfighter of Old West." Notably missing from the mourners was Sadie Earp. She said she had taken ill after Wyatt's death and could not go to Pierce Brothers' chapel in Los Angeles for the services. Grace Spolidoro and her mother served as witnesses of the cremation; Sadie, again, did not attend. "She wasn't sick, she was grief-stricken," Spolidoro said.

Sadie would soon grow very busy, watching over Lake and needling him to complete the book. And Lake would grow to mightily resent her interference. Lake and Wyatt had been partners in the book deal, and Sadie inherited the partnership, Wyatt's most valuable bequest. Sadie soon began shepherding the project, telling Lake how she wanted the book done. She wrote to Lake: "Several of our friends Mr. Lake tell us it will go big, but it must be a nice clean story, and we leave the rest to you." Sadie did not want to be mentioned—it could not have been a "nice clean story" if it had to detail her shifting affections between Behan and Earp, and of Wyatt's decision to abandon Mattie.[1]

Lake began discussions with Boston publisher Houghton Mifflin in March and completed the sale in September. During that period, Lake's relationship with Sadie went from friendly to quite sour. Lake attempted to broker a deal to sell her mining properties, but the effort fell through as the value of copper dropped. Sadie seemed to blame him for the failure and continued to complain about delays in the manuscript. She needed the money, she said, and she could not understand what was taking him so long.

Lake left for Tombstone in April and made remarkable discoveries. In the clerk of court's office he found the long-forgotten transcript of the Spicer hearing; he talked with old-timers and dug through the few remaining editions of the *Nugget* and the *Epitaph* that had survived Tombstone's various fires. The hearing transcript would provide the basis for much of his section on the gunfight.

Lake continued his correspondence with people in Kansas, building up a file on events. Unfortunately, some of the Kansas sources were far too generous in recalling Earp's deeds. In the days before copy machines, researchers had to copy stories from old newspapers by hand. On several occasions, the stories mailed to Lake were slightly different from the stories that appeared in the papers, and the shift of a few words turned Wyatt from a competent lawman to the great crimefighter of the plains. Lake would often marvel at Earp's modesty, unaware that for years Earp's old friends had inflated his legend.

In September, Lake came to an agreement with the *Saturday Evening Post*, then one of the most prestigious magazines in the land, for a three-part series on Earp's Kansas years. Lake quickly headed for an old-timers' reunion in Dodge City, where he picked up even more inflated tales. Earp had always been popular in Kansas; he had truly been one of the most respected peace officers in the wild cowtowns. It would have been a natural reaction to enhance the stories after his recent death.

"In Dodge, from more than 500 oldtimers who gathered for the reunion I learned much about Wyatt's days on the buffalo range, in Ellsworth, and as marshal in Wichita and Dodge," Lake wrote to Sadie Earp. "[Lake picked up] from many men who had known him many stories of his courage and his resourcefulness in the performance of his duty, not the least of which was the repeated assertion that 'Wyatt Earp was one peace officer who could not be swayed from any course he thought was right.' It would have done your heart good to have listened to the praise of him and the recollections of him by his loyal friends."[2]

After returning, Lake and Houghton Mifflin came to an interesting and curious decision. The saga of Wyatt Earp has two concurrent and complementary themes. First, it is the story of a man whose life encompasses the frontier experience—wagon trains, buffalo hunts, law in the cowtowns—and he is the central figure in the frontier's most storied event. Second is the lasting story of Tombstone, an event of biting importance that questions the foundations and fallacies of the American system of justice. Lake wrote to Sadie that he and Houghton Mifflin agreed that the early days on the plains were even more important than Tombstone.

Walter Noble Burns understood that Tomstone encapsulated far more significant basic truths than all the headbanging in all the cowtowns on the frontier. Lake would fall into it by good fortune.

As Lake continued work on the manuscript, his relationship with Sadie deteriorated. He knew Sadie had much to hide from her days in Tombstone, and she fought mightily to keep her secrets. Lake knew part of the story and sought help from Houghton Mifflin editor Ira Rich Kent, asking if he should tell the story of Sadie's involvement in the Earp–Behan feud. Lake added a handwritten note at the bottom of the letter: "Of course, if I so much as hint at all this in the Ms. Sadie is going to raise hell."[3]

Sadie did raise hell, no matter what Lake did. She went as far as consulting a lawyer about suing Lake.

On Kent's advice, Lake barely mentioned the conflict over an unnamed woman in Tombstone, then told of Wyatt's wooing Sadie in San Francisco years later. Throughout the writing, Sadie continually asked Lake for copies of the unfinished manuscript and beseeched him to hurry the book as she pleaded poverty. Late in 1930, both Lake and Sadie received a big surprise with the publication of *Saint Johnson*, a novel by William R. Burnett. A tale of brothers' vengeance in Tombstone, the book was clearly based on the Earp experience. Sadie accused Lake of stealing the story and writing a novel under a different name. Lake grew tired of the interruptions and accusations and wrote to Kent, "I'll put it this way now: I think that Mrs. Earp is very completely upset, mentally. . . . I feel sorry for her, very sorry. She is, however, the most suspicious person whom I have encountered."[4]

Angry and frightened, Sadie headed East to meet with Kent in Boston in early October. Kent wrote to Lake that Sadie had expressed her anxiety that the book should be a "nice, clean story," and that the incidents of rescuing a woman from a burning building and guarding a pay train were more important than the gunfights. Kent wrote, "It was plain to see that Mrs. Earp was deeply concerned about the matter. She sat at my desk for the better part of an hour, tears rolling down her cheeks in her emotion. She told me of various disagreements with you and with her refusal to meet your requests in some particulars." Kent consoled her and told her the revised version of the book would be more to her liking. Kent wrote, "She would much prefer that her husband's memory be left in as quiet a state as possible. I tried to show her that if there were to be any book at all, it must deal with the exciting episodes in which Earp played so important a part. It is obviously a situation calling for great tact, patience, kindliness and forbearance on your part."[5]

As Lake squabbled with Sadie, Kent and the editors at Houghton continued to implore the writer to shorten his manuscript, primarily by making cuts in the Tombstone section, and to contain himself in his idolizing. Other editors to whom Kent showed the manuscript "grew a little weary of having Earp presented in such a uniformly glowing light and they feel that the Tombstone incident has the air of being presented not quite ingenuously—that is, it evidently still seems a bit too much like a brief for the defense."[6]

Even when Lake toned down the praise, Earp came off as a candidate for sainthood. But the book read well—very well—and the editors at Houghton appreciated Lake's effort. Lake and Sadie anguished over the title. He suggested "Wyatt Earp: Gunfighter." She objected. Houghton representative Harrison Leussler came back with "Wyatt Earp: Frontier Marshal." Again Sadie complained.

"The title 'Wyatt Earp, Frontier Marshal,' I am not satisfied with. I would prefer much more that the title be just 'Wyatt Earp,' " she wrote Lake. "Thus far, what I have read of the story impresses me more as that of the blood and thunder type than a biography." Whether Sadie Earp liked it or not, "Frontier Marshal" stuck, and would continue to stick to Wyatt Earp.[7]

The series in the *Saturday Evening Post* appeared in November of 1930, priming America for the tale of a man who brought law to the frontier. In June of 1931, the book went into production. In August, Lake's relationship with Sadie reached the boiling point over her failure to return two working copies of his manuscript. He wrote to her, "Why did you do this? If, all through this job of producing and marketing Wyatt Earp's biography you had deliberately intended to hamper my work in every way possible you couldn't have done a much more thorough job of it."[8]

By the time the book appeared, Lake and Sadie Earp were struggling to maintain a shred of cordiality. She sent angry business letters followed by friendly little notes, inquiring about family and minor details. Lake would write to her that she was receiving bad advice on such things as movie rights and copyright laws. He suspected Flood was behind the misinformation, although he was never certain.

As publication neared, Lake began fearing he had wasted more than two years of his life and much of his money on the project. He thought the book would sell only about thirty-five hundred copies, and his half—after the split with Sadie—would not come close to covering his expenses. America was in the throes of the Great Depression, and people were not buying books as they had three years earlier. He had ominous expectations of failure about a project that once seemed certain of success.

In October of 1931, *Wyatt Earp: Frontier Marshal* began trickling into bookstores. Stuart N. Lake suddenly went from magazine writer to legend-maker. The saga of a brave lawman fighting for justice captured the hearts of America. It was the right book at the right time. In those dreary days of Depression and Prohibition, the streets of major cities had suddenly grown dangerous, with gangsters rattling machine guns and robbers heisting banks. Americans sensed a national crime wave and feared their neighborhoods had grown unsafe. With the likes of Al Capone, Bonnie and Clyde, John Dillinger, Baby Face Nelson, or any of their numerous imitators prowling around, safety was only an illusion, or at least that is what many people believed. Americans needed a hero, and *Wyatt Earp: Frontier Marshal* came galloping out of Boston.

Florence Finch Kelly summed up the appeal of the story in her *New York Times* book review: "That situation [in Tombstone] appears to have been not unlike Chicago's predicament, to say nothing of New York's, and what both those cities need seems to be a few Wyatt Earps."[9]

The saga met with instant success, selling out the first two print runs totaling seven thousand copies almost immediately. The sales made Lake and Sadie Earp solvent in the midst of the Depression, and Sadie kept planning. Motion pictures came with words now, and a talkie of the Wyatt Earp saga would cement the legend. Lake tried to sell the rights, with his agent suggesting Gary Cooper as "the living image of Wyatt Earp in his relentless youth."[10] Sadie kept writing him with suggestions and steaming at the content of the book. She grew so angry that she contacted attorney Nellie Bush to sue Lake. Bush declined the case.[11]

But before Hollywood found Wyatt Earp, Hollywood discovered Burnett's *Saint Johnson*—same story, different royalties. Wyatt Earp, with a different name, first appeared on the screen in the 1932 movie, *Law and Order*, with Walter Huston starring as the laconic Frame Johnson, riding into corrupt Tombstone. During filming, Sadie visited the Universal Studios lot to protest to Burnett, already known for his novel *Little Caesar*. Burnett recalled: "I talked to her for an afternoon, and she turned out to be a very nice woman. She realized I felt very strongly that Earp was a hero, a western hero, and we became friends."[12]

Even as the movie based on *Saint Johnson* went to the screen, *Frontier Mar-ʃhal* continued to build momentum. Lake had created a wonderful story of a man with few flaws. Through his discussions and correspondence with Earp, he had continued to ask the tough questions, as a journalist should. He asked about the incident in Wichita when Wyatt dropped his gun—Wyatt didn't want it in the book. He asked about the rumored stint as Andy Lawrence's bodyguard—Wyatt declined to discuss it. Lake gave no indication of knowing of Mattie's existence, and Wyatt apparently did not volunteer the information.

Earp did not make up stories so much as he covered them up, a natural human reaction. Not many folks would want their biography to include a discussion of their adolescent acne. Wyatt Earp had more than a few pimples to hide. Lake had compromised, ignoring the Wichita firing and leaving out other embarrassments. His letters to Earp show an earnest determination to tell an accurate story, with the difficult details covered; Earp wanted all blemishes ignored. Lake probably understood the logic in not exposing all his subject's flaws—"Wyatt Earp: Frontier Philanderer, Con Man, Gambler, and Marshal" would not have made nearly as appealing a title.

Lake also made a tactical decision, choosing to write the book as an interview with a series of first-person quotes and stories. He represented that most of the details came directly from his subject. In the foreword, Lake wrote: "Wyatt Earp was persuaded to devote the closing months of his long life to the narration of his full story, to a firsthand and a factual account of his career. It is upon this account that the succeeding pages are entirely based." Lake clearly used many sources for his information, then credited Earp, while adding quotes Earp never said. A decade later, Lake wrote to Rascoe explaining why he had falsified many quotes: "There had been so much erroneous matter printed about the Earp exploits, none ever put down in the order of cause and effect, that I was hunting for a method which would stamp mine as authentic. Possibly it was a form of 'cheating.' But, when I came to the task, I decided to [employ] the direct quotation form sufficiently often to achieve my purpose. I've often wondered if I did not overdo in this respect."[13]

It was cheating, and it was inaccurate. Because of Lake's overuse of the first-person device, Earp would be blamed—or credited—for making up or enhancing much of his own legend when actually most of the false details came from Lake and the Kansas old-timers who had spun some exaggerated yarns to Lake during his trip to Dodge City.

And there were fundamental mistakes. Lake had the gunfight take place inside the O.K. Corral, not in a vacant lot down the street. More misleading, he almost always cast Wyatt as the top-dog lawman in every situation, both in Dodge and in Arizona. Lake also made the outrageous claim that the cowboys fired the first two shots at the gunfight, while Wyatt consistently said he and one cowboy fired first.

Frontier Marʃhal emerged as the story of a white knight on horseback, defending the populace against corrupt officials and vile desperadoes. Lake erased the many shades of gray from Tombstone to create a conflict of good versus evil, rather than exploring the complex questions that actually existed. In Kansas, every minor incident turned into a confrontation for the ages. Earp's ancestry became a source of glory. Even Earp's weapon of choice became part of the image. By Lake's account, Earp received a long-barreled Colt as a gift from writer Ned Buntline, a pistol that gave him superior firepower to that of his foes.[14]

Many of the biographies of the day, especially of frontier heroes, were expected to be dramatic and exciting. Lake created a classic of the genre. Lewis Gannett's review in the *New York Tribune* said, "It has all the exciting qualities of a dime novel, the added value of authentic history, and the curious virtue that it might be used as a Sunday School text or a Hollywood scenario."[15]

Wyatt Earp emerged from the pages of *Frontier Marshal* as a hero who could do no wrong. Stuart N. Lake created a flesh-and-blood superhero, and he did it so convincingly that the majority of his readers believed unquestioningly. Many of Earp's old friends, sick of the false stories, congratulated Lake on his authenticity although they must have seen the many inaccuracies. Pronouncing the book "the most satisfactory story of the old West that has been published," John Clum wrote: "I have no doubt that this fine tribute to Wyatt Earp will be eagerly sought and widely read, and that the story will grow in popularity and interest with the passing years—thus securing for this foremost frontier marshal the public recognition and appreciation that his heroic services on behalf of the public welfare have so well merited."[16]

There were murmurs from a few doubters who didn't remember the stories quite that way. In 1934, Pink Simms, a former range rider who claimed to have known Earp, wrote a letter to writer Jay Kalez puzzling at the exploits. "Since Stuart Lake interviewed Wyatt Earp in Hollywood and wrote his articles . . . Earp has blossomed as a great western hero and a marvel with a revolver. I want to assure you that these stories presumed to have come from Wyatt himself have not a vestige of truth. It isn't like Wyatt to have told them and I often wonder if he did. He was alive when Walter Noble Burns' book was published, but he was dead when Lake's stuff came out. I never heard Wyatt talk like that; he was rather a quiet sort of person with many likable qualities."[17]

Down in Tombstone, James C. Hancock started spinning his own stories. He had been a teenager in Galeyville during the Earp period, hearing the cowboy version of Earp and accepting it. Of the Curley Bill killing, he said, "Wyatt must have had an extra dose of 'hop' when he dreamed that pipe dream, and his authors must have had several strong pulls at the same pipe."[18] Hancock came up with the most bizarre charge of all. "I have understood that Wyatt Earp was supposed to have left a publicity fund out of which any writer that would blow him up to the public as a great hero and lion was to be well paid. Surely some of them must have been working overtime and getting a bonus for they have turned out some of the most impossible and nonsensical stuff that was ever published and make the old time yellow back dime novel that was so popular in our boyhood days turn green with envy."[19] The thought of the impoverished Earps leaving a publicity fund is beyond absurdity, but Arizona old-timers who had grown up on the myth of Earp as villain believed that Lake had canonized a fraud.

BEFORE SADIE EARP BEGAN HER TROUBLES WITH LAKE, she faced an immediate problem: no arrangement had been made yet for burial of her husband. Earp's body was cremated after the services, and she kept the urn in her Los Angeles cottage for nearly six months. Then, in July, it was brought to the Marcus family plot at Hills of Eternity Cemetery in Colma, near San Francisco. For nearly three decades mystery would surround the final resting place of Wyatt Earp.[20]

Lake succeeded in selling the movie rights to Fox in 1932, sending Sadie a check for $3,375, half the profits. In the Depression, it was a tidy stake for the coming years. She protested quickly, writing to film agents Collier & Flinn that she would not allow the sale. Lake had to sweet-talk her into approval before the sale could be completed. The film *Frontier Marshal,* starring George O'Brien as "Michael Wyatt," appeared in 1934 and barely drew notice.

Sadie insisted to her relatives that she never received a penny from Lake. Hildreth Halliwell recalled Sadie complaining that the writer had cheated her out of her share and she had no money. More likely, the cash went quickly across the green felt tables in San Bernardino.

Sadie carried on for fifteen years after Wyatt's death, through good times and bad. She spent much time in Oakland visiting her sister, but most of her final years were spent in Los Angeles, complaining about her health or whatever other problems arose. At various times she angered other members of the Earp family, most notably Virgil's widow, Allie, also living in Los Angeles. During these years, Sadie made her own changes. She began referring to herself as "Josie," and signed Josie to her correspondence with her family, although her family had always called her Sadie. She told relatives and friends she grew up in a rich family — Sadie the baker's daughter became the offspring of a wealthy San Francisco merchant. Gradually, she became a most unwelcome visitor in the home of Wyatt's old friends the Welshes.

Christenne Welsh remembers Sadie coming to visit, usually two or three times a week, at dinnertime. "She was always broke and always begging. When we'd see her, we'd have to hide; we only had enough food for ourselves. She'd knock on the door and say in her high voice, 'I know you're in there, I know you're in there.'" The family ran into the bedroom and hid under the bed when they saw Sadie coming.[21] Elena Welsh Armstrong, Christenne's sister, recalls the voice as "high-pitched and sharp. It kind of grated on you. It was during the depression, and my mother was working very hard to feed us. She'd see it disappear when Sadie came and sat down at the table."[22]

Sadie fell into serious depression with the death of her sister Hattie in April of 1936. The ever-changing Sadie, now well into her seventies, again contacted Lake. "I am very lonely for my dear sister and it seems like I have nothing now to live for. My darling husband left me and now my best dear friend has gone on after. I am just miserable and so alone."[23]

Sadie Earp needed a new project in her life, and she found one. She had never been satisfied with Lake's vision of her husband. The Bold Knight of Tombstone had not been good enough to satisfy her belief in Wyatt's goodness. Around 1937, Sadie read an obituary notice of an Earp relative and looked up two sisters, Mabel Earp Cason and Vinnolia Earp Ackerman, both with some experience as writers, and approached them about the possibility of writing the story her way. By this time Sadie had grown more docile, and Jeanne Cason Laing, Mabel's daughter, affectionately recalled the woman who moved into her home: "She'd drive you nuts, but we all liked her. She was always interested in my sister Rae and me finding Mr. Right, and she'd talk to us about that. She made a scarf for me, hand sewn, when I graduated from high school. I remember her fondly."[24] However, the attempted book did not go well. Mabel Cason described the events in a letter to the Arizona Historical Society:

> We worked with her for four years, she was much of the time in our homes. We were very busy and didn't have time to check on all other possible avenues of information. My sister was in editorial work and I was teaching high school art besides maintaining a home for my college-age children. But we took voluminous notes, all in my sister's shorthand. We did all the research in source material that we could find. Houghton Mifflin Company, Publishers, through their agent in Los Angeles where we lived, encouraged us in this. But when we sent them the finished manuscript they asked for the complete Tombstone story. She simply would not give it to us. She had told us much about their time in Tombstone, how she had gone there with a theatrical troupe playing Gilbert and Sullivan's "HMS Pinafore" and that she had met Johnny Behan there and went back later with the understanding that they were to be married. . . . Finally he began running around with a married woman and neglecting her and she met Wyatt Earp. She never made any mention of his wife. . . .
>
> We finally abandoned work on the manuscript because she would not clear up the Tombstone sequence where it pertained to her and Wyatt.[25]

The surviving manuscript is a wonderful blend of trivialities and obfuscation, with long sections on Alaska and horse-racing days in San Diego and San Francisco. Sadie barely mentions her husband's involvement in gambling and saloonkeeping and ignores the controversial incidents in Idaho, simply telling of a berry-picking trip in the Coeur d'Alene country. Family pets are described in detail; long mining anecdotes are related. No good deed goes unmentioned, no alibi untold. She barely speaks of her time in Tombstone and says, "He never in all our years together described a gun battle to me. He considered it a great misfortune that he had lived in such a time and under such circumstances that guns had figured at all in his career."

Sadie spent four years trying to tell her story without ever getting to the best part. The Houghton Mifflin editors knew some of the details from Lake, and wanted the real story with all the juice and sizzle. Sadie Earp had secrets, and she took them to the grave.

Before she did, however, she still had much more to say. In 1939, Twentieth Century Fox decided to take another stab at *Frontier Marshal*, with Sadie hired to provide technical scrutiny. She immediately insisted on rewrites, according to the AP story:

> Mrs. Earp said her husband never would have hidden behind a safe while shooting it out with bandits. That was the crucial scene in the story called "Frontier Marshal." But, on Mrs. Earp's insistent say-so, this shooting scene was transferred to the famous O.K. Corral, where Randolph Scott, as Earp, will fight it right in the open with five armed opponents.
>
> Another scene Mrs. Earp didn't like was one where Scott tosses Binnie Barnes into a horse watering trough.
>
> "Mr. Earp would never have done a thing like that," she protested.

Miss Barnes explained the necessity of this horseplay and added that she didn't object to the dunking and was sure Mr. Earp wouldn't have minded so very much.[26]

While it strays far from the real story, the movie proved a surprise hit, both financially and artistically. Hearst newspaper reviewer Ada Hanifin called it the "dark horse of the year's westerns. It made the goal at the boxoffice, when the studio had marked it for an average 'B' run. . . . [it] projects a background of realism that camouflages a stereotyped Western formula, in a different setting. It is still a 'B' picture, but a very good 'B.'" Hanifin said Cesar Romero as Doc Holliday "has never given a better screen performance."[27]

Sadie Earp: movie consultant and budding writer. Things certainly picked up for the irascible widow in the late '30s. But something else attracted her attention. Allie, Virgil's widow, never on the best of terms with Sadie, started talking to a young writer named Frank Waters. Apparently Allie had become frustrated by Sadie's pretensions and the growing acclaim for Wyatt; Allie knew that Virgil had actually been the top lawman for most of their stay in Arizona. Allie had not been overly fond of Wyatt, either, and she completely adored Virgil.

Allie would visit Waters, pull a flask out of her high boots, and sit and talk a spell. "It didn't take long to discover that Aunt Allie was a character," Waters would later write. "At any provocation she would draw from the hip and fire a tall tale in a Western vernacular that was all Americana and a yard wide. She was hard and sentimental, with old-fashioned customs but startlingly original in thought, and always jovial. This jutting humor marked all her tales. In it was the eternal freshness and unvarying zest for life of those who in turmoil and tragedy remained young in a time when their world too was young."[28]

Waters began work on a most unusual manuscript that did not fit at all with the Earp image. As he continued, Sadie became aware of the project and raced to the Waters home. Frank Waters had left on a research trip to Arizona, but Sadie tried to convince Waters's mother and sister to promise he would not publish the manuscript. "My mother was a pretty calm person. She didn't get shaken up by Josephine," Waters said.[29] Waters completed his manuscript and put it in the files of the Arizona Pioneers' Historical Society, not to be published for more than two decades, when the legend of Wyatt Earp had grown beyond reality.

Sadie Earp had another cause remaining. In 1938 she brought suit against Emil Lehnhardt and Edna Stoddardt, her nephew and niece, claiming that they owed her 20 percent of the assets from the oil fields near Bakersfield they leased to Getty Oil. Sadie claimed Wyatt had saved the field for her sister, and that she deserved her portion of the profits. When Sadie could not document her case, the court dismissed the action. Jeanne Cason Laing recalled the unusual family dynamic: "They were always in court together, but they were basically close-knit. When they got out of court they were all friends again."[30]

Josephine Sarah Marcus Earp left her mark on Wyatt's saga. She had, indeed, been an important part of making the legend of Wyatt Earp stand as a nice, clean story. With little fanfare, in the midst of World War II, Josephine "Sadie" Earp died on December 20, 1944. Her death certificate said she had developed senility, and the newspapers did not cover any services. Her ashes were buried in Colma, under the gravestone she shared with her husband.

JOSEPHINE DID NOT SURVIVE TO SEE Hollywood change Wyatt from legend to myth. Although Lake's writings told Wyatt's story with exaggeration and an absence of controversy, they had a strong basis in fact. Hollywood versions often had only a scintilla of fact. Through the '30s and '40s, Hollywood was good to Wyatt Earp, filming three versions of the Earp legend in *Dodge City*, another *Law and Order*, and *Tombstone, the Town Too Tough to Die*. Only the third one actually used Earp's name, but all had a basis in the accounts of Lake and Burns.

John Ford, one of the great directors of his era, made a film of the Wyatt Earp story and turned it into a wonderful tale of good and evil. Released in 1946, *My Darling Clementine* captured the essence of the story without being burdened by either the facts or the furious social questions that swirled around Tombstone. It is considered by many film historians one of the great Westerns ever made, and Ford thought he got the story right or close to it. In a 1964 interview with fellow director Peter Bogdanovich, Ford said, "I knew Wyatt Earp. In the very early silent days, a couple of times a year, he would come up to visit pals, cowboys he knew in Tombstone; a lot of them were in my company. I think I was an assistant prop boy then and I used to give him a chair and a cup of coffee, and he told me about the fight at the O.K. Corral. So in "My Darling Clementine," we did it exactly the way it had been. They didn't just walk up the street and start banging away at each other; it was a clever military manoeuvre."[31] Ford did have a few things a little askew, such as killing off Doc Holliday and Old Man Clanton at the O.K. Corral, plus having the fight in the wrong location, but no one quibbles over details when a movie works.

Something else had happened during the '30s and '40s. Little pieces of Stuart Lake's book were appropriated as plots for dozens of B movies. The Johnny-Behind-the-Deuce affair, when Wyatt helped stand off a crowd bent on a lynching, showed up time and again, as did several other incidents. The trend would continue when TV found the Westerns in the 1950s and turned them into a nightly staple. In many ways, the life of Wyatt Earp and Stuart Lake's book, along with Owen Wister's *The Virginian*, were the greatest influences on how a generation viewed the frontier.

"Now there's a little bit of Wyatt in every frontier marshal on the air," Lake said in a 1959 interview. "Matt Dillon on 'Gunsmoke' is really Wyatt Earp. There never was a marshal by the name of Dillon in Dodge City—although many people think so."[32]

Where Lake erred on the facts, Hollywood compounded the error and delivered a very distorted portrait of the West that would baffle and frustrate the surviving old-timers. The frontier was wild; it was bloody; and it certainly was dangerous. But it was never anything like Hollywood fantasy. The reason the gunfight in Tombstone had drawn such attention at the time was because such things so rarely occurred. Drunks shot each other and lawmen chased down badmen, but marshals just never walked down the streets and shot it out with unconvicted and unindicted suspects. Americans had taken great pride in their legal system, and that pride carried onto the frontier where the law was held in the same esteem as it was in Boston. But before the frontier, Americans never truly had to confront the question of how to preserve order when the laws no longer functioned.

As Hollywood molded the frontier myth, so too grew the mythology surrounding Wyatt Earp. By 1955, eleven movies either used Earp as a character or were clearly based on the Earp saga. After *My Darling Clementine*, perhaps the most notable were a 1950 remake of *Law and Order*, starring Ronald Reagan, and the 1955 *Wichita*, with Joel McCrea in the Earp role.

In the last half of the 1950s, two separate Hollywood projects would raise the myth of Wyatt Earp to its peak. In 1955, producers Robert Sisk and Lew Edelman kicked off the TV series *The Life and Legend of Wyatt Earp*, with a plan to tell the truth. A year later, director John Sturges delivered *Gunfight at the O.K. Corral*, one of the most dynamic Westerns ever filmed. Both projects tried to tell the real story, but by then the real story had been overwhelmed by myth.

Sisk and Edelman wanted to produce the first truly adult Western on television. What's more, they wanted to make it historically accurate, something almost unheard of in TV fantasyland. The producers chose the story of the man considered the West's greatest gunfighter, the lawman who tamed three of the frontier's toughest towns, according to Lake's best-seller. By the early 1950s, Wyatt Earp had been glamorized in books and movies. And what better choice for a mature, historically correct Western than the true story of Wyatt Earp? With that plan came the birth of *The Life and Legend of Wyatt Earp*, which debuted on ABC in 1955 and owned its Tuesday time slot at 8:30 P.M. until the end of the 1960 season when the show left the air despite continuing high ratings.

To assure historical accuracy the producers hired Stuart Lake as a consultant, an ironic decision considering how Lake had embellished the tale. Perhaps the great irony is that no TV show has had a greater impact on rewriting American history than the show that tried to tell the truth. *The Life and Legend of Wyatt Earp* led to a surge of interest in the one-time marshal and set off a spate of research. Even as series star Hugh O'Brian was walking the streets of Hollywood's Dodge City or Tombstone, researchers were poring over yellowed newspapers to learn that some of Wyatt's great early adventures were more fantasy than fact, and that the crucial details of his love affairs and questionable deeds had been completely ignored in Lake's reverential biography. There was no secret wife, no firing in Wichita, no bunco arrest in Los Angeles, no conflict of opinion in Tombstone, and most of all no Sadie to help ignite the Arizona War. He was a hero the way Hollywood wanted it in the 1950s. And, through most of the run, they believed they had the story right, although the show gradually strayed further and further from the truth to provide more dramatic plots.

The impact of the Wild West TV series carried across the new West. The tourist trade picked up in Tombstone and led to a reconstruction of the town close to the way it was when Earp, Holliday, and the beguiling Sadie Marcus walked the streets. In Dodge City, the main street was renamed Wyatt Earp Boulevard. Towns that had cast aside their frontier foundations were happily moving back to their roots.

Hugh O'Brian had been the youngest drill instructor in the U.S. Marines at the end of World War II, serving under his real name, Hugh Krampe Jr. Moving to Hollywood after the war, he got a few small roles before landing the Earp part. The show was almost instantly a hit, finishing nineteenth in the ratings in 1957, sixth in '58, tenth in '59, and twentieth in '60, the final season. Toy

Buntline Specials became the weapon of choice for a generation of children mesmerized by the first adult Western. Soon after the show began, O'Brian gained
entree to the Hollywood social scene, where he made the acquaintance of a Hollywood legend who had met Earp many years earlier.

"About two months after the show started I was invited to go to a premier
by Rhonda Fleming. She was a big, well-known star, and absolutely gorgeous,
and here I had to borrow a tux from my agent," O'Brian recalled. "In those
days, any time they had a big opening like that, they always had a big dinner afterward at one of the Beverly Hills hotels. After the movie we went to the dinner
with all the wheels. When we went in, they kept walking us down near the front,
to the really top tables with the biggest stars. As we got to the table, John
Wayne stood up. He knew Rhonda, of course, because they'd worked together.
Then he turned and shook my hand and said, 'Hey, kid, you do a perfect Wyatt
Earp. I knew him, and you're terrific.'

"About three-quarters of the way through the dinner all the ladies at the
table got up and went to the ladies' room together. Wayne was across the table,
and he got up and came over next to me. 'No shit. I really think you do a great
job, and I knew him.' He also knew Stuart Lake. . . . He thought he [Earp] was
a terrific guy. He thought he was a very ballsy kind of guy that he tried to act
like in films. He said, 'I often think of Wyatt Earp when I play a film character.
There's a guy who actually did what I'm trying to do [in the movies].' He ad-
mired him very much."[33]

In so many movies, Wayne played the cool, tough lawman, slow to boil and
fast to act. Wayne had been an extra during the late '20s, then received his first
starring role in the film *The Big Trail*, in 1929, the year Earp died. Over the next
four decades Wayne personified the West in movie after movie, winning an
Academy Award for *True Grit* in 1969. Wayne's image of the West had been
shaped on studio back lots by a few chance meetings with the old marshal.
Wyatt Earp, who could never convince Hollywood to tell his story during his
lifetime, had his personality portrayed almost every time Wayne put on his Stet-
son and headed for the set.

THE LIFE AND LEGEND OF WYATT EARP inspired a new wave of interest in the
Tombstone saga, leading researchers to uncover the old unanswered questions
that had lingered since Earp rode out of Arizona. There had always been
naysayers who questioned the authenticity of Lake's account. As early as 1934,
Kansas historian Floyd B. Streeter began studying the arrest of Ben Thompson
in Ellsworth and found no corroboration for Lake's story. Eugene Cunningham's
classic 1941 *Triggernometry* relied on the Breakenridge version and presented an
unflattering portrait of Earp.

By the late '50s, the debate grew to high levels again. The rush began in several men's magazines and the new generation of Western pulps. The magazines
bought into the debate, publishing poorly researched stories and numerous old-
timer recollections. So many old-timers claimed to have witnessed the gunfight
in Tombstone that the city council must have put up bleachers along the side of
the vacant lot and had George Parsons selling popcorn.

In 1934, Raymond H. Gardner, writing under the moniker Arizona Bill, managed to sell his frontier recollections for national syndication. He claimed to have witnessed just about everything in the history of the West, including the events that led to the gunfight—he had the good sense to say he ducked when the bullets flew. Unfortunately, he also claimed to have joined the Arizona Rangers years before the force even existed.

Frank Waters gave a brief digest of Allie's memoirs in 1946 in his book *The Colorado*. He revealed the existence of Mattie and called Lake's effort "the most assiduously concocted blood-and-thunder piece of fiction ever written about the West, and a disgraceful indictment of the thousands of true Arizona pioneers whose lives and written protests refute every discolored incident in it."[34]

Two first-person memoirs appeared in the late '50s to further contribute anti-Earp fuel. Daniel Fore "Jim" Chisholm and Jack Ganzhorn provided inside stories that sound convincing but fall apart under scrutiny. The legend of Wyatt Earp has been continually plagued by false-memoir syndrome.

By the time the debunkers went into high gear, they had a vast reservoir of sources, ranging from the actual information Earp had covered up to one-sided Arizona newspaper stories to the many fallacious old-timer tales. The Earp myth had turned to miasma, with defenders and debunkers alike relying on information that was partly false, partly fabricated, and partly fraud.

As *The Life and Legend of Wyatt Earp* rode into its final seasons on television, sincere and intelligent debunking works began to appear. Frank Waters conducted further research. He had already talked to several Arizona old-timers and read some of the anti-Earp materials available. In 1960, he finally issued his biography of Allie, *The Earp Brothers of Tombstone*, which still stands as the classic debunking of the Earp legend. Waters's version is as one-sided as Lake's, offering the *Nugget*/cowboy view of events in Arizona and leaning heavily on the Sam Purdy stories. He also used the eminently unbelievable Jim Chisholm and the self-promoting Breakenridge as source material, and he added the tales of numerous old-timers who had received the anti-Earp dogma after most of Earp's businessmen supporters left town. The result was a well-written, convincing book presenting the anti-Earp view with intelligence and insight. Had Ike Clanton survived, he would have loved hearing it read to him. However, Allie probably would not have liked it at all.

Allie's relative, Hildreth Halliwell, lived with Allie for the last years of the old woman's life. In 1967, Halliwell wrote a letter describing the details of Allie's work with Waters:

> When Frank Waters mentions the other books being "a pack of lies" he was really speaking of his own book. I have even consulted an attorney about it but it would be so hard for me to prove that they are lies that it is hardly worth while to get upset about it. He write [*sic*] like Aunt Allie wanted him to publish the book when in fact she told him she would sue him if he did and you notice he waited until she had been gone almost 20 years before he did publish it. . . .
>
> I get so mad every time I think of what Frank Waters wrote after spending hours with Aunt Allie getting the true facts that I guess I go berserk. He read her part of his transcript and she told him if he printed it she would sue him so he waited

until 20 years after she was gone and then printed a lot of lies and now it would just be his word against mine so there is not much I can do, but seeth [*sic*].

No she did not hate Wyatt although she did not like him too well as he was a bit of a show off and took all of the credit for things that Uncle Virge really did, and according to Aunt Allie Wyatt was not too honest and that is the one thing Uncle Virge certainly was. Lake did not publish "Wyatt Earp, Frontier Marshall" [*sic*] until after Uncle Wyatt was gone either and there was very little truth in his book but he wrote it for the movies and that is what caused the national hullabaloo. Uncle Wyatt's third wife was still alive and went along with Lake (for the money), but Lake cheated her out of everything on the book, and she died very poor.[35]

During the next few years, Texas writer Ed Bartholomew presented a two-volume work on Earp revealing many of the flaws the ex-marshal had tried so hard to hide. Bartholomew discovered the horse-stealing, the firing in Wichita, and the dropped gun incident. This became the source of mockery, since Lake had quoted Earp as saying, "I have often been asked why five shots without reloading were all a topnotch gun-fighter ever fired, when his guns were chambered for six cartridges. The answer is, merely, safety. To ensure against accidental discharge of the gun while in the holster. . . . The number of cartridges a man carried in his six-gun may be taken as one indication of a man's rank with the gun-fighters of the old school. Practiced gun-wielders had too much respect for their weapons to take unnecessary chances with them; it was only with tyros and would-bes that you heard of accidental discharges."[36] The quote certainly made Earp appear silly when the debunkers pointed out that he had been guilty of dropping his gun and sending off a wild discharge. It is more than likely that Lake used his own words and attributed them to the one-time marshal.

Since Lake used the device of inserting first-person quotes in many places, critics—and even Allie—assumed Earp had simply lied to embellish his own legend. In the case of the Ben Thompson arrest in Ellsworth, Lake would later write to Robert Mullin that he had taken the story almost entirely from an old notebook belonging to Bat Masterson.[37] Earp had certainly mentioned it—he makes an oblique reference to it in a letter. But Masterson and Lake may well have combined to turn a small incident into a lollapalooza, as Lake did with the Clay Allison confrontation in Dodge City.

Lake died in 1964, about the time the debunkers went into full swing. He lived just long enough to see the accuracy of his book undermined and his credibility eroded. Ironically, continued research shows Lake was far more right than wrong, although he was certainly one-sided and given to exaggeration.

The debunkers succeeded in tarnishing the halo Lake had placed over Earp's head, and Hollywood reacted. The luster gradually fell off the Earp legend, and even John Ford ridiculed the old marshal somewhat in his 1964 *Cheyenne Autumn*. John Sturges's *Hour of the Gun* in 1967 portrayed a more vengeful and less noble Earp, and the 1971 *Doc* represents the debunkers' image of Earp and Holliday.

The Earp legend became even stranger as the years passed. In 1971, Wayne Montgomery claimed to have made a major discovery when he found the journals of his grandfather, O.K. Corral owner John Montgomery, and provided remarkable new information on the gunfight. Three years later, he gave the *Tomb-*

stone Epitaph a letter he claimed his grandfather had written to the *New York Herald* in 1902.[38] However, researchers discovered that the real John Montgomery had no descendants, and further investigation showed that Wayne Montgomery was not related to the O.K. Corral owner. The indefatigable Montgomery surfaced again in 1984 with the publication of his *Forty Years on the Wild Frontier.* By now, the author claimed descent from another John Montgomery altogether, a minor politician in Tombstone. This time the hoax received far less attention.

Wayne Montgomery was not the only hoaxer in the horde, and some even carried the surname Earp. In 1958, Virgil Edwin Earp, Newton's son, appeared on *$64,000 Question,* a popular TV show, and told lurid tales of how he helped Uncle Wyatt in Tombstone. Virgil Edwin claimed to have killed Indian Charlie and to have been sent on a vengeance trip to China to rub out an old enemy. "We Earps never know when someone out of the past will come looking for us. We had to kill a lot of men as lawmen and memories are long in the West," Virgil Edwin told reporters.[39] However, Virgil Edwin would have been about four when Indian Charlie died, a little young to be facing down outlaws. Another Earp, George, a distant cousin of Wyatt's, wrote a first-person story for *Reader's Digest* in 1960 detailing his participation in events that never occurred. With such an abundance of inaccurate sources available, it is no wonder the story fell into such a remarkable historical muddle.

Crime emerged as a social issue again in the America of the late 1980s and early 1990s, with debates focusing on the same issues that had torn Arizona apart a century earlier. America has never resolved one of the most fundamental questions of its legal system: In a nation of laws, should law reign supreme over public safety when the citizenry lives under constant threat? In 1882, Wyatt Earp made his own decision.

In the 1990s of drive-by shootings and gang warfare, the streets of some major cities became more dangerous than Tombstone ever was in the 1880s. Americans brought up the same old questions, trying to find solutions without compromising precious legal standards. With this backdrop, two box office movies and a TV project arrived on the market, retelling the tale of the marshal who made his own justice. It is inevitable that America rediscovers Wyatt Earp whenever lawlessness reigns.

Tombstone, starring Kurt Russell and Val Kilmer, showed up on Christmas Day of 1993. The original script by Kevin Jarre gave an authentic portrait of the West and told much of the Earp story as it had actually occurred. After a change of directors, the finished movie emerged as a jumble of authenticity and overdone violence; an interesting combination of facts and flaws. President Bill Clinton took a copy of the film with him to Russia to show as a symbol of American culture.

Six months later, Kevin Costner played the lead role in the Lawrence Kasdan production of *Wyatt Earp,* a film that seemed based more on past Earp movies than the story of Earp himself. Also in June of 1994, Hugh O'Brian reprised the role in a TV special, "Return to Tombstone," where clips from the old show were used to tell the story.

Probably no movie would have entirely satisfied the old-timers. They had lived the life, and cinema could never capture the intensity of reality. In 1930,

Fred Dodge wrote, "We old timers know that the battles fought for law and order in Tombstone were no moving picture affairs. Good men, who were our
friends, met wounds and death there. It is an offense to us and to them to repro-
duce these things as an entertaining spectacle, and incident, for it is not possible
to show what necessity lay back of them and made them inevitable."[40] Dodge
may not have liked it, but motion pictures have kept Tombstone alive and part of
American popular culture for more than a century.

After the movies returned Earp's name to prominence once again, a plaque
was placed at the site of Earp's former residence in Los Angeles in 1994, and city
councilman Nate Holden served as the main speaker. "Frankly, we could use
Wyatt Earp in America today. He was an incredible tall-in-the-saddle hero, a
mixture of great myth and fact, who should never be forgotten," Holden told the
crowd.

John Clum, George Parsons, Clara Brown, Bat Masterson, and Florence
Finch Kelly might all say the same thing. In fact, they did.

NOTES AND SOURCES

A note on spelling: Such names as McLaury, Philpott, and Borland were consistently misspelled in period sources. To avoid confusion, the spelling has been corrected in statements that would have been given orally and quoted directly from written sources. For example, information given during the Spicer hearing was presented orally, so the spelling of names has been corrected. Nicknames, such as Curley Bill, were spelled variously and have been made consistent except in direct written quotations. Aliases have generally been made consistent since the names cannot be confirmed. For example, Eliot Larkin Ferguson assumed the name of Pete Spence but it appears variously as Spence and Spencer on public records. Since this is not his real name, there is no accurate spelling.

CHAPTER 1. COWTOWN JUSTICE

1. Mrs. J. A. Rousseau, "Rousseau Diary: Across the Desert to California from Salt Lake City to San Bernardino in 1864," *San Bernardino County Museum Association Quarterly,* Winter 1958.

2. Stuart Lake's notes, 1928–1931, box 16, folders 5–8, Huntington Library, San Marino, Calif. Pages not numbered. Referred to in later references as Lake's notes.

3. Gary L. Roberts, "Wyatt Earp in Kansas," Gary L. Roberts Collection, 1989, p. 18.

4. Roberts, "Wyatt Earp in Kansas," p. 18 (quotes June 16, 1870, *Southwest Missourian*).

5. Ibid.

6. Ibid.

7. Richard Erwin, *The Truth about Wyatt Earp* (Carpenteria, Calif.: The O.K. Press, 1992), pp. 24–26.

8. Frank Murphy, "Why Cemeteries Became Boot Hills," *Los Angeles Times Sunday Magazine,* Oct. 23, 1932, p. 12.

9. Nyle Miller and Joseph Snell, *Why the West Was Wild* (Topeka: Kansas State Historical Society, 1968), p. 509.

10. *Ellsworth Reporter,* Aug. 8 and 15, 1957; Robert Dykstra, *The Cattle Towns* (New York: Knopf, 1968), pp. 136–41.

11. Miller and Snell, *Why the West Was Wild,* pp. 635–40.

12. Stuart N. Lake, *Wyatt Earp: Frontier Marshal* (Boston: Houghton Mifflin, 1931), pp. 91–92.

13. Floyd B. Streeter to W. S. Campbell, Oct. 14, 1950. W. S. Campbell Collection, box 91, folder 2, University of Oklahoma Western History Collection.

14. Bertha Hancock, "William Box Hancock Ms.," University of Oklahoma Western History Collection, 1934. The Hancock MS was written by Bertha Hancock, William's

wife, in 1934; however, the material seems uncorrupted by Lake's *Frontier Marshal.* Because it was written after Lake's book appeared, it cannot be considered absolute substantiation.

15. Mabel Earp Cason and Vinnolia Earp Ackerman, "She Married Wyatt Earp," C. Lee Simmons Collection, Sonoita, Ariz., undated but prepared in the late 1930s. Pages not consecutively numbered. It should be noted that material in the manuscript differs from that in a later treatment by writer Glenn G. Boyer. All references in this book are to the original manuscript.

16. Craig Minor, *Wichita, The Early Years* (Lincoln, Neb.: Bison, 1982), p. 110. West Wichita emerged as the gaming and brothel center in August of 1873 when Wichita's gamblers responded to a raid on a gambling house by moving most activities across the river, beyond the control of town officials.

17. Maurice Benfer, "Early Day Law Enforcement Problems in Wichita," *Wichita Eagle Sunday Magazine,* Jan. 21, 1929, p. 4, Gary L. Roberts Collection. Other quotes from Jimmy Cairns in this section also come from the interview.

18. Details on Earp's role in the Sanders affair are sketchy and somewhat contradictory. Snell and Miller, *Why the West Was Wild,* pp. 585–86, tells the story of the incident; the John Flood Manuscript (John Henry Flood Jr., "Wyatt Earp," Chafin Collection, Culver City, Calif., 1926) gives almost the same account and states that Earp became disturbed with Smith over his failure to act. Cairns's account says that he and Earp rounded up some of the troublemakers, a detail that is not included in other accounts. Lake, in *Frontier Marshal,* says Earp was not involved in the incident itself, and that the inefficiency of the police led to his being placed on the department.

19. Lake, *Wyatt Earp: Frontier Marshal,* pp. 118–21. The incident cannot be verified by outside sources. Lake says he was told the details by former Dodge City attorney Charles Hatton.

20. Miller and Snell, *Why the West Was Wild,* p. 147.

21. Virgil Earp dictation, Apr. 11, 1886, Bancroft California Dictations, Bancroft Library, Berkeley, Calif.

22. Miller and Snell, *Why the West Was Wild,* pp. 146–48.

23. Ibid., p. 491.

24. Ibid., p. 148.

25. Ibid., p. 150.

26. Ibid.

27. Ibid., pp. 151–52.

28. *Los Angeles Times,* Dec. 4, 1896.

29. *Atchison Daily Champion,* Apr. 6, 1876.

30. *San Francisco Examiner,* Aug. 16, 1896.

31. Robert K. DeArment, *Bat Masterson: The Man and the Legend* (Norman: University of Oklahoma Press, 1979), p. 9.

32. Stuart Lake's notes in the Huntington Library provide a chronology of this period. In letters, Lake said he took the chronology directly from Earp. However, Earp clearly gets confused on dates and is occasionally off by a year or two in his recollections.

33. While Earp's duties as a shotgun messenger on the shipment returning from the Black Hills have not been confirmed, the incident is noted in Lake's notes. However, express records indicate the route had been troubled by bandits, and such service would be fitting for a man with Earp's record (Erwin, *The Truth about Wyatt Earp,* pp. 85–86).

34. Snell and Miller, *Why the West Was Wild,* p. 153.

35. *Dodge City Times,* July 21, 1877.

36. Earp's real reason for traveling through Texas is the subject of some dispute. Big-Nose Kate said Earp and second wife Mattie passed through Fort Griffin while Earp

searched for a job; the 1896 *Examiner* stories identify the reason for the trip as chasing rustlers; some secondary sources say Earp traveled a gambling circuit. Stuart Lake's notes in the Huntington Library indicate that Earp told Lake the trip was indeed to pursue Roarke and Rudabaugh. Bat Masterson captured Rudabaugh on March 15, 1878, in Dodge City, before Earp received the wire in Joplin to return for the deputy job; he may have been pursuing Roarke or had other reasons for the trip. Adding to the puzzle, the *Ford County Globe* reported that Earp had "just returned from Fort Worth" when he took the assistant marshal post.

37. Bat Masterson and Jack DeMattos, *Famous Gunfighters of the Western Frontier* (Monroe, Wash.: Weatherford, 1982), p. 76. This book reprints a 1907 series in *Human Life* magazine.

38. *San Francisco Examiner,* May 11, 1882.

39. *Gunnison News-Democrat,* June 18, 1882.

40. *San Francisco Examiner,* Aug. 2, 1896. It should be noted that the *Examiner* series was written to glorify the events and that some quotes may have been enhanced or rephrased by the writer.

41. Joe Chisholm, "Tombstone's Tale," Jack Burrows Collection, San Jose, Calif., p. 113. Chisholm quotes a letter from Kate to writer Anton Mazzanovich. The story of Holliday's killing of Bailey appears in Lake's notes, but Kate's remarkable rescue does not appear. It should be noted that Lake quoted Earp as saying the *Examiner* writer had taken great liberties with the information on Holliday.

42. Eddie Foy, *Clowning through Life* (New York: E. P. Dutton & Co., 1928), pp. 113–14.

43. Hancock, "William Box Hancock Ms."

44. Snell and Miller, *Why the West Was Wild,* p. 298.

45. Bob Palmquist, "Who Killed Jack Wagner?" *True West* (October 1993), p. 14. Palmquist located the files of the Sughrue–Tarbox election fraud case in which Bat Masterson's reputation was questioned. Masterson testified he had indeed shot the men who killed his brother. This detail had eluded researchers who accepted the erroneous newspaper reports.

46. Roberts, "Wyatt Earp in Kansas," pp. 14–15. In addition to serving as deputy marshal, court records show that Earp served as a deputy sheriff at various times. It was not unusual for law officers to hold both commissions so their authority would be valid beyond their immediate jurisdictions.

47. Andy Adams, *Log of a Cowboy* (Boston: Houghton Mifflin, 1903), p. 191.

48. Snell and Miller, *Why the West Was Wild,* pp. 154–55; *San Francisco Examiner,* Aug. 2, 1896.

49. Foy, *Clowning through Life,* pp. 113–14. The *National Police Gazette,* Aug. 10, 1878, describes the source of the trouble as coming after Earp and one of the "cow-boys" had an altercation. Jeff Morey Collection.

50. Snell and Miller, *Why the West Was Wild,* p. 155.

51. *National Police Gazette,* Aug. 10, 1878.

52. Bat Masterson told a strikingly similar story in his 1907 *Human Life* magazine series (Masterson and DeMattos, *Famous Gunfighters,* pp. 30–31). Masterson said Earp arrested an unnamed alderman and kept him in jail overnight despite several protests.

53. Miller and Snell, *Why the West Was Wild,* pp. 25–27. Newspaper records indicate that Allison visited Dodge on both Aug. 6, 1878, and Sept. 5, 1878.

54. *San Francisco Examiner,* Aug. 16, 1896. Years later, cowboy Charlie Siringo, who had many frontier adventures real and imagined, would tell that he had innocently ridden into Dodge and been recruited into a group of Texans providing a guard for the lawman-hunting Allison. Siringo said he sat with the other Texans and waited, but Allison could

find no badges to puncture. The Texas guard may never have seen what happened quietly between Earp and Allison, or this could have been an incident on Allison's second visit when Earp was out chasing Indians. It could also have been the tactic often used by true-life Western writers of picking up a story and projecting themselves in the middle.

55. A typographical error in the *Examiner* story says "the same" instead of "a shame." When Lake told the story it emerged as one of the great encounters of the age. Earp's own description is far more believable. It should also be noted that Earp made the claims of Wright's plan in 1896 while Wright was still alive. Wright did not comment on Allison or any assassination attempt in his autobiography.

56. Isom Prentice "Print" Olive was a tough character indeed. His chase after the killers of his brothers inspired the character of Dan Suggs in the Pulitzer Prize–winning novel *Lonesome Dove* by Larry McMurtry.

57. DeArment, *Bat Masterson*, p. 117.

58. *San Francisco Examiner*, Aug. 16, 1896; DeArment, *Bat Masterson*, pp. 116–24; *Dallas Morning News*, Apr. 25, 1926. Lake's version of events is quite different from the account Earp gave to the *Examiner*, with Lake avoiding the story of how Earp allowed Kenedy to escape from the saloon.

59. Robert Wright, *Dodge City: The Cowboy Capital* (Wichita: Wichita Eagle Press, 1913), p. 175.

60. *Dodge City Times*, Oct. 26, 1878; *Ford County Globe*, Oct. 29, 1878.

61. DeArment, *Bat Masterson*, p. 124.

62. *Dodge City Times*, Dec. 7, 1878.

63. *Medicine Lodge Cresset*, June 5, 1879, exchange from *Ford County Globe*.

64. Miller and Snell, *Why the West Was Wild*, p. 157.

65. O. H. Marquis to Mabel Earp Cason, July 31, 1956, photocopy in C. Lee Simmons Collection, Sonoita, Ariz. Marquis was Blaylock's nephew and recalled family stories of his aunt.

66. Dodge City papers regularly refer to gambler John Tyler. While it cannot be confirmed that this is the same John Tyler who showed up in Tombstone later, gamblers often followed the money, and it is assumed to be the same person.

67. Lake's *Wyatt Earp: Frontier Marshal* is the only source for the details of this story; however, the *Medicine Lodge Cresset* of June 12, 1879, picked up the story: "A negro baby carried off the prize of being the handsomest child in Dodge City. We can't say that the ebony hue will be the prevailing color."

68. Hancock, "William Box Hancock Ms."

69. Madden to Lake, Nov. 6, 1928, Lake Collection, Huntington Library.

ℂ HAPTER 2. A NEW TOWN, A NEW BADGE

1. Wyatt Earp deposition, Lotta Crabtree will case, 1925, Harvard University Law Library.

2. Thomas H. Peterson Jr., "The Tombstone Stagecoach Lines, 1878–1903: A Study in Frontier Transportation" (master's thesis, University of Arizona, 1965), p. 35.

3. *San Diego Union*, July 14, 1880.

4. Fred Dodge presents an unusual problem because no Wells, Fargo records confirm his work for the company before 1890. However, newspapers openly identified him as working for Wells, Fargo in 1886, and he had a long and distinguished career with the company. In Carolyn Lake's *Undercover for Wells, Fargo* (Boston: Houghton Mifflin, 1964) he says his role was a secret, and it seems it was kept a secret from company records. Because of his later career, it seems highly unlikely he would fabricate his role in Tombstone.

5. George W. Parsons and Carl Chafin, ed., "The West of George Whitwell Parsons, 1880–1920." Entry date July 16, 1880.

6. Ibid.

7. *San Francisco Examiner,* Oct. 3, 1881.

8. *Tombstone Epitaph,* Mar. 18, 1881.

9. *New Southwest and Grant County Herald,* May 29, 1882.

10. John Pleasant Gray, "When All Roads Led to Tombstone," Arizona Historical Society Collection, Tucson, p. 100.

11. *San Francisco Examiner,* May 28, 1882; further Virgil Earp quotes in this chapter taken from May 27 and 28, 1882, *Examiner* stories.

12. Numerous period sources also confirm the McLaurys were in the business of purchasing rustled cattle for resale to butchers. The Nov. 3, 1881, *Arizona Weekly Star* published a letter from a McLaury defender who signed himself "Observer," saying: "They may have bought stolen cattle, and under their reputations were able to dispose of the same publicly in our markets."

13. B. M. Jacobs file, University of Arizona Special Collections, Tucson.

14. *San Francisco Examiner,* May 28, 1882; Forrestine Hooker, "An Arizona Vendetta: The Truth about Wyatt Earp and Some Others" (Southwest Museum, Los Angeles, 1920?), pp. 12–14.

15. *Weekly Epitaph,* Oct. 20, 1880.

16. *Tombstone Weekly Nugget,* Aug. 5, 1880; *Weekly Epitaph,* Aug. 7, 1881.

17. *Tombstone Weekly Nugget,* Aug. 5, 1880.

18. Phil Rasch, "A Note on Buckskin Frank Leslie" (Denver: 1954 Brand Book for the Denver Posse of the Westerners, 1954), pp. 197–216; *Weekly Nugget, Epitaph,* July–September 1880.

19. Wyatt Earp to Walter Noble Burns, Mar. 15, 1927, Burns Collection, University of Arizona Special Collections, Tucson.

20. *Tombstone Weekly Nugget,* Aug. 19, 1880.

21. *Epitaph,* Aug. 21, 1880, from *Tucson Star.*

22. *Tombstone Weekly Nugget,* Sept. 2, 1880.

23. *Daily Epitaph,* Aug. 27, 1881.

24. Mary Cummings to Lillian Raffert, Mar. 19, 1940, as quoted in Bob Boze Bell's *The Illustrated Life and Times of Doc Holliday* (Phoenix: Tri-Star Boze, 1995), pp. 107–8. Bell provided a copy of the original for confirmation.

25. Tuberculosis, then called consumption, was believed by most doctors to be hereditary, not contagious, until 1882, when Dr. Robert Koch isolated the tubercle bacilli. The writings of Dr. S. Adolphus Knopf helped make the knowledge of contagion widespread and led to a fear of consumptives who might spread the disease. No documentation could be located of attitudes toward victims of tuberculosis during Holliday's time in Kansas, New Mexico, and Tombstone.

26. *Tombstone Nugget,* Oct. 12, 1880.

27. *Territory of Arizona v. J. H. Holliday,* Cochise County Recorder's office, Bisbee, Ariz.

28. William Hunsaker to Lake, Oct. 2, 1928, Lake Collection, Huntington Library.

29. *Weekly Epitaph,* Aug. 21, 1880.

30. *Weekly Epitaph,* Sept. 11, 1880.

31. *Tucson Weekly Citizen,* Jan. 1, 1881.

32. Lake, *Undercover for Wells, Fargo,* p. 236.

33. Ibid., pp. 241–42.

34. *Arizona Daily Star,* Dec. 22, 1880.

35. *Tombstone Epitaph,* Oct. 31, 1880.

36. Analysis of Tombstone political turbulence done with the assistance of Carl Chafin, who has spent more than two decades studying the town's history and politics.

37. *San Francisco Examiner,* May 27, 1882.

38. *Tombstone Epitaph,* Nov. 8, 1880.

39. Minutes, Pima County Board of Supervisors, vol. 1, p. 424; research provided by Bob Palmquist.

40. While details on this deal are sketchy, such a deal is referred to in both the Flood MS (p. 138) and in Lake's *Frontier Marshal* (p. 245). The June 23, 1881, *Arizona Weekly Star* says Curley Bill "by a pretext and a political bargain, is turned loose on the community, since which time he has been a terror in the sections in which he mysteriously turns up," but gives no further details of the political bargain. Ike Clanton's position was most difficult, since he was being subpoenaed by Shibell to prove there was no fraud. If he lied on the stand, he would kill Curley Bill; if he told the truth he would admit to election fraud and probably go to jail. Ike apparently prepared to meet the process servers with guns (*Nugget,* Nov. 5, 1881), but Behan did not pursue the issue. Whether Earp and Paul sought Clanton's testimony is uncertain. Paul had the opportunity to serve him with a subpoena and did not, and Earp seems to have made no effort to bring Clanton to court.

41. Bob Palmquist, "Election Fraud, 1880—The Case of Paul v. Shibell," University of Arizona seminar paper, 1986, Palmquist Collection, Tucson.

42. *Arizona Weekly Star,* Jan. 20, 1881.

43. Palmquist, "Election Fraud, 1880."

44. *Tombstone Nugget, Epitaph,* Nov. 4, 5, 17, 1880.

45. Ibid., Nov. 17, 1880.

46. Ibid., Nov. 5, 1881.

47. Analysis of the incident comes from combining points of agreement in Hooker's "An Arizona Vendetta," Fred Dodge (in Lake, *Undercover for Wells, Fargo,* pp. 11–12), and Parsons. The quotes of Earp passing through town are from Dodge; the later quote is from Hooker.

48. *Tucson Citizen,* Feb. 5, 1932.

49. *Los Angeles Mining Review,* Mar. 23, 1901. Copy in Parsons scrapbooks, UCLA Special Collections.

50. Parsons to Lake, Oct. 25, 1928, Lake Collection, Huntington Library.

51. Walter Noble Burns notebooks, University of Arizona Special Collections.

52. *Tombstone Weekly Epitaph,* Jan. 17, 1881.

53. *Tucson Citizen,* Jan. 15, 1881.

54. Ibid., Jan. 22, 1881.

55. *Arizona Daily Star,* Dec. 28, 1880.

56. *San Francisco Exchange,* Feb. 16, 1882, from *San Jose Times.*

57. Ibid. The May 21, 1881, *San Francisco Daily Report* provides the first known report of Curley Bill's humiliation of the minister and says it occurred in Charleston. The *Report* also says that Bill with Jim Wallace "took in" Contention in March of '81 and "have several times taken Galeyville."

58. *Arizona Weekly Star,* Jan. 27, 1881.

59. Various memoirs and letters from James C. Hancock of Galeyville and later Paradise tell of the two different Curley Bills. Other old-timers, notably Melvin Jones, claim Curley Bill used both Graham and Brocious; however, Hancock said he knew the two different Curley Bills. In addition, there were other Curley Bills in the West, but none achieved the notoriety of the dance-master.

60. William M. Breakenridge, *Helldorado: Bringing Law to the Mesquite* (Boston: Houghton Mifflin, 1928), p. 227.

61. Ibid., pp. 227–28.

62. Emma Muir, "Shakespeare Becomes a Ghost Town," *New Mexico,* October 1948, p. 25.

63. *San Francisco Examiner,* Oct. 3, 1881.

64. *Arizona Weekly Star,* May 26, 1881 (includes account of shooting).

65. *Arizona Mining Journal,* July 9, 1881.

66. *San Diego Union,* Aug. 10, 1880.

67. *Arizona Weekly Star,* Mar. 3, 1881.

68. Wyatt Earp deposition, Lotta Crabtree will case, 1925, Harvard University Law Library.

69. *San Francisco Examiner,* Aug. 2, 1896.

70. Lake, *Wyatt Earp: Frontier Marshal,* pp. 253–54.

71. Masterson and DeMattos, *Famous Gunfighters,* pp. 55–56.

72. *San Francisco Examiner,* May 28, 1882.

73. *Tombstone Epitaph,* Apr. 16, 1881. The name had been such a source of irritation that legislator B. H. Hereford had suggested changing the name of the county to Huachuca.

74. Fremont initially appointed Republicans Lyttleton Price (district attorney), William Seamans (recorder), John Dunbar (treasurer), Abraham H. Emanuel (supervisor), Joseph Tasker (supervisor), and H. M. Matthews (coroner); and Democrats Behan (sheriff), Joseph Dyer (supervisor), J. H. Lucas (probate judge), Rodman Price (surveyor), and George Pridham (public administrator). The council rejected Seamans and Price, while Emanuel withdrew under pressure. Emanuel's withdrawal led to the appointment of saloonkeeper Milt Joyce, which gave the Democrats control of the board of supervisors. After Seamans's rejection, Fremont appointed Republican J. L. Redfern, who was also rejected. He finally capitulated and appointed Jones. Dunbar's brother, Thomas, was a legislator from Pima County and John Dunbar received bipartisan support. Surveyor Rodman Price's father, also Rodman, had served with Fremont in the military action that brought California into the possession of the United States, and later served as governor of New Jersey.

75. *Tombstone Epitaph,* May 14, 1881.

76. *Prescott Miner,* Feb. 21, 1881.

77. Researcher Barbara Grcar collected details on Josephine Marcus from San Francisco city directories and other records; Cason and Ackerman, "She Married Wyatt Earp," tells of Josephine Marcus's San Francisco days and joining the *Pinafore* troupe.

78. Details of the *Pinafore* story appear in the Oct. 21, 1879, *Los Angeles Herald;* the Oct. 22, 1879, *Santa Barbara Daily Press;* and the *Star* and *Citizen* through October, November, and December. The Oct. 5 *Daily Star* details the breakup of the original troupe in Casa Grande, and the Oct. 25 *Weekly Citizen* tells of Markham's arrival. It should be noted that none of the Los Angeles papers identify any of the performers as Josephine Sarah Marcus or Dora Hirsch. Former University of Arizona professor Pat Ryan identified May Bell as Josephine Marcus in his article "Tombstone Theatre Tonight," *The Smoke Signal,* Spring 1966, but fails to provide any substantiation. Because of the obvious time problems, it is apparent that Josephine Earp's version of events in "She Married Wyatt Earp" is inaccurate.

79. Lake to Ira Rich Kent, Feb. 13, 1930, bMS. Am. 1925 (1039) by permission of the Houghton Library, Harvard University. Further citation to Houghton Library.

80. *Tucson Citizen,* May 21, 1882.

81. *San Diego Union,* Mar. 9, 1881.

82. *Tombstone Weekly Epitaph,* Jan. 17, 1881.

83. *Tucson Weekly Citizen,* Apr. 3, 1881.

84. Ibid., June 5, 1881.

85. *Arizona Weekly Star*, Feb. 17, 1881.

86. *Tucson Weekly Citizen*, Feb. 13, 1881, and Apr. 10, 1881.

87. George H. Kelly, *Legislative History of Arizona, 1864–1912* (Phoenix: Manufacturing Stationers, 1926), pp. 98–101.

88. *Arizona Weekly Star*, Mar. 10, 1881.

89. Letter of L. Wollenberg to the *Prescott Miner*, Feb. 23, 1881.

90. *Prescott Daily Miner*, Mar. 17, 1881, from *Tombstone Gossip*, Mar. 17, 1881. Hints of an unofficial bounty on Curley Bill appear in several sources.

CHAPTER 3.   MURDER AND MADNESS

1. *Los Angeles Evening Express*, Oct. 22, 1881, Chafin Collection. Primary sources are contradictory on the exact location of the robbery, some indicating it happened before reaching Drew's Station, others saying after.

2. *Tombstone Epitaph*, Mar. 16, 17, 1881.

3. *San Francisco Examiner*, May 28, 1882; Forrestine Hooker, "An Arizona Vendetta: The Truth about Wyatt Earp and Some Others," Southwest Museum, Los Angeles, 1920? The account of Earp chasing a trail of pages from a dime novel comes from Hooker (pp. 23–24) and has not been substantiated by other sources.

4. *San Francisco Examiner*, May 28, 1882.

5. Ibid.

6. Ibid.

7. *Arizona Weekly Star*, Mar. 31, 1881, from *Tombstone Nugget*. It should be noted that the oft-picked-up quotation of King being "an important witness against Holliday" is false and did not appear in the *Nugget* or any other period source. The false quotation first appeared in Breakenridge's *Helldorado* and has been repeated in numerous books. This quotation has been the basis for much confusion in many secondary works.

8. *Tucson Weekly Citizen*, Apr. 5, 1881. Len Redfield, the rancher on whose ranch King was located, was hanged by a mob in Florence, Arizona, in September of 1883 after being accused of stage robbery and murder.

9. *Arizona Weekly Star*, Apr. 7, 1881, from *Tombstone Epitaph*.

10. Ibid.

11. *Tucson Citizen*, Mar. 27, 1881.

12. *San Francisco Exchange*, Mar. 17, 1881.

13. Jim Hume to Lida Munson, Mar. 1881, Hume Collection, Bancroft Library, Berkeley, Calif.

14. *San Francisco Examiner*, May 28, 1882.

15. *Arizona Weekly Star*, Mar. 3, 1880. Woods antagonized Tucson by attempting to ram through the Cochise County bill without the new county assuming a portion of Pima County's debt. The bill passed both state houses only to be vetoed by Governor Fremont, who ordered that Cochise must assume part of the debt. Woods further antagonized Tucson by supporting the bill to keep the state capital in Prescott rather than having it moved to Tucson.

16. *San Diego Union*, Aug. 28, 1881.

17. *Tombstone Nugget*, Nov. 17, 1881.

18. Ibid.

19. *Tombstone Nugget*, Nov. 13, 1881.

20. *Tombstone Epitaph, Nugget*, Nov. 13, 1881.

21. *San Francisco Exchange*, June 22, 1881, from *Tombstone Epitaph*. Mike Gray had indeed purchased his ranch from Curley Bill, as John Pleasant Gray confirmed in his memoirs. But the younger Gray accused the Hasletts of running something of an extortion

racket, trying to get more money from the Grays after they had already paid Curley Bill. Rumors circulated of Mike Gray serving as something of a crime boss for the cowboys, but this appears highly unlikely. The rumors were sparse and ended quickly. Parsons never mentioned any such thing in his diary and later became a friend of the family; he was not the sort to forgive a cowboy godfather. Gray did employ the cowboys on occasion and, while many of his dealings were of dubious ethical standards, there is not enough evidence to build him into a criminal kingpin.

22. *Tombstone Epitaph*, June 22, 1881. "Joe" would be identified as Sigman Biertzhoff in the *Epitaph's* July 23, 1881, edition.

23. Dialogue taken from Hooker's "An Arizona Vendetta."

24. *Tombstone Nugget*, July 19, 1881.

25. The actual events surrounding Virgil's appointment are uncertain. In Stuart Lake's notes in the Huntington Library is a cryptic note saying, "Ben Sippy elected Marshal after White couldn't handle the town, Citizens com. one met Wyatt one night, asked him to interview room—20 people. 'Virgil, want to put you in as the city marshal, to buy Ben Sippy off.' Took him for Virg. Wrong man. 'Ain't you Virg?' 'No, Wyatt.' Sent Virg in, talked bt. Sippy off, Virg. got job." Lake later wrote to Robert Mullin that the first indication of Sippy's failures came when the marshal just stood and watched during the Johnny-Behind-the-Deuce affair. None of this can be supported by documentation.

26. *Tombstone Nugget*, July 6, 7, 9, 10, 1881; not available is the July 8 *Nugget*, which apparently reported details of Kate's threats. The *Epitaph* did not report any court news for the period in question.

27. Wyatt Earp to Walter Noble Burns, Mar. 15, 1927, Burns Collection, University of Arizona Special Collections. Earp tells Burns that Holliday visited Leonard's shack at a location called "the Wells," and returned at 4 P.M., riding on a wagon with West Fuller's father, Henry Fuller. Earp says Holliday was playing faro at the time of the robbery.

28. Paula Mitchell Marks, *And Die in the West* (New York: Morrow, 1989), pp. 137–38.

29. *Arizona Weekly Star*, Aug. 25, 1881, from *Tombstone Nugget*. The question of who drove the stage is complicated by Fred Dodge's comment nearly a half-century later that he heard of the driver switch from passengers (*Undercover for Wells, Fargo*, p. 23) and by the Flood MS also telling of the driver switch. Unfortunately, the only known copies of the Flood MS may have been written before Wyatt Earp had the opportunity to read it and make corrections, and much of the Flood material is questionable. Mining engineer Robert A. Lewis claimed to have heard the story of the driver switch from Paul; however, there is no other record of Paul making such a statement. Lake's notes say, "Paul did not change seats," with three underlines under the *not* in a section that apparently came from an interview with Earp. All other known Earp interviews list Philpott as the driver at the time of the holdup.

30. *Tombstone Nugget*, Jan. 1, 1882.

31. *San Diego Union*, June 28, 1881.

32. The Flood MS tells a heroic tale of Wyatt crawling through fire to rescue a handicapped woman. Houghton Mifflin editor Ira Rich Kent wrote to Stuart Lake that Mrs. Earp had discussed the fire story with him and wanted it included in *Frontier Marshal*, Kent to Lake, Oct. 23, 1930, Houghton Collection, Houghton Library, Harvard.

33. *Tombstone Epitaph*, June 23, 1881.

34. Lake, *Undercover for Wells, Fargo*, pp. 34–35.

35. *San Diego Union*, June 23, 1881.

36. *Arizona Weekly Star*, June 23, 1881.

37. *Tucson Weekly Citizen*, May 22, 1881; *Tombstone Nugget*, June 9, 1881; Bowyer letter to Gosper, Sept. 17, 1881, National Archives, Chronological Files, State Box 12. A

Mar. 13, 1881, *Citizen* story lists McAllister as a partner in the People's Market with Tomlinson and Hicks, presumably either Milt or Joe Hicks.

38. Communications between Willcox and Division of the Pacific; copies at the Arizona State Library, Archives Division, Secretary of the Territory, box 2. Military observations of the cowboys preparing for attack is from National Archives, DOJ, RG60. Willcox wrote that Lieutenant Craig "believes that forty or fifty cow-boys of bad character are ready for action between Las Animas and Galeyville."

39. *Tombstone Nugget,* Aug. 3, 1881; story refers to Skull Canyon.

40. Joseph Bowyer to John Gosper, Sept. 17, 1881, National Archives.

41. Morales to Gosper, Aug. 10, 1881; Arizona State Library, Archives Division, Secretary of the Territory, box 2.

42. *Tombstone Epitaph,* Aug. 5, 1881, from the *Tucson Citizen.*

43. *Tombstone Epitaph,* Aug. 13, 1881.

44. *Arizona Weekly Star,* June 23, 1881.

45. *Tombstone Nugget,* June 9, 1881.

46. Breakenridge, *Helldorado,* pp. 229–30.

47. Eugene Cunningham to Jack Burrows, Aug. 10, 1953, Burrows Collection.

48. Muir, "Shakespeare Becomes a Ghost Town," p. 25. There is no record of Ringo ever killing a man in Arizona, though it is possible he participated in rustling and murder raids against the Mexicans. The oft-told story that Ringo killed a cowboy named Dick Lloyd is contradicted by newspaper reports that say a Camp Thomas bartender named O'Neil shot and killed Lloyd after Lloyd wounded one man and threatened to kill others. The Mar. 13, 1881, *Weekly Citizen* says a jury was quickly assembled and the case ruled justifiable homicide.

49. *San Francisco Examiner,* May 28, 1882.

50. Jack Burrows, *John Ringo: The Gunfighter Who Never Was* (Tucson: University of Arizona, 1987), pp. 81–82.

51. *Arizona Weekly Star,* Dec. 14, 1881.

52. Ringo to Pima County Courts, Craig Fouts Collection, San Diego, Calif.

53. *San Francisco Examiner,* Oct. 3, 1881.

54. Bob Palmquist, "A Man for Breakfast Every Morning: Homicide and the Law in Tombstone, 1880–1882," Palmquist Collection, Tucson. Graduate seminar paper, University of Arizona, 1991.

55. *Los Angeles Herald,* Nov. 18, 1881, from *Tombstone Nugget.*

56. Bowyer to Gosper, Sept. 17, 1881.

57. *San Francisco Weekly Stock Report,* Oct. 3, 1881.

58. Parsons and Chafin, "The West of George W. Parsons," Apr. 21, 1881.

59. *Tombstone Nugget,* as reprinted in *Arizona Weekly Star,* Sept. 1, 1881.

60. *Tombstone Nugget,* as reprinted in *Virginia City Territorial Enterprise,* Aug. 19, 1881. While there is little doubt the killings in Guadalupe Canyon were done by Mexicans, Will McLaury apparently believed Doc Holliday had some involvement. In his November 9 letter to D. D. Appelgate (Misc. MSS McLaury, New-York Historical Society), McLaury wrote: "It is now known that two other men who knew of the murder in the attempted robbery have since then been killed in Mexico. The report was by 'Greasers' but at the time they were killed Holliday was out of town 'said to be visiting Georgia.'" There are no other hints in period reports of any Earp or Holliday involvement in the Guadalupe Canyon massacre, and such involvement seems impossible. Billy Byers made no such accusation, and clearly said he saw Mexicans looting the bodies. John Pleasant Gray believed it was done by Mexicans. Ike Clanton never made any such accusation even when he was accusing the Earps of just about every unpleasant deed imaginable. The

story would lie dormant for six decades until being told again in Jack Ganzhorn's greatly exaggerated memoir *I've Killed Men,* first published in 1940, then again in 1971 in a fraudulent diary of O.K. Corral owner John Montgomery, then picked up by later writers.

61. *San Francisco Examiner,* Aug. 19, 1881.

62. *San Diego Union,* Aug. 28, 1881.

63. *Tombstone Epitaph,* Aug. 19, 1881.

64. *San Francisco Examiner,* Aug. 20, 1881.

65. *Tombstone Nugget,* Sept. 7, 16; Oct. 15, 1881.

66. *New York Tribune,* Aug. 25, 1881.

67. *San Francisco Examiner,* Oct. 3, 1881.

68. Frank Waters, *The Earp Brothers of Tombstone* (New York: C. N. Potter, 1960). Waters combines information from interviews with Allie Earp and various Tombstone old-timers. Although much of the detailed information is questionable, it is apparent that Wyatt and Sadie became friendly after her separation from Behan.

69. Lake to Kent, Feb. 13, 1930, Houghton Library, Harvard.

70. *San Francisco Examiner,* May 11, 1882.

71. Several letters to newspapers during late '81 and early '82 expressed a suspicion that Behan and the rustlers had some alliance with the cowboys. Wells, Fargo's Jim Hume came out and publicly made the charge to the *Police Gazette* and the *San Jose Times* (as quoted in the *San Francisco Exchange,* Feb. 16, 1882). On March 31, 1882, a letter-writer to the *Los Angeles Express* wrote: "It seems that the Earps believed (and not without cause) that the sheriff and party were exceedingly friendly with the cowboys, and it is certain the sheriff made no effort to detect the murderers of Earp." Several other letters expressed the same sentiment.

72. Burrows, *John Ringo,* p. 27.

73. *San Francisco Examiner,* May 11, 1882.

74. Ibid.

75. Fanny Kemble Wister, *Owen Wister Out West* (Chicago: University of Chicago Press, 1958), p. 220.

76. *Tombstone Epitaph,* Sept. 10, 1881.

77. *Tombstone Nugget,* Sept. 13, 1881.

78. *Tucson Citizen,* Mar. 25, 1881.

79. Lake, *Undercover for Wells, Fargo,* pp. 245–46. Later biographies of Earp and Breakenridge credited them with the investigative work. Both passed through glorifying biographers, however, while Dodge's version remains in a letter he wrote to Stuart Lake and stands as the sole first-person account of the events.

80. *Tombstone Nugget,* Oct. 22, 1881.

81. Parsons to Lake, Nov. 6, 1928, Lake Collection, Huntington Library.

82. *San Francisco Weekly Stock Report,* Oct. 3, 1881.

83. *Tombstone Epitaph,* Nov. 12, 1881, from *San Francisco Stock Report.*

84. *Arizona Weekly Star,* Oct. 13, 1881; *Tucson Weekly Citizen,* Oct. 9, 1881.

85. *Tombstone Nugget,* Nov. 17, 1881.

86. Jennie Robertson, as told to Cynthia Pridmore, "Memoirs of Jennie Robertson," Cynthia Pridmore Collection, Newport News, Va.

87. *Tombstone Epitaph,* Nov. 20, 1881.

88. Parsons and Chafin, "The West of George W. Parsons," Feb. 2, 1915.

89. Combines *Epitaph,* Nov. 22, 1881, with edited trial transcript (Pat Hayhurst, "Spicer Hearing Documents," Arizona Historical Foundation, Tempe, pp. 238–39). Hayhurst edited the original trial transcript as a WPA project in the 1930s. The original transcript has since disappeared and is believed to have been lost in a fire at Hayhurst's home.

Hayhurst deleted much material from his transcript. Original newspaper reports are the primary source of material on the Spicer hearing presented in this book.

90. Hooker, "An Arizona Vendetta," p. 76.

91. *San Francisco Examiner,* Mar. 23, 1882.

92. Ibid., Oct. 3, 1881.

93. Gosper to Blaine, Sept. 20, 1881, National Archives, DOJ, RG 60.

94. *San Francisco Examiner,* May 11, 1882.

95. The Aug. 28, 1881, *Tucson Citizen* identifies Morgan Earp as a member of Ed Byrnes's Top and Bottom gang, a collection of tinhorn gamblers who played a con game on train travelers stopping briefly at the depot. The report is most likely in error, since Morgan Earp served as Virgil's deputy at the time and arrested Byrnes on other charges. A later report in the May 24, 1882, *Las Vegas Optic* flatly denied any Earp involvement with the gang.

CHAPTER 4.   A MARCH TO DESTINY

1. *San Francisco Examiner,* Mar. 28, 1882.

2. *Tombstone Nugget,* Oct. 25, 1881; *Arizona Weekly Star,* Oct. 27, 1881.

3. *San Francisco Examiner,* Aug. 2, 1896.

4. Kate tells this story in many of her letters, including Mary Cummings's letter to Laffert, as quoted in Bell's *The Illustrated Life and Times of Doc Holliday.* The Earps' reason for summoning Holliday is never detailed, and some have speculated the brothers anticipated a fight and called him back to carry a gun. From information in the Flood and Hooker manuscripts and because of the Earps' seeming indifference to a fight early in the day of October 26, it seems more likely Wyatt would have called him back to salve Ike's suspicion about the Earps blabbing the deal. If, indeed, this was Earp's plan, it backfired when Holliday and Clanton bickered in the saloon. There is some question as to the mode of transportation. Wyatt says Doc arrived on the stage. Kate says they all took a buckboard, and she erroneously said they arrived on the night before the gunfight.

5. Wyatt Earp quotes taken from the *Tombstone Nugget,* Nov. 17, 1881. Several statements differ from later published versions.

6. *Tombstone Nugget,* Nov. 10 and 11, 1881, checked against *Epitaph* and Hayhurst versions.

7. *Tombstone Nugget,* Nov. 24, 1881.

8. Ibid.

9. Hayhurst, "The Spicer Hearing Documents," pp. 86–87.

10. Mary Cummings to Laffert, Mar. 19, 1940, as quoted in Bell's *The Illustrated Life of Doc Holliday,* pp. 106–8.

11. John Clum, "It All Happened in Tombstone," *Arizona Historical Review,* April 1929, pp. 46–72, Gary L. Roberts Collection.

12. *Tombstone Nugget,* Nov. 20, 1881.

13. *Tombstone Nugget,* Nov. 11, 1881; Campbell's recollection of Wyatt's words were that he called him a "cattle-thieving SOB, and now you have to fight."

14. *Tombstone Nugget,* Nov. 17, 1881.

15. Hayhurst, "Spicer Hearing Documents," p. 30.

16. *Tombstone Nugget,* Nov. 11, 1881.

17. Ibid., Nov. 17, 1881.

18. Ibid., Nov. 13, 1881.

19. Ibid., Nov. 17, 1881.

20. *Tombstone Nugget, Epitaph,* Nov. 3, 1881.

21. *Tombstone Nugget,* Nov. 20, 1881.

22. *Tombstone Epitaph,* Nov. 22, 1881.

23. *Tombstone Nugget*, Nov. 22, 1881.

24. *Tombstone Epitaph*, Nov. 3, 1881.

25. *Tombstone Nugget*, Nov. 5, 1881.

26. The time of the gunfight is uncertain. It must be remembered this occurred before times were standardized. Towns still operated on sun time, so different watches would have different times. Life in the 1880s was not so severely governed by the clock as it is today.

27. *Tombstone Nugget*, Nov. 5, 1881. It is important to note that King heard only a snatch of a conversation. The words from an unknown Earp may have been something to the effect of: "If they draw, let them have it," or "If they go for their guns, let them have it." That King heard this comment out of context must be considered.

28. *Tombstone Epitaph*, Nov. 23, 1881.

29. During the cross-examination of Behan, defense attorneys identified the location of the shot as coming from the east of Fly's gallery, not from the rear of the lot, to the south of Fly's, as is commonly misreported in various later accounts of the gunfight. Gunfight analyst Jeff Morey notes that this would make Billy Allen the prime suspect if such a shot was indeed fired.

30. Holliday's "You're a daisy if you have" comment is colloquial for "You're a good one if you have got me." The term "daisy" was popular in the 1880s and generally meant good.

31. *Tombstone Nugget*, Oct. 30, 1881. The chest wound to Frank McLaury was reported in the *Nugget* but not mentioned in the coroner's report, which listed only fatal wounds.

32. The exact course of Morgan's wound is uncertain. The *Epitaph* says the bullet entered the right shoulder; the *Nugget* says it entered the left.

33. *San Diego Union*, Nov. 3, 1881.

34. Ibid.

35. *Tombstone Nugget*, Nov. 8, 1881.

36. *Tombstone Nugget*, Nov. 12, 1881.

37. Inquest reports appeared in the Nov. 5, 1881, *Epitaph* and *Nugget*.

38. *Tombstone Epitaph*, Oct. 29, 1881.

39. *San Francisco Exchange*, Oct. 27, 1881.

40. *San Diego Union*, Nov. 3, 1881.

41. Ibid.

42. "Buck Fanshaw's Funeral" was a Mark Twain short story that originally appeared in *Roughing It*, in 1872. The story told of Virginia City honoring saloonkeeper Buck Fanshaw with a huge funeral ceremony at the instigation of one of his friends who wanted to give him a proper sendoff. The result was a massive cortege and mourning that hardly reflected Buck's place in life.

43. *San Francisco Exchange*, May 28, 1882.

44. *San Diego Union*, Nov. 3, 1881.

45. *Tombstone Nugget*, Oct. 30, 1881.

46. *Tombstone Epitaph*, Oct. 30, 1881.

47. *Tombstone Nugget*, Oct. 30, 1881.

ℂ HAPTER 5.   "I THINK WE CAN HANG THEM"

1. *Tombstone Nugget*, Oct. 30, 1881.

2. Ibid.

3. Hayhurst, "Spicer Hearing Documents," pp. 29–37. Allen testimony not available from other sources.

4. *Tombstone Nugget* and *Epitaph*, Nov. 23, 1881. Behan testimony.

5. *Tombstone Nugget,* Nov. 3, 1881.

6. *Arizona Weekly Star,* Nov. 3, 1881.

7. Ibid.

8. *Tombstone Nugget,* Nov. 4, 1881.

9. *Tombstone Nugget,* Nov. 5, 1881.

10. *Arizona Weekly Star,* Nov. 10, 1881.

11. McLaury to Appelgate, Nov. 9, 1881, Misc. MSS McLaury, William, The New-York Historical Society (hereafter cited as McLaury MSS).

12. McLaury to Greene, Nov. 8, 1881, McLaury MSS.

13. Ibid.

14. *Tombstone Nugget, Epitaph,* Nov. 8, 1881.

15. McLaury to Greene, Nov. 8, 1881, McLaury MSS.

16. McLaury to Appelgate, Nov. 9, 1881, McLaury MSS.

17. McLaury to Greene, Nov. 8, 1881, McLaury MSS.

18. McLaury to Appelgate, Nov. 9, 1881, McLaury MSS.

19. McLaury to Greene, Nov. 8, 1881, McLaury MSS.

20. McLaury to Appelgate, Nov. 17, 1881, McLaury MSS.

21. Gosper to Kirkwood, Nov. 29, 1881, as reprinted in "Lawlessness in Parts of Arizona," the 1882 presidential report to Congress. Copy in Gary L. Roberts Collection.

22. *Tombstone Nugget,* Nov. 10, 1881.

23. *Tombstone Nugget,* Nov. 13, 1881; the *Nugget* version differs from the Hayhurst transcript.

24. Ibid.

25. The change from "capture" to "kill" is noted only in the Hayhurst transcript and is not mentioned by either paper.

26. *Tombstone Epitaph,* Nov. 15, 1881.

27. Loan papers from University of Arizona Special Collections, Az. 196, vol. 122. Behan and Clanton secured the loan from the L. M. Jacobs Mercantile, which also ran a loan operation. Strangely, Clanton paid off the $500 loan on November 25, less than two weeks later. It can only be speculated that Will McLaury assumed much of the financial burden as the hearing progressed. Behan's financial dealings are most suspicious during this period. On November 1, he secured a personal loan from Jacobs for $500. Then on November 2 Behan and jailer Billy Soule took out a $200 loan. During Behan's testimony, asked if he had contributed money to the prosecution, he denied that he had.

28. *Rocky Mountain News,* Oct. 23, 1898.

29. "The Compiled Laws of Arizona Territory" (1877) state: "When the examination of witnesses on the part of the Territory is closed, the magistrate shall distinctly inform the defendant that it is his right to make a statement in relation to the charges against him (stating to him the nature thereof), that the statement is designed to enable him, if he see fit, to answer the charge, and to explain the fact alleged against him, that he is at liberty to waive making a statement and that his waiver cannot be used against him on the trial." The magistrate was to ask only questions of name, age, birth, length of residence, and occupation. The law was slightly amended in 1881 to provide for a defendant reserving his right to make his statement until after his supporting witnesses had been heard. The law applied only to preliminary hearings, not to open trial. It does not discriminate between reading a prepared statement and making an unprepared statement. It should be noted that later researchers have inaccurately used Spicer's allowing such a statement to show prejudice in favor of the defendant. Territorial law clearly provided this option and it was not questioned during the hearing. Legal research on this topic provided by Bob Palmquist.

30. In Earp's prepared statement, he said he heard about the death threats from Williams, Farmer Daly, Ed Byrnes, Charley Smith, and a man identified by the *Nugget* as

"Old Man Winter" and by the Hayhurst transcript as "Old Man Urrides." Earp also said there were three or four others who told him of the threats.

31. The words "pretty tight" appear only in the Nov. 17, 1881, *Epitaph.*

32. *Tombstone Epitaph* and *Nugget,* Nov. 17, 1881.

33. Earp's testimony taken from the Nov. 17, 1881, *Epitaph* and *Nugget.*

34. McLaury to Appelgate, Nov. 17, 1881, McLaury MSS.

35. Ibid., Nov. 9, 1881.

36. Ibid., Nov. 17, 1881.

37. *Tombstone Nugget,* Nov. 19, 1881. It should be noted that Spicer's decision strictly followed territorial law and was a clear ruling against the Earps. Later researchers, such as Ed Bartholomew, would charge that Spicer had clearly favored the Earps, but the refusal to allow Boyle's testimony without proper foundation could be considered evidence of Spicer's objectivity.

38. Virgil Earp does not make clear Wyatt Earp's actual appointment in his comments during the hearing. However, in the Mar. 28, 1882, *Examiner* story he says Wyatt served as a deputy U.S. marshal.

39. *Tombstone Nugget* and *Epitaph,* Nov. 20, 1881.

40. Ibid.

41. *Tombstone Nugget* and *Epitaph,* Nov. 24, 1881.

42. *Tombstone Nugget* and *Epitaph,* Nov. 28, 1881.

43. *Tombstone Epitaph,* Nov. 29, 1881.

44. *Tombstone Nugget* and *Epitaph,* Nov. 29, 1881.

45. *Tombstone Nugget* story taken from *Tucson Weekly Citizen,* Oct. 30, 1881.

46. Analysis by researcher Jeff Morey in various unpublished papers.

47. Morey has made a detailed analysis for a forthcoming book. In considering Morgan Earp's wound, Morey notes that the newspapers report opposite trajectories. The *Nugget* has a bullet ripping across Morgan's back from left to right, while the *Epitaph* says the shot traveled from right to left. Morey concludes that if the *Nugget* is right, Morgan was probably hit by a shot from his own party. Either Virgil's first shot at Frank McLaury or Wyatt's accidental discharge when wrestling with Ike Clanton is the most probable source for the left-to-right wound. If the *Epitaph* account is accurate, the probable shooter was Tom McLaury, as both Ike Clanton and Wyatt Earp placed Tom closest to the street, in the best position to inflict such a wound when Morgan was facing into the lot.

48. Lake's notes, Huntington Library.

49. *Tombstone Epitaph,* Dec. 30, 1881, from *Kansas City Star.*

50. The term "gunfight" presents some difficulty because of the imprecision of definitions. The shooting battle against Hoy in Dodge City was more an ambush and a response than a face-to-face gunfight. Lake's research notes also tell of a mysterious gun battle in Beardstown, Ill., in 1869 in which a Tom Piner referred to Earp as "California Boy," and the two drew. Earp shot Piner in the hip, and the fight ended. No further information has been discovered on this, and the story has not been confirmed from local newspapers.

51. *Tombstone Epitaph,* Dec. 30, 1881.

52. *San Diego Union,* Dec. 13, 1881.

53. *San Francisco Examiner,* May 11, 1882.

54. Williams said he heard Behan say to Virgil: "I heard you say, 'Boys, throw up your hands. I have come to disarm you,' when one of the McLaury boys said 'We will,' and drew his gun. The shooting then commenced." As reported in the Nov. 29, 1881, *Nugget.*

55. *Tombstone Nugget,* Dec. 1, 1881. The *Nugget* had good reason to not expect the grand jury to take action. When it was seated on November 22, lawyer Alexander

Campbell protested because several members were advocates of the Earps. Judge William Stilwell overruled the objection and seated a grand jury consisting of lumber dealer Lewis W. Blinn, tinsmith Charles W. Harwood, bookkeeper Edmond A. Harley, harness maker D. R. M. Thompson, clerk Max Marks, druggist Taliafero F. Hudson, merchant Abraham B. Barnett, lumber dealer William A. Harwood, merchant Dave Calisher, stage owner John D. Kinnear, merchant Rudolph A. Cohen, newspaper editor Oscar F. Thornton, speculator Sylvester B. Comstock, mining man/newspaper man Thomas R. Sorin, Wells, Fargo agent Marshall Williams, miner Frederick Restig, and trader George W. Buford. Several members—notably W. A. Harwood, Thornton, Williams, Comstock, Blinn, and Sorin—would be prominently identified with the pro-Earp business faction. Wyatt and Morgan Earp had served as shotgun messengers on Kinnear's stages. Research provided by Carl Chafin.

56. *Los Angeles Herald*, Dec. 1, 1881, from *San Bernardino Times*.

57. Chisholm, "Tombstone's Tale," p. 118. Chisholm quotes letter from Kate to Anton Mazzanovich.

ℭHAPTER 6.   TOMBSTONE IN TERROR

1. *Tombstone Epitaph*, Dec. 30, 1881.

2. John Clum, "It All Happened in Tombstone," *Arizona Historical Review*, October 1929, pp. 46–50. Further Clum quotes in this chapter from same story.

3. Gosper telegram to Arthur, Dec. 12, 1881, National Archives, Source-Chronological-President Files.

4. Clum, "It All Happened in Tombstone," p. 46.

5. *Tombstone Epitaph*, Dec. 16, 1881.

6. *Los Angeles Times*, Dec. 30, 1881.

7. John Clum, Clum scrapbooks, University of Arizona Special Collections.

8. *Tombstone Epitaph*, Dec. 16, 1881.

9. *Tombstone Nugget*, as reprinted in *Arizona Weekly Star*, Dec. 22, 1881.

10. Breakenridge, *Helldorado*, pp. 259–60.

11. *Tombstone Epitaph*, Dec. 24, 1881, from *San Francisco Exchange*.

12. *San Francisco Weekly Report*, Nov. 7, 1881.

13. *Tombstone Epitaph*, Aug. 8, 1880.

14. *Tombstone Nugget*, July 7, 1881.

15. *Tombstone Epitaph*, Dec. 9, 1881.

16. *San Francisco Exchange*, Dec. 16, 1881.

17. *Tombstone Nugget*, Dec. 21, 1881.

18. *Tombstone Epitaph*, Dec. 22, 1881.

19. Glenn G. Boyer, "Morgan Earp, Brother in the Shadow," *Old West*, Winter 1983, p. 20. Verified against copies of original letters in the Simmons Collection.

20. Hooker, "An Arizona Vendetta," pp. 47–48.

21. *San Francisco Examiner*, May 28, 1882.

22. *Tombstone Epitaph*, Dec. 29, 1881.

23. Ibid.

24. Will McLaury to Robert McLaury, Apr. 13, 1884. (McLaury MSS, William, New-York Historical Society). Will McLaury says in the letter that McMasters was one of the victims, probably because there were many erroneous newspaper reports of McMasters's death. Wyatt Earp said in the 1925 Lotta Crabtree deposition (Harvard Law Library) that McMasters died in the Philippines during the Spanish-American War.

25. Earp to Lake, undated, Lake Collection, Huntington Library.

26. *Phoenix Herald,* Dec. 30, 1881. There are semantic questions on the use of "deputy U.S. marshal" in this instance. Technically, only the territorial marshal had the authority to appoint deputies, while the deputies could appoint "possemen," who served as deputies to the deputy marshal. Newspapers in Arizona refer to Wyatt as a deputy marshal in earlier stories and later refer to his appointees as deputy marshals.

27. *Tombstone Nugget,* Jan. 1, 1882.

28. *Los Angeles Herald,* Jan. 3, 1882, from *Tucson Star.*

29. *San Francisco Stock Report,* from *Arizona Sentinel,* Yuma, Jan. 14, 1882.

30. *Tombstone Epitaph,* Dec. 25, 1881.

31. *Tombstone Nugget,* Jan. 1, 1882.

32. *Tucson Daily Star,* Jan. 14, 1882, exchange from *Prescott Democrat.*

33. *Tombstone Epitaph,* Jan. 10, 1882.

34. *San Francisco Exchange,* Jan. 9, 1882.

35. Lake, *Undercover for Wells, Fargo,* pp. 18–19. There is some confusion in the story. Fred Dodge says a double-barreled shotgun was taken from Hume. Earp would tell the *San Francisco Examiner* that the short shotgun had been taken from Charles Bartholomew, the driver of the other stage robbed. Contemporary newspaper accounts would tell of the two pistols taken from Hume without mentioning the shotgun. It seems more likely the shotgun would have been taken from the stage driver.

36. Ringo's arrest presents some problems, since numerous issues of both Tombstone papers for the key dates are missing and no actual record of his arrest could be located. He was identified by the *L.A. Times* as the prime suspect in a stage robbery, then identified in Tombstone papers as being on bail for robbery and jailed for more than a week in early February. He carried an $8,000 bail and was tried in territorial court on two charges. This indicates that the crime in question was probably more serious than robbing a poker game.

37. *Tombstone Weekly Epitaph,* Feb. 13, 1882.

38. John Boessenecker, interview by author, May 27, 1995. At time of publication Boessenecker was researching Wells, Fargo for a future book. Wells, Fargo had taken such action in January of 1881 by removing service from several California towns because the local citizenry had failed to halt stage robbery in the area. *San Francisco Report,* Jan. 14, 1881.

39. *Los Angeles Times,* Jan. 16, 1882.

40. *Arizona Daily Star,* Jan. 14, 1882, from *Prescott Democrat.*

41. Wyatt Earp's involvement in the Tombstone saloons has always been subject to some question. He certainly helped run the gambling concessions at the Oriental, and family members constantly identified him as a saloon owner. He said during the Spicer hearing that he held an interest in a faro game at the Golden Eagle as well.

42. *San Francisco Examiner,* May 28, 1882.

43. As usually happens with such events, a good story was blown up into a masterpiece. By the time John Pleasant Gray related it in his memoirs nearly sixty years later, the story came off as another confrontation for the ages, with Ringo riding into town, pulling off his red bandanna, and throwing it in the air. Ringo then told Wyatt Earp to take the other end and say when. Parsons's eyewitness report from the scene provides a more authentic version. Details on charges dropped from Marks, *And Die in the West,* p. 328; also, *Tucson Weekly Citizen,* Jan. 22, 1882.

44. *San Diego Union,* Feb. 4, 1882.

45. *Arizona Weekly Star,* Jan. 26, 1882, from *Nugget.*

46. *Tombstone Nugget,* Jan. 26, 1882.

47. *Tombstone Epitaph,* Jan. 26, 1882.

48. *Tombstone Nugget,* Jan. 26, 1882.

49. *Tombstone Nugget,* Jan. 26, 1882.

50. *Tombstone Epitaph,* Jan. 28, 1882.

51. Hooker, "An Arizona Vendetta," p. 47.

52. *Tombstone Nugget,* Feb. 16, 1882. According to entries in Parsons's diary, Maynard had a reputation as a local troublemaker. On the day of the Holliday–Ringo confrontation, Maynard and Earp ally Lou Rickabaugh "tried to kick each other's lungs out," Parsons wrote. Maynard got in a scrape with Dan Tipton on February 15, 1882, leaving Tipton with a cut over his eye. Maynard also started a saloon ruckus in November.

53. *Tombstone Epitaph,* Jan. 26, 1882.

54. Ibid., Jan. 27, 1882.

55. *Tombstone Nugget,* Jan. 28, 1882.

56. *San Diego Union,* Feb. 4, 1882.

57. *Tombstone Epitaph,* Feb. 2, 1882.

58. Ibid., Feb. 3, 1882.

59. *Tombstone Weekly Epitaph,* Jan. 29, 1882.

60. *Tombstone Nugget,* Jan. 31, 1882.

61. *Tombstone Epitaph,* Jan. 31, 1882.

62. *National Police Gazette,* Mar. 11, 1882.

63. *San Diego Union,* Feb. 4, 1882.

64. *Arizona Daily Star,* Feb. 5, 1882, from *Tombstone Nugget.*

65. Virtually the same comment is quoted in Hooker's "An Arizona Vendetta" and Lake's Sept. 10, 1928, letter to Judge Stilwell (Lake Collection, Huntington Library). The judge died without responding to confirm the remark.

66. Statements in Hooker's "An Arizona Vendetta" and in various writings of John Clum confirm the belief among Earp supporters that conviction of criminals had become impossible.

67. *Tucson Weekly Citizen,* Feb. 19, 1882.

68. Hayhurst, "Spicer Hearing Documents," Doc. 94, p. 5, Arizona Historical Foundation/Tempe.

69. *Tombstone Epitaph,* Feb. 11, 1882.

70. Byers File, Arizona Historical Society/Tucson.

71. Copy of mortgage papers from the Lee Simmons Collection. The papers show that Earp mortgaged property to James G. Howard.

72. Hooker, "An Arizona Vendetta," pp. 42–46.

73. Ibid.

74. *Tombstone Epitaph,* Dec. 10, 1881; *Tombstone Weekly Epitaph,* Feb. 13, 1882; "Lawlessness in Parts of Arizona, Message from the President of the United States," Congressional publication, Feb. 2, 1882, Gary L. Roberts Collection, Tifton, Ga.

75. *Tombstone Nugget,* Feb. 19, 1882.

76. *Arizona Daily Star,* Feb. 9, 1882. The term "sport" was used for both prostitutes and gamblers, and only the context leads to the conclusion that Williams left with a prostitute.

77. Boyer, "Morgan Earp, Brother in the Shadow," p. 20.

78. *Arizona Daily Star,* Mar. 10, 1882.

79. *Tombstone Nugget,* Feb. 28, 1882.

80. *San Diego Union,* Mar. 13, 1882.

81. Morgan Earp Inquest record, Arizona Historical Foundation; *Tombstone Nugget, Tombstone Epitaph,* Mar. 23, 1882.

82. Hooker, "An Arizona Vendetta," p. 48. Hooker tells details of Wyatt Earp's activities.

83. *San Diego Union,* Mar. 31, 1882.

84. Morgan's last words almost immediately became a subject of curiosity, and Wyatt refused to tell the onlookers. This led to several versions, the most interesting ap-

pearing in Lake's *Frontier Marshal* in a quote attributed to Earp. By this account, Earp says that Morgan had been interested in the afterlife, that he and Wyatt had previously discussed the subject and pondered whether a dying person had a vision of heaven, and that Morgan's last words were: "I guess you were right, Wyatt—I can't see a damn' thing." There is no confirmation, and Lake's notes do not report the conversation. More likely is the version quoted in the text, from Hooker's "An Arizona Vendetta." Sadie Earp recounted the final words as, "They got me, Wyatt, you be careful, don't let them get you," followed by "father, mother." Earp's comments to the *Gunnison News-Democrat*, June 4, 1882, as quoted in the text, indicate the Hooker version as the most likely.

CHAPTER 7. VENDETTA

1. *Denver Republican,* May 14, 1893.
2. Hooker, "An Arizona Vendetta," p. 57.
3. *Denver Republican,* May 14, 1893.
4. The "One for Morgan" comment comes from several sources, most notably Hooker's "An Arizona Vendetta." Its first known appearance came in Alfred Henry Lewis's 1905 book *Sunset Trail,* based on stories from Bat Masterson. Allie's carrying the pistol is described by Hildreth Halliwell. Halliwell, interview by Al Turner and Bill Oster, tape recording, University of Arizona Special Collections.
5. George Hand and Neil Carmony, ed., *Whiskey, Six-Guns & Red-Light Ladies* (Silver City, N.M.: High Lonesome, 1994), p. 228.
6. *Arizona Daily Star,* Mar. 21, 1882.
7. *Tucson Weekly Citizen,* Apr. 12, 1882. Includes details of Stilwell coroner's report.
8. *San Francisco Examiner,* May 28, 1882.
9. *Arizona Daily Star,* Mar. 21, 1882.
10. *Tombstone Nugget, Epitaph,* Mar. 23, 1882.
11. Ibid.
12. *Arizona Weekly Star,* Mar. 30, 1882.
13. While Earp generally avoided discussions of motives and emotions in later interviews, material in Hooker's "An Arizona Vendetta" indicates that Earp believed convictions against the cowboys were not possible. The letters of Judge B. L. Peel and other writers from the area show a similar consistency of thinking in the belief that no court could convict a cowboy.
14. Breakenridge, *Helldorado,* pp. 287–88.
15. *Arizona Daily Star,* Mar. 22, 1882, from *Tombstone Nugget.*
16. *Arizona Daily Star,* Mar. 25, 1882.
17. Alice Earp Wells, interview by Jack Burrows, 1956.
18. Wyatt Earp deposition, Lotta Crabtree estate trial, Harvard Law Library.
19. Ibid.
20. Breakenridge, *Helldorado,* pp. 297–98.
21. *Tombstone Nugget,* Mar. 31, 1882.
22. *Tucson Citizen,* Mar. 1, 1898.
23. This story grows with each telling. The Flood version says Indian Charlie turned and went for his guns; Hooker tells of a gunfight; and Lake makes it sound as if Earp and Charlie engaged in a fast-draw contest. Further information from Earp to Burns, Mar. 15, 1927, Burns Collection, University of Arizona Special Collections.
24. *Tombstone Weekly Epitaph,* Mar. 27, 1882.
25. *Arizona Daily Star,* Mar. 24, 1882.
26. Ibid., Mar. 31, 1882.

27. *San Francisco Weekly Exchange,* Mar. 23, 1882.

28. *San Francisco Examiner,* Mar. 23, 1882.

29. George Hand and Carl Chafin, ed., "One Hundred Days on the San Pedro: George Hand's Contention Diary," Chafin Collection, Culver City, Calif., 1989, p. 12.

30. Hooker, "An Arizona Vendetta," p. 60.

31. Various quotes from *Field and Farm,* Denver, Aug. 17, 1893, and *San Francisco Examiner,* Aug. 2, 1896, combine to tell Earp's story of the battle. The story is complicated because in 1893 and again in the initial *Examiner* story, Earp refers to Curley Bill using a Winchester rifle. In the *Examiner* story that followed a week later, Earp makes the correction and says Curley Bill used the shotgun stolen from Charley Bartholomew during the January Bisbee stage robbery.

32. *Denver Republican,* Mar. 22, 1882.

33. Hooker, "An Arizona Vendetta," p. 66; *Tombstone Weekly Epitaph,* Apr. 3, 1882.

34. *Tombstone Nugget,* Mar. 26, 1882. While the source is unidentified, the story is consistent with that told in Hooker's "An Arizona Vendetta" and identifies Wright and Kraker as delivering funds to Earp. This story becomes complex because Wright and Kraker later gave an interview to the *Epitaph* telling the cowboy version in which the Earp party's bullets did not connect with Curley Bill. The most likely scenario is that Wright and Kraker gave the story to the *Epitaph* to end suspicion that they were working with the Earps and avoid retribution.

35. *Tombstone Weekly Epitaph,* Mar. 27, 1882.

36. *San Francisco Exchange,* Mar. 27, 1882.

37. Lake, *Undercover for Wells, Fargo,* p. 239.

38. *New Southwest and Grant County Herald,* Apr. 29, 1882.

39. *Tucson Weekly Citizen,* Apr. 9, 1882.

40. *Sacramento Union,* Mar. 28, 1882.

41. *Tombstone Weekly Epitaph,* Apr. 10, 1882; Hooker, "An Arizona Vendetta," p. 74.

42. *Tombstone Weekly Epitaph,* Apr. 3, 1882.

43. *Los Angeles Herald,* Mar. 31, 1882, from *Tombstone Epitaph.*

44. *Tombstone Nugget,* Mar. 31, 1882.

45. Hooker, "An Arizona Vendetta," pp. 74–76; *Tombstone Epitaph,* Apr. 14, 1882. These two reports combine to tell the Hooker version of events at the ranch. Forrestine Hooker most likely took some detail from conversations with Henry Hooker, her father-in-law.

46. Hooker, "An Arizona Vendetta," p. 77.

47. *Tombstone Nugget,* Apr. 6, 1882; *Epitaph,* Apr. 5, 1882. The "lost Charlie Ross" was a child who was snatched from his Philadelphia home in 1874 and was falsely reported to have shown up all over the United States. This became a major news story through the 1880s as false leads constantly appeared. For details on Charlie Ross, see the *Cincinnati Enquirer,* July 9, 1884.

48. *Arizona Daily Star,* Apr. 6, 1882, from *Tombstone Nugget.*

49. Reminiscences of Henry Morgan, Arizona Historical Society/Tucson. Morgan says the Earps left a few minutes after mailing the documents. This presents a slight conflict with Halliwell's story of the dinner with Biddle; however, Morgan's imprecise "few minutes" could have been long enough for a quick dinner.

50. Halliwell interview.

51. *Tombstone Weekly Epitaph,* Apr. 24, 1882, from *San Francisco Exchange.*

52. *Tombstone Epitaph,* Apr. 14, 1882.

53. *New Southwest and Grant County Herald,* Apr. 22, 1882. Located by Robin Gilliam.

54. *Albuquerque Evening Review,* May 13, 1882.

CHAPTER 8.   LAW VERSUS ORDER

1. *Los Angeles Herald,* Mar. 28, 1882.

2. *Arizona Weekly Star,* Mar. 30, 1882. The Earp questions also confront another constitutional law principle: that law and government exist to prevent crime and punish wrongdoers vs. another that certain formal requirements must be followed in this process. Adherents of the first concept argue that society becomes unjust when the second concept becomes of paramount importance.

3. *Denver Republican,* May 22, 1882.

4. *Tucson Weekly Citizen,* May 21, 1882.

5. Dodge to Clum, Sept. 24, 1930, Dodge Collection, Huntington Library.

6. Angus Cameron, a retired editor at Knopf, tabulated Behan's bankbooks, which were in a private collection in the early 1960s. Cameron added the figures and says Behan's total earnings for a year were $40,000, a remarkable figure for a county sheriff in the 1880s. The original bankbooks were not available.

7. *Behan v. Goodfellow,* Arizona Historical Society, MS 180, box 17, folder 250. Located by Mario M. Einaudi of the AHS.

8. *San Francisco Examiner,* May 4, 1882.

9. *Arizona Daily Star,* May 7, 1882.

10. Undated *Nugget* from Tritle's scrapbook, Arizona Historical Society, MS 794; *Arizona Gazette,* May 18, 1882.

11. *San Francisco Exchange,* May 6, 1882; the *Exchange* picked up the *Epitaph* story and responded.

12. *Arizona Weekly Star,* Mar. 18, 1882.

13. *Denver Republican,* May 22, 1882; *Albuquerque Review,* May 13, 1882. Big-Nose Kate would later say the row came because Holliday objected to Wyatt's "steel shirt," or bulletproof vest, saying, "You should take the same chances I take. I'm out." This is a most unlikely story, notably because no "steel shirt" could stop a .45-calibre bullet. Holliday's drunken indiscretions provide a far more likely scenario.

14. DeArment, *Bat Masterson,* p. 225.

15. *Denver Tribune,* May 16, 1882.

16. *Rocky Mountain News,* May 16, 1882.

17. Ibid., May 21, 1882.

18. DeArment, *Bat Masterson,* p. 229.

19. *Rocky Mountain News,* May 25, 1882.

20. *Denver Republican,* May 27, 1882.

21. *Rocky Mountain News,* May 17, 1882.

22. *Arizona Daily Star,* May 18, 1882.

23. *Rocky Mountain News,* May 22, 1882.

24. *Denver Tribune,* May 20, 1882.

25. *Arizona Daily Star,* May 26, 1882.

26. *New Southwest and Grant County Herald,* May 27, 1882, from *Albuquerque Review.* Lake's notes say, "stage to Deming, Santa Fe to Albuquerque, —1 wk."

27. *Rocky Mountain News,* Oct. 23, 1898.

28. *Arizona Daily Star,* June 1, 1882.

29. Ibid., May 12, 1882.

30. *San Francisco Examiner,* May 27, 1882.

31. *Gunnison News-Democrat,* June 4, 1882.

32. Judd Riley interview, Lake Collection, Huntington Library, box 11, F. 41; *Gunnison News-Democrat,* June 18, 1882.

33. *Los Angeles Times,* Mar. 28, 1882.

34. *San Francisco Examiner,* May 27, 1882.

35. *Gunnison News-Democrat,* June 4, 1882.

36. *San Francisco Examiner,* May 27, 1882.

37. *San Francisco Call, Chronicle, Post, Examiner, Bulletin,* and *Report,* Aug. 2, 3, 1882; *San Francisco Report,* Sept. 6, 1882.

38. Langley's *San Francisco City Directory* lists the three Earp brothers residing at 406 Pine. The exact date of Wyatt Earp's arrival in San Francisco could not be determined.

39. *Denver Republican,* June 2, 1882.

40. Although the cause of Ringo's death will probably never be proven with certainty, there is little reason to link Earp to it. In 1893 he told the *Denver Republican:* "I never succeeded in finding Ringo. He got out of the country and was killed by somebody else." Both the Hooker MS and some versions of the Flood MS say he killed Ringo while leaving Arizona, which did not happen since Ringo was killed months after Earp left Arizona. The version of the Flood MS that Lake received does not include such a claim of killing Ringo, and Lake wrote to Hooker that Earp never told him he killed Ringo. After Lake wrote to Fred Dodge asking about the Hooker account, Dodge responded, "I am willing to bet . . . that she never got the Ringo end from Wyatt" (*Undercover for Wells, Fargo,* p. 239). There is no evidence to link Earp to the killing of Ringo, and it is logically and logistically unlikely that he made the long ride back from Colorado, did the killing, then returned to Colorado without being seen. It is also unlikely that Earp then kept this spectacular story secret for the rest of his life. It is impossible that Holliday participated in the death of Ringo. Court records use the term "In propria Persona" to indicate Holliday personally appeared in a Pueblo court two days before Ringo's death.

41. General assessment made through reading period newspapers and discussions with several Tombstone researchers, notably Carl Chafin.

42. Copy of revocation papers in the Bob Palmquist Collection; original from Cochise County Recorder's office, Bisbee, Ariz.

43. *Tombstone Epitaph,* Sept. 23, 1882.

44. Behan File, University of Arizona Special Collections.

45. Dake File, National Archives, DOJ, RG 60.

46. *Arizona Daily Star,* Sept. 15, 1882.

47. Rasch, "A Note on Buckskin Frank Leslie," p. 209.

48. *San Francisco Examiner,* Feb. 25, 1894.

49. Masterson and DeMattos, *Famous Gunfighters,* p. 57.

50. Miller and Snell, *Why the West Was Wild,* pp. 556–61.

51. Ibid., pp. 530–32.

52. Luke Short dictation, Mar. 19, 1886, Bancroft Texas Dictations, Bancroft Library, Berkeley, Calif.

53. *San Francisco Examiner,* Aug. 16, 1896.

54. Ibid.

55. *National Police Gazette,* July 21, 1883; *San Francisco Examiner,* Aug. 16, 1896.

56. Masterson and DeMattos, *Famous Gunfighters,* pp. 29–30.

57. Research and analysis on Earp in Idaho provided by Judge Richard G. Magnuson, who scoured Shoshone County records to gain an understanding of Earp's dealings in the Coeur d'Alene rush.

58. *Spokane Falls Review,* Apr. 5, 1884.

59. *San Francisco Call,* Dec. 7, 1896.

60. Ferguson's account of the incident is from a letter he wrote to Lee J. Rose signed Danny Miller. In a subsequent letter Miller identifies himself as Ferguson. Rose sent the

letters to Stuart Lake, and they are included in the Lake Collection (box 11, F.55) at the Huntington Library. Ferguson's account of the events is supported by *Spokane Falls Review*, June 20, 1884.

61. *Idaho Sun*, July 8, 1884.

62. *Aspen Daily Times*, Oct. 14, 1885.

63. Cason and Ackerman, "She Married Wyatt Earp."

64. Emma Walling, *Doc Holliday: Colorado Trials and Triumphs* (Snowmass, Colo.: Walling, 1994), p. 74. Quote appeared in *Denver Republican*, Dec. 25, 1887.

65. *Los Angeles Herald*, Feb. 3, 1887, citing source as *Police Gazette*.

66. Celia Earp Inquest, Arizona Department of Library, Archives Division; Pinal County Inquests; Filmfile 88.6.1.

CHAPTER 9. A FIGHT FOR HONOR

1. Lucius Beebe, "San Francisco Luxury Places," *Holiday Magazine*, April 1961, p. 38, Barbara Grear Collection. The date of the incident cannot be established.

2. *San Francisco Chronicle*, Apr. 29, 1893.

3. *Denver Republican*, Mar. 14, 1893.

4. Cason and Ackerman, "She Married Wyatt Earp."

5. Ibid.

6. *San Francisco Examiner*, Aug. 7, 1896.

7. *San Francisco Evening Bulletin*, Dec. 2, 1896.

8. *San Francisco Examiner*, Dec. 16, 1896. Spelling of *tony* changed from the original "tone."

9. *San Francisco Examiner*, Dec. 3, 1896.

10. *San Francisco Chronicle*, Dec. 3, 1896.

11. *San Francisco Evening Bulletin*, Dec. 3, 1896.

12. *San Francisco Examiner*, Dec. 3, 1896.

13. Ibid.

14. *San Francisco Chronicle*, Dec. 3, 1896.

15. *San Francisco Examiner*, Dec. 3, 1896.

16. Ibid., Dec. 4, 1896.

17. Cason and Ackerman, "She Married Wyatt Earp."

18. *San Francisco Call*, Dec. 4, 1896.

19. Ibid.

20. *San Francisco Bulletin*, Dec. 10, 1896.

21. *Los Angeles Herald*, Dec. 6, 1896, Associated Press report.

22. *San Francisco Evening Bulletin*, Dec. 5, 1896.

23. Ibid.

24. *San Francisco Call*, Dec. 15, 1896.

25. Ibid., Dec. 7, 1896.

26. *New York Morning Telegraph*, Jan. 6, 1910.

27. *San Francisco Chronicle*, Dec. 6, 1896.

28. *San Francisco Evening Bulletin*, Dec. 9, 1896.

29. *San Francisco Chronicle, San Francisco Evening Bulletin*, Dec. 9, 1896.

30. *San Francisco Evening Bulletin, San Francisco Examiner*, Dec. 10, 1896.

31. *San Francisco Chronicle*, Dec. 10, 1896.

32. *San Francisco Call*, Dec. 12, 1896.

33. *San Francisco Examiner*, Dec. 16, 1896.

34. *San Francisco Chronicle*, Dec. 16, 1896.

35. *San Francisco Examiner,* Dec. 16, 1896.

36. *San Francisco Evening Bulletin,* Dec. 17, 1896.

37. William D. McVey and Robert N. Mullin, "Wyatt Earp: Frontier Peace Officer," *The Chicago Brand Book of Westerners,* vol. 6, no. 9, 1949, p. 65, Gary L. Roberts Collection.

38. Charles Fernald, "Wyatt Earp in Alaska," *Chicago Posse of Westerners Brand Book,* vol. 8, no. 11, 1951, p. 82, Gary L. Roberts Collection.

39. Parsons and Chafin, "The West of George Whitwell Parsons," entry for Dec. 17, 1896.

40. *San Francisco Evening Bulletin,* Dec. 24, 1896.

41. Cason and Ackerman, "She Married Wyatt Earp."

42. *San Francisco Examiner,* Mar. 17, 1897.

43. Ibid., Mar. 18, 1897.

CHAPTER 10.   THE LAST FRONTIERS

1. Don Chaput, *The Earp Papers* (Encampment, Wyo.: Affiliated Writers, 1994), p. 185.

2. Halliwell interview; Peggy Greenberg interview with Roger S. Peterson, tape recording, Oct. 13, 1981, Roger S. Peterson Collection, Rocklin, Calif.

3. Cason and Ackerman, "She Married Wyatt Earp."

4. *San Francisco Call,* Apr. 30, 1900.

5. Chaput, *The Earp Papers,* p. 186.

6. Terrence Cole, ed., *Nome, City of the Golden Beaches* (Anchorage: Alaska Geographic Society, 1984), p. 76.

7. *Chicago InterOcean,* Sept. 16, 1900.

8. *Seattle Post-Intelligencer,* July 7, 1900.

9. Chaput, *The Earp Papers,* p. 186.

10. C. B. Glasscock, *Lucky Baldwin, The Story of an Unconventional Success* (Indianapolis: Bobbs-Merrill Co., 1933), pp. 282–85. Unruh, interviewed more than thirty years after the events, incorrectly recalled the name of Earp's saloon as the "Second Class." Actually, Earp ran the Dexter. The Second Class was a nearby operation.

11. Grace Welsh Spolidoro and Elena Welsh Armstrong, interview by author, tape recording, Nov. 8, 1994. Spolidoro told of Sadie Earp's gambling; Mabel Earp Cason quoted Sadie Earp as telling of Wyatt's affairs in an April 9, 1956 letter to Mrs. Beeson (photocopy from Simmons Collection).

12. *Los Angeles Express,* Dec. 12, 1901; Chaput, *The Earp Papers,* p. 188.

13. John Hays Hammond, "Strongmen of the Wild West," *Scribner's,* March 1925, p. 26. It should be noted that author Hammond recalled the mine guard incident from personal memories, while other stories in the piece he collected from other accounts.

14. Oral recollections of John Flood, as told to Robert Mullin, then to Jack Burrows. In Alaska, various records showing Wyatt and Sadie residing at different addresses make the stories seem likely.

15. *Los Angeles Herald,* Sept. 8, 1903.

16. Ibid., Sept. 9, 1903.

17. Entry for Sept. 19, 1903.

18. *San Francisco Call,* June 20, 1886.

19. *Sacramento Bee,* Sept. 12, 1958; A. M. King as told to Lea F. McCarty, "Wyatt Earp's Million Dollar Shotgun Ride," *True West,* August 1958, p. 16.

20. Entry for Oct. 14–15, 1910.

21. *Los Angeles Times*, Feb. 12, 1916; *San Bernardino Sun*, Jan. 26, 1916; *San Bernardino News*, Jan. 25, 1916. Lea McCarty, "Wyatt Earp's Burial Secret," *True West*, September–October 1957, p. 18. There is a slight inconsistency between Rasor's 1916 testimony and King's recollections. Rasor says Earp went to the tent and retrieved his gun. King says Earp only threatened to get a gun.

22. *Waymire v. Trona* trial transcripts, San Bernardino County courts.

23. *Los Angeles Times*, July 22, 1911.

24. Ibid.

25. Al Turner, "Wyatt Earp's Unique Faro Game," Chafin Collection, Culver City.

26. *Los Angeles Examiner*, July 28, 1911.

27. *Los Angeles Times, Herald, Examiner*, Sept. 28, 1911, court records. There is some question whether the prosecutor dropped the case or Judge Rose dismissed charges.

28. David Dempsey with Raymond P. Baldwin, *The Triumphs and Trials of Lotta Crabtree* (New York: Morrow, 1968), pp. 261–72.

29. Raoul Walsh, *Each Man in His Time* (New York: Farrar, Straus & Giroux, 1974), pp. 102–5.

30. Story came from John Flood, to Robert Mullin, to Jack Burrows. Flood often told this story, and it is orally repeated from several sources.

31. DeArment, *Bat Masterson*, p. 396, from *New York Morning Telegraph*, Oct. 9, 1921.

32. Earp to Hammond, May 21, 1925, Lake Collection, Huntington Library.

33. Earp to Hart, July 7, 1923, Hart Letters, Los Angeles Museum of Natural History.

34. Halliwell interview.

35. This story has been told and retold but lacks solid documentation. It was reprinted in *San Bernardino Sheriff's Office, 1853–1973* (San Bernardino: Sheriff's Employee Benefit Association, 1973), and told by Arthur M. King, among others.

36. Major Lois C. Welsh, Ret., interview with author, tape recording, Oct. 15, 1994.

37. John Henry Flood Jr., "Wyatt Earp," Chafin Collection, Culver City, Calif., 1926. Chafin has one of several copies of the Flood MS. Flood apparently wrote several drafts of the MS and made some changes in the different versions.

38. Earp to Hart, July 3, 1925, Hart Letters.

39. Anne Johnston to Hart, Feb. 21, 1927.

40. Hart to Flood, Jan. 31, 1927.

41. Earp to Burns, Mar. 15, 1927, Burns Collection, University of Arizona Special Collections.

42. Flood to Hart, Mar. 23, 1927, Hart Letters.

43. *San Francisco Chronicle*, Sept. 21, 1924.

44. *San Francisco Evening Bulletin*, Sept. 20, 1924.

45. Jack Armstrong to Gary L. Roberts, May 3, 1961, Gary L. Roberts Collection, Tifton, Ga. Armstrong worked as a rancher and served briefly as a special deputy with the Los Angeles Police Department.

46. Halliwell interview.

47. Roger S. Peterson, interview by Peggy Greenberg.

48. Lake to Burton Rascoe, Jan. 9, 1941, Lake Collection, Huntington Library.

49. Parsons to Dodge, Oct. 20, 1928, Dodge Collection, Huntington Library.

50. Clum to Dodge, Dec. 26, 1930, Dodge Collection, Huntington Library.

51. Earp to Lake, Nov. 26, 1928, Lake Collection, Huntington Library.

52. Lake to Dodge, Feb. 7, 1929, Lake Collection, Huntington Library; Cason and Ackerman, "She Married Wyatt Earp," provides a similar description of the death scene, quoting the final words as "supposing, supposing."

ⓒHAPTER 11.   LONG MAY HIS STORY BE TOLD

1. Josephine Earp to Lake, Sept. 19, 1928, Lake Collection, Huntington Library.

2. Lake to Josephine Earp, Nov. 9, 1929, Lake Collection, Huntington Library.

3. Lake to Kent, Feb. 13, 1930, Houghton Library, Harvard.

4. Ibid., Oct. 15, 1930.

5. Kent to Lake, Oct. 17, 1930, Houghton Library, Harvard.

6. Ibid., Mar. 17, 1931.

7. Josephine Earp to Lake, Jan. 27, 1931, Lake Collection, Huntington Library.

8. Lake to Josephine Earp, Aug. 23, 1931, Lake Collection, Huntington Library.

9. *New York Times,* Jan. 10, 1932.

10. Collier & Flinn Co., Ltd., list of available titles; Collier & Flinn correspondence file, Lake Collection, Huntington Library.

11. *San Bernardino Sun-Telegram,* June 25, 1961.

12. Pat McGilligan, *Backstory: Interviews with Screenwriters of Hollywood's Golden Age* (Berkeley: University of California Press, 1986), pp. 62–63.

13. Lake to Rascoe, Jan. 9, 1941, Lake Collection, Huntington Library.

14. The question of the Buntline Special remains an unsolved mystery. There is no tangible proof of the gun's existence. However, in 1929 Lake wrote letters to Alaskan newspapers trying to recover the gun, which makes it appear likely that he did not fabricate the weapon. If it did indeed exist, it seems more likely that it had a 10-inch barrel, as mentioned in Lake's notes, rather than the 12-inch barrel described in Lake's book. The 10-inch barrel would make it a more usable weapon.

15. *New York Tribune,* undated clipping in author's collection.

16. John Clum, "Review of Frontier Marshal," *Arizona Historical Review,* January 1932, p. 71. Copy from the Carl Chafin Collection.

17. Jay J. Kalez, "Texan Tamer," *Frontier Times,* May 1968, p. 29.

18. *Tucson Citizen,* Feb. 6, 1932.

19. *Tombstone Epitaph,* Feb. 19, 1937.

20. Hills of Eternity Cemetery, Colma, Calif., "Log of Burials." Wyatt and Josephine would both be cremated and buried under one tombstone. After a grave-robbing incident in 1957, a large seal would be put over the grave joining it to the nearby tombstone of Max Weiss to prevent further intrusions into the grave at the Jewish cemetery.

21. Welsh interview.

22. Armstrong interview.

23. Josephine Earp to Lake, undated, Lake Collection, Huntington Library.

24. Jeanne Cason Laing, interview by author, tape recording, Sept. 23, 1996.

25. Mabel Earp Cason to Eleanor Sloan, May 30, 1959, Arizona Pioneers Historical Society/Tucson.

26. *San Francisco Examiner,* July 16, 1939.

27. Ibid., July 29, 1939.

28. Waters, *The Earp Brothers of Tombstone,* p. 7. Waters told Carl Chafin of Allie's flask during a 1974 oral interview.

29. Frank Waters, interview by author, tape recording, Jan. 3, 1995.

30. Laing interview.

31. Peter Bogdanovich, *John Ford* (Berkeley: University of California Press; 1978), pp. 84–85.

32. *Oakland Tribune,* Feb. 8, 1959.

33. Wayne has also said that he was greatly influenced in his film portrayals by director John Ford, by stuntman/actor Yakima Canutt, and by actor Harry Carey.

34. Frank Waters, *The Colorado* (New York: Holt, Rinehart and Winston, 1946), pp. 224–27.

35. Halliwell to Sullivan, February 1967, Devere Collection, Tombstone, Ariz.

36. Lake, *Frontier Marshal*, pp. 42–43.

37. Lake to Mullin, Aug. 17, 1953, Lake Collection, Huntington Library.

38. Wayne Montgomery, "I Witnessed the O.K. Corral Fight," *True West*, February 1971, p. 18; *Tombstone Epitaph*, National Edition, Dec. 6, 1974.

39. *San Francisco Examiner*, Nov. 21, 1959.

40. Dodge to Clum, Sept. 24, 1930, Dodge Collection, Huntington Library.

BIBLIOGRAPHY

BOOKS

Adams, Andy. *The Log of a Cowboy.* Boston: Houghton Mifflin Co., 1903.

Bechdolt, Frederick R. *When the West Was Young.* New York: The Century Co., 1922.

Breakenridge, William M. (ghostwritten by William MacLeod Raine). *Helldorado: Bringing Law to the Mesquite.* Boston: Houghton Mifflin Co., 1928.

Burns, Walter Noble. *Tombstone: An Iliad of the Southwest.* New York: Doubleday, 1927.

Burrows, Jack. *John Ringo, The Gunfighter Who Never Was.* Tucson: University of Arizona Press, 1987.

Chaput, Don. *Virgil Earp: Western Peace Officer.* Encampment, Wyo.: Affiliated Writers of America, Inc., 1994.

———. *The Earp Papers.* Encampment, Wyo.: Affiliated Writers of America, Inc., 1994.

Cresswell, Stephen. *Mormons, Moonshiners, Cowboys & Klansmen.* Tuscaloosa and London: University of Alabama Press, 1991.

DeArment, Robert K. *Bat Masterson: The Man and the Legend.* Norman: University of Oklahoma Press, 1979.

DeMattos, Jack. *The Earp Decision.* College Station, Texas: Creative Publishing, 1989.

Dempsey, David, with Raymond P. Baldwin. *The Triumphs and Trials of Lotta Crabtree.* New York: Morrow, 1968.

Dykstra, Robert R. *The Cattle Towns.* New York: Knopf, 1968.

Erwin, Richard. *The Truth about Wyatt Earp.* Carpenteria, Calif.: The O.K. Press, 1992.

Foy, Eddie, and Alvin F. Harlow. *Clowning through Life.* New York: E. P. Dutton & Co., 1928.

Glasscock, C. B. *Lucky Baldwin, The Story of an Unconventional Success.* Indianapolis: Bobbs-Merrill, 1933.

Hand, George, and Neil Carmony, ed. *Whiskey, Six-guns & Red-light Ladies: George Hand's Saloon Diary, Tucson, 1875–1878.* Silver City, N.M.: High Lonesome Books, 1994.

Kelly, George H. *Legislative History of Arizona 1864–1912.* Phoenix: Manufacturing Stationers, 1926.

Kintop, Jeffrey M., and Guy Louis Rocha. *The Earps' Last Frontier.* Reno: Great Basin Press, 1989.

Lake, Carolyn. *Undercover for Wells, Fargo: The Unvarnished Recollections of Fred Dodge.* Boston: Houghton Mifflin Co., 1969.

Lake, Stuart Nathaniel. *Wyatt Earp: Frontier Marshal.* Boston: Houghton Mifflin Co., 1931.

Lyon, William H. *Those Old Yellow Dog Days: Frontier Journalism in Arizona 1859–1912.* Tucson: Arizona Historical Society Press, 1994.

Marks, Paula Mitchell. *And Die in the West: The Story of the O.K. Corral Gunfight.* New York: Morrow, 1989.

Martin, Douglas. *Tombstone's Epitaph,* rev. ed. Albuquerque: University of New Mexico Press, 1959.

Masterson, Bat, and Jack DeMattos. *Famous Gunfighters of the Western Frontier.* Monroe, Wash.: R. M. Weatherford, 1982.

McGilligan, Pat. *Backstory: Interviews with Screenwriters of Hollywood's Golden Age.* Berkeley: University of California Press, 1986.

Miller, Nyle H., and Joseph W. Snell. *Why the West Was Wild.* Topeka: Kansas State Historical Society, 1963.

Miner, H. Craig. *Wichita: The Early Years, 1865–80.* Lincoln: University of Nebraska Press, 1982.

Rothman, Sheila M. *Living in the Shadow of Death: Tuberculosis and the Social Experience of Illness in American History.* New York: Basic Books, 1994.

Walsh, Raoul. *Each Man in His Time: The Life Story of a Director.* New York: Farrar, Straus & Giroux, 1974.

Waters, Frank. *The Earp Brothers of Tombstone.* New York: Clarkson N. Potter, 1960.

Wister, Fanny Kemble. *Owen Wister Out West.* Chicago: University of Chicago Press, 1958.

Wright, Robert M. *Dodge City The Cowboy Capital and the Great Southwest.* Wichita: Wichita Eagle Press, 1913.

MAGAZINES

Beebe, Lucius. "San Francisco Luxury Places." *Holiday Magazine,* April 1961, p. 38.

Boyer, Glenn G. "Morgan Earp, A Brother in the Shadow." *Old West,* Winter 1983, p. 20.

Kalez, Jay J. "Texan Tamer." *Frontier Times,* May 1968, p. 29.

King, Arthur M., as told to Lea F. McCarty. "Wyatt Earp's Million Dollar Shotgun Ride." *True West,* August 1958, p. 16.

McCarty, Lea F. "Wyatt Earp's Burial Secret." *True West,* September–October 1957, p. 18.

Montgomery, Wayne. "I Witnessed the OK Corral Fight." *True West,* February 1971, p. 18.

Muir, Emma M. "Shakespeare Becomes a Ghost Town." *New Mexico Magazine,* October 1948, p. 25.

Palmquist, Bob. "Tombstone's Dogberry." *True West,* April 1987, p. 24.

——— . "Who Killed Jack Wagner?" *True West,* October 1993, p. 14.

UNPUBLISHED MANUSCRIPTS

Chisholm, Joe. "Tombstone's Tale." Typescript in the Jack Burrows Collection. Undated.

Gray, John Pleasant. "When All Roads Led to Tombstone." Typescript at the Arizona Historical Society. Undated.

Earp, Josephine, Mabel Earp Cason, and Vinnolia Earp Ackerman. "She Married Wyatt Earp: The Recollections of Josephine Earp." Copy of typescript in the C. Lee Simmons Collection, Sonoita, Ariz. Undated, believed to be about 1938.

Flood, John Henry Jr. "Wyatt Earp." Chafin Collection, Culver City, Calif., 1926.

Hancock, Bertha. "William Box Hancock Ms." Typescript at the University of Oklahoma Western History Collection, 1934.

Hand, George, and Carl Chafin, ed. "100 Days on the San Pedro, George Hand's Journal of 1882." Transcribed in 1988.

Hooker, Forrestine Cooper. "An Arizona Vendetta: The Truth about Wyatt Earp and Some Others." Typescript at the Southwest Museum, Los Angeles. Undated, believed to be about 1920.

Palmquist, Bob. "Election Fraud 1880: The Case of Paul v. Shibell." Seminar Paper, University of Arizona, 1986. Copy from Palmquist Collection.

———. "The Fight for the Tombstone Townsite." Seminar Paper, University of Arizona, 1988. Copy from Palmquist Collection.

———. "A Man for Breakfast Every Morning: Homicide and the Law in Tombstone." Seminar Paper, University of Arizona, 1991. Copy from Palmquist Collection.

Parsons, George W., and Carl Chafin. "The West of George Whitwell Parsons, 1880–1910." Copies of Parsons's diary entries provided by Chafin, who is transcribing fifty years of the diary. In process.

Pridmore, Cynthia. "The Recollections of Jennie Robertson, as told to her daughter, Cynthia Pridmore." Copy from Cynthia Pridmore Collection. Undated.

Roberts, Gary L. "Wyatt Earp in Kansas." Copy from Gary L. Roberts Collection, 1989.

INDEX

References to illustrations are in *italics*.

377